RESPONSIBLE BUSINESS

As sustainable development becomes an increasingly important strategic issue for all organizations, there is a growing need for management and executive education to adapt to this new reality. This textbook provides a theoretically sound and highly relevant introduction to the topic of socially and environmentally responsible business. The authors take a "competence-based approach" to responsible management education. The book aims to go beyond the traditional domains of teaching and towards the facilitation of learning across key competences. Each chapter in this book has a section dedicated to exercises that cover five core competences - know, think, do, relate, be - to enable self-directed transformative learning.

Drawing from the classic background theories such as corporate sustainability, business ethics, and corporate social responsibility, these concepts are applied to the most up-to-date practices. The book covers an international perspective, featuring cases from countries all around the world, has a strong theoretical basis, and fully integrates the topics of sustainability, responsibility, and ethics. The book includes a wide variety of tools for change at individual, company, and systemic levels resulting in both an essential resource for business students at all levels and a self-study, practical handbook for executives.

Alex Hope - Deputy Pro Vice-Chancellor and Associate Professor of Responsible Business, Newcastle Business School, Northumbria University, UK.

Oliver Laasch - Professor of Responsible Management at ESCP Berlin, adjunct professor in social entrepreneurship at the University of Manchester, and founder of the Center for Responsible Management Education.

The Principles for Responsible Management Education Series

Since the inception of the UN-supported Principles for Responsible Management Education (PRME) in 2007, there has been increased debate over how to adapt management education to best meet the demands of the 21st-century business environment. While consensus has been reached by the majority of globally focused management education institutions that sustainability must be incorporated into management education curricula, the relevant question is no longer why management education should change, but how.

Volumes within the Routledge/PRME book series aim to cultivate and inspire actively engaged participants by offering practical examples and case studies to support the implementation of the Six Principles of Responsible Management Education. Books in the series aim to enable participants to transition from a global learning community to an action community.

Revolutionizing Sustainability Education
Stories and Tools of Mindset Transformation
Edited by Ekaterina Ivanova and Isabel Rimanoczy

Principles of Sustainable Business
Frameworks for Corporate Action on the SDGs
Rob van Tulder and Eveline van Mil

Transforming Business Education for a Sustainable Future
Stories from Pioneers
Edited by Linda Irwin, Isabel Rimanoczy, Morgane Fritz, and James Weichert

Sustainability Beyond 2030
Trajectories and Priorities for Our Sustainable Future
Marco Tavanti and Alfredo Sfeir-Younis

Organizational Corruption, Crime and Covid-19
Upholding Integrity and Transparency in Times of Crisis
Edited by Agata Stachowicz-Stanusch, Wolfgang Amann, Christian Hauser, Matthias Kleinhempel and Shiv Tripathi

Responsible Business
Foundations of Ethical and Sustainable Management
Third Edition
Alex Hope and Oliver Laasch

For more information about this series, please visit: www.routledge.com/The-Principles-for-Responsible-Management-Education-Series/book-series/PRME

RESPONSIBLE BUSINESS

Foundations of Ethical and Sustainable Management

Third Edition

Alex Hope and Oliver Laasch

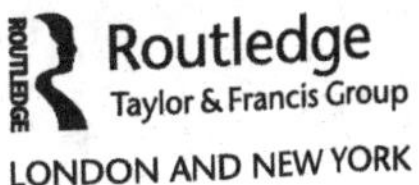

LONDON AND NEW YORK

Designed cover image: Getty Images

Third edition published 2025
by Routledge
4 Park Square, Milton Park, Abingdon, Oxon, OX14 4RN

and by Routledge
605 Third Avenue, New York, NY 10158

Routledge is an imprint of the Taylor & Francis Group, an informa business

First published 2016 by Greenleaf Publishing Limited
Second edition published by Routledge 2017

British Library Cataloguing-in-Publication Data
A catalogue record for this book is available from the British Library

ISBN: 978-1-032-89680-9 (hbk)
ISBN: 978-1-032-89450-8 (pbk)
ISBN: 978-1-003-54407-4 (ebk)

DOI: 10.4324/9781003544074

Typeset in Interstate
by SPi Technologies India Pvt Ltd (Straive)

CONTENTS

FIGURES

TABLES

INTRODUCTION TO THE THIRD EDITION

Much has happened in the areas of responsible business and management since the first edition of this book was published more than a decade ago in 2012 and the second edition in 2016. Relevant changes have happened not only in the content sphere, but also in terms of responsible management practice, and educational methods. We have lived through a global pandemic and geopolitical challenges such as the wars in the Ukraine and the Middle East have changed the landscape within which businesses operate internationally. Our understanding of global sustainability challenges such as climate change has evolved and the need for businesses to be part of the solution rather than the problem has become increasingly prominent. Despite, or perhaps because of these issues, more organizations than ever before are seeking to place the principles of responsible business at the heart of everything they do. The concepts introduced in this book are no longer relegated to the margins of business practice, rather they are becoming increasingly core to business practice. Many more business schools are aligning their curriculum with the UN Sustainable Development Goals, and both students and business leaders are seeking to understand how their business can be a force for good in the world. It is in this spirit that the 3rd edition of this book has evolved.

We have fully updated the book to ensure its continued relevance including new chapters on Climate Change, the Sustainable Development Goals, Equality, Diversity and Inclusion, Sustainable Economics, and Responsible Business Certifications. Existing chapters have been fully updated with new case studies, references, and sources where appropriate to ensure that they remain as relevant for business now, as they were in the previous editions. We have retained the structure that was introduced in the second edition with this new version having 24 chapters across seven sections designed to mirror important management tasks on the learning journey towards responsible business and management: A) Contextualizing, B) Conceptualizing, C) Managing, D) Strategizing, E) Implementing, F) Communicating, and G) Innovating.

In the "Contextualizing" section three chapters set out the critical interplay between the state of our planet, the stark realities of climate change, and the historical dynamics between business, society, and the environment. These chapters provide a foundational understanding of how deeply interconnected our global systems are, with a clear narrative that illustrates the urgent need for responsible business practices. As businesses stand at

DOI: 10.4324/9781003544074-1

the forefront of potential global transformation, this text underscores their capacity and responsibility to forge sustainable futures. We emphasize the role of innovative, sustainable business strategies in addressing the multifaceted challenges of our time, highlighting the essential shift towards practices that integrate environmental stewardship with economic and social prosperity – thereby ensuring the well-being of our planet and its inhabitants for generations to come.

The "Conceptualizing" section takes a deep dive into the foundational principles that underpin responsible and sustainable business practices. The four chapters explore the intertwined concepts of sustainability, responsibility, ethics, and the Sustainable Development Goals (SDGs), which collectively frame our understanding of what it means to operate ethically and sustainably in today's global economy. Readers are provided with a robust theoretical framework that not only explains the necessity of integrating ethical considerations into business practices but also demonstrates how these practices are indispensable for long-term success and societal well-being. As we discuss these concepts, we lay out the complexities of ethical decision making, the dynamics of corporate responsibility, and the imperative of aligning business strategies with the global goals for sustainable development.

In the "Managing" section we focus on the tangible aspects of implementing responsible management processes, emphasizing the importance of practice norms and the critical roles of equality, diversity, and inclusion in modern business environments. The three chapters provide practical insights into developing and sustaining ethical business practices through a detailed examination of responsible management processes, the reinforcement of practice norms, and the promotion of an inclusive corporate culture. We explore how businesses can operationalize their commitment to sustainability and social responsibility, addressing the complexities of translating ethical aspirations into actionable strategies. This section underlines the importance of not only adopting responsible management principles but also effectively managing their integration into daily business operations, thereby ensuring that these practices are not only endorsed but also enacted effectively across organizational levels.

The "Strategizing" section of this book addresses the crucial role of envisioning, sustaining economic practices, and strategic management in shaping the pathway to responsible business. These three chapters unravel the dynamics of aligning corporate strategies with sustainable and ethical business practices, offering a roadmap for integrating corporate responsibility deeply into business models. By exploring sustainable economics, we set out the economic underpinnings that support sustainable business practices, advocating for a business paradigm that aligns with long-term environmental and social goals. In the strategic management discourse, we dissect traditional approaches to corporate strategy, urging a shift towards models that integrate social and environmental dimensions with economic goals. Our aim is to emphasize the transformative approach businesses must adopt to not only envision but strategically execute responsible practices that ensure their operations contribute positively to society and the environment, reinforcing the notion that profitability and responsibility are not mutually exclusive but mutually reinforcing.

In the "Implementing" section we turn to the practical execution of responsible management across a company's internal functions and external supply chain relationships. This section explores how theoretical frameworks and strategies are put into practice, with a detailed focus on the challenges and successes of embedding responsible business practices across the main business, support functions, and extending into supply chain management. From the basics of implementation to the integration of such practices in every facet of business operations, this section offers an in-depth analysis of making responsibility a reality. By providing real-world examples and effective strategies, we seek to illustrate the tangible impact of responsible management on achieving sustainability and ethical integrity in business operations. Our discussion emphasizes that successful implementation requires not only commitment and resources but also a systemic approach that involves every stakeholder in the value chain.

The penultimate section of the book deals with "Communicating" and illuminates the critical role of communication in the context of responsible business practices, exploring various challenges and strategic approaches. We introduce effective communication methodologies that support the dissemination and implementation of responsible business values and practices both within and outside the organization and by examining key topics such as stakeholder engagement, responsible communication formats, and overcoming communication challenges, equip readers with the tools necessary to effectively articulate and reinforce ethical and sustainable initiatives. This section emphasizes the importance of integrating communication strategies throughout all levels of business operations to ensure transparency, consistency, and alignment with corporate social responsibilities as a means through which businesses can enhance their credibility, foster stakeholder trust, and ultimately, drive a genuine commitment to sustainable and responsible business practices. We underscore the strategic imperative of adept communication in not only conveying but also actualizing the principles of responsible business.

Finally, the "Innovating" section of this edition sets out the transformative processes necessary for achieving systemic, organizational, individual, and innovation-driven change within the context of responsible business. We focus on the necessity of innovative thinking in tackling the profound environmental, social, and ethical challenges faced today and emphasize the potential for significant change through the disruption of traditional business models and the embrace of sustainable development as a driver of innovation. Each chapter in this section articulates a different aspect of change – from individual behaviors and organizational shifts to systemic transformations and the role of innovation in facilitating these changes. In doing so we highlight the critical importance of creativity and innovation as catalysts for achieving sustainable and responsible business practices and encourage readers to think beyond conventional methods and to consider radical changes that align business operations with the urgent needs of our planet and society.

So how to make best use of this book? If you are an executive, we would propose you start with the section of the book which most suits your current need in responsible management learning. For instance, if you are currently developed into a strategic task, the strategizing section might be most relevant. If you are involved in affecting change for responsible business, the change sections make more sense. If you are an educator using this book as a textbook for your course, you might want to pick the most relevant chapters based on your course description. You might also want to review and possibly customize some of the end-of-chapter exercises to achieve a perfect fit. If you are a student, you have probably been told which parts of the book you are meant to cover. However, please do not let this fact keep you from browsing through the book. There are many things in here that you might find exciting, and you might even find that some of the exercises are quite fun!

Whatever background you come from and wherever you find yourself in your responsible management journey, we hope you will find good use for this book and that it may support you on your personal learning towards responsible business and management competence. Please feel free to let us know how it went, any time!

A Contextualizing

1 The State of the Planet

What is **responsible business**? A responsible business is a business that assumes its responsibilities in the social, environmental, and economic dimensions, ultimately contributing to sustainable development. Sustainable development is a development that "meets the needs of the present, without compromising the needs of future generations" (Brundtland, 1987, p. 24) and it is intrinsically linked with the state of our planet. Only if we live on a planet that provides the full human population (society) with the necessary (environmental) resources through an economic system that does not deplete these resources only then we will reach sustainable development. Thus, responsible business is at the heart of the relationship between business, society, and environment. The concept of responsible business aims is aimed at reaching a positive fit, a situation where businesses achieve a positive impact on society, environment, and the overall economy, without forfeiting profitability. However, there may be companies that can never achieve such a positive fit, due to the underlying nature of their business. Some of the terms used in relationship with responsible business are business sustainability, corporate citizenship, corporate social responsibility, and business ethics. Those terms are necessary background theories to responsible business, which will be explained with more detail in following chapters.

Responsible business pioneer

If there was a red carpet for responsible businesses, the company InterfaceFLOR with its late founder Ray Anderson would have walked it many times. As early as 1973 the company started producing carpet tiles, which had a considerably reduced environmental impact compared to the usually employed one-piece carpets. Interface had pioneered carpet recycling, is leading in employee diversity programs, and committed to reducing its environmental impact to – low and behold – Zero by 2020, a feat they achieved in 2019. They branded this goal "Mission Zero" and have since moved on to their Climate Take Back project which aims to reverse global warming by becoming a carbon negative enterprise by 2040 and develop processes and products that create a positive impact on the world (UNFCCC, 2023). Interface has also grown successfully in the economic dimension fueled by the differentiation provided by its environmental performance outstanding in the carpet industry, which is generally characterized as an economic sector outspokenly harmful to the natural environment (Interface, 2019).

DOI: 10.4324/9781003544074-3

The Planet as a Sick Organism

The problems humanity is facing are hard to ignore. Still, many people, organizations, and even governments do so; at least partly. Already in the mid-1960s, former NASA scientist James Lovelock and microbiologist Lynn Margulis developed the **Gaia hypothesis**, proposing the idea of Earth as a self-regulating organism; a sick organism, which is trying to fight off a harmful parasite: mankind (J. E. Lovelock, 1979; James Lovelock, 2006). The theory considering Earth or Gaia (Gaia is the word for the ancient Greek Earth goddess) a living organism as Lovelock proposed has been questioned. The more conventional perspective of the Earth systems science field, which considers Earth as an imbalanced mother system of environmental, social, and economic subsystems, explains today's issues and crisis-stricken planet. Issues such as global warming, poverty and the water and food crises are highly interlinked, convergent, and therefore even more difficult to solve. In the following section an overview of the various social, environmental, and economic issues or symptoms of the Earth crisis will be illustrated. The knowledge about the state of Earth will provide a sound basis for what responsible business should contribute to improving the "health" of the planet and the well-being of the people living on it.

Human climate relicts

Climate Relicts are small populations of species that managed surviving past eras of climate change in geographic "pockets" protecting them from the hardships of changing conditions (Zimmer, 2011). Human beings might become the next climate relicts. Lovelock (2009) in his book *"The vanishing face of Gaia: A final warning"* makes the case for human population surviving climate change of pockets such as some parts of Canada. Human beings might also have the ability to create man-made climate pockets.

While one might be concerned about the persistence of Earth as a whole, it should be highlighted that the planet is very likely to "survive". Without much doubt the living circumstances on Earth would be too hostile for humanity before the planet ceases to exist. Lovelock would argue that the planet will have healed itself. This reality is well-reflected in the very first definition of sustainable (Earth) development, which had been introduced above: A development that "(...) meets the needs of the present without compromising the ability of future generations to meet their own needs" (Brundtland, 1987, p. 24). Sustainable development aims at preserving the planet not primarily for the sake of itself, but for the sake of future generations of human beings to come.

The Economy-Society-Environment System

The issues and crises described are never potentially to be located completely in one of the three dimensions of society, environment, and economy. Eying closer, for instance, the poverty problem - people tend to see poverty as a purely social problem - one finds manifold interconnections also to environmental factors. On the one hand the root and very definition of poverty - the absence of wealth or money reveals the economic component of the issue.

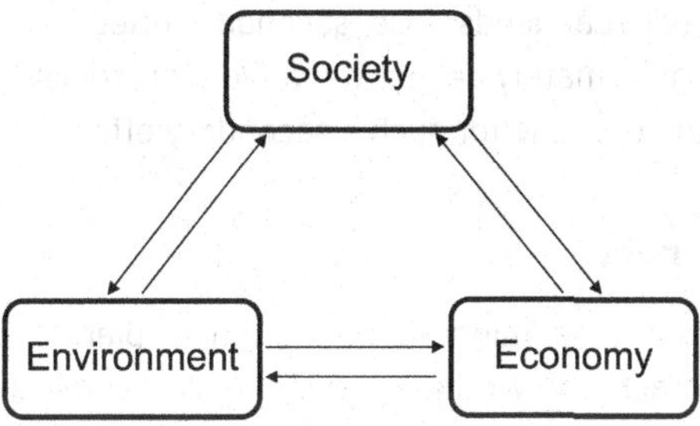

Figure 1.1 Global Interconnectedness of Economy, Society, and Environment.

This is why programs tackling poverty often have as many economic components such as micro-entrepreneurship, financial support, etc. as those programs also have social components, health, nutrition, and education. While the socio-economic link seems obvious, the link to the environmental dimension needs a little more explanation, while not being any less crucial. The World Bank (2001) in its document describing the organization's environmental strategy extensively illustrates the dynamics of environment and poverty. Deteriorating environmental conditions tend to negatively affect the poor over-proportionally strongly. The poorer population segments often earn their livelihoods in direct interaction with ecosystems, based on natural resources by working in fishery and agriculture. Environment is also an important health factor for poor communities. The number of people dying from diseases that could have been avoided with better environmental conditions equals the number of people dying from malnutrition. Often poor people are also more vulnerable to natural disasters such as droughts, hurricanes, and floods, which can often be related to causes related with environmental degradation. Figure 1.1 illustrates the ramifications of economy, society, and environment.

Cooking up diseases

Due to increased temperatures people are more likely to get sick. High temperatures cause an increase in parasites, bacteria, and viruses. The changing weather stimulates season-specific diseases to occur at any time of the year (Vanguardia, 2011).

Economy and Society

The relationship between economy and society is laden with conflicts, but also with enormous benefits for both sides. The economic system relies on society, people, as "human resources", an important input to its production activities. On the other hand, society is also the force fueling the economy by its purchasing power and peoples' role as consumers.

Then again economic activity has immense effects on society. Economic growth, if distributed equally and used wisely, leads to increased welfare and prosperity. The economy, single industries, or companies may also have negative effects on society. An example is the economic system's inherent tendency to fuel consumerism by massive marketing efforts. Criticism refers to often unnecessary consumption which creates artificial and often destructive wants, which distract from society's real needs. Also, secondary effects of economic activity on the natural environment often ultimately reflect negatively on society. The health effect of air pollution is one outstanding example for such a secondary effect.

Economy and Environment

Natural resources such as oil, ore, minerals, water, timber plants, and animals are the most basic inputs of economic activity. Whole bio-systems can serve as natural resource input such as in the case of eco-tourism. Without natural resources economic activity would have to stop. Throughout the history of modern economic activity, natural resources have been overused. An interesting example is the book *The Last Hours of Ancient Sunlight* (Hartman, 2001), which explains how the economic system is based on unsustainably using up "ancient sunlight" in the forms of fossil fuels such as coal and petroleum, which have been formed with the help of solar energy millions of years ago. Economic activity is increasingly shifting from non-renewable to renewable sources of energy and raw material. In 2006 Stern estimated the costs of switching to a low-carbon economy were estimated much lower (1–2% of the annual world GDP) than the costs caused by the consequences of sticking to the current CO_2 production patterns (5–20% of the annual world GDP) and further fueling climate change (Stern, 2008). More recently a study published in Nature Climate Change (Kikstra & Waidelich, 2023) takes a comprehensive approach to calculate the economically optimal emissions reductions and the resulting global temperature trajectories. It finds that the avoided damages from climate change mitigation are 1.5–3.9 times higher than the costs of mitigation. In other words, investing in climate solutions could save significantly in the long run from the effects of climate change.

On the other hand, the economy is exerting a strongly deteriorating influence on the world's natural environment. Not only using up natural resources, but also emissions and waste creation put stress on the world's ecosphere. It has been suggested that economic activity must not always have to result in a negative environmental impact. For instance, the movements of environmental entrepreneurship and natural capitalism aim at creating a basis for economic activity with added value for the environment (Lovins et al., 1999). Secondary effects of economy on the environment include the environmental impact of society's consumption of goods and services, produced by economic systems.

Society and Environment

Strictly speaking, the global human society is just one more species in the community of living things forming the world's biosphere. Nevertheless, the impact of society on the environment by far exceeds the impact of any other species that has ever lived on the planet. The reasons are both quantity and quality of human subsistence. Fueled by exploitative production methods and technological progress, the quantity of human beings living on Earth has by far exceeded the planet's biological carrying capacity. In 2007, it would have needed 1.5 Earths to sustainably provide the living ground for Earth's population in the long run. In 2023 that rose to 1.7 Earths (Earth Overshoot Day, 2022) seemingly on path to meet the WWF estimation that by 2050 this number will be up to two Earths (WWF, 2022). Behavior patterns harmful to the natural environment are also qualitatively unsustainable. In developed countries, the number of natural resources being used up to sustain those "developed societies" by far exceeds basic necessities. Developing countries, with their increasing middle-class follow suit in copying developed countries' unfortunate behavior patterns. Often environmental awareness, spirituality, and connection to living things get substituted by consumerist preferences.

Future consumption heavyweights

Due to their impressive quantitative growth, China and India are at the center of both economists' and sustainability scholars' attention. The qualitative development might even matter more than the mere population growth. For instance, India has increased its middle class over the last 15 years from 5 to 40% of the population; turning into the world's 5th largest consumer economy (Srivastava, 2023).

The natural environment provides manifold services to society. The Millennium Ecosystem Assessment (MA) (2005) provided an extensive overview on how human well-being depends on the integrity of biomes – the major types of ecosystems – that constitute the planet's ecosphere. Ecosystems influence human beings by providing a wide variety of different services; "**ecosystem services**". The following list illustrates the four main categories of ecosystem services and prominent examples for the services provided:

- **Provisioning services**: Provision of food, water, timber, fiber, etc.
- **Regulating services**: Regulated climate, floods, disease, wastes, water quality, etc.
- **Cultural services**: Influencing culture by providing recreational, aesthetic, and spiritual benefits, etc.
- **Supporting services**: The necessary support for the formerly mentioned three categories. Examples are soil formation, photosynthesis, nutrient cycling, etc.

The Millennium Ecosystem Assessment (MA) (2005) which had been conducted as early as 1987, estimated that the planet's 16 main ecosystems provide services with an average annual value of US$33 trillion to society and economy, while the global GDP was merely US$18 trillion (Costanza et al., 1997). In 2018 the WWF's Living Planet Index observed that nature underpins all economic activity worth an estimated US$125 trillion (Fleming, 2018). Comparing these facts, one easily comes to the solution that our society and the economic system providing the goods and services to satisfy society's need is highly inefficient. Another eye-opening interpretation of those numbers would be that eco-systems are providing more value to society than the economy does. A logical follow up question is: Why is society then supporting the growth of the economy and destroying the basis for the bigger value creation originating from the natural environment?

The probably most complete description of how "successful" we as humanity have been to destroy our own habitat comes from the thinking around "**planetary boundaries**" (Rockström et al., 2009). A multi-disciplinary team of scientists has outlined the "safe operating space for humanity" by looking at the critical values that our Earth system should not exceed for humanity to be able to live on Earth in the long run. These planetary boundaries were expressed in quantified thresholds. The following ten planetary boundaries were identified:

1. Climate change.
2. Rate of biodiversity loss.
3. Nitrogen cycle (part of a boundary with the phosphorus cycle).
4. Phosphorus cycle (part of a boundary with the nitrogen cycle).
5. Stratospheric ozone depletion.
6. Ocean acidification.
7. Global freshwater use.
8. Change in land use.
9. Atmospheric aerosol loading.
10. Chemical pollution.

While all boundaries were found to be narrowing rapidly, the most worrying ones were the first three for each of which the planetary boundary threshold has been exceeded dramatically. To quantify this situation, a safe planetary boundary was compared with the current value and with the value before the industrial revolution. For instance, the rate of biodiversity loss before the industrial revolution was 0 species per year. Whilst it is difficult to quantify the exact rate of biodiversity loss today due to the complex and multifaceted nature of the problem, The Living Planet Report by the World Wildlife Fund (WWF), which is published every two years provides an overview of global biodiversity and the health of the planet. The 2020 report showed that global populations of mammals, birds, fish, amphibians, and reptiles plunged by an average of 68% between 1970 and 2016, indicating a significant loss in biodiversity (WWF, 2022).

The Planet's Most Pressing Issues and Crises

As depicted in Table 1.1, many frameworks have been developed to describe, control, and solve the global social, environmental, and economic issues, and crises. The 17 UN Sustainable Development Goals (SDGs) are a set of 17 interconnected global goals designed to be a "blueprint to achieve a better and more sustainable future for all". Set in 2015 by the United Nations General Assembly and intended to be achieved by 2030, these goals are part of the 2030 Agenda for Sustainable Development. The SDGs built upon the United Nations Millennium Development Goals (MDGs) which described eight issues to be solved most urgently to erase poverty. Poverty is often seen a root-cause for many other global issues. Agenda 21 tackles the problems from a more generalized perspective, focusing on the necessary actions to ensure global sustainability (United Nations, 1993). The annually published World Development Indicators, established by the World Bank are divided up into People, Environment and Economy and deliver an extensive quantitative description of the State of the World (World Bank, 2023b).

A difficult fact about the issues and crises faced by the world is their highly complex structure. Aiming at economic, social, and environmental development separately or trying to

Table 1.1 Exemplary Global Development Frameworks

Framework	*Institution*	*Issues covered*
The Sustainable Development Goals (SDGs)	United Nations (ratified by all member states)	**Goal 1**: No Poverty **Goal 2**: Zero Hunger **Goal 3**: Good Health and Well-being **Goal 4**: Quality Education **Goal 5**: Gender Equality **Goal 6**: Clean Water and Sanitation **Goal 7**: Affordable and Clean Energy **Goal 8**: Decent Work and Economic Growth **Goal 9**: Industry, Innovation, and Infrastructure **Goal 10**: Reduced Inequality **Goal 11**: Sustainable Cities and Communities **Goal 12**: Responsible Consumption and Production **Goal 13**: Climate Action **Goal 14**: Life Below Water **Goal 15**: Life on Land **Goal 16**: Peace and Justice Strong Institutions **Goal 17**: Partnerships to achieve the Goal
Millennium development goals	United Nations (ratified by all member states)	**Goal 1**: Eradicate extreme poverty and hunger. **Goal 2**: Achieve universal primary education. **Goal 3**: Promote gender equality and empower women. **Goal 4**: Reduce child mortality rates. **Goal 5**: Improve maternal health. **Goal 6**: Combat HIV/AIDS, malaria, and other diseases **Goal 7**: Ensure environmental sustainability. **Goal 8**: Develop a global partnership for development
World development indicators	World Bank	**People**: e.g. wealth and consumption distribution, education, nutrition, health, labor **Environment**: e.g. agriculture, deforestation, biodiversity, air pollution, energy, water **Economy**: e.g. economic output, sectoral structure (manufacturing, commerce, services), consumption and investment, monetary indicators **States and markets**: e.g. business environment, stock market, tax policies, public services (military, transport, communication) **Global links**: e.g. trade, debt, commodities, financial flows, development aid, travel, and tourism
Agenda 21	United Nations	**Section I**: Social and Economic Dimensions **Section II**: Conservation and Management of Resources for Development **Section III**: Strengthening the Role of Major Groups **Section IV**: Means of Implementation

solve one issue at a time, in an isolated fashion is an easy mistake. The complex structure of the world's mega-issues can be summarized in five crucial characteristics:

- **Interlinked:** Issues are mutually interlinked and reinforcing.
- **Systemic:** Issues are not isolated phenomena, but rather based on systemic flaws in the relationship between business, society and environment.
- **Global:** Issues cannot be isolated locally but are global in both impact and potential solutions.
- **Resilient:** Issues have been threatening and known for a considerable amount of time but remained strong in spite of considerable solution efforts.
- **Convergent:** Joint issues development appears to move towards a planetary mega-crisis; a "show down".

The Brundtland Report by the World Commission on Environment and Development already in 1989 aimed to create awareness for the unique threatening structure of the global issues. The term used was "interlocked crises":

> ...the various global 'crises' that have seized public concern, particularly over the past decade. These are not separate crises: and environmental crises, a development crisis, an energy crisis: they are all one.
>
> (Brundtland, 1987, p. 17)

The CIA world factbook 2024 describes the global issues accurately. Under the "environment section" the world factbook notes that:

> large areas subject to overpopulation, industrial disasters, pollution (air, water, acid rain, toxic substances), loss of vegetation (overgrazing, deforestation, desertification), loss of biodiversity; soil degradation, soil depletion, erosion; ozone layer depletion; waste disposal; global warming becoming a greater concern.
>
> (CIA, 2024)

To achieve holistic, sustainable development it is of crucial importance to understand the main global issues and their mutual interconnectedness. Some of the most critical global issues and crises are described in the appendix of this chapter and summarized in the following Figure 1.2. Of course, such a summary can only provide a basic (and inevitably fragmentary) working knowledge of the most important challenges faced by humanity. Each topic

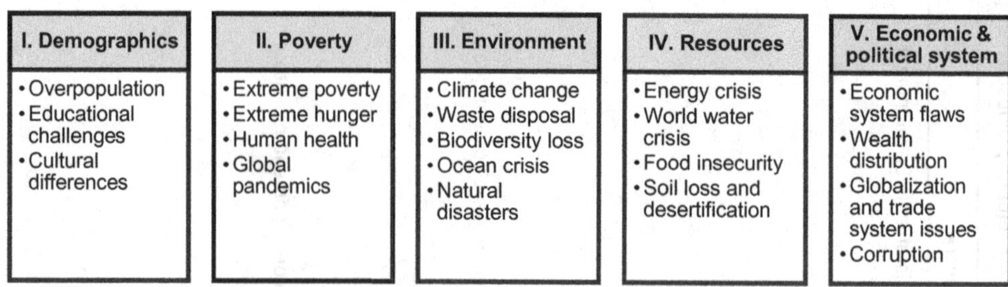

I. Demographics
• Overpopulation
• Educational challenges
• Cultural differences
II. Poverty
• Extreme poverty
• Extreme hunger
• Human health
• Global pandemics
III. Environment
• Climate change
• Waste disposal
• Biodiversity loss
• Ocean crisis
• Natural disasters
IV. Resources
• Energy crisis
• World water crisis
• Food insecurity
• Soil loss and desertification
V. Economic & political system
• Economic system flaws
• Wealth distribution
• Globalization and trade system issues
• Corruption

Figure 1.2 Planetary Mega Issues Overview.

constitutes an extensive domain of specialized knowledge to be acquired by managers aiming at contributing to mitigation and solution of the respective issue to be addressed by responsible business conduct.

Exercises

A. KNOW

Use the below multiple-choice questions to test your knowledge. Each answer may be wrong or right and there may be zero to four right or wrong answers per question:

1. Responsible business...
   a. ...aims at a positive fit, a situation achieving positive social and environmental impact. If necessary for achieving this positive impact, businesses should even accept to become unprofitable.
   b. ...is related to terms such as corporate citizenship and business ethics.
   c. ...is aimed at contributing to sustainable development.
   d. ...aims at managing the relationship between business, society, and environment.
2. The figure and explanation illustrating the mutual relationship between society, environment, and economy...
   a. ...describes how economy uses natural resources for the production of goods in the intersection between environment and society.
   b. ...is related to the three main dimensions of sustainable development.
   c. ...covers the human footprint on Earth in the relationship between society and environment.
   d. ...in one subsection describes so-called ecosystem services. This economic sector aims at providing services to improve the world's ecosystems.
3. The world's most severe issues and crises threatening life on planet Earth...
   a. ...are described in many frameworks such as the Sustainable Development Goals (SDGs), Millennium Development Goals (MDG) and the World Development Indicators (WDI).
   b. ...should be solved one-by-one.
   c. ...include poverty as one of the typical resource issues.
   d. ...include the fact that 1.1 billion people worldwide lack access to electricity.
4. The Gaia Hypothesis...
   a. ...considers Earth as an imbalanced mother system of environmental, social and economic subsystems.
   b. ...blames missing governmental interventions as the main problem for the Gaia phenomenon to occur.
   c. ...was developed by the ancient Greek philosopher Plato. He referred to Gaia, the ancient Greek Earth-goddess.
   d. ...has been proven wrong.

B. THINK

Look at the table in the appendix of this chapter which illustrates a set of planetary mega-issues in depth. Imagine a (feasible) scenario, a possible chain of events, where issues interact in a way that immediately threatens the survival of humanity on planet Earth.

C. DO

Think about one small thing you could do to stop being part of the problem and start being part of the solution to one of the planetary mega-issues. Then do it!

D. RELATE

Have a conversation with someone on one of the issues illustrated in the table in the appendix of this chapter which illustrates a set of planetary mega-issues in depth. Try to find out together what should be done to solve the issue focused. Document the position of your conversation partner(s).

E. BE

Watch a movie on the state of the planet such as the *11th Hour*, *An Inconvenient Truth*, *Before the Flood*, *A Life on Our Planet*, or similar. Write a short essay on how what you see relates to you and how it makes you feel.

Feedback

A. KNOW

Question 1

a. Right: Positive fit aims at achieving a positive social, environmental and economic system impact while being profitable. However, there may be companies that can never achieve such a positive fit, due to the underlying nature of their business.
b. Right: Those terms are important background theories of responsible business.
c. Right: The ultimate purpose of responsible business as framed in the context of this book is to contribute to sustainable development by becoming a sustainable business.
d. Right: The paragraph describing responsible business mentions it as having the business-society-environment relationship at its heart.

Question 2

a. Right: The Gaia hypothesis describes Earth as a sick mother system or organism.
b. Wrong: The Gaia hypothesis blames human society in general.
c. Wrong: The word Gaia as a matter of fact is ancient Greek, but Plato was not involved in the development of the hypothesis referring to the sickening planet. The Gaia hypothesis was developed by the scientists Lovelock and Margulis in the mid-1960s.
d. Wrong: The Gaia hypothesis has been developed by the scientists Lovelock and Margulis in the mid-1960s, during the modern period.

Question 3

a. Right: MDG and WDI are frameworks for the description of the worldwide issues and crises.
b. Wrong: Due to their interlinked structure, those issues and crises cannot be solved one-by-one.
c. Wrong: In the table describing the worldwide mega-issues and crises, poverty has been subsumed under "poverty issues".
d. Wrong: In the table section on the "future energy crisis" a similar (but different) figure of 1.5 billion people is mentioned. The figure of 1.1 billion people has not been mentioned and therefore is wrong.

Question 4

a. Right: The Gaia hypothesis describes Earth as a sick mother system or organism.
b. Wrong: The Gaia hypothesis blames human society in general.
c. Wrong: The word Gaia as a matter of fact is ancient Greek, but Plato was not involved in the development of the hypothesis referring to the sickening planet. The Gaia hypothesis was developed by the scientists Lovelock and Margulis in the mid-1960s.
d. Wrong: The Gaia hypothesis has not been proven wrong, but contested and complemented by other systemic approaches to the Earth system.

B. THINK

Level	*Anticipatory thinking*	*Notes*
+	Feasible scenario of multiple issues described that in its description reveals a profound level of anticipatory thinking.	
=	Feasible scenario involving multiple issues.	
–	No scenario of interacting issues has been developed, or the scenario is not feasible, either in terms of its threat-evoking mechanisms, or in in terms of its potential to wipe out humanity.	

C. DO

Level	*Taking initiative*	*Notes*
+	Initiative taken which is highly relevant to the mitigation of the issue. "If everyone would do this, the issue would be solved".	
=	Initiative taken, but it is not very relevant to the issue chosen.	
–	No initiative taken.	

D. RELATE

Level	*Collaborative problem solving*	*Notes*
+	A solution has been developed based on a process that involves meaningful input from both conversation partners.	
=	A solution has been developed, but it is mainly based on one dominant person's input.	
–	Conversation has not happened or no solution idea to the problem has been reached.	

E. BE

Level	*Emotional awareness*	*Notes*
+	Profound description of one's emotions regarding the state of the planet.	
=	Basic awareness of one's emotions regarding the state of the planet.	
–	No or little insight into own emotions regarding the state of the planet.	

Appendix: Planetary Mega-Issues

I. Demographic issues	
Overpopulation According to the OECD, "overpopulation refers to the exceeding of certain threshold limits of population density when environmental resources fail to meet the requirements of individual organisms regarding shelter, nutrition and so forth" (OECD, 2001).	Keeping up with the headcount All 8 billion of us should be included in the Guinness Book of World Records. In the 19th century world population reached the first billion; it took 130 more years to grow to 2 billion. The United Nations projects continued population increase but at a slowing rate, with estimates of reaching around 9 to 10 billion by 2050 (UNDESA, 2022). More people, less GDP per square kilometer The world population fits in a 410,000 square kilometer surface standing shoulder-to-shoulder. Many countries have both population and economic issues. In 2008 the less developed countries held 68 inhabitants per square kilometer with a GNI per Capita of US$5,150. Baby packages are landing in the wrong address Most fully developed countries, which are likely to provide a decent life to a child, are declining in fertility: In 2022, 143 million births per year were recorded, the majority of which were in less developed regions of the world (UNDESA, 2022).
Educational challenges ~ include a lack of education on manifold levels, most alarming is illiteracy, a problem mainly rooted in insufficient attendance at primary school level.	Increased, but still insufficient primary education Global progress towards universal primary education, as part of Sustainable Development Goal 4 (SDG 4), has faced significant challenges. As of 2023, UNESCO data indicates that the number of out-of-school children has increased by 6 million since 2021, totaling 250 million globally. The rise in out-of-school children is partly attributed to the exclusion of girls and young women from education in Afghanistan, contributing to global education stagnation (UNESCO, 2023a). School bells stop ringing too soon Globally, 16% of children and youth (covering primary to upper secondary) are not attending school. At primary level, one out of ten children worldwide are not in school. 122 million, or 48% of the out-of-school population are girls and young women. Sub-Saharan Africa accounts for close to 30% of all out-of-school children globally. One out of five African children are not attending school (19.7%). Only half of children attend upper secondary school (UNESCO, 2023b).
Cultural and ethnic issues ~ may be seen as a direct consequence of xenophobia, a psychological condition that results in a group of people trying to oppose everything or everyone that seems different from them.	Displaced by conflict More than 114 million people worldwide have been forced to flee their homes by the end of 2023, due to conflict, persecution and human rights violations according to the UN refugee agency UNHCR (United Nations, 2023). A country hungry and homeless Due to political instability, violent conflict and disastrous drought, Somalia is facing the biggest displacement of their people ever. Two in five children under five suffer from acute malnutrition. Some 3.8 million people are internally displaced, and a cholera outbreak is spreading in several areas (United Nations, 2024). 2010, the year of record discrimination According to the Equal Employment Opportunity Commission (EEOC), 2010 displayed the highest record of discrimination charges since 1997: A total amount of 99,922 charges was registered by the Office of Research, against the 95,402 in 2008, the last record year. Charges on race, sex, national origin, religion, and disability reached new top levels in 2010 (EEOC, 2011).

(Continued)

II. Poverty issues	
Extreme poverty ~ is defined by the World Bank in terms of purchasing power, as a daily income lower than US$2.15 per person (World Bank, 2022).	Less, but still overwhelming poverty After several decades of continuous global poverty reduction, a period of significant crises and shocks resulted in around three years of lost progress between 2020–2022. As of 2023 almost 700 million people around the world live in extreme poverty subsisting on less than US$2.15 per day, the extreme poverty line. Just over half of these people live in Sub-Saharan Africa (World Bank, 2023a). "Multidimensional poverty" Poverty does not only result in a lack of food or incomplete domestic services. Many other living conditions such as the education level can determine poverty- the term is "multidimensional poverty": Approximately 1.1 billion people experience such "multidimensional poverty" (UNDP and OPHI, 2023).
Extreme hunger ~also known as "chronic hunger" ~ is defined by a regular food intake that provides less than the essential energy requirement of 1800 kcal per day (FAO, 2011).	Famine is not declining Between 691 and 783 million people were facing hunger in 2022, reflecting an increase of 122 million since 2019, and nearly 670 million people are projected to still be facing hunger by 2030, signaling a significant setback in the global fight against hunger (World Health Organization, 2023a). Is agriculture the solution? Countries in protracted crises, dealing with long-term issues such as conflict or natural disasters, are particularly affected, housing around 20% of the world's undernourished population. Despite the critical role of agriculture in these countries, only about 3 to 4% of development and humanitarian assistance funds are allocated to this sector (World Health Organization, 2023a). Is repeated famine a systemic local problem? Regions such as the Horn of Africa, including Somalia, South Sudan, Yemen, and parts of Central America are facing systemic problems with repeated famines, exacerbated by conflict, climate change, and economic crises, with millions at risk of starvation and urgent humanitarian aid needed (World Food Programme, 2023).
Human health issues Human health according to the World Health Organization (WHO) is a state of complete physical, mental, and social well-being and not merely the absence of disease or infirmity.	Toxic air Air pollution continues to be a significant global health risk, contributing to an estimated 7 million premature deaths annually from both outdoor and household pollution (World Health Organization, 2023b). Nutrition is an issue in both developed and developing countries. nearly 39 million children under the age of 5 were overweight in 2020, a problem that is rising in low- and middle-income countries, while over 340 million children and adolescents aged 5–19 were overweight or obese in 2016. Concurrently, acute undernutrition, as indicated by wasting and severe wasting, affected 45.4 million children under 5 in 2020, signifying that malnutrition in various forms remains a global challenge for child health (UNICEF et al., 2023). Cancer, often a prevention problem Cancer caused nearly 10 million deaths in 2020 and by 2022 there were an estimated 20 million new cases and 9.7 million deaths. The global cancer burden is expected to rise by 77% by 2050, with prevention efforts and access to care remaining unequally distributed worldwide with the poorest least likely to seek treatment (World Heath Organization, 2022).

(*Continued*)

Global Pandemics

WHO defines a pandemic as a human disease that is new to a population, causes serious illness, and spreads easily and sustainably on a more than regional level (Seah, 2009).

New HIV/AIDS infections are declining; old infections still wreak havoc

By the end of 2022, approximately 39 million people were living with HIV globally, with 1.3 million new infections and 630,000 AIDS-related deaths in that year. Antiretroviral therapy was accessed by 29.8 million people, showing significant progress in treatment coverage since 2009. However, the majority of the global HIV burden is borne by the African region, with nearly two-thirds of all people living with HIV worldwide residing there (UNAIDS, 2023).

"Zoonosis" and poverty

The transmission of infectious diseases from animals to humans, known as zoonosis, continues to pose significant global health threats, with recent crises such as the COVID-19 pandemic and monkeypox outbreak underscoring this issue. Factors contributing to the spread of zoonotic diseases include environmental encroachment, climate change, and global connectivity, all of which create conditions that facilitate the spillover of pathogens from animals to humans (IAEA, 2022).

Are we creating a global pandemic incubator?

Species overpopulation, also of the human species is naturally controlled by diseases. Especially high-density population and environmental degradation favor the development of pandemic diseases (Pimentel et al., 1998). Both factors are defining characteristics of contemporary world development.

III: Environmental threats and degradation

Climate change

~ describes changes in the Earth's surface temperature and the related atmospheric phenomena. The term covers both global warming and global cooling. The recent debate focuses on global warming attributed to human production of greenhouse gases (GHGs).

Measuring CO_2 emissions

Global CO_2 emissions have continued to increase, reaching 36.8 gigatons in 2022, with an uptick of 1.1% in 2023. However, projections suggest a potential peak and subsequent decline by 2025, influenced by an upsurge in renewable energy, electrification of transportation, and extensive net-zero commitments by countries covering around 80% of emission. Despite this there remains a considerable decarbonization gap that needs to be closed to meet the 1.5° Celsius pathway outlined in international climate targets (Nivard et al., 2024).

Ecosystem overload!

By 2030, it is projected that humanity's demand on natural resources may require the ecological capacity equivalent to two Earths, reflecting a significant ecological deficit where consumption exceeds the planet's capacity to regenerate resources (Global Footprint Network, 2023).

Trees could be part of the solution but have become a problem.

Global forest loss in 2022 was 22.8 million hectares, with significant primary forest loss occurring in the Amazonas region of Brazil and reaching record highs in countries like Ghana and Bolivia. Indonesia, however, has seen a continued decrease in primary forest loss due to aggressive conservation strategies (FAO, 2022).

(Continued)

Waste disposal	
The European Commission defines waste as any substance or object which the holder discards, intends to or is required to discard (Chalmin & Gaillochet, 2009).	Where did all the waste go? Global waste production is projected to increase to 3.40 billion tones by 2050, doubling alongside population growth. Currently, about 33% of waste is not safely managed, with low-income countries collecting less than half of their waste. Waste-related emissions could rise to 2.38 billion tons of CO_2-equivalent by 2050 without sector improvements (World Bank, 2024)."North-south waste equality"? The disparity in waste production between high-income and low-income countries has widened in recent years due to varying consumption patterns. While high-income countries generate a disproportionately higher amount of waste per capita, the aggregate waste production in low-income countries has increased with their population growth. The global challenge remains to manage waste effectively, particularly in low-income countries where collection and recycling rates lag significantly behind those of high-income countries (World Bank, 2024). Toxic tech-toys Global e-waste is surging, with volumes projected to reach 74.7 million metric tons by 2030, with less than 20% currently being recycled properly. Electronic devices, including computers and monitors, are significant contributors to this waste, often containing hazardous substances like lead, which pose environmental and health risks if not managed responsibly (World Health Organization, 2023c).
Biodiversity loss	
Is a synonym for the degradation of the planet's natural environment reflected in the decrease of the number of species living in the planetary ecosystem (Vaughan et al., 2010).	Recently lost species Amphibians are the most threatened vertebrate class, with 40.7% of species globally threatened. There is an urgent need for conservation efforts to address emerging threats like climate change and protect these endangered species, especially in regions with high concentrations of threatened amphibians (Luedtke et al., 2023). Scaling ecosystem conservation By 2020, the number of protected ecosystems had expanded to encompass approximately 150,000 designated sites globally, a substantial increase from 2009–2010, when 67,000 protected areas were recorded, covering 12.7% of the world's land area and 7.2% of coastal waters (UNEP, 2021). Who is looking after the seas? As of 2022, legal environmental protection for water zones remains insufficient, with only 3.5% of exclusive economic zones and less than 1.5% of the total ocean area designated as protected areas, contributing to a 35% decline in freshwater species and a 25% decline in marine species, compared to a 24% loss among terrestrial species between 1970 and 2007 (UNESCO, 2023a).
Ocean crisis	
The term ~ describes the rapid degradation of the accelerated pollution and overfishing threatens to alter the natural conditions of oceans to a degree threatening the whole planetary ecosystem.	Floating graves Global dead zones with dangerously low oxygen levels, caused by fertilizer overuse, have continued to expand. In 2010, the Gulf of Mexico alone had around 7,776 square miles of dead zones, while the Baltic Sea developed a vast 145,000-square-mile dead area by 2022, indicating a persistent and concerning environmental issue (NOAA, 2022). Acid oceans – dead corals – destroyed ecosystems. Since the 19th century, the oceans have absorbed approximately one-third of human-emitted carbon dioxide, leading to a 30% drop in ocean pH levels over 170 years. This ocean acidification poses a severe threat to shell-building organisms, with coral reefs expected to face catastrophic decline by 2100, endangering marine ecosystems (Gattuso et al., 2018).

(Continued)

	Gloom and doom in fishery. According to a book released in 2010 by Daniel Pauly, a fisheries biologist at the University of British Columbia, the world's fish catch is prone to diminish by 20 to 30% by 2050 (Zimmer, 2011).
Natural disasters The World Bank defines "disaster" as a serious disruption of the functioning of a community or a society causing widespread human, material, economic or environmental losses that exceed the ability of the affected community or society to cope using its own resources (Parker, 2006).	Disastrous times In 2023, the human cost of natural disasters reached its highest since 2010, with over 62,000 lives lost, primarily due to a catastrophic earthquake in Turkey and Syria. Economic losses from such disasters also rose to US$380 billion, with a record number of 37 billion-dollar insured events signaling an increase in the frequency and intensity of medium-sized natural catastrophes (UNDRR, 2024). Building up natural disaster potential The frequency and intensity of natural disasters have surged, with a five-fold increase in climate-related events over the past 50 years, disproportionately affecting poorer countries. Advancements in early warning systems have reduced mortality, despite the rising economic costs, which have increased sevenfold since the 1970s. From 2000 to 2019, there were 7,348 major natural disasters, a significant rise from the 4,212 recorded between 1980 and 1999, with the latter period seeing a notable escalation in extreme weather events like floods and storms (United Nations, 2021). Disasters: Increasingly costly Natural disaster economic losses have risen sharply, with current figures indicating a sevenfold increase since the 1970s. The 2011 earthquake in Japan exemplifies this trend, causing losses equal to 3% of Japan's GDP (Our World in Data, 2023).
IV. Resource issues **Energy crisis** The ~ describes the problems being caused by energy scarcity and the various issues related to the world's energy supply from fossil fuel dependence to the dangers of nuclear energy.	Neither enlightened nor illuminated 200 years after the invention of the electric light bulb, illumination is far from having reached everybody's home. As of 2022, an estimated 771 million people still lack access to electricity, according to the International Energy Agency (IEA). This number rose in 2022 for the first time in decades due to the pandemic and global energy crisis (IEA, 2022a). The emission heavy-weight champion Although progress has been made, the energy sector still dominates global emissions at 75% in 2020, primarily driven by fossil fuels. This necessitates a significant acceleration in emission reductions to achieve net-zero by 2050 (IEA, 2022b). Could you cut down your personal energy consumption by 60%? The IEA suggests a reduction of energy consumption to a yearly level of 100 kWh per person. This means reducing global energy intensity by 40% by 2030. However, we may need to exceed this target due to increasing energy demands in developing countries (IEA, 2022b).
World water crisis The ~ is constituted by both problems in access to clean water and severe problems in managing excess and lack of water in floods and droughts.	"Virtual water" stress A study by the World Wildlife Fund (WWF) revealed that 71 countries were experiencing stress on their water resources due to the water consumption of so-called blue water through economic activities (WRI, 2023). Blue water is one type of so-called "virtual water", water being used throughout the production process, but not included in the final product. Blue water consumption remains a major contributor, with agriculture as the leading culprit in many regions.

(Continued)

	Water scarcity becomes omnipresent A 2005 study considered nine world regions and their water consumption. At that time, western Asia (166%) and North Africa (92%) had by far exceeded the "sustainable limits" of 70 of freshwater extraction. Southern (58%) and Central Asia (56%) along with the Caucasus (56%) were extremely close to reach the "water scarcity is approaching" level of 60% freshwater extraction Rural populations are more threatened In 2010 an estimated 141 million urbanities and 243 million rural dwellers continued to rely on unimproved sources for their daily drinking water needs (United Nations, 2011).
Food insecurity According to the FAO, food insecurity "exists when people lack access to enough safe and nutritious food, and therefore they are not consuming enough for an active and healthy life (FAO, 2011).	More people + less food =? There is a growing fear on how to feed the estimated world population of 9 billion people in 2050. According to the United Nations, up to 25% of the world food production may become "lost" by then as a result of climate change, water scarcity, invasive pests and land degradation (IPCC, 2022). Food-hunger-poverty dynamics It is impossible to analyze the topics of food prices, hunger, and poverty independently. The surge in food prices in 2008 resulted in a 50–200% increase in selected commodity prices, and drove 110 million people into poverty, adding 44 million to the group of world-wide undernourished (UNEP, 2009). Competing priorities; ecosystem vs. food A significant portion of all endangered birds and mammals face critical threats from unsustainable land use and agricultural expansion. These practices lead to habitat loss, fragmentation, and degradation, which are primary drivers of biodiversity decline.
Soil loss and desertification ~ are phenomena of a continued land degradation that due to among others climate change, unsustainable agriculture, and poor management of water resources (UNCCD, 2010).	The world-wide desertification trends. The period from 2010 to 2020 was declared the "UN Decade for Deserts and the Fight against Desertification". In the beginning of the 21st century, annually approximately 12 million hectares of land were lost, along with the possibility to produce 20 million tons of grain on those areas (UNCCD, 2010). Displaced by desert In 2005 the term "climate refugee" took importance when an official UN source declared that 50 million people would be displaced and homeless in 2010 due to extreme environmental conditions. In 2010 land degradation of dry land was recorded to affect 3.6 billion hectares around the world, an equivalent of 25% of the terrestrial surface. This environmental development jeopardizes the lives of at least 1 billion people in 100 countries (UNCCD, 2010). China's new deserts Some of the main reasons for increasing desertification are over-grazing and population pressure: By the end of the 20th century desertification in China had become more than alarming. Annually 1,400 square miles became deserts and some 24,000 villages in the north of the country have been abandoned giving way to drifting sand (Vidal, 2010).

(*Continued*)

V. Economic and political system issues	
Economic system flaws ~ in the context of this book are characteristics of the economic system impeding sustainable global development.	Infinite growth in a finite world. Doesn't this sound odd? Growth has always been and still is the main paradigm of the world economic system. Growth is omnipresent, such as GDP growth, revenue growth, and consumption growth. For instance, in 2010 the industrial production growth rate was an estimated 5.5%, world GDP grew by 4.9%. One indisputable fact is "raining on the parade" of the infinite growth paradigm. The economic system is embedded in a finite world of natural resources that had already reached its sustainable resource limits in 1975 when humanity's environmental footprint reached its sustainable limits. Currently we are using up 1.5 times the Earth's resources. It is only a matter of time until resources come to an end if we follow the current economic growth pattern (WWF International, 2020). The economy may voluntarily go into a maintenance or even a degrowth pattern or will be forced into degrowth by resource scarcity. Ignoring the true costs of economic activity What would happen if the average car would cost US$40,000 more than it does currently? This would be the estimated mark-up that has to be paid if the true cost (including social and environmental costs) of a car is considered. Demand would decrease drastically and so would car-usage-related pollution. True cost economics aims at including the external effects into prices (Halton, 2006). If including only the emissions of CO_2 into the cost accounting of the Standard & Poor's 500 companies, those corporations would incur an additional cost of 60 to US$93 billion per year; this is only the cost of emitting carbon (Serchuk, 2009). Those true costs are largely ignored in capitalist activity and neo-liberal economics. Petroleum addiction Historically, our reliance on fossil fuels has been staggering. A commonly cited figure illustrates that in the early 2000s, a single day's petroleum consumption could represent what took thousands of days to accumulate through natural processes. While petroleum remains crucial, the transition to a sustainable energy system requires rapidly shifting from fossil fuels towards renewable sources and enhanced energy efficiency.
Wealth inequalities ~ describe the difference in wealth between the poor and the rich on a national, regional, and international level.	Skewed wealth distribution According to the 2022 World Inequality Report, the top 10% of the global population owned around 76% of total wealth in 2021, while the bottom 50% held a mere 2% (Chancel et al., 2021). A whole continent left behind Africa continues to face significant wealth inequality challenges. According to the 2022 World Inequality Report, the top 10% of individuals in sub-Saharan Africa held 55% of total wealth (Chancel et al., 2021). Moreover, of the 35 countries currently classified as having "Low Human Development" on the Human Development Index (HDI), 33 are in Africa. This highlights the interconnectedness of economic inequality and broader development concerns within the continent (UNDP, 2022). Inequality even among the richest of the rich Reports continue to highlight the vast concentration of wealth within the highest financial echelons. While precise figures and definitions might vary across studies, recent data indicate that a small percentage of Ultra-High Net Worth Individuals (UHNWIs) control a disproportionate share of global wealth. For example, a 2023 report by Knight Frank found that UHNWIs (those with at least $30 million in investable assets) represented just 0.003% of the global population yet held around 13% of total global wealth (Harley, 2023).

(*Continued*)

Globalization and trade system issues	
~ describe systemic flaws in the global economic networks causing social and environmental issue and crises.	Global wage inequalities The 2010 Global Salary & Opinion Survey revealed that Chinese engineers receive, including bonus, overtime, etc., no more than 16% of the total amount salaried in the US. While annual payment in US amounts to US$107,300 for engineering jobs. Somebody in China doing the same work will on an average receive US$16,900 (EET, 2010). Illicit trade in hard times? The World Economic Forum declared in 2011 that illicit trade around the world reflected an overall value $1.3 trillion. At the same time, world GDP reached a 3% bottom; the lowest in the first decade of 21st century (World Economic Forum, 2011). Outsourcing – production and pollution Substituting domestic production by overseas labor, primarily in less developed countries, is one of the main pillars of international trade and globalization. While such behavior often makes profound money sense, the effect on global sustainability is questionable. Offshoring to and increased imports from developing countries have been accused of increasing CO_2 emissions by outsourcing activities to countries with lower environmental standards and by the increased need for CO_2-intensive transport activities (Black, 2005). Among many pieces of evidence for this mechanism, one is that between 1990 to 2008 emissions from most economically developed countries stabilized, while emissions from developing countries doubled. This development is suggested to be to a significant part due to an increase in imports from developing countries (Peters et al., 2011).
Corruption	
~ "any behavior in relation to persons entrusted with responsibilities in the public or private sector which violates their duties that follow from their status and is aimed at obtaining undue advantages of any kind for themselves or for others" (Council of Europe, 1995).	Bribery as export catalyst? At least US$0.1 billion per OECD member country was earned with the support of bribery in 2010. The OECD reported that among its 34 members and 4 additional parties a total amount of US$63.94 billion was exported with the support of bribery (OECD, 2011). Overwhelming world corruption The Corruption Perceptions Index 2010 included 178 countries. Nearly three quarters scored below 5 (on a scale from 0 to 10, 0 being the highest corruption level). Only 45 out of 178 countries were ranked above 5. No country received a perfect grade. Denmark, New Zealand, and Singapore achieved the high score of 9.3. Somalia ranked last with 1.1 (Transparency International, 2010). Lobbying = legal corruption? Lobbying activities, as an institutionalized form of corporate influence on political processes and decisions, is legal in most countries (Kaufmann & Vicente, 2005). For instance, in the USA the overall annual spending on lobbying has increased annually from an initial of US$1.44 billion in 1998 to US$ 3.51 billion in 2010 (Center for Responsive Politics, 2011).

References

Black, R. (2005). BBC NEWS. *BBC*. https://news.bbc.co.uk/2/hi/science/nature/4542104.stm

Brundtland, G. (1987). *Report of the World Commission on Environment and Development: Our Common Future* (A/42/427.). United Nations General Assembly.

Center for Responsive Politics. (2011). *Lobbying database*. Lobbying Database. https://www.opensecrets.org/lobby/

Chalmin, P., & Gaillochet, C. (2009). *From waste to resource: An abstract of the world waste survey 2009*. from veolia-environmentalservices.com: https://www.veolia-environmentalservices.com/veolia/ressources/files/1/927,753,abstract_2009_gb-1.pdf. veolia-environmentalservices.com

Chancel, L., Piketty, T., Saez, E., & Zucman, G. (2021). *The World Inequality Report*. World Inequality Lab. https://wir2022.wid.world/

CIA. (2024). *The world factbook*. Cia.org. https://www.cia.gov/the-world-factbook/countries/world/#environment

Costanza, R., d'Arge, R., de Groot, R., Farber, S., Grasso, M., Hannon, B., Limburg, K., Naeem, S., O'Neill, R. V., Paruelo, J., Raskin, R. G., Sutton, P., & van den Belt, M. (1997). The value of the world's ecosystem services and natural capital. *Nature*, *387*(6630), 253–260.

Council of Europe. (1995). *Programme of action against corruption*. Group of States against Corruption. https://www.coe.int/t/dghl/monitoring/greco/general/GMC96

Earth Overshoot Day. (2022, May 13). *Earth Overshoot Day home – #MoveTheDate*. Earth Overshoot Day. https://www.overshootday.org/

EEOC. (2011). *Charge statistics FY 1997 through FY 2022*. US EEOC. https://www.eeoc.gov/eeoc/statistics/enforcement/charges.cfm

EET. (2010). *2010 global salary and opinion survey*. https://pages.nxtbook.com/nxtbooks/cmp/eetimes112910/offline/cmp_eetimes112910.pdf

FAO. (2011). *Basic definitions: FAO*. https://www.fao.org/hunger/basic-definitions/en/

FAO. (2022). *The state of the world's forests 2022: Forest pathways for green recovery and building inclusive, resilient and sustainable economies*. Food & Agriculture Organization of the United Nations (FAO).

Fleming, S. (2018, October 30). *How much is nature worth? $125 trillion, according to this report*. World Economic Forum. https://www.weforum.org/agenda/2018/10/this-is-why-putting-a-price-on-the-value-of-nature-could-help-the-environment/

Gattuso, J.-P., Magnan, A. K., Bopp, L., Cheung, W. W. L., Duarte, C. M., Hinkel, J., Mcleod, E., Micheli, F., Oschlies, A., Williamson, P., Billé, R., Chalastani, V. I., Gates, R. D., Irisson, J.-O., Middelburg, J. J., Pörtner, H.-O., & Rau, G. H. (2018). Ocean solutions to address climate change and its effects on marine ecosystems. *Frontiers in Marine Science*, *5*. https://doi.org/10.3389/fmars.2018.00337

Global Footprint Network. (2023). *Ecological Footprint©*. Global Footprint Network. https://www.footprintnetwork.org/our-work/ecological-footprint/

Halton, C. (2006, June 14). *True cost economics: What it is and how it works*. Investopedia. https://www.investopedia.com/terms/t/truecosteconomics.asp

Harley, F. (2023). *The Wealth Report 2023*. Knight Frank. https://content.knightfrank.com/research/83/documents/en/the-wealth-report-wealth-populations-10198.pdf

Hartman, T. (2001). *The last hours of ancient sunlight: Waking up to personal and global transformation*. Hodder & Stoughton.

IAEA. (2022). *Zoonotic Disease Integrated Action (ZODIAC): Current status and future direction*. International Atomic Energy Agency. https://www.iaea.org/newscenter/news/zoonotic-disease-integrated-action-zodiac-current-status-and-future-direction

IEA. (2022a). *Access to electricity – SDG7: Data and Projections – Analysis*. IEA. https://www.iea.org/reports/sdg7-data-and-projections/access-to-electricity

IEA. (2022b). *World energy outlook 2022* (World Energy Outlook). OECD. https://doi.org/10.1787/3a469970-en

Interface. (2019). *Lessons for the future: The Interface guide to changing your business to change the world*. Interface. https://www.interface.com/content/dam/interfaceinc/interface/sustainability/emea/25th-anniversary-report/Interface_MissionZeroCel_Booklet_EN.pdf

IPCC. (2022). *Climate change 2022: Impacts, adaptation and vulnerability*. https://www.ipcc.ch/report/ar6/wg2/

Kaufmann, D., & Vicente, P. (2005). Legal corruption. *MPRA paper*. https://ideas.repec.org//p/pra/mprapa/8186.html

Kikstra, J. S., & Waidelich, P. (2023). Strong climate action is worth it. *Nature Climate Change*, *13*(5), 419–420.

Lovelock, J. (2009). *The vanishing face of Gaia: A final warning*. Basic Books.

Lovelock, J. E. (1979). *Gaia*. Oxford University Press.

Lovelock, James. (2006). *The revenge of Gaia*. Allen Lane.

Lovins, A. B., Lovins, L. H., & Hawken, P. (1999). A road map for natural capitalism. *Harvard Business Review, 77*(3), 145–158, 211.

Luedtke, J. A., Chanson, J., Neam, K., Hobin, L., Maciel, A. O., Catenazzi, A., Borzée, A., Hamidy, A., Aowphol, A., Jean, A., Sosa-Bartuano, Á., Fong G. A., de Silva, A., Fouquet, A., Angulo, A., Kidov, A. A., Muñoz Saravia, A., Diesmos, A. C., Tominaga, A., ... Stuart, S. N. (2023). Ongoing declines for the world's amphibians in the face of emerging threats. *Nature, 622*(7982), 308–314.

Millennium Ecosystem Assessment. (2005). *Millennium Ecosystem Assessment*. https://www.maweb.org/en/Synthesis.html

Nivard, M., Smeets, B., Tryggestad, C., van de Giessen, P., & van der Meijden, R. (2024). *Global Energy Perspective 2023: CO_2 emissions outlook*. McKinsey & Company. https://www.mckinsey.com/industries/oil-and-gas/our-insights/global-energy-perspective-2023-co2-emissions-outlook

NOAA. (2022). *Dead zone in the Gulf of Mexico*. NOAA Ocean Today. https://oceantoday.noaa.gov/deadzonegulf/

OECD. (2001). *Glossary of statistical terms*. https://stats.oecd.org/glossary/detail.asp?ID=1978

OECD. (2011). *Working group on bribery: 2010 data on enforcement of the anti-bribery convention*. https://www.oecd.org/dataoecd/47/39/47637707.pdf

Our World in Data. (2023). *Economic damage by natural disaster type*. Our World in Data. https://ourworldindata.org/grapher/economic-damage-from-natural-disasters

Parker, R. S. (2006). *Hazards of nature, risks to development*. World Bank Publications.

Peters, G. P., Minx, J. C., Weber, C. L., & Edenhofer, O. (2011). Growth in emission transfers via international trade from 1990 to 2008. *Proceedings of the National Academy of Sciences of the United States of America, 108*(21), 8903–8908.

Pimentel, D., Tort, M., D'Anna, L., Krawic, A., Berger, J., Rossman, J., Mugo, F., Doon, N., Shriberg, M., Howard, E., Lee, S., & Talbot, J. (1998). Ecology of increasing disease. *Bioscience, 48*(10), 817-826.

Rockström, J., Steffen, W., Noone, K., Persson, A., Chapin, F. S., 3rd, Lambin, E. F., Lenton, T. M., Scheffer, M., Folke, C., Schellnhuber, H. J., Nykvist, B., de Wit, C. A., Hughes, T., van der Leeuw, S., Rodhe, H., Sörlin, S., Snyder, P. K., Costanza, R., Svedin, U., ... Foley, J. A. (2009). A safe operating space for humanity. *Nature, 461*(7263), 472–475.

Seah, R. (2009). *What is a pandemic?* Flu Prevention and Treatments. https://www.flu-treatments.com/what-is-a-pandemic.html

Serchuk, D. (2009, June 3). *Calculating the true cost Of carbon*. Forbes. https://www.forbes.com/2009/06/03/cap-and-trade-intelligent-investing-carbon.html

Srivastava, S. (2023, January 17). *Market outlook: Where is the Indian market headed in 2023?* Mintgenie. https://mintgenie.livemint.com/news/markets/market-outlook-where-is-the-indian-market-headed-in-2023-151673517280862

Stamets, P. E. (2007). *The 11th hour* (L. Conners & N. Conners, Eds.). Warner Independent Pictures.

Stern, N. (2008). *The economics of climate change*. Cambridge University Press.

Transparency International. (2010, January 1). *2010*. Transparency.org. https://www.transparency.org/en/cpi/2010

UNAIDS. (2023). *Global HIV & AIDS statistics — Fact sheet*. www.unaids.org. https://www.unaids.org/en/resources/fact-sheet

UNCCD. (2010). *United Nations launches decade-long effort to tackle desertification*. https://press.un.org/en/2010/envdev1150.doc.htm

UNDESA. (2022). *World population prospects - Population Division - United Nations*. United Nations Department of Economic and Social Affairs. https://population.un.org/wpp/Graphs/Probabilistic/POP/TOT/900

UNDP. (2022). *Human development report 2021/2022*. United Nations Development Programme. https://hdr.undp.org/system/files/documents/global-report-document/hdr2021-22pdf_1.pdf

UNDP and OPHI. (2023). *Global Multidimensional Poverty Index 2023: Unstacking global poverty - Data for high-impact action*. United Nations Development Programme (UNDP), and Oxford Poverty and Human Development Initiative (OPHI). https://hdr.undp.org/system/files/documents/hdp-document/2023mpireportenpdf.pdf

UNDRR. (2024). *Uncounted costs - Data gaps hide the true human impacts of disasters in 2023*. United Nations Office for Disaster Risk Reduction. https://www.undrr.org/explainer/uncounted-costs-of-disasters-2023

UNEP. (2009, August 27). *The environmental food crisis*. UNEP – UN Environment Programme. https://www.unep.org/resources/report/environmental-food-crisis

UNEP. (2021). *Protected Planet Report 2020*. United Nations Environment Programme. https://www.unep.org/resources/protected-planet-report-2020

UNESCO. (2023a, September 13). *Education data release 2023*. United Nations Educational, Scientific and Cultural Organization. https://uis.unesco.org/en/news/education-data-release

UNESCO. (2023b, September 21). *250 million children out-of-school: What you need to know about UNESCO's latest education data*. United Nations Educational, Scientific and Cultural Organization. https://www.unesco.org/en/articles/250-million-children-out-school-what-you-need-know-about-unescos-latest-education-data

UNFCCC. (2023). *From mission zero to climate take back: How interface is transforming its business to have zero negative impact*. United Nations Climate Change. https://unfccc.int/climate-action/momentum-for-change/climate-neutral-now/interface#SnippetTab

UNICEF, WHO, & World Bank. (2023). *Levels and trends in child malnutrition*. Joint Child Malnutrition Estimates. https://iris.who.int/bitstream/handle/10665/368038/9789240073791-eng.pdf?sequence=1

United Nations. (1993). *Agenda 21*. United Nations.

United Nations. (2011). *Millennium development goals report 2011*. United Nations. https://www.un.org/millenniumgoals/pdf/%282011_E%29%20MDG%20Report%202011_Book%20LR.pdf

United Nations. (2021). *Climate and weather related disasters surge five-fold over 50 years, but early warnings save lives – WMO report*. UN News. https://news.un.org/en/story/2021/09/1098662

United Nations. (2023, October 25). *Over 114 million displaced by war, violence worldwide*. UN News. https://news.un.org/en/story/2023/10/1142827

United Nations. (2024). *Humanitarian partners seek US$1.6 billion to assist 5.2 million people in Somalia in 2024*. United Nations in Somalia. https://somalia.un.org/en/259189-humanitarian-partners-seek-us16-billion-assist-52-million-people-somalia-2024

Vanguardia. (2011). *Cambio climático puede incrementar enfermedades: especialista*. Vanguardia.com.Mx. https://www.vanguardia.com.mx/cambioclimaticopuedeaumentarenfermedadesespecialista-1064912.html

Vaughan, K., Starkey, N., Marshall, B., & Wreford, L. (2010). *WWF-UK policy position statement on: International climate change adaptation*. WWF. https://assets.wwf.org.uk/downloads/climate_change_adaptation.pdf

Vidal, J. (2010, December 14). Soil erosion threatens to leave Earth hungry. *The Guardian*. https://www.guardian.co.uk/environment/2010/dec/14/soil-erosion-environment-review-vidal

World Bank. (2001). *Making sustainable commitments: An environment strategy for the World Bank*. World Bank.

World Bank. (2022, September 16). *Fact sheet: An adjustment to global poverty lines*. World Bank; World Bank Group. https://www.worldbank.org/en/news/factsheet/2022/05/02/fact-sheet-an-adjustment-to-global-poverty-lines

World Bank. (2023a). *Poverty overview*. World Bank. https://www.worldbank.org/en/topic/poverty/overview

World Bank. (2023b). World Development Indicators [Data set]. In *World development indicators*. https://datacatalog.worldbank.org/search/dataset/0037712

World Bank. (2024). *Trends in solid waste management*. Worldbank.org. https://datatopics.worldbank.org/what-a-waste/trends_in_solid_waste_management.html

World Economic Forum. (2011). *Global risks 2011 sixth edition*. World Economic Forum. https://www.weforum.org/publications/global-risks-2011-sixth-edition/

World Food Programme. (2023). *A global food crisis*. World Food Programme. https://www.wfp.org/

World Heath Organization. (2022). *Cancer*. Fact Sheets. https://www.who.int/news-room/fact-sheets/detail/cancer

World Health Organization. (2023a). *122 million more people pushed into hunger since 2019 due to multiple crises, reveals UN report*. News. https://www.who.int/news/item/12-07-2023-122-million-more-people-pushed-into-hunger-since-2019-due-to-multiple-crises--reveals-un-report

World Health Organization. (2023b). *Air pollution*. Air Pollution. https://www.who.int/health-topics/air-pollution#tab=tab_1

World Health Organization. (2023c). *Electronic waste (e-waste)*. Fact Sheet. https://www.who.int/news-room/fact-sheets/detail/electronic-waste-%28e-waste%29

WRI. (2023). *Aqueduct Country Ranking*. World Resources Institute. https://www.wri.org/applications/aqueduct/country-rankings/
WWF. (2022). *Living Planet Report 2022*. WWF International.
WWF International. (2020). *Living Planet Report 2020*. WWF International.
Zimmer, C. (2011). *Climate relicts: Seeking clues on how some species survive*. Yale E360. https://e360.yale.edu/feature/surviving_climate_change_the_story_of_hardy_relicts/2437/

2 Climate Change

The issue of climate change has ascended to the forefront of global discourse in the 21st century, presenting multifaceted challenges and opportunities for businesses, governments, and civil society. In the contemporary business environment, characterized by complexity and rapid change, organizational leaders are compelled to confront various pressing issues, with climate change as a formidable challenge. A sophisticated grasp of climate science equips business leaders with the capacity to proactively identify and manage risks attributable to environmental variability, which may influence operational efficacy and profitability. Such comprehension is indispensable for adhering to regulatory frameworks as governments intensify environmental safeguarding measures. Moreover, applying climate-related insights enables businesses to foster innovation, thereby securing competitive advantages and aligning with the sustainable expectations of investors and consumers. Incorporating climate science into strategic planning is a potent mechanism for bolstering resilience, facilitating business adaptation, and ensuring prosperity in the face of evolving climatic conditions. In essence, integrating climate science principles into business practice transcends environmental custodianship, representing a commitment to the enduring vitality and success of the enterprise.

Climate Science

The Greenhouse Effect and Global Warming

The Earth's atmosphere contains a mixture of gases that help regulate the planet's temperature by trapping heat from the sun. This process, known as the greenhouse effect, is essential for maintaining a habitable climate on Earth. The process is illustrated in Figure 2.1.

The primary greenhouse gases include water vapor, carbon dioxide (CO_2), methane (CH_4), nitrous oxide (N_2O), and ozone (O_3). However, human activities, such as burning fossil fuels (coal, oil, and natural gas), deforestation, and intensive agriculture, have increased the concentration of greenhouse gases in the atmosphere, leading to an enhanced greenhouse effect and global warming (IPCC, 2022). This process has caused the Earth's average temperature to rise, with significant consequences for ecosystems, human societies, and the global economy.

DOI: 10.4324/9781003544074-4

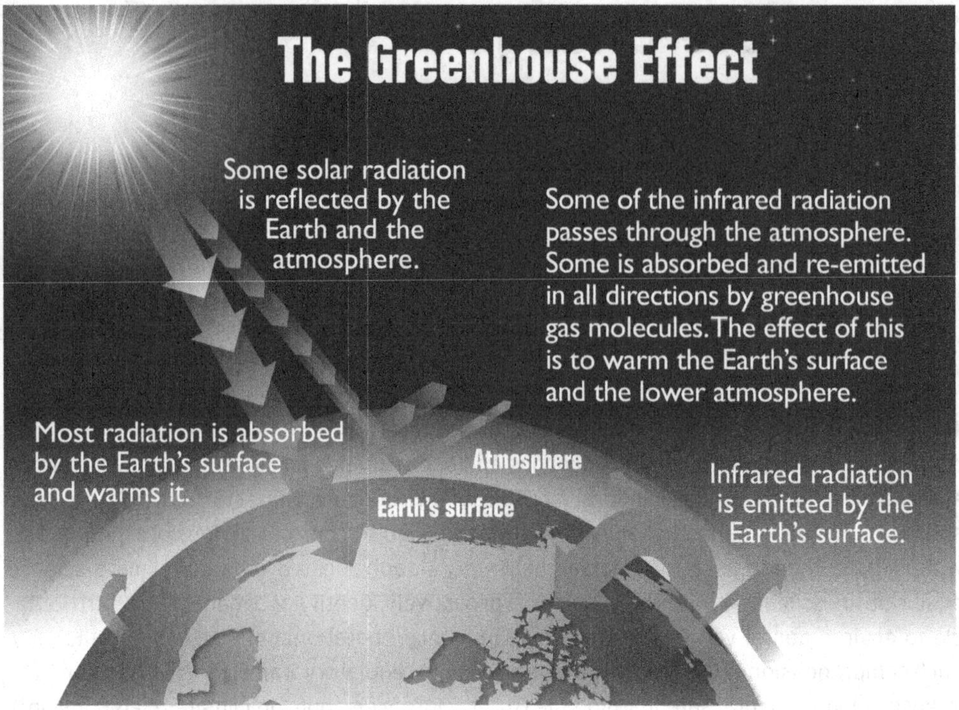

Figure 2.1 The Greenhouse Effect.

(US EPA, 2012)

Greenhouse gases differ significantly in their warming potentials and atmospheric lifetimes, which are pivotal factors in formulating strategies to mitigate climate change effects, as underscored by the Intergovernmental Panel on Climate Change (IPCC, 2022). Carbon dioxide (CO_2) is the predominant anthropogenic greenhouse gas, contributing to approximately 76% of human-induced warming (Friedlingstein et al., 2019). The combustion of fossil fuels, deforestation, and land-use changes are its primary sources, and it is characterized by an extensive atmospheric lifetime that allows it to affect global warming for centuries. Although methane (CH_4) represents only about 16% of human-induced warming (Saunois et al., 2020), it exhibits a more significant warming potential than CO_2 despite its relatively shorter atmospheric lifetime. Agricultural practices, waste management, and fossil fuel extraction and burning are the main contributors to methane emissions. Nitrous oxide (N_2O) accounts for roughly 6% of human-induced warming, and its warming potential, while lower than methane's, surpasses that of CO_2. The emission of N_2O is mainly due to agricultural activities, such as the use of fertilizers and manure management, as well as industrial processes and the combustion of fossil fuels (IPCC, 2022). Ozone (O_3), a secondary greenhouse gas, is generated in the atmosphere from complex chemical reactions involving other pollutants. It contributes to warming in the troposphere, whereas the depletion of stratospheric ozone, caused by human-made chlorofluorocarbons, has a net cooling effect on the Earth's climate. Lastly, fluorinated gases, employed in various industrial applications, make up a minor percentage of total greenhouse gas emissions but are significant due to their high warming potentials and lengthy atmospheric lifetimes (IPCC, 2022). Understanding the impacts of these gases is crucial for developing targeted and effective climate policies.

Business methane emitters

Agriculture and energy are the principal business sectors responsible for methane emissions. Agriculture, primarily through livestock and rice production, accounts for about one-fourth of anthropogenic methane emissions, with the energy sector, encompassing coal, oil, and natural gas operations, following closely. The International Energy Agency emphasizes the importance of mitigating methane emissions, highlighting the role of satellites in detecting otherwise elusive leaks. These two sectors are critical targets for implementing effective methane reduction strategies in business practices.

Climate Change Feedback Loops

Feedback loops play a crucial role in studying climate dynamics, acting as critical levers in the planet's climate system. The Intergovernmental Panel on Climate Change (IPCC) highlights the sensitivity of our climate to these feedback mechanisms, particularly the positive loops that exacerbate warming (IPCC, 2022). Notably, the ice-albedo effect results in a self-reinforcing cycle where melting ice uncovers darker surfaces, which absorb more heat and accelerate melting. Similarly, the thawing of permafrost liberates stored carbon dioxide and methane, significantly enhancing atmospheric greenhouse gas concentrations (Schuur et al., 2015). Additionally, the capacity of warmer air to hold more water vapor triggers a further increase in the greenhouse effect (Held & Soden, 2006). These feedback loops are not merely scientific curiosities but pivotal in shaping predictive climate models and formulating climate mitigation and adaptation strategies.

Climate Models and Projections

Climate models are mathematical representations of the Earth's climate system, including the atmosphere, oceans, land, and ice, which simulate the complex interactions between various components and processes (IPCC, 2022). They are essential tools for understanding past and present climate variability and for projecting future climate change under different greenhouse gas emissions scenarios. Several climate models, ranging from simple energy balance models to comprehensive Earth System Models (ESMs), incorporate detailed representations of biogeochemical cycles and human-induced changes to land use and land cover Fields (IPCC, 2022). Ensemble simulations, which combine the outputs of multiple models, account for uncertainties in model representation and provide a range of plausible future climate outcomes. Climate projections are often expressed in terms of Representative Concentration Pathways (RCPs) or Shared Socioeconomic Pathways (SSPs), which describe different trajectories of greenhouse gas emissions and concentrations based on various assumptions about future demographic, economic, and technological developments (IPCC, 2022). These scenarios help inform policymakers and stakeholders about the potential risks and consequences of different levels of climate change and the urgency of mitigation and adaptation efforts.

Climate Change Impacts

The impacts of climate change are wide-ranging and interconnected, affecting natural systems, human health, food production, and socioeconomic systems (IPCC, 2022). Some of the most significant observed and projected impacts include:

- **Temperature rise**: Global average temperatures have increased by approximately 1.1°C since the preindustrial era, with the last decade being the warmest on record. This temperature rise has consequences for ecosystems, agriculture, and human health and increases the frequency and intensity of heat waves.
- **Altered precipitation patterns**: Climate change affects precipitation patterns, leading to changes in the frequency, intensity, and duration of rainfall events, as well as increasing the risk of droughts in some regions. These changes can significantly affect water resources, agriculture, and flood risk management.
- **Melting ice and rising sea levels**: The accelerated melting of glaciers, ice caps, and polar ice sheets contributes to rising sea levels, threatening coastal communities and ecosystems and increasing the risk of storm surges and flooding. The global mean sea level has risen by about 0.2 meters since 1900 and is projected to continue accelerating.
- **Ocean acidification**: As the concentration of CO_2 in the atmosphere increases, the ocean absorbs more CO_2, leading to a decrease in ocean pH and a process called ocean acidification. This adversely impacts marine ecosystems, particularly calcifying organisms such as corals, shellfish, and plankton, which form the basis of many aquatic food chains.
- **Extreme weather events**: Climate change alters the frequency, intensity, and distribution of extreme weather events, including storms, floods, droughts, and wildfires. These events can cause significant damage to infrastructure, disrupt supply chains, and affect human health and well-being.
- **Loss of biodiversity**: The combination of climate change, habitat loss, and other human-induced pressures is driving a global decline in biodiversity, with potentially severe consequences for ecosystems and the goods and services they provide. This decline affects food security, water quality, and the resilience of natural systems to disturbances.
- **Climate change and human health**: Climate change impacts human health through various pathways, such as increased heat stress, the spread of vector-borne diseases (e.g., malaria and dengue fever), reduced air quality, and disruptions to food and water supplies. Vulnerable populations, including the elderly, children, and people with pre-existing health conditions, are particularly at risk (Figure 2.2).

Climate Change Mitigation and Adaptation

Mitigation refers to actions that reduce greenhouse gas emissions or enhance the capacity of natural systems to remove these gases from the atmosphere, ultimately limiting the magnitude of climate change (IPCC, 2022). Key mitigation strategies include transitioning to renewable energy sources, improving energy efficiency, promoting sustainable land-use practices, and developing and deploying low-carbon technologies. Adaptation involves adjusting human and natural systems to reduce vulnerability to the impacts of climate change

Figure 2.2 The Impacts of Climate Change.

and enhance resilience to future changes. Adaptation strategies vary depending on the specific risks and vulnerabilities of a given region, sector, or community. However, they may include improving infrastructure, implementing early warning systems for extreme weather events, and promoting sustainable water and land management practices. Both mitigation and adaptation are essential for addressing climate change, as even if emissions were to cease immediately, some impacts are already locked in due to the inertia of the climate system (IPCC, 2022). The effectiveness of these efforts depends on the level of international cooperation, the integration of climate policies with other policy areas, and the engagement of stakeholders from various sectors and levels of governance.

Climate Equity and Justice

Climate change disproportionately affects vulnerable populations, such as low-income communities, indigenous peoples, and small island developing states, due to their limited resources and adaptive capacity (IPCC, 2022). This disparity raises concerns about climate equity and justice, emphasizing the need for fair and inclusive climate policies that address the unequal distribution of risks, responsibilities, and benefits associated with climate change (Adger et al., 2017). Climate justice also encompasses the concept of historical responsibility, which recognizes that developed countries have contributed the most to greenhouse gas emissions over time and should, therefore, take a leading role in mitigating climate change and providing financial and technical support to developing countries (Roberts & Parks, 2007). The principle of common but differentiated responsibilities, enshrined in the United

Nations Framework Convention on Climate Change (UNFCCC), reflects this notion of climate justice. Addressing climate equity and justice is essential for building trust, fostering cooperation in international climate negotiations, and ensuring the long-term effectiveness and legitimacy of climate policies and actions at all levels.

Climate Change Communication and Public Perception

The conveyance of climate science to the public is a task of paramount importance, serving as the linchpin for raising awareness and catalyzing action, as Moser and Dilling (2011) advocate. However, the complexity of the science, the uncertainty that shadows it, and the political overtones that often color the discourse present formidable barriers, as noted by Weber and Stern (2011). Strategies to navigate these challenges and foster public engagement have emerged: framing the discourse to align with diverse values, utilizing visualization to clarify and connect, storytelling to personalize and emotionalize, and dialogue to democratize and co-create knowledge. These approaches are not mere adjuncts to climate communication; they are, at their core, essential for galvanizing the collective will and action needed to confront the climatic challenge effectively. In business leadership, the articulation and dissemination of climate science assume critical roles. Leaders are tasked with translating the complexities of climate change into actionable strategies that resonate with stakeholders' values and concerns. This translation involves framing the issue in terms relevant to business, such as risk management and growth opportunities, and employing visual and narrative techniques to make the abstract tangible and the impersonal personal. Moreover, leaders are called upon to facilitate dialogues engender trust and collaborative decision making. In essence, business leader's adept at communicating climate issues can drive change within their organizations and the broader community, steering collective efforts towards sustainable practices and solutions.

> **Negative perceptions of business**
>
> The mining sector provides a salient example of a business impacted by negative perceptions related to climate change. As climate awareness has grown, the environmental impact of mining has come under scrutiny, leading to reputational challenges for companies in this industry. Investors, increasingly attentive to sustainable practices, may shy away from businesses associated with high carbon emissions or environmental degradation, which can lead to financial risks, especially with the potential introduction of carbon pricing policies. This scenario underscores the importance of environmental responsibility and the tangible effects of public perception on business sustainability and viability.

Climate Change Education

The educational sphere has a significant role to play in the context of climate change, a role highlighted by UNESCO in 2017. Through education, individuals and societies acquire a foundational understanding of climate science and its intersection with human and natural systems. Such an understanding enables people to discern the multifaceted impacts of climate change, assess the strengths and weaknesses of various responses, and reflect on the deeper ethical considerations it raises. Moreover, education is the bedrock upon which critical thinking and problem-solving skills are honed, equipping individuals with the tools for informed action. Incorporating climate change education across diverse learning platforms and age groups is not just an educational imperative but a societal necessity, fostering a generation capable of navigating the complexities of climate change towards a sustainable and resilient future.

Climate Activism

Climate activism has gained significant momentum in recent years, driven by growing public awareness and concern about climate change Field's causes, impacts, and urgency (McKibben, 2019). Climate activists employ various strategies to advocate for more robust climate policies, raise public awareness, and challenge businesses and governments to take more ambitious and immediate action to address climate change. Critical drivers of climate activism include grassroots movements, non-governmental organizations (NGOs), and individual activists, who leverage social media, protests, direct actions, and shareholder activism to amplify their messages and influence decision-makers (Hadden, 2015).

Implications of Climate Activism for Business

The burgeoning clout of climate activism has substantial ramifications for the business sector, as delineated by Gunningham (2019). This movement plays a role in shaping public opinion, steering consumer preferences, molding investor expectations, and influencing regulatory frameworks, thus presenting businesses with challenges and prospects. Reputational risks arise for companies that neglect to disclose their climate stance or initiatives adequately, potentially branding them as indifferent or even antagonistic to climate concerns, as Linnenluecke and Griffiths (2015) observed. Conversely, those engaging constructively with climate issues may bolster their reputation and gain a competitive advantage. The implications on the market are palpable, with a consumer shift towards environmentally conscious products, pressuring businesses to innovate or face diminishing demand (Kautish & Sharma, 2020). Moreover, climate activism is spurring collaborative ventures to create sustainable solutions, aligning with transitioning to a low-carbon economy.

From an investment perspective, Eccles & Krzus (2018) highlight a trend where activism is spurring investors to demand more sustainable practices and transparency in climate-related corporate governance. Companies that ignore these calls may be financially disadvantaged, whereas those aligning with sustainable finance principles may enhance their capital prospects. Lastly, the regulatory landscape is not immune to activism's reach, with Hadden (2015) pointing out that activism catalyzes stringent climate policies. Companies that need to be equipped for these changes may incur additional costs and lose competitive ground. At the same time, those who preemptively adapt may find new opportunities and influence policy development to align with their strategic goals.

Business impacted by climate activism

A notable case where climate activism negatively impacted a business is British Petroleum (BP). Greenpeace's activism, including commissioning a consultancy to assess BP's climate risk and directly engaging shareholders, prompted a review of BP's climate strategy and subsequent public relations efforts to highlight renewable energy initiatives. Direct actions by Greenpeace activists, such as blocking BP's headquarters with solar panels and oil barrels, have also drawn public attention to the company's environmental practices. Moreover, the Royal Shakespeare Company ended its partnership with BP earlier than planned, citing the climate emergency and the concerns of young people as decisive factors influenced by climate activism. These incidents illustrate how climate activism can lead to significant reputational challenges and strategic shifts within major corporations.

Responding to Climate Activism: Strategies for Business

In the contemporary corporate arena, the influence of climate activism is driving businesses to adapt and innovate. A proactive stance involves dialogue with activists and NGOs, yielding insights into stakeholder expectations and emerging environmental trends. Companies are crafting comprehensive climate strategies integral to risk management and opportunity realization. Transparency in disclosing climate impacts is becoming a norm, satisfying shareholder demands and regulatory frameworks. Moreover, the market shift towards sustainability is spurring product and service innovation, aligning with consumer demand for environmentally responsible options. Engagement with policy development further allows businesses to influence and adapt to the evolving legislative context, ensuring strategic alignment with global climate objectives. Collectively, these approaches enable businesses to weather the challenges posed by climate activism and emerge as resilient, forward-thinking players in the movement towards a more sustainable economy.

In conclusion, understanding the intersections between climate science, climate activism, and business is essential for business practitioners and academics. As climate change continues to pose significant risks and opportunities for businesses across various sectors, companies must develop robust strategies, integrate climate risk management into their operations and decision-making processes, and demonstrate transparency and accountability in their climate-related disclosures and reporting. By doing so, businesses can build resilience, create value, and contribute to global climate change mitigation and adaptation efforts while navigating the challenges and opportunities associated with climate activism. Additionally, business education and research institutions are critical in equipping current and future business leaders with the knowledge, skills, and competencies to address climate change and drive the transition to a low-carbon and climate-resilient economy.

Climate Change and Business

Climate-Related Risks and Opportunities

Climate change presents both risks and opportunities for businesses across various sectors, which can be broadly categorized into two types: physical risks and transition risks (TCFD, 2017).

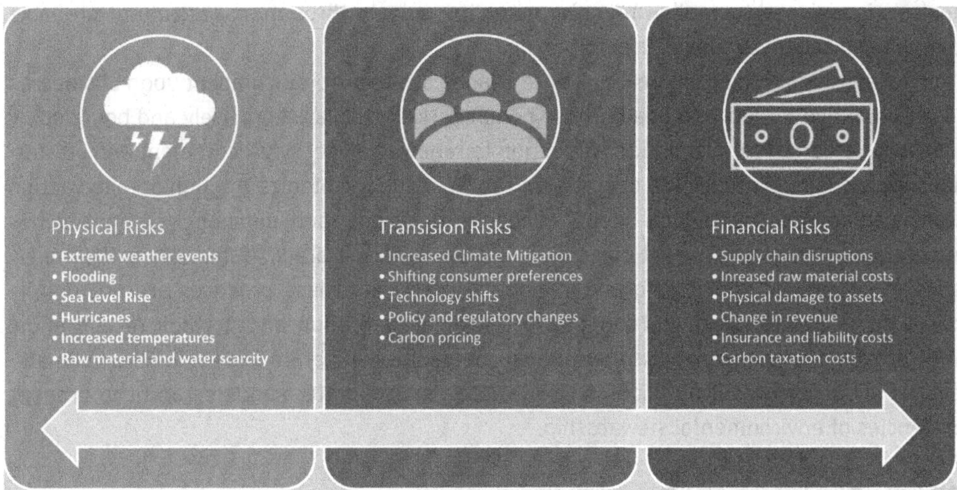

Physical Risks
• Extreme weather events
• Flooding
• Sea Level Rise
• Hurricanes
• Increased temperatures
• Raw material and water scarcity
Transision Risks
• Increased Climate Mitigation
• Shifting consumer preferences
• Technology shifts
• Policy and regulatory changes
• Carbon pricing
Financial Risks
• Supply chain disruptions
• Inreased raw material costs
• Physical damage to assets
• Change in revenue
• Insurance and liability costs
• Carbon taxation costs

Figure 2.3 Climate-Related Risks and Opportunities.

- **Physical risks**: These are the direct and indirect impacts of climate change on businesses, such as disruptions to operations, supply chains, and infrastructure due to extreme weather events, sea-level rise, or altered resource availability. Physical risks can lead to increased costs, reduced revenues, and decreased asset values, affecting a company's financial performance and competitiveness.
- **Transition risks**: These are the financial, regulatory, technological, and market-related challenges and uncertainties associated with the transition to a low-carbon economy. Transition risks may include policy measures (e.g., carbon pricing, emissions regulations), technological innovations (e.g., renewable energy, energy efficiency), and changing consumer preferences and market dynamics. Transition risks can create winners and losers, as businesses unable or unwilling to adapt may face declining demand, stranded assets, and reputational damage. At the same time, those who seize opportunities and innovate may gain a competitive advantage (Figure 2.3).

Businesses also face climate-related opportunities, such as developing new products and services, accessing new markets, improving resource efficiency, and enhancing brand reputation. Businesses can build resilience, create value, and contribute to global climate change mitigation and adaptation efforts by understanding and proactively addressing climate-related risks and opportunities.

Climate Change Strategy and Risk Management

In the vanguard of corporate strategy, the integration of climate risk management is emerging as an indispensable facet of organizational resilience and strategic foresight. The Task Force on Climate-related Financial Disclosures (TCFD) recommendations in 2017 serve as a touchstone, advocating for a rigorous evaluation of physical and transitional risks pertinent to climate change. This entails a systematic and recurring analysis of how climate perturbations might affect business operations, supply chains, and market dynamics. Using scenario analysis is a pivotal tool, allowing enterprises to navigate through a spectrum of probable climatic and socio-economic trajectories.

In establishing a comprehensive climate change strategy, it is incumbent upon businesses to set definitive targets and goals. These benchmarks, articulated precisely and bounded by time, span a gamut from emissions reduction to renewable energy procurement and bolstering supply chain fortitude. The operationalization of such strategies through detailed action plans demarcates the tactical steps, allocative decisions, and personnel responsibilities imperative for attaining the set objectives. Integral to this strategic framework is the imperative of continuous monitoring and evaluative practices. These practices are not merely oversight mechanisms but vital conduits for learning, adaptation, and strategic recalibration. They provide the empirical basis upon which companies can iterate and evolve their climate-related initiatives, ensuring alignment with internal corporate mandates and the broader exigencies of environmental stewardship.

Climate Disclosure and Reporting

Transparent disclosure and reporting of climate-related risks, opportunities, and performance are increasingly recognized as essential components of corporate accountability, stakeholder engagement, and sustainable finance (TCFD, 2017). By disclosing their climate-related information, businesses can demonstrate their commitment to addressing climate change and enhance their brand reputation and credibility: facilitate informed decision making by investors, lenders, insurers, and other stakeholders, enabling the efficient allocation of capital towards low-carbon and climate-resilient investments; comply with emerging regulatory requirements and voluntary reporting frameworks, such as the TCFD, the Global Reporting Initiative (GRI), or the Carbon Disclosure Project (CDP). Critical elements of climate-related disclosure and reporting include:

- **Governance**: Disclosing the company's governance structure, processes, and oversight mechanisms related to climate change, including the roles and responsibilities of the board of directors, management, and relevant committees.
- **Strategy**: Describing the company's climate change strategy, including its climate-related risks and opportunities, strategic priorities, and short, medium, and long-term goals and targets.
- **Risk management**: Providing information on the company's approach to identifying, assessing, and managing climate-related risks and opportunities, including its risk management processes, tools, and methodologies.
- **Metrics and targets**: Reporting on the company's key performance indicators (KPIs), metrics, and targets related to climate change, such as greenhouse gas emissions, energy consumption, water use, and waste generation. This may also involve disclosing the company's progress towards achieving its climate-related goals and targets and any challenges, successes, or lessons learned.

In addition to formal disclosure and reporting, businesses can engage with stakeholders through various channels, such as websites, social media, annual reports, or sustainability reports, to communicate their climate-related commitments, actions, and performance.

Climate Change Innovation and Collaboration

Innovation and collaboration are critical drivers of business success in the context of climate change, as they enable companies to develop and scale new solutions, technologies, and business models that contribute to the transition to a low-carbon and climate-resilient economy (Nidumolu & Prahalad, 2009).

Innovation: Businesses can invest in research and development (R&D), adopt cutting-edge technologies, and encourage a culture of innovation and creativity to develop new products, services, and processes that reduce greenhouse gas emissions, enhance resource efficiency, or help adapt to the impacts of climate change. Climate-related innovation includes renewable energy technologies, electric vehicles, energy-efficient building materials, or nature-based solutions for climate adaptation and resilience.

Collaboration: Businesses can engage in partnerships and collaborations with other companies, research institutions, governments, NGOs, and communities to share knowledge, resources, and expertise and to co-create innovative solutions to climate change challenges. Collaborative efforts can take various forms, such as industry consortia, public-private partnerships, or multi-stakeholder initiatives. They may focus on technology development, capacity building, policy advocacy, or market transformation.

By fostering innovation and collaboration, businesses can enhance their competitiveness and create value, contribute to broader societal goals, and drive systemic change towards a more sustainable and resilient future.

Innovating on climate challenges

The intersection of innovation and collaboration is vividly demonstrated by businesses tackling climate change. Carbicrete, a Montreal-based company, is transforming industrial waste into carbon-neutral concrete, addressing the significant emissions of the cement industry. Dutch designer Teresa van Dongen has harnessed olivine, a mineral with remarkable CO_2 absorption properties, to create a suite of carbon-capturing products. Swiss startup Climateworks is pioneering direct air capture technology to extract CO_2 directly from the atmosphere, offering a novel approach to mitigating excess atmospheric carbon.

Corporate Climate Leadership

Corporate climate leadership involves going beyond compliance with regulatory requirements and voluntary commitments to actively shape and drive the transition to a low-carbon and climate-resilient economy (Galpin & Whittington, 2012). Corporate climate leaders recognize the strategic importance and urgency of addressing climate change, and they are committed to integrating climate considerations into all aspects of their business, from strategy and operations to stakeholder engagement and external communications. In examining corporate environmental stewardship, specific characteristics emerge as hallmarks of climate leadership within the business realm. These entities are distinguished by their adoption of ambitious and scientifically grounded objectives to reduce greenhouse emissions and bolster

Figure 2.4 Attributes of Climate Leaders.

renewable energy utilization, thereby showcasing a solid commitment to international climate accords. Moreover, these leaders actively engage in advocacy and policy discourse to shape legislative frameworks conducive to sustainable transformation.

A comprehensive approach to climate leadership also extends to the systematic reconfiguration of supply and value chains, ensuring emissions reduction and resource efficiency are embedded across all operational dimensions. Accountability is another cornerstone characterized by transparent reporting of climate-related metrics, which allows for stakeholder scrutiny and reinforces the entity's dedication to climatic mitigation efforts. Additionally, fostering an organizational ethos oriented towards environmental cognizance, these leaders invest in their workforce, cultivating an intrinsic culture of sustainability and innovation. Collaborative endeavors, encompassing a broad spectrum of sectors and stakeholders, underscore their commitment to collective action, sharing best practices, and pursuing large-scale environmental change. Such attributes elevate a company's market standing and position it as a paragon of environmental responsibility, contributing to societal well-being and securing its long-term viability (Figure 2.4).

Net Zero

"Net Zero" refers to the balance between the amount of greenhouse gas (GHG) emissions produced and the amount removed from the atmosphere. In a net-zero scenario, all anthropogenic GHG emissions must be counterbalanced by carbon sequestration, effectively bringing the net emissions to zero (Rockström et al., 2017). The IPCC underscores the importance of achieving Net Zero to stabilize global temperatures, a key objective outlined in the Paris Agreement (UNFCC, 2015).

> **The Paris Agreement**
>
> Adopted in 2015 under the UNFCCC, the Paris Agreement aims to limit global warming to well below 2 degrees Celsius, preferably to 1.5 degrees, to mitigate climate change risks. Countries submit nationally determined contributions (NDCs) outlining emission reduction and adaptation plans committed to increasing ambition over time. The Agreement emphasizes financial support for developing nations and a balance between mitigation and adaptation efforts, representing a significant global commitment to a sustainable, low-carbon future (UNFCC, 2015).

The business sector is pivotal in transitioning to a Net Zero economy. Businesses significantly contribute to GHG emissions through operations, supply chains, and product life cycles. However, they also possess the resources, innovation potential, and economic influence to drive substantial changes in emission reduction strategies (Porter & Kramer, 2002). The pursuit of Net Zero can also stimulate innovation, leading to new business models and opportunities. Porter and Kramer's concept of shared value emphasizes that businesses can achieve economic success by addressing environmental and societal challenges. Net Zero strategies can enhance brand reputation, foster customer loyalty, and create new markets, offering a competitive edge.

Strategies for Achieving Net Zero in Business

In the journey towards achieving Net Zero, businesses embark on a multifaceted path, beginning with the essential step of understanding and managing their carbon footprint. This initial phase is akin to setting the coordinates for a long voyage, where tools such as the Greenhouse Gas Protocol act as navigational instruments, guiding companies in accurately charting their greenhouse gas emissions. As they move forward, businesses need to shift their energy paradigms. This transition is not just a mere change in energy sources but a transformative process of embracing renewable energy and enhancing energy efficiency. Like sailors adjusting their sails to harness the wind more effectively, companies recalibrate their operations to align with sustainable energy practices, a fundamental strategy for reducing emissions (OECD, 2023).

The journey then takes businesses beyond their immediate boundaries, reaching into the intricate networks of their supply chains. Here, they engage with suppliers to reduce upstream and downstream emissions, a task often more challenging than reducing direct operational emissions. This phase of the journey requires a collaborative effort, much like a fleet of ships working in unison, as supply chain emissions frequently surpass those of direct operations. Innovation and sustainable product design represent this voyage's creative and exploratory aspect. Companies invest in research and development, steering towards sustainable technologies and eco-friendly product designs. This commitment to innovation is a momentary effort and a continuous voyage towards long-term emission reductions, mirroring the spirit of explorers who continuously seek new horizons (Schaltegger & Wagner, 2011).

However, the path to Net Zero is fraught with challenges and barriers. Financial and economic constraints stand like formidable storms, with the substantial initial investment required for low-carbon technologies posing a significant barrier, especially for small and medium enterprises (SMEs). These financial headwinds can be particularly daunting, requiring careful navigation and resource management (Kolk & Pinkse, 2008). Technological limitations also present themselves as obstacles, much like uncharted waters. Industries such as aviation and heavy manufacturing encounter specific challenges in fully decarbonizing, necessitating innovative solutions and adaptations to navigate these limitations (Sharmina et al., 2021).

Finally, the journey is further complicated by the ever-evolving landscape of policy and regulatory frameworks. Like changing tides and shifting winds, these inconsistent climate policies across regions can make compliance and investment decisions complex, requiring businesses to be adaptable and resilient in their strategies (Rosenbloom & Markard, 2020). Collaboration among various stakeholders - governments, businesses, consumers, and NGOs - is essential for achieving Net Zero (Bonsu, 2020). Government policies can incentivize or mandate emission reductions, while consumers can drive demand for sustainable products, pushing businesses towards greener practices.

Achieving Net Zero is not merely an environmental imperative but a strategic business necessity in the context of climate change. While there are challenges, integrating Net Zero strategies aligns with long-term business resilience and sustainability. As businesses adapt and innovate to this imperative, they contribute significantly to the global effort against climate change, paving the way for a sustainable economic future. Transitioning to a Net Zero economy is a complex yet vital endeavor for the business sector. It involves a comprehensive overhaul of traditional business practices, innovative technologies, and active stakeholder engagement. The challenges, though significant, are surmountable with collaborative efforts and a commitment to sustainable development. As such, Net Zero emerges not only as an environmental goal but as a catalyst for economic transformation and sustainable growth in the business world.

Exercises

A. KNOW

Use the below multiple-choice questions to test your knowledge. Each answer may be wrong or right, and there may be zero to four right or wrong answers per question:

1. What is the primary purpose of the greenhouse effect...
   a. ...to increase global temperatures.
   b. ...to trap heat from the sun in Earth's atmosphere.
   c. ...to produce greenhouse gases.
   d. ...to reduce the habitability of Earth.

2. Which of the following is a direct physical risk of climate change for businesses...
   a. ...regulatory changes.
   b. ...technological innovation.
   c. ...disruptions due to extreme weather events.
   d. ...changing consumer preferences.
3. What is a key mitigation strategy to address climate change...
   a. ...reducing product prices.
   b. ...expanding urban development.
   c. ...transitioning to renewable energy sources.
   d. ...increasing fossil fuel consumption.
4. Which strategy is crucial for businesses in responding to climate activism...
   a. ...ignoring activist demands.
   b. ...engaging in dialogue with activists.
   c. ...focusing only on short-term profits.
   d. ...reducing employee benefits.
5. How do businesses contribute to climate change innovation...
   a. ...by avoiding new technologies.
   b. ...Investing in research and development for new solutions.
   c. ...Maintaining traditional business models.
   d. ...Reducing collaboration with other sectors.

B. THINK

Consider the climate change-related impacts in this chapter and list how these may relate to your business or a business you have worked for or are familiar with.

C. DO

Think about one specific action you could take in your own life to reduce your carbon emissions and mitigate some of the impacts of climate change.

D. RELATE

Have a conversation with someone in your business or your family about their perceptions of the current impacts of climate change. Are they affected? Is their business affected? Are they worried or hopeful about the future?

E. BE

How do you feel about climate change? Reflect upon your internal reactions to the challenges in the chapter and try to capture how it makes you feel and your attitudes to the overall development or single events. Can your reactions be impressed in feelings, motivations, moods, or attitudes? Do you react differently to different events or events in this history? How do you explain your reaction?

Feedback

A. KNOW

Feedback 1

a. Wrong: Global temperatures are increasing because anthropogenic greenhouse gas emissions exacerbate the greenhouse effect.
b. Right: The greenhouse effect is essential for maintaining a habitable climate on Earth by trapping heat from the sun.
c. Wrong: The greenhouse effect does not produce greenhouse gasses; instead, it is impacted by greenhouse gas emissions.
d. Wrong: The greenhouse effect is vital in regulating the temperature of the Earth for it to remain habitable. Anthropogenic greenhouse gas emissions are putting its ability to do so at risk.

Feedback 2

a. Wrong: Regulatory changes are an indirect risk for business as regulation exists to address climate change challenges rather than as a primary result of climate change.
b. Wrong: The greenhouse effect is essential for maintaining Earth's habitable climate by trapping sun heat.
c. Right: Physical risks include direct and indirect impacts like disruptions to operations due to extreme weather events.
d. Wrong: The greenhouse effect is vital in regulating the temperature of the Earth for it to remain habitable. Anthropogenic greenhouse gas emissions are putting its ability to do so at risk.

Feedback 3

a. Wrong: Reducing product prices would not impact climate change and may increase climate impacts by encouraging additional consumption.
b. Wrong: Expanding urban development may have a mixed impact on climate change. On the one hand, poorly designed urban infrastructure can increase climate-related impacts; on the other, the efficiencies associated with good urban development can reduce per-capita emissions.
c. Right: Transitioning to renewable energy sources is a key mitigation strategy for reducing greenhouse gas emissions.
d. Wrong: The International Energy Agency (IEA) warned in 2021 that the exploitation and development of new oil and gas fields must stop if the world is to stay within safe limits of global heating and meet the goal of net zero emissions by 2050.

Feedback 4

a. Wrong: Organizations who ignore stakeholder views, including those of activists, place themselves at reputational risk. Whilst activist demands by no means always to be met, a more proactive stance is more appropriate and valuable.

b. Right: A proactive stance in responding to climate activism involves dialogue with activists, yielding insights into stakeholder expectations.
c. Wrong: Focusing on short-term profit can lead to inherently unsustainable activities and is often why activists target companies.
d. Wrong: Reducing employee benefits brings a range of risks, such as alienating the workforce, reputational damage and an inability to recruit suitable staff.

Feedback 5

a. Wrong: The world is changing rapidly, and new technological solutions to climate change are emerging. Businesses that embrace technical change are likely to be included.
b. Right: Businesses contribute to climate change innovation by investing in research and development to develop new products and services.
c. Wrong: Business model innovation is a vital tool through which businesses can transform themselves to deal with business and societal risks such as climate change.
d. Wrong: Collaboration is a key to talking about climate change.

B. THINK

Level	*Anticipatory thinking*	*Notes*
+	Feasible scenario of multiple issues described that in its description reveals a profound level of anticipatory thinking.	
=	Feasible scenario involving multiple issues.	
–	No scenario of interacting issues has been developed, or the scenario is not feasible, either in terms of its threat-evoking mechanisms, or in in terms of its potential to wipe out humanity.	

C. DO

Level	*Taking initiative*	*Notes*
+	Initiative taken which is highly relevant to the mitigation of the issue. "If everyone would do this, the issue would be solved".	
=	Initiative taken, but it is not very relevant to the issue chosen.	
–	No initiative taken.	

D. RELATE

Level	Collaborative problem solving	Notes
+	A solution has been developed based on a process that involves meaningful input from both conversation partners.	
=	A solution has been developed, but it is mainly based on one dominant person's input.	
–	Conversation has not happened or no solution idea to the problem has been reached.	

E. BE

Level	Emotional awareness	Notes
+	Profound description of one's emotions regarding the state of the planet.	
=	Basic awareness of one's emotions regarding the state of the planet.	
–	No or little insight into own emotions regarding the state of the planet.	

References

Adger, W. N., Quinn, T., Lorenzoni, I., & Murphy, C. (2017). The social contract for climate risks. In *Institutional capacity for climate change response* (pp. 76–89). Routledge.

Bonsu, N. O. (2020). Towards a circular and low-carbon economy: Insights from the transitioning to electric vehicles and net zero economy. *Journal of Cleaner Production*, *256*(120659), 120659.

Eccles, R. G., & Krzus, M. P. (2018). Implementing the task force on climate-related financial disclosures recommendations: An assessment of corporate readiness. *Schmalenbach Business Review*, *71*(2), 287–293.

Friedlingstein, P., Jones, M. W., O'Sullivan, M., Andrew, R. M., Hauck, J., Peters, G. P., Peters, W., Pongratz, J., Sitch, S., Le Quéré, C., Bakker, D. C. E., Canadell, J. G., Ciais, P., Jackson, R. B., Anthoni, P., Barbero, L., Bastos, A., Bastrikov, V., Becker, M., ... Zaehle, S. (2019). Global carbon budget 2019. *Earth System Science Data*, *11*(4), 1783–1838.

Galpin, T., & Whittington, J. L. (2012). Sustainability leadership: From strategy to results. *The Journal of Business Strategy*, *33*(4), 40–48.

Gunningham, N. (2019). Averting climate catastrophe: Environmental activism, extinction rebellion and coalitions of influence. *King's Law Journal: KLJ*, *30*(2), 194–202.

Hadden, J. (2015). Climate justice activism. In *Networks in contention* (pp. 114–141). Cambridge University Press.

Held, I. M., & Soden, B. J. (2006). Robust responses of the hydrological cycle to global warming. *Journal of Climate*, *19*(21), 5686–5699.

IPCC. (2022). *Global warming of 1.5°C*. Cambridge University Press.

Kautish, P., & Sharma, R. (2020). Determinants of pro-environmental behavior and environmentally conscious consumer behavior: An empirical investigation from emerging market. *Business Strategy & Development*, *3*(1), 112–127.

Kolk, A., & Pinkse, J. (2008). Business and climate change: Emergent institutions in global governance. *Corporate Governance, 8*(4), 419–429.

Linnenluecke, M. K., & Griffiths, A. (2015). *The climate resilient organization*. Edward Elgar Publishing.

McKibben, B. (2019). The climate movement: What's next. *Opening reflections for a GTI forum. The great transition initiative*. https://greattransition.org/gti-forum/climate-movement-mckibben

Moser, S. C., & Dilling, L. (2011). Communicating climate change: Closing the science-action gap. In J. S. Dryzek, R. B. Norgaard, & D. Schlosberg (Eds.), *The Oxford handbook of climate change and society* (pp. 161–174). Oxford University Press.

Nidumolu, R., & Prahalad, C. K. (2009). Why sustainability is now the key driver of innovation. *Harvard Business Review*. https://www.businessandsociety.be/assets/ee902e549915b8586e8a8daa338e073e.pdf

OECD. (2023). *World energy outlook 2023*. OECD.

Porter, M. E., & Kramer, M. R. (2002). The competitive advantage of corporate philanthropy. *Harvard Business Review, 80*(12), 56–68, 133.

Roberts, J. T., & Parks, B. C. (2007). 8. Grandfathering, carbon intensity, historical responsibility, or contract/converge? In S. Bernstein, J. Brunee, D. Duff, & A. Green (Eds.), *A globally integrated climate policy for Canada*. University of Toronto Press.

Rockström, J., Gaffney, O., Rogelj, J., Meinshausen, M., Nakicenovic, N., & Schellnhuber, H. J. (2017). A roadmap for rapid decarbonization. *Science (New York, N.Y.), 355*(6331), 1269–1271.

Rosenbloom, D., & Markard, J. (2020). A COVID-19 recovery for climate. *Science (New York, N.Y.), 368*(6490), 447.

Saunois, M., Stavert, A. R., Poulter, B., Bousquet, P., Canadell, J. G., Jackson, R. B., Raymond, P. A., Dlugokencky, E. J., Houweling, S., Patra, P. K., Ciais, P., Arora, V. K., Bastviken, D., Bergamaschi, P., Blake, D. R., Brailsford, G., Bruhwiler, L., Carlson, K. M., Carrol, M., ... Zhuang, Q. (2020). The global methane budget 2000–2017. *Earth System Science Data, 12*(3), 1561–1623.

Schaltegger, S., & Wagner, M. (2011). Sustainable entrepreneurship and sustainability innovation: Categories and interactions. *Business Strategy and the Environment, 20*(4), 222–237.

Schuur, E. A. G., McGuire, A. D., Schädel, C., Grosse, G., Harden, J. W., Hayes, D. J., Hugelius, G., Koven, C. D., Kuhry, P., Lawrence, D. M., Natali, S. M., Olefeldt, D., Romanovsky, V. E., Schaefer, K., Turetsky, M. R., Treat, C. C., & Vonk, J. E. (2015). Climate change and the permafrost carbon feedback. *Nature, 520*(7546), 171–179.

Sharmina, M., Edelenbosch, O. Y., Wilson, C., Freeman, R., Gernaat, D. E. H. J., Gilbert, P., Larkin, A., Littleton, E. W., Traut, M., van Vuuren, D. P., Vaughan, N. E., Wood, F. R., & Le Quéré, C. (2021). Decarbonising the critical sectors of aviation, shipping, road freight and industry to limit warming to 1.5-2°C. *Climate Policy, 21*(4), 455–474.

TCFD. (2017). *Recommendations of the task force on climate-related financial disclosures*. Task Force on Climate-related Financial Disclosures.

UNFCC. (2015). *The Paris Agreement*. United Nations Climate Change. https://unfccc.int/process-and-meetings/the-paris-agreement

US EPA. (2012). The Greenhouse Effect. In: "Introduction", *Climate change indicators in the United States*, 2nd edition, Washington, DC, USA: US EPA, p. 3. EPA 430-R-12-004. https://www.epa.gov/climate-change

Weber, E. U., & Stern, P. C. (2011). Public understanding of climate change in the United States. *The American Psychologist, 66*(4), 315–328.

3 A History of Business, Society, and Environment

The historical development of responsible business is an endless source of insight and information for applying responsible management in practice. It comes as a surprise to many practitioners when they find out that the popular greenwashing term can be understood in depth when relating it to the classic Greek virtue ethics. Shockingly, for many philanthropists, stakeholder theory, which is the hailed management instrument of a socially responsible business, was designed as a profit-seeking strategic management instrument. Who would have guessed that the attractive LOHAS (Lifestyles of Health and Sustainability) market segment has a strong basis in the hippie movement? Sound knowledge of the historical landmark events of business, society and environment serves to achieve an understanding necessary to successfully managing the responsible business.

Important historical landmark facts are to be found mainly in economic history, general social history, labor history, and environmental history. The latter describes the interaction between human activity and the environment. In the following, historical events and developments will be described and analyzed in the light of responsible business. For responsible business to come to existence as we know it nowadays, the relationship between business, society, and environment had to run through three main phases of development, the *classic period*, the *modern period* the *progressive period* and the *contemporary period* described in Figure 3.1.

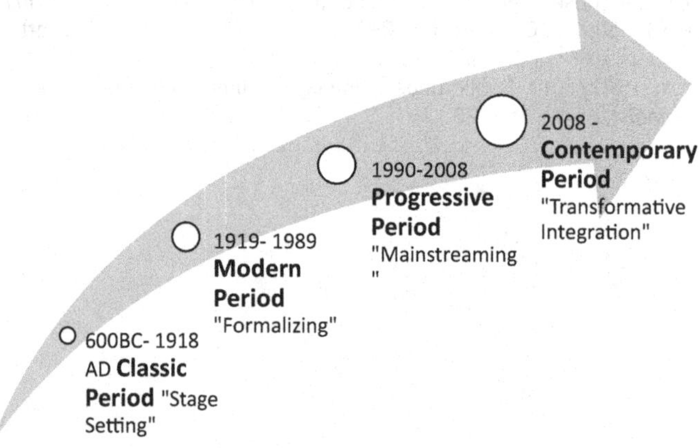

Figure 3.1 Historic Periods of the Relationship between Business, Society, and Environment.

DOI: 10.4324/9781003544074-5

The Classic Period: Setting the Stage

The classic period of the relationship between business, society, and environment is the time of the birth of many of the elements of today's status quo. Much of the philosophical basis, but also of today's unsustainable status quo has its origin in this period. The classic period sets the stage for where we are today (Figure 3.2).

The Roots of Business Culture and Responsible Business

During the classic period the stage was set for responsible business. The holy books of world religions such as the Bible [c. 1600 BC–100AD] and the Quran [c. 610–632] were written down and are still defining elements of regional business culture and the values applied in business conduct. The values promoted by the Bible are a basic driver of business philanthropy in the Americas and many regions of the old world. The Quran has largely influenced the practices of Islamic finance, which is one of the quickly emerging ethical and socially responsible investment trends (IMF, 2007). Islamic values are defining for businesses in Mid-East and large parts of Southeast Asia. Islamic values may sometimes clash with some of the Western causes in responsible management. For instance, diversity policies promoting gender equality, popular in Western responsible businesses are difficult to accept from an Islamic point of view. The thinking of Confucianism [c. 571–478] provides a common value construct for East-Asian business culture. Confucian thought's point of departure and most important value is the well-being of people or more generalized humanity as a whole. This very basic insight makes Confucianism highly conducive for the implementation of social responsibilities. Also, the second dominant Confucian core value of "righteousness" is positively-related to responsible business (Sprunger, 2011). A contemporary challenge is to adjust responsible business practices from a western approach to a truly global practice including all business regions, cultures, and philosophies of the world.

Figure 3.2 The Classic Period of Business, Society, and Environment.

An emergent responsible investment megatrend

"Islamic finance is limited to financial relationships involving entrepreneurial investment subject to the moral prohibition of interest earnings or usury (riba); money lending and direct or indirect association with lines of business involving anything forbidden (haram)" (IMF, 2007).

The Origins of (Business) Ethics

Ethical thinking as it is applied nowadays in business is the basis of responsible business. It is rooted in the ancient Greek philosophers' thought. The "band of three" [c. 469-322 BC] meaning the group of the three most influential Greek philosophers Plato, Socrates and Aristotle lay the foundation for non-consequentialist ethics, which judges right or wrong of an action not based on its outcome, but on the factors influencing the way the decision was made. Non-consequentialist ethics, often called deontological ethics includes the main streams of thought of virtue ethics, ethics of duties, and ethics of rights and justice. Virtue ethics judges by the righteousness of the character of the actor and finds its roots in Plato's and Aristotle's thinking. [469-322 BC]. Immanuel Kant's [1785] categorical imperative's first formulation advises to "Act only according to that maxim whereby you can, at the same time, will that it should become a universal law". Kant's work is often called the modern deontology (as opposed to the Greek classical deontology) or ethics of duty, as Kant describes it as the ultimate duty to of acting as good as if one's action should become generally applicable law (Hursthouse, 1999). John Locke's work on the ethics of rights, which has been published post-mortem [1689-1695], refers to the unalienable entitlements of people as they will later be described in greater detail in connection with the human rights movement (Chappel, 1994).

An extreme perspective on citizenship

Aristotle famously expressed that the one who does not take part in the community's affairs is either a beast or a god (Aristotle, 350 BC/2005)! The philosopher's call for active citizenship can be seen as representative of the ancient Greek contribution to today's civic activities and the topical corporate citizenship topic. What show should we consider companies not contributing to the community? Are they beasts or gods?

John Rawls' [1971] theory of justice leaded to the ethics of justice, which aims at fairness in both, the process leading to a decision and the outcome of the decision (Rawls, 1999). It is therefore a hybrid construction between consequentialist and non-consequentialist ethics. Outstanding streams of thought in consequentialist ethics (judging by the outcome of an action) are capitalist egoism based on Adam Smith [1776], and on utilitarian thinking by John Stewart Mill [1863]. Adam Smith in his work *The Wealth of Nations* (Smith, 1776/2008) draws a picture of a profit maximizing and therefore egoist business. Egoist ethics is ethics for the pursuit of self-interest. Egoism is the basis for today's discussion about what businesses should strive for, egoist profit maximization or profit optimization that benefits all involved stakeholders (Thielemann & Wettstein, 2008). Profit optimization reflects a utilitarian ethics as proposed by John Stewart Mill [1863] in his work *Utilitarianism* (Mill, 1863/2008). Utilitarian ethics aims at the search for the greatest amount of happiness possible, a rationale, which is reflected in current stakeholder management practices. Those main streams of ethical thinking are the philosophical basis of business ethics.

The Historical Roots of Today's Unsustainability

To understand today's economic world order and its effects on society and environment, historical phases of economic world history are of crucial importance. The age of discovery and colonization [1419–1660] was the starting point of today's wealth inequality between the northern and southern hemisphere, and of exploitative relationships between the first and the third world. It is the root of the need for today's sustainable and responsible supply chain management practices. The first industrial revolution [1730–1770] brought economic growth, which also caused a welfare increase for workers employed in the booming new industries. This increase in welfare in turn allowed for constant and rapid population growth, which is the basis for today's overpopulation and unsustainability of human existence on Earth. The second industrial revolution [1860–1914] not only brought an additional boost of world economic activity and negative impact on the environment, but also served as breeding ground for two of the most important characteristics of the problems being caused by today's economic activity. First, it gave birth to today's petroleum-based industry by the introduction of the internal combustion engine and petroleum-based plastics. Responsible business aims at achieving independence from the petroleum-based industry by technologies such as solar energy, alternative engines or kinetic local energy sourcing from wind, water, or even human movements. Responsible business practice also includes the constant reduction of the negative impact of petroleum-based plastics, including reduction in material and packaging, usage of plastics derived from renewable biomass, and recycling and biodegradability technologies. The second development is the birth of mass production most notably made possible by Henry Ford's development of the conveyor-belt-based assembly line. Mass-production is the technological basis of cheap products and the necessary condition for unsustainable consumerist behavior. Responsible management aims at fostering responsible, sustainable and ethical consumption patterns based on real needs rather than on superficial consumerist wants.

Ancient unsustainability

Human beings acted unsustainably long before the introduction of the fossil-fuel-based economy. The farming activity of irrigation in ancient Mesopotamia for example, increased the soil salinity to such levels that by the year 1700 BC, yields had decreased over 60%. As a result, wheat cultivation was abandoned completely (Tammilehto, 2008). The Easter Islands' ancient civilization, famous for their giant head-shaped stone sculptures also is supposed have become extinct because of the unsustainable use of the crucial scarce island resource: Wood (Foot, 2004).

The Development of Human and Labor Rights

Current responsible management standards such as the Global Compact framework and ISO 26000 strongly refer to human rights. The sub field of labor rights reflects the responsibility to one of businesses' most important interest groups, the employees. Human and citizen rights have been developed in a long line of historical events, documents and streams of thought. At least three classic statements of human rights lie in the British *Declaration of Rights* [1689], the *U.S. Declaration of Independence* [1776], and the *French Declaration of the Rights of Man and of the Citizen* [1789]. Those statements also serve to understand the field of corporate citizenship, as they illustrate basic civic rights and duties, which can be applied to corporate citizens as they can be applied to individual citizens. The labor rights and standards field has been developed by transferring human rights to the workplace and matching them with Marx' criticism [1867] of the capitalist system exploiting the working masses as described in "Capital" (Marx, 2000).

The Birth of Ecology

Human and labor rights, as part of the social component of responsible business, have gained early public attention. In contrast, the environmental component of responsible business was eyed closer for the first time during the 19th century. Inspired by the Darwin's evolutionary theories, the German biologist and philosopher Haeckel created the term Ecology [1866] describing the relationship between living organisms and their natural environment (Häckel, 1866/1988).

A Native American prophecy, the so-called Cree prophecy, in 1854 had first highlighted the harmful effects that human activity might have on ecology. The full prophecy draws an impressive early picture of environmental unsustainability of especially Western cultures. The prophecy deals with the consequences of ("white men's") greed, which can be interpreted as the search for profit maximization and consumerism. It describes a future state of environmental destruction characterized by the "earth being ravaged and polluted, the forests being destroyed, the birds would fall from the air, the waters would be blackened, the fish being poisoned in the streams, and the trees would no longer be ...". The prophecy even draws on the modern understanding of the environment being a necessary precondition for human survival when stating that "mankind as we would know it would all but cease to exist" ("Cree Indian prophecy", 2004, p. 1). The positive outlook of the prophecy was the advent of the so-called "rainbow warriors", which would lead the world to a sustainable situation, where "... all the peoples of all the tribes would form a new world of justice, peace, freedom and recognition of the Great Spirit [of nature] ("Cree Indian prophecy", 2004, p. 1)." This prophecy has later been adopted by the environmentalist movement. In retrospective it provides a very concise account of today's problems and potential solutions. As early as 1798, the British Economist Malthus provided a more scientific interpretation of humanity's future issues. His work on the world's demography suggests that constant population growth will exceed the Earth's carrying capacity. Malthus mentioned poverty and famine as potential results (Malthus, 1798/2011).

The Modern Period: Formalizing

The modern period of responsible management is characterized by an increasing formalization of responsible management in the form of international institutions, research, and practice applications. Important civic movements such as racial equality and the hippie and the environmentalist movements bring the relationship between business, society, and environment to the general society's attention (Figure 3.3).

Civic Movements

The late outliers of the second industrial revolution changed agriculture in such a profound way that it was called the "green revolution". In the middle of the 20th century [c. 1940-1970] the world witnessed a drastic increase in productivity of agricultural production based on new technologies and practices such as irrigation, fertilizers, and pesticides. Especially the two latter practices sparked an early environmentalist movement, which had long-lasting influences on later environmentalist activism. Rachel Carson's book *Silent Spring* moaned about the negative environmental and health effects of pesticides, one of the main enablers of the Green Revolution. As a matter of fact, the book title refers to the loss of biodiversity, most noticeable in the absence of birdsongs during springtime (Carson, 1962/2002).

Figure 3.3 The Modern Period of Business, Society, and Environment.

The African American civil rights movement [1955-1968] was the beginning point of the various non-discrimination movements. It later extended non-discrimination movements due to gender, sexual orientation, race-ethnicity, religion, physical handicaps, and age. The topic has entered into today's responsible business as the practice of diversity management. The hippie movement [1960-1970] integrated the environmental and equality movement fostering a liberal mindset, harmony with nature, respect, tolerance, and a search for spirituality. This spirituality and quest for holistic living reflects actual consumer tendencies towards sustainable living.

Activist with credentials

Born in 1907, Rachel Carson studied marine biology; received her MA in zoology; worked for the U.S. Bureau of Fisheries; and became one of the most influential people of the 20th century after publishing several books on nature, such as the famous *Silent Spring*, in which she calls "for a change in the way humankind viewed the natural world" (Lear, 1998).

Development of a Global Institutional Infrastructure

It is crucial for managing a responsible business successfully to know the international and regional norms and organizations providing an institutional framework for management conduct. As early as 1919 the International Labour Organization (ILO) was founded to promote workers' rights and well-being. ILO documents are until today the most important landmark standards for getting the employee stakeholder relationship right. The Universal Declaration of Human Rights [1948] is the modern version of the classically developed citizen rights. The declaration for the first time in history proposed a set of universally valid entitlements for all human beings on Earth. The declaration was developed by the United Nations and has served as a basis for the development of most of the subsequent standards applied in responsible business. In 1968 the so-called Club of Rome, an alliance of high impact business, society, academic, and political leaders, was founded with the purpose of fighting the unsustainability of human activity on Earth. An explosion of institutional infrastructure elements for responsible business and management took place throughout the progressive period as described in the next section's paragraph on institutional infrastructure.

Development of Practice Tools and of the Academic Discipline

Today's primary responsible business management tools began to be developed in the late 1960s. The tool of product lifecycle assessment aims at illustrating, measuring and managing environmental, social, and economic impacts of a product through sourcing and production to usage and the end of the useful lifecycle. Product life-cycle assessment had been first applied in a study by Teastley with The Coca Cola Company in 1969 (US Environmental Protection Agency, 2006; AGA, 2010). Corporate ethics was formalized as an academically accepted stream of applied ethics [1970-1980] and widely taught primarily in U.S. American business schools. The field of stakeholder management received broad academic attention with Edward Freeman's publication [1984] *Strategic Management: A Stakeholder Approach* (1984/2010). Stakeholder management has later been adopted as the main management tool of the responsible business movement.

In a parallel pattern to the responsible business practice tools, the academic understanding of responsible business evolved. According to Carroll, the publication of the book *The Social Responsibility of the Business Man* by Bowen in 1951 is recognized as the first publication explicitly describing responsible business (Carroll, 1999). However, there are also several articles in *Harvard Business Review* in the 1920s and 1930s documenting even earlier attention to the topic. After a sluggish growth of the academic coverage of responsible business, Nobel-Prize-winning economist Friedman brought controversial attention to corporate social responsibility in business and academic circles (Friedman M., 1970). His questioning of social business responsibilities in general is probably the most widely discussed statement in responsible business and still receives academic coverage more than four decades after its publication in the *New York Times Magazine* in 1970.

Only few years afterwards, birth was given to the modern sustainability movement. In 1972 the Club of Rome published *The Limits to Growth*, which reconnected to Malthus' classic forecasts of coming overpopulation (Malthus, 1798/2011). The publication was the starting point for the public recognition and academic coverage of the concept of **sustainable development** as defined by the report of the United Nations' World Commission on Environment and Development also titled the Brundtland Commission [1987] (Brundtland, 1987). The commission defined sustainable development as a "... development that meets the needs of the present without compromising the ability of future generations to meet their own needs". In the same year Barbier (1987) laid the ground for the popular Venn diagram, defining the three dimensions of sustainable development as being social, environmental, and economic development. This diagram later served to define those three dimensions as the pillars of sustainable development. The development of the concept of sustainable development was a very timely one as during the same period for the first time ever, humanity's ecological impact on the Earth overtook the planet's carrying capacity [1975] (WWF, 2010).

The Progressive Period: Mainstreaming

Throughout the progressive period of responsible business and management, the relationship between business, society and environment moved from being an accepted side-topic to a mainstream consideration for businesses, governments, and civil society. At the end of the progressive period, responsible business had become a worldwide social and business megatrend (Figure 3.4).

Issues, Scandals, and Crises

That responsible business was able to move mainstream can be attributed to a series of publicly highlighted business issues, crises, and scandals. The fashionable shoe company Nike was in constant struggle with civil society actors for alleged use of cheap and exploitative, so-called sweatshop labor. Nike's struggle with the activists on the issue went on for more than 20 years and served as a constant reminder of the harm that business behavior

Figure 3.4 The Progressive Period of Business, Society, and Environment.

perceived as irresponsible can do to a company and its reputation (Waller & Conaway, 2011). Corporate scandals have triggered off and fueled responsible businesses' move to mainstream. Another prominent example for this fact is the issue around the Brent Spar oil storage buoy operated by Shell [1995]. Greenpeace activists occupied Brent Spar in order to protest against the planned dumping of the platform into the Atlantic Ocean. Worldwide public attention rose to a degree where Shell service stations were boycotted on a large scale. One service station was even physically attacked in an arson attempt (Greenpeace, 2007). The Enron and WorldCom bankruptcies due to fraudulent accounting practices [2001-2002] not only brought down both companies, but also the world-renowned accounting consultancy Arthur Andersen (USA Today, 2005). The world financial and economic crises [2007] had severe social consequences globally. Recession, destruction of companies, subsequent job loss and an increase in poverty were only the most obvious outcomes. The reason of the crisis was a behavior that could have been avoided by good ethics and responsible business practices in the banking sector. The crisis was caused by a massive problem with the repayment of sub-prime loans, mortgages that could be sold at a higher price due to the considerably higher risk of payback.

The "Green Pop Culture"

In contrast to the negative coverage of constant social, environmental and economic issues, the progressive period has also seen the development in mainstream "pop-culture" of responsible business and issues related to it. Most prominently former US presidential candidate Al Gore enjoyed impressive global public attention with his movie *An Inconvenient Truth* [2006], which raised awareness for the issue and consequences of climate change (Guggenheim, 2006). The movie won two academy awards in 2007. Leonardo DiCaprio followed suit with *The 11th Hour* [2007], providing an extensive overview of the issues that threaten mankind's survival on Earth (Conners & Petersen, 2007). Those two Hollywood productions had been preceded by a long line of movies criticizing the negative impact of businesses on society and environment. In 2003 the movie and book both titled *The Corporation:*

The Pathological Pursuit of Profit and Power had translated the classic business ethics criticism of profit maximization to a fashionable and mass-accessible format (Achbar & Abbott, 2003). The movie maker Michael Moore had even produced three business-critical blockbusters in a period of 20 years. The latest Moore movie *Capitalism: A Love Story* covers the dubious role of the financial sector leading to the 2007 world economic crises (Moore, 2009). The movie *Supersize Me* [2004] became a modern classic by criticizing the fast-food industry for pursuing profits by promoting poor nutrition (Spurlock, 2004).

Last call

The 11th Hour is a film documentary that describes with reviews from more than 50 world leaders, the endangered natural state of the Earth. The film narrated by Leonardo DiCaprio, points to technology, social responsibility and conservation as key points to find a solution, although it is almost too late (Conners & Petersen, 2007).

Powered by broad public attention of social and environmental issues, sustainable, ethical and responsible living movement went main stream. The broadly accepted and researched LOHAS (Lifestyles of Health and Sustainability) consumer trend is subdivided into clearly defined sub-segments [2000]. The LOHAS market segment and with it sustainable consumption became a large-scale trend (NMI, 2011; NMI, 2010). A first sign of responsible business and products going mainstream became visible when Toyota launched the first mass-produced hybrid car, the PRIUS [1997]. Again, it was pop-culture pushing sustainable behavior and sales. Pictures of celebrities such as Leonardo DiCaprio, Sting, or Cameron Diaz posing with their Prius at the gas station were a decisive factor for the commercial success of more than 2 million cars sold in 2010. Another example is product RED promoted by the Singer Bono. Product RED offers mainstream corporations to introduce a co-branded RED product line, which donates a certain percentage of sales to the fight against AIDS in Africa (RED, 2011). RED was the first product-customized and global cause-related marketing campaign.

Development of High-Impact Institutions

During the modern period of responsible business, the institutional influence on responsible business behavior moved from marginalized initiatives to well accepted, high-impact mainstream institutions. In the following section, the most outstanding organizations and norms will be presented as they developed. The Foundation of the World Business Council for Sustainable Development (WBCSD) [1990] is probably the best example of how seriously responsible business began to be taken by major businesses. Today, WBCSD is a global sustainability player, led by the CEOs of around 200 companies, among others Toyota, Unilever, and Shell (Timberlake, 2006).

The governmental sector also started taking the topic very seriously. The [1992] Rio convention, known as the "Earth Summit", attracted representatives of over 172 governments including 108 heads of state. Outcomes were broad commitments to solving the world's most pressing problems, summarized in the Agenda 21. One-hundred-seventy-eight governments voted to adopt Agenda 21 and to follow the development goals divided into socio-economic factors, such as poverty, sustainable consumption and health, environmental factors, the strengthening of groups central to sustainable development and the measures necessary for implementation. Another important outcome of the Rio conference is the Rio Declaration on Environment and Development. The document summarizes the actions to be implemented to reach sustainable development stated in 27 principles (United Nations, 1997). In the follow-up conference [1997] the Kyoto protocol, the first global agreement for the global reduction of greenhouse gases was signed.

The International Organization for Standardization (ISO) mainstreamed the topic of environmental business responsibility by launching the now widely accepted ISO 14000 standard for environmental management [1995]. The ISO 26000 norm gives guidance on social responsibilities [2010] and is expected to further facilitate the implementation of responsible management for mainstream businesses and organizations of every kind. From 1999 onward, the United Nations increasingly focused on promoting responsible business. The Global Compact (GC), a voluntary initiative, which includes a self-commitment to ten responsible business principles, was founded in 2000. By 2010 GC had more than 6000 members, including many of the largest multinational companies. The United Nations Environment Program supports the foundation of the Global Reporting Initiative (GRI) by the Coalition for Environmentally Responsible Economies (CERES), which developed the GRI standard for sustainability reporting. GRI annual reports are nowadays available for most of the world's biggest enterprises and various other organizations. The eight Millennium Development Goals (MDG) were launched in 2005. They were quickly accepted as guidance for sustainable development. Sustainability also swapped over to the educational sector. The UN decade for Education for Sustainable Development (2005–2014) comprised extensive efforts of giving people the necessary competences to live more sustainable lives (DESD, 2011). The United Nations Principles for Responsible Management Education (PRME) (2007) identified management education as a crucial factor in shaping responsible businesses and aims at creating managers who can be change agents for a sustainable and inclusive economic system (PRME, 2011). The European Union also developed to become an institution at the forefront of the responsible business movement. Among others, the EU Corporate Social Responsibility Strategy and the EU Multi Stakeholder Forum have become role-models for regional initiatives for responsible business on a worldwide scale (Commission of the European Communities, 2006).

Training responsible managers

In 2007 the Principles for Responsible Management Education were developed, by deans, university presidents and representatives of leading educational institutions, with the support of the United Nations. By 2014 over 500 academic institutions had joined this initiative to educate a new generation of leaders than responsibly managing business for the good of the planet (UNPRME, 2011).

Megatrends of Flat Globalization and Interactive Transparency

The New York Times author and triple Pulitzer Prize winner Thomas L. Friedman described globalization in the 21st century as a flat globalization, where companies of any kind and size are able to compete on an international scale (Friedman T. L., 2005). Such a type of globalization increases the importance of internationally recognized and applied responsible business standards. A crucial factor in the then flat world had been information technology. The so-called information age begun with the mass-production of personal computers, but gained its importance for responsible business when the internet from 1995 onwards became a mass phenomenon. The internet has been a driver of responsible business for two main reasons. First, it facilitates an almost instant transparency about companies' positive and/or negative impacts. In combination with mobile-phone-based photography and internet connectedness, the news about an oil spill or an unethical remark of a frontline employee can go around the world instantly. It is easier for companies also to actively report social and environmental performance. Most companies have online sustainability, responsibility, and citizenship reports, which follow the Global Reporting Initiative standards. In 2004 the term Web 2.0 was coined by O'Reilly, describing a new internet age, characterized by a wide variety of new features such as interactivity, user-created content, and social networking. Web 2.0 enables a cheap and highly effective form of stakeholder dialog, which is the very basis of a successful responsible business (O'Reilly, 2005).

Focus Topic of Management Practice and Theory

Carroll's (1991) pyramid of corporate social responsibility for the first time clearly categorized the different types of responsibilities a company should fulfill. The four categories described are economic, legal, ethical, and philanthropic/discretionary responsibilities. The pyramid was a main component of a stream of research defining the different types of responsible business conduct such as, corporate social performance and corporate social responsiveness. Carroll's work is an important basis for the contemporary theoretical understanding and practice implementation of responsible business. The most conspicuous event showing how much responsible business had become a mainstream topic happened when the godfather of strategic management, Michael Porter and co-author NGO specialist Mark Kramer, published the article "Strategy and Society" (2006). The piece was published in the prestigious journal *Harvard Business Review*, which is appreciated by practitioners and academics. "Strategy and Society" shows, how much responsible business had moved mainstream; in this case mainstream in the field of strategic management. Another academic and business "superstar", Philip Kotler, a renowned academic in the marketing field had already integrated the responsible business topics of social and cause-related marketing into several textbooks. In 2004 he co-authored the best-selling book *Corporate Social Responsibility: Doing the Most Good for Your Company and Your Cause* (Kotler & Lee, 2004). Both publications show the integration of responsible business into classic business functions (strategy and marketing). They also gave rise to a general awareness of the business case for responsible business, describing the various ways how companies can benefit from behaving responsibly.

Another milestone for the mainstreaming of responsible business models is Muhammad Yunus' winning the Nobel Peace Prize in 2006. It was the first time that this prestigious award was given for a business model. The microbanking model represented by Yunus' Grameen Bank, profitably gave credits to millions of poor people in order to reduce poverty. The Grameen bank is often seen as an example for Prahalad's **bottom of the pyramid** theory, which postulates that businesses can tap into the potential of poor people and profitably integrate them into the market economy as suppliers, workers and consumers (Prahalad, 2010).

The Contemporary Period: Transformative Integration

The contemporary era of responsible business is characterized by a shift towards transformative change, marked by a fundamental rethinking of business purpose, integration of sustainability into core strategies, and strong leadership commitment. This shift reflects a growing recognition among companies of the need for systemic transformations to address the complex challenges facing society and the environment (Figure 3.5).

The Purpose of Business

In recent years, there has been a notable trend towards a fundamental rethinking of business purpose, driven by growing societal and environmental concerns. Scholars and business leaders alike have emphasized the need for companies to move beyond traditional profit-centric approaches and embrace a broader understanding of value creation that considers the interests of all stakeholders and the long-term sustainability of business activities. One significant development in this regard is the emergence of the "purpose-driven" business model, which prioritizes social and environmental impact alongside financial performance. Research by Eccles and Serafeim (2013) highlights the business case for purpose-driven

Figure 3.5 The Contemporary Period of Business, Society, and Environment.

companies, demonstrating that they tend to outperform their peers in terms of financial returns and resilience.

Moreover, the concept of "shared value", introduced by Porter and Kramer (2011), emphasizes the idea that creating societal value can also lead to competitive advantage. Companies that align their business strategies with societal needs and environmental stewardship can unlock new sources of innovation, growth, and profitability. Furthermore, the rise of environmental, social, and governance (ESG) investing has underscored the importance of sustainability considerations in business decision making. Investors are increasingly looking beyond short-term financial returns and assessing companies based on their ESG performance (Ioannou & Serafeim, 2019). This has prompted many businesses to integrate sustainability into their corporate strategies to attract investment and manage risk. Additionally, the COVID-19 pandemic has highlighted the interconnectedness between business, society, and the environment, prompting companies to reevaluate their purpose and role in addressing global challenges. Research by Bansal (2020) suggests that the pandemic has accelerated the adoption of purpose-driven practices, as companies recognize the importance of resilience, adaptability, and stakeholder engagement in navigating uncertain times.

Shared value

In their seminal 2011 *Harvard Business Review* article, Michael E. Porter and Mark R. Kramer introduce the concept of "shared value", a paradigm shift in business strategy that intertwines corporate success with societal welfare. Contrasting traditional corporate social responsibility (CSR), shared value embeds social and environmental benefits directly into a company's core business strategies and operations. This model identifies three primary avenues for creating shared value: Developing products and services that address societal needs while driving profitability, enhancing value chain efficiency in ways that benefit society and the environment, and fostering economic and social development in the communities where businesses operate. Porter and Kramer's shared value framework reimagines the role of business in society, suggesting that the most sustainable and scalable solutions to societal challenges are those that are integrally linked with a company's economic success.

Transformative Change

In the contemporary era of responsible business, a notable shift towards transformative change is observed, marking a departure from mere incremental improvements towards more profound and systemic transformations in business practices. This shift is underscored by an increasing recognition among companies that addressing pressing societal and environmental challenges requires more than just surface-level adjustments. Instead, it necessitates a fundamental rethinking and restructuring of business operations, strategies, and mindsets. Scholars argue that transformative change in responsible business involves not only complying with existing regulations or adopting green technologies but also redefining the very purpose and role of businesses in society (Stubbs & Cocklin, 2008). It entails moving beyond the pursuit of short-term profits to embracing a broader, long-term perspective that considers the interests of all stakeholders, including employees, communities, and future generations (Elkington, 1997).

Recent research has highlighted the importance of transformative change in driving sustainable business practices. For instance, Hahn and Kühnen (2020) argue that transformative change involves not only complying with existing regulations or adopting green technologies but also redefining the very purpose and role of businesses in society. This redefinition requires businesses to move beyond a narrow focus on profit maximization and embrace a broader, long-term perspective that considers the interests of all stakeholders, including employees, communities, and future generations.

Moreover, transformative change requires companies to integrate sustainability principles into their core business strategies, rather than treating them as peripheral or optional considerations (Hahn et al., 2014). This integration involves reexamining traditional business models, supply chains, and value propositions to ensure alignment with sustainability objectives (Kiron, 2012). Furthermore, scholars emphasize the importance of leadership in driving transformative change within organizations (Pratima Bansal & DesJardine, 2014). Effective leaders are not only visionary but also capable of mobilizing internal and external stakeholders, fostering innovation, and championing a culture of sustainability throughout the organization (Akrout, 2019). There is some evidence that companies are leveraging technology and innovation to drive transformative change. For example, research by Rasche and Waddock (2019) suggests that digital technologies such as blockchain and artificial intelligence can enable businesses to track and monitor their environmental and social impacts more effectively, leading to more sustainable outcomes.

Transformative Leadership

Leadership plays a pivotal role in catalyzing and sustaining transformative change within organizations, particularly in the context of responsible business practices. Effective leaders serve as architects of change, guiding their organizations towards more sustainable and socially responsible outcomes. They are not only visionary but also possess the ability to mobilize internal and external stakeholders, foster innovation, and champion a culture of sustainability throughout the organization. Recent research underscores the importance of leadership commitment in promoting transformative change. Akrout and Arnaud (2021) emphasize that leaders play a central role in shaping organizational culture and values, setting the tone for sustainability initiatives, and inspiring employees to embrace change. They argue that leadership commitment is crucial for overcoming resistance to change and driving meaningful progress towards sustainability goals. Other studies highlight specific leadership practices that are instrumental in promoting transformative change. For instance, Sosik and Jung (2018) emphasize the importance of authentic leadership, which involves leaders being true to themselves, fostering transparency, and building trust with their teams. Authentic leaders are able to inspire and motivate employees by demonstrating integrity, humility, and a genuine concern for social and environmental issues. Additionally, Avolio et al. (2009) highlight the role of transformational leadership in driving organizational change. Transformational leaders are able to articulate a compelling vision for the future, set ambitious goals, and empower employees to take ownership of sustainability initiatives. They create a supportive environment that encourages innovation, collaboration, and continuous learning, enabling organizations to adapt and thrive in a rapidly changing world. Finally there is evidence of the need for leaders to develop their emotional intelligence (EI) skills to effectively navigate the complexities of transformative change. Goleman et al. (2013) argue that leaders with high EI are better equipped to manage relationships, resolve conflicts, and inspire collective action towards shared sustainability objectives.

In summary, leadership plays a critical role in driving transformative change within organizations, particularly in the context of responsible business practices. Effective leaders are able to inspire and mobilize others, foster innovation, and champion a culture of sustainability. By demonstrating commitment, authenticity, and transformational leadership behaviors, leaders can pave the way for meaningful progress towards a more sustainable and socially responsible future.

Lisa Jackson, the Vice President of Environment, Policy, and Social Initiatives at Apple Inc., has emerged as a transformational leader in the realm of sustainability. Since joining Apple in 2013, Jackson has spearheaded a series of groundbreaking initiatives that have reshaped the company's approach to environmental stewardship and corporate responsibility. Her visionary leadership has been instrumental in driving Apple's transition to 100% renewable energy and setting ambitious targets for carbon neutrality. Beyond her environmental achievements, Jackson has also championed social and ethical initiatives within the company, advocating for diversity, inclusion, and data privacy. Her unwavering commitment to sustainability, coupled with her ability to inspire and mobilize others, has earned her recognition as one of the World's 100 Most Powerful Women by *Forbes* magazine and 35th in the *Fortune* magazine Most Powerful Women rankings (Fortune, 2023).

Data-Driven Decision Making

In the contemporary era of responsible business, there is a growing emphasis on data-driven decision making as a means to assess and improve environmental and social performance. Companies are increasingly leveraging advanced analytics and metrics to gather, analyze, and communicate data related to their sustainability initiatives. This data-driven approach not only enhances transparency but also enables organizations to identify opportunities for optimization and innovation. Recent research has highlighted the importance of data-driven decision making in driving sustainable business practices. For example, Gupta et al. (2018) emphasize the role of data analytics in helping companies measure and monitor their environmental impacts, identify areas for improvement, and track progress towards sustainability goals. By harnessing big data and machine learning techniques, companies can gain insights into complex environmental and social challenges, enabling them to make informed decisions and drive meaningful change.

Data-driven approaches are effective in promoting continuous improvement in sustainability performance. Companies that adopt data-driven decision-making processes are better equipped to identify inefficiencies, reduce waste, and optimize resource use, leading to enhanced environmental and social outcomes. This continuous improvement mindset is essential for organizations seeking to adapt and thrive in a rapidly changing business landscape while addressing pressing sustainability challenges. Furthermore, the use of data-driven decision making extends beyond internal operations to include supply chain management and stakeholder engagement. Research by Agrawal et al. (2023) highlight the importance of data transparency and collaboration across the supply chain to drive sustainability improvements and mitigate risks. By sharing data with suppliers and partners, companies can foster greater accountability and drive collective action towards shared sustainability objectives. It is clear that data-driven decision making is playing an increasingly important role in the contemporary era of responsible business, enabling companies to assess, monitor, and improve their environmental and social performance. By leveraging advanced analytics and metrics, organizations can enhance transparency, drive continuous improvement, and foster collaboration across the supply chain. This data-driven approach is essential for companies seeking to navigate complex sustainability challenges and create long-term value for stakeholders.

Resilience and Adaptation

In the contemporary era of responsible business, there is a growing recognition among companies of the need to build resilience in the face of environmental and social risks. This recognition stems from the increasing frequency and severity of climate-related events, natural disasters, and other sustainability challenges, which pose significant threats to business continuity and long-term viability. Companies are realizing that resilience is not only about mitigating negative impacts but also about adapting to changing circumstances and proactively managing risks. Recent research has underscored the importance of resilience and adaptation in driving sustainable business practices. For example, Smit et al. (2019) emphasize the need for companies to adopt a holistic approach to resilience, which includes identifying vulnerabilities, developing adaptive strategies, and building capacity to respond to and recover from disruptions. By investing in resilience-building measures, companies can enhance their ability to withstand shocks and maintain operations in the face of adversity.

Moreover, academic studies have highlighted the role of strategic foresight in enhancing resilience and adaptation. According to Burt et al. (2020), companies that anticipate and plan for future risks are better positioned to navigate uncertainty and seize opportunities for innovation and growth. By incorporating scenario planning, risk modeling, and other forward-looking techniques into their decision-making processes, companies can develop robust strategies that enable them to thrive in a volatile and unpredictable business environment. Furthermore, the concept of adaptive governance has emerged as a key framework for promoting resilience and adaptation in business operations. Research by Loorbach et al. (2017) highlight the importance of adaptive governance in fostering collaboration, learning, and innovation across organizational boundaries. By adopting flexible and participatory decision-making processes, companies can better respond to changing environmental and social conditions and co-create solutions with stakeholders.

Resilience and adaptation are becoming increasingly important considerations for companies in the contemporary era of responsible business. By recognizing and addressing environmental and social risks, companies can enhance their ability to withstand disruptions, seize opportunities, and create long-term value for stakeholders. This proactive approach to resilience-building is essential for companies seeking to thrive in a rapidly changing and uncertain world.

Exercises

A. KNOW

Use the below multiple-choice questions to test your knowledge. Each answer may be wrong or right and there may be zero to four right or wrong answers per question:

1. The classic period of the relationship between business, society and environment...
   a. ...among others comprizes the time of the industrial revolution.
   b. ...was a time of major importance for the development of human and labor Rights.
   c. ...mainly unfolded during the time from 1930 to 1950.
   d. ...is also called the era of "mainstreaming".
2. The modern period of the relationship between business, society and environment ...
   a. ...was the time of the African-American civil rights movement.
   b. ...was when the foundation of the World Business Council for Sustainable Development (WBCSD) took place.
   c. ...was the period between 1919 and 1990.
   d. ...is the era of mainstreaming the relationship between business, society, and environment.
3. The progressive period of the relationship between business, society and environment...
   a. ...gave birth to "The Green Revolution", a legendary movement of the major multinational businesses going "green".
   b. ...is not over yet.
   c. ...was when the central responsible business tool life-cycle assessment was developed.
   d. ...is the period, where topics related to business, society and environment began moving mainstream.
4. Today's unsustainability...
   a. ...is not a new phenomenon. Already in ancient Mesopotamia unsustainable agricultural practices caused problems in food production.
   b. ...is among others caused by the early discovery and colonization activities, as those activities have led to unsustainable migratory movements from the northern to southern hemisphere.

   c. ...is partly due to the birth of mass production, which enabled unsustainable consumption patterns.
   d. ...is partly due to a welfare increase during the first industrial revolution.

5. During the time when responsible business became a focus topic of management...
   a. ...Michael Porter developed the corporate social responsibility pyramid, which categorizes economic, legal, ethical, and philanthropic (discretionary) responsibilities.
   b. ...Mark Kramer is one of the co-authors of the article that highlighted the relationship between business and society.
   c. ...Muhammad Yunus won the Nobel Prize in Economic Science for his work with the Grameen bank.
   d. ...the awareness for the business case for responsible business was increased.

B. THINK

Rewriting history: Imagine what the world around you would look like if you lived in 50 years from today. Creatively write a fictitious history timeline from today to this imagined future.

C. DO

If you were in her shoes: Think about one point in time where the action of a person could have changed the course of history in a way that would have carried us into a more sustainable present. Describe the problem this person might have solved or the opportunity possibly realized and the actions you would have taken if you were this person.

D. RELATE

Open a conversation with someone you know about one of the historic events mentioned in this chapter. Exchange and document your knowledge and views on the meaning of these events with this person in order to better understand this event.

E. BE

How does this make you feel? Reflect upon your internal reactions to the above history of business, society, and environment. Try to capture how it makes you feel and what attitudes you have to the overall development or to single events. Can your reactions be impressed in feelings, motivations, moods, or attitudes? Do you react differently on different events or types of events in this history? How do you explain your reaction?

Feedback

A. KNOW

Feedback 1

a. Right: The first and the second industrial revolution as well as the agricultural "Green Revolution" fall into the classic period of the relationship between business, society and environment.

b. Right: The basics of human and labor rights can be found throughout the early British and French documents constituting basic citizen and human rights as well as Marx' works on the exploitation of workers by the capitalist system.

c. Wrong: 1930 to 1950 is the last stage of the classic period, but only represents a minor fraction of the overall period roughly ranging from 600 BC until 1950 AD.

d. Wrong: It is the progressive period that is characterized by a mainstreaming of the relationship between business, society and environment, while the classic period can be characterized by the term "stage-setting".

Feedback 2

a. Right: The main phase of the African-American civil rights movement roughly took place from 1955-1968.

b. Wrong: The WBCSD was founded at the very beginning of the progressive period.

c. Right: Those years reflect the progressive period.

d. Wrong: The era of mainstreaming is the progressive period.

Feedback 3

a. Wrong: "The Green Revolution" is related to efficiency improvements in food production due to improved agricultural methods during the early modern period.

b. Right: The progressive period and the "mainstreaming" of the relationship between business, society and environment began in 1990 and is in full process.

c. Wrong: Life-cycle assessment was developed during the modern period, together with business ethics and stakeholder management.

d. Right: It is also called the era of "mainstreaming".

Feedback 4

a. Right: The irrigation practices in ancient Mesopotamia proved unsustainable and finally lead to the abandonment of wheat cultivation.

b. Wrong: Discovery and colonization activities have contributed to today's global unsustainability, but mainly by the creation of wealth inequalities between the northern and southern hemisphere.

c. Right: Mass production lead to a decrease in prices and a higher consumption potential of people.

d. Right: The economic growth during the first industrial revolution increased peoples' welfare, which in turn supported a constant population growth based on the improved living conditions.

Feedback 5

a. Wrong: The pyramid was developed by Archie B. Carroll.
b. Right: The article was co-authored with Michael Porter as first author.
c. Wrong: In spite of being a finance professor, Yunus won the Nobel Peace Prize, not the Nobel Prize in Economics.
d. Right: Awareness of the positive business benefits from responsible business practices was increased by manifold publications such as "Business and Society" by Porter and Kramer.

B. THINK

Level	*Future-oriented thinking competence*	*Notes*
+	Illustration of a convincing future scenario and strong connection to today's situation through fictitious key events and developments.	
=	Illustration of a possible future with depth and grounds it in a strong argumentation.	
–	Little evidence of the ability to imagine a possible future in detail.	

C. DO

Level	*Problem and opportunity skills*	*Notes*
+	Feasible plan of action based in the recognition of a significant historic problem or opportunity.	
=	Plan of action based in the recognition of a historic problem or opportunity.	
–	No plan of action and/or no recognition of a historic problem or opportunity.	

D. RELATE

Level	*Collaborative knowledge creation competence*	*Notes*
+	Highly integrated shared knowledge about the event which attributes the origin of individual elements to the respective conversation partner.	
=	Equitable account of knowledge of all conversation partners, but little integration and attribution of individual elements to the respective conversation partner.	
–	Biased or unilateral account of knowledge.	

E. BE

Level	*Introspection competence*	*Notes*
+	Deep and thoughtful insight into internal states and processes, appreciating their causes.	
=	Basic insight into own internal states and processes.	
–	Little or no evidence of the ability to monitor and express insight into internal states and processes.	

Appendix: Historical Timeline

Table 3.1 Historic Events in the Relationship between Business, Society, and Environment

Period	*Event*	*Summary*	*Topic areas*
Classic Period: Stage Setting			
600 BC–100	Bible [Ƕ]	The scripture of the Bible defines values still prevalent in many Western businesses' morality.	-Business philanthropy
551–478 BC	Confucianism [Ƕ]	Confucianist thinking dominates business morality mostly in East-Asia.	-Welfare thinking
469-322 BC	Ancient Greece Philosophy and Citizenship [©]	Ancient Greece philosophers like Plato, Aristotle and Socrates are the grandfathers of modern ethical thinking. Also is the Greek "Polis" in its understanding of the city-state and community of citizens is the root of democracy and the understanding of citizenship.	-Virtue ethics -Corporate citizenship
610–632	Establishment of the Contents of the Quran [Ƕ]	The Quran's value construct largely influences the business morality in mid-eastern and many South-East-Asian countries.	-Islamic business -Islamic finance -Gender inequality
1215	Magna Carta [⌂]	The Magna Carta limited the arbitrary punishment powers of the king and conceded a basic freedom to "freemen".	-Citizen rights -Human rights
1419–1660	The Age of Discovery and Establishment of Colonial Empires [Ƕ]	The exploration and following colonial exploitation of the Americas, Africa, and Asia has led to many elements of today's world-wide imbalances in welfare.	-Third world poverty and exploitation -Racism -Sustainable supply chain management
1689	English Bill of Rights [⌂]	The ~ extended the rights of English citizens based on liberal thinking.	-Citizen rights -Human rights

(*Continued*)

Table 3.1 (Continued)

Period	*Event*	*Summary*	*Topic areas*
1730-1770 (approx.)	Industrial Revolution [Ꮀ]	The industrial revolution's technological achievements have led to increased welfare among workers and a subsequent explosion of the Earth's population. Also allowed the technological achievement for a large-scale exploitation and pollution of natural resources.	-Overpopulation -Pollution -Unsustainable economic development
1776	Book *The Wealth of Nations* by Adam Smith [©]	Adam Smith's book is often seen as the basis for economic thinking, capitalism and an incentive-based market economy. Smith's earlier book *The Theory of Moral Sentiments*, Smith first used the term "the invisible hand" to describe the forces of markets and also defines "self-love" (egoism) as the first motive for morality (Smith, 1776/2008).	-(Economic) egoist ethics -Market economy -Incentives
1785	Initiation of Kant's Categorical Imperative [©]	Kant in his work *Groundwork of the Metaphysics of Morals* proposes the "categorical imperative" as the ultimate decision-making instrument for defining moral behavior based on one's duties (Kant & Patton, 1785/2005).	-Ethics of duties -The categorical imperative of sustainability
1854	Cree Prophecy [©]	The ~ has been attributed to either an old native American woman of the Cree tribe or to Chief Seattle, eponym of the city Seattle. It states that due to the "white men's" greed destroying nature, there would be a time when mankind would almost cease to exist ("Cree Indian prophecy", 2004).	-Environmentalism-Unsustainability of "Western" lifestyles
1860-1914	Second Industrial (Technology) Revolution [Ꮀ]	The ~ sparked unprecedented economic growth fueled by inventions such as the assembly line, the internal combustion engine and the use of electricity. Also the petroleum industry was born in this period. The efficiency increase in production created the necessary precondition for a cheap mass production, which in turn raised average people's consumption possibilities.	-Mass production -Consumerism and materialism -Fossil-fuel-based industry

(Continued)

Table 3.1 (Continued)

Period	*Event*	*Summary*	*Topic areas*
1863	Publication of the Book *Utilitarianism* by John Stewart Mill [©]	Mill describes utilitarianism and the greatest overall happiness caused by a behavior as the main end of ethical decision making. Mill bases his arguments on the central idea of welfare and the "greatest happiness principle" proposed by Bentham (Mill, 1863/2008).	-Utilitarian ethics -Welfare thinking
1789	French Declaration on the Rights of Man and Citizen [⌂]	The ~ shifted universal rights from a pure citizen to a human rights approach, which grants natural right to any human being.	-Citizenship rights -Human rights
1798	Malthus publishes An Essay on the Principle of Population [©]	Malthus argued that a rise in the population would lead to an oversupply of labor and subsequent reduction of wages, which in turn creates poverty (Malthus, 1798/2011).	-Social unsustainability -Overpopulation -Poverty
1866	Ecology (Ernst Haeckel) [©]	Häckel coined the term ecology, describing the interrelation of the natural environment's elements, which served as a basis for the modern understanding of the term (Häckel, 1866/1988).	-Environmental management -Environmental unsustainability
1867	Publication Capital: Critique of Political Economy by Karl Marx [©]	Marx sees the exploitation of labor as the main motivation of capitalist behavior and therefore capitalism as intrinsically unsocial (Marx, 2000).	-Criticism of capitalism -Fair labor conditions -Exploitative labor
Modern Period: Formalizing			
1919	Foundation of the International Labour Organization [⌂]	The International Labour Organization (ILO) was founded after World War I for humanitarian, economic and political reasons. ILO has set the labor standards which are reference documents for the development of most of the actual norms for responsible business (ILO, 2000).	-International labor standards
1920	External Effects and Social Costs by Pigou in the Book *The Economics of Welfare* [©]	Pigou with his work on external effects, has laid the ground for the development of welfare and environmental economics, which are the economic theories, analyzing the social and environmental effects of economic activity (Pigou, 1920/2005)	-(Social) welfare economics -Environmental economics -Taxation of externalities

(*Continued*)

Table 3.1 (Continued)

Period	*Event*	*Summary*	*Topic areas*
1940–1960	The Green Revolution [Ᵽ]	During the ~ agricultural production experienced a dramatic increase in productivity based on automatization and the use of chemical substances.	-Unsustainable food supply -Biodiversity loss
1943	Publication of Maslow's Needs Pyramid in *A Theory of Human Motivation* [©]	Maslow's hierarchical needs pyramid explains the basic motivations of human beings (Maslow, 1943). Understanding Maslow's pyramid is fundamental to analyzing and changing consumerist behavior towards more sustainable ways.	-Consumerism -Sustainable living
1948	Universal Declaration of Human Rights [⌂]	The ~ developed after World War II is still the main reference document for the understanding of international, universal human rights.	-Human rights
1951	*The Social Responsibility of the Business Man*, Book by Bowen [©]	Bowen's book constitutes the point of departure of the modern understanding of corporate social responsibility (Bowen, 1953).	-Corporate social responsibility
1955–1968	African American Civil Rights Movement [Ᵽ]	The ~ has been a milestone for the achievement of the goal of racial non-discrimination which served as a basis for the general non-discrimination movement.	-Workplace diversity and inclusion -Civil rights
1960	Coase Theorem [©]	The Coase theorem describes how to internalize external costs by the attributing property rights to externalities; creating a market for externalities (Coase, 1960). A prominent example is "emission trading", where companies are given a certain maximum right to pollute. If the business does not use up this maximum amount, it can sell the emission rights not used other businesses that exceeded their emission limit.	-Environmental economics -(Social) welfare economics -Emission trading -Market-based solutions
1960–1970	Hippie Movement [Ᵽ]	The ~ with its promotion of liberal values, spirituality, proximity to nature and non-discrimination has been an important basis for many of the values pursued in responsible business. The modern Lifestyles of Health and Sustainability (LOHAS) movement shares much communality with the hippie mindset.	-Environmentalism -LOHAS markets -Diversity and inclusion

(*Continued*)

Table 3.1 (Continued)

Period	*Event*	*Summary*	*Topic areas*
1961	Book *Silent Spring* by Rachel Carson [©]	Rachel Carson criticizes the negative environmental and health effects of the green revolution in the agricultural sector (Carson, 1962/2002).	-Environmentalism
1968	Foundation of the Club of Rome [⌂]	The ~ brought together a group of diplomats, industry and civil society leaders and academics concerned about the economic and social activity overshooting the planet's environmental limits.	-Sustainable development -Overpopulation -Footprinting
1969	*Birth of the product Life-Cycle Assessment Methodology* [©]	The ~, a tool centrally applied in responsible management took place in a project headed by the researcher Tastley for The Coca Cola Company (US Environmental Protection Agency, 2006).	-Product life-cycle impact assessment -Cradle to cradle; recycling
1970	Friedman's *New York Times* Article The Social Responsibility of Business is to Increase Profits [©]	Friedman criticized social responsibility of a business from an economic perspective and also based on ideological reasons. A company as being a lifeless entity cannot have a responsibility, while companies' mangers might have a responsibility, but should not allocate financial resources to social causes as this means "stealing" money from business owners, employees and consumers (Friedman M., 1970).	-Corporate social responsibility -Philanthropy -Greenwashing -Principle-agent theory
1970–1980	*Development of Business (Corporate) Ethics* [©]	The ~ made the topic an academically recognized field of applied ethics, which lead to increased coverage of business ethics and the related topic of corporate governance throughout the business school curriculum.	-Business ethics -Corporate governance
1971	Book *A Theory of Justice* by John Bordley Rawls	The ~ was formalized the philosophical stream of thinking of ethics of justice, searching for fair decision-making procedures and outcomes (Rawls, 1999).	-Ethics of justice
1972	Publication of the Book *Limits of Growth* by the Club of Rome [©]	The ~ became a world bestseller by calling attention for a coming "overshoot"; a situation where world economy and society will be forced into decline by the resource limits of the planet (Meadows, Randers, & Meadows, 2005).	-Sustainable development

(*Continued*)

Table 3.1 (Continued)

Period	*Event*	*Summary*	*Topic areas*
1975	Humanity's Footprint on Earth Exceeds the Ecological Carrying Capacity [Ꮒ]	When the ~ the world society was barely aware of the problem. Corrective measures have not been taken sufficiently and humanities' ecological footprint kept growing, by far exceeding what Earth can bear in the long run.	-Unsustainability -Environmental footprint
1984	Book *Strategic Management: A Stakeholder Approach* by Edward Freeman [©]	The ~ for introduced the tool of stakeholder management, which is at the heart of managing responsible business. Freeman argued that a business cannot be successful without fulfilling the needs of "groups and individuals that can affect or are affected" by the business' activity stakeholders (Freeman, 1984/2010, p. 25).	-Stakeholders -Business case for responsible business
1987	Brundtland Report [©]	The United Nations "World Commission for Environment and Developments" ~, officially titled "Our common future", delivered the popular definition for sustainable development as a " ... development that meets the needs of the present without compromising the ability of future generations to meet their own needs" (United Nations, 1987).	-Sustainable development
1987	Barbier's Pillar Model of Sustainable Development [©]	~ formalized the three dimensions of sustainable development being social, environmental, and economic development (Barbier, 1987).	-Sustainable development
Progressive Period: Mainstreaming			
1990– 2001	Nike Sweatshop Issue [Ꮒ]	Nike being accused of employing sweatshop labor conditions in subsidiaries factories was picked up as a major issue by social activist groups. It showcased that companies' responsibilities do not end "at the factory door".	-Sustainable supply chain management -Exploitative labor -Social activism
1990	Foundation World Business Council for Sustainable Development (WBCSD) [⌂]	The ~ institutionalized high-level business leaders' commitment for a business contribution to sustainable development. WBCSD has designed the environmental management tool "eco-efficiency", aiming at simultaneously reducing environmental impact and costs of business' operations. WBCSD created the vision 2050 a roadmap towards a sustainable world economic system (Timberlake, 2006).	-Eco-efficiency -Business case

(*Continued*)

Table 3.1 (Continued)

Period	*Event*	*Summary*	*Topic areas*
1991	Archie B. Carroll's Responsibility Pyramid [©]	~ structured business responsibilities into the three categories of economic, legal, ethical and philanthropic/ discretionary responsibility (Carroll, 1991).	-Corporate social responsibility
1992	Rio Summit & Agenda 21 [⌂]	The United Nations Conference on Environment and Development (UNCED) also called Rio Summit served as breeding ground for several landmark institutions for sustainable development such as the Rio Declaration on Environment and Development, Agenda 21 and the Framework Convention on Climate Change (United Nations, 1997).	- Sustainable development -Climate change
1995	Brent Spar [Ꮋ]	Triggered off by the NGO Greenpeace's activist opposition to deep-sea dumping the oil platform Brent Spa, Shell received worldwide opposition to their business activities (Greenpeace, 2007).	-Activism -Environmentalism
1995-	Beginning of the "Information Age"; Internet becomes Public [Ꮋ]	The broad availability of the internet created the necessary condition for a new transparency including information on companies' responsible or irresponsible behavior.	-Transparency -Stakeholder engagement
1996	Publication ISO 14000 Standards on Environmental Management [⌂]	The ~ supports the implementation of environmental management systems and put companies' environmental impact on the management agenda.	-Environmental management
1997	Kyoto Protocol [⌂]	The ~ was the first internationally accepted agreement on the reduction of the emission of greenhouse gases, signed by the majority of the world's governments (UNFCCC, 2011).	-Climate change
1997	Toyota Presents the Mass-Produced Hybrid Car Prius [Ꮋ]	When ~, the first mass-produced alternative-engine powered car it is an important milestone as it shows that industries can reduce their independence from the fossil-fuel-based industry, while increasing their competitiveness and creating new markets.	-Sustainable innovation -Fossil-fuel-based industry -Green technologies
1999	Global Compact Foundation [⌂]	The ~ provides businesses a United Nations-backed platform to improve their social and environmental impacts based on ten principles (Global Compact, 2011).	-Institutionalization -Issues and causes

(*Continued*)

Table 3.1 (Continued)

Period	*Event*	*Summary*	*Topic areas*
1999	Global Reporting Initiative Launch [⌂]	The ~ created a standardized framework for reporting social, environmental and economic performance (Global Reporting Initiative, 2011).	-Institutionalization -Sustainability reporting
2000	Documentation of the LOHAS Market Segment [©]	The Lifestyles of Health and Sustainability (LOHAS) market is segmented into clearly defined sub markets such as sustainable living and eco-tourism (LOHAS Magazine, 2010).	-Sustainable consumption -Cause-related marketing
2000	Bursting of the "Dot-Com-Bubble" [Ꮒ]	The ~ and the massive economic damage done due to speculative stock market mechanisms highlighted the financial markets as one of the systemic problems of the capitalist system.	-Economic system malfunctions
2000-	Era of "Flat" Globalization [Ꮒ]	Thomas L. Friedman's description of the "flat world", where globalization becomes mass-accessible (Friedman T. L., 2005). The "flat world" enables a new type of global social- and environmental entrepreneurship.	-Sustainable entrepreneurship - Supply chain responsibility
2001–2002	Enron and WorldCom Scandals [Ꮒ]	The ~ triggered the collapse of several corporate giants due to unethical accounting and governance practices.	-Economic system malfunctions -Organizational governance
2004	Web 2.0 [Ꮒ]	The shift from the rather static internet 1.0 to the interactive ~ provides a platform highly conducive to enhanced stakeholder engagement (O'Reilly, 2005).	-Stakeholder engagement -Transparency
2004	Book *The Fortune at the Bottom of the Pyramid* by Prahalad [©]	The ~ cast light on the possibility to include poor people into the economic system, either as customers, employees or suppliers (Prahalad, 2010).	-Inclusive business
2005–2014	UN Decade of Education for Sustainable Development (2005–2014) [⌂]	The ~ highlights the importance of educating people in their private and professional life for sustainable behavior patterns (DESD, 2011).	-Institutionalization -Sustainability education
2005–2015	United Nations Millennium Development Goals [⌂]	The ~ summarize the most important goals necessary to combat poverty and have been adopted by the majority of the world's national governments (United Nations, 2011).	-Sustainable development -Issues & causes

(*Continued*)

Table 3.1 (Continued)

Period	*Event*	*Summary*	*Topic areas*
2006	European Union Corporate Social Responsibility Strategy [⌂]	The ~ has served as role model for many regional initiatives and clusters of responsible business. The Corporate Social Responsibility definition used in the ~ has been widely adopted (Commission of the European Communities, 2006).	-Corporate social responsibility -Responsible business clusters
2006	*Harvard Business Review* Article "Strategy and Society" by Michael Porter and Mark Kramer [©]	The ~ showcased how responsible business can co-created value for business and society when strategically aligned (Porter & Kramer, 2006).	-Business case -Strategic Corporate Social Responsibility
2006	Nobel Peace Prize for Muhammad Yunus and his Grameen Bank's Microfinance Program [⌂]	The ~ cast international attention to how innovative social business models can solve and/ or mitigate social and environmental issues profitably.	-Microfinance -Social business -Poverty alleviation -Business case
2006	Al Gore's *An Inconvenient Truth* Wins 2 Oscars [Ꮒ]	~. The movie educates about and calls for action against climate change and its world-threatening consequences (Guggenheim, 2006).	-Climate change
2006	Launch of Product Red, the First Mass-Customized Cause-Related Marketing Campaign [Ꮒ]	Product Red provides the platform for businesses to introduce "Red" product lines under their own brand names. A percentage of sales of Red-branded products is channeled to the cause of fighting AIDS in Africa (RED, 2011).	-Sustainable consumption -Cause-related marketing
2007-2008	World Financial and Economic Crises [Ꮒ]	The ~ and its social and economic consequences had been caused by the immoral business practice of "subprime lending"; selling loans with a high probability of not being paid back.	-Economic system failures
2007	Launch of the UN Principles for Responsible Management Education (PRME) [⌂]	The PRME are a quickly growing alliance of business schools worldwide, committing to educating responsible managers, committed with promoting sustainable development through their vocational activity (PRME, 2011).	-Sustainability education
2010	ISO 26000 on Social Responsibility [⌂]	The norm ~ aims at giving guidance for organizations to implement social responsibility.	-Institutionalization -Norms
2015	UN Sustainable Development Goals	Consists of 17 goals to be achieved for globally sustainable development.	-Global goals for sustainable development

(Continued)

Table 3.1 (Continued)

Period	*Event*	*Summary*	*Topic areas*
Contemporary Period: Transformative Integration			
2015	Paris Agreement	Landmark international treaty on climate change sets out a global framework to avoid dangerous climate change by limiting global warming to well below 2° Celsius.	-Climate Change
2015	Task Force on Climate-related Financial Disclosures (TCFD)	TCFD developed recommendations for more effective climate-related disclosures that could promote more informed investment, credit, and insurance underwriting decisions.	-Sustainable Finance
2016	The International Integrated Reporting Council (IIRC)	The IIRC framework promotes a more cohesive and efficient approach to corporate reporting, which has increasingly been adopted by organizations looking to communicate their sustainability efforts.	-Corporate Reporting
2018	EU Non-Financial Reporting Directive (NFRD)	This directive requires large companies to disclose information on the way they operate and manage social and environmental challenges, helping to enhance the transparency and accountability of businesses.	- Corporate Reporting
2019	Business Roundtable Redefinition of the Purpose of a Corporation	The Business Roundtable, an association of chief executive officers from major U.S. companies, redefined the purpose of a corporation to promote "An Economy That Serves All Americans", emphasizing stakeholder value over shareholder primacy.	-Responsible Business
2019	European Green Deal	This set of policy initiatives by the European Commission aims to make the EU's economy sustainable by turning climate and environmental challenges into opportunities across all policy areas.	-Climate Change -Environmental Policy
2020	Davos Manifesto	The World Economic Forum's Davos Manifesto 2020 reiterates the universal purpose of a company in the Fourth Industrial Revolution, focusing on stakeholder responsibility, social justice, and sustainability.	-Responsible Business

(*Continued*)

Table 3.1 (Continued)

Period	*Event*	*Summary*	*Topic areas*
2020	COVID-19 Pandemic	The global crisis has led to a heightened focus on corporate responsibility, particularly in terms of social welfare, health and safety, and economic sustainability.	-Global Shocks
2020	EU Taxonomy for Sustainable Activities	A classification system established by the European Union to guide investment towards environmentally sustainable economic activities.	-Sustainable Economics
2020	United Nations Principles for Responsible Banking	Launched by 130 banks from 49 countries, representing more than US$47 trillion in assets, these principles provide the framework for a sustainable banking system.	-Sustainable Finance
2021	Glasgow Climate Pact (COP26)	his agreement, reached at the 26th UN Climate Change Conference, included commitments from governments and businesses to accelerate action towards the goals of the Paris Agreement, influencing corporate climate policies and practices.	-Climate Change
2022	COP 27	The headline agreements from the conference were the establishment of a loss and damage fund and finalizing the details to implement the Santiago Network. It was also the first-time food security was recognized.	-Climate Change -Food Security
2028	COP 28	The conference closed with an agreement that signaled the "beginning of the end" of the fossil fuel era by laying the ground for a swift, just and equitable transition, underpinned by deep emissions cuts and scaled-up finance	-Climate Change -Fossil Fuels
2025	EU Corporate Sustainability Reporting Directive (CSRD)	This directive, once adopted, will extend the sustainability reporting requirements of the NFRD to all large companies and all listed companies in the EU.	-Corporate Reporting

Legend: Symbols used in the table divide the historical events and developments into the following three groups:

1) Ꞗ Major developments in world history impacting on responsible business and management
2) © Scientific developments impacting on responsible business and management
3) △ Institutional developments impacting on responsible business and management, including norms and organizations

References

Achbar, M., & Abbott, J. (Directors). (2003). *The corporation* [Motion Picture].

AGA. (2010). *Life cycle assessment (LCA)*. Retrieved August 30, 2011, from Grupo de analysis y gestion ambiental: https://www.etseq.urv.es/aga/Investigacion/LCA.htm

Agrawal, R., Wankhede, V. A., Kumar, A., & Luthra, S. (2023). A systematic and network-based analysis of data-driven quality management in supply chains and proposed future research directions. *The TQM Journal*, *35*(1), 73-101.

Akrout, H. (2019). Leading sustainable development: A survey on sustainable leadership literature. *Business Strategy and the Environment*, *28*(1), 156-170.

Akrout, H., & Arnaud, A. (2021). Leadership for sustainable development: A review of the literature and a research agenda. *Journal of Business Ethics*, *174*(2), 275-291.

Aristotle. (350 BC/2005). *Politics*. Stilwell: Digireads.com.

Avolio, B. J., Walumbwa, F. O., & Weber, T. J. (2009). Leadership: Current theories, research, and future directions. *Annual Review of Psychology*, *60*(1), 421-449.

Bansal, P. (2020). COVID-19 and the future of business. *Organization & Environment*, *33*(4), 433-440.

Bansal, Pratima, & DesJardine, M. R. (2014). Business sustainability: It is about time. *Strategic Organization*, *12*(1), 70-78.

Barbier, E. (1987). The concept of sustainable economic development. *Environmental Conservation*, *14*(2), 101-110.

Bowen, H. R. (1953). *Social responsibilities of the businessman*. New York: Harper.

Brundtland, G. H. (1987). *Presentation of the report of the World Comission on Environment and Development to UNEP's 14th governing council*. Nairobi.

Burt, G., Burt, S., & Rajakaruna, I. (2020). Strategic foresight for climate resilience: A review of climate change adaptation strategies for companies. *Business Strategy and the Environment*, *29*(3), 1226-1240.

Carroll, A. B. (1991). The pyramid of corporate social responsibility: Toward the moral management of organizational stakeholders. *Business Horizons*, *34*(4), 39-48.

Carroll, A. B. (1999). Corporate social responsibility a definitional construct. *Business & Society*, *38*(3), 268-295.

Carson, R. (1962/2002). *Silent spring*. New York: Houghton Mifflin.

Chappel, V. (1994). *The Cambridge companion to Locke*. Cambridge: Cambridge University Press.

Coase, R. H. (1960). The problem of social cost. *The Journal of Law & Economics*, *3*, 1-44. http://www.jstor.org/stable/724810

Commission of the European Communities. (2006). *Implementing the partnership for growth and jobs: Making Europe a pole of excellence of CSR*. Brussels: European Union.

Conners, N., & Petersen, L. C. (Directors). (2007). *The 11th hour* [Motion Picture]. Retrieved August 11, 2011, from amazon.com: https://www.amazon.com/11th-Hour-Leonardo-DiCaprio/dp/B00005JPXA

Cree Indian prophecy. (2004). *Cree Indian prophecy: Warriors of the rainbow*. Retrieved August 30, 2008, from Bird Clan of East Central Alabama: https://www.birdclan.org/rainbow.htm

DESD. (2011). *Decade of education for sustainable development*. Retrieved August 30, 2011, from https://www.desd.org/

Eccles, R. G., & Serafeim, G. (2013). The performance frontier: Innovating for a sustainable strategy. *Harvard Business Review*, *91*(5), 50-56, 58, 60, 150.

Elkington, J. (1997). *Cannibals with forks: The triple bottom line of 21st century business*. Capstone.

Foot, D. K. (2004). *Easter Island: A case study in non-sustainability*. London: Greenleaf. Retrieved October 2, 2011, from Greener Management International: https://goliath.ecnext.com/coms2/gi_0199-5944674/Easter-Island-a-case-study.html

Fortune. (2023, December 17). *Lisa Jackson*. Fortune. https://fortune.com/ranking/most-powerful-women/2020/lisa-jackson/

Freeman, R. E. (1984/2010). *Strategic management: A stakeholder approach*. Cambridge: Cambridge University Press.

Friedman, M. (1970, November 14). The only responsibility of business is profit. *New York Times Magazine*, p. 2.

Friedman, T. L. (2005). *The world is flat: A brief history of the twenty-first century*. New York: Picador.

Global Compact. (2011). *The United Nations Global Compact*. Retrieved August 30, 2011, from https://www.unglobalcompact.org/

Global Reporting Initiative. (2011). *Global Reporting Initiative*. Retrieved August 30, 2011, from https://www.globalreporting.org/Home

Goleman, D., Boyatzis, R., & McKee, A. (2013). *Primal leadership: Unleashing the power of emotional intelligence*. Harvard Business Press.

Greenpeace. (2007). *The Brent Spar*. Retrieved August 30, 2011, from Greenpeace International: https://www.greenpeace.org/international/en/about/history/the-brent-spar/

Guggenheim, D. (Director). (2006). *An inconvenient truth* [Motion Picture].

Gupta, A., Kumar, S., Kharb, R., & Joshi, R. (2018). The role of data analytics in sustainable supply chain management: A literature review. *Journal of Advances in Management Research, 15*(2), 206–229.

Hahn, R., & Kühnen, M. (2020). The role of corporate sustainability performance for economic performance: A global survey of executives. *Business Strategy and the Environment, 29*(4), 1467-1480.

Hahn, R., Kühnen, M., & Wilkesmann, M. (2014). Responsible leadership and stakeholder management: Influence pathways and organizational outcomes. *Academy of Management Perspectives, 28*(3), 255–274.

Häckel, E. (1866/1988). *Generelle morphologie der organismen*. Berlin: Gruyter.

Hursthouse, R. (1999). *On virtue ethics*. New York: Oxford University Press.

ILO. (2000). *ILO History*. Retrieved August 30, 2011, from International Labour Organization: https://www.ilo.org/public/english/about/history.htm

IMF. (2007, August). *The economics of Islamic finance and securitization*. Retrieved August 09, 2011, from imf.org: https://www.imf.org/external/pubs/ft/wp/2007/wp07117.pdf

Ioannou, I., & Serafeim, G. (2019). The consequences of mandatory corporate sustainability reporting: evidence from four countries. In Abagail McWilliams, Deborah E. Rupp, Donald S. Siegel, Günter K. Stahl, David A. Waldman (Eds.), *The Oxford Handbook of Corporate Social Responsibility* (pp. 452-489). Oxford University Press. https://doi.org/10.2139/SSRN.1799589

Kant, I., & Patton, H. (1785/2005). *Moral law: Groundwork of the metaphysic of morals*. New York: Routledge.

Kiron, D. (2012). Sustainability nears a tipping point. *Strategic Direction, 28*(7). https://doi.org/10.1108/sd.2012.05628gaa.012

Kotler, P., & Lee, N. (2004). *Corporate social responsibility: Doing the most good for your company and your cause*. Chichester: Wiley.

Lear, L. (1998). *Rachel Carson: Witness for nature*. Holt Paperbacks.

LOHAS Magazine. (2010). *LOHAS background*. Retrieved August 30, 2011, from *The LOHAS Magazine*: https://www.lohas.com/about

Loorbach, D., Frantzeskaki, N., & Avelino, F. (2017). Sustainability transitions research: Transforming science and practice for societal change. *Annual Review of Environment and Resources, 42*(1), 599–626.

Malthus, T. R. (1798/2011). *An essay on the principle of population: A view of its past and presents effects on human hapiness*. Forgotten Books.

Marx, K. (2000). *Das kapital*. Washington: Regnery.

Maslow, A. H. (1943). A theory of human motivation. *Psychological Review, 50*(4), 370–396.

Meadows, D. H., Randers, J., & Meadows, D. L. (2005). *Limits to growth: The 30-year update*. London: Earthscan.

Mill, J. S. (1863/2008). *Utilitarianism*. Forgotten Books.

Moore, M. (Director). (2009). *Capitalism: A love story* [Motion Picture].

NMI. (2010). *The 2010 LOHAS Global Reports*. Retrieved August 30, 2011, from The Natural Marketing Institute: https://www.nmisolutions.com/r_lohas_global.html

NMI. (2011). *The mainstreaming of sustainability in the U.S*. Retrieved August 30, 2011, from The Natural Marketing Institute: https://www.nmisolutions.com/r_lohas.html

O'Reilly, T. (2005). *What is Web 2.0: Design patterns and business models for the next generation of software*. Retrieved August 30, 2011, from O'Reilley Network: https://www.oreillynet.com/lpt/a/6228

Pigou, A. C. (1920/2005). *The economics of welfare: Volume 1*. New York: Cosimo.

Porter, M., & Kramer, M. (2006). Strategy and society: The link between competitive advantage and corporate social responsibility. *Harvard Business Review, 84*(12), 78–92.

Porter, M. E., & Kramer, M. R. (2011). The big idea: Creating shared value. *Harvard Business Review, 89*(1), 2.

Prahalad, C. K. (2010). *The fortune at the bottom of the pyramid: Eradicating poverty through profits we(5th anniversary edition)*. Upper Saddle River: Pearson.

PRME. (2011). *Principles of Responsible Management Education*. Retrieved August 30, 2011, from https://www.unprme.org/

Rasche, A., & Waddock, S. (2019). Global sustainability strategy in practice: Experiences from sustainability-oriented leaders. *Journal of Organizational Effectiveness: People and Performance, 6*(1), 2–20.

Rawls, J. (1999). *A theory of justice: Revised edition*. Cambridge: Harvard University Press.

RED. (2011). *The (RED) Idea*. Retrieved May 9, 2011, from RED: Designed to eliminate AIDS. https://www.joinred.com/aboutred

Smit, W., Wandel, J., & De Boer, J. (2019). The resilience spectrum: Three phases of adapting to environmental change. *Environment and Planning E. Nature and Space, 2*(4), 812–830.

Smith, A. (1776/2008). *An inquiry into the nature and causes of the wealth of nations*. Retrieved August 29, 2011, from The University of Adelaide Library Ebooks: https://ebooks.adelaide.edu.au/s/smith/adam/s64w/complete.html

Sprunger, M. (2011). *An introduction to Confucianism*. Retrieved August 29, 2011, from VI. Confucianism: The religion of social propriety: https://urantiabook.org/archive/readers/601_confucianism.htm

Spurlock, M. (Director). (2004). *Super size me* [Motion Picture].

Sosik, J. J., & Jung, D. I. (2018). *Full range leadership development: Pathways for people, profit, and planet*. Routledge.

Stubbs, W., & Cocklin, C. (2008). Conceptualizing a "sustainability business model". *Organization & Environment, 21*(2), 103–127.

Tammilehto, O. (2008, November). *A short history of unsustainability*. Retrieved August 11, 2011, from ymparistojakehitys.fi: https://www.ymparistojakehitys.fi/susopapers/Background_Paper_15_Olli_Tammilehto.pdf

Thielemann, U., & Wettstein, F. (2008). *The case against the business case and the idea of "earned reputation"*. St. Gallen: Institute for Business Ethics.

Timberlake, L. (2006). *Catalyzing change: A short history of the WBCSD*. Retrieved August 30, 2011, from World Business Council for Sustainable Development: https://www.wbcsd.org/DocRoot/acZUEFxTAKIvTsOKOtii/catalyzing-change.pdf

UNFCCC. (2011). *The Kyoto protocol*. Retrieved August 30, 2011, from United Nations Framework Convention on Climate Change: https://unfccc.int/kyoto_protocol/items/2830.php

United Nations. (1987). *Our common future*. United Nations, World Commission on the Environment and Development. New York: United Nations.

United Nations. (1997). *UN conference on environment and development (1992)*. Retrieved August 30, 2011, from United Nations: https://www.un.org/geninfo/bp/enviro.html

United Nations. (2011). *Millennium development goals*. Retrieved August 30, 2011, from https://www.un.org/millenniumgoals/

UNPRME. (2011). *Who developed the PRME?* Retrieved August 13, 2011, from unprme.org: https://www.unprme.org/the-6-principles/who-developed-prme/index.php

US Environmental Protection Agency. (2006). *Life cycle assessment: Principles and practice*. Ohio: US Environmental Protection Agency.

USA Today. (2005). *The rise and fall of WorldCom*. Retrieved August 30, 2011, from USA Today: https://www.usatoday.com/money/industries/telecom/2002-07-21-worldcom-chronology_x.htm

Waller, R. L., & Conaway, R. N. (2011). Framing and counterframing the issue of corporate social responsibility: The communication strategies of Nikebiz.com. *Journal of Business Communication, 48*(1), 83–106.

WWF. (2010). *Living planet report 2010*. Retrieved July 27, 2011, from footprintnetwork.org: https://www.footprintnetwork.org/press/LPR2010.pdf

B Conceptualizing

4 Sustainability

Understanding Sustainable Development

Readers of the earlier chapters, which described the state of the world, with all its issues, crises, human suffering, and environmental degradation, might arrive at simple, but fundamental questions: What can we do? Will we be able to stabilize and reverse the worrying state of the Earth? What is the cure?

Similar questions have led to the creation of the concept of sustainable development as an answer to the most pressing issues of the planet. Sustainable development is understood as a development that "(...) meets the needs of the present, without compromising the needs of future generations" (United Nations, 1987, p. 24). According to this definition, hence, sustainable development is a development, balancing present and future needs and sustaining today's resources for the future. Which are those resources? What is this capital that we have to sustain for future generations to live well?

A pragmatic definition

The Brundtland report defines sustainability with a strong focus on intergenerational justice or as the USA's first lady Michelle Obama put it in a speech in the White House, sustainable development has to do with "(...) the most important job - being a mom - and like mothers and fathers everywhere, the health and safety of our children is our top priority. This is what it is all about: The future" (Phillips, 2009.)

Barbier (1987) first described the three dimensions of sustainable development as a social, environmental and economic dimension, comprising different types of capital; social, environmental and economic capital. The economy is at the heart of a model of concentric circles that describes the interdependence of those three dimensions (Figure 4.1). The model shows how economic activity is restrained by the borders of society (the next bigger circle). If a company exceeds the borders of what society allows as acceptable economic activity it will lose its **license to operate**, meaning that society will force it to restrain its activity. This might happen, for instance, when consumers boycott a certain company due to a scandal, or when a company faces legal charges due to some societal or environmental damage done. Also is

DOI: 10.4324/9781003544074-7

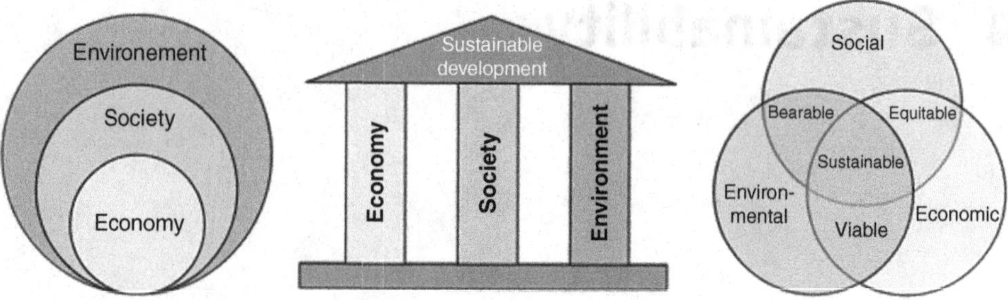

Figure 4.1 Main Graphic Concepts of the Three Dimensions of Sustainable Development. *United Nations (2005), Barbier (1987)*

the economy restrained by the society's labor force necessary for production and consumers' purchasing power. The biggest of the concentric circles is the environmental sphere, the planet, which constrains society in its growth. Unless we consider space colonization a viable option, the biological carrying capacity of the Earth is the final border for human population growth and economic growth alike.

Based on this graph the main variations describing the three dimensions of sustainable development have been developed. First, the famous pillar model conceptualizes how development can only be sustainable when balancing all three dimensions; co-creating and protecting social, environmental, and economic capital (United Nations, 2005). Second, a Venn diagram describes the different outcomes of unbalanced development (Barbier, 1987). For instance, a strong focus on joint economic and social development as has been observed in the People's Republic of China (with a stronger focus on the economic dimension) is equitable. It is an economic development, whose fruits are shared with people. Nevertheless, such a development pattern is not viable in the intersection between economy and environment. Environment is a necessary production input. Natural resources-based economic inputs such as steel and energy cannot keep up the pace with economic development. Such development neither is bearable in the relationship between society and environment. China's cities' air quality for instance is among the world's worst. Society - people - in cities largely suffer from pulmonary diseases. The outcomes of development are socially unbearable.

Elkington (1998) coined the term of the "triple bottom line", which translates the lofty sustainability concept to down-to-earth practice application. According to Elkington, in order to be sustainable, any activity has to produce a well-balanced triple bottom line between its social, environmental, and economic capital. In spite of the (financial-economic) "bottom line" being a business concept, the **triple bottom line** framework has been broadly accepted as a tool also for sustainable individual and governmental behavior. The basic assumption of the triple bottom line is that there are three kinds of capital, social, environmental and economic and that a sustainable activity has to protect or even renew all three types of capital in order to be called sustainable. In the frame of this book, we will describe the three main types of capital as follows:

- **Social capital** is any capital directly embodied in human beings. Social capital on the one hand comprises individual, so-called human capital including among others knowledge, skills, values and even physical health and personal well-being. On the other hand, social capital also comprises capital collectively created by interaction inside groups of human beings, such as joint values, culture, and collective welfare.

- **Natural (environmental) capital** comprises both renewable and non-renewable natural resources. Resources here should not be narrowly misunderstood as material production inputs, but also as non-material services provided by the natural environment such as the recreational value, realized while enjoying nature or flower pollination by bees.
- **Economic capital** can be expressed in monetary terms. It comprises tangible assets (often called man-made capital) such as machines or production facilities, intangible assets such as customer loyalty or brand value, and financial resources such as cash flows or a certain revenue margin. Economic capital can be attributed to an individual company or to the economic system as a whole.

Sustainable development and sustainability as a goal for businesses, civil society and government sectors has to fulfill two basic characteristics. A truly sustainable activity has to be characterized by balancing and sustaining all three types of capital. Balancing or horizontal sustainability creates a harmony between the social, environmental, and economic components of the activity. Vertical sustainability aims at sustaining - either protecting or even increasing - the social, environmental and economic capital involved for the future (Figure 4.2).

One might apply those two basic characteristics of analyzing sustainability for manifold types of activity. A law about to be passed by the government might be analyzed including its social, environmental, and economic consequences. Likewise, a certain consumption choice by a private individual might be analyzed. In the following two examples the importance of both vertical and horizontal sustainability will be illustrated for two activities in the business sector:

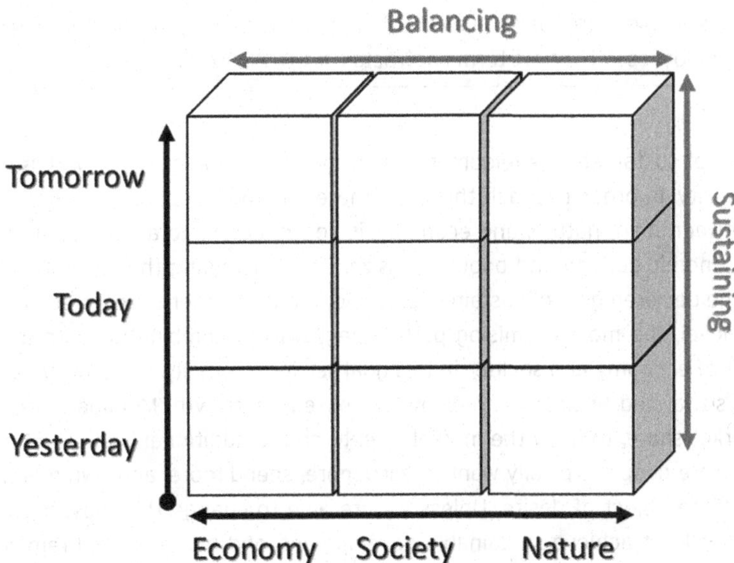

Figure 4.2 Tasks Necessary for Reaching Sustainability.

- **Donations and economic capital**: Should one consider a company that spends considerable amounts of money on donations for various good social and environmental causes a sustainable business? Most likely this company is creating social and/or environmental capital by its economic capital donations. Thus, the company is balancing well at least two out of three dimensions - types of capital - of horizontal sustainability. Then again, this company is not sustaining; respectively even decreasing the economic capital involved into the activity - spending money. Once the money is all spent, the donation campaign will cease to exist (the vertical dimension). It has not been sustained economically and therefore can neither sustain the creation of social and environmental capital in the future.
- **Short run profit maximization**: In the second example we look closer at a typical short-run profit maximizing company, exploiting natural resources and workers. While this company seems to be financially and economically sustainable, it is not harmonized, balanced with the environmental and social dimensions. Using up the environmental and social capital will finally have negative repercussions on what had seemed to be economically sustainable before. Workers might go on strike or leave the company completely. The environmental capital used for production might be used up. The business activity is not vertically sustainable in the long run, in none of the three dimensions of sustainable development.

From unsustainable behavior to global crisis

The 2007 subprime crisis with devastating effects on the global economy was based on unsustainable behavior. The root of the crisis - selling mortgages to people who were unlikely to pay back - was in itself economically unsustainable and morally wrong. In the aftermath the crisis also proved socially unsustainable as can be seen in the social capital destruction reflected in for instance massive job loss, mostly in the rather vulnerable employee groups such as youth, immigrants, lowly-skilled and older workers, and employees with short term contracts (OECD, 2009).

The final goal of sustainable development has to be to harmonically live within the Earth's carrying capacity. In order to reach this goal, there has to be a paradigm shift. To achieve harmony between man, nature, and economy, is contradictory to a continued quantitative growth of economic activity and population size. Even sustaining the current situation will not lead to the declared goal of sustainable development. In order to reach sustainability on a planetary level, the most promising path is degrowth in combination with a qualitative development of economy and society. In this goal setting one truly sees how big this task is. The current social and business paradigms are based on growth. Managers are trained to increase market share, to grow the market size, to create additional wants, and to increase revenues. Private people typically want to earn more, spend more, and own more. Limitless abundance is the object of desire. Unless we are able to change this most basic behavior patterns, we will not achieve sustainable development, and humanity will remain a highly endangered species destroying its own habitat.

An atypical business attitude

A region in the north of Argentina, famous for its impressive scenery, is eponymous of the outdoor clothing company Patagonia, which describes a very special vision of what abundance that might be just the right recipe for degrowth. The companies' owner Yvonne Chouinard explains as follows: "At Patagonia we choose to call them 'economies of abundance'. In an economy of abundance, there is enough. Not too much. Not too little. Enough. Most important, there is enough time for the things that matter: relationships, delicious food, art, games and rest. (...) At Patagonia, we are dedicated to abundance. We don't want to grow larger but want to remain lean and quick. We want to make the best clothes and make them so they will last a long, long time. Our idea is to make the best product so you can consume less and consume better" (Chouinard & Gallagher, 2004). Customers of Patagonia shops reported that cashiers even asked them: "Do you really need to buy this item?" (Wise, 2011).

Sectoral Contributions to Sustainable Development

In 2015, the United Nations communicated their current "masterplan" for reaching sustainable development, comprising 17 goals, and six central enablers for reaching these goals as illustrated in Table 4.1. As we can easily grasp from the picture, no single societal sector neither business, civil society, nor government will be able to reach these goals alone. Chapter 5 will examine the SDGs in more detail.

Table 4.1 United Nations Sustainable Development Goals 2015

1. End poverty in all its forms everywhere
2. End hunger, achieve food security and improved nutrition, and promote sustainable agriculture
3. Ensure healthy lives and promote well-being for all at all ages
4. Ensure inclusive and equitable quality education and promote life-long learning opportunities for all
5. Achieve gender equality and empower all women and girls
6. Ensure availability and sustainable management of water and sanitation for all
7. Ensure access to affordable, reliable, sustainable, and modern energy for all
8. Promote sustained, inclusive and sustainable economic growth, full and productive employment and decent work for all
9. Build resilient infrastructure, promote inclusive and sustainable industrialization and foster innovation
10. Reduce inequality within and among countries
11. Make cities and human settlements inclusive, safe, resilient and sustainable
12. Ensure sustainable consumption and production patterns
13. Take urgent action to combat climate change and its impacts
14. Conserve and sustainably use the oceans, seas and marine resources for sustainable development
15. Protect, restore and promote sustainable use of terrestrial ecosystems, sustainably manage forests, combat desertification, and halt and reverse land degradation and halt biodiversity loss
16. Promote peaceful and inclusive societies for sustainable development, provide access to justice for all and build effective, accountable and inclusive institutions at all levels
17. Strengthen the means of implementation and revitalize the global partnership for sustainable development

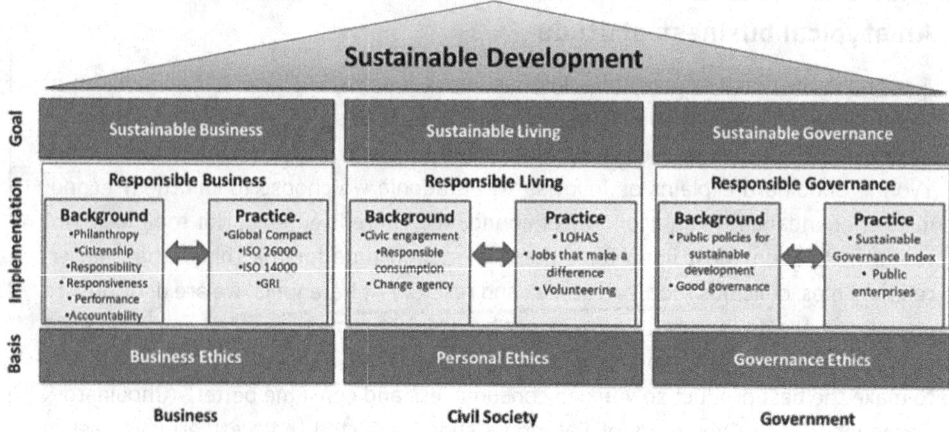

Figure 4.3 Sectoral Contributions to Sustainable Development.

To understand responsible business the model as illustrated in Figure 4.3 will be used to explain how the different societal sectors business, civil society, and government should contribute to sustainable development. In order to reach the final goal of sustainable development, the three main sectors of society have to reach a state of sustainability – socially, environmentally, and economically. The desired outcome is sustainable business for the business sector, sustainable living for civil society, and sustainable governance for the governmental sector.

Designing multi-sector solutions

Live Green Toronto is a program launched in 2007 by the city government, as a result of the Climate Change, Clean Air and Sustainable Energy action plan. The project works in association with both small and big businesses while hundreds of costumers using a system similar to a credit card receive benefits from the purchase of eco-friendly products. Live Green Toronto showcases the participation of all three sectors to jointly move towards a sustainable regional development (Live Green Toronto, 2011).

In order to reach the desired state of sustainable development, each sector has to implement a responsible practice aiming at sustainability. Responsibility here is defined as responsibility towards the ultimate goal of sustainable development. Responsible business is the practice of activities leading to the aspired outcome of being sustainable. The responsible practice for each sector is highly enhanced when based on sound ethical decision making, which is why Figure 4.3 bases every sector's activity on a specialized ethical framework such as business ethics, personal ethics, and governance ethics.

Sustainable Governance

On the way to reaching **sustainable governance**, the governmental sector has important contributions to make to the achievement of sustainable development. In order to achieve sustainable governance (or governance for sustainable development), the governmental sector's most powerful contribution consists of the making and implementation of laws and public policy measures for sustainable development. This governmental stage-setting function significantly influences both, civil society and business sectors. Government thus fulfills a support function in providing the regulatory and physical infrastructure for both sustainable business and sustainable living. The quality of public policies implemented to achieve responsible business have been divided into first generation (rudimentary implementation of responsible business activities), second generation (focus on priority sectors), and third generation (integration and mainstreaming) policies. Most countries worldwide display first- and second-generation public policies. Only the United Kingdom's public policy became classified a third-generation public policy framework, which is the highest classification (Bertelsmann Stiftung; GTZ, 2007).

Purposeful spending

The United Nations (UN) aims at actively promoting sustainable development by their procurement activities. In 2010 UN agencies spent more than US$14.5 billion. The UN claims to use their "purchasing power for good" (UNOPS, 2011b). The focus lies on supporting poorer countries in their development process by buying from them. In 2010 the UN's spending also focused strongly on furthering specific Millennium development goals such as reduction of child mortality and gender equality by their spending (UNOPS, 2011a).

The government and broad public sector also are important economic players. Public spending and public enterprises are main drivers of many industries such as construction, energy, and transportation. The public sector here can be a role model for private businesses, showcasing responsible management in their own organization. Many governments have done so, starting to focus on renewable energies, implementing sustainable sourcing policies, or defining energy efficiency standards for public housing. The sustainability of governments themselves is the subject of the Sustainable Governance Index (SGI). SGI covers main governmental performance indicators related to the social (e.g. welfare, and social inclusion), environmental (environment) and economic (e.g. economy, budgets, enterprises) dimensions of sustainability (SGI Network, 2011). The topic of good governance rather refers to the process of governance- public administration. Good governance is supposed to result in good outcomes. Issues of special concern are governance ethics, especially human rights, and corruption-related factors (UN ESCAP, 2011).

While the governmental sector does have a strong national power in creating legal and physical infrastructure, it also experiences major constraints in its potential to achieve sustainable development. One inhibiting factor is the speed of decision making, and implementation of changes that have already been decided upon. Due to mostly democratic and highly hierarchical structures urgent developments might not be implemented at the desired and urgently necessary pace. Especially in countries with a weak governmental structure, corruption and lacking knowledge also might be a factor leading to suboptimal outcomes. Governments also have been accused of being highly vulnerable to lobbying activities of companies and industries antagonizing sustainable development. Governments, while involved into diplomatic and supranational activities related to sustainable development, nevertheless exert the most significant influence on their own national territory. While most issues related to sustainable development are border-crossing and have a global impact. This narrow sphere of influence by governments makes an effective contribution more difficult. The later chapter on systemic change provides additional insights into what governments can do to contribute to sustainable development.

Sustainable Living

Sustainable (or unsustainable) living and what a world citizen makes out of his/her life is probably the most powerful force for or against change towards sustainable development.

Lifestyles influence consumption choices, which in turn define the demand for certain products and services. The quote "Every time you spend money, you're casting a vote for the kind of world you want", refers to so-called political consumption (Lappé & Lappé, 2002). It perfectly catches the essence of consumption which influences social and economic structures. The legal voting power of citizens also can exert an enormous influence over the public policies implemented for sustainable development. Sustainable living is not only about how to spend, but also how to earn the money spent. Sustainable living includes promoting sustainability throughout any job practiced by an individual and to "vote with the feet" if the employing organization is not conducive to improving its social and environmental footprint.

What are you owned by?

After its launch in 1999, the movie *Fight Club* became a cult classic showing the protagonist's particular way of dealing with his inconformity with society and consumerism. One of the quotes in the movie considered epic goes: "The things you own end up owning you" (Fincher, 1999).

Sustainable living refers to a personal lifestyle characterized by living a life, not exceeding the Earth's carrying capacity, to involve and actively promote change towards sustainability among individuals and organizations touching the spheres of one's life. In order not to exceed the personal footprint on the world's natural resources, sustainable living needs to be based on a certain change in behavior patterns, as individuals of middle and high economic purchasing power usually by far exceed the environmental footprint. The movement of simple living for instance promotes a lifestyle voluntarily focusing on the basic needs, while aiming at reducing personal dependence on superficial wants. Such simpler lives often lead to highly altered consumption patterns. So-called Freegans aim at totally avoiding consumerism and living from societies' leftovers. People living Lifestyles of Health and Sustainability (LOHAS), aim at changing their consumption patterns to more sustainable ways. The living and consumption styles related to sustainable living are manifold. Understanding those patterns is crucial for marketing sustainable products and will therefore be further explained in the chapters on communication in responsible business and management.

Activist or civic behavior is another facet of sustainable living, which aims at promoting sustainability in one's personal sphere of influence. Employing oneself as a change agent for sustainability can happen in either an individual pattern (as described in the first paragraph) or organized in some type of civil society organization. Civil society organizations, often interchangeably described as NGOs, may address many different social, environmental, political, or economic causes. A weakness of the civil society sector initiatives for sustainable development is the alleged lack of institutionalization, professionalization, and efficiency. The chapter on individual change illustrates tactics for reaching a sustainable living situation.

Sustainable Business

Sustainable business still is a utopia. To be truly sustainable, businesses would need to have a sustainable (at least neutral or even positive) impact throughout the social, environmental, and economic dimension. Some would argue that businesses can only become sustainable when the surrounding system is sustainable – a task possibly exceeding the influencing capability of an individual organization. However, a **responsible business** is a business that has made a commitment to reach this goal of becoming sustainable. On the way to this ultimate goal, responsible business conduct can very effectively contribute to sustainable development. A salient advantage of the business sector is its speed of decision making, based on a well-organized organizational structure, which allows businesses to quickly tackle any social, environmental, and economic issue at hand. Also, business is hardly constrained by national borders. Policies for sustainable development can be implemented simultaneously and on a global scale throughout business facilities in the most distinct locations. Also, the business sector has the financial means and mechanism of financial reproduction to put extensive policies in place and reproduce them on a large scale. Even more importantly, if business was able to make social and environmental responsibility a profitable part of its core business, the financial resources to contribute to sustainable development would become self-renewing and abundant.

A natural incentive

Imagine a business that develops a product to tap into a LOHAS market segment, let's say it starts to produce solar heaters. This business is likely to find out that this market segment is not only creating value for the goal of environmental sustainability, but is also highly attractive and profitable. A natural reaction then would be to invest even more resources into this venture. Automatically the businesses' contribution to sustainable development does grow in a parallel pattern with increased profit. However, such a natural incentive does not exist for all types of sustainable business activities. Some might require extensive investment with insecure returns. It is such activities that pose the biggest implementation challenge, and that are often regulated by laws forcing businesses to act sustainably or responsibly.

One of the most ambitious business sector initiatives for sustainable development is the World Business Council for Sustainable Development's (WBCSD) "Vision 2050", which aims at achieving in the year 2050, that 9 billion people will be able to "live well and within the limits of the planet" (WBCSD, 2010). The WBCSD Action 2020 strategy translated this vision into tangible direct actions along nine impact areas (e.g. climate change, ecosystems, and sustainable lifestyles) and five characteristics of the business solutions searched (e.g. beyond business as usual, scalable, impactful). But is following general principles enough? How do we know we have achieved the goal of sustainable business? There is a strong argument that a company can only claim to have become sustainable, based on an understanding of its own performance relates to the planetary boundaries described in the chapter on the status quo of the planet (Whiteman, Walker, & Perego, 2013). Only, if we can see the business in the context of the local and the planetary environmental systems can we reach an appreciation of the businesses' sustainability.

Disadvantageous characteristics of the business sector, when it comes to reaching sustainable business, are the inherent short-run profit maximization and the search for quick growth. One thing is for sure: However committed a business is to its ultimate responsibility for sustainable development, if its essence is the quest for constant quantitative growth (as opposed to qualitative improvement), in the long run, it will not and cannot be sustainable. As illustrated throughout this book, businesses and the economy have to start de-growing to a volume, where they serve the most important needs of a society of a size, which the planet can carry, efficiently and sustainably.

Current Developments

Since the previous edition of this book, sustainable development, particularly in the business sector, has undergone significant evolution and encountered various challenges. This development is primarily driven by the increasing recognition of the interconnectedness of economic growth, social inclusion, and environmental protection. One of the key developments in sustainable business practices has been the growing emphasis on environmental, social, and governance (ESG) issues in corporate strategies. Companies are increasingly integrating these factors into their business models, recognizing that sustainable practices can drive innovation, open new markets, and enhance their long-term viability. This shift in focus from reputation management to operational improvements and growth opportunities reflects a more pragmatic and business-oriented approach to sustainability. The adoption of the United Nations Sustainable Development Goals in 2015 has been a pivotal moment for sustainable development with many businesses seeking to align their strategies with the goals, recognizing their role in contributing to a sustainable future. This alignment not only helps address global challenges but also opens new opportunities for innovation and market development.

However, challenges persist. Despite growing awareness and initiatives, there is still a significant gap in integrating sustainability into core business operations. Many companies struggle to incorporate sustainability into supply chain management, budgeting, and key performance indicators (KPIs). Moreover, different industries face unique challenges and opportunities in sustainability, necessitating tailored strategies and solutions. Another critical issue is the role of sustainable development in promoting peace, justice, and strong institutions (SDG 16). The SDGs emphasize the importance of reducing violence, enhancing the rule of law, and developing effective and accountable institutions. This goal is particularly relevant for businesses operating in regions with conflict or weak governance, where they must navigate complex ethical and operational challenges. So, whilst sustainable development in the business sector has seen significant advancements, particularly in integrating ESG factors into corporate strategies and aligning with the SDGs, challenges remain in fully integrating sustainability into business operations and addressing industry-specific issues. Continued innovation, collaboration, and commitment from the business community are essential to overcome these challenges and achieve the ambitious targets set by the SDGs.

Exercises

A. KNOW

Use the below multiple-choice questions to test your knowledge. Each answer may be wrong or right and there may be zero to four right or wrong answers per question:

1. Sustainable development...
   a. ...in one of its primary concepts refers to the "three dimensions" of world development, state development and individual development.
   b. ...has been defined as a development that "satisfies all wants of present generations, while also enabling a luxurious life for future generations".
   c. ...in one of its main graphical representations defines joint economic and environmental development without social development as viable, while it is neither bearable, nor equitable and also not sustainable.
   d. ...does have a vertical and a horizontal dimension with the first describing persistence in time and the second describing the balance between social, environmental and economic development.
2. Sustainable governance...
   a. ...is the sectoral contribution to sustainable development by the governmental and public sector.
   b. ...comprises as one of its main functions is developing and implementing laws for sustainable development.
   c. ...also has an economic component, related to public enterprises.
   d. ...can have an immense influence by lawmaking and enforcement. Nevertheless, its effectiveness in contributing to sustainable development is often mitigated by a compared with the business sector low speed of decision making and influence on a rather narrow territory.
3. Sustainable business...
   a. ...is the sectoral contribution of the business sector to sustainable development.
   b. ...when contributing to sustainable development displays the two main advantages. First, especially multinational businesses have the capacity to make an impact in many countries in parallel. Second, businesses natural incentive for degrowth helps to reduce negative its impact.

c. ...can use its own to profit-seeking nature to co-create socio-environmental and business value.
d. ...connects to sustainable living for instance through the LOHAS market.

4. Sustainable living...
   a. ...is the sectoral contribution of the public sector to sustainable development.
   b. ...among others aims at having consumers making the right votes "with their wallets".
   c. ...comprises "voting with their feet", which in the context of this book is defined as quitting to work at a company that does not pay the highest wage in the market.
   d. ...is easy as only people living very luxuriously are likely to have an unsustainable footprint on the planet's systems.

B. THINK

Think about one sustainability issue such as water scarcity or poverty to understand how the civic, private, and public sectors may contribute to solving it. Make sure you appreciate how the three sectors relate instead of describing their contributions in isolation.

C. DO

Think about one concrete action that you could take to reduce negative environmental impact, or even to create a positive environmental impact. Repeat this action at least five times.

D. RELATE

Convince one person to change a concrete practice (e.g. printing, use of packaging, energy usage) to more sustainable ways.

E. BE

What does the topic of climate change mean to you? Then compare this appreciation with what it means to A) a Kenyan Fisherman, and B) the Brazilian head of state.

Feedback

A. KNOW

Feedback 1

a. Wrong: Society, environment, and economy are typically called the three dimensions of sustainable development.

b. Wrong: The main definition of sustainable development given by the Brundtland report defines a development that "(...) meets the needs of the present without comprising the needs of future generations". By no means is it a development that aims at satisfying neither today's nor future superficial wants, broadly exceeding peoples' basic needs to live a decent life.
c. Right: The concentric circles model, first used by Barbier in 1987 represents the described fact. Sustainable development can only be a joint social, environmental and economic development. Only if the three go together, development will be environmentally and socially bearable, economically and environmentally viable, and economically and socially equitable.
d. Right: The vertical and horizontal dimensions of sustainable development are its two basic defining characteristics.

Feedback 2

a. Right: Sustainable governance together with sustainable living and sustainable business is one of the three main necessary sectoral contributions to sustainable development.
b. Right: The most important contribution to sustainable development of the governmental sector is related to creating a legal infrastructure.
c. Right: Public enterprises are important economic players which as being significantly controlled by the governments are part of the governmental sector.
d. Right: While businesses are often characterized by a high speed of decision making and implementation as well as a multinational influence, governments often work at a slower pace and only on national territory.

Feedback 3

a. Right: Sustainable business, together with sustainable governance, is one of the three main necessary sectoral contributions to sustainable development.
b. Wrong: Businesses are naturally geared to growth. As a matter of fact, degrowth while being highly advantageous to reach sustainable development is not supported by the contemporary economic structure.
c. Right: The solar heater example illustrates a situation where the creation of environmental value is linked to profit-seeking activity.
d. Right: The Lifestyles of Health and Sustainability (LOHAS) market connects to sustainable living by proposing sustainable lifestyles, while LOHAS connects to sustainable business as a market segment prone to improve its socio-environmental impact.

Feedback 4

a. Wrong: The contribution to sustainable development of the public sector is called sustainable governance. Sustainable living is the contribution by civil society.
b. Right: A common quote by Lappé says "Every time you spend money, you're casting a vote for the kind of world you want". Consumption choices

automatically enforce or weaken companies and their respective impact on society and environment. Buying form sustainable businesses therefore gives power to the sustainable business movement, fostering sustainable development.

c. Wrong: "Voting with the feet" in the context of this book means to base the decision which company to work with on its social and environmental impact and/or improvements.

d. Wrong: Most people of middle-class socio-economic segments by far exceed what would be a sustainable footprint.

B. THINK

Level	*Multi-level analysis competence*	*Notes*
+	Solid description of each sectors distinct contribution and of the connection between the sectors.	
=	Solid description of each sectors distinct contribution.	
–	Little description of each sectors' distinct contribution to the issue.	

C. DO

Level	*Taking and sustaining action*	*Notes*
+	Action was taken and repeated at least five times.	
=	Action was taken.	
–	Action was either not identified or was identified but not taken.	

D. RELATE

Level	*Persuasion competence*	*Notes*
+	Adoption of new practice after application of persuasion.	
=	Adoption of practice in spite of little persuasion skill, or good persuasion skill, but no adoption of practice.	
–	Little evidence of persuasive skill and no adoption of more sustainable practice.	

E. BE

Level	*Ability to take different perspectives*	*Notes*
+	Profound level of insight into multiple perspectives displayed.	
=	Multiple perspectives evident in description.	
–	Evidence of singular perspective on climate change.	

References

Barbier, E. (1987). The concept of sustainable economic development. *Environmental Conservation, 14*(2), 101–110.

Bertelsmann Stiftung; GTZ. (2007). *The CSR navigator: Public policies in Africa, the Americas, Asia and Europe*. Eschborn: GTZ.

Brundtland, G. H. (1987). *Presentation of the report of the World Comission on Environment and Development to UNEP's 14th governing council*. Nairobi.

Chouinard, Y., & Gallagher, N. (2004). *Don't buy this shirt unless you need it*. Retrieved August 24, 2011, from Patagonia: https://www.patagonia.com/us/patagonia.go?assetid=2388

Elkington, J. (1998). *Cannibals with forks: The triple bottom line of 21st century business*. Gabriola Island: New Society Publishers.

Fincher, D. (Director). (1999). *Fight club* [Motion Picture].

Lappé, F. M., & Lappé, A. (2002). *Hope's edge: The next diet for a small planet*. New York: Tarcher/Penguin.

Live Green Toronto. (2011). *About Live Green Toronto*. Retrieved August 19, 2011, from toronto.ca: https://www.toronto.ca/livegreen/greenleaders_toronto_about.htm

OECD. (2009). *Impact of the economic crisis on employment and unemployment in the OECD countries*. Retrieved August 30, 2011, from Directorate for employment, labour and social affairs: https://www.oecd.org/document/63/0,3746,en_2649_33927_41727231_1_1_1_1,00.html

Phillips, M. (2009). *The world we leave our children*. Retrieved August 24, 2011, from The White House Blog: https://www.whitehouse.gov/blog/2009/02/26/world-we-leave-our-children

SGI Network. (2011). *Sustainable governance indicators 2001*. Retrieved August 24, 2011, from https://www.sgi-network.de/

UN ESCAP. (2011). *What is good governance?* Retrieved August 24, 2011, from United Nations Economic and Social Comission for Asian and the Pacific: https://www.unescap.org/pdd/prs/ProjectActivities/Ongoing/gg/governance.asp

United Nations. (1987). *Our common future*. United Nations, World Commission on the Environment and Development. New York: United Nations.

United Nations. (2005). *2005 World Summit outcome*. New York: United Nations.

UNOPS. (2011a). *Procurement and the Millennium Development Goals*. New York: United Nations.

UNOPS. (2011b). *2010 annual statistical report on United Nations procurement*. New York: United Nations.

WBCSD. (2010). *Vision 2050: The new agenda for business in brief*. Geneva: World Business Council for Sustainable Development.

Whiteman, G., Walker, B., & Perego, P. (2013). Planetary boundaries: Ecological foundations for corporate sustainability. *Journal of Management Studies, 50*(2), 307–336.

Wise, J. (2011). *There's no such thing as a sustainable business*. Retrieved August 24, 2011, from Jonathan Wise's sustainability scrapbook: https://jonathanwise1.wordpress.com/2011/01/31/theres-no-such-thing-as-a-sustainable-business/

5 Sustainable Development Goals

The introduction of the Sustainable Development Goals (SDGs) represents a pivotal moment in society's quest towards social, environmental and economic sustainability. They were developed as a framework to replace the outgoing Millennium Development Goals (MDGs) that guided international development from 2000 to 2015 (United Nations, 2015); the SDGs comprise a broad and ambitious set of 17 goals designed to address a wide range of global sustainability challenges. Their development followed an extensive process which relied on the collaboration of nations, civil society, and other stakeholders, which began following the Rio+20 Conference on Sustainable Development mandate in 2012 (United Nations Conference on Sustainable Development, 2012) and culminated in the adoption of the 2030 Agenda for Sustainable Development by all United Nations Member States in September 2015 (United Nations, 2015). The framework is based on the understanding that social, economic, and environmental issues are intrinsically linked and that progress towards sustainability requires an integrated approach, holistically applied (Griggs et al., 2013).

Historical Context and Evolution

The roots of the Sustainable Development Goals (SDGs) can be traced back to the 1972 United Nations Conference on the Human Environment held in Stockholm. This landmark event catalysed a global consciousness of the intricate relationships between human development and environmental protection. The concept of sustainable development continued to evolve, notably crystallized in the 1987 Brundtland Report, "Our Common Future", which defined sustainable development as meeting "the needs of the present without compromising the ability of future generations to meet their own needs" (World Commission on Environment and Development, 1987).

Millennium Development Goals

The Millennium Development Goals (MDGs), established in 2000, marked the first concerted international effort to set specific targets for poverty reduction, education, and health. The MDGs were a set of eight global development goals that all 191 United Nations member states at that time and at least 22 international organizations agreed to achieve by the year 2015.

DOI: 10.4324/9781003544074-8

Figure 5.1 The Millennial Development Goals (MDGs).

This ambitious program aimed primarily to confront the multifaceted nature of poverty. When assessed in retrospect, the narrative of the MDGs is one of both triumph and caution (Figure 5.1).

> **The MDGs and business**
>
> Levi Strauss & Co. integrated the Millennium Development Goals (MDGs) into their business strategy by requiring suppliers to support them through workplace policies, programs, and community outreach. This approach aimed to create positive local community impacts such as improved health and nutrition and provide access to bank accounts and financial literacy, which could lead to industry stability and sustainable product supply.

Success or Failure?

In the realm of poverty reduction, the achievements were striking. A target to diminish the ranks of those living in the most severe straits of impoverishment was reached with a commendable margin of time to spare. The incidence of extreme poverty, defined as subsistence on less than US$1.25 a day, plunged from 47% in 1990 to a lower though still troubling 14% in 2015. The education domain, particularly at the primary level, saw heartening advances. By 2015, enrolment figures in the developing parts of the world soared to 91%, a significant jump from the 83% recorded at the turn of the millennium. Gender equality took positive strides forward, with classrooms increasingly populated by girls and the corridors of power echoing more strongly with women's voices as they secured more excellent representation in parliamentary roles. A similar upward trajectory was observed in health-related measures. The mortality rate for children under five witnessed a steep fall, halving from 90 deaths per 1,000 live births in 1990 to 43 in 2015. Maternal health, too, saw substantial improvement, with the mortality ratio declining by nearly half on a global scale. Efforts to combat disease also bore fruit, particularly in the fight against HIV/AIDS, where the tide began to turn with a 40% drop in new infections from 2000 to 2013.

However, this narrative is tempered by the realization that the MDGs may have reached for the low-hanging fruit while leaving the more entrenched and complex branches of poverty untouched. Critics pointed out that the goals, in their targeted approach, skirted around the deep-seated structural factors that perpetuate poverty and inequality. The progress, while significant, was not uniform, with disparities in achievements across different regions and countries indicating that the development path is not a one-size-fits-all. This mixed legacy set the stage for a more nuanced and comprehensive sequel: The Sustainable Development Goals (SDGs). The SDGs were designed to pick up where the MDGs left off, aiming not only to continue the fight against poverty but to address its root causes and ensure prosperity and protection of the planet for future generations.

The Road to the SDGs

Recognizing these limitations, the international community embarked on a path towards a more inclusive and comprehensive framework. The Rio+20 Conference provided the mandate for an open working group to develop goals to build upon the MDGs and integrate social, economic, and environmental dimensions (United Nations Conference on Sustainable Development, 2012). The inclusive nature of the process involved an unprecedented level of public consultation and participation from a wide array of stakeholders (Le Blanc, 2015).

The Framework and Principles of the SDGs

The resultant 17 Sustainable Development Goals and 169 targets articulate a global agenda for transformative change by 2030 (United Nations, 2015). Unifying principles such as universality, integration, and indivisibility reflect a shift from a segmented approach to a systemic view of development challenges (Biermann et al., 2017) (Figure 5.2).

Figure 5.2 The Sustainable Development Goals.

Universality

Universality refers to the universal scope of the SDGs, meaning that they are not just targets for developing countries but apply to all countries. This versatile nature acknowledges that issues like climate change, inequality, and unsustainable consumption are global problems requiring action from all countries, regardless of their income level. This represents a shift from the MDGs, primarily focusing on the Global South. Universality in the SDGs calls for shared responsibility, recognizing that all countries have a part to play in promoting sustainable development.

Integration

Integration underscores the interconnectedness of the SDGs. Unlike the MDGs, which were often pursued in isolation, the integrated approach of the SDGs recognises that the goals are interdependent and that strategies to achieve one goal can support or hinder the achievement of others. For example, actions to reduce poverty (Goal 1) are inextricably linked to improving health (Goal 3), education (Goal 4), and reducing inequality (Goal 10). This integrated approach encourages policymakers to design strategies that simultaneously address multiple goals, reflecting a systemic view that considers economic, social, and environmental dimensions of development.

Indivisibility

Indivisibility suggests that all the SDGs should be treated equally crucial for our planet's well-being and inhabitants. This principle rejects prioritizing some goals over others, a common criticism of the MDGs, where the most accessible indicators often measure progress to quantify. The indivisibility of the SDGs means that neglecting one area can have adverse effects on others, reinforcing the need for a balanced approach to development.

The 17 Global Goals

The 17 SDGs are interconnected; the key to success on one will often involve tackling issues more commonly associated with another. Table 5.1 provides an overview of each goal:

Table 5.1 The 17 Global Goals

1. No Poverty:	This goal focuses on eradicating extreme poverty (people living on less than US$1.25 a day) and reducing the proportion of men, women, and children living in poverty in all its dimensions according to national definitions. It involves implementing social protection systems, ensuring equal rights to economic resources, and building the resilience of low-income people and those in vulnerable situations.
2. Zero Hunger:	This aims to end hunger and all forms of malnutrition by 2030. It includes promoting sustainable agriculture, achieving food security, improving nutrition, and ensuring that everyone has access to sufficient and nutritious food all year round.
3. Good Health and Well-being:	The goal here is to promote physical and mental health and well-being, and extend life expectancy by addressing major health priorities, including maternal and child health, communicable diseases, universal health coverage, and access to safe, effective, quality, and affordable medicines and vaccines for all.
4. Quality Education:	This goal aims to ensure inclusive and equitable quality education and promote opportunities for lifelong learning. Targets include free primary and secondary education, equal access to pre-primary education, and affordable technical, vocational, and higher education.
5. Gender Equality:	The objective is to end discrimination and violence against women and girls. This involves eliminating harmful practices such as child, early and forced marriage, and female genital mutilation and ensuring women's full participation in leadership and decision making.
6. Clean Water and Sanitation:	The aim is to ensure availability and sustainable management of water and sanitation for all. This includes achieving universal and equitable access to safe and affordable drinking water and sanitation and improving water quality by reducing pollution.
7. Affordable and Clean Energy:	This goal seeks to ensure access to affordable, reliable, sustainable, and modern energy services for all. It also aims to increase substantially the share of renewable energy in the global energy mix and improve energy efficiency.
8. Decent Work and Economic Growth:	The focus is on promoting sustained, inclusive, and sustainable economic growth, full and productive employment, and decent work for all. This includes reducing the proportion of youth not in employment, education, or training.
9. Industry, Innovation, and Infrastructure:	This goal is about building resilient infrastructure, promoting inclusive and sustainable industrialization, and fostering innovation. It includes increasing the access of small-scale industries to financial services and integrating them into value chains and markets.
10. Reduced Inequality:	The targets under this goal include progressively achieving and sustaining income growth of the bottom 40% of the population at a rate higher than the national average and eliminating discriminatory laws, policies, and practices.

(*Continued*)

Table 5.1 (Continued)

11. Sustainable Cities and Communities:	This goal aims to make cities and human settlements inclusive, safe, resilient, and sustainable. This involves enhancing inclusive and sustainable urbanization and ensuring that everyone has access to safe and affordable housing and basic services.
12. Responsible Consumption and Production:	The aim is to ensure sustainable consumption and production patterns. This involves promoting resource and energy efficiency, sustainable infrastructure, and providing access to basic services, green and decent jobs, and a better quality of life for all.
13. Climate Action:	This goal calls for urgent action to combat climate change and its impacts. This includes integrating climate change measures into national policies and planning and building resilience and adaptive capacity to climate-related disasters.
14. Life Below Water:	The aim is to conserve and sustainably use the oceans, seas, and marine resources for sustainable development. This includes preventing and significantly reducing marine pollution and overfishing and conserving at least 10% of coastal and marine areas.
15. Life on Land:	This goal aims to protect, restore, and promote the sustainable use of terrestrial ecosystems, manage forests sustainably, combat desertification, and halt and reverse land degradation and halt biodiversity loss.
16. Peace and Justice Strong Institutions:	The goal is to promote peaceful and inclusive societies for sustainable development, provide access to justice for all, and build effective, accountable institutions at all levels.
17. Partnerships for the Goals:	This goal recognizes that the SDGs can only be realized with a strong commitment to global partnership and cooperation. It focuses on strengthening the means of implementation and revitalizing the global partnership for sustainable development.

Targets and Indicators

The SDGs are accompanied by a set of targets and indicators that provide a framework for measuring and tracking progress. Each SDG has specific targets, which are measurable and action-oriented objectives. There are 169 targets in total for all 17 goals. A set of indicators are used to assess the progress towards these targets. Indicators are data points that provide evidence about the state or change of an aspect related to a target. They are tools for measurement that can quantifiably assess a particular concept, such as the proportion of the population living below the national poverty line or the mortality rate for children under five years of age. Each target has at least one indicator, and more than 230 are combined for all the marks. These indicators are established by the Inter-Agency and Expert Group on SDG Indicators (IAEG-SDGs) and are used to monitor progress, inform policy, and ensure accountability. The indicators are typically quantitative, but some are qualitative.

The indicators are classified into three tiers based on their level of methodological development and the availability of data at the global level:

Tier 1: The indicator is conceptually clear, has an internationally established methodology, and countries regularly produce data.

Tier 2: The indicator is conceptually straightforward and has an internationally established methodology, but data are only sometimes produced by countries.

Tier 3: The indicator still needs an internationally established methodology or standards.

The targets and indicators are designed to be integrated and inseparable, reflecting the complex and interlinked nature of the goals. To be effectively achieved, they require collaboration across sectors and actors, including governments, international organizations, the private sector, and civil society. For example, Goal 1, "No Poverty", has targets ranging from reducing by at least half the proportion of men, women, and children of all ages living in poverty to implementing appropriate social protection systems and measures for all. Indicators for these targets include the proportion of the population living below the national poverty line or the proportion of the total government spending on essential services such as education, health, and social protection.

The Global Indicator Framework was adopted by the UN General Assembly on July 6, 2017, and is used by UN Member States to report progress towards the SDGs. The United Nations Statistics Division oversees the framework, ensuring that data is collected and used to measure progress and inform policy.

Implementation and Progress

The implementation of the Sustainable Development Goals (SDGs) is a comprehensive process that involves multiple stakeholders at both the global and local levels. The United Nations spearheads the overarching framework, providing guidance and monitoring progress through various platforms and reports. Individual countries are primarily responsible for adopting and integrating the goals into their national development agendas and policies.

National governments typically establish SDG-focused committees or working groups to align the goals with existing strategies, laws, and budgets. These entities often include representatives from civil society, academia, the private sector, and other relevant stakeholders, ensuring a multi-sectoral approach. The private sector plays a critical role by aligning its business practices with SDGs, investing in sustainable solutions, and innovative partnerships. Civil society organizations contribute by advocating for SDG implementation, holding governments accountable, and driving community-based initiatives. Academia contributes through research and evaluation of SDG-related programs and policies. International organizations, including the World Bank and various UN agencies, provide support through expertise, financial resources, and capacity building (Figure 5.3).

Monitoring and evaluation mechanisms are integral to this process, with countries expected to report on their progress using a set of globally agreed indicators. Voluntary National Reviews (VNRs) are presented at the High-Level Political Forum on Sustainable Development, the central platform for follow-up and review of the SDGs at the global level. This multi-stakeholder, multi-level approach reflects the SDGs' complexity and ambition, requiring concerted effort and collaboration across borders, sectors, and disciplines to achieve the 2030 Agenda.

Challenges and Criticisms

While the SDGs have been celebrated for their breadth and ambition, they have also faced criticism. Concerns have been raised about the feasibility of implementation, potential conflicts between goals, and issues of accountability and measurement (Stafford-Smith et al., 2017). A primary concern is their ambitious and broad scope, which can be overwhelming for implementation and measurement. Critics argue that the 169 targets and over 230 indicators might dilute focus and resources. Additionally, there is a critique regarding the need for a

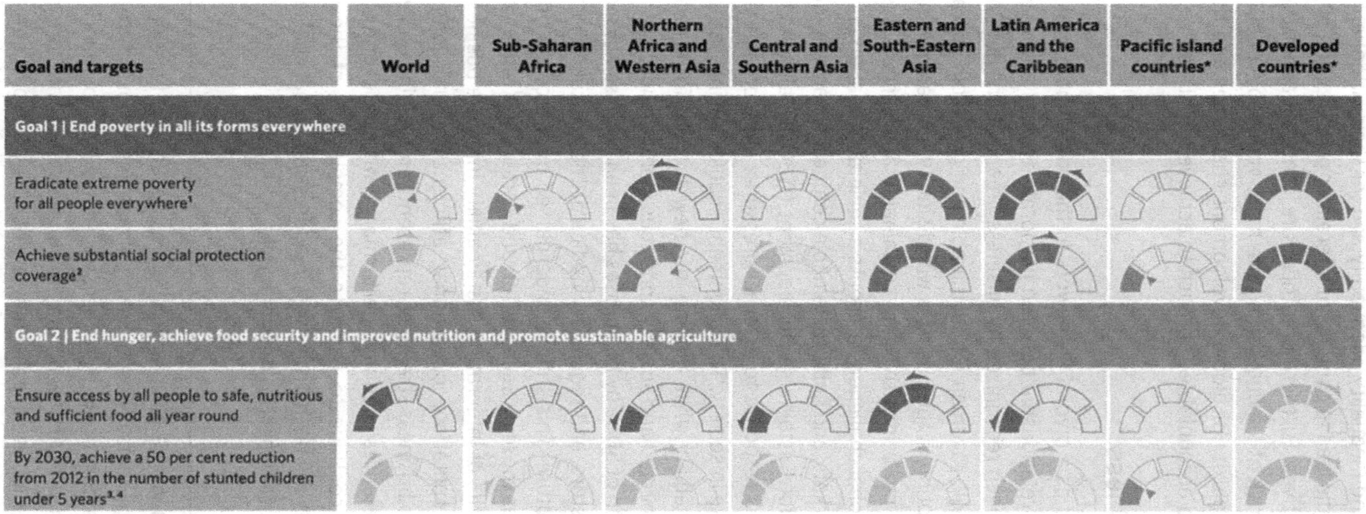

Goal and targets	World	Sub-Saharan Africa	Northern Africa and Western Asia	Central and Southern Asia	Eastern and South-Eastern Asia	Latin America and the Caribbean	Pacific island countries*	Developed countries*
Goal 1 | End poverty in all its forms everywhere								
Eradicate extreme poverty for all people everywhere[1]								
Achieve substantial social protection coverage[2]								
Goal 2 | End hunger, achieve food security and improved nutrition and promote sustainable agriculture								
Ensure access by all people to safe, nutritious and sufficient food all year round								
By 2030, achieve a 50 per cent reduction from 2012 in the number of stunted children under 5 years[3,4]								

Figure 5.3 Extract from The Sustainable Development Goals Progress Chart 2022. (*UNSTATS, 2022*)

precise, enforceable mechanism for achieving these goals, leading to questions about their practicality and effectiveness. The SDGs have also been criticized for failing to address the root causes of poverty and inequality adequately and for their potential reliance on private-sector funding, which could lead to conflicts of interest or prioritization of profit over sustainable development objectives. Furthermore, there are concerns about the uneven progress across regions and the risk of leaving behind the most vulnerable populations. These criticisms highlight the complexity of global development challenges and the need for a more integrated, inclusive, and accountable approach to achieve the SDGs.

The SDGs and Business

The SDGs have emerged as a pivotal framework in the contemporary global business environment, reshaping the relationship between corporate entities and societal development. They have increasingly been recognized by business organizations not only as a moral compass but also as a strategic roadmap for sustainable and profitable operations. SDGs' growing importance and adoption in the business world signify a paradigm shift from traditional profit-centric models to more inclusive and sustainable approaches. Businesses recognize that addressing these global challenges presents a societal obligation and an opportunity to innovate, create new markets, and build sustainable competitive advantages. As noted by the World Business Council for Sustainable Development (WBCSD), aligning business strategies with SDGs is not merely a response to external pressures but a proactive approach to redefining the role of business in society. This alignment enables businesses to contribute meaningfully to global sustainability while tapping into new avenues for growth and resilience in an increasingly interconnected and socially conscious market landscape.

Moreover, the adoption of SDGs by businesses has been catalysed by a growing awareness among consumers, investors, and regulatory bodies of the critical role corporations play in shaping a sustainable future. This shift is underpinned by a growing body of evidence, as outlined in studies such as those by Sachs (2015) and Porter and Kramer (2011), which demonstrate the tangible benefits of integrating sustainability into core business practices, including enhanced brand reputation, operational efficiencies, and long-term profitability. Integrating the SDGs into business strategies represents an evolving understanding of corporate success, one that balances economic performance with social and environmental stewardship. As businesses continue to navigate the complexities of the 21st century, their commitment to the SDGs will be instrumental in addressing global challenges and pivotal in shaping the future of sustainable business practices.

The UN Global Compact is a voluntary initiative encouraging businesses worldwide to adopt sustainable and socially responsible policies and report on their implementation. It aligns its strategic goals with the Sustainable Development Goals (SDGs) by emphasising ten human rights, labor, the environment, and anti-corruption principles. The Compact aims to mobilise a global movement of sustainable companies and stakeholders to create the world we want, thus contributing to achieving the SDGs through responsible business practices.

Corporate Social Responsibility (CSR) and the SDGs

The evolving concept of Corporate Social Responsibility (CSR) in the context of the Sustainable Development Goals (SDGs) marks a significant shift in how businesses approach societal and environmental challenges. Traditionally viewed as a voluntary mechanism for societal contribution, CSR has transformed into a strategic tool aligned with the broader objectives of sustainable development. This transformation moves away from traditional philanthropic activities, advocating for integrating social and environmental concerns into core business operations and strategies. Schaltegger and Wagner (2011) emphasise that CSR, underpinned by SDGs, extends beyond charity, requiring businesses to embed sustainable practices into their operational fabric.

In addressing the alignment of CSR with SDGs, the concept of materiality has gained prominence. Companies are focusing on the most relevant SDGs to their business, ensuring that their CSR efforts align with their business objectives and global sustainability challenges. For instance, an energy sector corporation might focus its CSR initiatives on Affordable and Clean Energy (Goal 7) and Climate Action (Goal 13), as highlighted by Eccles et al. (2014). This focus ensures a meaningful impact, where corporate efforts are directed towards areas where they can exert the most influence. Another critical aspect of this evolved CSR approach is the emphasis on innovative partnerships and collaboration. The achievement of SDGs necessitates collaborative efforts across sectors involving governments, NGOs, and other stakeholders. Austin and Seitanidi (2012) highlight that emphasising Partnerships for the Goals (Goal 17) underscores the importance of collaborative efforts in CSR strategies to tackle complex sustainability challenges.

Measuring and communicating the impact of CSR activities aligned with SDGs has also become a focal point for businesses. Standardized reporting frameworks like the Global Reporting Initiative (GRI) and the United Nations Global Compact have been instrumental. These frameworks enable companies to transparently report their contributions towards the SDGs, enhancing accountability and stakeholder trust, as explored by Kolk (2016). Moreover, integrating SDGs into CSR is not limited to external strategies but also involves fostering a sustainable corporate culture. This approach includes employee engagement in CSR initiatives, vital for creating a motivated workforce and a sustainable corporate culture. Glavas and Kelley (2014) discuss how employee involvement in CSR activities related to SDGs fosters a sense of purpose and commitment, contributing to overall corporate sustainability.

Integrating SDGs into Corporate Strategy

Integrating Sustainable Development Goals (SDGs) into corporate strategy represents a paradigm shift in how businesses approach sustainability and social responsibility. This integration is not merely an ethical imperative but has become a strategic necessity in modern business.

Understanding the Business Case for SDGs: The first step in integrating SDGs into corporate strategy is to recognise their relevance to business operations and growth, according to Scheyvens et al. (2016), the SDGs provide a framework for businesses to identify and address their operations' social and environmental impacts, which in turn can drive innovation, open new markets, and enhance brand value. This alignment is not just beneficial for society and the environment but also contributes to long-term business success.

Strategic Alignment with SDGs: Companies must assess which SDGs are most relevant to their business context. As noted by Sachs (2015), this involves evaluating the company's core activities, supply chain, and operational footprint to identify where they can make the most significant impact. For instance, a corporation in the manufacturing sector might focus on SDG 9 (Industry, Innovation, and Infrastructure) and SDG 12 (Responsible Consumption and Production), seeking ways to innovate in product design and manufacturing processes to reduce environmental impact.

Setting Targets and Measuring Impact: Effective integration of SDGs into corporate strategy requires setting clear, measurable targets and regularly monitoring progress. KPMG (2017) emphasises the importance of businesses establishing specific, quantifiable goals aligned with the SDGs to ensure accountability and transparency in their sustainability efforts.

Engaging Stakeholders: Stakeholder engagement is crucial in aligning corporate strategies with SDGs. As Porter and Kramer (2011) argued, creating shared value involves understanding the needs and challenges of various stakeholders, including employees, customers, suppliers, and the broader community. This engagement helps identify material issues related to SDGs and fosters collaboration and partnership, which are essential for achieving these goals.

Embedding SDGs in Corporate Culture: Integrating SDGs into a company's culture is vital. As highlighted by Bocken et al. (2014), fostering a culture of sustainability within the organisation encourages innovation and commitment among employees towards achieving the SDGs, making them an integral part of the company's identity and operations.

SDG Integration in Action

Greggs, a prominent UK food-on-the-go retailer, has integrated the SDGs into its corporate strategy by establishing The Greggs Pledge. Launched in 2021, The Greggs Pledge is the company's first complete sustainability plan, underscoring its commitment to positively impacting society and the environment. The Greggs Pledge is structured around three strategic pillars: building stronger, healthier communities, making the planet safer, and being a better business. These pillars are supported by ten specific commitments that align with the ambitions of the SDGs, with Greggs focusing on the areas where it believes it can make the most significant difference. Greggs Corporate| Our strategy

The Future of the Sustainable Development Goals (SDGs) Post-2030

As we look towards the future of the Sustainable Development Goals (SDGs) beyond 2030, it is essential to consider the evolving landscape shaped by various challenges and the lessons learned during implementing these goals. The journey of the SDGs has been marked by imbalances and trade-offs, where progress has been uneven across different regions. Developing countries, grappling with basic needs like clean water and energy, contrast sharply with developed countries, where the focus is more on responsible consumption and production. The COVID-19 pandemic has further complicated the path towards achieving the SDGs. It has led to a marked decline in global SDG performance, adversely impacting poverty, health, education, and economic stability. This setback calls for strategies that are resilient and adaptable to unforeseen global challenges (Zhao et al., 2022).

The focus is shifting towards a more nuanced approach to SDG implementation. Prioritization and focused acceleration are key, drawing lessons from previous global goals like the Millennium Development Goals. This involves strategically selecting targets based on criticality and feasibility and integrating actions into mainstream planning frameworks. Localization emerges as a crucial element in this future trajectory. Having played a pivotal role in responding to the COVID-19 crisis, local governments are now recognized as essential in achieving SDG goals. Support for local actions and the application of SDGs at the city level are increasingly seen as vital to success (Persson, 2022).

Moreover, there is a growing recognition of the need to move beyond anecdotal evidence towards best-practice interventions. This shift entails a detailed evaluation of interventions that can significantly impact SDG performance and create synergies. The aim is to identify strategies that accelerate action and ensure transformative change. In summary, the post-2030 era for the SDGs will likely be characterised by an adaptive, localized, and evidence-based approach, drawing on past lessons while addressing present and future challenges.

Exercises

A. KNOW

Use the below multiple-choice questions to test your knowledge. Each answer may be wrong or right, and there may be zero to four right or wrong answers per question:

1. What was the main focus of the Millennium Development Goals (MDGs)?
   a. ...Climate change.
   b. ...Sustainable agriculture.
   c. ...Poverty reduction.
   d. ...Gender equality.
2. What does the principle of "Universality" in SDGs refer to?
   a. ...Goals are only for developing countries.
   b. ...Goals apply to all countries, irrespective of income level.
   c. ...Only universal problems like climate change are addressed.
   d. ...Each country can choose their own goals.
3. Which conference led to the mandate for the Sustainable Development Goals (SDGs)?
   a. ...The 1972 United Nations Conference on the Human Environment.
   b. ...The 1987 Brundtland Report Conference.
   c. ...The Rio+20 Conference on Sustainable Development in 2012.
   d. ...The United Nations Millennium Summit in 2000.

4. What is the primary role of indicators associated with the Sustainable Development Goals?
    a. ...To provide financial assistance for goal implementation.
    b. ...To establish new targets every year.
    c. ...To provide evidence about the state or change of an aspect related to a target.
    d. ...To replace outdated targets with new ones.
5. How have businesses recognized the importance of the Sustainable Development Goals (SDGs)?
    a. ...As a regulatory compliance requirement.
    b. ...As a moral compass and a strategic roadmap for operations.
    c. ...As a temporary trend in social development.
    d. ...As a means to reduce taxation.

B. THINK

Consider the SDG framework and list how many of the SDGs relate to the activities of your business or a business that you have worked for or are familiar with.

C. DO

Think about which SDG you relate to the most from a personal point of view. Consider what actions you could take in your own life or within your community to advance the goals it represents, such as volunteering for local initiatives, advocating for policy changes, or making lifestyle choices that reduce your environmental footprint. Reflect on how you can contribute to achieving this goal through daily actions, collaboration, and awareness-raising to drive positive change.

D. RELATE

Talk with someone in your business or your family about the SDGs. Are they aware of them in their professional and/or personal lives? If not, explain them in the best way you are able. Do they think they provide a helpful framework through which to advance society? Do they think that there are too many or too few SDGs?

E. BE

How do you feel about the SDGs as a universal call to action? Do you think they are an effective way to get governments and organizations to consider sustainable development? Do you feel hopeful? Focus on your internal reactions to the challenges set out in the chapter and try to capture how it makes you feel and your attitudes to the overall development or single events. Can your reactions be impressed in feelings, motivations, moods, or attitudes? Do you react differently to different events or events in this history? How do you explain your reaction?

Feedback

A. KNOW

Feedback 1

a. Wrong: Climate change was not explicitly addressed in the Millennium Development Goals.

b. Wrong: Whilst the concept of sustainable agriculture can be implicitly linked to the Millennium Development Goals (MDGs), particularly under Goal 1: Eradicate Extreme Poverty and Hunger, and Goal 7: Ensure Environmental Sustainability it was not an explicit feature.

c. Right: The MDG's primary aim was for poverty reduction with a view that in doing so, the other issues would also be addressed by proxy.

d. Wrong: Gender equality was not the focus of the Millennium Development Goals; rather, it was one of the eight interlinked goals intended to address the various facets of global development.

Feedback 2

a. Wrong: Whilst many of the challenges typified by the SDGs are experienced more acutely by developing countries, developed countries are also impacted and must act.

b. Right: "Universality" means the SDGs apply to all countries irrespective of income level.

c. Wrong: Arguably each of the SDGs is a universal problem

d. Wrong: Each country must assess their progress against each of the 17 SDGs. Whilst some will be more material to a country than others, the universality of the goals means that they are intrinsically linked.

Feedback 3

a. Wrong: The 1972 United Nations Conference on the Human Environment also known as the Stockholm Conference, was the first major international conference to focus on environmental issues at the global level.

b. Wrong: The 1987 Brundtland Report, officially titled "Our Common Future", was not the outcome of a specific conference but a publication by the World Commission on Environment and Development (WCED), chaired by Gro Harlem Brundtland.

c. Right: The SDGs were born from the mandate of the Rio+20 Conference, marking the start of their development process.

d. Wrong: The outcome of this summit was the adoption of the United Nations Millennium Declaration, which outlined a series of time-bound targets that came to be known as the Millennium Development Goals (MDGs).

Feedback 4

a. Wrong: The SDG indicators do not provide financial assistance for goal implementation. Finance is raised through public, private, and third-sector means at local, national, and international levels.

b. Wrong: The SDG indicators are not typically established yearly; they are fixed benchmarks intended to guide progress towards the goals by the target year 2030.
c. Right: The SDG indicators are data points that provide evidence about the state or change of an aspect related to a target. They are not meant for financial assistance; they do not establish or replace new targets annually.
d. Wrong: The SDG indicators do not replace outdated targets with new ones annually. Instead, the indicators serve as a set of globally agreed measurements to track progress towards the specific targets from up to 2030.

Feedback 5

a. Wrong: The SDGs do not have any statutory or regulatory compliance requirements.
b. Right: Businesses have increasingly recognized SDGs as a moral compass and a strategic roadmap for sustainable and profitable operations, reflecting a shift from profit-centric models to sustainable approaches.
c. Wrong: The SDGs are not a temporary trend in social development. Work is already underway to develop a new framework for global development following their expiration in 2030.
d. Wrong: The SDGs have no direct bearing on taxation.

B. THINK

Level	*Anticipatory thinking*	*Notes*
+	You can identify multiple SDGs that directly relate to the example business.	
=	Some of the SDGs relate to the example business.	
–	You are unable to relate any of the SDGs in a business context.	

C. DO

Level	*Taking initiative*	*Notes*
+	You have identified one or more SDGs that you relate to and can identify actions which you can take to contribute to its advancement.	
=	You have identified one or more SDGs that you relate to but are unable to identify any specific actions.	
–	You don't see how the SDGs relate to you in your personal life.	

D. RELATE

Level	*Collaborative problem solving*	*Notes*
+	The person you have spoken with has heard of the SDGs, or if not, you were able to make them aware through a discussion of what you have learned in this chapter.	
=	The person was unaware of the SDGs, and you were unable to explain to them such that they became aware.	
–	Conversation has not happened or no solution idea to the problem has been reached.	

E. BE

Level	*Emotional awareness*	*Notes*
+	Profound description of one's emotions regarding the SDGs and the likelihood of their success.	
=	Basic awareness of one's emotions regarding the SDGs and their implications.	
–	No or little insight into own emotions regarding SDGs and their implications.	

References

Austin, J. E., & Seitanidi, M. M. (2012). Collaborative value creation: A review of partnering between non-profits and businesses: Part I. Value creation spectrum and collaboration stages. *Nonprofit and Voluntary Sector Quarterly*, *41*, 726–758.

Biermann, F., Kanie, N., & Kim, R. E. (2017). Global governance by goal-setting: The novel approach of the UN Sustainable Development Goals. *Current Opinion in Environmental Sustainability*, *26–27*, 26–31.

Bocken, N. M. P., Short, S. W., Rana, P., & Evans, S. (2014). A literature and practice review to develop sustainable business model archetypes. *Journal of Cleaner Production*, *65*, 42–56.

Eccles, R. G., Ioannou, I., & Serafeim, G. (2014). The impact of corporate sustainability on organizational processes and performance. *Management Science*, *60*(11), 2835–2857.

Glavas, A., & Kelley, K. (2014). The effects of perceived corporate social responsibility on employee attitudes. *Business Ethics Quarterly: The Journal of the Society for Business Ethics*, *24*(2), 165–202.

Griggs, D., Stafford-Smith, M., Gaffney, O., Rockström, J., Ohman, M. C., Shyamsundar, P., Steffen, W., Glaser, G., Kanie, N., & Noble, I. (2013). Policy: Sustainable development goals for people and planet. *Nature*, *495*(7441), 305–307.

Kolk, A. (2016). The social responsibility of international business: From ethics and the environment to CSR and sustainable development. *Journal of World Business*, *51*(1), 23–34.

KPMG. (2017). *The Road Ahead: The KPMG Survey of Corporate Responsibility Reporting 2017*. KPMG International.

Le Blanc, D. (2015). Towards integration at last? The Sustainable Development Goals as a network of targets. *Sustainable Development*, *23*(3), 176–187.

Persson, Å. (2022). *Guest article: What do we need to save the SDGs ahead of 2030?* https://sdg.iisd.org/commentary/guest-articles/what-do-we-need-to-save-the-sdgs-ahead-of-2030/

Porter, M., & Kramer, M. R. (2011). Creating shared value. *Harvard Business Review*, *89*(1/2), 62–77.

Sachs, J. D. (2015). *The age of sustainable development*. Columbia University Press.

Schaltegger, S., & Wagner, M. (2011). Sustainable entrepreneurship and sustainability innovation: Categories and interactions. *Business Strategy and the Environment*, *20*(4), 222–237.

Scheyvens, R., Banks, G., & Hughes, E. (2016). The private sector and the SDGs: The need to move beyond 'business as usual'. *Sustainable Development*, *24*(6), 371–382.

Stafford-Smith, M., Griggs, D., Gaffney, O., Ullah, F., Reyers, B., Kanie, N., Stigson, B., Shrivastava, P., Leach, M., & O'Connell, D. (2017). Integration: The key to implementing the Sustainable Development Goals. *Sustainability Science*, *12*(6), 911–919.

United Nations. (2015). *Transforming our world: the 2030 Agenda for Sustainable Development* (A/RES/70/1.). United Nations.

United Nations Conference on Sustainable Development. (2012). *The future we want* (A_RES_66_288). United Nations. https://www.un.org/en/development/desa/population/migration/generalassembly/docs/globalcompact/A_RES_66_288.pdf

UNSTATS (2022) *Sustainable Development Goals Progress Chart 2022*. Statistics Division, Department of Economic and Social Affairs, United Nations. Available at: https://unstats.un.org/sdgs/report/2022/progress-chart-2022.pdf (accessed March 2024).

World Commission on Environment and Development. (1987). *Our common future*. Oxford University Press.

Zhao, W., Yin, C., Hua, T., Meadows, M. E., Li, Y., Liu, Y., Cherubini, F., Pereira, P., & Fu, B. (2022). Achieving the Sustainable Development Goals in the post-pandemic era. *Humanities & Social Sciences Communications*, *9*(1), 258.

6 Responsibility

One of the main terms used for responsible business is corporate social responsibility (CSR). Through forecasting coming developments in corporate social responsibility, Windsor (2001) raised significant doubts about how CSR would develop in theory and practice. About ten years later corporate social responsibility or responsible business in all its facets and varieties has become stronger than ever. Windsor for sure was right in the prediction that the traditional term and understanding of CSR would change. Today, notions such as responsible business, corporate responsibility, corporate citizenship, or business sustainability are used almost interchangeably, especially in business practice.

In spite of the often-confusing use of vocabulary, business practitioners and scholars agree upon one point: Social and environmental business performance is a mainstream business megatrend, no matter if called responsible business, CSR, corporate citizenship, philanthropy, or business sustainability. The following quotes illustrate the scale and scope of this megatrend.

The responsibility imperative and revolution

2010 *Harvard Business Review* article "The sustainability imperative": Most executives know that how they respond to the challenge of sustainability will profoundly affect the competitiveness – and perhaps even the survival – of their organizations" (Lubin & Esty, 2010, p. 2).

- Accenture and Global Compact CEO study (2010): 93 percent of CEOs are convinced that sustainability will be **critical for the future success of their business.** 96 percent believe it should be deeply integrated into companies' strategy and operations (Lacey, Cooper, Hayward, & Neuberger, 2010).
- Academy of management executive (2002, p. 132) "Responsibility: The new business imperative" state: "A wide range of **stakeholders is pushing companies** to respond in a more responsible way (…)" (Waddock, Bodwell, & Graves, 2002).
- Hollender & Breen in the book "The responsibility revolution": "The voices of business establishment have come to recognize eight key drivers (…) that make **responsible**

DOI: 10.4324/9781003544074-9

corporate behavior an imperative. Not only are they persistent, they are predominant, and they will endure for decades to come" (Hollender & Breen, 2010).

- Edwards in the book "The **sustainability revolution**": "A revolution of interconnections. The sustainability revolution provides a vital new approach to tackling the issues confronting the world today" (Edwards, 2005, p. 9).

From Responsible Business and Management to Sustainable Business and Development

What is responsible and sustainable business? How are they different? In the context of this book, **sustainable business** as described in Figure 6.1 is the aspired goal of shaping a business that strongly contributes to sustainable development; a business with at least a neutral socio-environmental impact - or even better a positive one. **Responsible business** instead describes businesses that have made a commitment and implemented activities aiming to reach the goal of sustainable business. Responsibility here means a commitment to reaching the status of a sustainable business and the ultimate responsibility of (collaboratively with governmental and civil society sectors' contributions) reaching sustainable development. **Responsible management** refers to management process, tools, and activities necessary to achieve the goal of sustainable business.

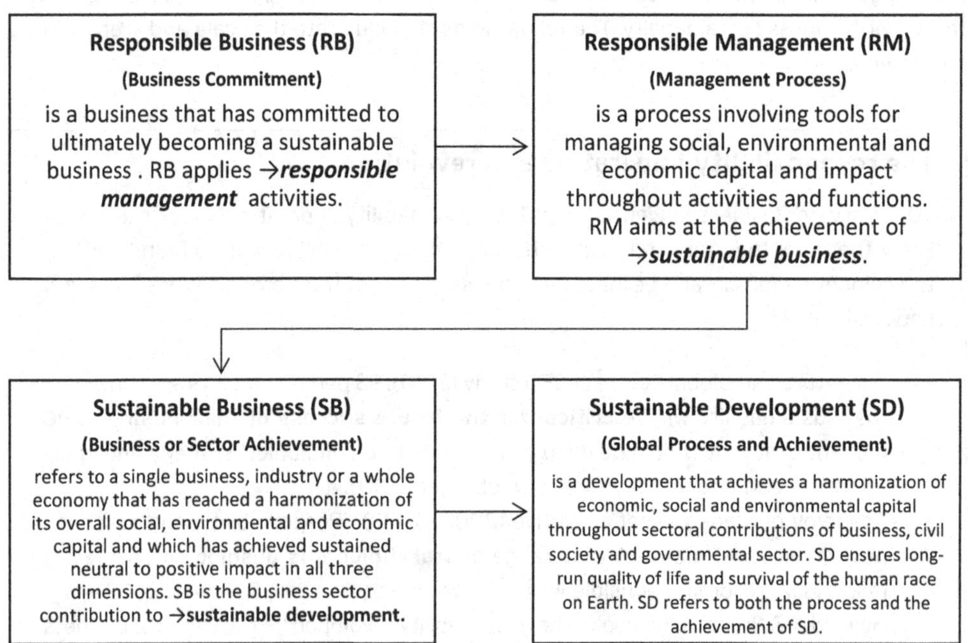

Figure 6.1 Dynamics and Definitions of Responsible Business, Responsible Management, Sustainable Business, and Sustainable Development.

This conceptualization of responsible and sustainable business at first sight might sound different from the traditionally established definitions. Nevertheless, at closer sight, it is a highly open and inclusive view which embraces the majority of historical and contemporary understanding of the relationship between business, society, and environment. The final responsibility of reaching sustainable development can be seen as a categorical imperative (not to be confused with Kant's categorical imperative) for evaluating each and every action a business takes. If aligning all business activity can become the main maxim of decision making in business, it will automatically lead to also fulfilling the responsibilities to various stakeholders; to create value for society, environment, and economy alike. However, it has to be noted that this very narrow instrumental (responsibility as instrument for sustainability) working definition of responsible business and management may be complemented by a wider understanding. The wider understanding sees responsible management as a management embracing principles of sustainability, responsibility, and ethics (Laasch & Conaway, *Principles of responsible management: Glocal sustainability, responsibility, ethics*, 2015).

Fruits on a sustainable business mission

The British fruit smoothie company Innocent's responsible business commitment reads like a textbook definition: "We take responsibility for the impact of our business on society and the environment, aiming to move these impacts from negative to neutral or (better still) positive. It's part of our quest to become a truly sustainable business where we have a net positive effect on the wonderful world around us" (Innocent, 2012).

Background Frameworks of Responsible Business

A wide variety of theoretical and practice-oriented management frameworks have been developed to describe the management of responsible business. The main academically discussed frameworks include the topics of business philanthropy, corporate citizenship, and corporate social responsibility (see Figure 4.2). In the following paragraphs an explanation of each framework will carve out the distinct features and contributions to responsible business practice (Figure 6.2).

Business Philanthropy: Altruistic Giving

Business philanthropy has been one of the first and, for a long time, the prevailing framework for responsible business. Philanthropy in translation of its ancient Greek roots means "Love for mankind". This basic motivation of altruistic, meaning selfless giving for the good of mankind, is philanthropy's distinct feature. In the following, we will see how many things that are called philanthropic might actually not be an act motivated by altruistic love for mankind. Topical variations such as strategic philanthropy (Porter & Kramer, 2002) are not to be subsumed under the umbrella of philanthropic activities. By definition there is no such thing as strategic philanthropy. Philanthropy instrumentalized for the achievement of

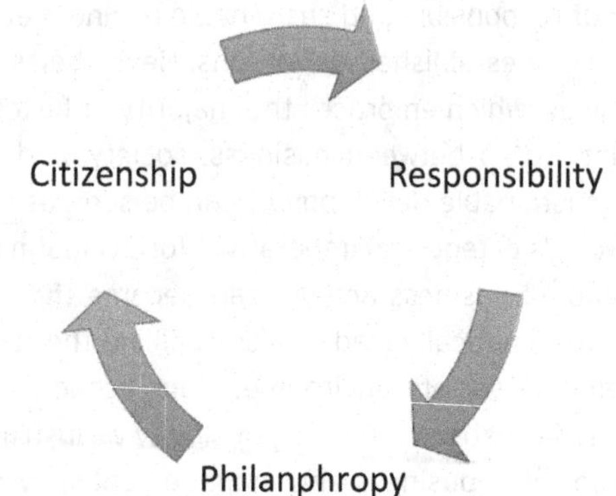

Figure 6.2 Background Frameworks of Responsible Business.

competitive advantage is not altruistic; and therefore, not philanthropic. Also venture philanthropy, capital provided to power ventures with social value added, cannot be completely altruistic as there is an intended return on the capital invested involved.

> **Philanthropy, the divine fire**
>
> It was the ancient Greeks and their saga of the god Prometheus sharing Zeus' divine fire with mortals that gave birth to the concept of "philanthropia".

The moral philosophy of egoism defined earlier in this book, is often seen as opposite to altruism. We had made a point that actions, which seem to be altruistically or philanthropically motivated come from an egoist motivation. It is important to highlight that this lack of altruistic motivation does not necessarily have to be interpreted negatively. As a matter of fact, it will be argued later that a philanthropic motivation leads to suboptimal results in responsible business.

"The age of philanthropy", as Visser (2010) puts it is as old as civilized mankind. Ever since the term has been coined in ancient Greece around 2500 BC, affluent individuals and institutions have been involved in charitable giving. Many religions expect their followers to share wealth in a selfless manner. Until today many charitable activities are religiously motivated. In modern times, industrial philanthropists such as Microsoft's Bill Gates, or CNN's Ted Turner have grabbed the headlines by donating literally billions of dollars of their private property to good causes (Visser, 2010). Individual philanthropic giving as described in the preceding lines is one form of philanthropic activity in the business field. Another type is institutional giving, which in the business sector usually is organized by corporate foundations.

Corporate Citizenship: The Company as Political Actor and Part of the Community

Corporate citizenship (CC) has been used as a very topical buzzword. In this paragraph we will pursue the concept back to its roots in order to find out what the distinct features in comparison to corporate social responsibility are. Crane and Matten (2010) define three different views on how corporate citizenship can be understood.

- **Limited view**: CC = corporate philanthropy.
- **Equivalent view**: CC = corporate social responsibility.
- **Extended view**: CC recognizes the extended political role of the corporation in society.

In the following, CC will be described in its extended view, which most clearly reveals its distinct features. In the extended view, companies are considered another civic actor of a certain community - a citizen. How community is defined in a specific case constitutes the scale of the respective citizenship activities. A company could be defined as a citizen of the local community in which its facilities are located, the national community, or even the global community. Citizenship brings about rights and responsibilities. Governments often are not able to completely fulfill all the responsibilities towards their citizens. Companies in many areas may support governmental functions, if they accept and assume their political role in society by strengthening the three basic citizen rights (Marshall, 1977).

- **Social rights**: Create social welfare for other citizens of the community. A company could establish community centers to provide education, invest in physical infrastructure, and provide volunteering opportunities.
- **Civil rights**: Ensure the protection of unalienable entitlements. Companies can make a commitment to respect human rights throughout all their interactions with any kind of stakeholder.
- **Political rights**: Support political activism. Companies can support political activity of their stakeholders by for instance giving employees leave time for political engagement.

Honing skills and doing even more good

Supporting employees to make an impact in the community is at the heart of corporate citizenship. The topic-talk of the day is skill-based volunteering (SBV), where employees base their contributions on personal strengths and skills (Hands On Network, 2011). Volunteering also trains in skills important to their job performance. Eighty-three percent of volunteers state that their engagement improved their leadership skills, 78 percent communication skills, 62 percent problem solving, 57 percent organization and multitasking and 52 percent marketing skills (Women's Way, 2006).

Among the three types of citizen entitlements, companies are probably the most strongly engaged in the promotion of social welfare and the protection of human rights. The connection with responsible business as understood in this book is very obvious when CC is defined as the "... aspirational metaphor for business to be part of developing a better world" (McIntosh, 2010, p. 89). This understanding of CC as business activities for an improved world community goes in accordance with the formerly applied definition of responsible business being activities with the ultimate responsibility of reaching the sustainable development of the world.

Corporate (Social) Responsibility: Fulfilling Stakeholder Responsibilities

The object of study of **corporate social responsibility** is business conduct that acts upon the various social responsibilities a business has towards it's **stakeholders**. The most complete and inclusive definition of corporate social responsibility (CSR) stems from the European Union's development of a regional focus, a pole of excellence on CSR (Commission of the European Communities, 2006).

> *Corporate social responsibility (CSR) is a concept whereby companies integrate social and environmental concerns in their business operations and in their interaction with their stakeholders on a voluntary basis. It is about enterprises deciding to go beyond minimum legal requirements and obligations stemming from collective agreements in order to address societal needs. Through CSR, enterprises of all sizes, in cooperation with their stakeholders, can help to reconcile economic, social and environmental ambitions.*

This definition embraces the most salient points of the concept. "Responsibility to whom?" might we ask. The answer is that business responsibility is defined by the different "stakeholders" that a company is connected with. The responsibilities towards those stakeholders might be of an "economic, social or environmental" nature. Organizational responsibility is not only a topic for big corporations. "Enterprises of all sizes" can "integrate" responsible business practices into their operations. It is important to highlight the "voluntary basis" of such responsibilities. If a company is coerced by legal or societal pressure into adopting desirable practices, this is cannot be counted as a responsibility that the company has accepted actively.

A long-established framework for the description is the CSR pyramid developed by Carroll (1991). The pyramid proposes a sequence of levels of responsibilities as described in the following:

- **Economic** responsibilities: The company does what is necessary to survive economically.
- **Legal** responsibilities: The company does what is required by the law.
- **Ethical** responsibilities: The company does what is considered moral behavior by stakeholders and broader society.
- **Philanthropic/discretionary** responsibilities: The company exceeds basic expectations and chooses freely to engage with additional responsibilities.

Those stages of responsibilities illustrate how corporate social responsibility is intertwined with other background theories presented throughout this chapter. Philanthropy and business ethics are here presented as two sub-topics under the broad umbrella of corporate social responsibility. So is law, which contradicts the European Union definition, which had defined corporate social responsibility as a responsibility above the sphere of legal requirements. This inclusiveness of corporate social responsibility towards related topics has served to define it as an umbrella term for responsible business management frameworks (Matten & Moon, 2004).

During the years of academic refinement of the term *corporate social responsibility (CSR1)*, researchers have developed manifold very similar terms, which in practice are often used interchangeably. Knowing those terms and their differences opens up access to a rich field of research, which is why those terms will be illustrated briefly. Clarkson (1995) has provided an excellent framework for understanding the finer differences. *Corporate social responsiveness (CSR2)* refers to the characteristic posture and reaction towards social issues. The level of a company's responsiveness can be categorized into one of the following four stages:

- "**Defensive**: Deny responsibility. Doing less than required".
- "**Reactive**: Admit responsibility, but fight it. Doing the least that is required".
- "**Accommodative**: Accept responsibility. Doing all that is required".
- "**Proactive**: Anticipates responsibility. Doing more than is required".

Clarkson also describes *corporate social performance (CSP)*, which refers to a company's performance in the direct relationship to one, several, or all of its stakeholder groups. This is why CSP has also been described as stakeholder performance. Corporate social performance is less well-defined than corporate social responsiveness. Carroll describes CSP as a cube bringing together the four types of responsibilities covered in Carroll's pyramid, the four different levels of responsiveness and several different stakeholder types. According to Carroll, such a combination of tools for describing a company's responsible behavior is most fit to categorize a businesses' overall social performance (Carroll, 1979).

Wiggling responsiveness

It is fascinating how one and the same company's corporate responsiveness can vary throughout time and different responsibility areas of the same business. Walmart, for instance, has implemented an extensively praised supplier code and assessment, considerably improving their sustainability throughout the company's massive supply chain. This progressive activity has all the characteristics of a highly advanced proactive activity (Walmart, 2009). Only few years before, in 2005, Walmart had been criticized for questionable business practices involving their competitors and employees. Filmmaker Robert Greenwald had attacked Walmart in the movie "The high cost of low price". Because of Walmart's denial of those responsibilities, this particular behavior would be characterized as "defensive" (Greenwald, 2005).

The term corporate social responsibility has many flaws. As summarized by Laasch and Flores (2010), the word "corporation" excludes businesses of other legal forms and sizes. The word "social" neglects the environmental and economic responsibilities of the business. By using the term "responsibility" the business automatically is guided into a mode of compliance (with responsibilities), which fails to reflect the immense opportunities related to responsible business. In recent years amendments to those semantical inconsistencies have been made. For instance, Grayson and Hodges (2004) introduced the term corporate social opportunity. The contemporary use of Corporate Responsibility, which many practitioners have come to use, avoids the exclusion of environmental and economic responsibilities, by referring to responsibility in general. The ISO 26000 standard applies the term "organizational responsibilities", instead of referring to mere "corporate" responsibilities and this way opens the topic up to businesses of all types and sizes (ISO, 2010). So does the term responsible business as applied in this book. Nevertheless, those adjustments remain incomplete. In later chapters "three-dimensional management" will be proposed as an alternative, fully avoiding those semantical flaws.

"This is only for big corporations"

Small and medium enterprises (SMEs) due to the "corporation" focus might be considered to have an intuitive barrier in embracing the concept and implementing responsible business activities. Already in 2002, a survey through 5 European countries revealed that 48 percent of very small, 65 percent of small and even 75 percent of medium-sized businesses had been involved into social causes. Business cases highlighted included a wide variety of SMEs from a Polish construction company to an Austrian chocolate manufacturer (Mandl, 2005).

The Death of Corporate Social Responsibility?

The discourse surrounding corporate social responsibility has undergone significant transformation in recent years, leading some scholars to assert that traditional CSR is effectively "dead". This perspective is rooted in a comprehensive critique of CSR's efficacy and relevance in the modern context of sustainable development and responsible business practices as we have seen. In response to these criticisms, the concept of creating shared value (CSV) has gained prominence as touched upon in Chapter 3. Introduced by Porter and Kramer (2011) CSV advocates for the integration of social and environmental considerations directly into business strategies and operations. Contrasting with the often-peripheral nature of CSR, CSV posits that companies can generate economic value in ways that also produce value for society, thereby addressing its challenges. This approach necessitates a rethinking of business practices and models to align social and economic objectives more closely.

Simultaneously, the rise of sustainability and Environmental, Social, and Governance (ESG) criteria represents a more integrated approach to responsible business conduct. ESG emphasizes measurable, transparent criteria, compelling companies to incorporate these considerations into their decision-making processes (Eccles & Klimenko, 2019). This framework is often perceived as more robust and comprehensive than traditional CSR. Moreover, there is a discernible shift towards purpose-driven business models. This paradigm shift involves redefining the core purpose of a company to align with societal and environmental welfare. Such an approach transcends the traditional domain of CSR, re-envisioning the *raison d'être* of a company with a focus on long-term sustainability and ethical considerations as central to business success (Henderson & Steen, 2015). Additionally, increasing regulatory requirements around sustainability and responsible business practices, coupled with escalating pressures from various stakeholders - including consumers, employees, and investors - are impelling companies to adopt more holistic and integrated approaches (Scherer & Palazzo, 2011). This development reflects a broader consensus that responsible business practices must be deeply ingrained in corporate culture and operations, moving beyond the optional or ancillary status that CSR has traditionally occupied.

ESG: A pillar in modern business

Environmental, Social, and Governance (ESG) criteria are standards used to evaluate a company's ethical impact and sustainability practices. Environmentally, it assesses the company's stewardship of nature; socially, it considers relationships and ethical practices affecting employees, suppliers, customers, and communities; and governance relates to company leadership, audits, internal controls, and shareholder rights. Increasingly important to investors, ESG criteria guide investment decisions and corporate strategies, emphasizing long-term sustainable growth over short-term gains.

Whilst CSR as a concept has not been entirely abandoned, it is undergoing significant evolution. The transition towards CSV, ESG, and purpose-driven business models indicates a more nuanced and integrated approach to responsible business. This evolution seeks to address the limitations of traditional CSR, aiming for a more substantive and impactful convergence of business and societal goals.

Exercises

A. KNOW

Use the below multiple-choice questions to test your knowledge. Each answer may be wrong or right and there may be zero to four right or wrong answers per question:

1. Responsible business...
   a. ...includes sustainable development as one of the background management frameworks.
   b. ...includes philanthropy as one of the background management frameworks. Philanthropy includes both organizational and individual giving.
   c. ...includes main practice frameworks for its management such as the Global Compact, ISO 26000, and the SGI.
   d. ...as one main element aims at managing stakeholder relationships.
2. Corporate citizenship (CC)...
   a. ...in its equivalent view equals corporate philanthropy.
   b. ...as one of the central ideas sees companies as political actors with the responsibility to improve their respective communities.

c. ...defines community as strictly the community (in the sense of a settlement) that the company operates in locally.
d. ...aims at the company promoting and supporting the three main citizen rights.

3. Corporate social responsibility (CSR)...
   a. ...has been defined by Archie B. Carroll in a pyramid model.
   b. ...in its definition by the European Union among others defines corporate social responsibility by the interaction with stakeholders. Corporate social responsibility in this definition primarily aims at compliance with local and international laws.
   c. ...is related to the topic of corporate social performance. It is defined as high corporate social performance when a company proactively reacts even before stakeholders claim a certain activity from the company.
   d. ...is a flawless description of an organization's social, environmental, and economic responsibilities.

4. Imagine a company refuses to talk to the members of the local community who have gathered at the gates of one of their factories after a chemical spill. This is an example of...
   a. ...philanthropic responsibility.
   b. ...of an accommodative response.
   c. ...high corporate social responsiveness.
   d. ...a defensive response.

B. THINK

Inform yourself about the British Petroleum oil spill in the Gulf of Mexico and make a list of the main stakeholders affected by the disaster. Think about how each of them was affected by the oil spill and rank them based on the level of negative consequences they had to suffer.

C. DO

Find a company's corporate responsibility report online and review it. Write a short brief which explains what concrete actions you would take to improve the company's corporate social performance.

D. RELATE

Find a company's social network presence (e.g. on Facebook, LinkedIn, Twitter, or YouTube; some companies have independent social networks or Blogs) ask them a question in an ongoing conversation there. If necessary, try it several times until you receive an answer and are able to reply to it. Try to draw others into the conversation.

E. BE

Think about someone in your sphere of influence (anyone there is a stakeholder by definition) who might benefit most from something you could do. Then do it and reflect on how it made you feel.

Feedback

A. KNOW

Feedback 1

a. Wrong: Sustainable development is the intended outcome to which sustainable business aims at contributing to.
b. Right: Both forms of giving fall into the broad category of philanthropy.
c. Wrong: The Sustainable Governance Index (SGI) is a norm primarily applying to the field of responsible governance.
d. Right: One of the main activities in responsible business is stakeholder management.

Feedback 2

a. Wrong: The limited view describes CC as corporate philanthropy. In the equivalent view, it equals corporate social responsibility.
b. Right: Community thinking and seeing the company as a political entity are central elements of CC.
c. Wrong: The understanding of community in CC varies largely from small local communities to the even the world community.
d. Right: Companies being good citizens should protect and promote the social, civil, and political rights of their stakeholders.

Feedback 3

a. Right: The four steps of the pyramid of corporate social responsibility are 1) economic, 2) legal, 3) ethical, and 4) discretionary/philanthropic responsibilities.
b. Wrong: The European Union definition aims at fulfilling voluntary responsibilities, which exceed the basic legal requirements and expectations of society.
c. Wrong: Proactive reactions are part of the corporate social responsiveness framework, which describe a company's mode of reaction to stakeholder claims.
d. Wrong: The term CSR in all its three words is flawed. "Corporation" excludes other business and organization forms, "Social" does not include environmental and economic responsibilities, and "Responsibility" excludes opportunity.

Feedback 4

a. Wrong: If this was a philanthropic responsibility the company would do something good for their stakeholders without anyone asking them to do so.
b. Wrong: An accommodative response is when a company "does all that is required". Here a minimum requirement would be to speak and listen to the stakeholders.
c. Wrong: High corporate social responsiveness would be if the company responds either in an accommodative or even in a proactive fashion. In this case their response is defensive.
d. Right: By not speaking to stakeholders the company denies their responsibility, which is a defensive response.

B. THINK

Level	*Analyzing social consequences*	*Notes*
+	Wide appreciation of stakeholders affected and well-reasoned, sensible appreciation of the different degrees of impact.	
=	Wide appreciation of the stakeholders affected.	
–	Narrow or no appreciation of the breadth of stakeholders affected.	

C. DO

Level	*Improvement and adaptation skills*	*Notes*
+	Feasible and well thought-through actions to increase corporate social performance, based on a deep understanding of the company status quo as outlined in the corporate responsibility report.	
=	Either a good appreciation of the company status quo or concrete actions to improve its corporate social performance.	
–	Little appreciation of the company status quo and no concrete actions to improve its corporate social performance.	

D. RELATE

Level	*Initiating and sustaining multilateral dialogue*	*Notes*
+	Ongoing conversation with multiple partners.	
=	Bilateral dialogue with company.	
–	No communication established.	

E. BE

Level	*Caring attitude*	*Notes*
+	Someone has been cared for and the reflection shows a deeper inclination towards caring.	
=	Someone has been positively affected.	
–	No evidence someone has been cared for.	

References

Carroll, A. B. (1979). A three-dimensional conceputal model of corporate performance. *Academy of Management Review*, *4*(4), 497–505.

Carroll, A. B. (1991). The pyramid of corporate social responsibility: Toward the moral management of organizational stakeholders. *Business Horizons*, *34*(4), 39–48.

Clarkson, M. B. (1995). A stakeholder framework for analyzing and evaluating corporate social performance. *Academy of Management Review*, *20*(1), 82–117.

Commission of the European Communities. (2006). *Implementing the partnership for growth and jobs: Making Europe a pole of excellence of CSR*. Brussels: European Union.

Crane, A., & Matten, D. (2010). *Businesss ethics* (3rd Edition). New York: Oxford University Press.

Eccles, R. G., & Klimenko, S. (2019). The investor revolution. *Harvard Business Review*, *97*(3), 106–116.

Edwards, A. R. (2005). *The sustainability revolution: Portrait of a paradigm shift*. Gabriola Island: New Society Publishers.

Grayson, D., & Hodges, A. (2004). *Corporate social opportunity!: Seven steps to make corporate social responsibility work for your business*. Sheffield: Greenleaf.

Greenwald, R. (Director). (2005). *The high cost of low price* [Motion Picture].

Hands On Network. (2011). *Skills-based volunteering*. Retrieved August 27, 2011, from Hands on Network: https://www.handsonnetwork.org/nationalprograms/skillsbasedvolunteering

Henderson, R., & Steen, E. (2015). Why and how businesses must address sustainability. In *Sustainable development goals and sustainable supply chains in the post-global economy* (pp. 35–53). Springer.

Hollender, J., & Breen, B. (2010). *The responsibility revolution: How the next generation of businesses will win*. San Francisco: Jossey-Bass.

Innocent. (2012). *Being sustainable*. Retrieved March 3, 2012, from Innocent: https://www.innocentdrinks.co.uk/us/being-sustainable

ISO. (2010). *International Standard ISO 26000: Guidance on social responsibility*. Geneva: International Organization for Standardization.

Laasch, O., & Conaway, R. N. (2015). *Principles of responsible management: Glocal sustainability, responsibility, ethics*. Mason: Cengage.

Laasch, O., & Flores, U. (2010). Implementing profitable CSR: The CSR 2.0 business compass. In M. Pohl, & N. Tolhurst, *Responsible business: How to manage a CSR strategy successfully* (pp. 289–309). Chichester: John Wiley & Sons Ltd

Lacey, P., Cooper, T., Hayward, R., & Neuberger, L. (2010). *A new era of sustainability: UN global compact-Accenture CEO study 2010*. Accenture Institute for High Performance.

Lubin, D. A., & Esty, D. C. (2010). The sustainability imperative. *Harvard Business Review*, May 2010, 1–9.

Mandl, I. (2005). *CSR and competitiveness: European SMEs good practice*. Vienna: Austrian Institute for SME Research.

Marshall, T. H. (1977). *Class, citizenship, and social development: Essays*. Chicago: The University of Chicago Press.

Matten, D., & Moon, J. (2004). Corporate social responsibility education in Europe. *Journal of Business Ethics*, *54*, 323–337.

McIntosh, M. (2010). Citizenship. In W. Visser, D. Matten, M. Pohl, & N. Tolhurst, *The A-Z of corporate social responsibility* (pp. 89–93). Chichester: Wiley.

Porter, M., & Kramer, M. (2002). The competitive advantage of corporate philanthropy. *Harvard Business Review, 80*(12), 56–68.

Porter, M. E., & Kramer, M. R. (2011). The big idea: Creating shared value. *Harvard Business Review, 89*(1), 2.

Scherer, A. G., & Palazzo, G. (2011). The new political role of business in a globalized world: A review of a new perspective on CSR and its implications for the firm, governance, and democracy. *Journal of Management Studies, 48*(4), 899–931.

Visser, W. (2010). *The age of responsibility: CSR 2.0 and the new DNA of business*. Chichester: Wiley.

Waddock, S. A., Bodwell, C., & Graves, S. B. (2002). Responsibility: The new business imperative. *Academy of Management Executive, 47*(1), 132–147.

Walmart. (2009). *Standards for suppliers*.

Windsor, D. (2001). The future of corporate social responsibility. *The International Journal of Organizational Analysis, 9*(3), 225–256.

Women's Way. (2006). *Power skills: How volunteering shapes professional success*. Philadelphia: Women's Way. Retrieved August 27, 2011, from World Volunteer Web: https://www.worldvolunteerweb.org/news-views/news/doc/leadership-skills-linked-to.html

7 Ethics

What is Business Ethics?

Business ethics is the study of morally right or wrong decisions in a managerial and business context. Why are such decisions so fundamentally important for business conduct in general? Why is business ethics the very basis for responsible business? According to Crane and Matten (2010b, p. 46) "(...) business ethics can be seen as the analytical tool that managers and others can use to understand, conceptualize and legitimize the moral status of corporate policies, strategies and programs". Business ethics supports a concise reflection of what the business is doing, what it should or should not do, and therefore builds the foundation for any subsequent business activity from mainstream management to the implementation of responsible business policies.

The terms ethics and morality are often used interchangeably, which from a conceptual perspective is wrong. Understanding the difference between ethics and morality supports a clearer understanding of concrete issues in practice. Figure 7.1 describes ethics and morality as two mutually affecting components of the same reasoning and decision-making process. The philosophical foundation of *ethics* provides the tools for deciding about right or wrong in an ethical dilemma situation. Ethics is based on philosophical decision-making schemes, while *morality* describes what is considered right or wrong, based on the application of those schemes in concrete situations, cultures, or environments. One could also say that ethics is the tool for developing morality, while morality is the outcome of the ethical decision-making process. The moral outcome of ethical decisions can take manifold forms such as a group values, a written code of ethics, or a certain culture of do's and don'ts inside a specific group of people.

Codes of morality?

In 2007, 85% of the first listed 100 companies in the London-based FTSE stock index had codes of ethics. While the term codes of "ethics" suggest that such a code provides ethical reasoning mechanisms, the contents rather illustrate a pre-fixed set of moral rules - do's and don'ts for certain situations; strictly speaking those documents should rather be called codes of morality (IBE, 2011).

DOI: 10.4324/9781003544074-10

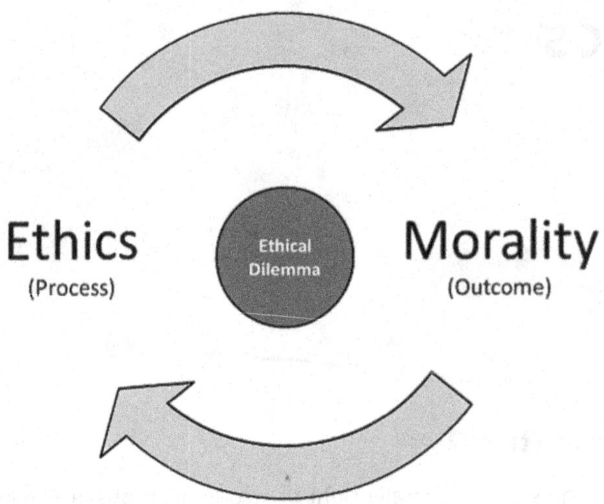

Figure 7.1 The Relationship between Ethics and Morality.

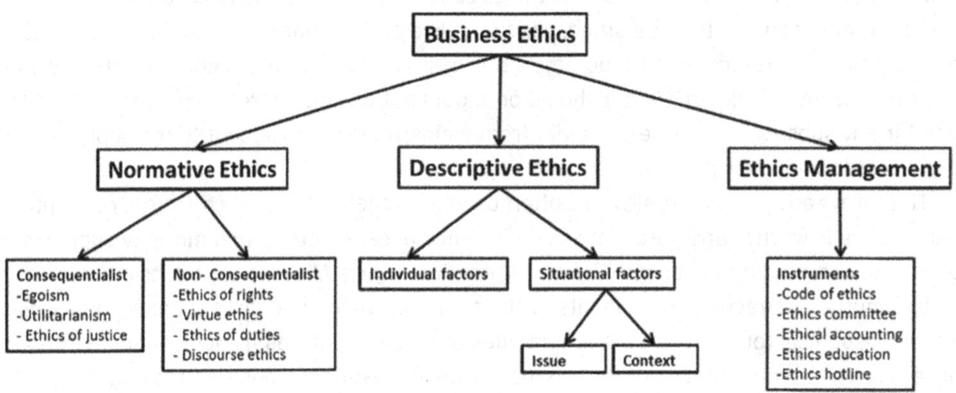

Figure 7.2 Domains of Business Ethics.

Based on Crane and Matten (2010a)

Morality without ethics is a static product of rules, which as time goes by automatically will become out of date. This is why ethical reasoning should not only create a certain morality, but also should constantly be applied in order to re-check if morality still reflects the ethical reasoning it was originally based on. Also, *ethics without morality* does not live up to the full potential of ethical reasoning, as it lacks application. A philosophical ethical debate, which is not translated into a practice application has at best theoretical value.

Figure 7.2 illustrates how business ethics can be subdivided into three main domains following a structure as outlined by Crane and Matten (2010a). The first and most commonly considered domain is *normative business ethics*, which aims at providing guidance on the right or wrong for an ethical decision in a business context. Normative ethics is often erroneously equated with the whole business ethics field, forgetting about the second domain of descriptive business ethics and the third, which is ethics management. *Descriptive business ethics* aim at understanding and describing the "why" of an ethical decision, scrutinizing individual and situational factors important for understanding why a certain business actor decides one way or another. *Ethics management* is concerned with the institutional implementation of tools that ensure "good ethics" and to avoid ethical misconduct. Examples of such tools are among others codes of ethics, ethics officers, and ethics hotlines. In this chapter we will focus on the first domain, normative business ethics, while the later section on the responsible management process will provide deeper insight into the managerial implications of descriptive ethics and ethics management.

Not all decisions have an ethical component. Crane and Matten (2010a) define three main characteristics of ethical decisions as summarized in Figure 7.3. Only if a decision is ethically relevant, has potential effect on others, and involves a choice to be made, one can talk of an ethical decision. However, not all ethically right or wrong behaviors are related to an ethical dilemma. Wrong behaviors in business might, for instance, be compliance problems, where people know what is right, but do not act upon it.

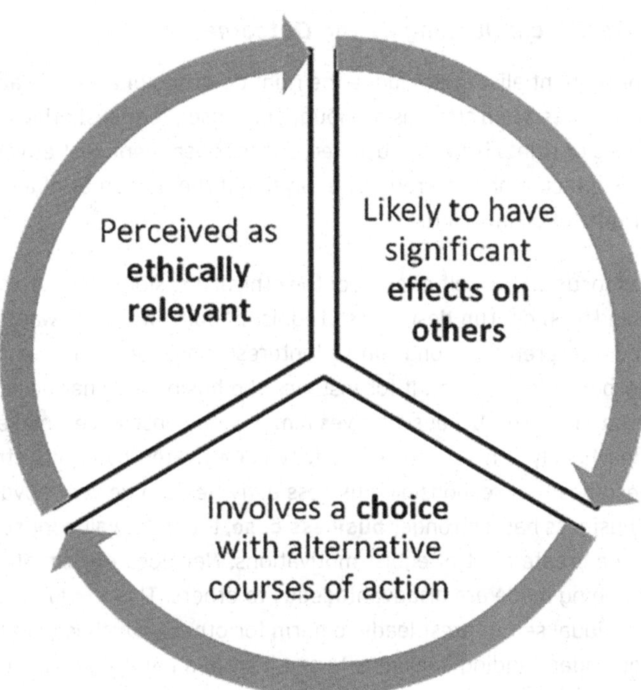

Figure 7.3 Characteristics of Ethical Dilemma Situations.

Based on Crane and Matten (2010a)

Normative Business Ethics: Making Right Decisions

What is the right decision? What should be done? What shouldn't? Normative business ethics as framed in this book does NOT provide a definite answer to those questions. Instead, it provides a set of reasoning mechanisms, which in turn lead to a diverse set of potential answers. Such an approach is called ethical pluralism, as opposed to moral absolutism, which postulates that there can only be one absolutely right solution to an ethical dilemma. The pluralist line-up of different ethical solutions to a certain problem should not lead to a moral ambiguity in the sense of "anything goes", but instead enable managers to evaluate a solid basis of different ethical alternatives; a very "pragmatic perspective" as proposed by Crane and Matten (2010a). In communicating responsible business, understanding those alternatives also helps to understand the different types of reasoning applied by a company's stakeholder and helps to shape answers corresponding to the respective reasoning applied. In the following the main streams of ethical reasoning will be divided into consequentialist (outcome oriented) and non-consequentialist (not outcome oriented) ethics. In the academic tradition, those two categories have often been used in a very narrow definition, applying to only few of the streams of ethical reasoning. In this book the literal understanding of the term will be applied in order to provide a practical categorization of important streams of ethical thought which will result in either consequentialist or non-consequentialist ethics.

Consequentialist Ethics: Judging by the Outcome

Proponents of consequentialist ethics judge the right or wrong of a certain action by its outcomes - its consequences. Main streams of thought in consequentialist ethics are egoism and utilitarianism. Ethics of rights is here subsumed under consequentialist ethics. As framed in this book, it judges ethical right or wrong by analyzing if the outcomes of a decision respect the unalienable rights of all involved.

- **Egoist ethics** focus on the self-interest of the ethical decision-maker. This interest might on the one hand be short-run-desire-based egoism; "doing what one wants". Self-interest might also be interpreted as long-run self-interest. Thus, egoism does not necessarily contradict responsible business. If for instance the business owner decides to donate a certain amount of money, because it gives him a good conscience - makes him feel better - this superficially "philanthropic" activity is motivated by egoist ethics. The more obvious it becomes that responsible business activities can be very advantageous, that responsible business has a stronger **business case**, the more value for society and environment will be created out of egoist motivations. Nor does egoism always mean that the decisions being made are disadvantageous to others. This would only be true, if the pursuit of individual self-interest leads to harm for others, which is not always the case. Important for understanding egoism is to see it from a neutral perspective. Yes, egoist decision making does involve a certain danger of leading to negative consequences for others. Nevertheless, it can become a powerful tool for doing good, when there is a win-win situation, where the pursuit of self-interest also creates value for others.

> **Egoists, genetically altruistic**
>
> *The Selfish Gene*, a book published in 1975 by the British evolutionary biologist Richard Dawkins argues that altruistic behavior is in the genes. From an evolutionary perspective it makes sense to be good to others as this behavior increases the likelihood of reproduction and genetic survival in the long run. Thus, egoism or selfishness even on a genetic level of interpretation may lead to a behavior perceived as altruistic (Dawkins, 1976).

- **Utilitarianism** aims at creating maximum utility or welfare for all groups and individuals affected by a decision. In contrast to egoism, the right decision is not the one making the decision-maker "maximum happy", but the one creating the greatest happiness for all involved (Mill, 1863/2008). This so-called "Greatest Happiness Principle" has found very modern applications in responsible business. The responsible business management tool of stakeholder management facilitates a consideration of all effects that a certain business activity has on the various groups "that can affect or are affected" (Freeman, 1984/2010, p. 25). The topical discussion about maximizing stakeholders' value instead of maximizing shareholders' value is a discussion of utilitarian versus egoist ethics arguments.
- **Ethics of rights** consider a decision right when its outcome does not harm the unalienable rights and entitlements of the groups and individuals involved. The most common theory of ethics of rights is the field of citizen and human rights. The Universal Declaration of Human Rights is the most recent document defining human rights (United Nations, 2011). Ethics of rights has recently been extended to include special fields such as the rights of future and unborn generations, animal rights, and rights of nature as a whole.

Non-Consequentialist Ethics: Judging by Intrinsic Qualities

Non-consequentialist streams of normative ethical thinking can be based on various factors not being the outcome of the action or decision. Ethical right and wrong is based on intrinsic qualities of the decision such as on the motivation (ethics of duties), the virtuous characteristics of the actor (virtue ethics), or the fairness (ethics of justice) of a decision and action.

- **Ethics of justice** follows the maxim of fairness. Fairness comprises the two domains of fair outcomes and fair procedures leading to those outcomes (Crane & Matten, 2010a; Rawls, 1999). Thus, ethics of justice has components of both consequentialist and non-consequentialist ethics. Consequentialist outcome-oriented justice aims at "everybody getting what (s)he deserves". The non-consequentialist procedural justice instead follows the purpose of appreciating what a fair outcome is and at implementing the adequate process leading to this outcome.
- **Virtue ethics** defines a right decision by the virtuous character of the actor or decision-maker. Good decisions are the ones that have been made by a person of virtuous

character. When focusing on virtue ethics, in order to foster good ethical decisions, character education increases in importance. While the other streams of ethical thought can be learnt and understood on an intellectual level, virtue ethics requires a profound effort of character building. A conceptual flaw of virtue ethics is that there is hardly a generally accepted set of virtues one should possess. The underlying question is: What is a virtuous character?

- **Ethics of duties** is based on the adherence to higher rules and principles. Ethics of duties means the duty or responsibility to adhere to those higher rules. Such rules are not given. Human beings should be able to derive those rules themselves. Kant's set of three maxims is the most commonly known framework for developing such higher principles for any situation given. According to Kant every action to be considered right and good has to comply with the following three points (Kant & Patton, 1785/2005):
    1. *Would you want your action to become **universally lawgiving**? Would you wish everybody else to act the same way?*
    2. *Do you treat **human beings as means or as an end**? It is desired not to use human beings for a certain purpose, but instead to align your action for the good of humanity and every individual human being.*
    3. *Act as if by your action what you do would automatically **become a natural law**.*

Fairness in executive remuneration?

A controversial topic in the fairness debate is the topic of executive payment. Is it fair that among the S&P 500 companies a CEO in 2010 on average earned US$11,358,445? This sum equaled the annual wage of 342 average US American workers (AFL-CIO, 2011).

Applying Normative Ethics

While the former mentioned streams of normative ethical thought cannot be complete, they provide a powerful toolset for ethical decision making which in the following will be applied on a concrete case.

***News of the World*, freshly hacked**

The traditional, 168-years-old British newspaper *News of the World* (NoW) shut down in 2011. The reason was revelations about phone hacking of allegedly thousands of mailboxes of politicians, celebrities, and even of a kidnapped girl. The activities had lasted several years. Sean Hoare, a former NoW reporter was quoted with "Everyone knew. The office cat knew". Imagine you are a newly-hired mid-level manager of *News of the World* and coincidentally find out about the phone hacking activity. Due your strong values and to past congruent application of ethics in your private and professional life, this situation poses a serious dilemma. What would be the right thing to do? (CBC News, 2011; Sabbagh, 2011; New Statesman, 2010)

Table 7.1 Applying Pluralistic Ethical Decision Making on the NoW Case

Reasoning	*Core question*	*Typical considerations*
Egoism	Which decision is in my best interest?	Will I be fired for whistle blowing? Will other companies want to hire me if I am perceived as a "traitor"? Will my colleagues be mad at me and give me a hard time? Will the general public see me as a hero?
Utilitarianism	What is the best decision for all involved?	Is the overall effect among all people affected by the hacking, positive or negative? Is the harm done to the victims of the hacking smaller or bigger than the suffering of the people out of job their jobs when NoW collapses?
Ethics of rights	How do I avoid harming human rights?	How can I best avoid that NoW keeps violating the right of privacy? How is NoW's freedom of press and the newspapers' readers' right on information involved?
Ethics of justice	What is the fairest solution?	Is it fair that NoW is making business by harming the hacking victims?
Virtue ethics	Does the actor have a virtuous character?	Is NoW generally a good ("virtuous") newspaper? Is the hacking done out of good or bad intentions?
Ethics of duties	Does the action comply with the requirements of being universally lawgiving and considering human beings involved as ends?	Would I want all newspapers to start hacking mailboxes? Does the NoW use people or does it intend to help people by its hacking activities? What would I want others in my situation to do? By which decision do I involve people as ends and not as means for my own benefit?

Table 7.1 sums up the likely recommendations given by the streams of ethical reasoning described throughout the preceding sections. Imagining you were a NoW employee who had found out about the questionable phone hacking practices. What might be the typical considerations stemming from the different types of ethical reasoning?

Contemporary Approaches to Business Ethics

In the realm of business ethics, prior decades have been characterized by several pivotal developments that reflect a paradigmatic shift in how businesses approach ethical considerations. These developments, influenced by global economic challenges, technological advancements, increased focus on corporate social responsibility, and evolving societal expectations, signify a more integrative and comprehensive approach to business ethics.

Despite the challenges and changes discussed in Chapter 6, a notable trend has been the greater emphasis on CSR and ethics. This shift is not merely rhetorical but has seen CSR becoming an integral part of core business strategies. Companies are increasingly held accountable for their impact on society and the environment, beyond just financial performance. This has led to a more holistic approach to business ethics, encompassing issues such as environmental sustainability, social justice, and ethical labor practices (Carroll & Brown, 2018). Concurrently, there has been a heightened focus on sustainability and environmental ethics. The urgency of addressing climate change and environmental degradation has compelled businesses to integrate sustainability into their ethical frameworks. This encompasses adopting sustainable practices, reducing carbon footprints, and engaging in environmental stewardship. Such measures are reflective of the growing awareness among businesses of their role in contributing to sustainable development goals (Schaltegger & Burritt, 2018).

The rapid advancement of technology has also introduced new ethical challenges. Developments in artificial intelligence (AI), big data, and social media have raised significant concerns related to data privacy, cybersecurity, and the ethical use of AI. This necessitates the development of new ethical guidelines and policies to address these emerging challenges (Martin, 2019). Similarly, increased demands for transparency and accountability represent another critical development. Partly driven by regulatory changes and public expectation, businesses are now more focused on demonstrating their commitment to ethical practices through reporting and compliance mechanisms. This has led to the development of more robust ethics and compliance programs within organizations (Crane & Glozer, 2016).

The significance of ethical leadership and culture has also been increasingly recognized in this era. Leaders are expected to set the tone for ethical behavior within organizations and to foster a culture of integrity. This involves not just adhering to legal requirements but also embodying the values and principles that define the ethical stance of the organization Lastly, globalization has brought to the fore complex ethical challenges arising from operating in diverse cultural and regulatory environments. This has led to a greater focus on understanding and navigating cross-cultural ethical issues and developing global ethical standards that can be applied across different jurisdictions (Antunez et al., 2024).

These developments collectively signify an evolution in the landscape of business ethics. They underscore the increasing recognition of ethical considerations as integral to business success and sustainability. The emphasis has shifted towards creating value for a broader set of stakeholders, including employees, customers, communities, and the environment. This holistic approach underscores the interconnectedness of economic, social, and environmental issues and highlights the necessity for responsible and sustainable business practices.

Exercises

A. KNOW

Use the below multiple-choice questions to test your knowledge. Each answer may be wrong or right and there may be zero to four right or wrong answers per question:

1. Business ethics...
   a. ...is a synonym for business morality.
   b. ...comprises the three main domains of normative and descriptive ethics and ethics management.
   c. ...in its sub-domain normative business ethics primarily aim at understanding why people make bad or good decisions in ethical dilemma situations.
   d. ...is a mere synonym for ethics management.

2. Normative ethical theories...
   a. ...in this book has been subdivided into consequentialist and non-consequentialist ethical theories.
   b. ...include ethics of duties mainly based on the thinking of John Stuart Mill.
   c. ...include virtue ethics, which is rooted in ancient Greek philosophy. Virtue ethics is a typical consequentialist theory.
   d. ...includes egoism, the opposite of altruism. In egoist ethics, the intended outcome is one's own good. Somebody motivated by egoist thinking would for instance never donate money to a good cause.
3. Imagine in the retail corporation you are working in it has become a common practice that buyers ask suppliers to forfeit money in exchange for the renewal of their supplier contract. Which of the following sentences commenting the situation would be (a) statement(s) that is made from a descriptive ethics perspective?
   a. I think the reason why the buyers act this way is that they have high pressures to keep a high margin. Paying the money the suppliers are owed would reduce their margin.
   b. This practice is wrong as it is not fair that suppliers are not paid what they are owed.
   c. I think we need a buyer code of conduct that explicitly states that such behaviour is forbidden.
   d. Business is as it is. It is perfectly legitimate to drive a hard bargain!

B. THINK

Imagine you work in a company's HR department and have found out that it is a common practice to systematically pay less than is contractually agreed to some employees to save the company money. Whenever single employees find out, it is justified as an "accounting mistake" and the difference is paid. Apparently, the practice is widely known in the senior management team, and is approved by them, as the company is currently in a difficult economic situation. It is apparent that any major issue or scandal impacting in further loss of customer confidence might lead to bankruptcy. What would you do?

C. DO

Look up one company's code of ethics and inform yourself about the typical ethical issues in the company's industry, past ethical issues encountered by the company (e.g. through news coverage), and potential ethical issues.

D. RELATE

Think about one situation where you thought you knew what the ethically right thing to do was, but you did not speak up so people ended up doing the wrong thing. Get in touch with the people involved, tell them what you think would have been the right thing, and why you did not tell them back then.

E. BE

Reflect on how you make your ethical decisions? Think about several occasions where you had to make a morally difficult decision. What were the main thoughts and arguments leading to the decision you finally took? Can you recognize any of the above normative theories or decision-making principles as dominant in the way you made these decisions?

Feedback

A. KNOW

Feedback 1

a. Wrong: Business ethics as ethics in general refers to the mechanism of making right or wrong decisions, while morality rather focuses on values of specific individuals, groups and situations, which are the outcomes of the ethical decision-making process.
b. Right: The three main domains of business ethics mentioned in the question are illustrated in the figure titled "domains of business ethics".
c. Wrong: This description refers to descriptive ethics, while normative ethics aims at providing reasoning mechanisms that aim at normatively defining right or wrong for any given situation.
d. Wrong: Ethics management is a sub-domain of business ethics, which deals with the management instruments necessary to reach "good ethics" in an organization.

Feedback 2

a. Right: Mainstream philosophy aims at more complex subdivisions of normative ethics. For the pragmatic, management-focused purpose of this book the division between outcome based (consequentialist) and not-outcome-based (non-consequentialist) ethics has been made.
b. Wrong: Ethics of duties is mainly based on the thinking of Kant. John Stuart Mill is the grandfather of utilitarianism.
c. Wrong: Virtue ethics as basing the reasoning for right or wrong on the actors' virtuous, good character is non-consequentialist theory.
d. Wrong: Egoist ethics explicitly includes that someone acts for her/his own self-interest, but nevertheless creates a positive outcome for others. Someone donating money might for instance do so for the egoist motivation of the desire to feel like a good person.

Feedback 3

a. Right: This statement aims to describe the reasons underlying the (unethical) behavior.
b. Wrong: The question about right or wrong is made from a normative ethics position, not from a descriptive ethics stance.
c. Wrong: This statement describes a management instrument (a code of ethics) to manage the behavior in a way that leads to the buyers doing the right thing, which is typical for the domain of ethics management.
d. Wrong: No assumption about the reasons of the unethical behavior is made. The statement legitimizes the behavior.

B. THINK

Level	*Moral reasoning*	*Notes*
+	Decision based on higher principles such as justice, fairness, or the categorical imperative, possibly going beyond established societal norms with exemplary statements such as "I don't care what people think - it is the right thing to do" or "I cannot do it, as it is against a fundamental human rights principle".	
=	Decision based on arguments and motivations related to social conformity, with exemplary statements such as "I will do it if it is legal", or "what will people think?".	
–	Decision based on arguments and motivations related to avoiding punishment, and achieving direct reward, with exemplary statements such as "what's in for me?" and "I do it if I am sure not to be caught".	

C. DO

Level	*Using ethics management tools*	*Notes*
+	Code has been corroborated or adapted, based on a demonstrated deep understanding of ethical issues encountered in company and industry.	
=	Code has been corroborated or adapted.	
–	Code has neither been corroborated nor adapted.	

D. RELATE

Level	Asserting one's moral concerns	Notes
+	Moral concern has been voiced, and learning about how to make sure to voice concerns in similar future situations has been realized.	
=	People have been contacted and the moral concern has been voiced.	
–	Situation has not been identified and/or people have not been contacted.	

E. BE

Level	Reflecting on own decision making	Notes
+	Deep introspection into own ethical decision-making patterns and a link to underlying ethical theories or values.	
=	Basic introspection into own ethical decision-making patterns.	
–	Reflection has not happened or not led to introspection.	

References

AFL-CIO. (2011). *Executive paywatch*. Retrieved August 28, 2011, from 2011 executive paywatch: https://www.aflcio.org/corporatewatch/paywatch/

Antunez, M., Ramalho, N., & Marques, T. M. (2024). Context matters less than leadership in preventing unethical behaviour in international business. *Journal of Business Ethics, 192*(2), 307–322.

Carroll, A. B., & Brown, J. A. (2018). Corporate social responsibility: A review of current concepts, research, and issues. In *Business and Society 360* (pp. 39–69). Emerald Publishing Limited.

CBC News. (2011). *CBC news: World*. Retrieved August 26, 2011, from News of the World to shut down: https://www.cbc.ca/news/world/story/2011/07/07/newscorp-hacking.html

Crane, A., & Matten, D. (2010a). *Businesss ethics* (3rd Edition). New York: Oxford University Press.

Crane, A., & Matten, D. (2010b). Business ethics. In W. Visse, D. Matte, M. Pohl, & N. Tolhurst, *The A to Z of corporate social responsibility*. Chichester: Wiley.

Crane, A., & Glozer, S. (2016). Researching corporate social responsibility communication: Themes, opportunities and challenges. *The Journal of Management Studies, 53*(7), 1223–1252.

Dawkins, R. (1976). *The selfish gene*. Oxford: Oxford University Press.

Freeman, R. E. (1984/2010). *Strategic management: A stakeholder approach*. Cambridge: Cambridge University Press.

IBE. (2011). *How many companies have codes?* Retrieved August 28, 2011, from Institute of Business Ethics: https://www.ibe.org.uk/index.asp?upid=71&msid=12#17

Kant, I., & Patton, H. (1785/2005). *Moral law: Groundwork of the metaphysic of morals*. New York: Routledge.

Martin, K. (2019). Ethical implications and accountability of algorithms. *Journal of Business Ethics, 160*(4), 835–850.

Mill, J. S. (1863/2008). *Utilitarianism*. Forgotten Books.

New Statesman. (2010). *New Statesman*. Retrieved August 28, 2011, from NYT: Cameron's chief media adviser Andy Coulson "actively encouraged" NoW phone-hacking: https://www.newstatesman.com/uk-politics/2010/09/former-reporter-knew-coulson

Rawls, J. (1999). *A theory of justice: Revised edition*. Cambridge: Harvard University Press.

Sabbagh, D. (2011, July 8). *Guardian*. Retrieved August 28, 2011, from Phone hacking: How News of the World's story unravelled: https://www.guardian.co.uk/media/2011/jul/08/news-of-the-world-phone-hacking

Schaltegger, S., & Burritt, R. (2018). Business cases and corporate engagement with sustainability: Differentiating ethical motivations. *Journal of Business Ethics*, *147*(2), 241–259.

United Nations. (2011). *History of the document*. Retrieved August 28, 2011, from The universal declaration of human rights: https://www.un.org/en/documents/udhr/history.shtml

C Managing

8 Responsible Management Process

Three-Dimensional Management for the Triple Bottom Line

How does one manage a responsible business? As defined beforehand, the ultimate goal of responsible business must be to contribute to sustainable development. The three dimensions of sustainable development are social, environmental, and economic. Therefore, any management activity in a responsible business has to create value in all three dimensions, achieving performance and creation of capital, of all three kinds. Responsible management always has to be three-dimensional management. Elkington (1998) described this aspired management outcome as the triple bottom line, in contrast to traditional businesses' single bottom line of financial value. **Three-dimensional management** (or 3D management) is the integrated management process aiming at the creation of a sound triple bottom line. In the following, responsible management and 3-dimensional management will be used synonymously (Figure 8.1).

Social, environmental, and economic capital can be impacted inside and outside the company. Social value outside the company could, for instance, be social welfare created by a donation to a local school, while internal social value could be increased job-satisfaction of employees. Outside environmental value could be reflected by the reduction of environmental impacts of a zero-waste facility, while internal environmental value might be the improvement of an office's internal atmospheric environment by the application of sustainable architecture. External economic value of a certain business activity could be the economic benefit created for a supplier by a certain company, while a typical internal economic value could be the profit created from a business activity. Value here should not to be confused with a person's or a group's values, referring to a set of moral standards. Value instead refers to a positive or negative effect of a certain action along the lines of external and internal effects as they are used in welfare and environmental economics. Accordingly, value refers to an effect in social, environmental, and economic capital.

Managing blended value

John Elkington, the creator of the term "triple bottom line" (TBL) describes sustainable business as a "multidimensional challenge", defined by the basic task to manage social, financial, and environmental (three-dimensional) value at a time (Elkington, 2011).

DOI: 10.4324/9781003544074-12

This task, which could also be called the management of "blended value" (Emerson, 2003) is the very basis of three-dimensional management. The difference between the two terms is that the TBL describes the desired outcome, while three-dimensional management describes the management process.

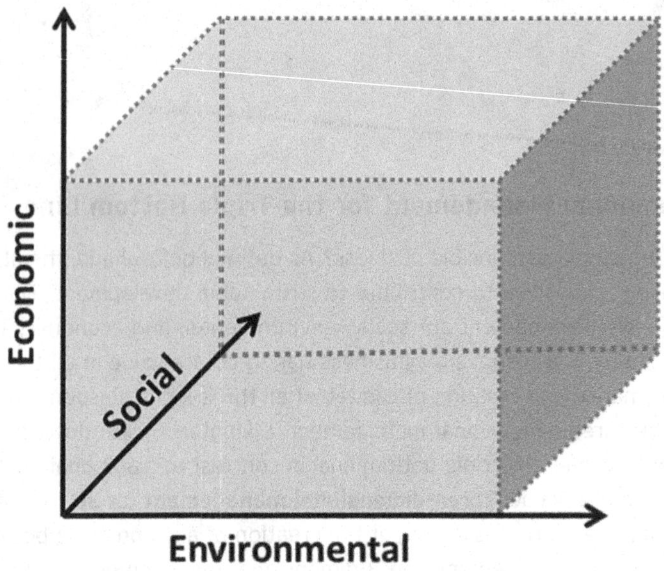

Figure 8.1 Three-Dimensional Management for the Triple Bottom Line.

Value creation is a highly interlinked process. Often one type of value automatically leads to another. A wage increase for workers (positive economic value) leads to an increase in the welfare of families (positive social value). The workers might be able to take their families on vacation, which in turn might lead to an additional amount of CO_2 emissions of the transportation used to reach the holiday destination (negative environmental value). Also, the external and internal creations of value are highly connected. The activity leading to the creation of a certain value does not have to be realized in the same location as the value created. Porter and Kramer (2006) describe in their concept of inside-out and outside-in linkages how company internal factors create value outside the company (inside-out linkages) and external factors lead to value creation inside the company (outside-in linkages). Value creation can also be understood in the light of the three different types (social, environmental, economic) of capital as illustrated in the chapter on sustainability. A positive value reflects an increase, a negative value a reduction in the respective capital. Table 8.1 provides an exemplary overview of different types of positive and negative value that might be created in the conduct of an average business.

Why talk about responsible business in such a lifeless and technical way? Is responsible business not all about exciting topics such as saving the planet, combating poverty, and being a good person and moral manager? Yes it is. Still, in order to reach those goals, management

Table 8.1 Classifying Value Creation into Internal, External, Social, Environmental, and Economic

	Internal	*External*
Social	(+) Employee satisfaction (–) Number of accidents (+) Diversity indicators (+) Direct employment	(+) Customer satisfaction (+) Healthiness of products (+) Community well-being (+) Indirect employment
Environmental	(+) Lighting and air quality (+) Biodiversity in facility (+) Gardening (–) Land use	(–) CO_2 emissions (–) Water discharged (–) Waste disposed (–) Biodiversity loss
Economic	(+) Revenue (+) Profit (+) Wages paid (+) Stock value	(–) Competitor destruction (+) Supplier economies (+) Regional economic development (+) Innovation spillovers

is in urgent need of a meta-perspective, which allows for understanding, measurement, and management of the effect of the responsible management process as described in the following paragraphs.

Immediate versus intergenerational responsibilities

In the preceding paragraph we have gotten to know sustainable development as a development that allows for the survival of the human race on planet Earth, as the ultimate goal of every responsible business. Do the working conditions in a third-world factory affect humanity's possibilities for survival on Earth? Does it really matter if another species, let's say the polar bear is extinct? Even more cynical: Wouldn't it be great for the survival of humanity to keep the majority of the world population in poverty? Poor people have the smallest average environmental footprint.

What does this ultimate responsibility to sustainable development mean? What responsibilities should and shouldn't a business assume? To answer this question, it helps to review the Brundtland definition (United Nations, 1987) of sustainable development mentioned in the preceding chapters. The definition refers to the goal of fulfilling the present generations' needs and to create a situation where also future generations can fulfill their own needs too. Thus, for a responsible business, taking this ultimate responsibility to contribute to sustainable development seriously means assuming two kinds of responsibilities; immediate and intergenerational responsibilities.

- **Immediate responsibilities** aim at fulfilling the needs of stakeholders with immediate claims in a humanistic approach of maximizing stakeholder welfare. For instance, that includes poor peoples' right to increase their standard of living. It also includes fair, healthy, and safe working conditions. Immediate responsibilities should also include responsibilities not necessarily instrumental to human well-being. To fulfill immediate responsibilities, a company needs to go beyond the question of "What do people need?" and include the rights of natural objects and natural beings, beyond their value for people. Even if the survival of polar bears might possibly not be instrumental to human well-being neither today, nor in the future, responsible businesses should assume the responsibility to protect natural entities beyond their instrumental value.

- **Intergenerational responsibilities** aim to ensure humanity's survival on Earth and to maintain and restore today's resources for future generations. Intergenerational responsibilities pragmatically follow the question: "What do we need for the future?"

Responsible business and management requires one to address both kinds of responsibilities and to balance the fulfillment of current needs with the one of future needs.

The Responsible Management Process

The **responsible management process**, as framed in this book is aimed at the management of social and environmental business performance. Three-dimensional management requires three main elements of the responsible management process, and a management instrument as depicted in Figure 8.2. Those four are omnipresent in any responsible management activity. Thus, they could be called **trinity of responsible management**. The actor or agent of a 3D management activity is the first element and executes 3D management. Actors might

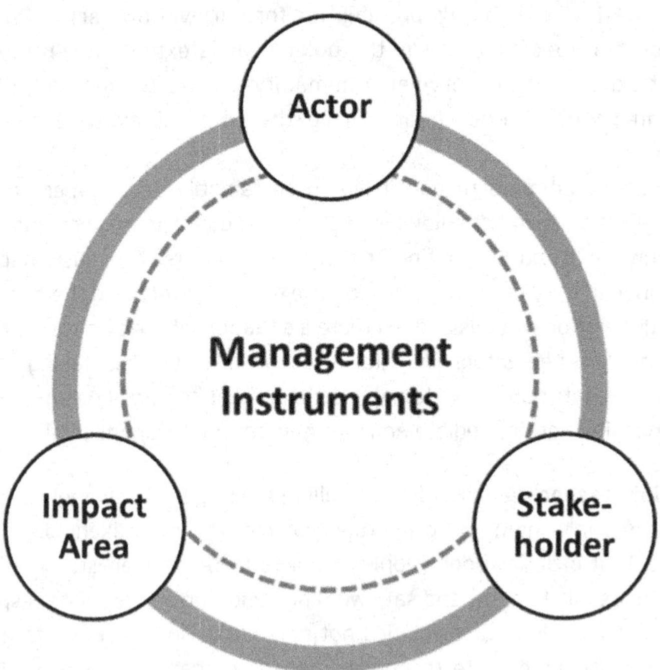

Figure 8.2 The Responsible Management Process Trinity.

be a corporation, an entrepreneur, an NGO, or also a government agency. The impact to be made on social, environmental, or economic issues (element two) involved in the management process are manifold and may require substantial and diverse specialist knowledge. Issues might for instance be CO_2 emissions, demographic diversity, and global warming. Stakeholders (element three) are the groups that "can affect or are affected" (Freeman, 1984/2010, p. 25) by the business in general and more specifically by the 3D management activity at hand. The **responsible management instrument** is the specific administrative tool applied to a certain responsible management activity.

To manage responsible business, it makes sense to split a company's overall activity for the good of society and environment into single manageable responsible management activities. Once such a list or portfolio of single responsible management activities is established, it is of crucial importance to deeply understand the three main elements and the management instrument applied in the activity at hand. Imagine three different responsible management activities such as the ones described in the following examples:

- **Green packaging technology**: The Mexican bakery and pastry products manufacturer Bimbo is in the vanguard of the biodegradable plastic packaging movement. As one of the first companies in Latin America, Bimbo in 2008 introduced a biodegradable polyethylene wrapping for bread products. In 2010 the company implemented the first biodegradable metalized packaging for many pastry products (Ortiz, 2008).
- **Responsible consumption**: The Danish beer brewery multinational Heineken aims at promoting the responsible consumption of alcohol. As part of this activity, Heineken lobbies against drunk driving in South Korea, which has experienced a strong cultural bias towards such behavior. The campaign has led to more than 2000 people directly pledging not to drink and drive and more than 3 million people who learned about the campaign via news media. Heineken also promoted similar activities among its local competitors and lobbied the South Korean government (Heineken, 2011).
- **Employee workplace inclusion**: The US American company Hewlett Packard is highly involved into the promotion of diversity and inclusive labor practices among its employees. The company has implemented a broad set of related practices such as an extensive non-discrimination policy, flexible work hours, and the creation of employee networking activities for often marginalized groups (HP, 2011b; HP, 2011a).

Table 8.2 provides an overview of the analysis of the key elements of the three 3D management activities introduced as the trinity of responsible management. The table reveals how different the basic parameters of each are and how management must adapt. In the following the three constituting elements of responsible management will be characterized one-by one. The table also includes the management instruments mainly applied in each respective activity.

Actors

Actors of a specific responsible management activity might be either a single manager or an organization in charge of a specific responsible management activity. When management is seen in its simplest understanding of "organizing and applying given resources for the

Table 8.2 Elements and Management Instruments of Exemplary Responsible Management Activities

Activity	*Actor*	*Stakeholder(s)*	*Impact area*	*Management instrument*
Biodegradable packaging	Bimbo	Natural environment	Waste reduction	Sustainable innovation
Promotion of responsible alcohol consumption	Heineken	Consumers, competitors, government, civil society	Drunk driving	Social marketing
Promotion of diversity and inclusion	Hewlett Packard	Employees	Workplace inclusion	Sustainable human resources management

achievement for a predefined goal", it becomes clear that the management process does not exclusively apply to a business environment (McNamara, 2011). There are also management activities in civil society organizations, governments, and other organizational actors. In this book, as dealing with responsible business, the clear focus is on management in a business context. Nevertheless, it is important to learn about how organizational parameters change when responsible management is executed by organizational actors other than businesses.

As illustrated in Table 8.3, there are three main organization types and individuals affiliated to those organizations typically administrating responsible management activities. It is important to know the main differences among actors from the three sectors, business, government, and civil society, in order to successfully manage collaborations for a common cause between those actors. The potential reasons for conflict are as great as the structural

Table 8.3 Types of Organizational Actors and Their Main Characteristics

Organizational actor type	*Primary motivation*	*Management characteristics*	*Resources and strengths for sustainable development*
Business	Economic (profit)	Quick reaction to trends and opportunities High effectiveness and efficiency Pragmatism Often little professionalization in the social and environmental field	Financial resources Frequent international outreach Quick response capacity
Civil society organization (CSO)	Social, Environmental, Economic (depends on specific CSO focus)	High motivation for achievement of announced social and environmental goals Strong idealism Often little professionalization	High cause - knowledge High cause - motivation Cost-effective contribution
Governmental sector	Social (welfare)	Hierarchical and often sluggish reaction to external developments	Legislative power Institutional mandate to better social and environmental causes

differences. For instance, businesses sometimes refrain from teaming up with civil society organizations (CSOs) due to the low level of CSO professionalization. Often collaborators, especially in smaller CSOs join the organization due to their idealistic motivation to help the cause, but do not necessarily have a professional background in the field or operational activities covered by the organization. Also, very often CSOs are run by volunteers, whose main job comes first in terms of commitment and available time. CSOs on the other hand may see a conflict in company's profit drivenness, which not always goes in accordance with promoting a CSO's cause. Also, if profit is the main priority of an organization, the attention it may pay to topics not directly affecting the financial bottom line may be very limited. In the relationship between businesses and governmental institutions, businesses often perceive governmental institutions as reacting sluggishly in the management process.

In spite of those differences, collaboration between those three different actor groups is absolutely necessary to achieve the goal of sustainable development. Only with the three types of actors' complementary types of contribution, the ultimate goal of sustainable development can be reached.

While the preceding paragraph focused on organizational actors for sustainable development, one should not underestimate the potential power for change individual actors, so-called change agents, have. The chapter on individual change extensively covers the role of individual actors as change agents for a more sustainable society in all three sectors, business, government, and civil society.

Actors for freedom of speech in China

The fight for an improvement of human rights in China has found many agents acting together from all three sectors of the global society. In the governmental arena, for instance, the German foreign minister Guido Westerwelle during his inaugural visit in 2007 made human rights, especially freedom of speech, a primary topic (Welt, 2010). The world's biggest search engine Google, as a representative of the business sector, pulled out of China as a reaction to ongoing censorship and hacking attempts in early 2010 (Lee, 2011). The human rights activist Liu Xiaobo, representing the civil society sector, received the Nobel Peace Prize while still in a Chinese prison in 2010 (Appiah, 2010). In late 2011 the Chinese government announced forthcoming efforts to further develop and explain "Chinese-style" human rights. Freedom of speech is not a focal point of the program (El Mundo, 2011).

Stakeholders

Stakeholders are all groups, individuals, and also non-human entities (such as animals, plants, and future generations) that "can affect or are affected" (Freeman, 1984/2010, p. 25; Buchholtz & Carroll, 2008). Stakeholders may be affected by any activity of any of the actors characterized in the last paragraph, which means any such activities have stakeholders. In the following section it will primarily be referred to stakeholders of businesses and economic activities in general.

Business stakeholders typically are employees, customers, communities, civil society organizations, governments, suppliers, shareholders, and competitors. Competitors are the most frequently forgotten stakeholders. Probably due to the antagonistic relationship to competitors, companies tend not to consider competitors as stakeholders. Nevertheless, a company and its competitors do have a strong mutual relationship. Many activities in responsible business strongly affect competitors and, on the one hand, responsible business is a strong differentiation factor against competitors, and on the other hand, many industry-wide movements towards responsible business require considerable industry-internal collaboration between competitors.

Stakeholders, let's play

Gamification is the newest trend in engaging with stakeholders. Sustainable development actors increasingly use games to foster awareness and sustainable behavior. Examples include the collaborative simulation "World without oil" (Peters, 2011). Jane McGonigal claims that the state of mind reached in while gaming can solve most of the world's problems by reaching "epic wins" and change peoples' behavior towards more sustainability (McGonigal, 2010).

For a better understanding of the basic characteristics of stakeholders and how to manage the stakeholder relationship, Table 8.4 describes the characteristics of some important stakeholder groups. It is conspicuous that the list of typical stakeholders includes governments, civil society organizations (CSOs), and companies, which beforehand had been described as actors of 3D management. Depending on the responsible management activity at hand any of those organization types mentioned might either be an actor or a stakeholder of a certain responsible management activity. Imagine, for instance, a company's donation campaign to a CSO such as Doctors without Borders. If one takes the perspective of the person managing the campaign from the inside of a for-profit business, the respective actor would be the company, and the stakeholder would be the CSO. If one takes the perspective of a manager in charge of fundraising inside the CSO Doctors without Borders, the actor is the CSO and the company becomes a stakeholder of this fundraising activity.

Table 8.4 Typical Stakeholders and Their Characteristics

Stakeholder	*Mutual interests*	*Typical issues/causes*
Customers	*Customers*: High-quality products, satisfaction of consumption wants and needs *Business*: Maximum willingness to pay, brand loyalty	Product security Sustainable consumption Consumer boycotts Sales and lending practices
Employees	*Employees*: Good work, high wage, professional fulfillment *Business*: Motivation, productivity, loyalty, human capital	Work-life balance Labor conditions and fair wage Workplace inclusiveness Labor union association Ethical misconduct of employees

(*Continued*)

Table 8.4 (Continued)

Stakeholder	*Mutual interests*	*Typical issues/causes*
Owners	*Owners*: Return on investment, investment security, influence over company *Business*: Funding, liberty in use of funds	Corporate governance Accounting practices Socially responsible investment Transparency
Civil society organizations (CSOs)	*CSO*: Influence on businesses' behavior, cooperation for funding *Business*: Minimum CSO influence, cooperation for issue know-how, association for credibility	Variable issues, depending on CSO's focus Contributions to society (citizenship) Community involvement
Competitors	*Competitor*: Gain competitive advantage, collaborate to share the burden of sustainability *Business*: Gain competitive advantage, collaborate to share the burden of sustainability	Industry sustainability initiatives Sustainable innovation products Collusion/oligopolies Fair competition
Suppliers	*Supplier*: Long-run relationships, high sales volume, high price, independence *Business*: Long-run relationships, high sales volume, low price, high-quality relationship	Labor conditions Exploitative contracting Supply chain inclusiveness Responsible sourcing
Governments	*Government*: Regulation and taxation, businesses' contribution to society, business support of governmental-institutional interests *Business*: Minimum taxation and regulation, governmental support for own interest	Legal compliance Corruption/lobbying Privatization Monopolies Relationship governmental legislation – business standards

Impact Area

When we talk about where impacts are made, responsible business jargon often includes the terms **issues**, **causes**, and crisis. What do those terms exactly mean? How can one characterize their internal relationship? An issue describes a social, environmental, or economic factor, which has the latent potential to cause problems or even result in a crisis if ignored. A cause is an issue that a company has started to mitigate or solve. Issues a company faces can, for instance, be the environmental impact of its operations, the job satisfaction created among its employees, customer protection, and supply chain sustainability. The difference between an issue and a cause is simple, but very significant for communication and motivational purposes. A cause is an issue a company is positively involved in; an issue on the way to mitigation or even solution. This difference is highly important when it comes to communicating an organization's responsible business activity. In order to convey a positive picture of a business, it makes sense that whenever justified by good socio-environmental performance to talk about the solutions (causes) and not only about the problems (issues), which the company faces. There might even be responsible management activities that address a cause that has never been an issue (problem) to the company. For instance, Deutsche Bank is very active in the promotion of arts and culture (cause). The topic never constituted a problem (issue) for the company and for sure would, if ignored, not have resulted in negative consequences, much less in a crisis. So, we can unify the topics of issues and causes under the umbrella of impact areas, certain themes under which we can make a certain type of impact, be it positive or negative.

The business case for high-level inclusion

The issue of discrimination based on ethnicity, race, religion, physical abilities, gender, and sexual preferences is a widespread problem in many businesses. This issue has become a common cause when companies make an effort to counteract discriminatory behaviors and structures. Non-discrimination policies have become a mainstream business topic best-known under the term "inclusion". A diversity topic that has received special attention is gender diversity. While 72% of corporate level leaders believe that gender diversity increases financial performance, the measurement for an extraordinary diversity performance is an above 15% share of women in C-level leadership positions, which appears distant from an equal 50:50 leadership share between men and women (McKinsey, 2010).

In order to identify how important a certain issue is to stakeholders and to an actor of responsible management, the concept of materiality is applied. The Global Reporting Initiative (GRI) defines materiality by the two factors of how much an issue is important to the inside of a company and how much it matters to the outside. Internal factors include, for instance, the actual financial impact and risk posed by the issue or how much the respective issue is aligned with the businesses' values, goals, and core competencies. External factors comprise, for instance, the degree of stakeholder interest into the issue, as well as future challenges of the industry and the planet (GRI, 2011). To analyze how much an issue matters, companies frequently use a graph split up into the two axes of external and internal importance as proposed by the GRI. The international NGO AccountAbility instead proposes a set of five tests to detect the materiality of a certain issue. The tests go in accordance with the GRI framework, but give more detailed advice (Zadeck & Merme, 2003).

A 2010 survey among CEOs of Global Compact member companies revealed that the social and environmental issues seen most material by companies are education, climate change, and poverty, followed by diversity, access to clean water and sanitation, and food security (Lacey, Cooper, Hayward, & Neuberger, 2010). While CEO priorities within sustainability have evolved since 2010, issues such as education, climate change, and poverty remain at the forefront. The 2023 Accenture & UN Global Compact CEO Study (Accenture, 2023) underscores this ongoing concern, ranking climate action, inclusive growth, and resource stewardship among the areas CEOs globally see as most crucial for creating long-term value. Interestingly, when comparing those issues at the heart of company executives with the threatening global issues as described in Chapter 1, one finds out that CEOs are very aware of the importance of those topics. Seeing them as material means an implicit commitment by the companies to get active in making them their causes and solving them. For a hands-on materiality assessment, please see the materiality assessment section of the chapter on strategic management.

Picking the Right Responsible Management Instrument

Responsible management instruments for the management of integrated social, environmental, and economic performance, 3D management instruments, fall into two broad categories. First, **specialized responsible management instruments** have been developed for and tuned in to the creation of social and environmental business performance. Those

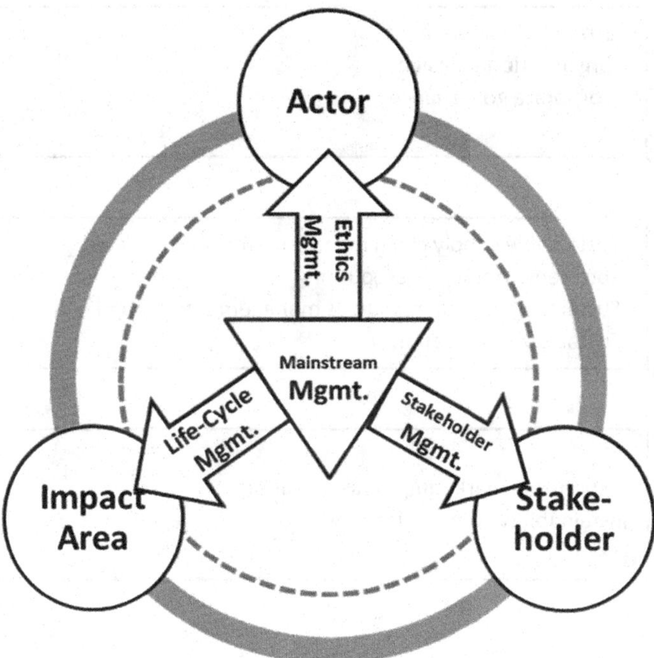

Figure 8.3 Specialized Responsible Management Instruments.

instruments comprising stakeholder management, life-cycle management, and ethics management are new to mainstream business management. Specialized 3D management instruments are fundamental to managing responsible business. As illustrated in Figure 8.3, each of the three specialized responsible management instruments corresponds to one of the three main elements of the responsible management trinity. In most 3D management activities, all three specialized responsible management instruments are applied, while the second category of management instruments finds rather punctual application.

The second category is **mainstream responsible management instruments**. Those instruments are well-known business management instruments such as accounting, marketing, or innovation that have been re-interpreted in order to additionally enhance economic performance in order to create social and environmental performance or value. Some examples for such instruments are sustainable innovation, cause-related marketing, or socio-environmental accounting. While the specialized responsible management instruments each correspond to one of the three main elements of the responsible management process and thus are omnipresent in any responsible management activity, the mainstream management instruments change depending on the specific functional area of a company that the responsible management activity is located in. The responsible management process will now be divided into three main processes as described in Figure 8.4. The following chapters will cover the mainstream management instruments in additional depth.

The main goal of the first process, planning, is to design responsible management activities that are neatly aligned with the organization's strategic infrastructure such as the vision and mission statements, the strategy development process, and the implemented corporate, business-unit and function strategies. The strategic management process fulfills the function

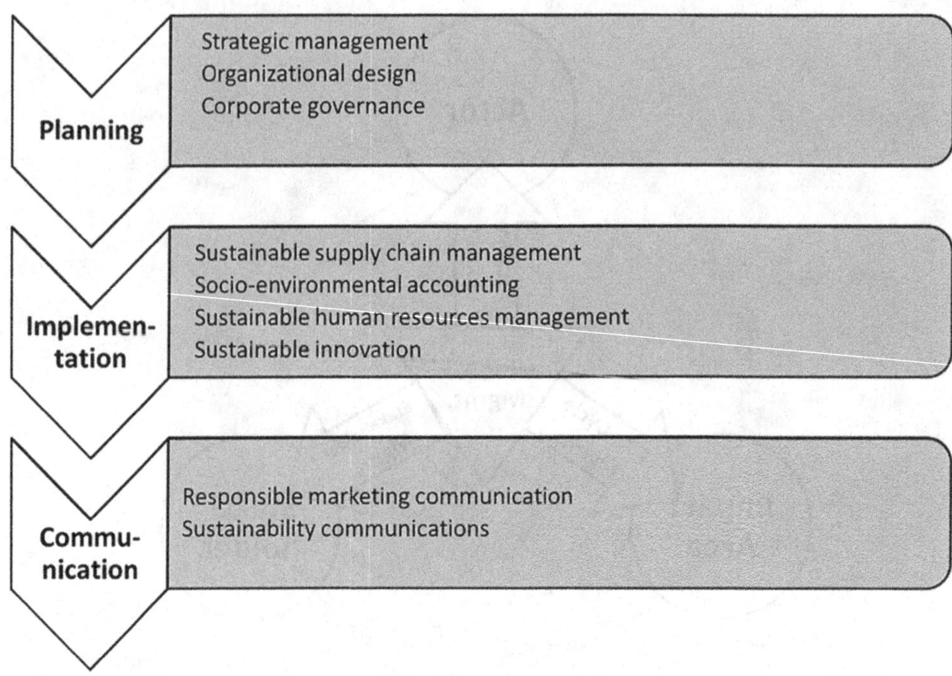

Figure 8.4 The Mainstream Management Process and Exemplary Management Instruments Applied.

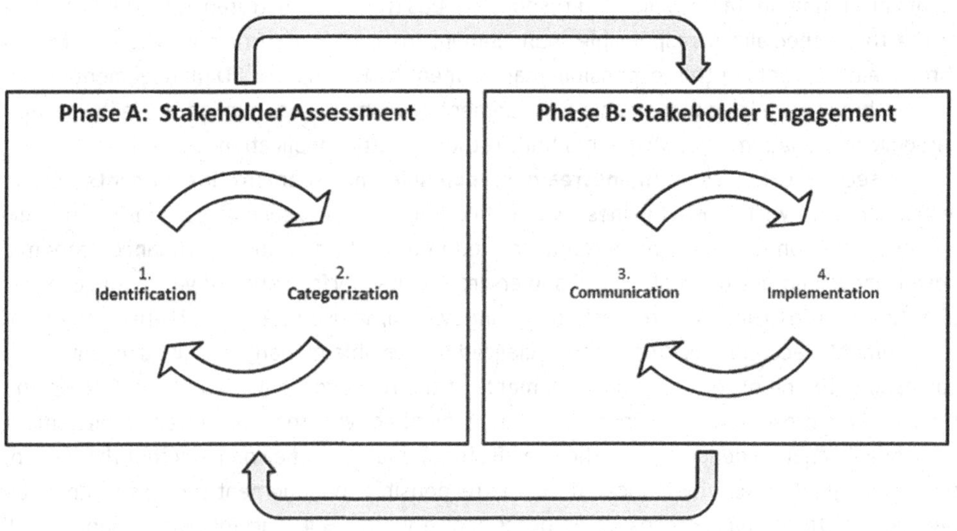

Figure 8.5 The Stakeholder Management Process.

of the brain and guiding light of an organization and all its activities. The second process is the implementation and realization of responsible business practice throughout all business functions and hierarchical levels. The realization process includes not only the main business functions (e.g. logistics and production) involved in the resource transformation process, but also the support functions (e.g. human resources and innovation) enabling this process. The third process fulfills the function of communicating with the various stakeholder groups during the responsible management process. Communication instruments are, for instance, social- and cause-related marketing, sustainability reporting, and codes of ethics. It is important to realize that these processes do not necessarily have to happen in the sequenced suggested by the figure. For instance, an exchange with stakeholders might lead to a new strategic position, which then leads to the realization of new practices. Or the other way around, a new set of socially responsible practices might lead to a rethinking of strategy and a parallel communication effort.

However, the above sequencing may be of high value under certain conditions. In many cases planning has to be the first step. Many companies have tried to do "some philanthropy" in a rather disconnected way from the core-business and without a long-run strategy. The result has often been unsatisfactory for both stakeholders and the business. Such strategically unaligned activities not only lack high-level management support, but also are seen as an extra that can be downsized, whenever resources have to be reassigned for "more strategic" activities. Sound implementation of responsible management practices has to come before the communication of social and environmental topics. "Social" and "eco" claims when unsubstantiated by organizational practice are quickly perceived as so-called "greenwashing", a situation where a business focuses more on "talking responsibility" than actually "walking it". Greenwashing has the potential to create considerable reputational havoc. Later sections of this book will extensively cover these stages, while we will cover the specialized responsible management instruments, stakeholder management, life-cycle impact management, and ethics management with greater detail in the following sections.

Stakeholder Management

Stakeholders and the relationship with them exert significant influence on both business and stakeholders. The role of **stakeholder management** is to optimize this mutual influence. Do governments oppose or support your business? Do activist groups boycott or endorse? Are employees motivated or frustrated? Do the media idolize or bash what you are doing? All those opposing stakeholder behaviors are factors that can make or break a business. Stakeholder management is the management tool which aims at managing stakeholder relations to the best of both the business and stakeholders. It sounds overly simplistic, but how stakeholders affect the business very much depends on how the business affects stakeholders. To cite a commonplace: "You get what you give". This is why the very purpose of stakeholder management is to create value for a businesses' stakeholders and to enable them in turn to create value for the business.

How to achieve such mutual value creation? The stakeholder management process consists of two phases, each comprising two main activities for successful stakeholder management. Phase A is the stakeholder analysis and consists of 1) identifying and 2) categorizing

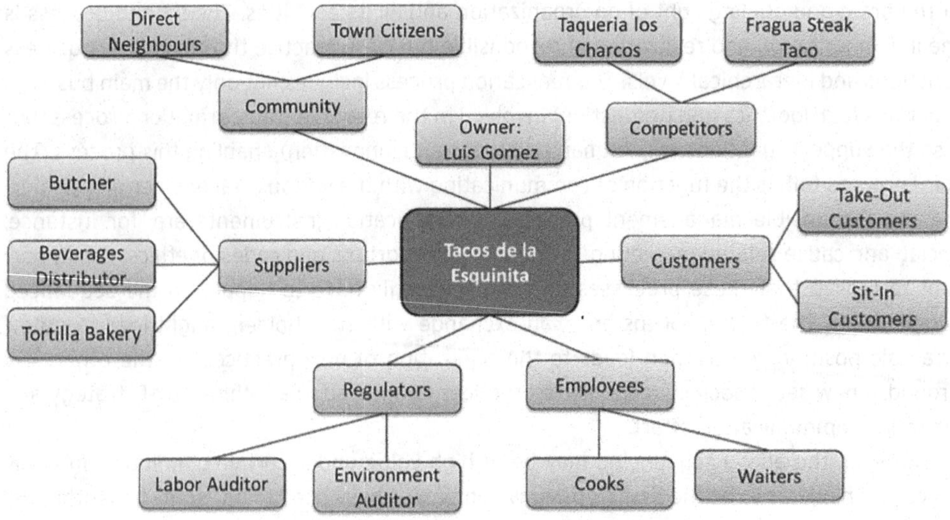

Figure 8.6 Exemplary Stakeholder Map of a Taco Restaurant.

the groups a company affects or is affected by. Phase B, the stakeholder engagement consists of 3) communication with stakeholders and 4) implementing actions based on the outcomes of steps 1–3. In the following, the two phases of the stakeholder management process will be illustrated in greater detail.

The first step of the stakeholder assessment phase consists of identifying stakeholders of an organization. Usually, this is done by establishing a stakeholder map. Stakeholder maps can be very general or highly specific, from merely showing the direct obvious connections to covering various levels of stakeholders. At this stage of the analysis it also makes sense to define the mutual relationship between each respective stakeholder and the company. Figure 8.6 illustrates such a graph for the fictional case of a Mexican Taco business which will be further described later in this book.

Should stakeholders rule the (world of) business?

Stakeholder theory is an exciting field for criticism of the very basic foundations of typical capitalist enterprises. For instance, the concept of stakeholder democracy proposes that stakeholders should have the say about the fate, activities, and the mere survival of businesses, not shareholders or owners (Matten & Crane, 2005). Another revolutionary approach is to make a switch from shareholder value-based management, a central instrument in financial management, to stakeholder value-based management. Interestingly, there is evidence that a focus on stakeholder value can also be instrumental in creating shareholder value.

The second step is to categorize stakeholders in order to better understand their position and importance to the organization. Many different stakeholder categorization schemes have been developed. Each provides a different clue for understanding stakeholders, their impact on and relationship to the organization. Table 8.5 provides an overview of the most

Table 8.5 Stakeholder Categories

Definition/Stakeholder characteristic	*Examples*	*Analysis criteria*
1) Internal: Stakeholder located inside the company. 2) External: Stakeholders located outside the company.	1) Employees; shareholders 1) Government; competitors	Physical location of stakeholder and proximity to company structure and mainstream business activities. (Freeman, 1984/2010, pp. 8-13, 216; ISO, 2010, p. 15; Buchholtz & Carroll, 2008, p. 27)
1) Primary: Stakeholders directly involved in transactions with the company. 2) Secondary: Stakeholder with an indirect relationship with the company.	1) An employee of a company; the natural environment affected by operations 2) The family of a company's employee; an environmental interest group	Proximity of relationship (Clarkson, 1995)
1) Social: An individual or group of human beings currently alive. 2) Non-social: Non-human entities and individuals and groups not living in the present.	1) Today's society; an environmental activist group 2) Future generations; the natural environment	Stakeholder (Buchholtz & Carroll, 2008, pp. 86-88; Fitch, 1976, p. 39)
1) Powerful: Stakeholders having the potential to "impose their will" on the company. 2) Legitimate: Stakeholders with a legitimate claim. 3) Urgent: Stakeholders issuing an urgent claim.	1) A CEO; a major single client; a critical supplier 2) An employee asking for legal wage and benefits; a community member being negatively affected by the company's operations 3) An ecosystem imminently threatened in existence by the company's operations; customers to be negatively affected by a manufacturing error of a product	Importance (salience) of stakeholder: The most important stakeholder is the one that combines most of the three stakeholder characteristics. No characteristic: Non-stakeholder One characteristic: Latent stakeholder Two characteristics: Expectant stakeholder Three characteristics: Definite stakeholder (Mitchell, Agle, & Wood, 1997, pp. 874-875)
1) Core: Stakeholders without which the company is not able to survive. 2) Strategic: Stakeholders crucial for success of the company. 3) Environmental: Stakeholders neither important for survival nor for success of the company.	1) A key employee 2) A strong competitor 3) An activist group unrelated to the business and its impacts	Significance of impact on company (Clarkson et al, 1994 as cited in Buchholtz & Carroll, 2008)
Potential for Threat: Stakeholder has a high potential to harm the company. Potential for Cooperation: Stakeholder has a high potential to cooperate with the company.	1) Competitor introducing a sustainable innovation product that will gain immense market share 2) An NGO with an excellent reputation, willing to support a company's responsible management efforts	Potential impact of stakeholder: Impacts might be positive or negative. (Freeman, 1984/2010, p. 143; Savage, Nix, Whitehead, & Blair, 1991)

Definitions given have been slightly altered from the original sources in order to create a coherent stakeholder classification framework.

commonly used approaches. A study showed that in the companies' perception the stakeholders exerting the highest influence are consumers, followed by employees and governments on the third rank. Interestingly investors scored only seventh (Lacey, Cooper, Hayward, & Neuberger, 2010). Such a general prioritization of stakeholder importance, based on managers' intuitive perception, is a good starting point to then applying stakeholder categorization tools for a more detailed picture.

After stakeholders have been identified and categorized, an organization should be clear about which stakeholder to engage with (or not) with which goal. Phase B of the stakeholder management process is the stakeholder engagement consisting of two additional steps. Step three, communicating with stakeholders fulfills important functions such as gathering information on stakeholder claims, attitudes, ideas, propensity to collaboration, and many others. Stakeholder communication can serve to refine the results achieved from the stakeholder assessment phase and serves as a basis for the subsequent step. During the fourth and last step companies implement activities to satisfy stakeholder needs. Steps three and four should be repeated in an interlinked fashion in order to gather feedback from stakeholders on the process of implementation and on the quality of the outcome. The chapters on main and support functions will provide extensive guidance on the implementation step, while the communication chapters can be seen as a manual for successful stakeholder communication.

Life-Cycle Impact Management

The physical product life-cycle model[1] depicts all stages of a product from the extraction of the first raw material, through the various stages of production, through use and finally the end of the product's useful lifetime. The management instrument **life-cycle impact management** aims to simultaneously optimize the impact throughout all of those stages. The first stage of application is life-cycle assessment, analyzing and depicting the overall social, environmental, and economic performance from "cradle to grave". If the product can be recycled, the circle closes and the life-cycle management process could even be described as ranging from "cradle to cradle" (McDonough & Braungart, 2002).

Life-cycle management is most related with the impact element of the responsible management process. This is due to the life-cycle's capacity to capture any kind of social, environmental, and economic impact throughout all issues at any stage of a product's life cycle. Thus, the life-cycle model has the capacity to holistically describe and manage any beneficial or adverse effect on any social, environmental, or economic issue. One might be confused as to why the life-cycle instrument shifts the focus from a complete responsible business to the mere product. The idea is that if one can assess the individual impact of all products of a company, throughout all life-cycle stages, this assessment at the same time reflects the overall impact of the company as a whole. A main advantage is that life-cycle assessment does not stop at the company gate or considers the mere production process. Instead, the tool delivers a holistic picture of all impacts created directly or indirectly by the product or service upstream (in its use) or downstream (in sourcing activities).

LCA for THC?

Life-cycle assessment (LCA) can be a tool for unusual, even illegal products. The Cannabis legalization debate is implicitly conducting a (rather confusing) life-cycle assessment of the plants' impact on society. Proponents and opponents of the drug's legalization discuss impacts of mainly two life-cycle stages. Concerning the "usage" stage, pro- and anti-legalization groups debate about the health and addiction impacts of the drug and the supposed medical effects of its active substance, THC. During the "production and sourcing" phase, the main negative impacts are the severe outcomes of criminal activity, such as over tens of thousands of deceased people in the Mexican fight against drug cartels ongoing since 2005 (Messerli, 2011; BBC, 2011).

The physical product life cycle consists of three major phases as described in Figure 8.7. The first phase, the production stage, can be subdivided into the production external to the company throughout its supply chain and the company internal production process. The usage stage describes employment of the product until the end of its useful lifetime. At the end of its useful lifetime (the third phase), a product can either be disposed or lead to another useful lifetime. This last step is called revalorization - giving the product back a certain value. Revalorization does not always have to mean to go back to the raw material. Alternatives are to repair, refurbish, disassemble, or reuse the same product. Table 8.6 provides an exemplary list of positive and negative impacts made throughout the life-cycle stages.

The life-cycle management process consists of three main stages as illustrated in Figure 8.8. During the life-cycle mapping stage, a company lists all social, environmental, and economic impacts created at every stage of the life cycle as shown in Table 8.6. During the second stage, the stage of impact evaluation, impacts created are analyzed with the goal of

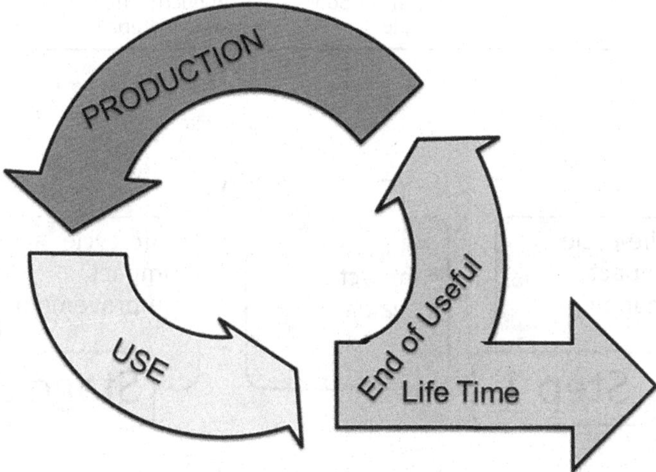

Figure 8.7 The Physical Product Life Cycle.

Table 8.6 Exemplary Impacts throughout the Life Cycle

Life-cycle stage		*Examples of positive (+) and negative (–) impacts*		
		Social	*Environmental*	*Economic*
Production	External sourcing	(–) Supply-chain labor conditions (+) Poverty reduction by inclusive supply chains	(–) Exploitation of natural resources (+) Environmental impact exceeding local standards	(–) Destruction of local industries (+) Support of developing countries
	Internal Production	(–) Factory labor conditions (+) Socio-economic welfare effects	(–) Waste produced (+) Energy surplus production (e.g. internal wind energy plant)	(–) Net-value destruction due to unsustainable practices (+) Economic spillover effects on local clusters and business environment
Use		(–) Harmful or insecure products (+) Satisfaction of customer needs (and wants)	(–) Energy, water, gas usage (–) Planned redundancy	(–) Running expenses (+) Service and repair
End of useful life	Disposal	(–) Waste as health risk (+) Ease of "throwing away"	(–) Packaging waste (–) Product/component toxicity	(–) Rest-value destruction by ultimate disposal (+) The waste business
	Revalori-zation	(–) Complexity and effort of revalorization (e.g. waste separation) (+) Re-usage as cost-saving for factor for poor people	(–) Reuse, refurbishment, recycling (+) Lower energy intensity of recycling compared to production from virgin materials	(–) Cost of reverse logistics of product recovery (+) Income from selling recycled materials

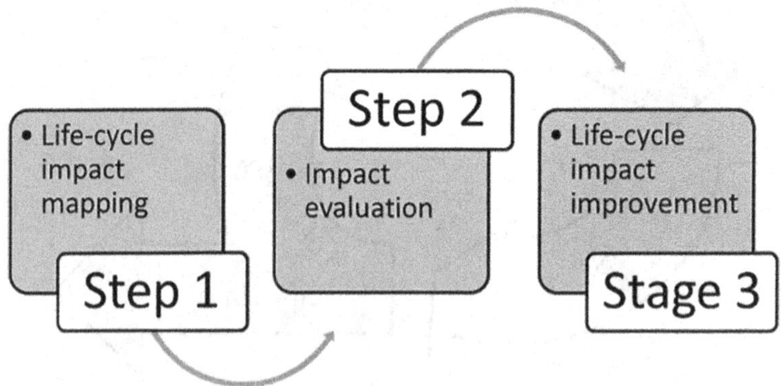

Figure 8.8 The Life-Cycle Management Process.

normatively evaluating how positive or negative a certain impact is. In the same step, the impacts that should be altered are identified. In the third and final stage of impact improvement, concrete changes for the improvement of the overall life-cycle impact are planned and implemented. Such changes might attach to any impact at any life-cycle stage. Examples might be improving working conditions throughout the supply chain, increasing the eco-efficiency of the in-house production process, designing a product that consumes less energy during its usage, or assuring that the product can be fully recycled at the end of its useful life. Life-cycle management might even lead to the complete substitution of a very negative-impact product type by another one with an improved 3D performance.

Ethics Management

Ethics management is the managerial application of business ethics and aims at increasing the amount of a company's right or desirable ethical decisions on an individual employee level as well as on the overall organizational level. Thus, ethics management aims at creating both ethically good employees and good organizations. Ethics management is the management instrument focusing on the ethical decision making of actors in responsible business.

The ethics management process consists of three main steps as illustrated in Figure 8.9. First, the typical ethical issues throughout an organization's characteristic activities and impacts (along the whole product life cycle) have to be identified and analyzed. Second, one should decide on the desired "most ethical" decision for every dilemma encountered. In order to define the ethically "best choice" one should systematically analyze the dilemma drawing upon the normative ethical theories described in the preceding chapter. For many of the ethical issues, and morally wrong behaviors, there might actually be a clear idea of what is right or wrong. In this case a dilemma evaluation is not necessary. The focus here should be on understanding why individuals engage in unethical behavior in spite of knowing what would be right, and on applying the right management instruments to foster right behaviors.

The third step is to apply descriptive business ethics on every dilemma situation in order to fully understand why a certain actor does or does not reach desirable decisions in practice. Factors influencing ethical behavior in practice might either be individual - directly related to the actor - or situational - related to factors external to the actor.

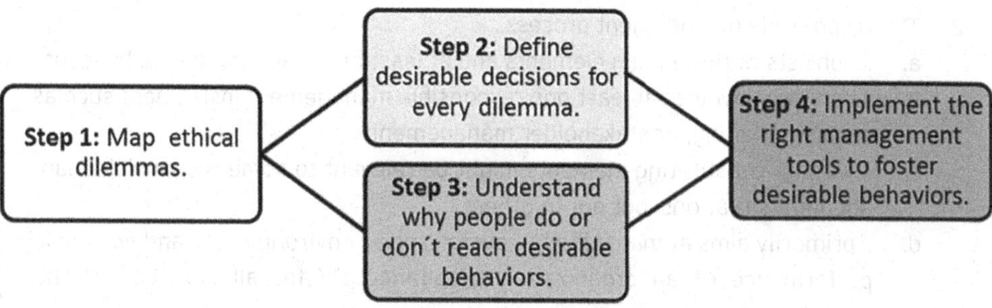

Figure 8.9 The Ethics Management Process.

The fourth and final step is to apply ethics management tools in order to support the making of desired ethical decisions. Typical ethics management tools are for instance ethics education, codes of ethics, ethics officers, and hotlines. A more seldom-applied, but highly effective tool is social marketing, defined as marketing for behavior change. The deployment of ethics management tools must attach to the individual and situational factors identified as crucial in step three of the ethics management process.

The power of the CECO

The highest job function in ethics management is the so-called chief ethics and compliance officer (CECO). CECOs cover far-reaching responsibilities. Based on a working knowledge of their company's strategy, processes, policies, and risks, a CECO develops standards and monitors good ethical conduct throughout a whole company. Among US-based companies, 87% of the CECOs regularly report on the state of ethics and compliance to the company's Chief Executive Officers (CEOs) (ECOA; ERC, 2011).

Exercises

A. KNOW

Use the below multiple-choice questions to test your knowledge. Each answer may be wrong or right and there may be zero to four right or wrong answers per question:

1. 3-Dimensional value creation...
   a. ...in a responsible business happens internally and externally, leading to social, environmental, and economic value.
   b. ...as a business-internal economic value might include for instance increased sales income from sales of a more sustainable product.
   c. ...is related to inside-out, outside-in linkages. Porter and Kramer describe an outside-in linkage as the effect a company's business activity has on its surrounding environment.
   d. ...provides a meta-perspective as an important analytical basis throughout the responsible management process.

2. The responsible management process...
   a. ...consists of three main elements and at least one management instrument.
   b. ...centrally involves at least one responsible management instrument such as social marketing, or stakeholder management.
   c. ...with its constituting elements might be relevant to some responsible management situations, but not to others.
   d. ...primarily aims at managing the overall social, environmental, and economic performance of an organization simultaneously for all activities of the organization.

3. Actors...
   a. ...may for instance be a company, a government agency, or a civil society organization.
   b. ...from different sectors should not collaborate, as their primary motivations and management characteristics are inherently incompatible.
   c. ...include businesses, which are well equipped to contribute to sustainable development among others due to their quick response capacity and international outreach.
   d. ...as mentioned in the chapter include so-called CSOs, chief security officers.

4. Stakeholders...
   a. ...of an organization can be fully identified by thinking about who are the groups and individuals that affect the company.
   b. ...do not include competitors, as they are the "enemies" of the business.
   c. ...include future generations as so-called social stakeholders.
   d. ...a CSO can be either actor or stakeholder in a certain responsible management activity.

5. Issues...
   a. ...are latent problems, which might turn into crises if unattended.
   b. ...once they are addressed become a cause.
   c. ...help to understand an impact area, which makes them one of the basic elements of the responsible management process.
   d. ...may be addressed by the management instrument life-cycle impact management.

6. Responsible management instruments...
   a. ...may be specialized or mainstream management instruments.
   b. ...may also be called 3D management instruments.
   c. ...are for instance corporate citizenship and sustainable development.
   d. ...include for instance sustainable innovation, a management instrument that the bakery business Bimbo used in their packaging technology.

B. THINK

Imagine you are a company fleet manager of a large logistics company. You have been tasked to make a decision on whether to adopt alternative fuels for your vehicles. Think through the topic of bio diesel usage for your company, based on extensive research of the sustainability, responsibility, and ethics aspects of their use. Make a decision about adoption.

C. DO

Conduct a life-cycle assessment for a product of your choice. Make sure you are able to access information on the product's impacts. Localizing information on different stages and impact types from multiple websites will most likely be necessary.

D. RELATE

Talk with someone you know well about a typical ethical issue encountered in her/his work environment. Ask about ethics management tools in place in this job and discuss what other ethics management tools could possibly help to manage the situation.

E. BE

Think about one situation where you had to manage (this could be either in a private or a professional role). How do you think you did? How would others describe what you did well and/or where you didn't? What could have been done better? Do you think your management activity would be described as "responsible" management? Why, or why not?

Feedback

A. KNOW

Feedback 1

a. Right: Value creation in a responsible business includes both external and internal value throughout all three dimensions.
b. Right: Increased sales from a sustainable innovation product is an internal economic business value.
c. Wrong: Outside-in linkages are effects inside the company, caused by developments in the company's environment.
d. Right: 3D value creation creates a value neutral analytical basis or meta-perspective.

Feedback 2

a. Right: The three main elements of the responsible management process are actor, impact, and stakeholder. Management instruments might be specialized responsible management and/or mainstream management instruments.
b. Right: Without such an instrument, it would not be a management process. The responsible management process might involve one or many specialized or mainstream responsible management instruments.
c. Wrong: The three constituting elements are called the "trinity" of responsible management, as they can be found in any responsible management activity.

d. Wrong: The purpose of 3D or responsible management is to create sustainable management results for single activities involving social, environmental, and economic capital.

Feedback 3

a. Right: Actors in responsible management do not necessarily have to be only companies. It could be any type of organization and also individuals.
b. Wrong: While different sectoral actors show different characteristics that might make collaboration difficult, they also have valuable complementary resources and strengths, which make collaboration for sustainable development promising and necessary.
c. Right: The two strengths mentioned are correct. Another strength mentioned is the financial endowment of businesses.
d. Wrong: CSO stands for civil society organization.

Feedback 4

a. Wrong: In order to fully identify all stakeholders of an organization, one has to think about both types of groups and individuals, the ones that affect the organization and even more importantly the ones who might not affect the organization, but are affected by it.
b. Wrong: Competitors strongly affect the business and are strongly affected by it. They are stakeholders.
c. Wrong: Future generations are classified as non-social stakeholders, as they are not currently-living human beings.
d. Right: A manager inside a civil society organization would see the CSO as an actor, while the CSO is seen as a stakeholder if the responsible management activity is controlled from a business, which involves the CSO in its activities.

Feedback 5

a. Right: Not attending to an issue such as discrimination might lead to a crisis if, for instance, consumers start boycotting (crisis) a company for misconduct (issue).
b. Right: An issue is a mere problem, while a cause is a problem addressed for mitigation or solution.
c. Right: The other two elements are actors/agents and stakeholders.
d. Right: Life-cycle impact management is the management instrument managing the impacts of an organization throughout its various issues.

Feedback 6

a. Right: The two different groups of instruments are specialized responsible management instruments (stakeholder, life cycle, and ethics management) and mainstream management instruments (e.g. sustainable innovation, social marketing) that have been re-interpreted to also manage social and environmental impacts.

b. Right: Responsible management and 3D management (the management of the social, environmental, and economic dimension) are used synonymously.

c. Wrong: Both are background theories of responsible business. Responsible management instruments are for instance stakeholder management, cause-related marketing, and social accounting.

d. Right: Bimbo used sustainable innovation to become a pioneer in the biodegradable packaging business.

B. THINK

Level	Dealing with complexity	Notes
+	Decision is well grounded in an appreciation of the complexity of the topic.	
=	Decision has been made, but based on an incomplete grasp of the complexities and competing issues.	
–	Little capture of the complexities and competing issues around biofuels.	

C. DO

Level	Using (LCA) management tools	Notes
+	Complete representation of all major life-cycle impacts across all life-cycle stages.	
=	Sensible, but incomplete representation of major product life cycle impacts across all stages.	
–	Incomplete life-cycle assessment, not covering all three stages of the life cycle.	

D. RELATE

Level	Orienting others	Notes
+	Successful orientation of the other towards additional ethics management tools and options.	
=	Appreciation of issue and context, but no guidance given	
–	No appreciation of the ethical issue and its context.	

E. BE

Level	Awareness of own performance and limitations	Notes
+	Well evidenced account of awareness of own performance and limitations.	
=	Convincing account of either performance or limitations.	
–	No convincing account of neither performance nor limitations in this situation.	

Note

1 Products' physical life-cycle should not be confused with their business life-cycle as illustrated in the later section on Research, Development, and Innovation.

References

Accenture. (2023). *The 12th United Nations Global Compact-Accenture CEO Study*. Accenture & UN Global Compact. https://unglobalcompact.org/library/6103

Appiah, K. A. (2010). *Why I nominated Liu Xiaobo*. Retrieved October 12, 2011, from Foreign Policy: https://www.foreignpolicy.com/articles/2010/10/08/why_i_nominated_liu_xiaobo

BBC. (2011). *Q&A: Mexico's drug-related violence*. Retrieved October 14, 2011, from BBC: https://www.bbc.co.uk/news/world-latin-america-10681249

Buchholtz, A. K., & Carroll, A. B. (2008). *Business and society* (7th Edition). Scarborough, Canada: Cengage.

Clarkson, M., Starik, M., Cochran, P., & Jones, T. M. (1994). The Toronto conference: Reflections on stakeholder theory. *Business and Society*, *33*(1), 82.

Clarkson, M. B. (1995). A stakeholder framework for analyzing and evaluating corporate social performance. *Academy of Management Review*, *20*(1), 82–117.

ECOA; ERC. (2011). *The release of statistics on ethics and enforcement decisions: A joint report to the U.S. Department of Justice*. Ethics Resource Center.

El Mundo. (2011). *Derechos humanos 'a la china' para 2012*. Retrieved October 12, 2011, from El Mundo: https://www.elmundo.es/elmundo/2011/08/26/solidaridad/1314356293.html

Elkington, J. (1998). *Cannibals with forks: The triple bottom line of 21st century business*. Gabriola Island: New Society Publishers.

Elkington, J. (2011). *What is the triple bottom line?* Retrieved October 14, 2011, from Big Picture TV: https://www.bigpicture.tv/?id=3456

Emerson, J. (2003). The blended value proposition: Integrating social and financial results. *California Management Review*, *45*(4), 35–51.

Fitch, H. G. (1976). Achieving corporate social responsibility. *The Academy of Management Review*, *1*(1), 38–46.

Freeman, R. E. (1984/2010). *Strategic management: A stakeholder approach*. Cambridge: Cambridge University Press.

GRI. (2011). *Materiality*. Retrieved October 10, 2011, from Global Reporting Inititative: https://www.globalreporting.org/ReportingFramework/G3Online/DefiningReportContent/LowerBlock/Materiality.htm

Heineken. (2011). *Korea: Responsible consumption*. Retrieved October 12, 2011, from Heineken sustainability report: https://www.sustainabilityreport.heineken.com/best-practices/index.html

HP. (2011a). *Policies and practices that support diversity*. Retrieved October 12, 2011, from HP diversity & inclusion: Policies and practices: https://www8.hp.com/us/en/hp-information/about-hp/diversity/policies.html

HP. (2011b). *Diversity and inclusion*. Retrieved October 12, 2011, from HP corporate information: https://www8.hp.com/us/en/hp-information/about-hp/diversity/index.html

ISO. (2010). *International Standard ISO 26000: Guidance on Social Responsibility*. Geneva: International Organization for Standardization.

Lacey, P., Cooper, T., Hayward, R., & Neuberger, L. (2010). *A new era of sustainability: UN global compact-Accenture CEO study 2010*. Accenture Institute for High Performance.

Lee, M. (2011). *Analysis: A year after China retreat, Google plots new growth*. Retrieved October 12, 2011, from Reuters: https://www.reuters.com/article/2011/01/13/us-google-china-idUSTRE70C1X820110113

Matten, D., & Crane, A. (2005). What is stakeholder democracy? Perspectives and issues. *Business Ethics: A European Perspective, 14*(1), 6–13.

McDonough, W., & Braungart, M. (2002). *Cradle to cradle: Remaking the way we make things*. San Francisco: North Point Press.

McGonigal, J. (2010). *Gaming can make a better world*. Retrieved October 12, 2011, from Ted: Ideas worth spreading: https://www.ted.com/talks/jane_mcgonigal_gaming_can_make_a_better_world.html

McKinsey. (2010). *Mc Kinsey global survey results: Moving women to the top*. McKinsey.

McNamara, C. (2011). *Management*. Retrieved October 12, 2011, from Free management library: https://managementhelp.org/management/terms.htm

Messerli, J. (2011). *Should marijuana be legalized under any circumstances?* Retrieved October 14, 2011, from Balanced Politics: https://www.balancedpolitics.org/marijuana_legalization.htm

Mitchell, R. K., Agle, B. R., & Wood, D. J. (1997). Toward a theory of stakeholder salience: Defining the principles of who and what really counts. *Academy of Management Review, 22*(4), 853–886.

Ortiz, S. (2008). *Bimbo a la vanguardia en empaques*. Retrieved October 12, 2011, from CNN Expansión: https://www.cnnexpansion.com/manufactura/actualidad/2008/08/28/bimbo-a-la-vanguardia-en-empaques

Peters, A. (2011). *Using gamification to make the world a better place*. Retrieved October 12, 2011, from GreenBiz.com: https://www.greenbiz.com/blog/2011/07/03/using-gamification-make-world-better-place?page=0%2C2

Porter, M., & Kramer, M. (2006). Strategy and society: The link between competitive advantage and corporate social responsibility. *Harvard Business Review, 84*(12), 78–92.

Savage, G. T., Nix, T. W., Whitehead, C. J., & Blair, J. D. (1991). Strategies for assessing and managing organizational stakeholders. *Academy of Management Executive, 2*, 61–75.

United Nations. (1987). *Our common future*. United Nations, World Commission on the Environment and Development. New York: United Nations.

Welt. (2010). *Westerwelle mahnt in China Menschenrechte an*. Retrieved October 12, 2011, from Welt Online: https://www.welt.de/politik/article5855385/Westerwelle-mahnt-in-China-Menschenrechte-an.html

Zadeck, S., & Merme, M. (2003). *Redefining materiality: Practice and public policy for effective corporate reporting*. London: Accountability.

9 Practice Norms

The norms and frameworks guiding responsible business conduct are many. In the following some of the most recognized and prominently applied norms will be presented to provide an overview and point of departure for further study and practice application. Leipziger lists differing terms which all can be subsumed under the umbrella term "norm". Norms, such as codes, standards, principles, values, guidelines, framework agreements may differ considerably in scope and scale, stakeholder, issues, and industry foci and in the methods of development (Leipziger, 2010, p. 37). In day-to-day management practice it does not make a big difference, though, what category one puts a specific norm into. The important value lies in understanding a norm's contribution to responsible management practice. Norms' areas of application differ considerably. Norms can be categorized by their coverage of different issues and stakeholders (broad or narrow) and their focus on either an intended outcome or the implementation process. Figure 9.1 sums up some of the most important norms based on those two categories mentioned: Process versus outcome focus and broad versus narrow coverage.

Norms for responsible business, additionally to the criteria used in the last section, can also be classified into a wide variety of additional types. *Industry and sector initiatives* focus on a specific type of business, instead of providing advice for businesses in general. *Cause-focused norms*, such as the Forest Stewardship Council for the protection of forests, focus on single or a narrow set of causes. Initiatives might be *global*, such as the Global Compact, or *local* such as the "Empresa Socialmente Responsible" organization in Latin America. Some norms might provide a **certification or label**, such as the ISO 14000 or even provide *benchmarking or rankings*, such as the Dow Jones Sustainability Index. *Background norms* such as the Universal Declaration of Human Rights offer a very basic frame for responsible business behavior, while guidance norms such as the ISO 26000 aim at concise hands-on advice. *Networking initiatives*, such as the Principles for Responsible Management Education provide strong connections and interactions between members. Table 9.2 in the Appendix illustrates the characteristics of some of the main norms in responsible business. The detailed description of the table focuses on four of the most frequently applied norms, the Global Compact, the Global Reporting Initiative, ISO 14000, and ISO 26000.

DOI: 10.4324/9781003544074-13

	Outcome orientation	Process orientation
Broad coverage	•Global Compact (GC) •World Business Council for Sustainable Development (WBCSD) •Millennium Development Goals (MDG) •Dow Jones Sustainability Index (DJSI) •Guidelines for Multinational Enterprises •Empresa Socialmente Responsible (ESR)	•AA 1000 Series •ISO 26 000 •ISO 14 000 •Natural Step Framework •Global Reporting Initiative (GRI) Guidelines
Narrow coverage	•Leadership in Energy and Environmental Design (LEED) •FSC certified forest products •Fair Trade Standards and Label •Energy Star	•ILO Declaration on Fundamental Principles and Rights at Work •Rio Declaration on Environment and Development •Universal Declaration of Human Rights •CERES Principles •SA 8000 •Business Principles for Countering Bribery •Equator Principles (EPs) •Carbon Disclosure Project (CDP) •Principles of Responsible Management Education (PRME)

Figure 9.1 Classifying Responsible Business Norms.

A norm against war?

The Extractive Industries Transparency Initiative (EITI) has developed the EITI Principles and Criteria, which aim at fostering transparency in the number of natural resources extracted and usage of the revenues generated (EITI, 2009). One of the initiative's candidate countries is the Democratic Republic of Congo (DRC), which at the beginning of the 20th century had suffered the second Congo War, also called "Coltan War". Five point four million people perished during the war and of its consequences (EITI, 2011). It has been the deadliest conflict since World War Two. The war had largely been financed by the extraction of natural resources, mainly of Coltan, a mineral crucial in the production of many consumer electronics, from computers to MP3 players. DRC holds 80% of the world's Coltan resources, meaning that for instance most of the cell phones used by consumers around the world were indirectly financing the tragedy in the Congo (John & Hepinstall, 2011; Bavier, 2008; cellular-news, 2011; Dizolele, 2006). The conflict has also been called the "PlayStation War", when the console's producer Sony became entangled in the happenings (Lasker, 2008). Could a norm such as the EITI principles really mitigate or even solve such a conflict-laden situation?

United Nations-Influenced Norms

The United Nation's (UN) strong background in the promotion of human rights and its engagement for social, environmental, and economic causes for the good of the world community has made the UN take a strong interest into responsible business. Two of the most influential UN powered norms are the 10 Global Compact principles and the Global Reporting Initiative Guidelines for establishing sustainability reports, which has been developed in collaboration with the CERES organization.

Global Compact

The 10 Global Compact (GC) principles cover a broad range of issues. In 2011, more than 6000 companies and organizations had pledged to adhere to the Global Compact Principles. Among them are many of the world's most influential multinational enterprises such as BMW, PepsiCo, and Microsoft. The ten principles read as follows:

Human Rights

* *Principle 1: Businesses should support and respect the protection of internationally proclaimed human rights; and*
* *Principle 2: make sure that they are not complicit in human rights abuses.*

Labour

* *Principle 3: Businesses should uphold the freedom of association and the effective recognition of the right to collective bargaining;*
* *Principle 4: the elimination of all forms of forced and compulsory labour;*
* *Principle 5: the effective abolition of child labour; and*
* *Principle 6: the elimination of discrimination in respect of employment and occupation.*

Environment

* *Principle 7: Businesses should support a precautionary approach to environmental challenges;*
* *Principle 8: undertake initiatives to promote greater environmental responsibility; and*
* *Principle 9: encourage the development and diffusion of environmentally friendly technologies.*

Anti-Corruption

* *Principle 10: Businesses should work against corruption in all its forms, including extortion and bribery* (UNGC, 2011).

Companies covering those ten principles are supposed to make considerable contributions to some of the world's most pressing social and environmental problems by improving their social and environmental performance. GC subscriber organizations are encouraged to "share information on progress" periodically. Despite those positive points, the Global Compact has been criticized on a handful of issues. Critics commonly state that GC is not binding enough. Commitment to the principles is on a voluntary basis and therefore can hardly be enforced. A related criticism is that of "bluewashing", referring to the blue color of the United Nations flag. The GC is accused of being used as an easy tool to appear socially- and environmentally responsible to the outside, but not necessarily implementing such behavior to the inside (Bandi, 2007). The flexible structure of the GC must not necessarily be seen as a weakness. Proponents of the GC state that the norm must be very general and non-enforcing to be able to provide a broadly applicable and worldwide platform for responsible business practice (Leipziger, 2010, p. 37).

GC is highly interrelated with various other United Nations-powered initiatives (further illustrated in Table 9.1). GC is also seen as the business pendant of the Sustainable Development Goals (SDGs). As a matter of fact, compliance with the GC principles is likely to support the achievement of the SDGs.

Global Reporting Initiative

The Global Compact and Global Reporting Initiative (GRI) are highly complementary norms. On a continuum from broad guidance to specific advice, GC and GRI are exactly on the opposite extremes. GRI delivers a concise set of guidelines on how to establish reports that are comparable, consistent, and of high utility (Leipziger, 2010, p. 490). Many companies of all sizes, industries, and regions have established periodic GRI reports, covering social and environmental business performance. The extension of such report's ranges from approximately 40 to 150 pages. Report quality can be rated by independent organizations following the GRI standard. Deep-diving into GRI-based responsibility reports can be a never-ending source of highly consistent information and inspiration. To maximize the learning from such reading, understanding the GRI guidelines is crucially important (Figure 9.2).

The GRI reporting standards can be broadly divided into two main topic areas. The first area of principles and guidance (options for reporting) support's businesses' process of defining report contents, quality, and boundaries within the options available. Defining *report content* is based on the materiality-assessment as described before. Among the contents, potentially to be included, organizations should focus on fulfilling the principles defined in the following:

- **Materiality Principle**: *"The information in a report should cover topics and indicators that reflect the organization's significant economic, environmental, and social impacts, or that would substantively influence the assessments and decisions of stakeholders"*.
- **Stakeholder Inclusiveness Principle**: *"The reporting organization should identify its stakeholders and explain in the report how it has responded to their reasonable expectations and interests"*.
- **Sustainability Context**: *"The report should present the organization's performance in the wider context of sustainability"*.
- **Completeness**: *"Coverage of material topics and indicators and definition of the report boundary should be sufficient to reflect significant economic, environmental, and social impacts and enable stakeholder to assess the reporting organization's performance in the reporting period"*.

(Leipziger, 2010, pp. 498–502)

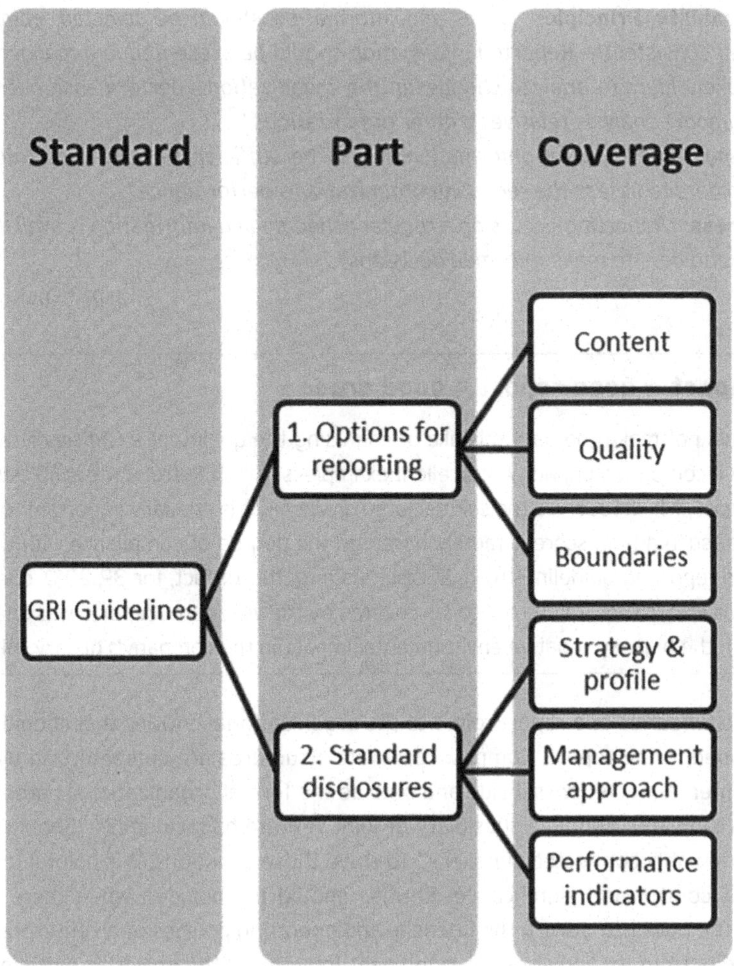

Figure 9.2 Main Components of the GRI Guidelines.

Integrated reporting

The reporting trend goes towards integration. Many annual reports are now integrated reports, which jointly cover social, environmental, and mainstream financial performance. Such triple-bottom-line reports reflect the overall trend of an increasing convergence and integration of responsible and mainstream management (GRI, 2010).

To define the *quality* of a report, organizations are invited to follow the guidelines described in the next paragraph:

- **Balance Principle**: *"The report should reflect positive and negative aspects of the organization's performance to enable a reasoned assessment of overall performance"*.

- **Comparability Principle**: *"Issues and information should be selected, compiled, and reported consistently. Reported information should be presented in a manger that enables stakeholders to analyze changes in the organization's performance over time and could support analysis relative to other organizations".*
- **Accuracy**: *"The reported information should be sufficientl accurate and detailed for stakeholders to assess the reporting organization's performance".*
- **Timeliness**: *"Reporting occurs on a regular schedule and information is available in time for stakeholders to make informed decisions".*

(Leipziger, 2010, p. 505)

Bad impact + good report = good grade

One should not make the easy mistake of confusing the quality of a GRI report with the quality of a company's impact. An excellent example is British Petroleum's 2010 "sustainability review", which received the self-declared grade A+. It is crucially important to understand that such a high score is merely based on the degree of compliance with the here illustrated reporting guidelines (GRI, 2006b). As a matter of fact, for BP, 2010, due to the massive oil spill in the Gulf of Mexico (as covered by the very same report), was one of the years with the highest negative environmental impact in the company's history (BP, 2011).

Setting the *boundaries* of a report refers to the organizational entities that should or should not be included in the report. Complex corporate structures are characterized by different degrees of interconnectedness inside and outside the formal organizational borders. Typical questions arising are "Should a subsidiary or joint venture be included?" "Should we report activities of a highly connected supplier?" To solve those questions, it is helpful to apply the principles of control and significance. Entities should be included when there is control defined as "the power to govern the financial and operating policies of an enterprise so as to obtain benefits from its activities" or significant influence, "the power to participate in the financial and operating policy decisions of the entity, but not the power to control those policies "(Leipziger, 2010, p. 509). To specifically define which entity to include or not the GRI G3 guidelines propose an easy-to-use and practical decision tree (GRI, 2006a, p. 18).

Who was reporting most?

The statistics on sustainability reporting following the Global Reporting Initiative (GRI) are impressive. The annual growth rate in the overall number of GRI reports from 2001-2010 was 50.1%. European businesses account for the highest number of reports (45%) followed by Asia (20%), and Latin America and North America (14% each). The country accounting for the single biggest quantity of reports is the USA (10%), followed by Spain (9%), and Brazil and Japan (7% each). The industries reporting most in total numbers are financial services (250) and the energy sector (145), the ones reporting least are tobacco (3) and toys (1). In total, 1800 companies issued GRI sustainability reports in 2010 (GRI, 2010).

While the first area of the guiding principles aims at supporting and providing guidance on different options for reporting, the second area of *standard disclosures* informs about the required topic areas to be covered in a compulsory manner. In the following, the three main standard disclosure areas are described:

- **Strategy and Profile**: *"Disclosures that set the overall context for understanding organizational performance such as its strategy, profile, and governance".*
- **Management Approach**: *"Disclosures that cover how an organization addresses a given set of topics in order to provide context for understanding performance in a specific area".*
- **Performance Indicators**: *"Indicators that elicit comparable information on the economic, environmental, and social performance of the organization".*

(GRI, 2006a)

The Global Reporting Initiative guidelines leading to sustainability reports might be perceived as extensive and complex. Nevertheless, being able to read, understand, evaluate, and communicate an organizations' social, environmental, and economic performance report is an invaluable step towards successful and responsible management.

Sustainability reporting is a quickly developing topic, which is why we would like to direct your attention to two very recent developments. First, the above information is based on the G 3.1 reporting guidelines. Since December 31, 2015, new *G4 reporting guidelines* are required for GRI reports. However, the basic reporting principles above remain valid. What mainly changes with the G4 reporting guidelines are pieces of content in the standard disclosure lists, particular impact areas to be covered, which we have not presented above (GRI, 2014a, 2014b). Second, there is a strong trend towards *integrated reporting*. Integrated reporting refers to reports that cover the financial annual report and the sustainability report together. The idea is that integrated reporting will also reflect in integrated thinking and doing ultimately leading to both financial stability and social, environmental, and economic sustainability (IIRC, 2013). While we strongly support this aspiration behind integrated reports, we also see a danger of a loss in depth of sustainability reporting, if the integrated report is seen as a substitute to GRI reports. The typically 5–20 pages explicitly dedicated to sustainability or corporate responsibility in integrated reports provide a much shallower picture than a 60–100 page GRI report can.

Guidelines by the International Standardization Organization (ISO)

The International Standardization Organization (ISO) is an international organization, widely accepted for its standards in the most diverse fields. It is for this international recognition that the ISO standards most relevant for responsible business will be explained here. The ISO 14000 series on environmental management systems has become the internationally most applied norm for managing business' operations' environmental performance. The ISO 14000 was launched in 1996. The ISO 26000 standard on social responsibility (also ISO SR) is a recent product of the responsible business boom, which after its publication in 2010 has quickly gained both recognition and extensive criticism. Both norms, while issued by the same institution differ widely in outreach, coverage, and structure. While management systems developed using the ISO 14000 standard can be audited and certified, the ISO 26000 does not aim at direct certification. The ISO 26000 aims at providing guidance on the vocabulary and basic structure of social responsibility. The standard also aims at defining the very topic of Social Responsibility.

> **Where did the ISO 26000 come from?**
>
> The ISO SR was developed through the collaboration of the six main stakeholder groups: Industry; government; labor; consumers; nongovernmental organizations; and service, support, research, and others. A geographical- and gender-based balance of participants was ensured to avoid biases. The process was led by experts from ISO members (national standards bodies–NSBs) and from liaison organizations, associations representing business, consumers, or labor, or inter-governmental or nongovernmental organizations. In July 2010, the ISO working group on Social Responsibility had 450 participating experts and 210 observers from 99 ISO member countries and 42 liaison organizations (ISO, 2012).

ISO 26000

The ISO26000 standard on social responsibility, often abbreviated as ISO SR, is subdivided into seven clauses, each covering different aspects of social responsibility. In the following, helpful aspects of the norm will be punctually illustrated (ISO, 2010).

- **Clause 1 (Scope)**: Interestingly, the norm applies to any kind of organization and therefore veers away from the narrow understanding of social responsibility only applying to businesses.
- **Clause 2 (Terms, definitions, abbreviations)**: The definitions used for the ISO SR have been both hailed and criticized. On the one hand, for instance, the definition of "Social Responsibility" provides a highly inclusive and integrated understanding of responsible business subjects such as ethics and transparency. The definition also defines sustainable development as the intended outcome of social responsibility in line with the understanding assumed in this book. Further positive features are that the document defines the stakeholder relationship as a core piece of the responsible management process, the alignment with norms, law, and international frameworks, and the focus on "mainstreamed" integration of responsible business into the organization's main activities. The document also avoids the common European Union definition's narrow focus on voluntary initiatives by including compulsory legal aspects as part of the responsibilities. The overall evaluation of this definition is positive. Unfortunately, other concepts such as "stakeholders" have been unnecessarily altered. Defining a stakeholder by the "interest" taken in the organization lacks the reciprocal relationship "affects or is affected" of the commonly accepted definition by Freeman (1984/2010, p. 25). Definitions of terms related to SR range from "a" as in "accountability" to "v" as in "vulnerable groups".
- **Clause 3 (Understanding)**: This section describes a "colorful bunch" of interesting, but loosely structured pieces of background knowledge such as the historical development,

actual external conditions, and the relationships between social responsibility and sustainable development.

- **Clause 4 (Principles of SR)**: ISO SR defines seven principles of social responsibility as universal to a responsible organization, while admitting that those seven principles cannot be a definite and ultimate list. The text also mentions subject- (synonymous to what we called issue, cause, and impact area before) related additional principles. The first three subject-comprehensive principles are accountability, transparency, ethical behavior. Principles four to seven refer to respecting stakeholder interests, law, international norms of behavior, and human rights. While those principles can be central to a responsible organization, it remains sometimes structurally unclear. For instance, it is hard to understand why human rights is mentioned twice, once as an overarching principle of SR and then again in Clause 6 as a subject area.
- **Clause 5 (Fundamental practices)**: The ISO SR defines two fundamental practices for SR. First, the acceptance that recognizing the social responsibility of business includes the two steps of first recognizing the concrete characteristics of a specific organization's responsibilities, and of a second step identifying and engaging with stakeholders. While those two practices are undoubtedly fundamentally important, one can easily identify other fundamentally important practices such as impact and life-cycle management.
- **Clause 6 (Core subjects)**: Core subjects are supposed to "(...) cover the most likely economic, social and environmental impacts" (ISO, 2010, p. 15). The seven core subjects proposed are organizational governance, human rights, labor practices, the environment, fair operating practices, consumer issues, and community involvement and development. What is questionable about these core subjects is their supposed exhaustiveness. It remains subject to a detailed check-up of the coverage of typical organizational impacts to verify the exhaustiveness of the seven core subjects. The homogeneity of the subjects identified is not given. While for instance the subject of human rights is an "across-stakeholder" subject, others such as consumer issues and labor practices each refer to one specific stakeholder (consumers and employees). The ISO SR mixed up a stakeholder categorization with the identification of issues. As described in the three elements of responsible management, stakeholders might be related to various issues and issues are likely to relate to many stakeholders.
- **Clause 7 (Integrating SR)**: Integrating SR as proposed by the norm is characterized by a loosely connected set of "good practices" such as voluntary initiatives, including organizational characteristics and communicating SR. In improving the integration of those good practices, they may become an important source of advice for the "how" of implementing SR in an integrated manner and not just as an unconnected add-on.

The ISO SR solves many of the common definitional problems and has created a sound basis for the future development of a common language in the field of social responsibility. Main inconsistencies still to be resolved for ISO SR to make up to achieve its potential is to resolve definitional and structural inconsistencies in the framework such as the double coverage of human rights, the stakeholder definition inconsistent with the long-established understanding, and the intuitively inconsistent subordination of environmental issues under a social responsibility construct.

From converging norms to legislation

Norms for responsible business are increasingly complementary instead of competing. For instance, the ISO SR and the GRI work well together as seen in this official statement of both organizations "GRI provides the most suitable guidelines to support organizations interested in reporting on the topics covered by ISO 26000" (GRI, 2010a, p. 4). Such convergence might even result in legislative pressure for application. The GRI in its 2010 summit officially declared the goal to make sustainability reporting mandatory by 2015 for all large and medium-sized companies in OECD countries (GRI, 2010b).

ISO 14000

While the ISO26000 is primarily focusing on social topics, the ISO 14000 standard for the development of environmental management systems extensively covers the environmental responsibility of a company's operations. The ISO 14000's methodology is arranged around the following six steps for the implementation of an environmental management system:

1. *Environmental policy*
2. *Planning*
3. *Implementation and operation*
4. *Checking a corrective action*
5. *Management review*
6. *Continual improvement*

The rigorous methodology allows for audit and certification of the implementation of environmental management systems. It has been criticized that the norm and certification does not include benchmarks for what should be considered a "good" environmental impact. The certification merely refers to the installation of the environmental management system. This could create a misleading impression of all ISO 14000 certified organizations automatically being "clean enterprises", while the certification means that such an organization does have a management system in place, which might improve its environmental impact; but not necessarily to a degree that it would be considered environmentally friendly.

Exercises

A. KNOW

Use the below multiple-choice questions to test your knowledge. Each answer may be wrong or right and there may be zero to four right or wrong answers per question:

1. Practice norms...
   a. ...among others include corporate citizenship and sustainable development.
   b. ...include for instance the Global Reporting Initiative (GRI), a set of ten standards aiming at improving multinationals' collaboration for topics such as human rights and good environmental performance.

c. ...include for instance the ISO 14000, which aims at improving organizational social responsibility.
d. ...include the GRI which also covers the balance principle, aiming at companies' reporting not only positive, but also negative aspects of their performance.

2. Someone is criticizing that a company's corporate responsibility report did not cover a major environmental scandal the company was involved in during the year, and which is of highest interest to the stakeholders. The person is implicitly criticizing that the company had not applied the...
   a. ...materiality principle.
   b. ...completeness principle.
   c. ...balance principle.
   d. ...timeliness principle.

3. You hear from a colleague that your company has adopted this new standard which has a strong focus on human rights and labor practices, but which also covers anti-corruption. Which standard is she most likely talking about?
   a. Global Compact Principles.
   b. ILO Standard.
   c. Universal Declaration of Human Rights.
   d. ISO 14000.

B. THINK

Imagine you are the managing director of a small enterprise, and you would like to formalize your responsible business agenda by adopting a norm. Evaluate the value of several distinct norms for your company, based on a set of criteria you choose.

C. DO

Review the points of the Universal Declaration of Human Rights and identify one reality that interferes with one of these rights in your environment. Often human rights abuses can be quite small things that occur in daily life, either in the private or professional context. Write an action plan outlining what would need to happen to change this situation, including one step you can take to its mitigation. Take the step!

D. RELATE

Look up a company's Global Compact (GC) report and compare it with the news coverage about the company. Find one point where the company apparently has acted against one of the ten GC principles. Get in touch with the company to let them know that you have studied their efforts to abide by the GC principles, but that you would like to better understand why they acted against them in this specific case.

E. BE

Write your personal professional norm. It could include principles such as "I will never be involved in corruption" or "I will always treat everyone I work with friendliness and respect". Make sure your personal professional norm reflects both your values and elements related to work culture and profession.

Feedback

A. KNOW

Feedback 1

a. Wrong: Both are background theories of responsible business. Practice norms include for instance the ISO 26000 or the Extractive Industries Transparency Initiative.
b. Wrong: The description given fits the Global Compact. GRI provides guidelines for the reporting of social, environmental, and economic business performance.
c. Wrong: ISO 14000 aims at environmental performance, while ISO 26000 focuses on organizational social responsibility.
d. Right: The balance principle is one out of four principles to define the quality of sustainability reports.

Feedback 2

a. Right: The issue appears of high materiality to the stakeholders which is why it would have to be included.
b. Right: The completeness principle says that all material issues must be covered.
c. Wrong: The balance principle says that both positive and negative topics must be covered in a balanced manner. To make a statement about balance the person would have had to look at all topics covered.
d. Wrong: No statement about the regularity and timely provision of the report has been made.

Feedback 3

a. Right: The description perfectly fits the ten Global Compact Principles, while not mentioning the environment part.
b. Wrong: The International Labour Organization (ILO) standard focuses exclusively on labor-related topics.
c. Wrong: The Universal Declaration exclusively focuses on human rights. Some of the other topics might be covered indirectly.
d. Wrong: The ISO 14000 is a series of norms on environmental management.

B. THINK

Level	*Multi-criteria analysis*	Notes
+	Decision was made and explained well, based on an adequate set of criteria.	
=	Decision was made, but criteria do not appear adequate for the situation.	
–	Decision was not made, or only single norms and single criteria were considered.	

C. DO

Level	*Actioning change skills*	Notes
+	Own action taken as part of a feasible larger action plan.	
=	Feasible action plan, based on a fair understanding of the observed human rights issue.	
–	No action plan or no fair appreciation of a human rights issue.	

D. RELATE

Level	*Appreciative feedback skill*	Notes
+	Feedback given on fair appreciation of both general, and press-covered incident GC performance.	
=	Feedback given on fair appreciation of either general, or press-covered incident GC performance.	
–	No feedback based on appreciation of neither general GC performance, nor performance in the press-covered case.	

E. BE

Level	*Responsible professional identity*	Notes
+	Personal values and professional factors deeply reflected in personal norm.	
=	Personal values or professional factors well reflected in personal norm.	
–	Norm does neither reflect personal values, nor professional considerations.	

Appendix: Responsible Business Norms

Table 9.1 Overview Responsible Business Norms

Norm	*Organization*	*Type*	*Description*
Broad Coverage + Outcome Orientation			
Global Compact (GC) Principles	United Nations Global Compact	Global + network norm	Network of over 20,000 businesses and stakeholder institutions, self-committing to the ten Global Compact Principles.
Content Areas	Human and labor rights, environment, corruption.		
World Business Council for Sustainable Development (WBCSD)	WBCSD	Network	WBCSD is a CEO-led business initiative with a joint agenda for sustainable business, focusing on the business case for sustainable development (WBCSD, 2011).
Content Areas	Work program includes focus areas (e.g. ecosystems, development, climate), sector projects (e.g. buildings, energy, water), systems solutions, and capacity building for sustainable development.		
The Sustainable Development Goals (SDGS)	United Nations	Global + guidance	The Sustainable Development Goals (SDGs) are a collection of 17 interconnected global goals established by the United Nations in 2015. They aim to create a more just and sustainable future for people and the planet by 2030.
Content Areas	Poverty, hunger, education, gender equality, health, environment, development partnership, education, economic growth, industry, inequality, cities, peace.		
Dow Jones Sustainability Indexes (DJSI)	Dow Jones Indexes/ Sustainable Asset Management (SAM)	Global + benchmarking	Rigorous and highly selective ("best-in class approach") assessment based on extensive catalogue of hard indicators, which must be improved constantly. DJSI is mostly used as a responsible investment benchmarking system (DJSI, 2011). A norm with similar approach and importance is the London-based FTSE 4 Good Index.
Content Areas	**1. Economic Dimension**: Corporate governance, risk and crisis management, codes of conduct, compliance, bribery, customer relationship management, brand management, privacy protection, environmental reporting. **2. Environmental Dimension**: Environmental policy/management system, operational eco-efficiency. **3. Social Dimension**: Social reporting, labor practices, human capital development, talent attraction and retention, corporate citizenship and philanthropy, standards for suppliers, stakeholder engagement (SAM Research AG, 2010).		
Guidelines for Multinational Enterprises	Organisation for Economic Co-operation and Development (OECD)	Global + guidance	Extensive set of responsible business recommendations for multinational enterprises unequaled in its broad coverage of social, environmental, and ethical issues (OECD, 2011).
Content Areas	The guidelines cover concepts and principles, general policies, disclosure, human rights, employment and industrial relations, environment, combating bribery, bribe solicitation and extortion, consumer interests, science and technology, competition, and taxation.		

Empresa Socialmente Responsible (ESR)	Centro Mexicano para la Filantropía (CEMEFI)	Distinction, local standard, label	First implemented in Mexico, ESR has evolved as a widely applied responsible business label throughout Latin America. Based on an evidence-based self-evaluation, businesses of all sizes may be awarded with the ESR distinction on a yearly basis. The ESR label is widely recognized among consumers (CEMEFI, 2011). ESR in the context of this overview represents many local norms that have gained importance throughout the world by responding to local issues, and specific responsible business culture.
Content Areas	1. Quality of life inside the business; 2. Business ethics; 3. Community involvement; 4. Relationship to the natural environment; 5. Ethics, communication, and promotion of sustainable consumption.		
Broad Coverage + Process Orientation			
AA 1000 Series	AccountAbility	Guidance, certification	AA 1000 is a series of three standards describing basic tasks of responsible management. The Accountability Principles **(APS) standard** describes the basic principles of accountability (materiality, responsiveness, completeness, and inclusivity). The **assurance standard (AS)** describes the process of externally assuring a company's information on responsible business. The **stakeholder engagement standard (SES)** provides detailed guidance on the stakeholder engagement process (AccountAbility, 2011).
Content Areas	Accountability, assurance, stakeholder engagement.		
ISO 26000	International Standardization Organization (ISO)	Guidance	The ISO 26000 aims at providing guidance on the social responsibilities of organizations, its elements, concepts, and vocabulary.
Content Areas	***Clause 1 (Scope)*** : Any kind of organization independent of size, legal form, etc. ***Clause 2 (Terms, definitions, abbreviations)***: Attempt to standardize language used. ***Clause 3 (Understanding)***: Background knowledge. ***Clause 4 (Principles of SR)***: Seven principles of social responsibility, universal to a responsible organization. ***Clause 5 (Fundamental practices)***: 1) Acceptance recognizing the social responsibility of business; 2) Identifying and engaging with stakeholders. ***Clause 6 (Core subjects)***: Seven core subjects proposed: Organizational governance, human rights, labor practices, the environment, fair operating practices, consumer issues, and community involvement and development. ***Clause 7 (Integrating SR)***: "good practices".		

(Continued)

Table 9.1 (Continued)

Norm	*Organization*	*Type*	*Description*
ISO 14000	International Standardization Organization (ISO)	Guidance + certification	The ISO 14000 provides an easy to apply and certifiable methodology for establishing environmental management systems (ISO, 2012). A comparable standard is the European Environmental Management and Accounting Scheme (EMAS).
Content Areas	Six steps for implementing an environmental management system: 1. Environmental policy; 2. Planning; 3. Implementation and operation; 4. Checking a corrective action; 5. Management review; 6. Continual improvement.		
Natural Step Framework	The Natural Step	Guidance	The Natural Step Framework takes a systemic approach guiding organizations, governments, and individuals towards sustainable behavior, based on four system conditions that must be met to reach sustainable development and create a sustainable society (The Natural Step, 2011).
Content Areas	Problems to be solved: 1. Concentrations of substances extracted from the Earth's crust; 2. Concentrations of substances produced by society; 3. Degradation by physical means; 4. Society, people are not subject to conditions that systemically undermine their capacity to meet their needs.		
Global Reporting Initiative (GRI) Guidelines	CERES, United Nations	Guidance, ranking	The GRI guidelines provide a standardized framework for the establishment of businesses' high-quality sustainability reports (Global Reporting Initiative, 2011). Report quality is assessed through the application of different levels (from A to C) for reports.
Content Areas	**Guidance** for a) defining report content; b) report boundary setting. **Principles** for a) defining report content; b) report quality. **Standard disclosures** are a) profile; b) management approach; c) performance indicators.		
Narrow Coverage + Outcome Orientation			
Leadership in Energy and Environmental Design (LEED)	US Green Building Council	Guidance, certification, ranking, label	LEED provides a ranking system to assess buildings' environmental and health performance. Ranking levels range from certified, silver, and gold to platinum (U.S. Green Building Council, 2011).
Content Areas	Impacts of buildings in a) design; b) construction; c) operations.		
FSC certified forest products	Forest stewardship council (FSC)	Label	FSC certified forest products comply with ten principles assuring an above-average social and environmental impact of such products in forestry activities during product sourcing and elaboration (Forest Stewardship Council, 2011). The marine stewardship council (MSC) certification is a similar approach for seafood products.

Content Areas	1. Compliance 2. Land tenure and use 3. Indigenous peoples' rights 4. Well-being of forest workers and local communities 5. Equitable sharing of benefits 6. Environmental impact of logging 7. Forest management plan 8. Monitoring and assessment of social and environmental impacts 9. High conservation value forests 10. Restoration and conservation of natural forests.		
Fair Trade Standards and Label	Fairtrade International	Global, cause-focused, label	Fair trade certifications may be generic standards that must be met by all fair-trade producers and traders (Fairtrade International, 2011).
Content Areas	Fair trade principles: –Pay a price to producer that aims to cover the costs of sustainable production: The Fairtrade minimum price. –Pay an additional sum that producers can invest in development: The Fairtrade Premium. –Partially pay in advance when producers ask for it. –Sign contracts that allow for long-term planning and sustainable production practices.		
Energy Star	U.S. Environmental Protection Agency and the U.S. Department of Energy	Label	The Energy Star initiative consists of several programs from building certification to industrial process improvement and its flagship program, the electronic product certification initiative. All programs aim at saving "money and protect the environment through energy efficient products and practices" (U.S. Environmental Protection Agency, 2011).
Content Areas	Guiding principles for product label: 1) Significant energy savings 2) Complies with features and performance demanded by consumers 3) Price-add up (if exists) is compensated by financial savings in reasonable time 4) General availability of applied technology also to competitors 5) Energy performance can be measured and verified 6) Label when applied differentiates the product and is visible for consumers		

(*Continued*)

Table 9.1 (Continued)

Norm	*Organization*	*Type*	*Description*
Narrow Coverage + Process Orientation			
ILO Declaration on Fundamental Principles and Rights at Work	International Labour Organization (ILO)	Global, cause-focused, background document	ILO is a "'tripartite' United Nations agency that brings together representatives of governments, employers, and workers to jointly shape policies and programmes promoting decent work for all" (ILO, 2012).
Content Areas	Fundamental Principles and Rights at Work: (a) Freedom of association and the effective recognition of the right to collective bargaining (b) The elimination of all forms of forced or compulsory labor (c) The effective abolition of child labor (d) The elimination of discrimination in respect of employment and occupation		
Rio Declaration on Environment and Development	United Nations Environment Program (UNEP)	Background document	The Rio Declaration is a landmark document, addressing a broad variety of declarations and practices all aiming to achieve sustainable social and environmental world development (UNEP, 2012).
Content Areas	The 27 Rio Principles (P):**P1**: Role of humans; **P2**: Sovereignty of states; **P3**: Right to development; **P4**: Environmental protection and development; **P5**: Poverty eradication; **P6**: Least-developed are priority; **P7**: State cooperation for ecosystem protection; **P8**: Unsustainable production and consumption; **P9**: Sustainable development capacities; **P10**: Public participation; **P11**: National environmental legislation; **P12**: Economic system; **P13**: Compensation for victims; **P14**:Prevent environmental dumping; **P15**: Precautionary principle; **P16**: International environmental costs; **P17**: Environmental impacts assessment; **P18**: Disaster notification; **P19**: Notification practice; **P20**:Vital role of women; **P21**: Youth mobilization; **P22**: Vital role of indigenous people; **P23**: Oppressed people; **P24**: Warfare; **P25**: Peace, development, environmental protection; **P26**: Environmental disputes; **P27**: Cooperation between state and people.		
Universal Declaration of Human Rights	United Nations	Background document, global	The Universal Declaration of Human Rights is the most widely accepted list of rights to which all human beings are universally entitled. The last three out of the declaration's 30 articles are not rights, but duties (United Nations, 2012).

Content Areas	The contents of the 30 articles of the Universal Declaration of Human Rights can be summarized as follows (HREA, 2012): 1. Everyone is free, and we should all be treated in the same way. 2. Everyone is equal despite differences in skin color, sex, religion, language for example. 3. Everyone has the right to life and to live in freedom and safety. 4. No one has the right to treat you as a slave nor should you make anyone your slave. 5. No one has the right to hurt you or to torture you. 6. Everyone has the right to be treated equally by the law. 7. The law is the same for everyone, it should be applied in the same way to all. 8. Everyone has the right to ask for legal help when their rights are not respected. 9. No one has the right to imprison you unjustly or expel you from your own country. 10. Everyone has the right to a fair and public trial. 11. Everyone should be considered innocent until guilt is proved. 12. Everyone has the right to ask for help if someone tries to harm you, but no-one can enter your home, open your letters, or bother you or your family without a good reason. 13. Everyone has the right to travel as they wish. 14. Everyone has the right to go to another country and ask for protection if they are being persecuted or are in danger of being persecuted. 15. Everyone has the right to belong to a country. No one has the right to prevent you from belonging to another country if you wish to. 16. Everyone has the right to marry and have a family. 17. Everyone has the right to own property and possessions. 18. Everyone has the right to practice and observe all aspects of their own religion and change their religion if they want to. 19. Everyone has the right to say what they think and to give and receive information. 20. Everyone has the right to take part in meetings and to join associations in a peaceful way. 21. Everyone has the right to help choose and take part in the government of their country. 22. Everyone has the right to social security and to opportunities to develop their skills. 23. Everyone has the right to work for a fair wage in a safe environment and to join a trade union. 24. Everyone has the right to rest and leisure. 25. Everyone has the right to an adequate standard of living and medical help if they are ill. 26. Everyone has the right to go to school. 27. Everyone has the right to share in their community's cultural life. 28. Everyone must respect the "social order" that is necessary for all these rights to be available. 29. Everyone must respect the rights of others, the community, and public property. 30. No one has the right to take away any of the rights in this declaration.

(Continued)

Table 9.1 (Continued)

Norm	*Organization*	*Type*	*Description*
CERES Principles	Coalition for Environmentally Responsible Economies (CERES)	International, background standard	Triggered by the *Exxon Valdez* oil spill of 1989, CERES launched the CERES Principles to promote environmentally responsible business behavior, which served as a basis for many subsequent norms. In 2010 the CERES principles were transformed and updated through the document *The Ceres roadmap for sustainability* (Ceres, 2012).
Content Areas	The Ceres Principles: 1) Protection of the biosphere; 2) Sustainable use of natural resources; 3) Reduction and disposal of wastes; 4) Energy conservation; 5) Risk reduction; 6) Safe products and services; 7) Environmental restoration; 8) Informing the public; 9) Management commitment; 10) Audits and reports.		
SA 8000	Social Accountability International (SAI)	International standard, certification	SA 8000 is a widely applied standard for responsible labor practices that can be integrated into existing management systems. SA 8000 provides an extensive definition section of terms central to workplace responsibilities of both direct and indirect employees (SAI, 2008).
Content Areas	**Definitions**: Company, personnel, worker, supplier/subcontractor, sub-supplier, corrective and preventive action, interested party, child, young worker, child labor, forced and compulsory labor, human trafficking, remediation of children, home worker, SA 8000 worker representative, management representative, worker organization, collective bargaining. **Requirement topics**: 1. Child labor; 2. Forced and compulsory labor; 3. Health and safety; 4. Freedom of association and right to collective bargaining; 5. Discrimination; 6. Disciplinary practices; 7. Working hours; 8. Remuneration; 9. Management systems.		
Business Principles for Countering Bribery	Transparency International	Global, cause-focused	The Business Principles for Countering Bribery provide an action plan to combat bribery as one of the most widespread forms of corruption in businesses. Participating businesses make a board-level commitment to the values of integrity, transparency, and accountability, to prohibit bribery in any form and to implement a formal program to counter bribery (Transparency International, 2009). Cause-wise related norms are the United Nations Convention against Corruption and the OECD Anti-Bribery Convention.
Content Areas	Program topics: 1) Bribes; 2) Political contributions; 3) Charitable contributions and sponsorships; 4) Facilitation payments; 5) Gifts, hospitality, and expenses.		
Equator Principles (EPs)	Equator Principles Association (EPA)	Global, industry initiative	The EPs are an initiative of the financial sector that "are a credit risk management framework for determining, assessing and managing environmental and social risk in project finance transactions" (EPA, 2012). The EPs in the context of this summary are introduced as an example for an industry-focused norm. Other popular examples include the *Extractive Industries Transparency Initiative (EITI)*, the *Retail Environmental Sustainability Code*, and the *Responsible Care Initiative* by the International Council of Chemical Associations.

Content Areas	Principles to be applied by Equator Principles Financial Institutions (EPFIs): P1: Review and categorization P2: Social and environmental assessment P3: Applicable social and environmental standards P4: Action plan and management system P5: Consultation and disclosure P6: Grievance mechanism P7: Independent review P8: Covenants P9: Independent monitoring and reporting P10: EPFI reporting		
Carbon Disclosure Project (CDP)	Carbon Disclosure Project	Global network, reporting	The CDP is an investor centered organization, promoting the disclosure of carbon and water impacts through five independent programmes, of which underneath will be highlighted the Carbon Action Program and the Supply Chain Program (Carbon Disclosure Project, 2012).
Content Areas	**Carbon Action Program**: "A vanguard group of 35 investors with US$7.6 trillion assets under management are asking the world's largest companies to demonstrate that they are managing carbon effectively". **Supply Chain Initiative**: "Global corporations aim to understand the impacts of climate change across the supply chain, harnessing their collective purchasing power to encourage suppliers to measure and disclose climate change information".		
Principles of Responsible Management Education (PRME)	United Nations Global Compact	Global network, cause-focused	The PRME are an open international network of business schools that have made a self-commitment to seven principles with the joint purpose of promoting responsible management education (PRME, 2023).
Content Areas	**P1: Purpose**: We advance responsible management education to foster inclusive prosperity in a world of thriving ecosystems. **P2: Values**: We place organizational responsibility and accountability to society and the planet at the core of what we do. **P3: Teach**: We transform our learning environments by integrating responsible management concepts and practices into our curriculum and pedagogy. **P4: Research**: We study people, organizations, institutions, and the state of the world to inspire responsible management and education practice. **P5: Partner**: We engage people from business, government, civil society, and academia to advance responsible and accountable management education and practice. **P6: Practice**: We adopt responsible and accountable management principles in our own governance and operations. **P7: Share**: We share our successes and failures with each other to enable our collective learning and best live our common values and purpose.		

References

AccountAbility. (2011). *AccountAbility: Setting the standard for corporate responsibility and sustainable development*. Retrieved November 20, 2011, from https://www.accountability.org/

Bandi, N. (2007). *United Nations Global Compact: Impact and its critics*. Geneva: Covalence.

Bavier, J. (2008). *Congo war-driven crisis kills 45,000 a month: Study*. Retrieved October 15, 2011, from Reuters: https://www.reuters.com/article/2008/01/22/us-congo-democratic-death-idUSL2280201220080122

BP. (2011). *Sustainability review 2010*. London: British Petroleum.

Carbon Disclosure Project. (2012). *Carbon Disclosure Project*. Retrieved January 15, 2012, from https://www.cdproject.net/en-US/Pages/HomePage.aspx

Cellular-News. (2011). *Coltan, gorillas and cellphones*. Retrieved October 15, 2011, from cellular-news: https://www.cellular-news.com/coltan/

CEMEFI. (2011). *Empresa Socialmente Responsable*. Retrieved November 20, 2011, from https://www.cemefi.org/esr/

Ceres. (2012). *The Ceres Principles*. Retrieved January 15, 2012, from https://www.ceres.org/about-us/our-history/ceres-principles

Dizolele, M. P. (2006). *In focus: Congo's bloody coltan*. Retrieved October 15, 2011, from Pulitzer Center: https://pulitzercenter.org/video/congos-bloody-coltan

DJSI. (2011). *Dow Jones Sustainability Indexes*. Retrieved November 6, 2011, from https://www.sustainability-index.com/07_htmle/assessment/overview.html

EITI. (2009). *The EITI principles and criteria*. Retrieved October 15, 2011, from Extractive Industries Transparency Initiative: https://eiti.org/eiti/principles

EITI. (2011). *Democratic Republic of Congo*. Retrieved October 15, 2011, from Extractive Industries Transparency Initiative: https://eiti.org/DRCongo

EPA. (2012). *Equator Principles*. Retrieved January 15, 2012, from https://www.equator-principles.com/

Fairtrade International. (2011). *Fairtrade International*. Retrieved November 20, 2011, from https://www.fairtrade.net/

Forest Stewardship Council. (2011). *FSC certification*. Retrieved November 20, 2011, from https://www.fsc.org/

Freeman, R. E. (1984/2010). *Strategic management: A stakeholder approach*. Cambridge: Cambridge University Press.

Global Reporting Initiative. (2011). *Global Reporting Initiative*. Retrieved August 30, 2011, from https://www.globalreporting.org/Home

GRI. (2006a). *Sustainability reporting guidelines*. Amsterdam: Global Reporting Initiative.

GRI. (2006b). *GRI application levels*. 2006: Global Reporting Initiative.

GRI. (2010). *GRI sustainability reporting statistics*. Amsterdam: Global Reporting Inititative.

GRI. (2010a). *GRI and ISO 26000: How to use the GRI guidelines in conjunction with ISO 26000*. Amsterdam: Global Reporting Initiative.

GRI. (2010b). *The Amsterdam global conference on sustainability and transparency*. Amsterdam: Global Reporting Initiative.

GRI. (2014a). *Overview of changes in standard disclosures from G3 to G4 guidelines*. Amsterdam: Global Reporting Initiative.

GRI. (2014b). *G4 sustainability reporting guidelines: Frequently asked questions*. Amsterdam: Global Reporting Initiative.

HREA. (2012). *Simplified version of the Universal Declaration of Human Rights*. Retrieved January 15, 2012, from https://www.hrea.org/index.php?base_id=104&language_id=1&erc_doc_id=5211&category_id=24&category_type=3&group=

IIRC. (2013). *The International Integrated Reporting Framework*. International Integrated Reporting Council.

ILO. (2012). *International Labour Organization: Promoting jobs, protecting people*. Retrieved January 15, 2012, from https://www.ilo.org/

ISO. (2010). *International Standard ISO 26000: Guidance on social responsibility*. Geneva: International Organization for Standardization.

ISO. (2012a). *International Organization for Standardization*. Retrieved January 15, 2012, from ISO 14000 essentials: https://www.iso.org/iso/iso_14000_essentials

ISO. (2012b). *ISO 26000 - Social responsibility*. Retrieved January 15, 2012, from International Organization for Standardization: https://www.iso.org/iso/iso_catalogue/management_and_leadership_standards/social_responsibility/sr_iso26000_overview.htm#sr-7

John, M., & Hepinstall, S. (2011). *U.S. buyers shun "conflict minerals" in Congo's east*. Retrieved October 15, 2011, from Reuters: https://www.reuters.com/article/2011/10/05/congo-democratic-minerals-corrected-idUSL5E7L31S720111005

Lasker, J. (2008). *Inside Africa's PlayStation war*. Retrieved October 15, 2011, from Toward Freedom: https://towardfreedom.com/home/content/view/1352/1

Leipziger, D. (2010). *The corporate responsibility codebook*. Sheffield: Greenleaf.

OECD. (2011). *OECD guidelines for multinational enterprises: 2011 Edition*. Retrieved November 20, 2011, from https://www.oecd.org/dataoecd/43/29/48004323.pdf

PRME. (2023). *The Seven Principles*. UNPRME; Principles for Responsible Management Education. https://www.unprme.org/what-we-do/

SAI. (2008). *Social Accountability 8000*. New York: SAI.

SAM Research AG. (2010). *Corporate sustainability assessment questionnaire*. Zurich.

The Natural Step. (2011). *Principles of sustainability*. Retrieved November 11, 2011, from The Natural Step: https://www.naturalstep.org/

Transparency International. (2009). *Business principles for countering bribery*. Berlin.

U.S. Environmental Protection Agency. (2011). *About ENERGY STAR*. Retrieved November 20, 2011, from https://www.energystar.gov/

U.S. Green Building Council. (2011). *What LEED is*. Retrieved November 11, 2011, from LEED: https://www.usgbc.org/DisplayPage.aspx?CMSPageID=1988

UNEP. (2012). *United Nations Environment Programme*. Retrieved January 15, 2012, from https://www.unep.org/

UNGC. (2011). *The ten principles*. Retrieved October 15, 2011, from United Nations Global Compact: https://www.unglobalcompact.org/AboutTheGC/TheTenPrinciples/index.html

United Nations. (2012). *The Universal Declaration of Human Rights*. Retrieved January 15, 2012, from https://www.un.org/en/documents/udhr/

WBCSD. (2011). *About WBCSD*. Retrieved November 6, 2011, from WBCSD: Business solutions for a sustainable world: https://www.wbcsd.org/about.aspx

10 Equality, Diversity, and Inclusion

In the realm of responsible business, the concepts of Equality, Diversity, and Inclusion (EDI) stand as pillars that uphold the ethical and practical framework within which modern businesses operate. The articulation of Equality, Diversity, and Inclusion (EDI) within academic and organizational contexts can vary, reflecting these concepts' complexity and evolving nature. Diversity, equality, and inclusion are often discussed in tandem, emphasizing the need for a varied workforce, equitable practices, and a culture that embraces differences (Shore et al., 2011). The inclusion of "Belonging" to form DEIB (Diversity, Equality, Inclusion, and Belonging) represents a deeper understanding of inclusion's psychological and emotional aspects. As noted by Walton and Cohen (2007), the sense of belonging can significantly impact the well-being and performance of individuals in an institution. The different terminologies, whether EDI or DEIB, underscore specific aspects of the broader objective but share a common goal: Creating inclusive environments where everyone has equitable access to opportunities and feels valued and integral to the social fabric (Barak, 2014). This goal aligns with the principles of social justice, advocating for dismantling systemic barriers and cultivating practices that promote equality and mutual respect (Young, 1990). In essence, while the terminology may differ, the underlying pursuit of these concepts is to foster a society in which all individuals, irrespective of their background, identity, or ability, can thrive and contribute to their fullest potential (Ely & Thomas, 2001) (Figure 10.1).

Equality in a business context is fundamentally about ensuring that all employees are provided with equal opportunities and are not subjected to discrimination based on gender, race, age, disability, sexual orientation, religion, or other personal attributes. It is a commitment to creating a level playing field where decisions, opportunities, and treatment are based solely on merit, free from the influence of bias or stereotypes. Adherence to legal standards such as the Equality Act 2010 in the UK and implementing fair policies in recruitment, promotion, pay, and training are critical to achieving true equality in the workplace.

On the other hand, diversity involves acknowledging, valuing, and effectively leveraging the differences in the workforce. These differences span a broad spectrum, including race, gender, age, ethnicity, sexual orientation, physical abilities, religious beliefs, and socioeconomic status. Embracing diversity means moving beyond mere tolerance to celebrate and harness these differences, which can drive innovation, creativity, and business success. For businesses, this means creating a workforce that reflects the diversity of the market and

DOI: 10.4324/9781003544074-14

Figure 10.1 Equality, Diversity, and Inclusion Word Cloud.

society. Research consistently shows that diverse teams are more creative and effective in problem-solving, providing a clear business advantage.

EDI exemplar

Accenture, a global leader in professional services, exemplifies a notable success in the domain of EDI. Their approach is distinguished by a multifaceted strategy that includes targeted recruitment practices aimed at enhancing workforce diversity, comprehensive training to cultivate an inclusive corporate culture, and dedicated initiatives supporting various marginalized groups. The effectiveness of Accenture's EDI initiatives is evidenced by their consistent recognition in external rankings including *The Times* and Business in the Community (BITC) Top 50 Employers for Gender Equality 2023 and regularly topping the FTSE Diversity and Inclusion Index which ranks over 12,000 companies globally and identifies the top 100 publicly traded companies with the most diverse and inclusive workplaces, as measured by 24 metrics across four key pillars.

Inclusion complements these concepts by ensuring people feel valued, respected, and supported. It is about cultivating an environment where all employees can thrive and contribute to their fullest potential, actively combating conscious and unconscious bias, fostering a sense of belonging, and ensuring that all voices are heard and considered. Inclusive businesses are characterized by leadership that embraces diversity, inclusive policies, and a culture where differences are accepted and seen as an asset. The interconnectedness of EDI is crucial to understand. Equality lays the foundation for diversity by ensuring fair treatment and opportunity access. Diversity brings a range of perspectives and skills essential for innovation and market relevance. Inclusion allows diverse individuals to work together harmoniously, maximizing the benefits of diversity.

The dimension of "Belonging" within the diversity, equity, and inclusion (DEI) paradigm is increasingly recognized as a critical component of influential organizational culture and practice. Belonging extends beyond mere presence or representation to encapsulate the experiential aspect of being a valued member of a community or organization. According to a synthesis of psychological theories by Baumeister and Leary (1995), the innate human need for belonging is satisfied through frequent, positive interactions within a framework of long-term, caring relationships. This sense of belonging can significantly influence an individual's engagement, productivity, and overall job satisfaction (Hagerty et al., 1992).

Organizations that foster a sense of belonging acknowledge diversity, strive for equity, and create environments where individuals feel personally connected, supported, and integral to the collective identity (Cheryan et al., 2009). This inclusive approach is associated with enhanced organizational commitment and individual well-being (Allen, 2010). Consequently, when individuals perceive that they belong, they are more likely to contribute authentically and leverage their unique perspectives for the organization's benefit (Kahn, 1990). Belonging, therefore, is not merely a supplement to DEI but a transformative element that completes the experience of inclusion by ensuring that individuals are seen, heard, affirmed, and valued. Figure 10.2 based on the work of Burnette (2019) demonstrates how each element represents a different piece of the full human experience. Addressing only one or two of these falls short on developing a sense of belonging.

In the context of responsible business, EDI goes beyond a moral imperative; it is a business necessity. It aligns with corporate social responsibility and sustainability goals, enhancing a company's ethical stature and social responsiveness. Businesses embracing EDI are perceived as more honest, socially responsible, and better equipped to face global challenges. Adopting EDI contributes to a positive brand image and employee satisfaction and impacts productivity and profitability. While the benefits of EDI are significant, its practical implementation presents challenges. It requires a profound commitment from leadership and a shift in organizational culture. The challenge is addressing biases and institutional barriers to create a genuinely inclusive environment. However, the opportunities are immense. Harnessing EDI can create a dynamic, innovative, and resilient business capable of thriving in a diverse and globalized market.

Historical Context and Evolution of EDI

The landscape of EDI within the corporate sphere has been shaped by a confluence of historical movements and legal milestones, evolving through various stages of societal transformation. The origins of EDI can be traced back to the labor movements of the early 20th century,

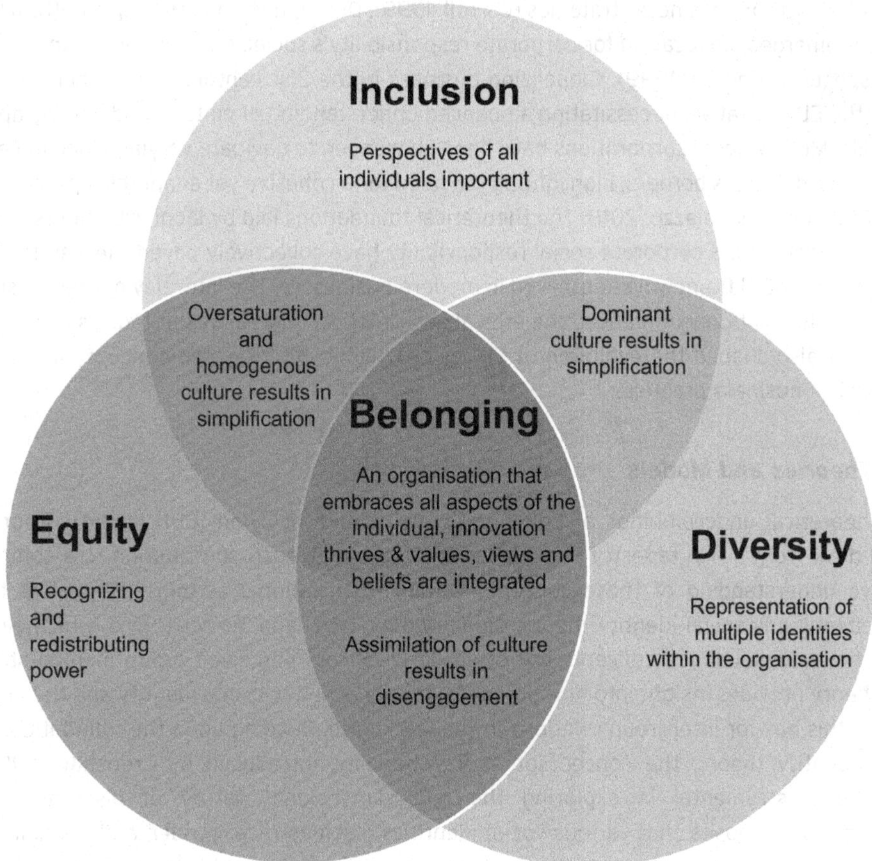

Figure 10.2 Diversity, Equity, Inclusion, and Belonging.
Based on Burnette (2019)

which set the groundwork for workers' collective bargaining rights, championing principles of fair labor and equitable treatment (Kaufman, 2002). These movements laid the initial foundations for what would become a broader push towards workplace equality. The mid-20th century civil rights movement marked a significant pivot point, with legal strides such as the Civil Rights Act of 1964 in the United States prohibited employment discrimination based on race, color, religion, sex, or national origin (Civil Rights Act, 1964). This pivotal legislation underscored the ethical imperative for equality and set a legal precedent that would influence global business practices. Feminist theory further contributed to the EDI discourse, mainly through the works of scholars such as bell hooks (1982) and Simone de Beauvoir (1949), who articulated the intersections of gender and power dynamics within societal structures, urging a revaluation of women's roles in both the public and private sectors.

The emergence of business ethics and corporate social responsibility paradigms in the late 20th century brought about a shift in business practices. This period saw an increasing awareness that responsible business conduct entailed profitability and incorporating ethical principles into core business strategies (Carroll, 1999). During this time, the triple bottom line concept emerged, advocating for corporate responsibility's social, environmental, and financial aspects (Elkington, 1999). Globalizing business in the 21st century has further complicated the EDI narrative, necessitating a nuanced understanding of cultural and demographic diversity. Multinational corporations have been challenged to navigate varying legal and ethical standards across borders, highlighting the need for a cohesive yet adaptable approach to the EDI (Scherer & Palazzo, 2011). The theoretical foundations laid by labor, civil rights, feminist movements, and corporate social responsibility have collectively paved the way for the contemporary EDI frameworks observed in modern businesses. The interplay of these historical forces has not only influenced the ethical and practical imperatives of today's corporate world but also shaped the evolution of EDI as a dynamic, multifaceted concept integral to responsible business practice.

Key Theories and Models

The theoretical underpinnings of Equality, Diversity, and Inclusion (EDI) in the corporate world draw from a rich tapestry of social science research, each contributing to a comprehensive understanding of these concepts within organizational settings. Central to this understanding is social identity theory, pioneered by Tajfel and Turner (1979), which elucidates how individual self-concepts are often derived from perceived group memberships. This theory provides insight into how personal identity is tied to group identity and the implications this has for intergroup relations in the workplace. Building upon the foundations of social identity theory, the concept of intersectionality, introduced by Crenshaw (1989), has been instrumental in exploring the multi-dimensional nature of discrimination. Intersectionality posits that various social identities, such as race, gender, and class, intersect to create unique experiences of advantage and disadvantage. This framework has been particularly transformative in recognizing the complex realities faced by individuals who navigate multiple marginalized identities, compelling organizations to adopt more nuanced and inclusive EDI policies.

The contact hypothesis, proposed by Allport (1954), suggests that under certain conditions, interpersonal contact is one of the most effective ways to reduce prejudice between majority and minority group members. This hypothesis has significant implications for organizational diversity training programs, suggesting that facilitated contact between diverse employees can enhance mutual understanding and cooperation. These theoretical frameworks are complemented by Cox's diversity-validating model (1993), which argues that an organization's multicultural environment can improve the well-being of its employees and overall performance. Cox's model advocates recognizing and celebrating cultural differences as a cornerstone of effective EDI strategies.

Moreover, contemporary EDI discourse has been informed by the principles of distributive and procedural justice theories. As articulated by Adams, distributive justice concerns the fairness of outcomes received. In contrast, as Walker Field (1975) discussed, procedural justice concerns the right of the processes that lead to these outcomes. In an organizational context, these concepts of justice inform the fairness of HR practices and policies, shaping the perceptions and attitudes of employees towards their employer. Together, these theories

Table 10.1 Summary of Common EDI Theories

Diversity management theory	Cox	1993	The theory suggests that effective diversity management enhances organizational performance and competitiveness.
Social identity theory	Tajfel and Turner	1979	The theory suggests that shared traits lead to social identities and distinct group behaviors.
Intersectionality theory	Crenshaw	1989	The theory acknowledges that discrimination and inequality are influenced by various identity facets such as race, gender, and sexual orientation.
Inclusive leadership theory	Nembhard and Edmondson	2006	The theory posits that leaders are key in fostering workplace EDI through nurturing an inclusive culture.
Diversity training theory	Pendry et al.	2007	This theory suggests that organizations can achieve diversity and inclusion objectives through training and education initiatives.

and models provide a robust framework for understanding the complexities of EDI in the business environment. They offer a rationale for implementing EDI initiatives and a strategic guide for organizations seeking to foster a truly inclusive workplace (Table 10.1).

Legislative Frameworks

The promulgation of laws and regulations has been instrumental in implementing Equality, Diversity, and Inclusion (EDI) within the business sector. This legislative corpus serves as a legal scaffold that shapes the contours of EDI by delineating the obligations and rights of employers and employees alike.

In the United States, the Civil Rights Act of 1964 emerged as a watershed in anti-discrimination law, prohibiting employment discrimination on multiple grounds (Civil Rights Act, 1964). This act laid the groundwork for subsequent legislation protecting specific employee rights. The Americans with Disabilities Act of 1990 (ADA) represented another significant advancement, mandating reasonable accommodations in the workplace for individuals with disabilities (Americans with Disabilities Act of 1990, Pub. L. No. 101-336, 104 Stat, 1990). The enactment of the ADA signaled a broadening of the understanding of discrimination to include the systemic barriers faced by individuals with disabilities. The United Kingdom codified its commitment to EDI through the Equality Act 2010, consolidating previous anti-discrimination laws into one act. This comprehensive legislation provides a framework for equality encompassing protected characteristics such as age, disability, gender reassignment, marriage and civil partnership, pregnancy and maternity, race, religion or belief, sex, and sexual orientation (Equality Act, 2010). The European Union has proactively enacted directives such as the Employment Equality Directive (2000/78/EC), which sets a precedent for non-discrimination in the workplace based on religion or belief, disability, age, and sexual orientation (Establishing a General Framework for Equal Treatment in Employment and Occupation, 2000). This directive underscores the commitment of member states to foster an inclusive labor market.

The legislative landscape is further enriched by international conventions and declarations, such as the United Nations' Universal Declaration of Human Rights (United Nations, General Assembly, 1948), which, although not legally binding, has influenced global norms relating to equality and non-discrimination. Furthermore, the International Labour Organization's (ILO) Declaration on Fundamental Principles and Rights at Work (1998) commits member states to respect and promote principles and rights in four categories: Non-discrimination concerning employment and occupation (International Labour Organization, 1988). While much of the discourse on EDI is often centered on Western legislation, countries in the Global South have also made significant strides, often reflecting unique cultural and socio-economic contexts. In Latin America, Brazil stands out with its Statute of Racial Equality (Estatuto da Igualdade Racial [Statute of Racial Equality], 2010), which seeks to combat racial discrimination and promote equality, particularly for Afro-Brazilians, who have historically faced significant barriers (Estatuto da Igualdade Racial [Statute of Racial Equality], 2010). This statute is part of a broader trend in the region where countries address inequalities stemming from their diverse ethnic compositions and colonial legacies.

African nations, with their rich tapestries of ethnic and cultural diversity, have also been proactive. Post-apartheid South Africa has established one of EDI's most progressive legal frameworks through the Employment Equity Act (1998). The act aims to achieve equity in the workplace by promoting equal opportunity and fair treatment in employment by eliminating unfair discrimination (Employment Equity Act, No. 55, 1998). In Asia, India's landmark Rights of Persons with Disabilities Act (2016) represents a comprehensive approach to addressing the challenges faced by individuals with disabilities, aligning with the United Nations Convention on the Rights of Persons with Disabilities (The Rights of Persons with Disability Act, 2016). This act reflects a global shift towards a more inclusive view of disability rights. The ASEAN Human Rights Declaration (2013), while not legally binding, reflects the collective commitment of Southeast Asian nations to the principles of human rights, which implicitly includes aspects of equality and non-discrimination in the workplace (Renshaw, 2013). Middle Eastern countries, too, are gradually incorporating EDI principles into their legal systems. For example, the United Arab Emirates has implemented anti-discrimination laws prohibiting discrimination based on religion, belief, sect, faith, creed, race, color, or ethnic origin (Federal Decree-Law No. (2) of 2015 on Combating Discrimination and Hatred, 2015). Despite these developments, countries in the Global South often need help with unique challenges, including enforcing EDI laws, which may be hindered by economic constraints, political instability, and deeply ingrained social norms. Nevertheless, the Global South's legislative efforts demonstrate a growing recognition of the importance of EDI in achieving social and economic development.

EDI in Business Organizations

In the contemporary business milieu, the Equality, Diversity, and Inclusion triad has emerged as a pivotal axis around which organizations orient their cultural, strategic, and operational endeavors. Integrating EDI within the corporate structure is more than a compliance agenda; it embodies a strategic imperative that fosters innovation, drives performance, and enhances ethical reputation.

Equality in the organizational context is premised on the equitable treatment of all employees, ensuring that opportunities for growth, development, and advancement are accessible irrespective of an individual's inherent or acquired characteristics. It is anchored in the principle of meritocracy, where talent and effort determine professional trajectories unimpeded by prejudice or systemic barriers (Kalev et al., 2006). Organizations championing equality benefit from a motivated, engaged, and committed workforce to the entity's success. Diversity extends this narrative by valuing the heterogeneity of the workforce. It involves recognizing and appreciating the myriad dimensions of difference, including but not restricted to race, gender, age, ethnicity, sexual orientation, and disability. Diverse organizations leverage this multiplicity to harness a broader spectrum of ideas, perspectives, and approaches to problem-solving (Page, 2007). Such organizations are better equipped to navigate the complexities of global markets and are more attuned to the needs and aspirations of a diverse customer base. Inclusion is the strategic element that actualizes the potential of diversity. It involves creating an organizational ethos where differences are accepted and integral to the organizational fabric. Inclusive organizations craft environments where employees feel valued and empowered to contribute to their fullest potential (Barak, 2014). Such inclusivity is positively correlated with higher levels of innovation, employee satisfaction, and retention, as it fosters a culture of respect and collaboration.

Various strategic, ethical, and compliance-oriented motivations underpin the enactment of EDI within business organizations. Strategically, companies that embrace EDI are positioned to outperform their peers by capitalizing on a broader array of market opportunities and creative innovations (Herring, 2009). Ethically, businesses are increasingly expected to reflect the societal values of fairness and justice within their internal operations and broader engagements with stakeholders (Brammer et al., 2007). Compliance with legislative mandates also necessitates a commitment to EDI, as businesses strive to meet the standards set forth by anti-discrimination laws and equality frameworks. Despite its strategic significance, the operationalization of EDI is fraught with challenges. Cultural inertia, unconscious biases, and institutionalized norms can impede the translation of EDI from policy to practice (Ely & Thomas, 2001). Moreover, the dynamic and evolving nature of societal norms around diversity and inclusion necessitates organizations maintaining an ongoing commitment to learning, adaptation, and dialogue. In sum, EDI represents a comprehensive paradigm through which business organizations can enhance their competitive advantage and affirm their commitment to social responsibility and ethical excellence. It is a multifaceted construct requiring nuanced understanding and a proactive approach to embed within the corporate ethos and practice.

Benefits and Challenges of EDI for Businesses

The benefits of EDI in business are extensive and substantiated by empirical research. Cox and Blake (1991) posit that diversity is a business asset that enhances creativity and problem-solving by pooling various perspectives and solutions. Barta, Kleiner, and Neumann (2012) also provide evidence that companies with more diverse top teams were top financial performers, underscoring EDI's economic incentives. Furthermore, Roberson (2006) argues that an inclusive work environment can increase job satisfaction, reduce turnover, and improve productivity by fostering employees' sense of belonging and value. Hewlett, Marshall, and Sherbin (2013)note that such environments tend to be more innovative due to the variety of experiences and perspectives that can spark creativity and drive innovation. EDI also aligns with the principles of corporate social responsibility, enhancing a company's reputation and brand (Aguinis & Glavas, 2012). In today's socially conscious market, customers and clients often make choices based on a company's commitment to social values, including EDI.

Despite the clear advantages, businesses need help in implementing effective EDI policies. One of the primary hurdles is resistance to change. Traditional corporate cultures can be deeply entrenched, and attempts to alter the status quo may encounter opposition (Dobbin & Kalev, 2016). Overcoming such resistance often requires significant cultural transformation and sustained commitment from leadership. Another challenge is the complexity of measuring EDI outcomes. Compared to more straightforward business metrics, the impact of EDI initiatives can be difficult to quantify, posing a challenge for organizations seeking to assess progress and impact (Kaplan & Donovan, 2013). Additionally, implementing EDI strategies can be costly, requiring investment in training, policy development, and, sometimes, structural changes to the organization. Small and medium-sized enterprises may find these costs prohibitive (Jonsen et al., 2013). Finally, businesses operating globally may need help with the variability of EDI across different cultural and legal landscapes. What constitutes fair and inclusive practices in one country may need to align with the norms or laws of another, complicating the implementation of universal EDI policies (Shen et al., 2009).

Metrics and KPIs to Measure EDI Effectiveness

In the strategic pursuit of Equality, Diversity, and Inclusion (EDI), business organizations often turn to metrics and Key Performance Indicators (KPIs) to gauge the effectiveness and impact of their initiatives. The judicious application of these measures can yield a granular understanding of progress and illuminate pathways for ongoing improvement. Metrics and KPIs serve as the compass by which organizations navigate the complex terrain of EDI, providing quantifiable benchmarks against which to assess outcomes and strategies. The development of these measures is rooted in the recognition that EDI objectives, while qualitatively rich, benefit from quantitative scrutiny to ensure accountability and focused action (Kaplan & Donovan, 2013).

Regarding equality, organizations may track the gender pay gap as a critical metric, offering insights into the parity of remuneration across genders—a quantifiable reflection of the principle of equal pay for equal work (Metcalf & Rolfe, 2010). Recruitment and promotion rates disaggregated by gender, ethnicity, age, and other demographic factors can also serve as KPIs, illuminating potential biases or barriers within talent management processes (Kalev et al., 2006). Diversity metrics often encompass compositional analyses, such as the percentage of employees from underrepresented groups at various organizational levels. When tracked over time, such measures can indicate the effectiveness of diversity recruitment initiatives and the inclusiveness of promotion practices (Richard, 2000). Moreover, the diversity of suppliers and contractors can extend the purview of these metrics beyond the immediate organization, reflecting a commitment to a broad-based diversity (KPMG, 2014).

Inclusion metrics are more nuanced, capturing the qualitative aspects of the workplace environment. Employee surveys that assess perceptions of inclusivity, belonging, and equitable treatment can yield valuable data, translating subjective experiences into actionable intelligence (Barak, 2014). Another significant KPI is the rate of participation in EDI training and development programs, which indicates an organizational commitment to fostering an inclusive culture (Roberson, 2006). Beyond internal measures, external recognition in the form of awards or certifications for EDI practices can also serve as KPIs, providing a benchmark of an organization's standing against industry standards or societal expectations (Bersin, 2015). While these metrics and KPIs provide a mechanism for evaluation and accountability, they are not without challenges. The selection of appropriate measures, data interpretation, and insights integration into strategic decision making require a sophisticated understanding of EDI's goals and the organization's operational context (Kochan et al., 2003). Furthermore, the dynamic nature of EDI goals necessitates that KPIs evolve in tandem with organizational objectives and societal shifts.

The Athena SWAN Charter

The Athena SWAN Charter, established in 2005 by the Equality Challenge Unit in the UK, represents a pioneering accreditation framework dedicated to the advancement of Equality, Diversity, and Inclusion (EDI) within higher education and research. Participating institutions commit to a rigorous self-assessment process, developing action plans to promote gender equality and remove obstacles faced by women. Accreditation levels—Bronze, Silver, and Gold—reflect the maturity of an institution's EDI practices. Athena SWAN's framework has become a benchmark for excellence in EDI, encouraging systemic and cultural changes that foster an inclusive academic environment where all can thrive (Advance HE, 2020).

Strategy Development for EDI Alignment with Business Objectives

Developing a strategy for Equality, Diversity, and Inclusion (EDI) that aligns with business objectives is crucial for organizations seeking to integrate these values into their core operations. An effective EDI strategy supports a company's commitment to social justice, enhances its competitive edge, fosters innovation, and improves its standing with various stakeholders.

The formulation of an EDI strategy begins with a clear articulation of the business's vision and the role that EDI plays in achieving that vision. As Thomas and Ely (1996) suggest, viewing diversity through enhancing organizational capability underpins the strategic value of EDI initiatives. Aligning EDI objectives with business goals requires a deep understanding of how diversity drives market growth, fosters creativity, and enhances team problem-solving capabilities.

A comprehensive EDI strategy encompasses a range of components, including policy development, leadership engagement, employee involvement, and continuous learning. Sabharwal (2014) emphasizes the importance of having policies that articulate clear goals and provide a framework for implementation. These policies must be dynamic and responsive to the evolving understanding of what EDI entails within the organization's context. Leadership commitment is pivotal to the success of any EDI strategy. Leaders must embody the principles of EDI and actively promote these values within the organization. As Ely and Thomas (2001) argue, when leaders demonstrate a commitment to diversity, they set a tone that resonates throughout the organization, fostering a culture of inclusion. This involves not only rhetorical support but also the allocation of resources and the establishment of accountability mechanisms.

Employee involvement is another critical aspect of strategy development. By engaging employees at all levels in the conversation around EDI, organizations can ensure that the strategy reflects diverse perspectives and has broad-based support. Involving employees in the development and execution of EDI initiatives can also increase their commitment and foster a sense of ownership over the outcomes (Kochan et al., 2003). Moreover, an EDI strategy should include provisions for continuous learning and adaptation. As Cox (1993) points out, the learning organization continually transforms to embrace diversity better. This means providing training and development opportunities and creating channels for feedback and dialogue that allow for the ongoing refinement of EDI initiatives (Figure 10.3).

A strategic approach to EDI also necessitates a robust evaluation mechanism to assess the impact of EDI initiatives. Metrics and KPIs must be identified to measure progress against EDI objectives and to ensure that these initiatives contribute positively to the organization's performance (Kaplan & Donovan, 2013). In essence, an EDI strategy aligned with business objectives is integrated into the fabric of the organization's operational and strategic plans.

Figure 10.3 The EDI Development Process.

Based on Raja (2021)

It is informed by a clear understanding of EDI's value to the organization and is characterized by policies and practices that foster an inclusive and diverse workplace.

Fostering an Inclusive Corporate Culture

At the heart of fostering an inclusive corporate culture lies the concept of organizational change towards inclusivity, which is a shift that moves beyond mere workforce diversity. It is about creating a work environment where all individuals are treated fairly, have equal access to opportunities, and can contribute fully to the organization's success. Schein (2011) posits that organizational culture is a pattern of shared basic assumptions that a group learns as it solves its problems of external adaptation and internal integration. In this light, fostering an inclusive culture necessitates addressing the observable behaviors and the underlying values and beliefs that inform them. Ely and Thomas (2001) argue that leveraging diversity and fostering inclusivity can significantly enhance group functioning. However, this requires organizational leaders to cultivate an environment where differences are tolerated and viewed as a potential source of strength and enrichment. This involves acknowledging and celebrating differences and recognizing the unique contributions that individuals from varied backgrounds bring to the table.

A key aspect of cultural change is engagement from the top. Leaders must not only espouse the virtues of inclusivity but also embody them in their actions and decisions. The leadership approach exemplifies "inclusive leadership", which Bourke and Dillon (2016) define as a set of behaviors promoting involvement, respect, and connection where diverse groups can thrive. Creating an inclusive culture also involves rethinking and, if necessary, redesigning organizational processes to ensure they are inclusive. This can mean anything from reviewing hiring and promotion practices to ensuring that meeting structures and communication processes allow diverse voices to be heard. Roberson's (2019) inclusive behaviors and challenging processes and practices may hinder EDI efforts. In addition to inspiring and motivating, leaders are responsible for integrating EDI into the organization's strategic framework. This involves ensuring that EDI considerations are reflected in decision-making processes, resource allocation, and business planning. Nishii and Özbilgin (2007) suggest that when leaders incorporate EDI into the organization's core strategy, it sends a powerful message about its importance, and this strategic emphasis helps align EDI initiatives with business goals.

Leaders also play a crucial role in creating an environment where EDI can thrive. This involves actively working to eliminate discrimination and bias, both implicit and explicit, and creating systems that promote fairness and equality. Shore et al. (2011) note that leaders must foster an inclusive climate where diversity is accepted and celebrated to achieve superior organizational outcomes. Furthermore, leaders must also be accountable for EDI outcomes. This requires the establishment of clear metrics and KPIs to assess the impact of EDI initiatives and the willingness to adjust strategies based on these outcomes, according to Homan et al. (2015), accountability mechanisms are essential to ensure that EDI efforts are symbolic and translate into real progress. Effective leadership in promoting EDI also extends beyond the organization's internal operations. Leaders must engage with external stakeholders, including customers, suppliers, and the wider community, to promote EDI principles.

By doing so, leaders can enhance the organization's reputation and demonstrate its commitment to social responsibility (Mors, 2011).

Leadership for EDI

A prominent business leader who has been at the forefront of advancing Equality, Diversity, and Inclusion (EDI) is Rosalind Brewer, the CEO of Walgreens Boots Alliance. Brewer has been a vocal advocate for EDI throughout her career, which includes her tenure as the COO of Starbucks and CEO of Sam's Club. She has consistently leveraged her leadership roles to drive forward initiatives aimed at increasing representation, fostering inclusive environments, and supporting supplier diversity. Her commitment to EDI has been recognized by her inclusion on lists of top business leaders and influencers, and she is often cited as a trailblazer for her active role in promoting diversity and inclusion within the corporate sphere. Brewer's actions and influence underscore the importance of executive leadership in championing EDI within organizations (MasterClass, 2023).

Emerging Trends in EDI within the Business Context

In the dynamic business landscape, the domain of Equality, Diversity, and Inclusion (EDI) is continually evolving, propelled by new societal norms, technological advancements, and global economic shifts. Recognizing EDI's strategic importance has prompted organizations to adapt and innovate, leading to novel trends that redefine how EDI is conceptualized and implemented.

One of EDI's most significant emerging trends is the deepening integration of technology into diversity initiatives. The rise of artificial intelligence and machine learning presents novel opportunities to mitigate unconscious bias in recruitment and promotion processes. Algorithms and analytics are increasingly employed to ensure job advertisements reach a diverse candidate pool and to develop blind recruitment processes focusing on skills and competencies, as Kim and Kim (2020) highlighted. However, this trend also necessitates vigilance to ensure that biases are not inadvertently encoded into the technology. Another trend is the growing recognition of intersectionality within workplace EDI efforts. Organizations are moving beyond single-axis approaches that focus on one aspect of identity, such as gender or race, to more nuanced understandings that recognize the complexity of overlapping social identities. This shift aligns with Crenshaw's (1989) seminal work, which laid the foundation for intersectional analysis and is crucial for comprehensively addressing systemic inequality.

The globalization of business has ushered in an increased focus on cultural intelligence and global diversity management. With operations spanning multiple continents, companies embrace global EDI standards while tailoring their approaches to fit local cultural contexts. Leaders are expected to exhibit cultural intelligence–the capability to function effectively across national, ethnic, and organizational cultures, as per the research of Earley and Mosakowski (2004). Sustainability and social responsibility have become intertwined with EDI initiatives. The United Nations' Sustainable Development Goals (SDGs), particularly those related to gender equality and reduced inequalities, have been instrumental in this convergence. Businesses are increasingly aligning their EDI strategies with broader sustainability and social responsibility goals, recognizing the interdependence of these objectives (Rasche et al., 2013).

Moreover, there is a growing trend towards employee-driven EDI initiatives. Employees organize in groups, such as Employee Resource Groups (ERGs) and affinity networks, to advocate for change and support one another. These groups have become a powerful force for promoting EDI from within the organization, as they provide platforms for voices that might otherwise go unheard (Roberson, 2019).

Finally, the narrative around EDI is expanding to include a focus on mental health and well-being. As the conversation around workplace health becomes more sophisticated, EDI efforts encompass initiatives to support mental health, recognizing that psychological safety is integral to an inclusive work environment (Williams et al., 2020). These emerging trends signify a transformative phase in EDI within the business context. As organizations navigate these trends, they face balancing innovation with the ongoing commitment to fundamental EDI principles. The future of EDI in business will likely be characterized by a blend of technological sophistication, intersectional approaches, cultural intelligence, sustainability alignment, employee advocacy, and a holistic view of well-being, all of which will require organizations to be agile, empathetic, and strategic.

Exercises

A. KNOW

Use the below multiple-choice questions to test your knowledge. Each answer may be wrong or right, and there may be zero to four right or wrong answers per question:

1. What does the term "DEIB" stand for in the context of workplace equality?
   a. ...Diversity, Equity, Inclusion, and Belonging.
   b. ...Diversity, Empowerment, Integrity, and Balance.
   c. ...Diversity, Equality, Inclusion, and Bias.
   d. ...Diversity, Efficiency, Innovation, and Business.
2. Which of the following best defines "diversity" in a business context?
   a. ...Uniformity in employee skills and experiences.
   b. ...Variety in employee backgrounds and perspectives.
   c. ...Adherence to traditional business practices.
   d. ...Consistency in employee behavior and attitudes.
3. What is the primary challenge in implementing Equality, Diversity, and Inclusion (EDI) in businesses?
   a. ...Decreased profitability.
   b. ...Resistance to change and cultural transformation.
   c. ...Overemphasis on technology.
   d. ...Lack of legal support.

4. Which of the following is a key aspect of the "Belonging" dimension in DEIB?
   a. ...Strict adherence to corporate policies.
   b. ...Frequent positive interactions within a framework of long-term caring relationships.
   c. ...Maintaining traditional organizational hierarchies.
   d. ...Emphasis on individual achievements over team success.

5. Which legislation marked a significant pivot point for workplace equality in the United States?
   a. ...Civil Rights Act of 1964.
   b. ...Equality Act 2010.
   c. ...Employment Equity Act 1998.
   d. ...Americans with Disabilities Act 1990.

B. THINK

Consider the concept of EDI in the context of a business you have worked for or are familiar with. Can you identify the moral or ethical case for considering EDI in this workplace?

C. DO

Make a note of the key challenges relating to Equality, Diversity, and Inclusion that impact a business you have worked for or are familiar with. Can you identify some solutions to these challenges that could be implemented by the organization?

D. RELATE

Talk with someone in your business or your family about EDI, preferably someone of a different gender, ethnicity, or ability. Discuss if there are any EDI-related challenges that they have been faced with or that have affected people around them.

E. BE

How do you feel about the issues raised through the EDI lens? Can you place yourself in the position of others and see challenges from their perspective? Do you think organizations are doing enough to address EDI issues? Focus on your internal reactions to the challenges set out in this chapter and try to capture how it makes you feel and your attitudes to the overall EDI agenda. Can your reactions be expressed in feelings, motivations, moods, or attitudes? Do you react differently to different events or events in this history? How do you explain your reaction?

Feedback

A. KNOW

Feedback 1

a. Right: DEIB is an acronym for Diversity, Equity, Inclusion, and Belonging. This term reflects the evolving nature of workplace equality by adding the aspect of "Belonging", which emphasizes the psychological and emotional facets of inclusion.
b. Wrong: Diversity, Empowerment, Integrity, and Balance is incorrect.
c. Wrong: Diversity, Equality, Inclusion, and Bias is incorrect.
d. Wrong: Diversity, Efficiency, Innovation, and Business is incorrect.

Feedback 2

a. Wrong: Diversity is the opposite of uniformity.
b. Right: Diversity in a business context refers to the variety of employee backgrounds and perspectives, including race, gender, ethnicity, and other characteristics. This variety is seen as an asset to drive innovation and creativity.
c. Wrong: Taking a proactive stance on diversity often requires a shift in business practices.
d. Wrong: Diversity is about celebrating the differentiation of employee behavior and attitudes.

Feedback 3

a. Wrong: Research has confirmed that a focus on EDI within a company can lead to improved productivity and thus an increase in profitability.
b. Right: The primary challenge in implementing EDI in businesses is overcoming resistance to change and achieving cultural transformation. This involves altering entrenched corporate cultures to embrace diversity and inclusion, resistance to change, and cultural transformation.
c. Wrong: EDI does not rely on technology.
d. Wrong: While there are some legal implications in implementing EDI, they may be seen as enablers rather than challenges.

Feedback 4

a. Wrong: Adherence to corporate policies does not directly relate to belonging.
b. Right: The "Belonging" dimension emphasizes the importance of frequent positive interactions within a framework of long-term caring relationships. This fosters a sense of belonging, which is vital for individual engagement and productivity.
c. Wrong: In some cases, traditional organizational hierarchies may need to be reviewed to address belonging issues.
d. Wrong: Team success and belonging go hand in hand.

Feedback 5

a. Right: The Civil Rights Act of 1964 in the United States was a landmark legislation prohibiting employment discrimination based on race, color, religion, sex, or national origin, marking a significant pivot point in the journey towards workplace equality.
b. Wrong: The Equality Act 2010 applies to the UK and forms the basis of anti-discrimination law in mostly England, Scotland, and Wales.
c. Wrong: The Employment Equity Act 1998 applies in South Africa and aims to achieve equity in the workplace by promoting equal opportunity and fair treatment in employment by eliminating unfair discrimination.
d. Wrong: The Americans with Disabilities Act of 1990 mandates reasonable accommodations in the workplace for individuals with disabilities in the US.

B. THINK

Level	*Moral imagination*	*Notes*
+	You can identify the case for ethical and moral importance of incorporating EDI into workplace practices.	
=	You prioritize legal and regulatory EDI considerations over the moral and ethical.	
–	You are unable to grasp the moral, ethical, and legal reasons for incorporating EDI into workplace practices.	

C. DO

Level	*Taking initiative*	*Notes*
+	You have identified one or more EDI challenges and associated actions that can be taken to enhance EDI in your organization or one with which you are familiar.	
=	You have identified one or more EDI challenges but are unable to identify any specific actions.	
–	You are unable to identify any actions relating to EDI.	

D. RELATE

Level	Collaborative problem solving	Notes
+	You have started a conversation on EDI with someone at work, your study group, or friends and family who is of a different gender, ethnicity, or ability and considered some of the key challenges which they face at work, study, or home.	
=	You have started a conversation on EDI with someone at work, your study group, or friends and family who is of a different gender, ethnicity, or ability but not identified challenges.	
–	Conversation has not happened at all.	

E. BE

Level	Emotional awareness	Notes
+	Profound description of your thoughts and emotions regarding EDI and their implications.	
=	Basic awareness of one's emotions regarding EDI and their implications.	
–	No or little insight into own emotions regarding EDI and their implications.	

References

Advance HE. (2020). *Athena Swan Charter*. Advance HE. https://advance-he.ac.uk/equality-charters/athena-swan-charter

Aguinis, H., & Glavas, A. (2012). What we know and don't know about corporate social responsibility: A review and research agenda. *Journal of Management, 38*, 932–968.

Allen, T. D. (2010). *The mentoring advantage: Creating the next generation of leaders*. Davies-Black.

Allport, G. W. (1954). *The nature of prejudice*. Addison-Wesley.

Americans with Disabilities Act of 1990, Pub. L. No. 101-336, 104 Stat. (1990).

Barak, M. (2014). *Managing diversity: Toward a globally inclusive workplace*. Sage Publications.

Barta, T., Kleiner, M., & Neumann, T. (2012). Is there a payoff from top-team diversity. *McKinsey Quarterly, 12*(April), 65–66.

Baumeister, R. F., & Leary, M. R. (1995). The need to belong: Desire for interpersonal attachments as a fundamental human motivation. *Psychological Bulletin, 117*(3), 497–529.

Bersin, J. (2015). Why diversity and inclusion will be a top priority for 2016. *Forbes*.

Bourke, J., & Dillon, B. (2016). *Six signature traits of inclusive leadership*. Deloitte University Press.

Brammer, S., Millington, A., & Rayton, B. (2007). The contribution of corporate social responsibility to organizational commitment. *The International Journal of Human Resource Management, 18*(10), 1701-1719.

Burnette, K. (2019, January 21). *Belonging: A conversation about equity, diversity & inclusion*. Krys Burnette. https://www.krysburnette.com/blog/belonging-a-conversation-about-equity-diversity-amp-inclusion

Carroll, A. B. (1999). Corporate social responsibility: Evolution of a definitional construct. *Business & Society*, *38*, 268–295.

Cheryan, S., Plaut, V. C., Davies, P. G., & Steele, C. M. (2009). Ambient belonging: How stereotypical cues impact gender participation in computer science. *Journal of Personality and Social Psychology*, *97*(6), 1045–1060.

Civil Rights Act, Pub. L. No. 88-352, Stat. 241. 78 (1964).

Cox, T. (1993). *Cultural diversity in organizations: Theory, research and practice*. Berrett-Koehler.

Cox, T. H., & Blake, S. (1991). Managing cultural diversity: Implications for organizational competitiveness. *The Academy of Management Perspectives*, *5*(3), 45–56.

Crenshaw, K. (1989). Demarginalizing the intersection of race and sex: A black feminist critique of antidiscrimination doctrine. *University of Chicago Legal Forum*, *1989*(1), 8.

de Beauvoir, S. (1949). *The second sex*. Trans. H. M. Parshley. Jonathan Cape.

Dobbin, F., & Kalev, A. (2016). Why diversity programs fail. *Harvard Business Review*, (July/August 2016).

Earley, P. C., & Mosakowski, E. (2004). Toward culture intelligence: Turning cultural differences into a workplace advantage. *The Academy of Management Perspectives*, *18*(3), 151–157.

Elkington, J. (1999). *Cannibals with forks: The triple bottom line of 21st century business*. Capstone.

Ely, R. J., & Thomas, D. A. (2001). Cultural diversity at work: The effects of diversity perspectives on work group processes and outcomes. *Administrative Science Quarterly*, *46*(2), 229–273.

Employment Equity Act, No. 55, 55 (1998). https://www.gov.za/documents/employment-equity-act

Equality Act, 15 (2010). https://www.legislation.gov.uk/ukpga/2010/15/contents

Establishing a General Framework for Equal Treatment in Employment and Occupation, 2000/78/EC § Employment Equality Directive (2000).

Estatuto da Igualdade Racial [Statute of Racial Equality], 12.288 (2010). https://adsdatabase.ohchr.org/IssueLibrary/ESTATUTO%20DE%20LA%20IGUALDAD%20RACIAL%20(Brazil).pdf

Federal Decree-Law No. (2) of 2015 on Combating Discrimination and Hatred, 2 (2015).

Hagerty, B. M., Lynch-Sauer, J., Patusky, K. L., Bouwsema, M., & Collier, P. (1992). Sense of belonging: A vital mental health concept. *Archives of Psychiatric Nursing*, *6*(3), 172–177.

Herring, C. (2009). Does diversity pay?: Race, gender, and the business case for diversity. *American Sociological Review*, *74*(2), 208–224.

Hewlett, S. A., Marshall, M., & Sherbin, L. (2013). How diversity can drive innovation. *Harvard Business Review*, *91*(12), 30–30.

Homan, A. C., Buengeler, C., Eckhoff, R. A., van Ginkel, W. P., & Voelpel, S. C. (2015). The interplay of diversity training and diversity beliefs on team creativity in nationality diverse teams. *The Journal of Applied Psychology*, *100*(5), 1456–1467.

hooks, b. (1982). *Ain't I a woman*. South End Press.

International Labour Organization. (1988). *Declaration on Fundamental Principles and Rights at Work*. International Labour Office.

Jonsen, K., Tatli, A., Özbilgin, M. F., & Bell, M. P. (2013). The tragedy of the uncommons: Reframing workforce diversity. *Human Relations: Studies towards the Integration of the Social Sciences*, *66*(2), 271–294.

Kahn, W. A. (1990). Psychological conditions of personal engagement and disengagement at work. *Academy of Management Journal*, *33*(4), 692–724.

Kalev, A., Dobbin, F., & Kelly, E. (2006). Best practices or best guesses? Assessing the efficacy of corporate affirmative action and diversity policies. *American Sociological Review*, *71*(4), 589–617.

Kaplan, S. N., & Donovan, M. A. (2013). Measuring and communicating the value of diversity and inclusion. In *The 2013 Diversity and Inclusion Conference* (pp. 1–22).

Kaufman, B. E. (2002). The theory and practice of strategic HRM and participative management: Antecedents in early industrial relations. *Human Resource Management Review*, *12*(4), 505–533.

Kim, Y. J., & Kim, J. (2020). Algorithmic transparency and accountability in AI for recruitment: Insights from the hiring process at a large technology company. *Computers and Society*.

Kochan, T., Bezrukova, K., Ely, R., Jackson, S., Joshi, A., Jehn, K., Leonard, J., Levine, D., & Thomas, D. (2003). The effects of diversity on business performance: Report of the Diversity Research Network. *Human Resource Management*, *42*(1), 3–21.

KPMG. (2014). *A new vision of value: Connecting corporate and societal value creation*. KPMG International.

MasterClass. (2023). *Rosalind Brewer on diversity and inclusion in the workplace*. MasterClass. https://www.masterclass.com/articles/diversity-and-inclusion-in-the-workplace

Metcalf, H., & Rolfe, H. (2010). Barriers to employment for Pakistanis and Bangladeshis in Britain. *Work, Employment and Society, 24*, 627–647.

Mors, M. L. (2011). Innovation in a global consulting firm: When the problem is too much diversity. *Strategic Direction, 27*(1). https://doi.org/10.1108/sd.2011.05627aad.001

Nembhard, I. M., & Edmondson, A. C. (2006). Making it safe: The effects of leader inclusiveness and professional status on psychological safety and improvement efforts in health care teams. *Journal of Organizational Behavior: The International Journal of Industrial, Occupational and Organizational Psychology and Behavior, 27*(7), 941–966.

Nishii, L. H., & Özbilgin, M. F. (2007). Global diversity management: Towards a conceptual framework. *The International Journal of Human Resource Management, 18*(11), 1883–1894.

Page, S. E. (2007). *The difference: How the power of diversity creates better groups, firms, schools, and societies*. Princeton University Press.

Pendry, L. F., Driscoll, D. M., & Field, S. C. (2007). Diversity training: Putting theory into practice. *Journal of Occupational and Organizational Psychology, 80*(1), 27–50.

Raja, A. (2021). Blog: Journey to better equality, diversity and inclusion in your organisation. *Reading Voluntary Action*. https://rva.org.uk/article/blog-journey-to-better-equality-diversity-and-inclusion-in-your-organisation/

Rasche, A., Waddock, S., & McIntosh, M. (2013). The United Nations Global Compact: Retrospect and prospect. *Business & Society, 52*, 6–30.

Renshaw, C. S. (2013). The ASEAN Human Rights Declaration 2012. *Human Rights Law Review, 13*(3), 557–579.

Richard, O. C. (2000). Racial diversity, business strategy, and firm performance: A resource-based view. *Academy of Management Journal, 43*(2), 164–177.

Roberson, Q. M. (2006). Disentangling the meanings of diversity and inclusion in organizations. *Group & Organization Management, 31*(2), 212–236.

Roberson, Q. M. (2019). Diversity in the workplace: A review, synthesis, and future research agenda. *Annual Review of Organizational Psychology and Organizational Behavior, 6*(1), 69–88.

Sabharwal, M. (2014). Is diversity management sufficient? Organizational inclusion to further performance. *Public Personnel Management, 43*(2), 197–217.

Schein, E. H. (2011). *Organizational culture and leadership, Cafescribe* (3rd ed.). Jossey-Bass. https://books.google.co.uk/books?hl=en&lr=&id=Mnres2PIFLMC&oi=fnd&pg=PR9&dq=Schein,+E.+H.+(2010).+Organizational+culture+and+leadership+(4th+ed.).+San+Francisco,+CA:+Jossey-Bass.&ots=oqbrleOuLj&sig=kPI72RNsXSpbJSgEoPxb8GL227M

Scherer, A. G., & Palazzo, G. (2011). The new political role of business in a globalized world: A review of a new perspective on CSR and its implications for the firm, governance, and democracy. *Journal of Management Studies, 48*(4), 899–931.

Shen, J., Chanda, A., D'Netto, B., & Monga, M. (2009). Managing diversity through human resource management: An international perspective and conceptual framework. *The International Journal of Human Resource Management, 20*(2), 235–251.

Shore, L. M., Randel, A. E., Chung, B. G., Dean, M. A., Holcombe Ehrhart, K., & Singh, G. (2011). Inclusion and diversity in work groups: A review and model for future research. *Journal of Management, 37*(4), 1262–1289.

Tajfel, H., & Turner, J. C. (1979). An integrative theory of intergroup conflict. In W. G. Austin & S. Worchel (Eds.), *The social psychology of intergroup relations* (pp. 33–47). Brooks/Cole.

The Rights of Persons with Disability Act, (2016).

Thomas, D. A., & Ely, R. J. (1996). Making differences matter: A new paradigm for managing diversity. *Harvard Business Review, 74*(5), 79–90.

United Nations, General Assembly. (1948). *Universal Declaration of Human Rights* (G.A. Res. 217A (III), U.N. Doc. A/810). United Nations. https://www.un.org/en/about-us/universal-declaration-of-human-rights

Walton, G. M., & Cohen, G. L. (2007). A question of belonging: Race, social fit, and achievement. *Journal of Personality and Social Psychology, 92*(1), 82–96.

Williams, M., Phillips, K. W., & Hall, E. V. (2020). Tools for change: Boosting the retention of women in the STEM pipeline. *Journal of Research in Gender Studies, 10*(1), 11–75.

Young, I. M. (1990). *Justice and the politics of difference*. Princeton University Press.

D Strategizing

11 Sustainable Economics

Sustainable economics has emerged as a cornerstone in the evolving landscape of responsible business practices. This chapter delves into the intricate relationship between economic sustainability and business ethics, shedding light on how enterprises can thrive while fostering a more sustainable and equitable world. As businesses grapple with the dual challenges of economic performance and social responsibility, sustainable economics offers a framework for reconciling these objectives. At the heart of this discussion lies the recognition that traditional economic models, primarily driven by short-term gains and resource-intensive practices, are increasingly untenable in the face of global challenges such as climate change, resource depletion, and social inequality (Elkington, 1997; Raworth, 2017). Sustainable economics represents a paradigm shift, advocating for an economic system prioritizing long-term viability, environmental stewardship, and social well-being.

The significance of sustainable economics extends beyond mere theoretical discourse; it has profound implications for how businesses operate and interact with society. In the context of a responsible company, it necessitates re-evaluating business models, strategies, and goals, aligning them with sustainability principles and ethical considerations (Schaltegger & Burritt, 2018). This chapter aims to unpack these principles and explore their application in the business realm. By integrating sustainable economics into their core operations, businesses can mitigate their environmental and social impacts and unlock new opportunities for growth and innovation. This approach aligns with the growing demand from consumers, investors, and regulators for greater corporate responsibility and transparency (Ioannou & Serafeim, 2019). It also reflects a broader societal shift towards values-based commerce, where success is measured in financial terms and social and environmental contributions (Kramer & Porter, 2011).

Definition and Evolution: The Sustainable Economy

The sustainable economy represents a transformative economic theory and practice concept that seeks to harmonize the interplay between economic growth, environmental stewardship, and social equity. At its core, a sustainable economy is characterized by its commitment to meet the needs of the present without compromising the ability of future generations to

DOI: 10.4324/9781003544074-16

meet their own needs, a principle famously outlined in the Brundtland Report (Brundtland, 1987). This definition underscores the necessity of balancing economic activities with ecological limits and social well-being.

> **The Brundtland Report**, known as "Our Common Future", was published in 1987 by the World Commission on Environment and Development (WCED), chaired by Gro Harlem Brundtland. It is a seminal document that significantly shaped the global understanding and development of sustainable development. The report introduced the classic definition of sustainable development as "development that meets the needs of the present without compromising the ability of future generations to meet their own needs". This definition foregrounded the interconnectedness of economic growth, environmental protection, and social equity, providing a blueprint for sustainability that continues to inform policy, practice, and academic discourse on sustainable development globally (Brundtland, 1987).

Tracing the historical development of the sustainable economy requires delving into various interdisciplinary fields, including environmental ethics, economics, and social theory. The roots of sustainable economics can be found in the ecological movements of the 1960s and 1970s, which brought to light the consequences of unchecked industrial growth and resource exploitation. Seminal works like Rachel Carson's *Silent Spring* (Carson, 1962) and the Club of Rome's report *The Limits to Growth* (Meadows et al., 1972) played pivotal roles in sparking a global discourse on sustainability.

The 1980s marked a significant evolution in the concept, where sustainability began to be seen as an environmental and integrated economic issue. The Brundtland Report's definition of sustainable development provided a foundation for linking economic development with environmental and social concerns. This period also saw the emergence of concepts like the "Triple Bottom Line" introduced by John Elkington in 1994, which advocated for businesses to focus on social and environmental concerns as much as financial profits (Elkington, 1997). In the subsequent decades, the concept of a sustainable economy has continued to evolve, influenced by growing concerns over climate change, resource scarcity, and social inequality. Contemporary scholars and practitioners have expanded the scope of sustainable economics to include ideas like the circular economy, which emphasizes the reuse and regeneration of resources (Stahel, 2016), and the sharing economy, which focuses on collaborative consumption (Botsman & Rogers, 2010). These models reflect a shift towards systems thinking in economics, where the interconnections between environmental, social, and economic factors are fundamentally recognized.

The 21st century has thus seen sustainable economics move from a fringe idea to a mainstream economic agenda, with governments, corporations, and international organizations increasingly adopting sustainability principles. This shift is driven by a growing consensus that long-term economic prosperity is inextricably linked to environmental health and social equity. As such, the sustainable economy of today is viewed not only as a moral imperative but as a practical necessity for ensuring the resilience and viability of our global economic system in the face of mounting challenges.

Is it all about growth?

The concept of "Degrowth" challenges the traditional focus on economic growth, advocating for a reduction in production and consumption to protect the environment, promote social equity, and sustain natural resources. This concept suggests that true progress and well-being lie not in material wealth but in living within ecological limits, fostering resilient communities, and prioritizing quality of life over economic expansion. Degrowth emphasizes sustainable lifestyles, local economies, and renewable resources, aiming to redefine success by harmonizing human activities with the planet's health and advocating for a shift towards a more equitable and sustainable future. Critics of degrowth argue that reducing economic activity could lead to negative impacts on employment, innovation, and the ability to fund public services, potentially exacerbating poverty and inequality in the short term. They question the feasibility of degrowth in a globalized economy and emphasize the need for technological solutions and green growth strategies to address environmental challenges without sacrificing economic development.

Fundamental Principles of a Sustainable Economy

The sustainable economy is underpinned by core principles that redefine the conventional understanding of economic success. These principles, such as the circular economy, renewable resources, and social equity, form a financial system that seeks harmony between human activities and the planet's ecological balance. The circular economy represents a significant departure from the traditional linear model of "take, make, dispose of". It envisions a regenerative approach where waste is minimized, and materials are continuously cycled back into the economy. This model emphasizes the importance of designing products for longevity, reuse, and recyclability, fundamentally challenging the prevailing throwaway culture. Pioneers in this field, like Ellen MacArthur, argue that a circular economy reduces environmental impact and offers economic opportunities through innovative business models (MacArthur et al., 2015).

Renewable resources are another cornerstone of sustainable economics. Unlike finite fossil fuels, renewable resources such as solar, wind, and hydropower sustainably meet our energy needs. The shift towards renewables is an environmental imperative and an economic strategy to create resilient and diverse energy systems. Jacobson and Delucchi (2011) highlighted that transitioning to 100% renewable energy is technically feasible and economically advantageous, offering a pathway to mitigate climate change while spurring economic growth. Social equity is integral to the concept of a sustainable economy. This principle emphasizes that economic development should be inclusive, equitable, and accessible to all members of society. It challenges the disparities and injustices often accompanying financial growth, advocating for fair distribution of resources, opportunities, and benefits. As Sachs (2015) points out, sustainable development requires addressing the needs of both present and future generations, which includes tackling poverty, inequality, and social exclusion.

Collectively, these principles propose a transformative shift in how we conceive and manage economic activity. They advocate for a systemic change that aligns financial processes with ecological limits and social needs. Thus, the sustainable economy is not just a theoretical construct but a practical roadmap for creating an economically prosperous, environmentally sustainable, and socially just world.

Global and Local Perspectives on Sustainable Economics

The application and interpretation of sustainable economics exhibit significant variation across different geographical regions and cultures, reflecting the global diversity of environmental, economic, and social contexts. This diversity is critical in understanding how sustainable economic principles are adapted and implemented to meet local needs and conditions while contributing to global sustainability goals. Sustainable economics often focuses on technological innovation and efficiency improvements in the Global North, mainly Europe and North America. Countries like Germany and Denmark are at the forefront of integrating renewable energy and sustainable practices into their economic systems, driven by policy initiatives and public awareness of environmental issues (Renn et al., 2017). These regions have also pioneered the circular economy concept, with the European Union implementing comprehensive strategies to promote waste reduction and resource efficiency (Geissdoerfer et al., 2017).

Conversely, sustainable economics is frequently intertwined with development challenges in the Global South, including poverty alleviation, access to clean energy, and sustainable agriculture. For instance, in many African countries, sustainability initiatives focus on responsibly leveraging natural resources to drive economic growth and improve living standards while addressing issues like climate change and biodiversity loss (Mensah, 2019). Latin America strongly emphasizes the social dimensions of sustainability, with movements advocating for indigenous rights and equitable resource distribution (Escobar, 2011). Emerging economies like China and India present another unique perspective, balancing rapid economic growth with sustainability challenges. China, for instance, has invested heavily in renewable energy and sustainable urban development as part of its transition towards a more sustainable economic model (Zhang et al., 2017). India's approach to sustainable economics focuses on sustainable livelihoods, combining traditional knowledge with modern practices to achieve economic and environmental objectives (Agarwal, 2013).

At the local level, sustainable economic practices are often deeply rooted in traditional and indigenous knowledge systems. Communities worldwide have long practised forms of sustainable living guided by principles of harmony with nature and community well-being. These local practices provide valuable insights into sustainable resource management and community resilience, offering models to inform broader economic strategies (Berkes, 2009).

In summary, the global and local perspectives on sustainable economics reflect a rich tapestry of approaches and practices. They demonstrate that while the principles of sustainable economics are universal, their application is highly context-specific and shaped by regional environments, cultural values, and socio-economic conditions. This diversity underscores the importance of considering local realities in the global pursuit of sustainable economic development.

Theoretical Frameworks Underpinning Sustainable Economics

Various theoretical models undergird sustainable economics, offering distinct perspectives on how economies can be structured to balance environmental sustainability, social equity, and economic viability. Among these models, Doughnut Economics and the Triple Bottom Line have emerged as particularly influential in shaping contemporary understanding and practice.

Doughnut Economics, a model conceptualised by Kate Raworth, presents a radical rethinking of economic priorities. This model is visualised as a doughnut, with the inner ring representing the minimum standards for human life based on the United Nations' Sustainable Development Goals and the outer ring symbolising the ecological ceiling beyond which lies planetary degradation (Raworth, 2017). The space between these rings, the "safe and just space for humanity", represents the ideal zone where sustainable development should occur. This framework challenges the traditional focus on GDP growth and advocates for an economy within these ecological and social boundaries. Doughnut Economics presents a compelling framework for sustainable development, visualised as a doughnut-shaped space defined by planetary boundaries and social foundations. Its strength lies in its holistic perspective, integrating environmental limits with social needs (Raworth, 2017). However, the model's broad scope can pose challenges in practical application, particularly in translating its conceptual boundaries into specific policy measures and business strategies (Figure 11.1).

The Triple Bottom Line (TBL), introduced by John Elkington in the mid-1990s, is another foundational model in sustainable economics. It expands the conventional accounting framework to encompass profit, people, and the planet. This model advocates that businesses should measure their success not only in terms of financial performance (profit) but also in terms of their social (people) and environmental (planet) impact (Elkington, 1997). The TBL framework has been instrumental in encouraging businesses to adopt more sustainable practices by redefining how success is measured in the corporate world. The Triple Bottom Line model is lauded for introducing the concept of sustainability into mainstream business practice. Emphasizing profit, people, and the planet have encouraged businesses to consider social and environmental impacts alongside financial performance (Elkington, 1997). Despite its widespread adoption, critics argue that the Triple Bottom Line can lead to trade-offs between its three pillars, often with the economic aspect taking precedence. Furthermore, measuring and comparing social and environmental impacts alongside financial returns remains complex (Figure 11.2).

Beyond these, some other models and frameworks contribute to understanding sustainable economics. For instance, the Circular Economy concept challenges the traditional linear model of consumption and waste. It promotes a closed-loop system where resources are reused, remanufactured, and recycled to minimize waste and reduce the environmental impact (Geissdoerfer et al., 2017). This model has gained traction in policy and business circles as a viable approach to sustainable economic growth. The Shared Value concept, proposed by Michael Porter and Mark Kramer, is another influential framework. It suggests that businesses can generate economic value in a way that also produces value for society by addressing its challenges. This approach sees social problems as opportunities for corporate innovation, profitability, and competitive advantage (Kramer & Porter, 2011). Shared Value shifts the focus from corporate social responsibility to integrating social issues into core business strategies.

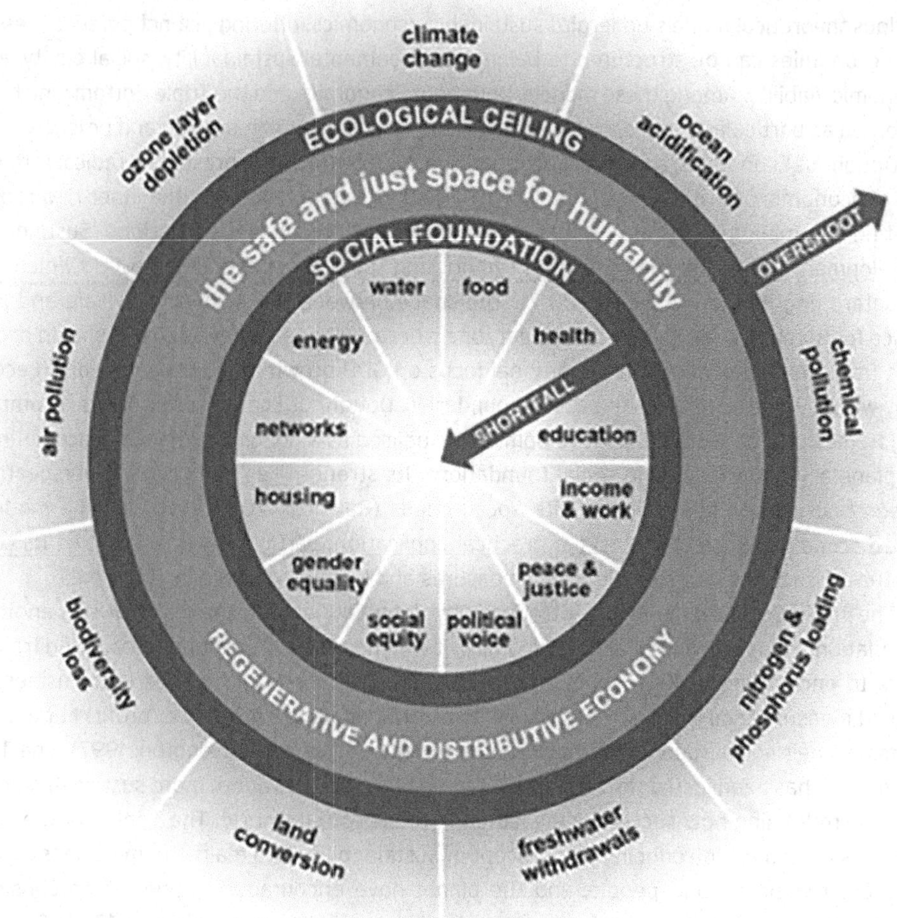

Figure 11.1 Donut Economics.

Based on Raworth (2017)

The Green Economy framework has also gained prominence in recent years, particularly following its endorsement by the United Nations Environment Programme (UNEP). This model emphasizes transitioning towards economic activities that promote environmental health, resource efficiency, and social inclusivity. It advocates for sustainable consumption and production, low-carbon technologies, and green infrastructure. The Green Economy is a pathway to sustainable development, balancing economic growth with environmental stewardship (UNEP, 2011). The framework is particularly relevant in addressing contemporary environmental challenges such as climate change and resource depletion. It promotes a transition towards low-carbon, resource-efficient, and socially inclusive economic growth (UNEP, 2011). The Green Economy's focus on practical policy measures and technological solutions is a significant strength. However, this model can be criticized for overly relying on

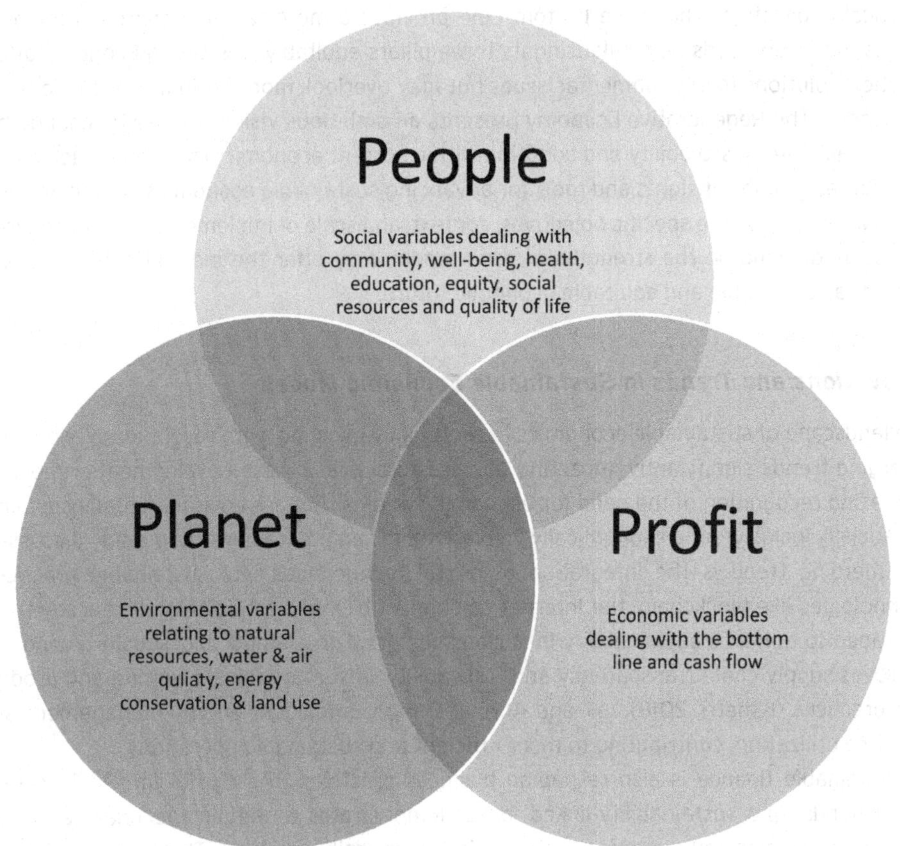

Figure 11.2 The Triple Bottom Line.

Based on Elkington (1997)

technological fixes and market mechanisms, which may not address deeper systemic equity and power dynamics issues.

In addition, the 'Regenerative Economy' notion goes beyond sustainability and aims to create systems that restore and revitalize their sources of energy and materials. Proposed by John Fullerton and others, this framework draws inspiration from living systems and nature's principles. It focuses on holistic, systemic change where economic activities contribute to the regeneration of ecosystems, communities, and cultures. This approach emphasizes resilience, adaptability, and the interconnectedness of social, environmental, and economic health (Fullerton, 2015). The challenge with the Regenerative Economy is its ambitious scope, which may make it difficult to implement on a large scale. Additionally, the model's emphasis on systemic change requires a paradigm shift in thinking and practice, which can be a significant barrier in traditional economic and political structures.

Whilst Doughnut Economics offers a comprehensive framework that aligns economic activity within ecological and social boundaries, its broad scope can be challenging in practical application. The Triple Bottom Line provides a more tangible approach for businesses but often needs help balancing its three pillars equitably. The Green Economy offers practical solutions to environmental issues but may overlook more profound systemic social challenges. The Regenerative Economy presents an ambitious vision for holistic change but faces challenges in scalability and adoption within current economic paradigms. Each model contributes valuable insights and tools for advancing sustainable economics, and their applicability depends on the specific objectives, context, and scale of implementation. A combined approach, drawing on the strengths of each model, may offer the most effective pathway towards a sustainable and equitable economic future.

Innovations and Trends in Sustainable Economic Models

The landscape of sustainable economics is continually evolving, with recent innovations and emerging trends significantly impacting business practices. These developments reflect an increasing recognition of the need for economic systems that are environmentally sustainable, socially inclusive, and economically viable. Other than the frameworks already discussed, an emerging trend is the integration of digital technologies into sustainable practices. Technologies like blockchain, the Internet of Things (IoT), and artificial intelligence (AI) are leveraged to enhance sustainability in various sectors. For example, blockchain technology improves supply chain transparency and traceability, ensuring ethical sourcing and production practices (Kshetri, 2018). IoT and AI enable more intelligent energy management and resource utilization, contributing to more efficient and sustainable operations.

Sustainable finance is also reshaping business practices. The rise of impact investing, green bonds, and sustainability-linked loans demonstrates a shift in the financial sector towards supporting environmentally and socially responsible projects. This trend is driven by a growing recognition of the financial risks associated with unsustainable practices and the opportunities presented by green and social investments (Sachs et al., 2019). Aligned with this, inclusive business models are gaining momentum, where companies focus on creating shared value by addressing social problems through their core business activities. This approach goes beyond corporate social responsibility; it involves designing products and services that serve underserved or marginalized communities, thereby contributing to social equity and economic inclusion (Porter & Kramer, 2011).

Sustainable Finance can be integrated into company strategy. Patagonia, a US-based outdoor clothing company has a commitment to sustainability which is deeply embedded in its corporate ethos, extending beyond environmental stewardship to encompass a broader range of ethical considerations. A notable instance of this commitment is the launch of its in-house venture fund, Tin Shed Ventures, which invests in environmentally and socially responsible start-up companies (Patagonia, 2024). This initiative underlines Patagonia's dedication to fostering sustainable innovation and supporting a new generation of responsible businesses (Patagonia, n.d.).

In the realm of policy and governance, there is an increasing move towards integrating sustainability into regulatory frameworks. Governments and international organizations are implementing policies that incentivize sustainable practices and penalize unsustainable ones. For instance, the European Union's Green Deal aims to make Europe climate-neutral by 2050, significantly influencing business operations and investment decisions within the region (The European Green Deal, 2019). These innovations and trends reshape businesses' operations, driving a transition towards more sustainable and responsible economic practices. They reflect a growing understanding that sustainable economics is not just a theoretical ideal but a practical necessity for long-term business success and societal well-being.

Core Components of a Sustainable Business Model

In the evolving landscape of sustainable business, specific core components are essential for creating economically viable, environmentally sound, and socially responsible models. These components–value creation, stakeholder engagement, and resource utilization–are integral to designing and implementing business practices that align with the principles of sustainable development.

Value Creation: Sustainable business extends beyond the traditional economic parameters to encompass environmental and social value. This broader perspective redefines value, emphasizing long-term benefits over short-term gains. According to the Shared Value concept by Porter and Kramer (2011), businesses can generate economic value in a way that also produces value for society, addressing its challenges and needs. This approach necessitates product, service, and business model innovation to meet societal needs while achieving profitability. An example is the development of sustainable products that reduce environmental impact while meeting consumer demands, thereby creating value for both the business and society.

Stakeholder Engagement: Is crucial in sustainable business models. It involves involving various stakeholders–customers, employees, suppliers, communities, and investors–in the business process. This engagement is not only about communication but also about incorporating stakeholder insights and concerns into business decisions. O'Riordan and Fairbrass (2008) emphasize that effective stakeholder engagement can improve sustainability outcomes, as it helps businesses understand and address their operations' social and environmental impacts. Engaging with stakeholders also builds trust and strengthens the business's social license to operate.

Resource Utilization: Sustainable business models focus on efficiency and environmental stewardship. It involves the prudent use of natural resources, minimizing waste, and adopting practices such as recycling and renewable energy use. The Circular Economy model, advocated by the Ellen MacArthur Foundation (2015), highlights the importance of designing out waste and regenerating natural systems. This approach reduces the environmental footprint and can lead to cost savings and innovation as businesses find new ways to use resources more efficiently and sustainably.

These core components–value creation, stakeholder engagement, and resource utilization–are not standalone but deeply interconnected. A sustainable business model that effectively integrates these components can harmoniously balance economic growth, environmental protection, and social welfare. Such models are pivotal in driving the transition towards a more sustainable and resilient economic future.

Design Process of Sustainable Business Models

In the intricate and systematic development of sustainable business models, an approach marked by strategic depth and iterative refinement, coupled with consistent stakeholder feedback, is paramount. This developmental journey, akin to a scholarly inquiry, unfolds through several distinct but interconnected phases, each contributing critically to aligning business practices with the overarching principles of sustainability. The process is illustrated in Figure 11.3.

The initial phase, Identifying Opportunities for Sustainability, resembles the foundational stage of a research project where businesses thoroughly examine their operations, supply chains, and prevailing market trends. This phase is akin to the literature review in academic research, where a deep understanding of the current situation is crucial. Bocken et al. (2014) emphasize the importance of this stage as a cornerstone for comprehending the existing business model and identifying critical areas for integrating sustainability.

Progressing to Stakeholder Mapping and Engagement, one can draw parallels to the methodology section in academic research. In this phase, businesses identify and categorize various stakeholders—analogous to selecting research methods and participants. This

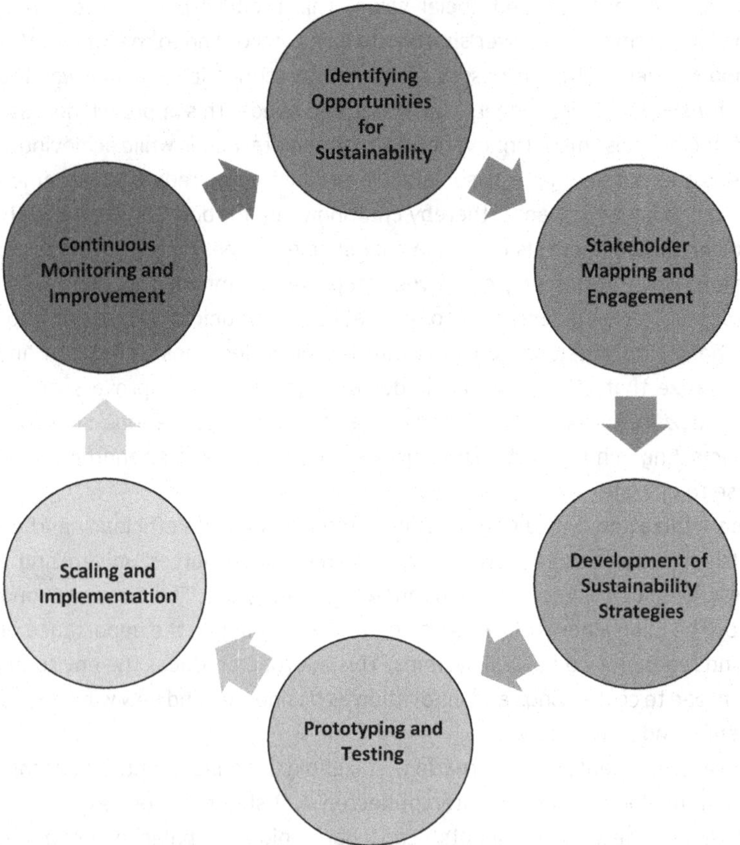

Figure 11.3 Sustainable Business Model Design Process.

engagement is not merely a procedural step; instead, it is akin to gathering empirical data. It involves actively incorporating stakeholder insights into the business decision-making process. O'Riordan and Fairbrass (2008) underscore the significance of this engagement, equating it to the critical process of data collection and analysis in research, ensuring the business model is responsive to the multifaceted impacts and opportunities of its operations.

Subsequently, businesses formulate specific strategies in the Development of Sustainability Strategies, like developing research hypotheses. This stage involves the creation of innovative products, services, and business models tailored to address identified sustainability opportunities. Porter and Kramer (2011) articulate that these strategies should aim to create shared value, mirroring the academic process of hypothesis testing where theoretical concepts are applied to practical scenarios.

Prototyping and testing these sustainability strategies is analogous to the experimental phase in scholarly research. This stage involves developing and trialling model prototypes, facilitating learning and adaptation based on real-world feedback and performance metrics. Bocken et al. (2014) highlight the experimental nature of this phase, which is essential for refining and validating the sustainability aspects of the business model. The Scaling and Implementation phase can be likened to disseminating research findings. Here, the tested and refined sustainable business models are implemented on a broader scale, necessitating strategic planning and resource management akin to publishing and advocating research findings in the academic community. Finally, the Continuous Monitoring and Improvement phase resonates with the ongoing nature of academic research. Sustainable business models require constant evaluation and adaptation to respond to evolving environmental conditions, stakeholder expectations, and market dynamics, much like academia's continuous learning and development process.

The design process of sustainable business models is reflective of an academic endeavor characterized by rigorous analysis, methodical strategy development, empirical testing, and continuous refinement. This approach demands a profound comprehension of the interrelationships among economic, environmental, and social factors and a dedication to perpetual enhancement, ensuring the realization of an economically sound business model conducive to a sustainable and equitable future.

Best Practices and Strategies for Implementing Sustainable Business Models

Implementing sustainable business models is multifaceted, demanding a strategic approach that intertwines environmental stewardship, social responsibility, and economic viability. The practices and strategies for this implementation draw from diverse real-world examples and scholarly insights, charting a course for organizations to align with contemporary sustainability standards.

A pivotal practice in this realm is the integration of sustainability into corporate governance and strategic planning. This involves embedding sustainability principles at the highest decision-making levels, ensuring that these principles permeate every aspect of the organization. A prime illustration of this is seen in Unilever's Sustainable Living Plan. This comprehensive strategy sets ambitious targets to decouple business growth from environmental impact while enhancing social impact, embodying the principle of sustainability as a core business strategy rather than a peripheral concern (Unilever, 2021). Innovation plays a critical role in the journey towards sustainability. It encompasses product or service innovation, processes, and business models. Tesla's efforts in revolutionising the automotive industry with electric vehicles and renewable energy solutions exemplify this strategy. By challenging the traditional automotive business model, Tesla demonstrates the potential and viability of sustainable transport, marking a significant stride in business model innovation (Tesla, 2020).

Unilever's Sustainable Living Plan, inaugurated in 2010, epitomizes a strategic paradigm shift in corporate sustainability. This comprehensive initiative aims to dissociate corporate growth from environmental impact, whilst augmenting social welfare. Central to its strategy are objectives to enhance health and well-being for over a billion individuals, diminish the environmental impact of its products, and improve livelihoods within its supply chain. This plan is aligned with the United Nations Sustainable Development Goals, embodying a holistic approach to the triple bottom line: People, planet, and profit. Unilever's approach transcends traditional corporate social responsibility, embedding sustainability into the core business model, thereby fostering innovation and securing long-term viability (Unilever, 2021).

The importance of stakeholder engagement and collaboration cannot be overstated. Sustainable business practices often necessitate working with a diverse range of stakeholders, including but not limited to suppliers, customers, communities, and even competitors. Patagonia's approach to engaging its supply chain in ethical and environmentally sound practices while collaborating with various organizations on environmental advocacy underscores the value of this engagement (Patagonia, 2024). Transparency and accountability form another cornerstone of sustainable business practices. Companies are increasingly expected to be transparent about their sustainability performance and impacts in today's context. Through its annual sustainability reports, Microsoft details its progress towards carbon neutrality and responsible sourcing, exemplifying the transparency that modern stakeholders demand (Microsoft, 2022).

Adapting sustainability strategies to local contexts is essential, particularly for multinational corporations. This involves tailoring approaches to each location's unique environmental, social, and regulatory landscapes. Nestlé's implementation of local sustainability programs customized to the needs and challenges of their communities is a case in point (Nestlé, 2022). Last, the measurement and management of sustainability performance are critical. Adopting frameworks such as the Global Reporting Initiative (GRI) (Global Reporting Initiative, 2024) and the Sustainability Accounting Standards Board (SASB) (SASB, 2018) aids businesses in standardizing and benchmarking their sustainability impacts. These tools facilitate the internal management of sustainability performance and communicate commitments and progress to external stakeholders, fostering a culture of continuous improvement.

These practices and strategies illustrate the nuanced approach to implementing sustainable business models. They highlight the need for a holistic view beyond mere compliance or superficial initiatives, advocating for deep-rooted business operations changes. By embracing these strategies, companies can navigate the complexities of sustainability, paving the way for innovation, resilience, and a positive contribution to society and the environment. Implementing sustainable business models is akin to a strategic symphony, where various elements must harmonize to create a sustainable, resilient, and equitable business practice. The journey is continuous, requiring ongoing commitment, adaptation, and innovation, but the rewards are substantial—for the business, society, and the planet.

Integrating Sustainable Economics into Business Practice

Integrating sustainable economics into business practice represents a significant shift from traditional business models focused primarily on profitability to models that equally prioritize environmental stewardship and social well-being. This transition is both a challenge and an opportunity for businesses in the contemporary world. At the forefront of this integration is the challenge of redefining corporate objectives. Traditional business models have primarily emphasized shareholder value, often at the expense of environmental and social considerations. However, the sustainable economic model necessitates a broader perspective. As eloquently put by Porter and Kramer (2011), businesses must look beyond profit maximisation to value creation for a broader set of stakeholders. This shift involves rethinking corporate strategies, objectives, and performance indicators to encapsulate sustainability goals.

Adopting a Systems Thinking approach is another critical aspect of this integration. Sustainable economics is not just about individual sustainable practices but about understanding and addressing the complex interdependencies within business operations and the broader environment. Meadows (2008) emphasizes the importance of systems thinking in identifying leverage points in systems where small changes can lead to significant impacts. This approach requires businesses to holistically analyze their supply chains, operations, and product lifecycles, considering the long-term impacts on the environment and society.

Systems Thinking is a holistic approach crucial for responsible business, emphasizing the interconnectedness of a company with its wider ecological, social, and economic environment. It shifts the focus from individual components to the more extensive system, acknowledging that business decisions have ripple effects across the entire network. Critical aspects of systems thinking in business include understanding the complex interplay between different elements, recognizing feedback loops, and considering long-term impacts over immediate gains. This approach helps businesses develop sustainable strategies that align with broader societal goals, fostering resilience and long-term viability (Wright & Meadows, 2009).

Cultural and organizational change within businesses is essential for effective integration. Sustainable economics requires a cultural shift within organizations, where sustainability becomes a core corporate ethos. Schaltegger and Wagner (2017) described that this involves developing new policies and practices and fostering a culture where employees at all levels are committed to sustainability goals. Training, leadership commitment, and employee engagement drive this cultural change. Similarly, innovative financing and investment management play a pivotal role in integrating sustainable economics into business practice. Traditional financing models often overlook environmental and social risks and opportunities; however, as Sachs et al. (2019) note that sustainable financing–which includes green bonds, sustainable loans, and impact investing–is gaining traction. These financial instruments allow businesses to access capital for sustainable projects, incentivizing and facilitating the transition to sustainable business practices.

Enhanced regulatory compliance is a crucial aspect of this integration. While regulatory compliance is a baseline, sustainable economics encourages businesses to go beyond compliance to become leaders in sustainability. This proactive approach involves adhering to existing environmental and social regulations, anticipating future trends and regulations, and voluntarily adopting higher standards. Vogel (2007) argues that businesses can gain a competitive advantage by exceeding regulatory requirements, improving their reputation, and reducing risks associated with unsustainable practices.

Integrating sustainable economics into business practice is a multifaceted process that requires fundamentally rethinking corporate objectives, adopting systems thinking, cultural and organizational change, innovative financing, and a proactive approach to regulatory compliance. This integration represents a paradigm shift in businesses' operations, potentially driving significant positive impacts on society and the environment. By embracing sustainable economics, businesses can contribute to the global sustainability agenda and uncover new opportunities for innovation, growth, and competitive advantage. This transformative journey is not without its challenges, but the evolving landscape of global business and increasing stakeholder expectations make it a necessary and rewarding pursuit. In essence, integrating sustainable economics into business practice is not just about implementing a set of isolated initiatives but about embedding sustainability into the very DNA of the organization. It requires a holistic and strategic approach, encompassing every aspect of business operations and decision making. As businesses navigate this journey, they become part of a more significant movement towards a more sustainable, equitable, and prosperous future.

Emerging Opportunities in Sustainable Economics: A Future Perspective

Focusing on the latest literature from the past two years, several emerging opportunities in sustainable economics within the business context are shaping the future landscape. These opportunities, reflecting the latest trends and innovations, are crucial for businesses seeking to align with sustainable development while exploring new avenues for growth and innovation. One notable area of future growth is the advancement of "Digital Sustainability". Recent literature points towards the increasing role of digital technologies in enhancing sustainable business practices. This includes using big data and analytics to improve resource efficiency, applying blockchain for supply chain transparency, and AI-driven environmental monitoring and management solutions. Integrating these technologies presents opportunities for businesses to innovate in sustainability tracking, reporting, and improvement (Bohnsack et al., 2022).

Another significant opportunity lies in the development of sustainable urban infrastructure. With urbanization continuing rapidly, there is a growing need for sustainable solutions in urban development. This includes green building practices, sustainable urban planning, and integrating renewable energy systems in urban settings. Recent studies emphasize the potential for businesses to create sustainable cities, addressing challenges related to energy, waste, and transportation (Ferrer et al., 2018). The expansion of the economy is also emerging as a critical area. The economy uses renewable biological resources to produce food, energy, and industrial goods. Recent advancements in biotechnology and the increasing demand for sustainable products are driving opportunities in this sector. Businesses can innovate in bio-based materials, biofuels, and biodegradable products, contributing to a more circular economy Marshall et al (2022).

Similarly, ecosystem services and biodiversity markets present an innovative area for business engagement. The recent emphasis on valuing and protecting ecosystem services and biodiversity is leading to the development of new markets. Businesses can explore opportunities in ecosystem restoration, conservation finance, and biodiversity credits, aligning economic activities with environmental stewardship (Goldstein, 2021).

Last, the shift towards sustainable consumerism is creating new market opportunities. With increasing consumer awareness and demand for sustainable products, businesses can innovate in sustainable product design, ethical sourcing, and green marketing. Research indicates a growing market segment of environmentally conscious consumers, opening avenues for businesses to cater to this demographic while promoting sustainable consumption patterns (Niinimäki, 2021).

Exercises

A. KNOW

Use the below multiple-choice questions to test your knowledge. Each answer may be wrong or right, and there may be zero to four right or wrong answers per question:

1. What does the concept of "sustainable economics" emphasize?
   a. ...Maximizing short-term profits.
   b. ...Focusing solely on environmental conservation.
   c. ...Balancing economic growth with environmental stewardship and social equity.
   d. ...Prioritizing industrial growth over resource management.
2. What does the "circular economy" model emphasize?
   a. ...A linear model of consumption.
   b. ...Minimizing waste and cycling materials back into the economy.
   c. ...Sole focus on renewable energy.
   d. ...Maximizing resource extraction.

3. Which concept focuses on creating economic value that also benefits society?
    a. ...Profit Maximization.
    b. ...The Shared Value Concept.
    c. ...Traditional Corporate Governance.
    d. ...Linear Economic Models.
4. Which approach is essential for integrating sustainable economics into business practice?
    a. ...Avoiding stakeholder engagement.
    b. ...Focusing solely on short-term profitability.
    c. ...Adopting systems thinking.
    d. ...Maintaining traditional business models.
5. How does the concept of Doughnut Economics visualize sustainable development?
    a. ...As an unlimited growth model.
    b. ...By prioritizing financial growth over environmental concerns.
    c. ...Ignoring social equity.
    d. ...Through a doughnut-shaped space defined by planetary boundaries and social foundations.

B. THINK

Imagine you are the finance director of an organization, and you would like to transition from your business-as-usual ways of working to embrace sustainable economics. How would you begin the process?

C. DO

Review the core components of a sustainable business model: Value creation, stakeholder engagement, and resource utilization. Map out how these apply to the business model of your current organization, or one with which you are familiar. Can you identify any strengths and weaknesses that pertain to the organization? How may you accentuate the strengths and mitigate the challenges?

D. RELATE

Consider Unilever's Sustainable Living Plan. Review the current performance of the company and assess how the plan has contributed to their financial and non-financial results. Are you able to relate aspects of their success or performance with the plan?

E. BE

Consider the concept of degrowth. How do feel about it? Do you believe that is a viable alternative to sustainable economic growth? Is it a realistic proposition in today's global economy?

Feedback

A. KNOW

Feedback 1

a. Wrong: A focus on maximizing short-term profits does not align with sustainability thinking.
b. Wrong: Focusing solely on environmental conservation is too narrow. Social and Economic considerations must be addressed too.
c. Right: Sustainable economics is about harmonizing economic growth with environmental stewardship and social equity, as outlined in the chapter.
d. Wrong: Prioritizing industrial growth over resource management will not result in sound economic management.

Feedback 2

a. Wrong: A linear model of consumption is the traditional focus which does not consider reuse of waste as a resource.
b. Right: A circular economy model is about minimizing waste and ensuring materials are reused, remanufactured, or recycled, contrasting with the linear "take, make, dispose of" model.
c. Wrong: Renewable energy may feature in an organization's sustainability efforts but is not the sole focus of a circular economic model.
d. Wrong: Maximizing resource extraction is likely to lead to an uneconomically sound business model.

Feedback 3

a. Wrong: A focus on profit maximization usually only benefits shareholders and executives rather than society more generally.
b. Right: The Shared Value Concept, as described by Porter and Kramer, focuses on creating economic value that also benefits society.
c. Wrong: Traditional Corporate Governance can be narrow in its focus and as such does not extend to creating benefits for society.
d. Wrong: Linear Economic Models can be wasteful and not provide enhanced social and economic benefits.

Feedback 4

a. Wrong: Stakeholder engagement is essential to the success of any organization.
b. Wrong: Focusing solely on short-term profitability does not enable organizations to meet its social and environmental responsibilities.
c. Right: Adopting systems thinking is essential for integrating sustainable economics into business practice, recognizing the interconnectedness of various business aspects.
d. Wrong: Maintaining traditional business models preserves business-as-usual and fails to recognize the changing nature of the world today.

Feedback 5

a. Wrong: Donut economics acknowledges that there are limits to growth and planetary boundaries.

b. Wrong: Social, economic, and environmental concerns are all considered equally.

c. Wrong: The model places social equity at its core.

d. Right: Doughnut Economics visualizes sustainable development as a doughnut-shape space, with the inner ring representing social foundations.

B. THINK

Level	*Sustainable economic transitions*	*Notes*
+	You begin with stakeholder mapping and engagement ensuring buy in of key internal and external stakeholders.	
=	You prioritize the development of sustainability policies and begin their implementation.	
–	You don't know where to begin and decide to continue with business-as-usual.	

C. DO

Level	*Core components of a sustainable business model*	*Notes*
+	You have identified one or more strengths or weaknesses inherent in your organizations business model and considered actions that extenuate or mitigate these.	
=	You have identified one or more strengths or weaknesses inherent in your organizations business model but are unable to identify any specific actions.	
–	You are unable to identify any strengths or weaknesses inherent in your organizations business model.	

D. RELATE

Level	Sustainable living plan	Notes
+	You have considered Unilever's Sustainable Living Plan and related their performance with aspects of the plan.	
=	You have considered Unilever's Sustainable Living Plan and reviewed their performance but are not able to relate any success or challenge with the plan.	
–	You have not considered Unilever's Sustainable Living Plan, or you have not reviewed their performance.	

E. BE

Level	Growth or degrowth?	Notes
+	Thoughtful consideration and description of your thoughts and emotions regarding degrowth.	
=	Basic understanding of the concept of degrowth and unable to form an opinion.	
–	No or little insight into own thoughts regarding degrowth and its implications.	

References

Agarwal, B. (2013). *Food security, productivity, and gender inequality* (R. J. Herring, Ed.). Oxford University Press.

Berkes, F. (2009). Indigenous ways of knowing and the study of environmental change. *Journal of the Royal Society of New Zealand, 39*(4), 151–156.

Bocken, N. M. P., Short, S. W., Rana, P., & Evans, S. (2014). A literature and practice review to develop sustainable business model archetypes. *Journal of Cleaner Production, 65*, 42–56.

Bohnsack, R., Bidmon, C. M., & Pinkse, J. (2022). Sustainability in the digital age: Intended and unintended consequences of digital technologies for sustainable development. *Business Strategy and the Environment, 31*(2), 599–602.

Botsman, R., & Rogers, R. (2010). *What's mine is yours: The rise of collaborative consumption*. HarperBusiness.

Brundtland, G. (1987). *Report of the World Commission on Environment and Development: Our Common Future* (A/42/427). United Nations General Assembly.

Carson, R. L. (1962). *Silent spring*. Houghton Mifflin.

Elkington, J. (1997). *Cannibals with forks: The triple bottom line of 21st century business*. Capstone.

Escobar, A. (2011). Sustainability: Design for the pluriverse. *Development (Society for International Development), 54*(2), 137–140.

Ferrer, A. L. C., Thomé, A. M. T., & Scavarda, A. J. (2018). Sustainable urban infrastructure: A review. *Resources, Conservation, and Recycling, 128*, 360–372.

Fullerton, J. (2015). *Regenerative capitalism: How universal principles and patterns will shape our new economy*. Capital Institute.

Geissdoerfer, M., Savaget, P., Bocken, N. M. P., & Hultink, E. J. (2017). The circular economy - A new sustainability paradigm? *Journal of Cleaner Production*, *143*, 757–768.

Global Reporting Initiative. (2024). *GRI - Universal standards*. GRI. https://www.globalreporting.org/standards/standards-development/universal-standards/

Goldstein, B. (2021). Ecosystem services and biodiversity markets: New business frontiers. *Ecosystem Services Journal*.

Ioannou, I., & Serafeim, G. (2019). The consequences of mandatory corporate sustainability reporting: evidence from four countries. *Harvard Business School Research Working Paper No. 11-100*.

Jacobson, M. Z., & Delucchi, M. A. (2011). Providing all global energy with wind, water, and solar power, Part I: Technologies, energy resources, quantities and areas of infrastructure, and materials. *Energy Policy*, *39*(3), 1154–1169.

Kramer, M. R., & Porter, M. (2011). Creating shared value. *Harvard Business Review*, *89*(1/2), 62–77.

Kshetri, N. (2018). Blockchain's roles in meeting key supply chain management objectives. *International Journal of Information Management*, *39*, 80–89.

MacArthur, E., Waughray, D., & Stuchtey, M. R. (2015). *The circular economy*. McKinsey & Company.

Marshall, D., O'Dochartaigh, A., Prothero, A., Reynolds, O., & Secchi, E. (2022). Why businesses need to embrace the bioeconomy. *MIT Sloan Management Review*, *64*(2), 13–15.

Meadows, D. H. (2008). *Thinking in systems: A primer*. Chelsea Green Publishing.

Meadows, D. H., Meadows, D. L., Randers, J., & Behrens, W. W. (1972). *The limits to growth: A report for the Club of Rome's project on the predicament of mankind*. Universe Books.

Mensah, J. (2019). Sustainable development: Meaning, history, principles, pillars, and implications for human action: Literature review. *Cogent Social Sciences*, *5*(1), 1653531.

Microsoft. (2022). *2022 Environmental Sustainability Report*. Microsoft Corporation. https://query.prod.cms.rt.microsoft.com/cms/api/am/binary/RW15mgm

Nestlé. (2022). *Creating Shared Value and Sustainability Report 2022*. Nestlé. https://www.nestle.com/sites/default/files/2023-03/creating-shared-value-sustainability-report-2022-en.pdf

Niinimäki, K. (2021). Sustainable consumerism: New directions and opportunities. *Journal of Cleaner Production*.

O'Riordan, L., & Fairbrass, J. (2008). Corporate social responsibility (CSR): Models and theories in stakeholder dialogue. *Journal of Business Ethics*, *83*(4), 745–758.

Patagonia. (2024). *Environmental & Social Footprint - Patagonia*. https://www.patagonia.com/our-footprint/

Patagonia. (n.d.). *Tin Shed Ventures – Patagonia's venture capital fund*. TinShedVentures. Retrieved 26 January 2024, from https://www.tinshedventures.com/approach/

Porter, M. E., & Kramer, M. R. (2011). The big idea: Creating shared value. *Harvard Business Review*, *89*(1), 2.

Raworth, K. (2017). *Doughnut economics: Seven ways to think like a 21st-century economist*. Chelsea Green Publishing.

Renn, O., Lucas, K., Haas, A., & Jaeger, C. (2017). Sustainability and resilience in the European Union: A case study of the German energy transition. *European Journal of Futures Research*, *5*(1), 1–11.

Sachs, J. D. (2015). *The age of sustainable development*. Columbia University Press.

Sachs, J. D., Woo, W. T., Yoshino, N., & Taghizadeh-Hesary, F. (2019). Importance of green finance for achieving sustainable development goals and energy security. *Handbook of Green Finance*, 3–12. https://doi.org/10.1007/978-981-13-0227-5_13

SASB. (2018, August 3). *SASB Standards overview*. SASB. https://sasb.org/standards/

Schaltegger, S., & Burritt, R. (2018). Business cases and corporate engagement with sustainability: Differentiating ethical motivations. *Journal of Business Ethics*, *147*(2), 241–259.

Schaltegger, S., & Wagner, M. (2017). Managing and measuring the business case for sustainability: Capturing the relationship between sustainability performance, business competitiveness and economic performance. In *Managing the business case for sustainability* (pp. 1–27). Routledge.

Stahel, W. R. (2016). The circular economy. *Nature*, *531*(7595), 435–438.

Tesla. (2020). *Impact Report. Tesla, Inc.* https://www.tesla.com/ns_videos/2020-tesla-impact-report.pdf

The European Green Deal. (2019). *European Commission*. European Commission.

Towards a Circular Economy: Business Rationale for an Accelerated Transition. (2015). Ellen MacArthur Foundation.

UNEP. (2011). *Towards a green economy: Pathways to sustainable development and poverty eradication*. United Nations Environment Programme.

Unilever. (2021). *Unilever Sustainable Living Plan 2010 to 2020*. https://www.unilever.com/files/92ui5egz/production/16cb778e4d31b81509dc5937001559f1f5c863ab.pdf
Vogel, D. (2007). *The market for virtue: The potential and limits of corporate social responsibility*. Brookings Institution Press.
Wright, D., & Meadows, D. H. (2009). *Thinking in systems*. Earthscan.
Zhang, Y., Li, H., Zhang, X., Wang, F., & Weber, R. (2017). The rise of South-South trade and its effect on global CO_2 emissions. *Nature Communications*, *8*(1), 1–6.

12 Envisioning Responsible Business

Effective moves towards responsible business must be bold, disruptive, and visionary. Old-established management wisdom in many cases must be altered significantly, if not abandoned completely to keep pace with the rapid degradation of humanity's habitat. To make tangible strides towards becoming a truly responsible business and reaching the goal of becoming a sustainable business, there is no place for superficial and unaligned management moves. Questions must be made putting the very foundations, procedures, values, and wisdoms to a test—a sustainability test. The two most fundamental questions are 1) What is the businesses' **primary motivation** and objective? Profit or non-profit (e.g. furthering a certain cause, being a virtuous business)? 2) What is the responsible businesses' **development strategy**? Growth or non-growth (e.g. maintenance of actual business or even degrowth)?

There is a responsible business strategy for every company. Even the aggressively economic growth seeking and profit maximizing type will find a responsible business strategy going along with those basic drivers at least in the short and medium run. However, they might be well-advised to also rethink these basic characteristics in the long run. Both drivers' primary motivation and development strategy are not fixed and thus may change through time. A purely profit maximizing company for instance might, with a change in organizational culture, become a company beginning to focus rather on its virtuous characteristics. It must be remarked that the conceptualization of primary motivation and development strategy is one that we find particularly helpful in the context of responsible business for sustainable development. However, there may be many other valuable ways of envisioning responsible business, especially in different contexts.

Primary Motivations for Becoming a Responsible Business

Businesses' primary motivations for responsible business as depicted in Figure 12.1 can be subdivided into two types: Profit motivation and non-profit motivations. It must be stressed that those two types are not mutually exclusive. A motivation here refers to a primary motivation, which leaves ample room for subsequent secondary motivations. A business might for instance primarily be motivated by increasing profitability but aim at doing so by furthering social and environmental performance—a typical non-profit motivation. The other way

DOI: 10.4324/9781003544074-17

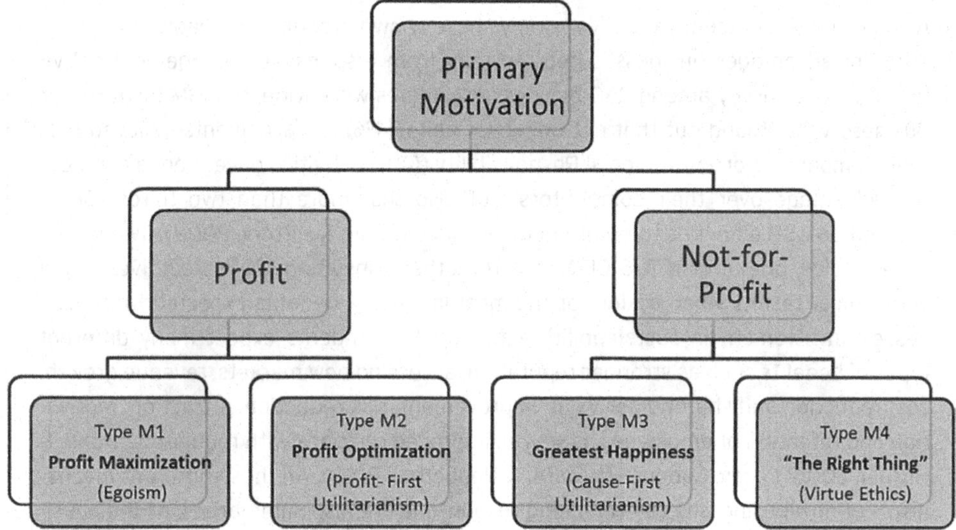

Figure 12.1 Primary Motivations for Responsible Business.

around a social enterprise with the primary goal of reducing poverty might realize that such an endeavor may only have the intended effect—reducing poverty—when being economically viable; and profitable.

"The business case"

The central question for the validity of profit motivation for responsible business is: "Is responsible business profitable? The inevitable answer is: "It depends". Research of quantitative links between socio-environmental business performance and financial performance has provided positive, negative, and neutral results. However, most of the research suggests a positive relationship between responsible behaviors and profits (Griffin & Mahoon, 1997; Orlitzky, Schmidt, & Rynes, 2003; Roman, Hayibor, & Agle, 1999).

While academia still searches for the proverbial philosopher's stone, practice seems to be fairly convinced that being a responsible business pays off. The Corporate Responsibility Officers Association asked if the respondents' companies can prove that they increased profits by being responsibly; 68.5% confirmed that responsible business has proven profitable, while 31.2% stated they could not measure it. Only 0.3% had found responsible business activities to be unprofitable (Corporate Responsibility Magazine, 2010). As early as 2002, the World Business Council for Sustainable Development (2002) had stated that:

> ...pursuing a mission of sustainable development can make our firms more competitive, more resilient to shocks, nimbler in a fast-changing world, more unified in purpose, more likely to attract and hold customers, and the best employees, and more at ease with regulators, banks, insurers and the financial market.

A wide variety of recent executive surveys have shown breadth and magnitude of the different advantages businesses hope to reap from responsible management activities. During a survey among 250 business executives worldwide, the IBM Institute for Business Value found out that not only over half (54%) of participants believed that their companies Corporate Social Responsibility (CSR) activities gave them a competitive advantage over their competitors, but also that more than two thirds (68%) focused on CSR activities to create new revenues (Pohle & Hittner, 2008). Two worldwide studies, one among 766 CEOs and the other consulting 1200 executives found very similar results when asking for the most important benefits expected from businesses' involvement in sustainability activities. Respondents expect many different types of benefits such as stronger reputation, accessing new markets, revenue growth, cost reduction and shareholder value improvement, risk reduction, attraction, motivation and retention of employees as well as improved relations with regulators (Pohle & Hittner, 2008; Lacey, Cooper, Hayward, & Neuberger, 2010). All those different mechanisms of how businesses can win being responsible are also summarized as the "business case" for responsible business.

A profit motivation for engaging with responsible business is strongly based on the achievement of a sound business case for responsible business and can be subdivided into two categories. A business motivated by profit maximization follows an egoist ethical decision making and will only engage in responsible business practices if there is no other activity or investment opportunity more profitable than making a commitment to responsible business activities (Thielemann & Wettstein, 2008). Also, might such a profit maximizing business be tempted to behave irresponsibly always when the irresponsible business activity promises higher profits (Vogel, 2005)? Carr (1968) even claims that the business context is characterized by a generally lower morale than the private context and that profit maximization leads to irresponsible behavior.

Irresponsible profit maximization in practice

Germany's leading poultry brand Wiesenhof, which translates "meadow farm", has made the slogan "Responsibility for people, animals and environment" its public credo (PHW, 2011). In 2011, a report by public German television showed a different picture. The report starts with the words "Pictures which are not directed at the general public; pictures that provide insight into a system with profit as the first priority". The documentary "The Wiesenhof System" claims that the only and ultimate priority of the company is profit and gives evidence by showcasing cost-reducing, but barbarous farming practices, cost-efficient, but inhumane working conditions, and depletion of local groundwater resources (Anthes & Verheyen, 2011).

Fortunately, nowadays the business context has become very favorable to responsible business being the highest-profit alternative. As illustrated in the box on the business case for responsible business, the reasons for believing that responsibility will pay-off are manifold and there is sound evidence for a profit maximizing business to believe that business responsibility makes maximum money sense.

Responsible profit maximization in practice

An interesting example of how profit maximization can lead to a role-model responsible business activity is the birth story of the Toyota Prius, the world's first mass-produced alternative engine-powered car. The primary motivation of Toyota to venture into the Prius was a concern about the future profitability of the car business because of rising oil prices and environmental damage, a typical profit maximization rationale (Taylor, 2006). In hindsight, the move towards the Prius was one of the cornerstones of Toyota's market leader position in the worldwide auto industry (Laasch & Flores, 2010).

In contrast to a business striving for maximum profit, the one striving for profit optimization will not aim at maximum profit as the only goal. A profit-optimizing business will aim at maximum profit, while paying attention to the parallel second-order condition of acting responsibly, so long as in acting responsibly such a profit optimizing business will make the most profitable choice. One could also call profit optimization profit-first utilitarianism, as the company will always aim at creating as much social, environmental, and economic value as possible (the "greatest happiness principle") while favoring profit and economic value creation first.

Profit optimization in practice

An impressive example of such a profit-optimizing responsible business is Procter & Gamble's (P&Gs) approach to social and environmental business performance. Instead of talking about responsibilities, P&G refers to opportunities in sustainable behavior. P&G in 2007 aimed at drastically increasing its percentage of sustainable innovation products in their portfolio (Laasch & Flores, 2010). P&G has seen a shared opportunity between society, environment, and the company's profit in so-called sustainable innovation products with an improved social and/or environmental impact. The opportunity for society and environment lies in the immense environmental impact that the consumer-packaged goods company has in the use phase of its products, such as detergents, nappies, and grooming products. The business opportunity for P&G lies in seizing the immense market opportunity (roughly 75% of the overall market) in the so-called "sustainable mainstream customers" segment (Procter & Gamble, 2011).

Businesses primarily motivated by non-profit objectives can be subdivided into the ones aiming at creating the greatest happiness among all their stakeholders and the ones aiming at achieving virtuousness and doing "the right thing".[1] One might be tempted to say that those two types of motivation do not sound very much like a traditional business motivation. As a matter of fact, those motivational patterns can rather be found among social or environmental entrepreneurial ventures, not traditional businesses indeed.

Businesses operating based upon the greatest happiness motivation usually start up with the urgent drive to mitigate or solve a pressing social or environmental issue, which is why they make this issue their cause and the very core of all business activity. Such "cause-driven businesses" interestingly are often quick-growth, high-revenue ventures as the possibility to make the greatest impact on the cause, to achieve greatest happiness, are inseparably married to the growth success of such a business. One could also call this business motivation for responsible management "cause-first" utilitarianism. Such businesses might be very successful economically to mitigate their cause. Cause-first, then profit.

Greatest happiness in practice

TOMS Shoes for instance started up with the greatest happiness principle as its very initial motivation. The TOMS founder was searching for a business solution to giving shoes to poor children in Argentina and later all over the world. The company's founder Blake Mycoskie describes the initial thought for founding the company as "What if I started a shoe company and every time I sold a pair of shoes, I gave a pair away? And that way, as long as I keep selling shoes, those kids will have shoes for the rest of their life. ... This was when I decided, I am going to build this into the most successful, profitable, and charitable shoe company in the world" (TOMS Shoes, 2009).

While a business is aimed at creating greatest happiness measure fulfillment externally, by how much good it has done, a business primarily being motivated by improving its virtuousness is rather focusing on its internal acts and how to live up to the values the business stands for. Such a business might rather focus on the qualitative than the quantitative aspects of its responsible business activities.

Virtuousness in practice

The UK-based smoothie business Innocent carries virtuousness in its name. The whole brand image is based on virtuous "innocent" products and operations. Smoothies are made of "pure crushed fruits and juices. No added sugar. No concentrates" (Design Council, 2010; Innocent Drinks, 2008). This virtuous value of purity is complemented by a "...non-corporate attitude, a sincere commitment to the cause and creative thinking" as additional virtues (CSA, 2011). When Innocent sold a minor stake to The Coca Cola Company to finance its European growth activities in 2009, a central point in the agreement was that the Innocent values and the existing labor structures would remain untouched (Sweney, 2009).

Development Strategies for Becoming a Responsible Business

Being responsible can be pursued in two drastically distinct underlying business strategies, permeating any subsequent business decision. Figure 12.2 illustrates the main **development strategies** for responsible business subsumed under the headings of growth and non-growth strategies. A growth-oriented responsible business strategy will aim at quantitatively increasing the business in the economic dimension, in market share, profit, and revenue. Growth might be pursued at all costs or responsibly. Non-growth strategies aim at qualitative development of the business, which could lead to a maintenance of the company's economic status quo or even to a degrowth situation, a shrinking of the businesses' economic size. A voluntarily degrowing business sounds counter-intuitive in a traditional capitalist-competitive economy. As a matter of fact, an arduous discussion questioning the compatibility of degrowth and capitalism is in full swing (Martínez-Alier, Pascual, Vivien, & Zaccai, 2010; Foster, 2011). Nevertheless, degrowth of consumption patterns, and economic activity has been identified as a prerequisite for sustainable world development. The chapter on systemic change will further illustrate the enablers, inhibitors, and scenarios of a degrowing world economy.

A business pursuing a growth "at all costs" strategy will only apply responsible management if it is providing the most attractive growth opportunity. Many traditional businesses from mining to alcohol, weapons and junk food may be categorized as displaying growth at-all-cost strategies. An expansion of those businesses due to their indisputably negative footprint always has negative effects on society and/or the environment; and thus leads to the destruction of social, environmental, and economic capital. Often such companies are over-proportionally active in responsible management activities, mostly superficially "doing good things", media-attractive, but largely unrelated to the overwhelming negative effects of the company's core-business. Such behavior can be explained with the so-called license to operate. Businesses being perceived as largely irresponsible might experience serious resistance against their growth efforts or even against their mere resistance. Figuratively

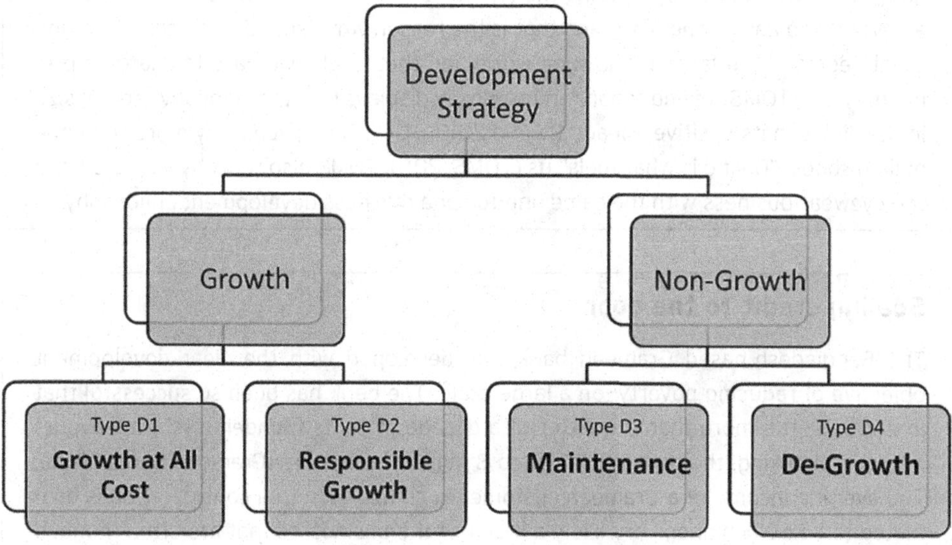

Figure 12.2 Development Strategies for Responsible Business.

speaking, society might withdraw their social license to operate (Gunningham, Kagan, & Thornton, 2002).

Growth at all costs in practice

Marketing among children is an important element of McDonald's growth strategy. A 2011 pledge to "fire Ronald McDonald" may be interpreted as a social uproar against the irresponsible- "growth at all costs" strategy of marketing unhealthy junk food to the ones most vulnerable to such marketing activities–children. The letter was jointly signed by 550 health professionals and organizations (Jargon, 2011). McDonald's on the other hand conducts extensive responsible management activities largely in line with the company's growth strategy. The company's responsibility report claims what McDonald's "is made of", presenting an extensive list of topical responsible management practices which reads as follows: "Nutrition and Wellbeing, sustainable supply chain, environmental responsibility, employee experience, and community" (McDonald's, 2011).

A responsible growth strategy aims at combining responsible management activity and company growth. The match seems to provide a highly promising mechanism. As seen in the box on the business case, responsible management activities have an outstanding potential to be market openers, to create new revenues and innovation. Nevertheless, a growth strategy can only lead to a sustainable business if the growth strategy is based on a sound positive social, environmental, and economic impact of the business activity which is being increased.

Responsible growth in practice

Entrepreneur Blake Mycoskie impressively "reveals his company's very basic development strategy, which aims at achieving growth, based on a positive social and economic business impact. By creating the one-for-one model with TOMS we have created a never going away benefactor and that is the reason why I spend as much time hiring great people in the fashion and shoe world and that is why we have to charge a premium price". TOMS "giving report" impressively displays how the company grew in size in parallel with its positive impact. By mid-2010, TOMS had given away more than one million shoes. "Giving is what fuels" us (TOMS, 2011). TOMS also recently ventured into the eyewear business with the same one-for-one business development philosophy.

Scaling credit to the poor

The Bangladesh-based Grameen bank was developed with the clear development objective of reducing poverty–on a large scale. The bank has been so successful that in 2009, a little more than a quarter of a decade after its founders first endeavours into microbanking, the bank had close to 8 million customers (Grameen Bank, 2011b). The average income of a Grameen customer in comparison to a control group is estimated to be 50% higher, very likely a result of the businesses that are often founded with the credit from Grameen Bank (Grameen Bank, 2011a).

Slowly, maintenance strategies for responsible business become a visible phenomenon. Businesses aiming at maintenance of their economic scope usually have accepted their negative impact on society and environment related to relentless growth. Maintenance often sees qualitative improvements as an alternative to total economic growth. Sustainability thinking makes increased profitability through unchanged size an ever more attractive option.

Maintenance strategy in practice

The company Patagonia, a world leader in outdoor clothing, displays a somewhat different perspective on their development strategy towards responsible business. "We don't want to grow larger but want to remain lean and quick. We want to make the best clothes and make them so they will last a long, long time. Our idea is to make the best product so you can consume less and consume better. Every decision we make must include its impact on the environment. We want to zero in on quality" (Chouinard & Gallagher, 2004). The outdoor clothing company aims at becoming a truly virtuous responsible business, transforming its basic processes and culture towards more sustainable ways. Patagonia's "Footprint Chronicles" give insight into the extensive effort being made to transparently transform the business from the inside, beginning with its products. Patagonia's development strategy arises from the insight "... that everything we do as a business ... leaves its mark on the environment. There is still no such thing as sustainable business" (Patagonia, 2011).

Probably the least common strategy for a typical market-economy business is responsible degrowth. Businesses might realize that the only possibility to become a sustainable business in the long run is to reduce its scale. Degrowth is perhaps the most complex strategic approach to responsible business development. Companies reducing size in most cases also need to reduce the number of staff, a move with potentially severe social consequences. Degrowth often goes against the most basic incentives of a competitive market system; the business that shrinks is perceived to have lost in competition. Reducing market share, reducing revenues, reducing business units, reducing the product line, or even actively decreasing the market goes against the very basis of the free market: Competition.

Baby steps towards degrowth in practice

While Unilever does not aim at degrowing the economic business volume, the company at least aims at de-coupling their economic growth from their negative environmental impact. The company's plan reads as follows: "We will decouple our growth from our environmental impact, achieving absolute reductions across the product lifecycle. Our goal is to halve the environmental footprint of the making and use of our products" (Unilever, 2010). If these commitments contribute to an overall degrowth of the company's environmental impact, one will need to scrutinize if this halving of impact refers to the relative impact per product or the total impact of all the company's products.

Examples displaying large scale degrowth efforts of companies are hard to find. Nevertheless, there are hints of at least partial degrowth activities. For instance, "responsible consumption" has become a common cause of many alcohol companies. Telling your customers to consume responsibly and avoid addictive consumption patterns implicitly means to recommend consumers to consume less. Nevertheless, such efforts only display partial degrowth, which does not ensure the overall degrowth of the company.

A cautionary tale

The Body Shop, a pioneering ethical brand established nearly 50 years ago in Brighton, UK, by Dame Anita Roddick, has faced challenges in maintaining its ethical image in an evolving market, and in early 2024 went into administration placing 2200 jobs at risk. Initially lauded for its stand against animal testing and commitment to sustainable practices, the brand struggled to keep pace with changing consumer expectations and market dynamics. Today's competitive landscape demands continuous innovation and adaptation, aspects where The Body Shop faltered, leading to its decline. The brand's experience underscores the importance of evolving ethical stances and business strategies to remain relevant and competitive, highlighting the need for continual reinvention in both product offerings and ethical commitments.

Making Responsible Business Commitments

The first step towards making a commitment to responsible business must be to make a conscious decision on the basic parameters of what the company's way towards sustainable business should be. What should be the primary motivation, profit or not? How should we develop the business, growing or not? Those basic questions, which define the conditions of responsible business conduct, are of crucial importance. The answers given drastically change how responsible business activities will be implemented. It sounds very drastic, but there *is* a strong case for drastic decisions due to the urgency of becoming sustainable. If a company is not able to become a sustainable business while growing, a growth strategy coupled with whatever good deeds on the way cannot reflect truly responsible business practice. Figures 12.3 and 12.4 illustrate the different types of businesses emerging from combining the basic parameters of responsible business described in the preceding section. For instance, a business primarily motivated by profit and growth is a "business as usual", while a company with the primary motivation to create the "greatest happiness" and aiming at responsible growth is a so-called "responsibility superstar" due to its often star-like rise. A business aiming at maintenance and profit optimization is titled "Utilitarian Capitalist", while a company degrowing and motivated by being a virtuous business is described as a "Pure Virtue Business". Figure 12.4 is a self-analysis tool to categorize businesses' basic parameters of responsible business strategy.

Only the company that has identified those basic parameters of its long run perspective can credibly commit to responsible business. Anything else could be unsubstantiated and hollow talk. The two most fundamental components of a formal commitment to responsible business must be its primary motivation and its development strategy. The technicalities of

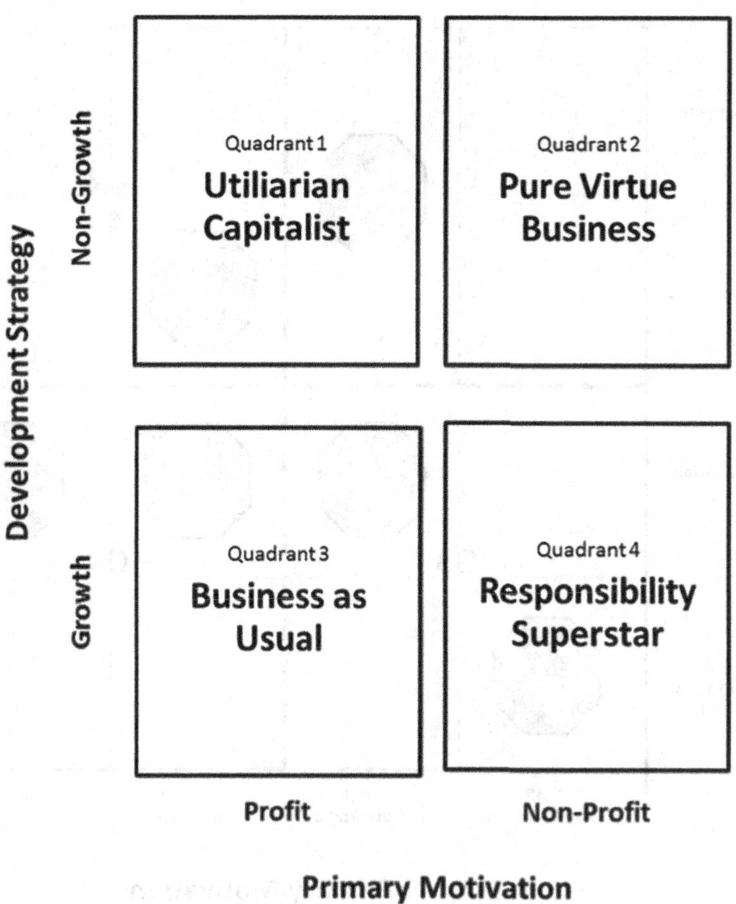

Figure 12.3 Responsible Business Categories and Self-Assessment.

committing to responsible business, what communication instruments to use and how to design such a commitment from a communication perspective will be covered in the chapters on communicating in responsible business. Nevertheless, already at this point two crucial best-practices in making a responsible business commitment need to be highlighted. Without those two points, commitments made have the tendency to be paper tigers without effecting real change inside the company.

1) **Show high-level leadership** and make living up to the commitment a priority! If responsible business is taken seriously a company making a commitment to it has profound changes ahead. Only if the responsible businesses change is signaled from the very top of the organization such changes are possible. A large-scale survey among responsibility officers revealed that 77% of companies had made a commitment to ethical-responsible values by their leadership team, while only 63% regularly communicate this commitment, only 61% of the C-level leaders showed personal action based on those values and even then only half of the leaders would turn down a business offer that contradicts the

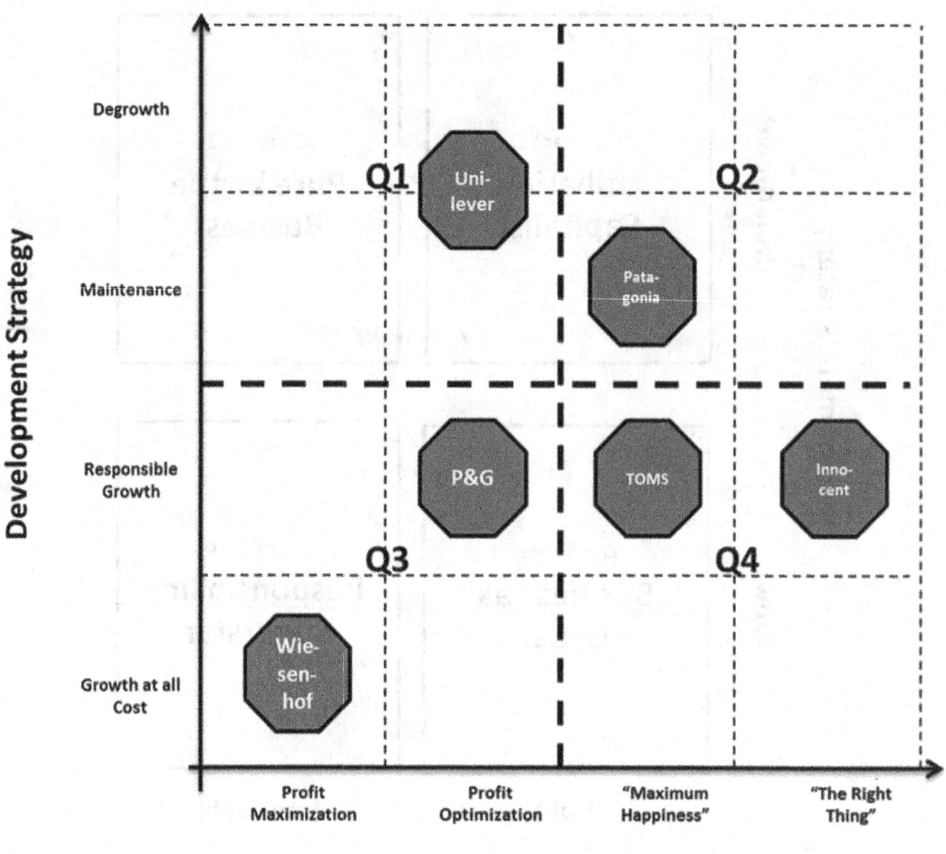

Figure 12.4 Responsible Business Parameters.

responsible business commitment (Corporate Responsibility Magazine, 2010). Interestingly, 42% of CEOs care personally for their companies' commitment to responsible business. When being asked about why they had acted on responsible business, the third biggest driver of such activity is the personal motivation of the CEO (Lacey, Cooper, Hayward, & Neuberger, 2010). With such broad personal commitment doors are open to get the C-level leadership team on board when planning and making responsible business commitments. Corporate responsibility officers perceived strategic planning of sustainability to be the No. 1 point on their responsible business agenda (Corporate Responsibility Magazine, 2010).

2) **Extensively involve stakeholders** into drafting the commitment and achieve co-commitments! If stakeholder consultation is important for the management of responsible business, it is even more so when setting the most basic parameters and making a commitment. Tuning in the business' motivation and development perspective on stakeholder interest saves the trouble a business might run into if its main stakeholders have not bought into the businesses' commitment. Drafting the commitment is also an

excellent opportunity to achieve upfront co-commitments from the most important stakeholders. Such joint commitments are especially efficient among industry peers, to improve a whole industry's or sector's initiative. For instance, automotive companies increasingly collaborate in the development of new environmentally friendly technologies. Co-commitments may also be used to make important allies to permanently bring the business on the way towards becoming a sustainable business.

Asking stakeholders "What should we be?"

The Monterrey Institute of Technology, one of the world's largest private university systems, uses its mission statement as an instrument to commit to responsible business. The mission statement focuses on the profile of graduates (the product of the institution), who should be formed to be become change agents for sustainable development, be ethical, and to act with integrity. The mission statement translates into concrete strategies, and implementation tasks, which are personally endorsed by the university's president (ITESM, 2011). The mission had been developed in a one-year-lasting stakeholder consultation process involving 14,850 individual stakeholders such as students, employees, professors, governmental and business leaders, and families (ITESM, 2010).

Exercises

A. KNOW

Use the below multiple-choice questions to test your knowledge. Each answer may be wrong or right and there may be zero to four right or wrong answers per question:

1. Primary motivations of business...
   a. ...may be subdivided into profit and non-profit motivations.
   b. ...may include a profit motivation. For a profit motivation for responsible business to make sense, there must be a so-called business case for responsible business.
   c. ...may include profit optimization, which describes a situation where a business is purely motivated by generating maximum profit as its only goal.
   d. ...may include a motivation to create the "greatest happiness" and to "be virtuous". Both motivations are mostly found among traditional businesses.
2. Development strategies for responsible business...
   a. ...may be subdivided into profit and non-profit approaches.
   b. ... include, for instance, degrowth strategies.
   c. ... include, for instance, growth-at-all-cost strategies.
   d. ...includes Patagonia as an example for a growth-at-all-cost strategy.

3. The four responsible business categories...
   a. ...include the "Responsibility Superstar", a business that combines a non-profit motivation with a non-growth development strategy.
   b. ...include the "Pure Utilitarianism" business.
   c. ... serve to combine business motivation and development strategy to four stereotypic responsible business categories.
   d. ...may be used to better understand a business' basic motivation and development perspective towards responsible business.

B. THINK

Imagine you are working in an electronic goods company such as Samsung or Philips and your boss, the head of sourcing, asks you to give him a recommendation on whether he should accept a batch of minerals used for mobile phone screens of which the origin is unknown. How do you deal with the incomplete information you have and what is your advice?

C. DO

Imagine you are working in an investment company and one of your main investors wants to invest into a company that is mainly motivated by "doing the right thing". The investor is highly sensitive to "Greenwashers" and wants to make sure the motivation of the company identified is "pure". A good starting point for identifying such a company are the databases of networks of sustainable, responsible, and ethical companies, such as BCorp, UNGC, or the WBCSD. Develop a tool to make your assessment decision explainable to your investor.

D. RELATE

Write a short description of a responsible business practice that has inspired you and publish it through a social network. Try to formulate the message in a way that inspires others to take similar actions.

E. BE

Analyze one occasion that you considered as a personal success. What do you think was your primary motivation? Was it to get most out of it for yourself? To get most for yourself while also thinking about others? To make all involved as happy as possible? To do "the right thing", based on some higher principles? Something else?

Feedback

A. KNOW

Feedback 1

a. Right: A profit motivation can further be subdivided into profit maximization and optimization, while a non-profit motivation may be subdivided into a "Greatest happiness" and doing "The right thing" motivation.
b. Right: If there was no business case for responsible business, a profit motivation would not make sense as there would not be any profit to be made from responsible business.
c. Wrong: Profit maximization aims at maximum profit, while profit optimizing businesses aim at maximizing profit only if this behavior does not lead to irresponsible behavior.
d. Wrong: Those motivational patterns are rather typical for social and environmental entrepreneurial ventures, than for traditional businesses.

Feedback 2

a. Wrong: Development strategies are either growth or non-growth based.
b. Right: Degrowth is one of the non-growth strategies.
c. Right: A growth-at-all-cost strategy for responsible business will only apply to responsible business if it provides the most attractive growth alternative.
d. Wrong: Patagonia was used as an example for a maintenance development strategy.

Feedback 3

a. Wrong: A "Responsibility Superstar" business has a strong growth development strategy.
b. Wrong: Such a business is not mentioned.
c. Right: The four categories are "Business as Usual", "Responsibility Superstar", "Utilitarian Capitalist", and "Pure virtue business".
d. Right. As outlined in the chapter, this is the purpose of the four responsible business types.

B. THINK

Level	*Dealing with incomplete information*	*Notes*
+	Judgment made after successfully applying strategies for dealing with incomplete information.	
=	Reasonable judgment based on incomplete information given in the text.	
–	No judgment made, due to insecurity about how to deal with incomplete information.	

C. DO

Level	*Developing tools*	*Notes*
+	Company has been identified based on a rigorous and transparent process based on the developed tool.	
=	Company has been identified applying a reasonable argument.	
–	No company has been identified.	

D. RELATE

Level	*Inspiring others*	*Notes*
+	Message has the strong potential to inspire others to take similar action.	
=	Message gives a fair account of what is special about the responsible business practice.	
–	Message does not allow others to understand what is special about the practice.	

E. BE

Level	*Developing critical distance to own actions*	*Notes*
+	Impartial evaluation identifying deeper behavioral and motivational structures.	
=	Impartial evaluation of the situation like an outside observer.	
–	Description appears entangled with self-justification and a "clouded view" of oneself.	

Note

1 The terms used here are derived from the main ethical reasoning frameworks as described in Chapter 3.

References

Anthes, M., & Verheyen, E. (Directors). (2011). *ARD Exklusiv: Das System Wiesenhof* [Motion Picture].

Carr, A. Z. (1968). Is business bluffing ethical? *Harvard Business Review*, *46*(1), 143–153.

Chouinard, Y., & Gallagher, N. (2004). *Don't buy this shirt unless you need it*. Retrieved August 24, 2011, from Patagonia: https://www.patagonia.com/us/patagonia.go?assetid=2388

Corporate Responsibility Magazine. (2010). *The state of corporate responsibility: Setting the baseline*. Retrieved September 4, 2011, from Corporate Responsibility Magazine: www.thecro.com

CSA. (2011). *Richard Reed: Co-founder of Innocent drinks*. Retrieved October 15, 2011, from CSA Celebrity Speakers: https://www.speakers.co.uk/pdf/Richard_Reed

Design Council. (2010). *Innocent drinks: Creative culture and strong brand*. Retrieved October 15, 2011, from Design Council: https://www.designcouncil.org.uk/innocent

Foster, J. B. (2011). Capitalism and degrowth: An impossibility theorem. *Monthly Review*, *62*(8). Retrieved September 6, 2011, from Monthly Review: https://monthlyreview.org/2011/01/01/capitalism-and-degrowth-an-impossibility-theorem

Grameen Bank. (2011a). *Breaking the vicious cycle of proverty through microcredit*. Retrieved October 15, 2011, from Grameen Bank: https://www.grameeninfo.org/index.php?option=com_content&task=view&id=25&Itemid=128

Grameen Bank. (2011b). *Historical data series in USD*. Retrieved October 15, 2011, from Grameen Bank: https://www.grameeninfo.org/index.php?option=com_content&task=view&id=177&Itemid=503

Griffin, J. J., & Mahoon, J. F. (1997). The corporate social performance and corporate financial performance debate: Twenty-five years of incomparable research. *Business and Society*, *36*(1), 5–31.

Gunningham, N., Kagan, R. A., & Thornton, D. (2002). *Social license and environmental protection: Why businesses go beyond compliance*. London: Centre for the Analysis of Risk and Regulation; London School of Economics and Political Science.

Innocent Drinks. (2008). *Innocent: Tasty little drinks*. Retrieved October 15, 2011, from Innocent Drinks: https://innocentdrinks.co.uk/resourceupload/approved/ty3rsaw8jumfixbsOou7v50o.jpg

ITESM. (2010). *Diagrama del proceso general*. Retrieved October 15, 2011, from Tecnológico de Monterrey: https://www.itesm.edu/wps/wcm/connect/ITESM/Tecnologico+de+Monterrey/Nosotros/Principios%2C+vision+y+mision/Proceso+de+definicion+de+la+Mision+2015/Diagrama+del+proceso+general/

ITESM. (2011). *Mission*. Retrieved October 15, 2011, from Tecnológico de Monterrey: https://www.itesm.mx/2015/english/mission.html

Jargon, J. (2011). *McDonald's under pressure to fire Ronald*. Retrieved September 6, 2011, from The Wall Street Journal: https://online.wsj.com/article/SB10001424052748703509104576329610340358394.html

Laasch, O., & Flores, U. (2010). Implementing profitable CSR: The CSR 2.0 business compass. In M. Pohl, & N. Tolhurst, *Responsible business: How to manage a CSR strategy successfully* (pp. 289–309). Chichester: John Wiley & Sons Ltd.

Lacey, P., Cooper, T., Hayward, R., & Neuberger, L. (2010). *A new era of sustainability: UN global compact-Accenture CEO study 2010*. Accenture Institute for High Performance.

Martínez-Alier, J., Pascual, U., Vivien, F.-D., & Zaccai, E. (2010). Sustainable de-growth: Mapping the context, criticisms and future prospects of an emergent paradigm. *Ecological Economics*, *69*, 1741–1747.

McDonald's. (2011). *McDonald's 2010 corporate responsibility report*. Retrieved September 6, 2011, from Mc Donald's corporate social responsibility: https://www.aboutmcdonalds.com/mcd/csr/report.html

Orlitzky, M., Schmidt, F. L., & Rynes, S. L. (2003). Corporate social and financial performance: A meta-analysis. *Organization Studies*, *24*(3), 403–441.

Patagonia. (2011). *The footprint chronicles*. Retrieved September 6, 2011, from https://www.patagonia.com/us/footprint/index.jsp

PHW. (2011). *PHW: Working for a better life*. Retrieved September 9, 2011, from https://www.phw-gruppe.de/

Pohle, G., & Hittner, J. (2008). *Attaining sustainable growth through corporate social responsibility*. Somers: IBM Institute for Business Value.

Procter & Gamble. (2011). *Consumer insight*. Retrieved September 4, 2011, from P&G sustainability: https://www.pg.com/en_US/sustainability/products_packaging/our_approach.shtml

Roman, R. M., Hayibor, S., & Agle, B. R. (1999). The relationship between social and financial performance. *Business and Society*, *38*(1), 109–125.

Sweney, M. (2009). *Innocent drinks offer a taste to Coca-Cola*. Retrieved October 15, 2011, from The Guardian: https://www.guardian.co.uk/business/2009/apr/06/innocent-drinks-sell-stake-coca-cola

Taylor, A. (2006). *Toyota: The birth of the Prius*. Retrieved June 12, 2011, from CNN money: https://money.cnn.com/2006/02/17/news/companies/mostadmired_fortune_toyota/index.htm

Thielemann, U., & Wettstein, F. (2008). *The case against the business case and the idea of "earned reputation"*. St. Gallen: Institute for Business Ethics.

TOMS. (2011). *Giving report*. TOMS.

TOMS Shoes. (2009). *TOMS: A history*. Retrieved September 5, 2011, from YouTube: https://www.youtube.com/watch?v=PTQsQUu1Ho8

Unilever. (2010). *The plan: Small actions, big differences*. Retrieved June 6, 2011, from Unilever sustainable living plan: https://www.uslp.unilever.com/wp-content/uploads/2010/10/UnileverSustainabilityPlan2.pdf

Vogel, D. J. (2005). Is there a market for virtue? The business case for corporate social responsibility. *California Management Review*, *47*(4), 19.45.

13 Strategic Management

Analyzing the Status Quo

The precondition for crafting effective strategies, and the first part of the strategic management process is to develop a sound appreciation of the status quo. Only if we know where we are, we can find the path that leads us to where we want to be. In the following two sections, we will look at tools invaluable to understanding the status quo, SWOT analysis, materiality assessment, and portfolios of responsible business activities.

Responsible Business SWOT Analysis

After making a basic broad commitment to responsible business, the next step is to check the breeding ground for different strategic alternatives. This analysis can be subdivided into two basic spheres. First, in the business-internal sphere, the analytical focus lies on internal factors such as processes, culture, and capabilities. Second, the external sphere can be subdivided into the businesses' industry environment including suppliers, customers, industry competition, substitutes and new entrants (Porter, 1980). The external macro environment includes the factors surrounding and permeating industries such as technologies, norms and legislation, culture, natural environment and demographics. In the following the most commonly used integrative tool for considering both environments, the **responsible business "SWOT analysis"** will be applied. The first two letters (S) strength and (W) weaknesses refer to analyzing the internal business dimension, while (O) opportunities and (T) threat refers to the external dimension. Figure 13.1 further illustrates the responsible business SWOT analysis tool.

Analyzing the internal business environment first, typical strengths helpful for implementing responsible business activities are for instance a strong internal business culture, fostering social and environmental business performance. Procter & Gamble, for instance, had begun to strongly improve its socio-environmental business performance as early as 1992 (P&G, 2006). As a result, the company was internally well-prepared to take on a challenge to seize the goal of producing US$50 billion in revenues from sustainable innovation products from 2007 to 2012 (Laasch & Flores, 2010). Also, mainstream business resources may be capitalized for responsible management. For instance, Walmart's highly efficient logistics and warehousing system allows for a concise estimation and handling of food products that do not fulfill Walmart's quality standards. It is only through the logistics of this

DOI: 10.4324/9781003544074-18

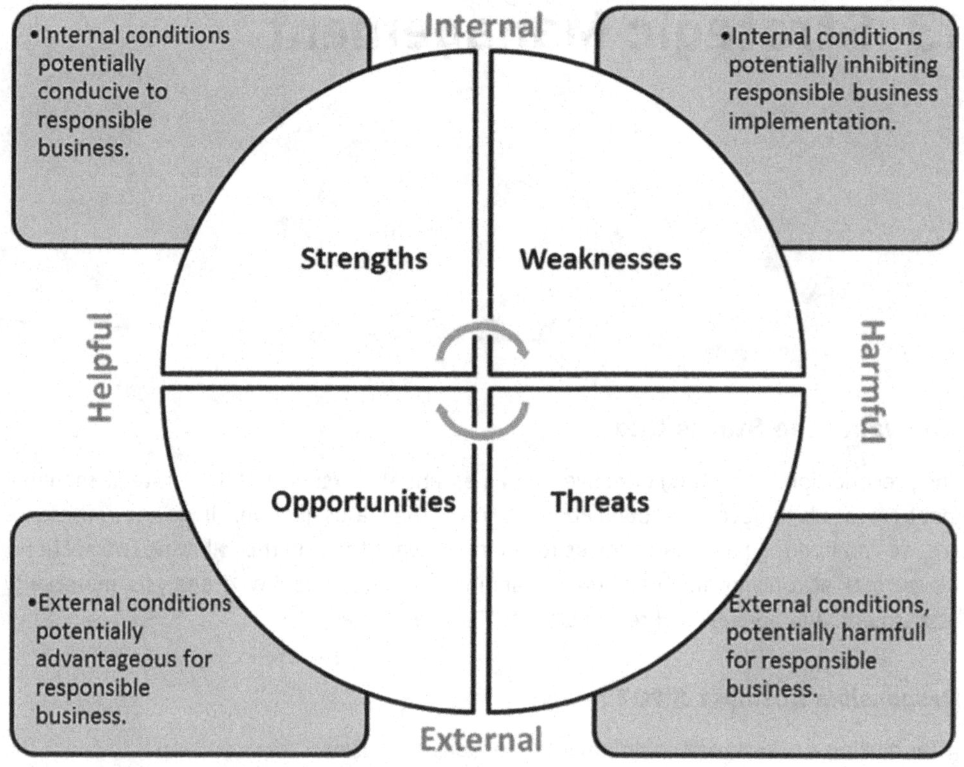

Figure 13.1 Responsible Business SWOT Analysis.

system that Walmart is able to make a commitment to donate US$2 billion in cash and kind by 2015. The company annually donates 1 million pounds of food, most of which products that otherwise would have ended up in the trash (Walmart, 2011). Other internally positive conditions might be an internally existent management system standard (such as for quality, safety or environment) that can be adapted to integrate responsible management. Also, a personal conviction of individuals in the company may be a condition highly conducive to drafting a viable and scalable strategy for implementing responsible business conduct.

Mountain guide for climbing "Mount Sustainability"

One of the most powerful internal strengths for successfully implementing responsible business is high-level visionary leadership and commitment. One of the most impressive leaders for responsible business is InterfaceFLOR's late CEO Ray Anderson. He had been inspired by Hawken's (1993) book *The Ecology of Commerce* in the mid-1990s and ever from this point on had pushed his company to always new heights of responsible business. The self-declared medium-run goal is to rise to the top of "Mount Sustainability". InterfaceFLOR has committed to becoming a truly sustainable business with zero negative impact by 2020 (Anderson, 2009).

Internal conditions with the potential to inhibit responsible business conduct - weaknesses - might for instance be that the core business in its very basic characteristics does not leave much room for becoming sustainable in the long run. For instance, the extractive industry, or any business involved into the life-cycle of petroleum-based products will find it difficult to achieve environmental sustainability in the long run. In order to get there, a drastic change of the very core business and processes would be required. British Petroleum's (BP) slogan "Beyond Petroleum" superficially indicates a shift away from the immanently unsustainable petroleum-based core business. Whether this aspiration has been followed by real-life changes has largely been questioned (Baker, 2007; Greenpeace, 2010). Another internal inhibitor typically encountered is the very human tendency to resist change, however virtuous the aspired goal may be. Truly changing a business to more responsible ways requires extensive shifts in structure, processes, work patterns, and even attitudes. Change is usually work-intensive. In the chapter on changing businesses and other organizations an extensive toolset to dealing with change towards more responsible ways will be provided.

Factors of the external business environment play a crucial role in responsible business conduct. The sustainability megatrend rapidly "changes the rules of the game" and creates threats for the unprepared and offers opportunities for the prepared. External opportunities are manifold. New markets open up such as the Lifestyles of Health and Sustainability (LOHAS) market or the bottom of the pyramid (BOP) market catering to the poor. Green technology is another rapidly growing boom market. External opportunities also lie in governmental support for sustainable business - be it grants or know how - and the search of investors for socially responsible investment opportunities.

Typical external threats related to business responsibility include restraining legislation related to ethics, society or environment. There is also an omnipresent threat to lose customers, employees, and investors, due to their search for more responsible business alternatives. The broad environmental and societal issues also may develop into a tangible business threat. The Coca Cola Company for instance ventured into a broad US$17 million-funded water protection program in collaboration with the World Wildlife Fund. Water scarcity is an imminent threat to Coca Colas water-intensive production process and the water-intensive sugar-cane production, providing one of the soft-drink producer's main resources input.

Materiality Assessment

In the chapter on managing responsible business, the three most salient specialized responsible management instruments have been defined. It is those very three instruments, ethics management, stakeholder, and life-cycle management, that deliver the basic insight necessary to understanding a company's impacts, ethical risks, and stakeholders. As illustrated in Chapter 3, bringing those three assessments together, a company is able to define the **"materiality"** -importance - of engaging in a certain responsible management activity.

Materiality consists of a business and a stakeholder dimension. The business dimension comprises both importance and impact of a certain issue to the business, while the stakeholder dimension does the same thing jointly for all stakeholder groups. The fictional case of typical Mexican Taco corner restaurant, "Tacos de la Esquinita" (as illustrated in Figure 13.2)

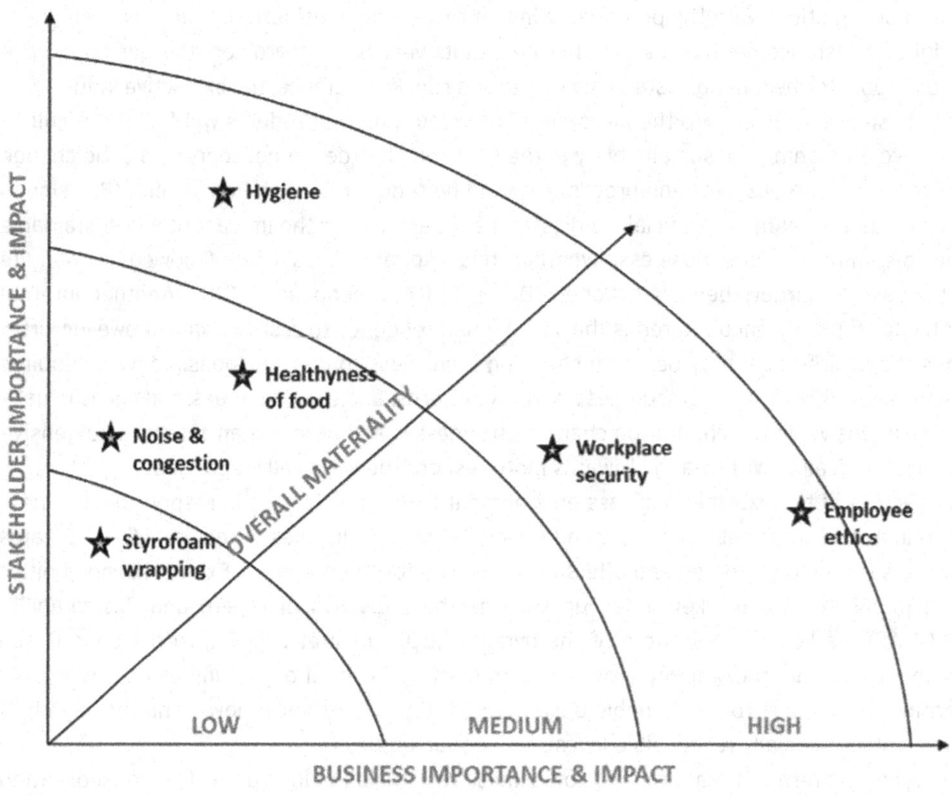

Figure 13.2 Materiality Assessment for a Taco Business.

will be used to further illustrate how a materiality analysis might be conducted in practice. It might be helpful to review the Taco businesses' stakeholder map in the previous chapter on managing responsible business.

Issues at the Tacos

The owner of Tacos de la Esquinita Jose-Luis Gomez, for a long time had been concerned about various latent impact areas of his business. Among others the noise and congestion from the intensive customer traffic, and the environmental impact of Styrofoam packaging have recently caught his attention. To find out which issue he should take care of first, Luis talked to the main stakeholders of his business, mainly employees, customers and neighbors. The most important, most material, issues identified were hygienic aspects, the security of his taco-makers (a lot of heat and sharp instruments) and several employees' bad ethics which had resulted in upset customers and financial losses when waiters had defrauded considerable amounts of money charged to customers. In spite of its low immediate materiality, Luis also decided to act upon the Styrofoam packaging, aiming to proactively react to a pending legislation soon banning Styrofoam in general throughout all Mexico.

Table 13.1 Excerpt of "Tacos de la Esquinita's" Responsible Business Portfolio

A. Mapping		*B. Analysis*		*C. Outcomes*	
Issue	*Main stakeholders*	*Materiality level*	*Main related SWOT factor*	*Responsible management actions*	*Indicators*
Styrofoam	Customers Environment	Low	(T)hreat: Looming legislation to ban Styrofoam	Implement alternative packaging technologies Use Styrofoam only for take-out meals	Percentage of overall servings in Styrofoam Total amount of Styrofoam used
Congestion and noise	Neighbors Customers	Intermediate	(T)hreat: Neighbors obstructing business	Offer home service	Monthly amount of "angry neighbor incidents"
Employee ethics	Employees Customers	High	(W)eakness: Low work satisfaction	Decrease stress level by hiring additional waiters Improve control mechanisms	Percentage of monthly employee immorality incidents

Responsible Business Portfolio

A basic prerequisite for planning the responsible management process is to have a clear picture and continuous assessment of issues related to the business. A **responsible business portfolio** establishes such an inventory (similar to a risk portfolio), which supports the ongoing responsible management and planning process by providing information on every issue materiality, interrelatedness, potential or taken actions, and the businesses' performance in every issue. Table 13.1 provides an excerpt of the taco business described in the preceding paragraph's responsible business portfolio.

A responsible business portfolio sums up a first mapping of issues and of the involved stakeholders, then an analysis of the entities mapped and finally provides a summary related to the potential responsible business alternatives and outcomes. This scheme rather than claiming exhaustiveness provides a basic scaffold open to adjustments depending of each respective businesses' situation and practice.

Strategic Management Processes

Figure 13.3 illustrates how step 1 (defining the basic prerequisites) and step 2 (understanding the status quo) interrelate with every business' components related to classic strategic management. The ultimate goal of the strategic management process for a responsible business is to shape a customized **sustainability strategy**, aiming at the ultimate goal of becoming a sustainable business. A sustainability strategy must be deeply integrated with the organization's mainstream strategy. In the best case they should be one. Thus, vision, mission, and value have to be informed by the responsible business planning, including social and environmental in addition to economic factors. So does the strategy development process and the

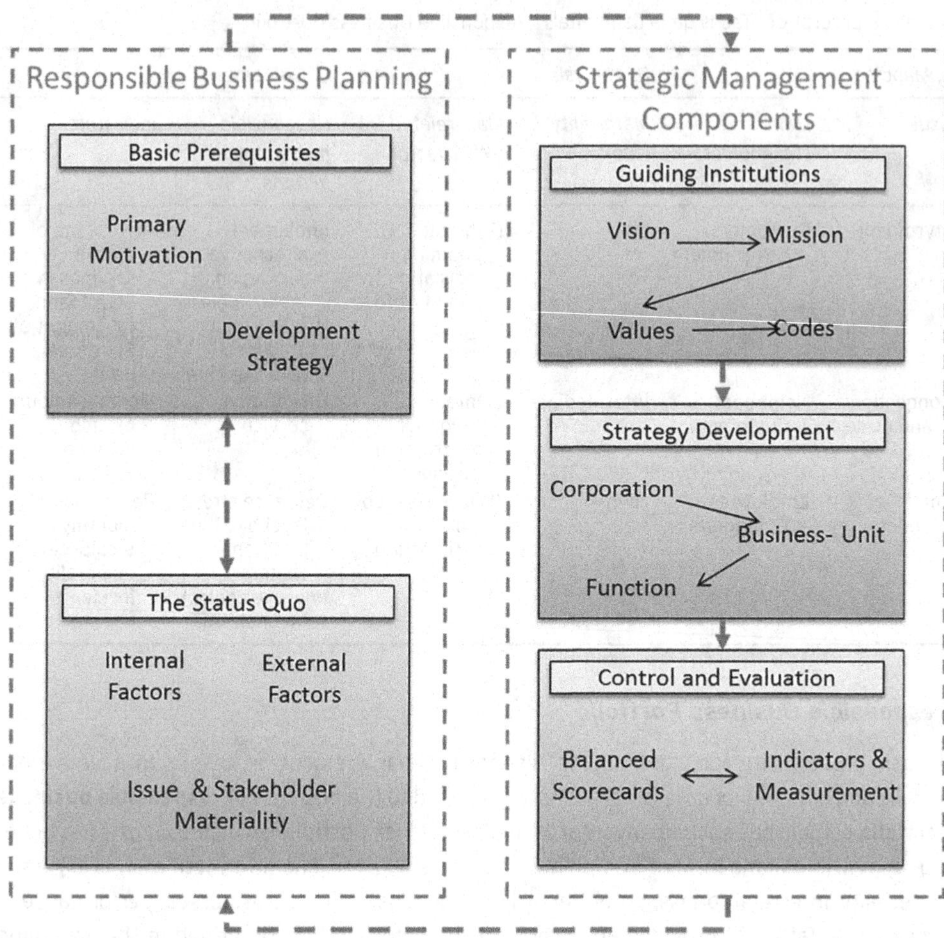

Figure 13.3 Dynamics of Responsible Business Planning and Mainstream Strategic Management Components.

control and evaluation tools. In the following the three main components of the strategic management will be described while highlighting their main interrelations with responsible business.

Vision and mission and value statements of business are the strategic guidance statements - lighthouses of business conduct. Thus, a responsible business strategy ultimately aiming at becoming a truly sustainable business has to begin with tuning in those very guiding institutions. Vision statements describe what a company ultimately aims to become. Hence, the company's vision statement should contain the goal of becoming a sustainable business, customized to what this would look like for this particular company. Companies' mission statements instead aim at describing what the company is and does, it's practices, typical customers, products and processes.

Guiding light or just creative writing?

The company Enron that finally threw in the towel after probably the largest accounting scandal in world history, as a matter of fact, had a very well-developed mission statement. The text was centered on the four key values of respect, integrity, communication, and excellence (Business Library, 2002). As a matter of fact, the scandal showed a reality that was contradictory to the values aspired. Responsible business statements have to strongly reflect a true commitment to an aspired and achievable business reality.

Mission statements provide an excellent possibility to define how responsible business practices should be implemented. Company value statements are a natural extension of the mission statement, describing "how to do business", providing the underlying values, principles, cultural and ethical guidance. It is recommended to not separate the mainstream business/financial guiding institutions from the responsible-business-related ones. Some companies have drafted impressive plans covering social and environmental business elements, which are presented on beautiful, responsible business homepages. Unfortunately, those documents are often isolated from the respective mainstream financial/economic instruments. As extensively described in previous chapters, a sustainable business is the one that balances and integrates social, environmental, and economic business performance. Thus, such integration as illustrated in Table 13.2 has to begin in the guiding institutions.

Table 13.2 Integrating Mainstream and Responsible Business throughout Strategic Guidance Institutions

Strategic guidance statement	*Responsible business function*	*Typical contents*
Vision Statement	Describes a vision of what the achieved sustainable business should ultimately look like.	Achievement through growth, maintenance, or degrowth. Main motivation by profit (financial value creation) or non-profit (maximum happiness, virtue).
Mission Statement	Describes the actual responsible business conduct to be implemented in the day-to-day business and necessary to achieve the vision.	Main causes and stakeholders addressed. Management focus on growth, non-growth; profit, non-profit. Main activity areas necessary to implement responsible business.
Values Statement	Is an important benchmark document for drafting aspired business culture and describes the values that company employees should use to guide their actions.	Values conducive to responsible management conduct: transparency, ethical behavior, respect, accountability, responsibility, etc.
Codes of Conduct and Ethics	Defines aspired behaviors for the business at large or in areas of key importance.	Definition of aspired processes, behaviors in areas crucial to becoming a responsible business for each respective business. Examples include general codes of ethics, supplier codes, sourcing codes, sales ethics, finance, accounting etc.

Business strategies should follow companies' guiding institutions. The main reference document to be followed in *strategy development* should be the mission statement. Strategies usually become developed on the three different levels. On the broadest level, corporate strategies aim at managing and integrating several business units operating in distinct markets. Business unit strategies aim at achieving competitive advantages on single markets by strategically positioning the company's products and brands. The narrowest level called functional strategies tunes in single business functions such as marketing, accounting, and human resources on supporting the higher-level strategies.

Responsible business strongly influences strategy development on all three levels. In the **corporate level strategy** many companies aim at responsible diversification of their business portfolio by acquiring or developing new units with above-average social and environmental performance. The Coca Cola Company, for instance, tried to buy up the German eco-lemonade producer Bionade and invested in shares of the British natural smoothie producer Innocent (The Local, 2009; Sweney, 2009). Clorox developed the Green Works environmentally friendly cleaners' business unit (Green Works, 2011). L'Oreal bought the organic cosmetics pioneer The Body Shop (Bones, 2006). On the **business unit strategy** level, companies aim at improving their strategic positioning, based on either low cost or differentiation (Porter, 1985). Reducing costs (low-cost competition) by for instance eco-efficiency measures such as reducing packaging and energy usage may facilitate a substantial reduction in product prices. Responsible business may also be harnessed to differentiate product offers. Car manufacturers increasingly aim at differentiating their product with "eco-features". The hybrids, hydrogens, electrics, and fuel efficient have become omnipresent marketing terms for automakers. Each **functional level strategy** contributes differently to the overall strategy of a business. For instance, PepsiCo strongly focuses on inclusiveness diversity in its human resources function and claims that this policy strongly enhances its innovative potential, which in turn contributes to the company's overall strategy (HR Voice, 2010). Deutsche Bank's (DB) product-development department created Microfinance Invest, the then first private-customer-focused microfinance-based investment fund. Microfinance invest has been an important contribution to DB's product development strategy (DB, 2010).

Racing to the top?

Many main industry incumbents have begun to increasingly compete on sustainability. Prominent examples are for instance UPS and FedEx, P&G and Unilever, and Coca Cola and Pepsi. The Coca Cola Company for instance announced a 30% plant-based PET bottle in 2009; Pepsi in 2012 raised the bar with its 100% plant-based bottles (Gallisa, 2011). Car manufacturers are outgunning each other in the fight for the alternative engine standard of the future. Construction companies overbid each other in the most sustainable housing, aiming at a zero-sum emission construction or even "climate positive houses" that reduce CO_2 emissions. Such "races to the top" are important drivers of innovation towards more responsible industries and maybe even towards a sustainable economic system.

Traditional strategic management aims at creating competitive advantage above competitors with the ultimate goal of achieving above-average returns (Hitt, Ireland, & Hoskisson, 2007). For responsible business, such above average-returns, profit, can only represent one out of several intended final outcomes of the strategic management process. To become a sustainable business, the strategic management goal structure is multi-dimensional and consists of above-average social, environmental and – of course – also economic business performance (profit versus non-profit motivations) and of the type of development to be achieved (growth versus non-growth). This is why also *strategy evaluation and control* mechanisms have to reflect those multiple dimensions.

Controlling and evaluating strategy is most commonly conducted by the development of **performance indicators** reflecting the aspired outcomes to be achieved by the strategies implemented. Performance indicators for responsible business are social, environmental, and economic (financial). Financial indicators are for instance total revenues, profit margin and shareholder value created. Environmental performance indicators may be related to environmental resource efficiency such as water usage, CO_2 emissions and toxicity. Often environmental indicators are expressed as footprints such as "trees per ton of paper" and "liters of water per cup of coffee produced". Social indicators largely depend on the main social causes the company focuses on. For a company aiming at improving primary education, a social indicator might be the literacy rate of communities operated in; for a business aiming at employee well-being, organizational climate surveys may measure changes in job satisfaction. A common practice is to rather measure activity (e.g. volunteering hours, money donated, and responsibility budget) for social and environmental causes instead of the actual outcome of those activities. Whenever possible it is preferable to measure realized outcomes instead of activities with hard to estimate real-life repercussions.

Indicators for responsible impact

Unilever's "Sustainable Living Plan" has achieved to bring down lofty slogans to down-to-earth tangible indicators. For instance, the ideal of "enhancing livelihoods" translates into the tangible goal of sourcing 100% of agricultural materials sustainably, which in turn is translated into the integration of at least 500,000 smallholder farmers into the company's supply chain by 2020. Another concrete indicator is to employ 7500 micro-entrepreneurs throughout the value chain by 2015. The indicators mentioned are only two examples out of 50 aimed at the achievement of concrete goals for both society and the environment (Unilever, 2010b).

Sustainability balanced scorecards (SBCs) aim at strategically planning social, environmental, and economic business performance. SBCS provide a management system that integrates not only profit and non-profit goals, but also long-run and short run thinking (Figge, Hahn, Schaltegger, & Wagner, 2002). The original balanced scorecard model had been invented by Kaplan and Norton (1996) to get away from short run profit thinking, which they reflected as an inadequate indicator for business performance and direct the attention to

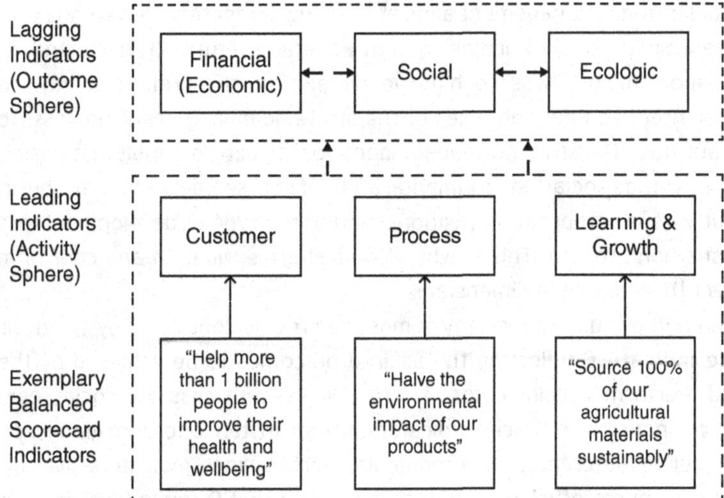

Figure 13.4 Sustainability Scorecards Applied on Unilever's Sustainable Living Plan.

long-run profit drivers. Figure 13.4 combines the classic four scorecard perspectives 1) financial performance; 2) customers; 3) internal processes; 4) growth and learning with two additional sustainability perspectives of environmental and social performance. The model is then used to analyze Unilever's (2010a) "Sustainable Living Plan's" effect on the company's balanced scorecard and subsequently on its strategy. The plan's three main activity areas can be neatly subdivided under the three lagging scorecard indicators. The customer perspective is influenced by the goal to use Unilever products to improve (mainly customers') health and well-being. The ambitious goal to halve the company's environmental impact mostly refers to the internal operations' impact. The goal of sourcing 100% of agricultural materials sustainably falls into the perspective of organizational learning and growth, as its main goals involves the training of small farmers and micro-entrepreneurs to form a crucial part of the company's upstream and downstream supply chain. All goals are aimed to be fulfilled by 2020, a 10-year period from the establishment of the plan in 2010. The sustainability balanced scorecard model has been adjusted extensively to many different settings, out of which Figure 13.4 just represents one design that works for the Unilever case (Hansen & Schaltegger, 2014). Every company is well advised to design a balanced scorecard best fitting their settings.

In the following chapters on the implementation of responsible business and management, we will see how to translate balanced scorecard objectives into real-life practice throughout any business function inside and even to the businesses' supply chain outside the company.

Business Models

The concept of **business model** is used to reflect a company's realized strategy (Casadesus-Masanell & Ricart, 2010). A business model describes the essence of a business, the basic logic of everything it does. So, if we are to know if a responsible business strategy has truly become a business reality we have to see if it is reflected in its business model. The most dominant understanding of business models' elements is one that divides the business model into the following four main functions (Osterwalder, Pigneur, & Smith, 2010; Osterwalder, 2004):

1. **Value proposition** describes what value the company offers.
2. **Value creation** describes the structures, processes and actors involved in creating the value offered.
3. **Value delivery** describes the different customer segments, the relationship to them, and the channels applied to offer the value to them.
4. **Value capture** describes how the company retains a certain amount of economic value (the profit), based on the costs and revenues realized.

It is visible in the above points, how dominant for-profit thinking as main motivation and customers as main stakeholders are in the mainstream business model concept. In a responsible business, where sustainability, responsibility, and ethics are also dominant themes, a business model structure as outlined above cannot provide the full appreciation of the logic of a responsible business. Mainstream, for-profit business and responsible business elements have to be combined which often leads to hybrid businesses so-called hybrid organization. These businesses combine hybrid characteristics from both mainstream and responsible business, following a profit, and a not-for profit logic in parallel (Battilana, Lee, Walker, & Dorsey, 2012; Haigh & Hoffman, 2012). If we are to build such hybrid organizations, the business model thinking has to reflect the non-mainstream business factors of sustainability, responsibility, and ethics. This reflects in a number of changes in business model thinking. For instance, instead of thinking about a mainly economic value proposition for only customers, a more holistic idea of value has to be adopted. In responsible business the value to be considered also includes value for other stakeholders, such as the work satisfaction of employees in a company that is a great place to work, the community contribution of a locally involved business, or possibly a positive environmental value for the local ecosystem, for instance in the case of a recycling business. It is shared value between multiple stakeholders and blended social, environmental, and economic value. This then translates into the three other business model functions of creation, delivery, and capture. Figure 13.4 further illustrates the questions to be asked for integrating mainstream and responsible business in a business model. As the business models of responsible businesses are strongly influenced by specific environmental factors, Figure 13.5 also includes three sections aimed at the appreciation of the moral, stakeholder, and triple equity systems the company is embedded in Figure 13.7 in the Appendix of this chapter includes a blank version of this business model canvas for you to draw on and to design a vision of your responsible business.

The above canvas model is an idealized structure aimed at facilitating the business model design process "on a blank sheet of paper". It is immensely helpful as simple model of the business as it may be used to communicate to the many different business stakeholders (Baden-Fuller & Morgan, 2010; Doganovaa & Eyquem-Renault, 2009). However, we are rarely presented with such a blank sheet of paper, unless we are trying to design a business venture that is not in existence yet. Existing business models are often complex activity systems with multiple connections and feedback loops among these activities (Casadesus-Masanell & Ricart, 2010; Zott & Amit, 2010). The reality is much messier than then neat business model

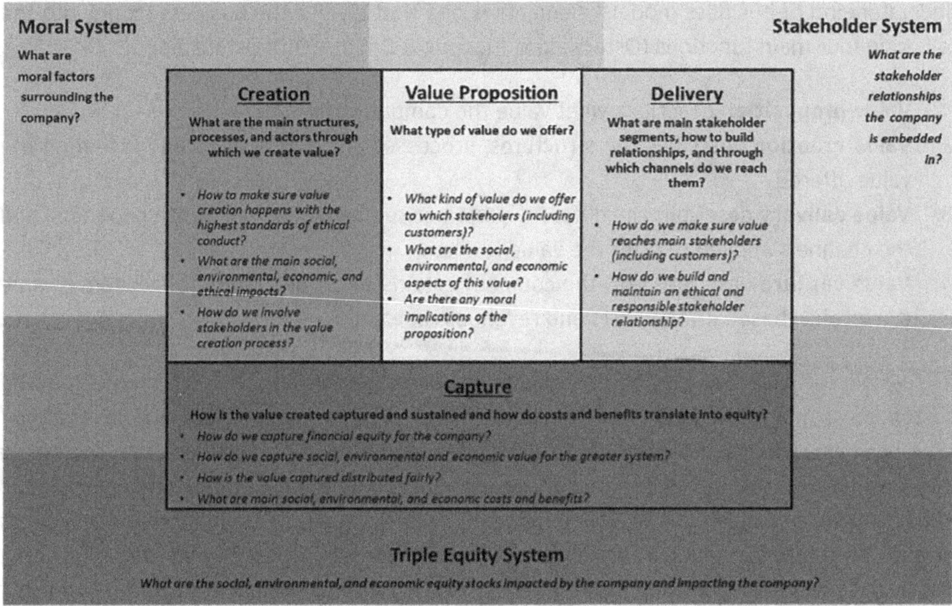

Figure 13.5 Questions to Be Asked when Designing Business Models for Responsible Business Loosely.

Based on Osterwalder, Pigneur, and Smith (2010)

canvas. Accordingly, if we want to consider both an idealized perfect business model and its current status quo, we need an additional tool geared towards showing this messy reality.

Imagine, for instance, an existing business like TOMS, the innovative company we had introduced in the last chapter. TOMS unique quick growth from having a disruptive business idea to becoming a global player in the fashion industry is often attributed to its business model. Figure 13.6 provides a basic impression of the activity system that has led to this success. While the figure does not put the different functions of the business model into boxes as neatly as the canvas model does it, the four main business model functions are still visible. We see, for instance, that TOMS achieves both an economic value capture for the business in the form of a premium margin, and a social value capture as the shoes donated have variable lasting social impacts. For instance, they improve the health of beneficiaries, and they enable kids to go to school for which shoes are often an entry requirement in developing countries. We may also appreciate the delivery mechanism of "shoe runs" and a multiple-value proposition to three main stakeholders. The customer value proposition consists of a stylish pair of shoes and the warm feeling of having done good by buying them. The beneficiaries, mostly kids, benefit from receiving a pair of shoes which may improve their health of give them access to social opportunities, such as visiting school. The third value proposition is towards employees who, working in TOMS, may get a chance to do good through their job which they would possibly find only in few other companies in the fashion industry.

Business models are higher level descriptions of all of the activities realized in the different company functions all of which will be described with greater detail in the following chapters.

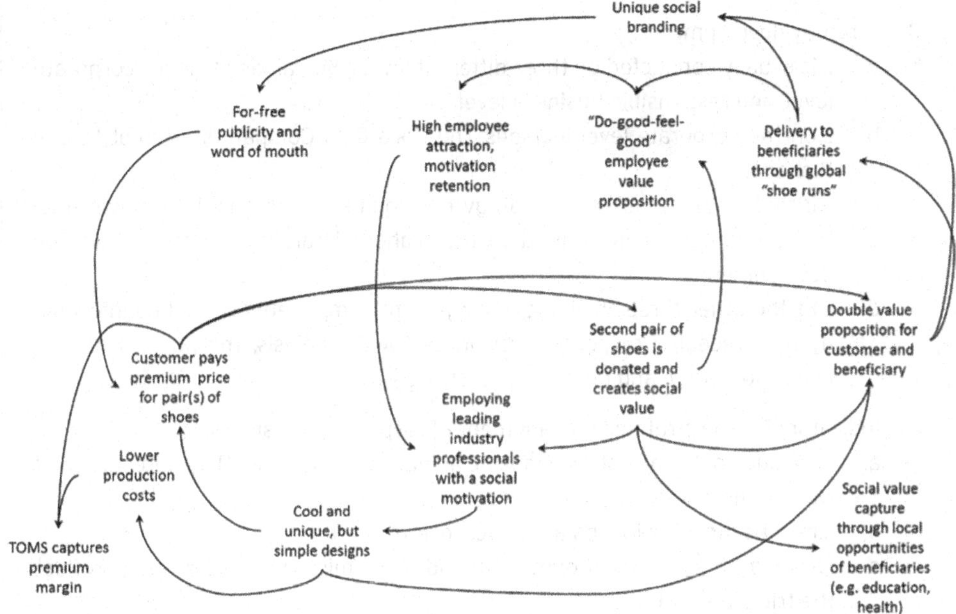

Figure 13.6 Feedback Loops in the TOMS Business Model Activity System Loosely.

Based on Casadesus-Masanell and Ricart (2010)

Exercises

A. KNOW

Use the below multiple-choice questions to test your knowledge. Each answer may be wrong or right and there may be zero to four right or wrong answers per question:

1. A responsible business SWOT analysis...
   a. ...abbreviates the words Sustainability-Weakness-Organizational-Tactics
   b. ...may include a CEO opposing responsible business as a harmful internal factor.
   c. ...helps to analyze an organization's external and internal conditions.
   d. ...supports subsequent strategy development.
2. Materiality...
   a. ...helps to define how important a certain issue should be.
   b. ...has been illustrated by a "Taco example". In this example, workplace security was one of the "most material" issues.
   c. ...combines business importance and impact with stakeholder importance and impact.
   d. ...may be one component reflected in a responsible business portfolio.

3. Strategy development...
   a. ...is usually conducted on three different levels: Sustainability level, corporate level, and responsible business level.
   b. ...on the corporate level includes The Coca Cola Company's attempt to buy Bionade.
   c. ...includes functional level strategy development. The goal is to have functional strategies contributing to the higher hierarchical levels of strategy development.
   d. ...as the other three strategic management components should be informed by the preceding responsible business SWOT analysis, the businesses' primary motivation and development strategy.
4. Indicators for the strategic management of responsible business...
   a. ...include social indicators. One social indicator might be "The percentage of workers unionized".
   b. ...may be included in a balanced scorecard.
   c. ...should be social, environmental, and economic. Those dimensions reflect the triple bottom line.
   d. ...are different for every business, depending on the specific causes it focuses on.
5. The balanced scorecard
   a. ...has originally been developed to avoid short-run profit thinking as the primary driver of business.
   b. ...integrating responsible business indicators has been illustrated by Unilever's Sustainable Living Plan.
   c. ...reflects outcomes and activities in its indicators.
   d. ...is an instrument for strategy control and evaluation.
6. Business models...
   a. ...typically have the five elements of value proposition, value offer, creation, delivery, and capture of value.
   b. ...are best described through the business model canvas if we want to fully appreciate the "messy reality" of an existing business.
   c. ...are reflections of a company's realized strategy.
   d. ...for responsible business are typically hybrids between "mainstream" and responsible business activities.

B. THINK

Imagine two competitors are secretly conspiring to fix their product prices. What moral implications can you think of? Explain why you think the points you mention are morally relevant.

C. DO

Think about an own idea for a responsible business and use the business model canvas to describe the big picture of your idea. You will find a blank canvas model in the Appendix of this chapter.

D. RELATE

Imagine you were in charge of rewriting a big tobacco company's vision statement so that it brings the company onto a responsible business path. Meet with three other people to jointly come up with a statement that serves this purpose.

E. BE

Use the SWOT tool analysis to develop a personal action plan for you to become a responsible manager.

Feedback

A. KNOW

Feedback 1

a. Wrong: SWOT stands for Strength-Weaknesses-Opportunities-Threats.
b. Right: Such a CEO would be an organizational weakness for responsible business conduct.
c. Right: Internal conditions are strength and weaknesses, while external conditions are threats and weaknesses.
d. Right: The appreciation of relevant internal and external environments is a necessary precondition for crafting viable strategies.

Feedback 2

a. Right: A materiality analysis does so by estimating an issues' importance to the business and stakeholders.
b. Right: Workplace security, employee ethics, and hygiene were in the highest materiality category.
c. Right: Both categories are used to define the materiality of a certain issue.
d. Right: Including materiality in a responsible business portfolio helps to categorize the various issues and causes of a business.

Feedback 3

a. Wrong: The three levels of strategy development are 1) corporate level; 2) business unit (or market) level; and 3) functional level.
b. Right: The buying attempt is an example for how companies on the corporate level try to achieve a responsible diversification.

c. Right: The functional level strategy should contribute to the business unit level strategy by either contributing to a product differentiation or a low-cost strategy.
d. Right: As shown in Error! Reference source not found. responsible business planning and mainstream strategic management are highly interconnected.

Feedback 4

a. Right: Membership in labor unions might be an indicator in the social topic area work and labor rights.
b. Right: The traditional balanced scorecard model categorizes indicators in four perspectives, potentially covering many social and environmental indicators.
c. Right: In spite of the triple-bottom line not being mentioned explicitly, those three performance dimensions perfectly reflect the triple bottom line concept.
d. Right: Indicators are different for each cause.

Feedback 5

a. Right: To develop long-run indicators for business success was Kaplan and Norton's goal when developing the balanced scorecard model.
b. Right: The sustainable living plan's three main macro-indicators each may be categorized in one of the three non-financial scorecard perspectives.
c. Right: As shown in the figure of a balanced scorecard, it has an outcome and an activity sphere.
d. Right: The balanced scorecard fulfils both functions, to control if the strategy is working and to evaluate if it is the right strategy to reach set goals.

Feedback 6

a. Wrong: Value offer and proposition is the same thing.
b. Wrong: The business model canvas is a tool that primarily idealizes an aspired business model to be created.
c. Right: The closer the business model is to the company's strategy, the more it may be called a "realized strategy".
d. Right: The mixed elements of mainstream and for responsible business lead to hybrid organizations.

B. THINK

Level	*Moral imagination*	*Notes*
+	Account of wider moral implications only accessible with deeper argument outlined in description.	
=	Account of moral implications not at plain sight, but easily accessible.	
–	Account of the "obvious" moral implications "at plain sight".	

C. DO

Level	Using specialized tools	Notes
+	Tool has been used to its full potential.	
=	Tool has been used correctly, but might have been put to more effective use.	
–	Tool has been used incorrectly, leading to little helpful outcomes.	

D. RELATE

Level	Co-design competence	Notes
+	An adequate vision statement has been designed and it shows that it has been co-designed integrating multiple distinct perspectives on the company.	
=	A vision statement has been designed that appears adequate to provide direction towards becoming a responsible company.	
–	No feasible vision statement has been designed.	

E. BE

Level	Fortitude (matching actions and capability)	Notes
+	Planned actions are congruent with well-developed appreciation of capacity understood through the SWOT analysis.	
=	Planned actions and capability (SWOT) are both well described, but appear incongruent.	
–	Unrealistic, non-transparent, or incomplete picture through SWOT analysis.	

Appendix: Business Model Canvas

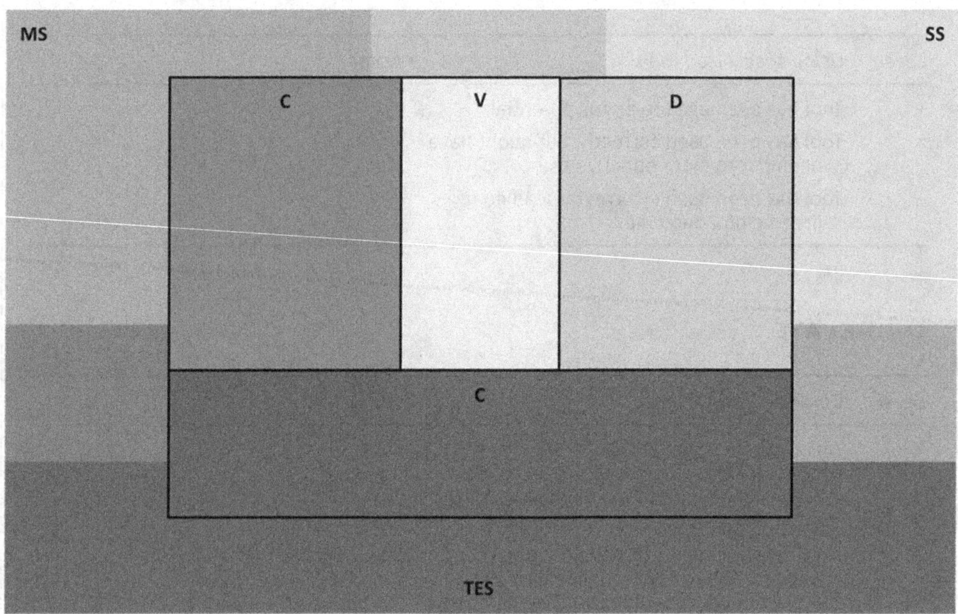

Figure 13.7 Responsible Business Model Canvas in Blank.

References

Anderson, R. (2009, November 30). Ray Anderson, Interface: Climbing mount sustainability. *Ethical Corporation*. (T. Webb, Interviewer) Retrieved October 16, 2011, from Ethical Corporation: https://www.ethicalcorp.com/%5Btermalias-raw%5D/podcasts/ray-anderson-interface-climbing-mount-sustainability

Baden-Fuller, C., & Morgan, M. S. (2010). Business models as models. *Long Range Planning*, *43*, 156–171.

Baker, M. (2007). *British Petroleum*. Retrieved October 15, 2011, from Mallenbaker.net: https://www.mallenbaker.net/csr/CSRfiles/bp.html

Battilana, J., Lee, M., Walker, J., & Dorsey, C. (2012). In search of the hybrid ideal. *Stanford Social Innovation Review*, *10*(3), 49–55.

Bones, C. (2006). *Taking over an ethical business*. Retrieved October 15, 2011, from BBC News: https://news.bbc.co.uk/2/hi/business/4817814.stm

Business Library. (2002). *Missed mission: Watch out!* Retrieved October 15, 2011, from Business Library: https://findarticles.com/p/articles/mi_m0DTI/is_5_30/ai_96892217/

Casadesus-Masanell, R., & Ricart, J. E. (2010). From strategy to business models and onto tactics. *Long Range Planning*, *43*(2), 195–215.

DB. (2010). *DB Microfinance Invest No.1*. Retrieved October 15, 2011, from Deutsche Bank Group: https://www.db.com/us/content/en/1181.html

Doganovaa, L., & Eyquem-Renault, M. (2009). What do business models do? Innovation devices in technology entrepreneurship. *Research Policy*, *38*, 1559–1570.

Figge, F., Hahn, T., Schaltegger, S., & Wagner, M. (2002). The sustainability balanced scorecard: Linking sustainability management to business strategy. *Business Strategy and the Environment*, *11*, 269–284.

Gallisa, R. (2011). *How Pepsi and Coke's plant-based bottle wars affect manufacturers*. Retrieved October 14, 2011, from GreenBiz: How Pepsi and Coke's Plant-Based Bottle Wars Affect Manufacturers

Green Works. (2011). *Home*. Retrieved 28 May, 2011, from Green Works: https://www.greenworkscleaners.com/

Greenpeace. (2010). *Recapping on BP's long history of greenwashing*. Retrieved October 15, 2011, from Greenpeace USA: https://www.greenpeace.org/usa/en/news-and-blogs/campaign-blog/recapping-on-bps-long-history-of-greenwashing/blog/26025/

Haigh, N., & Hoffman, A. J. (2012). Hybrid organizations: The next chapter of sustainable business. *Organizational Dynamics*, *41*, 126–134.

Hansen, E. G., & Schaltegger, S. (2014). The sustainability balanced scorecard: A systematic review of architectures. *Journal of Business Ethics*. doi:10.1007/s10551-014-2340-3

Hawken, P. (1993). *The ecology of commerce*. US: HarperCollins.

Hitt, M. A., Ireland, R. D., & Hoskisson, R. E. (2007). *Strategic management: Competitiveness and globalization* (7th ed.). Mason: Thomson Southwestern.

HR Voice. (2010). *Developing diversity ignites innovation*. Retrieved October 15, 2011, from HR Voice: https://www.hrvoice.org/developing-diversity-ignites-innovation/

Kaplan, R. S., & Norton, D. P. (1996, January–February). Using the balanced scorecard as a strategic management system. *Harvard Business Review*, *74*(1), 75–85.

Laasch, O., & Flores, U. (2010). Implementing profitable CSR: The CSR 2.0 business compass. In M. Pohl, & N. Tolhurst, *Responsible business: How to manage a CSR strategy successfully* (pp. 289–309). Chichester: John Wiley & Sons Ltd.

Osterwalder, A. (2004). *The business model ontology: A proposition in a design science approach*. Lausanne: University of Lausanne.

Osterwalder, A., Pigneur, Y., & Smith, A. (2010). *Business model generation*. Chichester: Wiley. Retrieved January 19, 2012, from https://www.businessmodelgeneration.com/downloads/business_model_canvas_poster.pdf

P&G. (2006). *A company history*. Retrieved October 15, 2011, from Procter & Gamble: https://www.pg.com/translations/history_pdf/english_history.pdf

Porter, M. (1980). *Competitive strategy: Techniques for analizing industries and competitors*. New York: The Free Press.

Porter, M. (1985). *Competitive advantage: Creating and sustaining superior performance*. New York: The Free Press.

Sweney, M. (2009). *Innocent drinks offer a taste to Coca-Cola*. Retrieved October 15, 2011, from The Guardian: https://www.guardian.co.uk/business/2009/apr/06/innocent-drinks-sell-stake-coca-cola

The Local. (2009). *Coca-Cola looking to buy Germany's Bionade*. Retrieved October 15, 2011, from The Local: https://www.thelocal.de/money/20090731-20957.html

Unilever. (2010a). *The plan*. Retrieved September 10, 2011, from Unilever sustainable living plan: https://www.sustainable-living.unilever.com/

Unilever. (2010b). *Health and hygiene*. Retrieved October 15, 2011, from Unilever sustainable living plan: https://www.sustainable-living.unilever.com/the-plan/health-hygiene/

Walmart. (2011). *Building the next generation Walmart: 2011 global responsibility report*.

Zott, C., & Amit, R. (2010). Business model design: An activity system perspective. *Long Range Planning*, *43*(2), 216–226.

E Implementing

14 Implementation Basics

Good Implementation Practices

Advice on how to become a responsible business and how to implement responsible management activities has been given extensively. There are not only qualitative "step-by-step approaches", but also quantitatively supported best practice reports.[1] The often extensive, and in the worst case confusingly rich body of knowledge on the best practices in implementing responsible management, can be boiled down to a rather narrow set of principles. In the following we will focus on the three principles we consider most crucial for truly moving a business towards becoming sustainable.

Transformative and Aligned

If a business truly aims at becoming sustainable, which means having at least zero or even positive impact, implementation of responsible business necessarily has to be transformative. Profound change for most businesses is inevitable in a large majority of cases. Most likely, "sacred cows" of business as usual will have to be slaughtered. If the criteria of "planet sense" are applied jointly with the conventional "money sense" rationale, long-established evaluations might change drastically. For instance, it might be necessary to change or abandon a highly profitable, but unsustainable core process. A long-serving high-level executive's profit-first mindset might make a replacement necessary. One of the company's cash-cow products might, while being a financial pillar, be unacceptable from a sustainability perspective.

To over-protect disadvantageous elements of a company's status quo is one commonly made mistake and obstacle to successful responsible business conduct. The opposite extreme is to aim at implementing responsible business activities which are completely unaligned with the strategy and capabilities of the company. Responsible business has immense potential to strengthen strategy and core business as has been shown in the box on the business case for responsible business in a previous chapter. Thus, a deep integration of responsible management activities throughout an organization's strategic infrastructure, as described in the strategic management chapter is a must.

DOI: 10.4324/9781003544074-20

Embedded, Measured, and Controlled

A typical mistake being made in many businesses first implementing responsible management activities is to misperceive them as nice add-ons but separate from core-business. Responsible management should be deeply embedded, not merely "bolted-on" (Laszlo & Zhexembayeva, 2011, p. 100). Bolted-on responsible business activities are often costly, not very credible, and as a result mostly short-lived. Only when embedded into existing business functions responsible management becomes a tangibly contributing element of the business structure.

Another typical problem resulting from responsible management implemented as a pure add-on is that it often is not treated with the same rigorous management practices as any other business activity would be, an outcome of which is often non-satisfying results. Results of responsible management as is the case in any other management activity need to be measured, controlled, and regulated in order to be successful. The sustainability scorecard model presented in the strategic management chapter and this chapter's section on accounting and finance provide rich insight into how to implement an indicator and control system for responsible management.

Scoring climate performance

The Climate Counts scorecard is a tool customized for companies of many sectors, that makes your performance for or against climate change tangible, visible, and manageable. Additionally, companies can submit their scorecard results, which will then be made public. Companies of the same sector are able to benchmark their climate performance against their peers. Let the climate-competition begin! (Climate Counts, 2012).

Systemic and Collaborative

Silo mentality is one of the most experienced pitfalls in responsible management. Responsible management must take the overall system of social, environmental, and economic factors into consideration. Collaboration with the most different stakeholder groups inside and outside the company is indispensable. Of special operational importance is the need to connect all of the company's functional departments into a coherent responsible management system. Such holistic and collaborative management systems take different shapes and forms and need to be tuned in to each respective company's specific conditions. There are many helpful resources for developing such a management system for your company.

- The **ISO 26000 norm on social responsibility** (ISO, 2010) aims at providing a background framework for developing more specific company management systems.
- Blackburn (2007) proposes so-called **sustainability operating systems** (SOS), which integrate social, environmental, and economic factors.
- Laszlo and Zhexembayeva (2011) recommend a **sustainability management system** that is embedded into all business functions and highly aligned with the company's strategy.

- Waddock and Bodwell (2007) propose **total responsibility management** based on quality management thinking.
- Morsing and Oswald (2009) illustrate how to use **mainstream management systems** for responsible business.

How can you plan a responsibility management system that connects all the different functional departments of a company to the best of business, society, and environment? An initial step is to map a specific responsible management activity including all responsible management instruments throughout the involved functional departments and the management outputs expected by each function. Such a responsible management map is an excellent first step to plan the organizational architecture of a company's responsible management system, defining processes, responsibilities, and aspired outcomes.

"AIDS is your business"

Is the title of an article which appeared in *Harvard Business Review* in 2003. The article starts off with "If you've got global operations, you've got an HIV-infected workforce. Doing something about it will save lives- as well as money" (Rosen, et al., 2003, p. 80). As a matter of fact the cost of HIV/AIDS cases inside for instance South-African companies were surveyed to be 0.5 to 3.6 times an annual salary of a worker. Cost included into the calculation were for instance "sick leave; productivity loss; supervisory time; retirement, death, disability, and medical benefits; and recruitment and training of replacement workers" (Rosen, et al., 2004, p. 317). With such a well-documented case for doing well by doing good, it is not surprising that many multi-national companies such as the beer brewer Heineken have become active in fighting AIDS/HIV for the good of both their employees and their families (Borght, et al., 2006).

The example of implementing a HIV/AIDS program on-site will be used to exemplify the system of different functions collaborating as a coherent system of functional mainstream management instruments (see Figure 14.1). The starting point has to be the activity of providing a HIV/AIDS prevention, screening, and treatment program - a typical activity for the responsible management instrument of sustainable human resources management. The aspired outcome of this activity is to achieve a lower infection rate and the recovery from the disease's symptoms for already infected employees. Another major outcome is the protection of the company's human resources, motivation of employees, and improved employee attraction and retention rates. The management instrument of social accounting keeps track of resources used and outcomes achieved. This information is then used as feedback for the management process and is covered in a sustainability report. The sustainability communication tool then uses the data raised to create goodwill among strategic stakeholders of the company. Of course, this description, while providing a first systemic approach, is strongly reduced in complexity. In the following sections, functional mainstream management instruments as the ones used in this example will be illustrated with further detail to provide

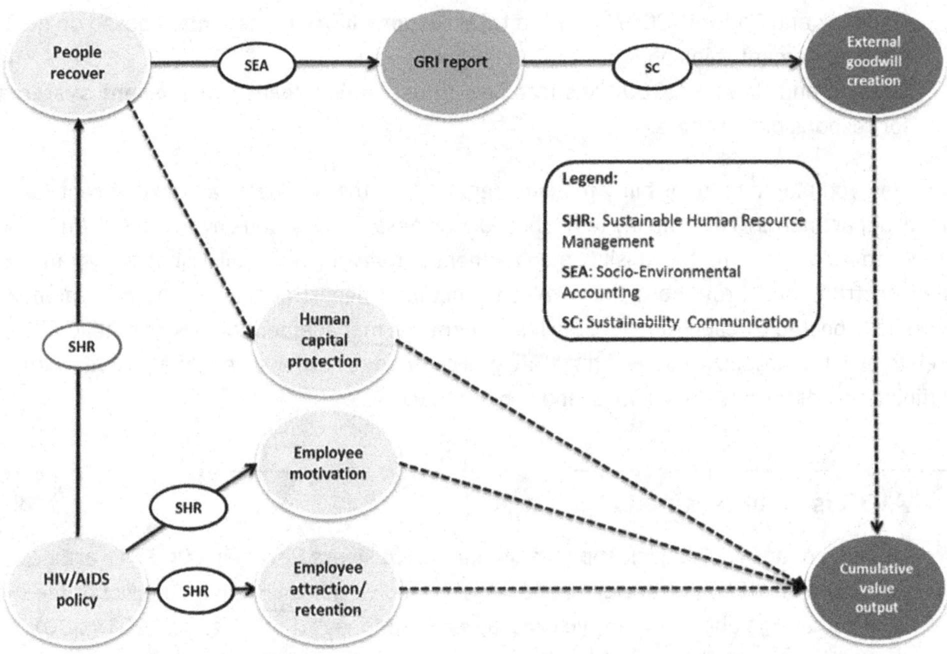

Figure 14.1 Mapping a Responsible Management Sub-System.

readers with an extensive toolset for successfully managing the responsible business in all its systemic interconnectedness.

Mainstream Responsible Management Instruments

Implementing responsible management activities throughout all functions and departments of a business is a highly complex task. Successful implementation requires a profound understanding of both the mainstream management function and of the responsible management instruments that may be deployed in each function. Using the **value chain** model (Porter, 1985), functions can be divided into primary activities (also called primary or line functions) and support activities or functions. Primary functions are directly involved into the process of handling inputs, transforming them into a product or service, marketing and selling it to customers, and providing after-sales service. Support functions, also called staff functions, support the primary functions process. Typical support functions are human resources, finance, accounting, etc. Figure 14.2 describes the main functions of a business as they are illustrated in the remainder of this book.

It is important to bear in mind that responsible management instruments can be subdivided into two groups as illustrated before. The first group is so-called **mainstream responsible management instruments**, which have been developed by adapting mainstream management functions for social and environmental value creation. The second group is specialized instruments, which have been developed based on pure responsible management tasks **(specialized responsible management instruments**). Specialized responsible management instruments, as explained before, are crucially important for informing decisions

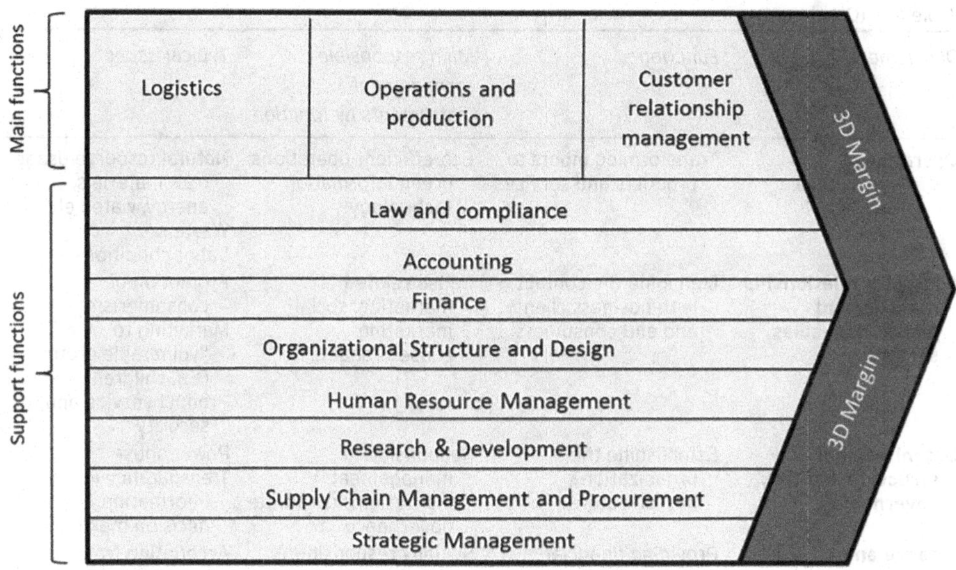

Figure 14.2 Mainstream Management Functions in a Company's Value Chain.

Adapted from Porter (1985)

being made inside functional departments of businesses. Those three specialized instruments (ethics management, stakeholder management, life-cycle management) provide the bigger context of sustainable business. Nevertheless, the main practical work to move a company towards becoming a sustainable business is with mainstream responsible management instruments that can neatly be subsumed under existing functional departments of businesses. At least as important as the management tools deployed inside business functions are the typical social, environmental, and ethical issues to be found in the functions. Table 14.1 covers both management instruments and typical issues.

Table 14.1 Responsible Management Instruments Used in a Company's Functions in Order of Appearance in this Book

Department	*Function*	*Main responsible management instruments by function*	*Typical issues*
Strategic management	Setting the company's strategic direction and parameters	Strategic responsible management	Monopoly power Aggressive strategies
Logistics	Making inputs available to the production process and delivering products and services to customers	Sustainable logistics; green logistics	Environmental impact of packaging (waste) and transportation (emissions) Accidents in road transportation Congestion, noise, infrastructure deterioration

(*Continued*)

Table 14.1 (Continued)

Department	*Function*	*Main responsible management instruments by function*	*Typical issues*
Operations	Transforming inputs to products and services	Eco-efficient operations; green information technology	Natural resource usage (raw materials, energy, water, etc.) Waste Labor conditions
Customer relationship management (marketing, sales, service)	Managing the contact with business clients and end-consumers	Cause-related marketing; social marketing; cause-branding	Promotion of consumerism Marketing to "vulnerable groups" (e.g. children) Product service and security
Organizational structure, control, governance	Establishing the organization's infrastructure	Responsible management institutions; corporate governance	Power abuse Transparency in information flow and decision making
Finance and accounting	Providing financial resources; planning and documenting resource usage and resulting outputs	Socially responsible investment; sustainability accounting; inclusive pricing and costing; sustainability reporting	Accounting fraud and corruption Measurement of social-environmental performance
Human resources management	Managing employee relations	Responsible human resources management; employee volunteering; sustainability training and empowerment	Work and contractual issues Work-life balance
Research and development	Innovating products and processes	Sustainable innovation; bottom of the pyramid products; sustainable process innovation	Product safety Planned redundancy
Legal and compliance department	Complying with norms and legislation	Environmental and social norms and compliance	Legal compliance Fair contracts
Procurement	Procuring inputs necessary for production	Sustainable procurement; inclusive and sustainable supply chain management; fair trade	Ethical procurement Fair trade Corruption
Communication	Communicating activities and outcomes	Stakeholder communication; codes of conduct; sustainability trainings; sustainability vision/ mission statements; issues- and crisis communication; social marketing; cause-related marketing	Truthfulness Transparency

Who is managing responsible business activities in a company?

Which functions should be involved? The answer is simple: ALL! For instance, take a look at the sustainability report of the Indian Tata Motors Company. Tata's development and marketing teams brought the Tata Nano, the first US$2000 car, a milestone for low-income classes to enjoy safe and cost-effective transportation. The human resources, procurement, and finance departments are instrumental in fulfilling Tata's stakeholder mission "to create an organization that people enjoy working for, doing business with and investing in". In this simple example of the company's responsible business activities, five departments are involved.

(Tata Motors, 2010)

Exercises

A. KNOW

Use the below multiple-choice questions to test your knowledge. Each answer may be wrong or right and there may be zero to four right or wrong answers per question:

1. Good practices in implementing responsible business...
    a. ...include for instance that implementation should be transformative. Transformative means that the company has to transform business practices to become a responsible business. Those changes should never affect established institutions or generation of profit.
    b. ...include for instance that implementation should be embedded (part of the main business structure) and controlled (applying rigorous management practices).
    c. ...include a systemic implementation. An important tool for this good practice is the establishment of a responsible management system.
    d. ...include the mapping of management instruments deployed and the outcomes created by them.
2. Implementing responsible management throughout company functions and departments...
    a. ...usually involves so-called mainstream responsible management instruments such as ethics management.
    b. ...involves both the implementation in support functions (e.g. operations and logistics) and main functions (e.g. human resources and finance).
    c. ...for instance, the research and development department involves both implementing the responsible management instrument of sustainable innovation and ensuring product safety as one of the typical issues encountered in this department.

   d. ...involves both knowledge of main responsible management instruments of the respective function and issues typically encountered in the function.

3. The Mexican cinema chain Cinepolis has integrated responsible business key performance indicators across the four areas of its balanced scorecard through which the company and its executives evaluate their success. This is a direct example of...
   a. ...a systemic and collaborative approach to responsible business implementation.
   b. ...transformative and aligned responsible business implementation.
   c. ...embedded and controlled responsible business implementation.
   d. ...an organizational control mechanism.

B. THINK

Identify one responsible business activity from a case (e.g. the OIKOS case collection among many other sources) and translate what you find into a map similar to the one in this chapter describing the HIV/AIDS initiative of Heineken.

C. DO

Download a company's corporate social responsibility or corporate sustainability report and try to identify at least one activity of the company located in each of the functions of the value chain model illustrated above and describe how they fit together in the big picture of responsible business.

D. RELATE

Probably your professional background or goals will make you more interested in one or another function (e.g. human resources, strategy, or accounting) of a company. Search online and possibly offline for a group of people that best reflects your interest (e.g. through groups on professional networks like Facebook and LinkedIn; through professional associations like the "responsible sourcing network", or the "sustainable banking network"; or also through students' associations for responsible business like NetImpact or OIKOS). Get in touch with the group and become part of their network.

E. BE

A good practice for responsibility and sustainability measures is to embed and control them. Think about one thing you could do to lead a more responsible and/or sustainable life. Design a control mechanism to ensure you do it correctly and repeatedly for a predefined period of time. Then do it!

Feedback

A. KNOW

Feedback 1

a. Wrong: Transformation towards responsible business often requires managers to question practices.
b. Right: As illustrated in the beginning of this chapter, embeddedness is a basis of good practice in responsible business and management.
c. Right: As illustrated in the beginning of this chapter, systemic implementation, for instance, through an integrated management system is a basis of good practice in responsible business and management.
d. Right: Such mapping is a basic precondition for the good practices of both systemic and embedded activities.

Feedback 2

a. Wrong: Ethics management is not a mainstream responsible management instrument, but a specialized responsible management instrument.
b. Wrong: The concrete functions mentioned do not correspond to the type of function they are used to exemplify. For instance, logistics is not an example of a support function, but of a main function.
c. Right: This point is reflected in depth in the table on responsible management instruments used in different company departments.
d. Right: This point is reflected in depth in the table on responsible management instruments used in different company departments.

Feedback 3

a. Right: The balanced scorecard connects different functions of the business which makes it collaborative and systemic. However, we learn little from the text about the connections to and collaboration with external stakeholders.
b. Right: As the balanced scorecard is a strategic instrument that applies to the whole business anything that is on it is automatically aligned with the overall business strategy.
c. Right: The balanced scorecard is a control instrument, and as it applies to all kinds of departments in the business, anything that is on it is embedded into the company.
d. Right: The balanced scorecard and the key performance indicators on it are organizational and managerial control mechanisms.

B. THINK

Level	Reducing complexity through structuring	Notes
+	Case has been described and its understanding enhanced in comparison to written text.	
=	Case has been described adequately and accessibly through map.	
–	Case has not been captured adequately in map.	

C. DO

Level	Holistic activity analysis	Notes
+	All of the value chain functions have been matched and they have been described interdependently.	
=	Most value chain functions have been independently matched with at least one activity mentioned in the report.	
–	No or few activities and value chain functions have been matched convincingly.	

D. RELATE

Level	Participating in the community	Notes
+	Evidence of participation in the community.	
=	Community identified, but no contact has been made.	
–	Community has not been identified.	

E. BE

Level	Self-direction competence	Notes
+	Activity and control mechanisms are in place and there is evidence of their functioning in action.	
=	Feasible activity and control mechanisms are in place.	
–	Activity and control mechanisms are either not feasible or not in place.	

Notes

1 For a qualitative approach see for instance Grayson and Hodges. An excellent quantitative study has been provided by the *Corporate Responsibility Magazine*.

References

Blackburn, W. R. (2007). *The sustainability handbook: The complete management guide to achieving social, economic and environmental responsibility*. Washington: Earthscan.

Borght, S. V., Wit, T. F., Janssens, V., Loeff, M. F., Rijckborst, H., & Lange, J. M. (2006). HAART for the HIV-infected employees of large companies in Africa. *The Lancet, 368*, 547–550.

Climate Counts. (2012). *Scorecard overview*. Retrieved January 18, 2012, from Climate Counts: https://www.climatecounts.org/scorecard_overview.php

ISO. (2010). *International Standard ISO 26000: Guidance on Social Responsibility*. Geneva: International Organization for Standardization.

Laszlo, C., & Zhexembayeva, N. (2011). *Embedded sustainability: The next big competitive advantage*. Stanford: Stanford University Press.

Morsing, M., & Oswald, D. (2009). Sustainable leadership: Management control systems and organizational culture in Novo Nordisk A/S. *Corporate Governance*, 9(1), 83–99.

Porter, M. (1985). *Competitive advantage: Creating and sustaining superior performance*. New York: The Free Press.

Rosen, S., Simon, J., Vincent, J. R., MacLeod, W., Fox, M., & Thea, D. M. (2003). AIDS is your business. *Harvard Business Review, 81*(1), 80–87.

Rosen, S., Vincent, J. R., MacLeod, W., Fox, M., Thea, D. M., & Simon, J. L. (2004). The cost of HIV/AIDS to businesses in southern Africa. *AIDS, 18*, 317–324.

Tata Motors. (2010). *Wheeling innovation: Corporate sustainability report 2009-2010*.

Waddock, S., & Bodwell, C. (2007). *Total responsibility management: The manual*. Sheffield, UK: Greenleaf Publishing.

15 Main Business Functions

Logistics

Logistics include both inbound and outbound logistics. *Inbound logistics* are concerned with delivering inputs to the production process, while *outbound logistics* delivers finished products and services to the customer. On the one hand, logistics are often outsourced, which suggests that the topic should rather be covered under supply chain management. On the other hand, in a responsible management context, logistics is so intimately linked with a businesses' main functions that it makes sense to cover both in an interlinked fashion. Logistics are also a crucial part of the management of world-wide supply chains as will be described in chapter on supply chain management.

Bring your own mug!

Since 1985 Starbucks has been encouraging customers to have their beverage filled into their own re-usable mug. The company even rewards this effort with a 10% discount on any beverage bought. This example of outbound logistics shows how simple it can be to reduce your logistics impact (in this case the paper used and waste made). By 2015 Starbucks had aimed to use 10% of re-usable or recyclable cups (Starbucks, 2011).

Depending on the product and production process, logistics can be very intensive in natural resources and harmful for the environment. Typical environmental issues are noise, air pollution, traffic congestion, land use (the land occupied by roads, railways, airports), and, mostly, excessive packaging. Typical negative social impacts of logistic activity are road accidents and pulmonary diseases. The logistic network leading to most products are connected worldwide and involve extensive and complex transportation activities. In order to move logistics activities towards sustainability, it is helpful to understand the typical conflicts of interest between efficient logistics and sustainable development. The following list includes some of the most salient paradoxes of "green logistics" as they have been described by Rodrigue, Slack, and Comtois (2001). It has to be remarked that service logistics typically involve different structures and impacts from the logistics of products.

DOI: 10.4324/9781003544074-21

- **Minimizing costs**: A crucial competitive factor of logistics is the ability to provide transportation at the lowest cost possible. This is contrasted by the urgent need to internalize external environmental costs mentioned above. Internalization of those external costs would increase costs of the logistics activity immensely.
- **Speed, flexibility, reliability**: Speed flexibility, and reliability are basic requirements for logistics networks. Unfortunately, the means of transportation fulfilling those requirements (such as planes and trucks) also do more harm to the environment than the less desired alternatives (such as ships and trains).
- **Hub and spoke**: The usage of centralized hub and spoke logistical networks creates a highly concentrated negative impact at the center of logistic networks.
- **Warehousing and just-in-time logistics**: The just-in-time movement has drastically reduced the amount of goods stored. A result is that much of the storage has been transferred "to the streets", increasing the overall amount of goods in movement and their negative environmental impact.
- **E-commerce**: Small, individual shipments are required by the logistical structures of the rapidly increasing e-commerce. Such methods significantly decrease the efficiency of logistics due to more packaging and the need for customized transportation efforts. However, for instance, the weekly online grocery shop is on average much more eco-efficient than when customers drive to the shop with their own cars.

What's so bad about a left turn?

The car motor is idling using gasoline while you wait for the cars in the opposite lane to pass. Right turns are just more eco-efficient and prevent unnecessary emissions. The logistics enterprise UPS has taken the consequence and implemented a formal program to minimize the number of left turns taken by their delivery drivers. Multiplying this single effort by the 95,000 delivery trucks of the company's fleet, the impact, both environmental and economic, is enormous (Lovell, 2007).

Actions to mitigate the negative impact of logistics take many forms, which can be subdivided into two basic approaches: First, reducing the impact of logistic activities, while maintaining or growing the volume, and second reducing the logistics volume. In the following paragraphs, you find some typical practices which may result in one of the approaches mentioned or in some cases combine both:

- **Transport impact transparency**: The social and environmental impact of transportation is often hidden. While many products are labeled by the country of origin, this only provides a superficial impression of the overall transport activities necessary. Some industries and single companies have started to increase the transparency of their impact. Food miles, which describe the distance traveled by food products, are a good example.

- **Eco-efficient logistics**: Eco efficiency aims at improving the ratio between economic output and required input of natural resources. For the logistics sector this ratio is highly important. Eco-efficient logistics aim at reducing the environmental impact of a given logistic activity. The weakness of the methodology is that it does not aim at reducing the overall amount of harmful activity, but rather keeping (or even increasing) economic activity, while making each logistic output unit (such as kilometers traveled, items transported, etc.) more eco-efficient. The cumulative negative impact might not be reduced at all.
- **Reverse logistics**: Recycling only works if products at the end of their useful life-cycle are transported back to be re-integrated into the production process. This is the main task of reverse logistics, which makes it a crucial part of a circular and sustainable economy. Reverse logistics may also have ecological downsides, such as in the case of returns management. Many companies provide convenient financial and logistic take-back schemes for unsold goods. Such returns management systems create an incentive to order more goods than are actually used.
- **E-commerce (retailing) logistics**: Increasingly traditional logistic activities are altered and often substituted by new business models. E-commerce has often been described as more environmentally friendly, due to the reduction of resource-intensive bricks-and-mortar store networks. It is not yet certain if this trend leads to more or less environmentally friendly logistics. Research suggests that the home-delivery services connected to e-commerce are less polluting than customers picking up the bought item in the shop themselves (Edwards, McKinnon, & Cullinane, 2010).
- **Servitization logistics**: Complementing or substituting products by services often reduces the necessity to transport a physical product. Servitization models are, for instance, "repair instead of replace" and "rent instead of own". The section on Customer Relationship Management will cover servitization in greater depth.
- **Local production and consumption networks**: Increasingly, local production and consumption networks substitute the need for extensive global logistics networks and activities. Such a development is not necessarily always more sustainable. Focusing only on the environmental impact, in some cases, local production is actually less sustainable than foreign production plus importation. For instance, in food products, the reason may lie in local differences in productivity and refrigeration efforts (AEA Technology, 2008).

Local production vs. global logistics

The central Mexican city of San Luis Potosí has been ranked as the world-wide third most promising global free trade zone just behind Shanghai and Dubai. One of the main reasons: Its great logistics infrastructure and location (Financial Times, 2010). On the other hand, the city also sees the opposite movement. Local production and consumption is a focus topic. The initiative "Puro Potosino", which roughly translates to "purely from San Luis Potosí" has taken local production to the next level. Several hundreds of enterprises of all sizes, all located inside the city have created a local network of interconnected businesses rendering many international logistic efforts pointless. A broad variety of products is mainly sourced, produced, and sold locally (H Ayuntamiento San Luis Potosí, 2011). The newest development is an industrial park of over 100 businesses mainly from the food sector, moving even closer together to create a unique local production network (Global Media, 2011). Positive effects are not only reducing environmental impact from logistics, but also strengthening the local economic development, creating jobs and welfare.

Operations and Production

The terms operations and production management are often used interchangeably. In the following **operations management** will be used as the activities of managing the operational level of a business, in contrast to the non-operational (strategic or planning) activities. Operations management aims at reaching strategic objectives by achieving operational efficiency (minimum resource usage) and effectiveness (maximum value creation for customers) throughout all business functions. **Production management** instead takes a rather narrow focus on the core manufacturing process (see Table 15.1). This section will cover operations management and production management as both, in terms of responsible management, share similar characteristics. Often, operations management includes supply chain management (SCM) and the management of innovation and technology (R&D). Because of the special importance of those two topics for responsible business and management, they will be covered as stand-alone sections.

While the social and environmental impact of operations can be immensely negative (depleting resources, dangerous for workers, polluting, etc.) the most basic goals of operations management and the goals of a responsible business seem to be highly compatible on

Table 15.1 Strategic, Operations, and Production Management

Management level	*Strategic management*	*Operations management*	*Production management*
Description	Planning, strategic infrastructure and goal setting for the company as a whole	Managing intra-departmental and inter-departmental efficiency and effectiveness	Managing core manufacturing processes from raw material to finished product, often on a local scope and from a floor-level perspective
Aspired Goal	Strategic competitiveness	Business processes quality	Manufacturing process efficiency
Departments	Supra-department, organizational level	All	Mainly production and logistics
Typical Job Positions	Staff functions such as sustainability officer, vice-president sustainability	Line functions such as sustainability manager	Environment health and safety (EHS) manager/ supervisor
Typical Tools	Sustainability balanced scorecards and key performance indicators (KPIs)	Sustainability operating systems (SOS); total responsibility management	Eco-efficiency; environment-health-safety frameworks

Job titles may differ widely depending on organizational structure, history, and size.

a managerial level. Some responsible business managers even go so far to say that "sustainability and operational excellence" are "one goal not two"; that one cannot be reached without the other due to considerable synergies (Hutchins, 2010, p. 1; Kleindorfer, Singhal, & Van Wassenhove, 2005). Thus, it is not surprising that many of the approaches to responsible operations are derived from well-known and long-established approaches in operations management. Operational efficiency becomes re-interpreted as eco-efficiency; total quality management becomes total responsibility management; general management systems serve as a blueprint for sustainable operating and environmental management systems.

In the following some of the most common approaches to sustainable operations management are summarized. Most of them have been adapted from well-known operations management tools, which are working under the parameters of a businesses' established processes and structures. In the later section on research, development, and innovation, tools for the proactive change of existing structures are examined. The approaches summarized in the following are a valuable tool set for improving businesses' social and environmental performance at the operational level (Table 15.2).

- **Compliance to EHS management**: Probably the most extensive implementation of responsible business in operations is the one legally required in most regions. If not required by local law, certain behaviors towards the environment and for employee safety have become a fixed element of business operations. Usually, such activities are subsumed under the term of compliance. At the local level, compliance often translates into the job position of **Environment health and safety (EHS)** managers or supervisors.

Table 15.2 Operations Approaches to Responsible Management

Approach	*Responsible management instruments*	*Goal*	*Stakeholders involved*	*Typical advantages achieved*
Compliance & damage reduction	EHS management; cleaner production	Comply with normative requirements	Through employees for government; and normative organizations	↓Accidents/ environmental damage → ↓Operational risk, law suits
Operational efficiency	Eco-efficiency	Efficiency	Through employees	↓Resource consumption→ ↓Cost
Quality management	Total responsibility management; environmental Kaizen	Quality/customer satisfaction	Through employees for customers	↑Product quality→ ↑Customer satisfaction
Management systems	ISO 14000, ISO 26000; EMAS	Process integration and control	Through managers and employees	Increasing capacity to manage preceding approaches
Metrics & benchmarking	e.g. GRI indicators	Ensure measurability and manageability	Through managers and independent research institutions	Increase capability of goal-based responsible management.

The main goal of EHS management is usually to avoid events with high negative impacts (such as accidents and chemical spills or toxic emissions) from happening. EHS management is a well-established part of the operational risk management process.

- **Operational efficiency to eco-efficiency**: A main focus of operational management is to achieve operational efficiency; to ensure the minimum required resource usage for a given output. Efficiency is achieved when the amount of waste (waste = unused resources) is minimized. Minimizing (natural) resource usage and avoiding waste (pollution) almost sound like an environmentalist's jargon and, as a matter of fact, operational efficiency is highly aligned with improving environmental business performance. The responsible management tool of **eco-efficiency** aims at spotting and attacking areas of improvement for both better environmental performance and economic cost reduction (WBCSD, 1999). Eco-efficiency methodologies can often be integrated into existing management practices such as lean manufacturing and management.
- **Total quality management (TQM) to total responsibility management**: While efficiency has a process focus, quality management rather strives for customer satisfaction as its ultimate purpose. As a matter of fact, in an operational management context, quality is commonly understood as anything that contributes to satisfaction and value. Total quality management (TQM), the Six Sigma framework, the ISO 9000 series, and Kaizen are common management tools used to meet or exceed customer expectations. In responsible management, the customer satisfaction focus has been broadened to a general stakeholder satisfaction focus. The way to achieving stakeholder satisfaction is fulfilling the responsibilities towards stakeholders. The term "**total responsibility management**" (TRM) is born. The goal of TRM is to achieve maximum quality in responsible management out of all operations of an organization (Waddock, Bodwell, & Graves, 2002; Waddock & Bodwell, 2004). A quality management-based approach to environmental performance is environmental Kaizen, which establishes a continuous improvement process aiming at better environmental performance (Szell, 2004).

In order for the operational management instruments mentioned to work well, companies need to embed those instruments in two additional basic tools. The establishment of hard, tangible metrics measuring social, environmental, and economic business performance is a must for any subsequent management activity. Operations must also be embedded into the company's overall management system to work in a truly integrated, efficient, and effective manner.

- **Metrics and benchmarking**: A common prejudice is that social and environmental performance is not measurable. This is not true. In the chapter on support functions, the field of sustainability accounting will be highlighted to show how to develop sustainability metrics. Many companies use social and environmental **metrics** such as employee satisfaction for an employee welfare program, water usage per product for water protection programs, or male-female employee ratios to measure the progress of gender diversity initiatives. After the development of metrics, those measurements can be used in many ways adding value to responsible management in operations. One of the most important applications after controlling success is the establishments of benchmarks, either internally between different company facilities or externally, comparing with other businesses such as industry peers. An excellent benchmarking tool is the (often quantifiable) required-disclosures system by the Global Reporting Initiative, which can easily be accessed through companies' sustainability reports

- **Operations Management systems** connect a companies' departments through shared procedures, coordination, and information channels. Social and environmental factors for the management of business responsibility can often be integrated into existing management systems. Practices to do so vary; as do terms used for such systems. The longest-established are environmental management systems such as the ISO 14000 standards and the European Environmental Management and Auditing Standard (EMAS). While the ISO 26000 on social responsibility does not officially aim at establishing a management system standard, it nevertheless often is used as one. Blackburn (2007) integrates social and environmental topics by proposing a "sustainability operating system (SOS)".

How can there ever be zero waste?

Isn't it amazing that many companies announce zero-waste to landfill goals for their factories? How can those companies measure the achievement of this goal? The Greenbiz website provides a thrilling insight into seven companies and their "journey to zero waste". Successful practices include recycling, re-usage, inverse logistics of giving packaging to suppliers, and of course the re-design of processes in order to avoid creating waste in the first place (Lehrer, 2011).

Customer Relationship Management

The departments of a company in direct contact with customers are marketing, sales, and service. Those three departments as they are primarily in touch with customers are typically summarized as **customer relationship management (CRM)**. Those three functions are crucial for a good relationship with clients as one of the most influential stakeholders. In order to responsibly manage the customer relationship both a preventive and a proactive perspective needs to be assumed.

Preventively, harm that could possibly be done by CRM needs to be avoided. The list of potential negative effects is long. Most prominently, marketing usually tends to reinforce consumerism and an unnecessary overconsumption, which in turn creates adverse effects on the natural environment. Marketing may also be subject to manifold ethical conflicts. Marketing fast-food to children, promoting unhealthy-beauty ideals, and untruthful claims about products are only a few out of many potential areas of ethical conflicts with responsible management. Sales staff have often been accused of selling to maximize their own remuneration, instead of considering the best interest of their customers. Bad after-sales service, resulting in faulty products and decreased product lifetimes does not only decrease consumer satisfaction, but also speeds up the product turnover rate, boosting the negative environmental impacts from production and disposal.

Creating the wrong wants

The negative health effects of smoking are well known. As a result, tobacco marketing has long been restricted aggressively. There are many other side-effects among tobacco customers. For instance, in Mexico, the poorest households spend more money on tobacco than on healthcare. Marketing has the power and responsibility to promote viable and healthy consumption patterns (Miera-Juárez, Jiménez-Ruíz, & Reynales-Shigematsu, 2011). Recently, e-cigarettes have begun to be marketed. While not being healthy per-se, they are often considered a less unhealthy alternative, a fact that has also been picked up in the marketing efforts and corporate responsibility departments of major international tobacco companies.

In spite of the often-extensive criticism of the marketing, sales, and service functions, those departments do have at least as much potential to do good as much as to do bad. The field of **social marketing** for instance aims at using marketing methods, in order to achieve a behavior change to the good of society and environment; to encourage people to quit smoking, to stop using your car, or to save water. Social marketing does not sell a product, but it "sells behavior change". This approach is very different from **cause-related marketing**, which connects a product's sale to a good cause. TOMS shoes donate a pair of shoes every time consumers buy a pair. Danone in Mexico donates a percentage of the sales income from their products to a child-cancer foundation. The Product RED initiative allows multiple brands to associate with their cause of fighting HIV/AIDS in Africa, if those brands commit to donating a fair share of products' sales revenue. The communication chapters will provide deeper insight into the nuts and bolts of both marketing tools. **Servitization** is another promising tool applied in responsible management in customer relations. Servitization aims at substituting products with services, in order to reduce negative environmental and often also economic and social impacts. Ownership of a car for instance can be substituted by car sharing, which significantly decreases the environmental impact and ownership costs.

Many consumer tendencies and markets have been associated with responsible business. The world-wide Lifestyles of Health and Sustainability (LOHAS) market comprises a wide variety of market segments, which are associated with an improved social and environmental performance of the products being sold in them. Ecotourism, alternative energy, sustainable mobility, socially responsible investment are just a few of the market segments falling into the overall LOHAS market (LOHAS Magazine, 2010). The Bottom of the Pyramid (BoP) market is another world-wide phenomenon calling for responsible marketers' attention. As a matter of fact, marketing has traditionally worked to the medium to high income groups. BoP instead calls for marketing to the poor, a largely unattended market. Allowing low-income households to be included into the economic system is not only an important task to alleviate the consequences of poverty, but also provides an attractive and fresh market. Over four billion people worldwide live below the poverty line (Prahalad, 2010). In order to access those markets, the marketing management strategy needs to be adjusted; often drastically. The well-known four Ps of the marketing management process provide a helpful framework for

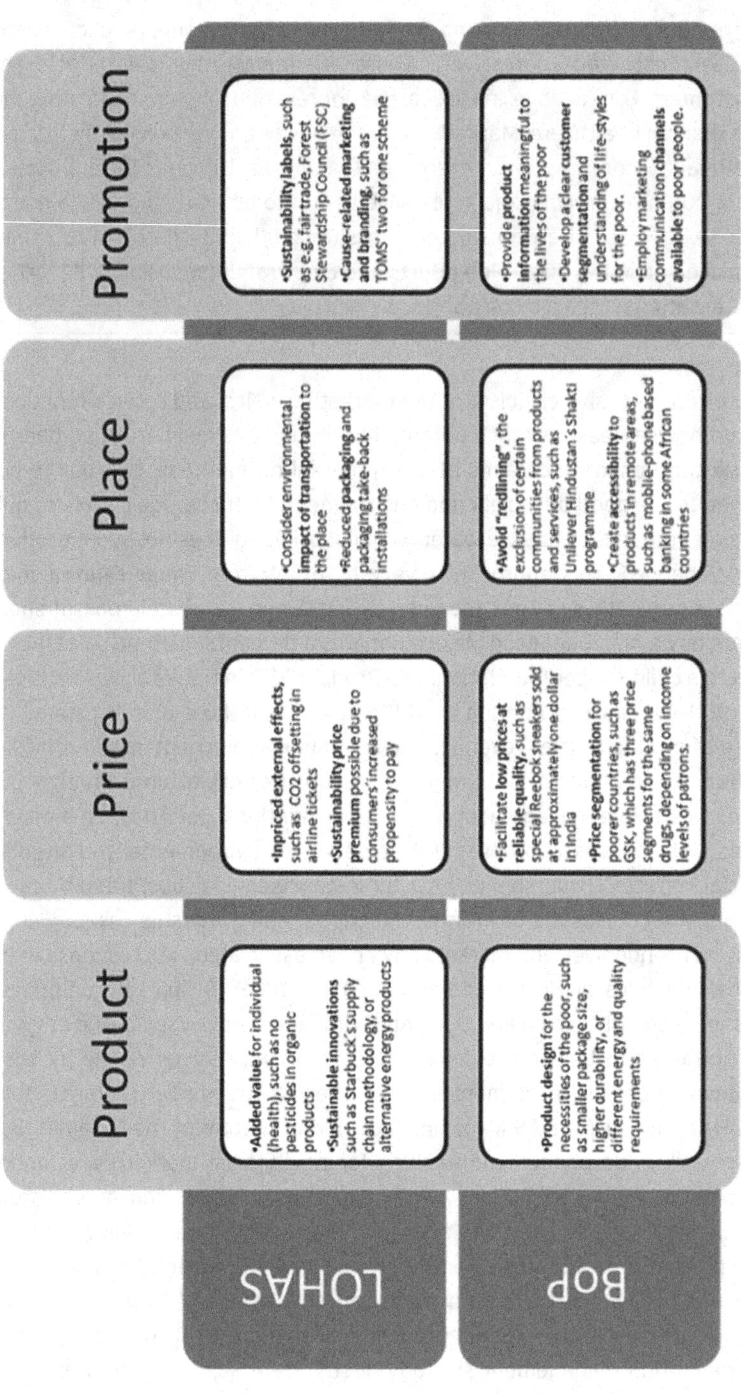

Product
Price
Place
Promotion
LOHAS
•Added value for individual (health), such as no pesticides in organic products
•Sustainable innovations such as Starbuck's supply chain methodology, or alternative energy products
•Inpriced external effects, such as CO2 offsetting in airline tickets
•Sustainability price premium possible due to consumers' increased propensity to pay
•Consider environmental impact of transportation to the place
•Reduced packaging and packaging take-back installations
•Sustainability labels, such as e.g. fair trade, Forest Stewardship Council (FSC)
•Cause-related marketing and branding, such as TOMS' two for one scheme
BoP
•Product design for the necessities of the poor, such as smaller package size, higher durability, or different energy and quality requirements
•Facilitate low prices at reliable quality, such as special Reebok sneakers sold at approximately one dollar in India
•Price segmentation for poorer countries, such as GSK, which has three price segments for the same drugs, depending on income levels of patrons.
•Avoid "redlining", the exclusion of certain communities from products and services, such as Unilever Hindustan's Shakti programme
•Create accessibility to products in remote areas, such as mobile-phone based banking in some African countries
•Provide product information meaningful to the lives of the poor
•Develop a clear customer segmentation and understanding of life-styles for the poor.
•Employ marketing communication channels available to poor people.

Figure 15.1 Applying the Four Ps on LOHAS and BoP Markets.

analyzing the necessary adjustments to be made in order to assess the new markets with responsible characteristics.

Figure 15.1 exemplarily shows how the four Ps (product, price, place, promotion) have been applied by companies, in order to shape solutions to the LOHAS and BoP market. Analyzing the four Ps of a company's existing product portfolio with an eye on the products' social and environmental performance may bring drastic improvements of the products' social, environmental, and economic performance.

Exercises

A. KNOW

Use the below multiple-choice questions to test your knowledge. Each answer may be wrong or right and there may be zero to four right or wrong answers per question:

1. Responsible management in logistics and operations...
   a. ...involves conflicts of interest between efficient logistics and sustainable development. An example is that logistics aims at offering transportation at the lowest cost possible, while sustainable development requires internalizing external costs.
   b. ... involves among the actions to mitigate the negative impact of logistics, so-called reverse logistics, which follows the primary goal of creating a local production and consumption network.
   c. ...includes among the actions to improve the social and environmental impact at the operational level, to move from mainstream operational efficiency to eco-efficiency.
   d. ...would require establishing indicators for measuring social, environmental, and economic business performance alike. Unfortunately, social and environmental performance cannot be measured quantitatively.
2. The marketing service and sales function, responsible management...
   a. ...involves the deployment of the tool social marketing, which aims to increase product sales by connecting it to a good cause.
   b. ...may attach marketing activities to social and environmental consumer movements such as the LOHAS consumer tendency.
   c. ...may attach marketing activities to the "BOP" (Basic Organic Products) market.
   d. ...involves manifold responsibilities towards customers stemming from the function's close relationship with customers.
3. Car2Go, a subsidiary of Daimler AG (the producer of car brands such as SMART, Maybach, and Mercedes-Benz) has established a car-sharing network in European and North American cities. This is an example of...
   a. ...a BoP market.
   b. ...servitization.

c. ...approaching a LOHAS market.
d. ...of a local production and consumption network.

B. THINK

Total responsibility management is based on the idea that companies should optimize the quality of their product or service for all stakeholders. Think of one situation where two company stakeholders would have very distinct ideas about the quality of a product. Then come up with changes to the product or services which reconcile these distinct requirements.

C. DO

The EMAS environmental management framework is based on the Plan-Do-Check-Act cycle to improve environmental performance. Run through the process in one area of activity either in your private or professional life. You will find more background information on the PDCA cycle on the EMAS website.

D. RELATE

Visit a businesses' environment (e.g. the area around a factory, or a shop) in person and try to unearth the links of how the business relates to its social, environmental, and economic local environment.

E. BE

Imagine you are the hygiene manager of a food poultry processing factory. Any time you have a doubt about a potential hygiene risk the production stops which causes your colleagues pressure in keeping up with their goals. How would that make you feel, and how would you cope with the situation?

Feedback

A. KNOW

Feedback 1

a. Right: This is an excellent example for typical conflicts experienced.
b. Wrong: Reverse logistics and local production and consumption networks are two distinct activities to mitigate the negative impact of logistics.
c. Right: Moving from mainstream operational efficiency to eco-efficiency includes environmental impacts into efficiency thinking, which in turn supports the environmental dimension of responsible business and management.
d. Wrong: The text provides many examples for excellent quantitative metrics.

Feedback 2

a. Wrong: Social marketing is to use marketing to change individuals' behavior for the good of society.

b. Right: In the chapter we mentioned both the BoP and the LOHAS market segments as relevant new markets.

c. Wrong: BOP stands for bottom of the pyramid market and refers to consumers of low income at the bottom of the income pyramid.

d. Right: This is right. However, while being customer focused, the customer relationship function could well also be reinterpreted as a stakeholder relationship function, if we consider the value proposition to our main stakeholders, our product.

Feedback 3

a. Wrong: There is no indication that users of the carsharing are located at the bottom of the economic wealth pyramid.

b. Right: Daimler moves from producing and selling a product (a car), to providing the service of having a car available (carsharing).

c. Right: While carsharing is not necessarily a health topic, the more eco-efficient usage of cars when shared is often related to a more sustainable lifestyle.

d. Wrong: The cars are still produced somewhere else and shipped to the location. So production and consumption are not in the same place.

B. THINK

Level	*Reconcile divergent perspectives*	*Notes*
+	Identification and reconciliation.	
=	Identification of divergent perspectives, but no reconciliation.	
–	Divergent perspectives have not been identified.	

C. DO

Level	*Application of management tools*	*Notes*
+	Cycle has been applied correctly and environmental performance has been improved.	
=	Cycle has been applied correctly.	
–	Cycle has not been applied correctly.	

D. RELATE

Level	*Ability to learn about local needs and impacts*	*Notes*
+	Deep appreciation of multiple relationships of the business to its locality.	
=	Basic ("obvious") appreciation of the relationship of the business to its locality.	
–	No relationship between business and its locality visible.	

E. BE

Level	*Moral agency*	*Notes*
+	Answer expresses a commitment to involve in moral agency no matter what.	
=	Answer expresses a commitment to balance moral agency and environmental pressures.	
–	Answer expresses an avoidance of moral agency when faced with potential opposition.	

References

AEA Technology. (2008). *Comparative life-cycle assessment of food commodities procured for UK consumption through a diversity of supply chains - FO0103*. United Kingdom: Department for Environment Food and Rural Affairs (DEFRA).

Blackburn, W. R. (2007). *The sustainability handbook: The complete management guide to achieving social, economic and environmental responsibility*. Washington: Earthscan.

Edwards, J. B., McKinnon, A. C., & Cullinane, S. L. (2010). Comparative analysis of the carbon footprints of conventional and online retailing. *International Journal of Physical Distribution and Logistics Management*, *40*(1/2), 103-123.

Financial Times. (2010). Global free zones of the future 2010/2011 winners. *FDI Intelligence*, 21-26.

Global Media. (2011). *Avanza Parque industrial Puro Potosino [The Puro Potosino industrial park makes progress]*. Retrieved November 2, 2011, from Global Media: https://www.globalmedia.mx/sanluis/ver_noticia.php?id=38767

H Ayuntamiento San Luis Potosí. (2011). *Programa Puro Potosino [Program Purely Potosí]*. Retrieved November 2, 2011, from H Ayuntamiento San Luis Potosí: https://sanluis.gob.mx/puropotosino/index.php

Hutchins, G. (2010). *Sustainability and operational excellence: One goal, not two*. London: Atos.

Kleindorfer, P. R., Singhal, K., & Van Wassenhove, L. N. (2005). Sustainable operations management. *Production and Operations Management*, *14*(4), 482-492.

Lehrer, J. (2011). *7 Success stories from the journey to zero waste*. Retrieved January 18, 2012, from Greenbiz: https://www.greenbiz.com/blog/2011/11/18/7-success-stories-journey-zero-waste?page=0%2C1&utm_source=GreenBuzz&utm_campaign=80b3699a77-GreenBuzz-2011-11-21&utm_medium=email

LOHAS Magazine. (2010). *LOHAS background*. Retrieved August 30, 2011, from The LOHAS magazine: https://www.lohas.com/about

Lovell, J. (2007). *Left-hand-turn elimination*. Retrieved January 18, 2012, from New York Times Magazine: https://www.nytimes.com/2007/12/09/magazine/09left-handturn.html

Miera-Juárez, B. S., Jiménez-Ruíz, J. A., & Reynales-Shigematsu, L. M. (2011). *Las repercusiones del consumo de tabaco en la distribución del gasto de los hogares mexicanos*. Mexico City: Instituto Nacional de Salud Pública.

Prahalad, C. K. (2010). *The fortune at the bottom of the pyramid: Eradicating poverty through profits (5th anniversary edition)*. Upper Saddle River: Pearson.

Rodrigue, J.-P., Slack, B., & Comtois, C. (2001). Green logistics (the paradoxes of). In A. Brewer, K. Button, & D. Hensher, *The handbook of logistics and supply-chain management* (London). Pergamon/Elsevier.

Starbucks. (2011). *Make a difference*. Retrieved January 18, 2012, from Starbucks: https://www.starbucks.com/thebigpicture

Szell, G. (2004). Environmental Kaizen: Environmental protection as a process. In G. Szell, & K. Tominaga, *Environmental challenges for Japan and Germany: Interdisciplinary and intercultural perspectives* (pp. 253–268). Frankfurt: Peter Lang.

Waddock, S., & Bodwell, C. (2004). Managing responsibility: What can be learnt from the quality movement? *California Management Review*, *47*(1), 25–38.

Waddock, S. A., Bodwell, C., & Graves, S. B. (2002). Responsibility: The new business imperative. *Academy of Management Executive*, *47*(1), 132–147.

WBCSD. (1999). *Eco-efficiency: Creating more value with less impact*. Geneva: World Business Council for Sustainable Development.

16 Support Functions

The previous chapter was focused on responsible business and management in companies' main functions directly involved into the production and delivery of products and services. This chapter will describe how to integrate responsible business and management into the functions of a company supporting this process, such as law and compliance, finance, and human resources.

Law and Compliance

Compliance is not one of the business functions usually considered central. Most definitions of responsible business and its sub-fields of social and environmental responsibilities take the topic beyond mere legal compliance. Why should one then think of the law and compliance department, when managing responsible business? The answer becomes obvious, when responsible management is understood as the management of the triple bottom line; of performance in the three dimensions society, environment, and economy. Responsible management is largely influenced by a breathtaking variety of compulsory laws (often called **hard law**), regulations and voluntary norms and standards (also called **soft law**) to comply with. Environmental and labor legislation, antitrust law, human rights, and international norms and standards are just some examples for how norms set the baseline for social and environmental business performance (Sobczak, 2006). This also goes in accordance with Carroll's (1991) popular pyramid model of business responsibilities, which describes legal responsibilities as a part of the responsible business concept.

Legislation that will transform business

"Obeying the law" sounds easy at first sight but becomes very complex when taken on in practice. Just understanding which laws apply to your job position, your function, your business, your industry, and to the locations of your company, including all branches, your suppliers and customers is a highly complex task. Before assuming any voluntary responsibility with stakeholders in responsible business, a company is well-advised to check if compulsory, legal responsibilities have been fulfilled. An important part of this law mapping task is to keep up with new legislation in responsible

DOI: 10.4324/9781003544074-22

business. The following trends are two world-wide movements in legislation that will transform how we do business. In 2011, the Australian clean energy act, which forces the country's 500 worst-polluting companies to pay a tax on carbon emissions, has been widely discussed (BBC, 2011). As a matter of fact, *carbon taxes* have long been an element of legislation in many countries from the European Union to India and South Africa. They increasingly become a legal standard around the world. Another strong trend is the increase in a company's sustainability reporting duties, which is an important external driver for responsible business (Ioannou & Serafeim, 2011). The trend moves towards *mandatory sustainability reporting* (UNEP; KPMG, 2006). The Global Reporting initiative has made public the commitment that from "2015, all large and medium-size companies in OECD countries and large emerging economies should be required to report on their Environmental, Social and Governance (ESG) performance and, if they do not do so, to explain why (GRI, 2011, p. 1)".

The job position of the **compliance officer**, representing businesses' compliance function, probably describes best how responsible business and law intersect. Compliance officers' function is to ensure conformity of the company's actions with both compulsory law and voluntary norms. Knowing hard and soft law is important for compliance job functions, and obeying the law becomes the baseline for responsible managers throughout all job functions. For instance, production managers will need to comply with environmental legislation in terms of waste treatment or emissions. Human resources professionals need to know and apply labor regulations. Anti-corruption, especially anti-bribery legislation, is an important factor for procurement managers. Consumer protection and product safety norms are a basic parameter of activities for professionals among others in research and development, marketing, and sales. Figure 16.1 describes some of the most salient areas of hard law as it applies to responsible management practice. For important soft-law applications, please review the list of norms in in the earlier chapter on responsible business norms.

Companies are not only obeying, but also making norms and "laws" applying to employees and other stakeholders, such as suppliers, shareholders or even consumers. The manifestation of such norms can take various forms from soft procedures to codes of conduct or firm contractual agreements. Such norms need to be constantly checked for consistence with external norms and with their ethical viability. The two basic approaches for establishing those norms are either to base them on values or on compliance. *Values-based programs* consist of an approach support the development of values and employee ethics, preventing from misconduct, while *compliance-based programs* work with consistently monitored and enforced concise rules. Both approaches show results in reducing misconduct, while there is evidence, that values-based programs achieved better results (Weaver & Treviño, 1999).

"Should Trees Have Standing?" is the controversial title of a highly recognized scientific paper from 1972. The author promotes the idea that natural objects should have rights, which then can be translated in concrete legislation (Stone, 1972). Obviously, that has not happened in the forty years since then. The question is why? What would happen if there was a "Universal Declaration of Nature's Rights" suggested to be as inviolable as human rights? What would happen if animals, plants, rivers, mountains, oceans, and whole eco-systems had the same rights for existence and integrity as human beings? The *deep ecology* movement has long postulated such rights and their practice implementation, which is based on the protection of the environment as an end, rather than a necessary precondition for peoples' well-being and survival (Naess, 1973). What companies can do despite lacking legislation is to at least provide non-human nature with the same attention as a stakeholder as human beings (Starik, 1995).

By stakeholder
E. g. consumer protection, employee rights, corporate governance (shareholders), procument legisation (suppliers)

By function
E.g. regulation for the management of dangerous substances (logistics), Sarbanes Oxley Act (accounting), emissions requirements (production)

By dimensions
Social, environmental, economic legislation

By industry
E.g. anti-money laundering (banking), extractives industry act (mining)

By issue
E.g. antitrust law (competition), climate & water protection, anti-corruption

By scope
Global, regional, national, local legislation

Figure 16.1 Classifications of Hard Law Important for Responsible Management.

Accounting

Accounting is typically done for two main purposes, to either provide numbers for the internal managerial process or to report externally. First, *managerial accounting* is often also called controlling and follows the maxim of "What cannot be measured cannot be managed". This is not exclusively true for financial accounting. Measuring and documenting social and environmental factors is an indispensable basis for successfully managing the responsible business. The second purpose of accounting is to create documentation for required external *reporting and tax* purposes. Also, this purpose is transferable to responsible management. Companies are increasingly required to inform about their social and environmental performance, as they are in terms of their economic performance (GRI, 2011). Accounting for responsible management has to be an integrated social, environmental, and economic (three-dimensional) accounting, also called **sustainability accounting** (Bent & Richardson, 2003). The Global Reporting Initiative, described in the chapter on responsible business and management norms, has made it their goal to establish required reporting for medium and big companies of OECD countries by 2015. Many local legislators have begun to require social and environmental reporting of companies located in their area of influence.

Figure 16.2 illustrates main elements of the accounting process. Activities and performance (outcomes) are first measured and then documented. The documentation then usually triggers feedback by both managers and general stakeholders, which in turn influences the activities of the company and ultimately the social, environmental, and economic performance achieved. A central role throughout the accounting process is played by **sustainability indicators**, well-defined social, environmental, and economic entities, which can be observed, measured, and managed (Keeble, Topiol, & Berkeley, 2003). The number of accidents happening in a company might be a *social indicator*, reflecting workplace security, which in turn is a highly important building stone to assume responsibilities for employee stakeholders. An *environmental indicator* frequently used is the amount of CO_2 produced by production activities. An **economic indicator** is, for instance, the return on investment. Indicators are valuable to both main purposes of accounting illustrated before. Indicators

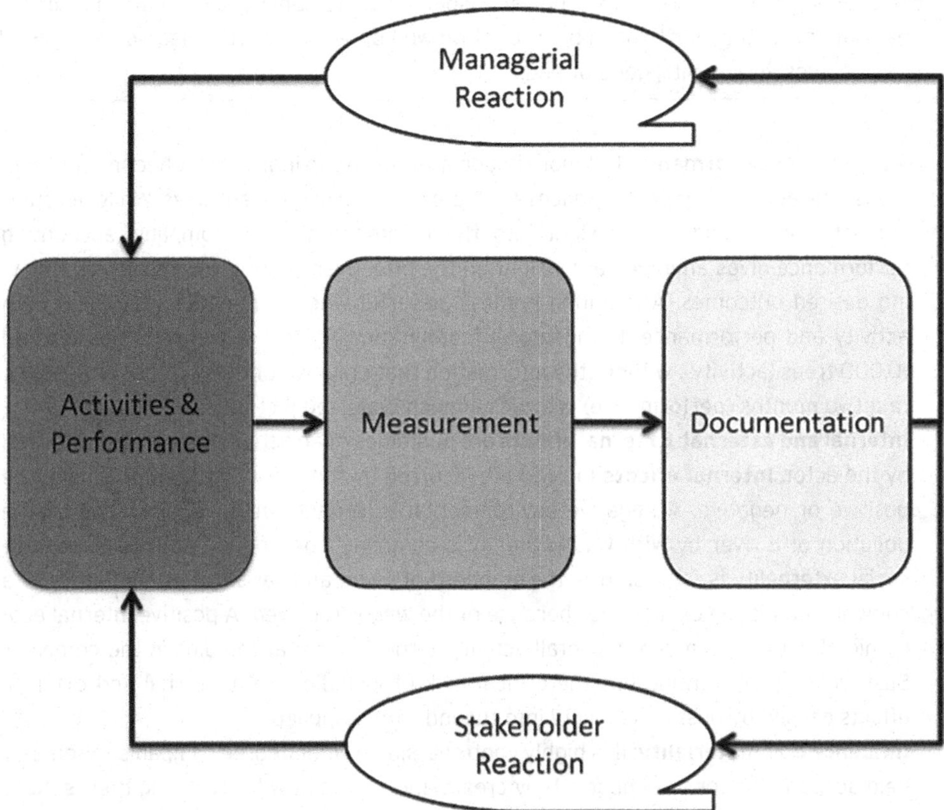

Figure 16.2 Basic Elements of the Sustainability Accounting Process.

help to adjust management activities, are the basis for **sustainability scorecards**, and can be used to evaluate and give incentives to single managers, projects, business functions and even may capture whole companies' triple bottom line performance. Indicators also provide tangible units to report and evaluate reported data. The following bullet points provide a quick checklist highlighting critical considerations to be made in order to develop powerful indicators.

Sustainability accounting grows with time and with responsible business

Going from purely financial accounting to the integration of social, environmental, and economic indicators may be quite a complex process. For instance, the Argentinean natural gas business, Gas Natural Fenosa describes it as an evolution. The company published its first sustainability report in 2005 and has since then evolved from a Global Reporting Initiative C ranking first to a B and finally to an A+ ranking[1] in 2009 and 2010. The company stresses that each of the over 100 indicators covered in the reports should not be seen as a mere figure, but as a whole management process, a team, and extensive policies (Ambito.com, 2011; Gas Natural Fenosa, 2011). This statement reflects very well another important aspect of sustainability accounting: As with financial accounting, sustainability accounting well-done is a mirror image of company's practices and results, good or bad.

- **Activity and performance**: Is it more important to develop indicators reflecting three-dimensional *activities* or *performance*? Both are valuable in different ways. While accounting activities provides an insight into the commitment of a company, accounting performance gives an important insight on the effectiveness of the company in achieving desired outcomes. Accounting is most powerful when it provides insight on both activity and performance. For instance, merely knowing that a company has planted 10,000 trees (activity), without the information that only two of those trees survived the first two months (performance) provides a much-distorted picture.
- **Internal and external: External effects** are outcomes of an activity that are not incurred by the actor. **Internal effects** instead are incurred by the actor. Those effects might be positive or negative. A negative environmental externality might for instance be the pollution of a river by with wastewater of a company's production activity. A positive social externality is for instance, the standard of living and satisfaction, the family of a company employee experiences because of the wages received. A positive internal economic effect of a company's overall activity is the profit that remains in the company. Sustainability accounting has the critical task of including both internal and external effects caused by business activity into the indicators applied.
- **Influence and materiality**: It is highly controversial to what degree companies should be held accountable for the impacts they create and assess how far reaching their **sphere of influence** is. Typical questions for defining a company's sphere of influence might be

"Are we able to improve the sustainability performance of our suppliers?" and "Are we able to influence the health of the eco-systems close to our production facilities?" The sphere of influence is defined as the potential influence a company has. Defining **materiality**, as illustrated in the strategy chapter, refers to the process of assessing how important single issues are to a certain business and its stakeholders. Effective sustainability accounting must include indicators for all material issues of a business within a sphere of influence as broad as possible. Even if a company finally decides to not assume **accountability** for indicators in their sphere of influence, it is important for managerial decisions to monitor factors that can potentially be influenced.

- **Measurability and monetarization**: It is a common prejudice to say that environmental and social topics are those "soft factors" that cannot be measured. However, there exist more than 80 well-established and standardized sustainability performance indicators, all of them quantitatively measurable (GRI, 2006). It has been supposed to translate also social and environmental indicators into monetary units; the process is called **monetarization**. The main advantage of monetarization lies in the creation of a common unit for measurement and comparison of different impacts and to create the basis for integrating social and environmental factors in the financial management of a company. Critics highlight the potential inaccuracies in transforming non-monetary indicators to monetary terms.

Sustainability accounting cannot be an end in itself. It should be used as a necessary condition to monitor and improve a company's activities and performance in order to move it towards becoming a truly **sustainable business**. To fulfill this function, outcomes of the accounting process must be made accessible to both, managers, and a broad set of external stakeholders. The chapter on norms has provided deeper insight on how to establish GRI reports covering the outcomes of the accounting process. The chapters on communication will illustrate how to communicate such outcomes. For both it is of crucial importance that those outcomes have run through an external verification and review process, a so-called **assurance**, which assesses the quality of the accounting process conducted and of its outcomes.

Finance

The goal of financial management is to maximize financial business performance indicators such as stockholder and shareholder value and profits. As has been discussed before, there has been a long ongoing debate on the relationship between social and financial business performance (see side-bar "The Business Case"). Interestingly, some prominent financial management scholars have adopted the view that there is not even a conflict between financial value and social value creation. A leading financial management textbook even argues that maximizing "stock value also benefits society" (Erhardt & Brigham, 2010, p. 11). In business ethics, maximizing financial performance is often seen as the main "root of evil" leading to unethical business conduct (Thielemann & Wettstein, 2008). Whichever argument one tends to support, one fact remains clear: Financial functions and financial management are

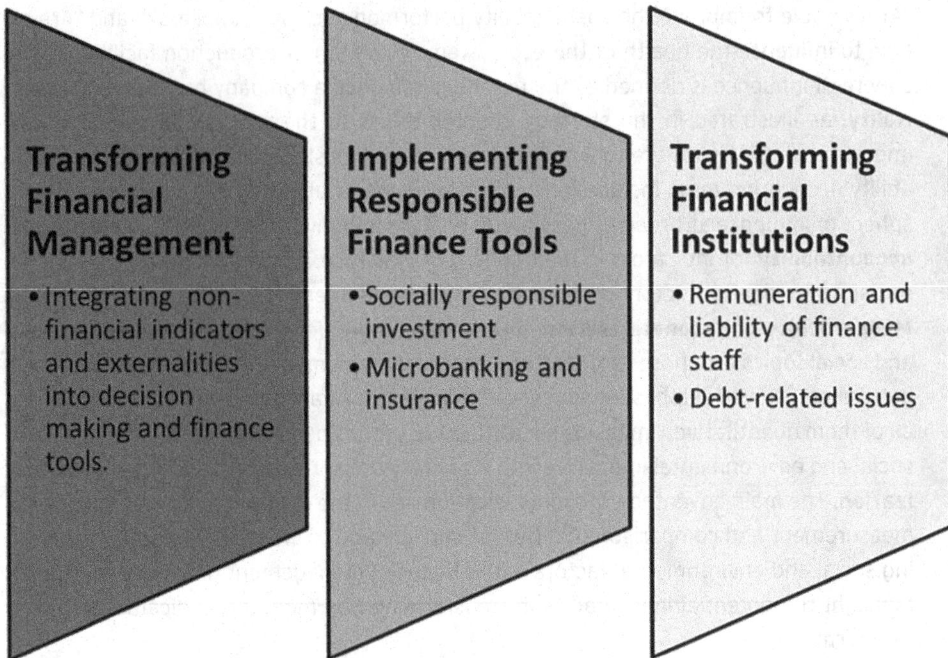

Figure 16.3 Activity Areas of Responsible Management in Finance.

central target areas for responsible management. Responsible management in finance can be sub-divided in three main areas of interest as illustrated in Figure 16.3. First of all, *financial management*, which primarily deals with money, is the lifeblood of every business and needs to be transformed towards more responsible ways, if the company as a whole is to be made first responsible and ultimately sustainable. Second, there are also *responsible finance tools*, such as socially responsible investment and microfinance that have the potential to strengthen the finance function, while creating value for society and environment. Third, it is important to scrutinize and transform the structure of *financial institutions*, in order to ensure the social, environmental, and economic sustainability of the financial industry as a whole. The focus in the following section will be on activity areas one and two, while area three will be covered in the chapter on changing systems.

The processes and parameters given by financial management largely define how decisions in business are made. Inquiries like "Is this profitable?", "How risky is this?", "Do we have budget for this?" "How much does it cost us?" are some centrally important questions that influence decision making in companies. Often those questions cannot be answered satisfactorily for responsible management advocates. The reason is that the crucial social and environmental components of responsible management are partially new to the field of finance, which at its core is concerned about the economic and financial dimensions. Thus, *transforming financial management* to align it with social and environmental value creation is key to getting responsible management right. The following list provides an initial overview of important, required action areas to establish responsible financial management.

- ***Inclusion***: Including *social and environmental, external, and internal* indicators into the financial management process is a crucial task for achieving well-informed and responsible outcomes. Effective sustainability accounting as illustrated in the last section is a necessary condition for the integration of socio-environmental factors with economic factors inside and outside the company. Inclusion can be reached, if the company conducts an extensive impact assessment of all its activities and then monetarizes those impacts so that they can be included in the calculation of financial key indicators. For instance, the project to build a road through the Peruvian Amazon might seem a financially viable alternative, if contrasting the rather small cost of road construction with the great economic opportunities provided by the project. The outcome of such an assessment might change drastically when taking into consideration the destruction of valuable eco-systems and the damage done to native communities losing their basis for subsistence.
- ***Integration***: Social and environmental factors need to be integrated into vocabulary and frameworks used in financial management: For instance, in addition to an economic value added, there is a need also to analyze the social and environmental value added. The term shareholder value might partially become substituted by stakeholder value. There might be a social and an environmental return on investment (ROI) in addition to the normally used financial ROI.
- ***Harmonization***: Maximization of financial indicators is usually conducted in a short run fashion. Sustainability is about maximizing the economic, social, and environmental value in the long run, and about sustaining that value n. This is why responsible finance that aims at leading to a sustainable business must find a balance between short-, medium-, and long-run indicators when evaluating performance.

In a simplistic description, the financial management process can be divided into the three phases that are described in Figure 16.4. Throughout those phases, manifold responsible business topics find application. During the *raise money* stage, paying attention to responsible business topics can lead to tangible advantages. Fundraising becomes easier because of good social and environmental performance. Sustainability indices such as the *Dow Jones Sustainability Index*, the *FTSE4Good*, or the Mexican *IPC Sustentable* provide information on companies' sustainability performance. Based on those and other sources of sustainability information, socially responsible investors aim at financing responsible companies' operations. A special type of responsible investment focusing on entrepreneurs are so-called "angel investors", affluent individuals who financially support start-ups. Increasingly angel investors focus on entrepreneurial ventures with added social and environmental value. For established companies with social, environmental, or ethical issues, activist investors are an important topic. Activist investors usually buy a minority share of a company in order to have a speaking right in stockholders' meetings. They then use this right to speak up to influence other shareholders and company leadership's decisions. Often shareholder activism is used to aggressively lobby changes towards a better social, environmental, and ethical business performance.

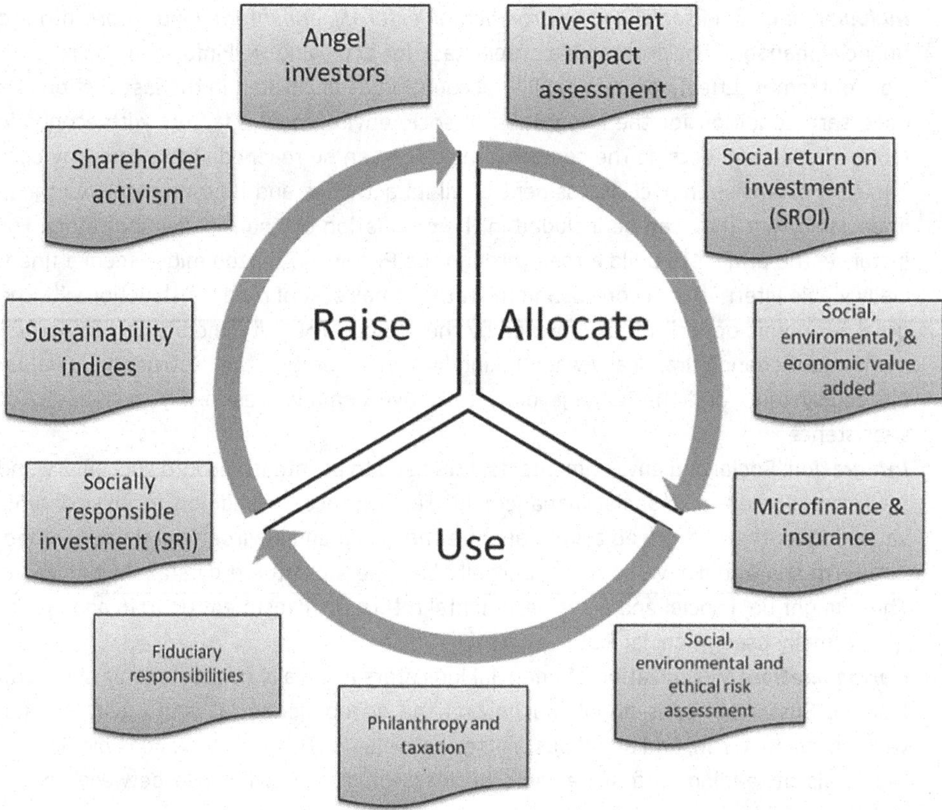

Figure 16.4 Responsible Management Topics throughout the Financial Management Process.

Redefining return on investment

One of the most important financial indicators is the return on investment (ROI). Traditionally the ROI is understood as the profit made from a certain amount of money invested (e.g. 30% of annual profit on an investment at the stock market). Two variants of ROI are especially important for responsible business. The ROI on social and environmental projects is an important indicator to understand. If you actually have a business case for your responsible business activity, then the results often can be monetarized (e.g. an increase in profit from sales of 40% through a cause-related marketing campaign). You could call this percentage a "return on responsible business". Such numbers will go a long way in explaining to stakeholders thinking in financial terms (e.g. investors, owners, managers), why you act responsibly. For stakeholders focusing on the social and environmental impacts made by businesses (e.g. NGOs and governments), it is important to be able to provide an *environmental* or *social return* on investment. Such an E-ROI or S-ROI can take various forms, depending on the respective social (S-) and environmental (E-) activity. A reforestation campaign, for instance, could use trees planted per dollar spent as E-ROI. The S-ROI of a gender diversity campaign could calculate the number of women hired per dollar spent on the campaign.

When companies *allocate money* to business activities, they usually align their allocation priorities with the company's strategy and the potential economic value added by each activity. To allocate money to the right project leading to a responsible business, those selection criteria need to include additional factors. Projects need to go through a rigorous assessment of their social and environmental impacts and ethical risks. Helpful concepts for such an assessment are the social and economic value-added frameworks (Bent & Richardson, 2003). Such an assessment allows for considering the triple bottom line of single company activities and the assignation of budgets, instead of the single financial bottom line, considered traditionally. Attractive areas of activity are microbanking and microinsurance programs. Both companies from the financial sector and non-financial sectors have increasingly used those frameworks to add value to their operations and at the same time reduce poverty.

When companies *use money* earned from business' operations, the basic options are either to disburse it to owners or to re-invest. In the case of disbursement, owners might decide to spend the money or re-invest themselves. Responsible ventures and businesses might be attractive investment opportunities. When companies re-invest, they might do so internally, or investing by acquiring other companies as part of the business' diversification strategy. So have done major mainstream corporations. For instance, the cleaning products giant CLOROX bought Burt's Bees, a natural cosmetics producer, L'Oreal bought The Body Shop, and The Coca Company invested in shares of the smoothie producer Innocent. Generally, such investments are likely to yield a high return as well as low risk. The high return can be explained by those businesses' operations in the rapidly growing markets related to social and environmental topics. Lower risk stems from the companies' focus on doing good business socially, environmentally, and ethically. Many risks are so-called social environmental and ethical (SEE) risks, which are reduced when explicitly focusing on SEE topics. Some companies such as CLOROX also justify such acquisitions by the need to learn from the acquired businesses about how to become a responsible business.

Organizational Structure and Design

Organizational structure and design are management tasks that are central to responsible business. Companies that aim at ultimately becoming a sustainable business often require substantial change of their organizational structure to reach this goal. Central questions are, for instance, "Which job functions, departments and institutions should be empowered to lead the change towards more responsibility?", "What is the role of individuals in a responsible company?", "What role, responsibilities, and power does the organization provide stakeholders with?" "What processes need to be changed to become a responsible business?" As reflected in many of the preceding questions, the management task of **organizational structure and design** is to determine roles, power, responsibilities, information flows, and processes inside a company (see Figure 16.5).

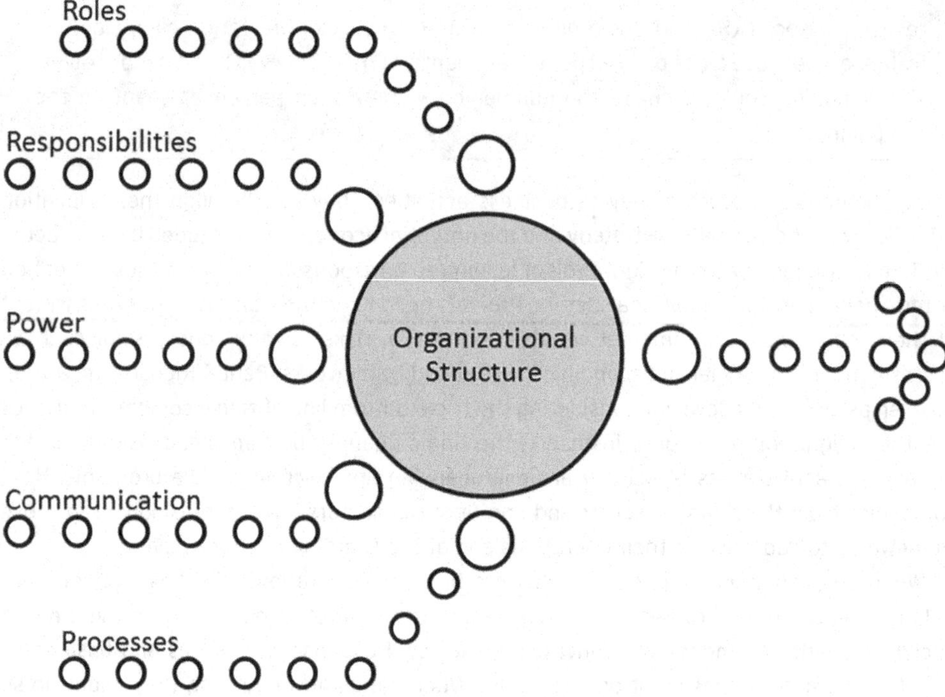

Figure 16.5 Elements of Organizational Structure.

Spotting responsible business throughout the organizational institutions and structure

Do businesses really consider responsible business in their organizational institutions? Among the world's biggest corporations' 96% have a formal corporate responsibility (CR) function. This number increases with organization size. Among the businesses without such a function, 66% mention that CR is integrated into other functions as the reason for the absence of a stand-alone function. Company boards increasingly (41%) include designated members for CR topics (Corporate Responsibility Magazine, 2010). The C-level leaders in charge of such departments widely vary in names. Examples are, for instance, the well-known Chief Compliance Officer or the Chief Sustainability and Responsibility Officers. Other versions include the Chief Reputation and Sustainability Officer and the Chief Visionary Officers (Vives, 2011).

Resulting from the basic task description it becomes clear that organizational design and structuring has the power to question and change the basic structure of the firm. It can either be an inhibitor, preventing or considerably slowing down the development of a responsible business, or a strong catalyst creating an internal business structure, conducive to assuming stakeholder responsibilities. In the following a checklist for organizational structure change towards responsible business provides basic starting points for facilitating responsible business through organizational structure.

- Has your organization **established and empowered institutions** promoting responsible business? Examples for such institutions range from codes of conduct and ethics, responsibility budgets, corporate foundations, responsibility hotlines, whistle-blowing mechanisms, to whole departments in charge of responsible business. It is of critical importance not only to establish such institutions, but also to provide them with the necessary power to exert a significant influence. Empowerment features, for instance, consist of a salient position in organizational hierarchy, a big budget, and support and proximity to high-level leaders.
- Has your organization created high-impact **job positions** in charge of responsible business as main task of their job description? The titles Global Sustainability Director, Vice President Responsible Business, Chief Responsibility Officer all reflect an increasing trend to assign c-suite individuals in charge of developing responsible businesses.
- Has your organization re-defined the **role and power of main stakeholders** throughout the organizational structure? Responsible business must have stakeholders at its core. How does your company institutionalize stakeholder engagement and equip stakeholders with the power to take part in shaping and managing the organization? Examples of providing stakeholders with central roles are boards of directors representing primary internal and external stakeholders, inclusion of stakeholders into core processes, and the creation of channels for exchange with stakeholder groups.
- Does your organization facilitate **criticism, innovation, and disruptive change**? Hierarchies and power structures can be a serious impediment to change towards becoming a responsible business. Whistle-blowing and proposal mechanisms for employees help to create a critical culture inside the company that brings problematic areas to the attention of decision-makers. Transformation to responsible business is only possible if innovation is furthered and structures are flexible enough to facilitate disruptive change, instead of inhibiting it. The chapter on changing organizations provides a deeper insight on how to achieve such change by illustrating the tools of change management.

Corporate governance

The term **Corporate governance** refers to the rules, mechanisms and institutions that regulate and control businesses. The main difference between organizational structure and corporate governance lies in the governance topic's focus on managing the **principle-agent relationship** that exists between the managers and owners of a company. In the traditional understanding of corporate governance, the aim is to ensure that managers in companies act in the best interest of owners. A main conflict is that owners usually aim at maximizing profits, while managers prefer to maximize their personal well-being. Managers might for instance prefer less-risky investments, in order to protect their own jobs, prefer higher compensation than justified, and might strive for personal power against the best interest of maximizing profits.

A *progressive understanding* of corporate governance is based not on a narrow owner perspective, but on assuring that managers act in the best interest of a broader set of stakeholders. The principle-agent relationship between managers and society as a whole is to be managed. Such a progressive understanding is rather aligned with the businesses' overall responsibilities instead of the narrow set of responsibilities towards owners (Freeman & Reed, 1983). The contemporary understanding of corporate governance, as illustrated for instance in the OECD Principles of Corporate Governance, usually is a mixture of traditional and progressive understanding (OECD, 2004).

Governance is about the way companies are controlled externally and internally (see Figure 16.6). *External control* in the traditional understanding stems from mechanisms of the financial market. If management is not able to ensure above-average returns on owners' investment in the company two regulation mechanisms get active. Either owners will replace the existing management, or the company will be bought by new owners that have detected that it is underperforming. Also new owners would replace the old management. External control in the progressive understanding consists of increasing stakeholder opposition to the activities in which the company is not acting in the stakeholders' best interest; stakeholders would revoke the company's **social license to operate.**

Companies' main *internal control* mechanisms can be subdivided into three main topics (Hitt, Ireland, & Hoskisson, 2007). *Ownership structure* of companies might, for instance, be characterized by individual, family, or conglomerate ownership, or by large institutional owners such as banks or governmental institutions. This structure largely influences the power and preferences of owners. The *board of directors* might consist of a mixture of internal and external individuals to balance interests. Also, the double function of many CEOs, simultaneously serving as chairman of the board has been criticized as the "fox guarding the hen-house" situation, compromising the board's control function. *Executive compensation* is considered an important tool for aligning manager's interest and stockholders' interest. High performance-based compensation packages are a typical practice, which on the other hand is often questioned because

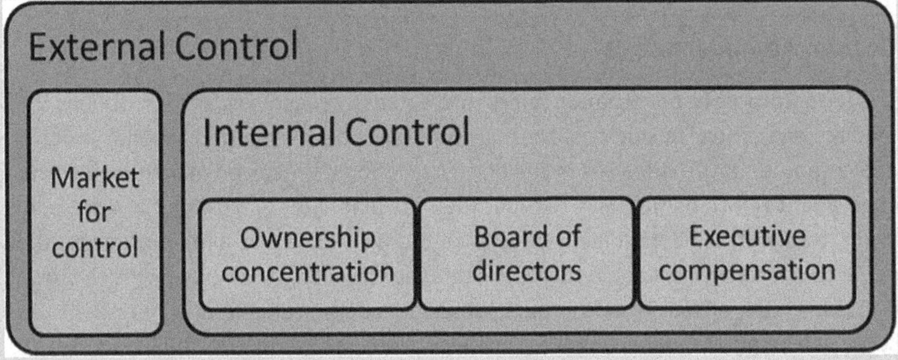

Figure 16.6 Control Mechanisms and Governance.

of a lack of fairness in comparison with the much lower wages of average employees. The high manager wages resulting from good performance have often brought about aggressive criticism from employees and civil society in general. Control mechanisms for good corporate governance operate in a constant stress field between narrow shareholder responsibilities and the broader responsibility to remaining stakeholders and society as a whole.

Human Resources Management

Human resources (HR) and responsible business are interlinked in a symbiotic relationship. HR needs responsible business as much as responsible business needs HR. Responsible business activities throughout many surveys has been shown to support and enrich the work of HR management (see Figure 16.7).

How does responsible business support HR? Responsible business covers many causes related to companies' responsibilities towards employees, which are also core to the activity of the HR department. Responsible business, for instance, means improvement of workplace health and security, increased work satisfaction and human development, assurance of a healthy work-life balance, promotion of diversity, equal opportunities, and fair wages. Key performance indicators of HR management may be positively influenced by employees' perception of working for a responsible company. One indicator typically influenced positively is the motivation of employees. Also, the attraction of prospective employees by a company's reputation of providing a responsible, "great place to work" is a factor positively affecting the work of the HR department. In addition to this, the employee retention rate is typically increased and the turnover rate reduced by becoming a responsible business. Low turnover rates and higher work motivation usually result in tangible cost savings throughout the

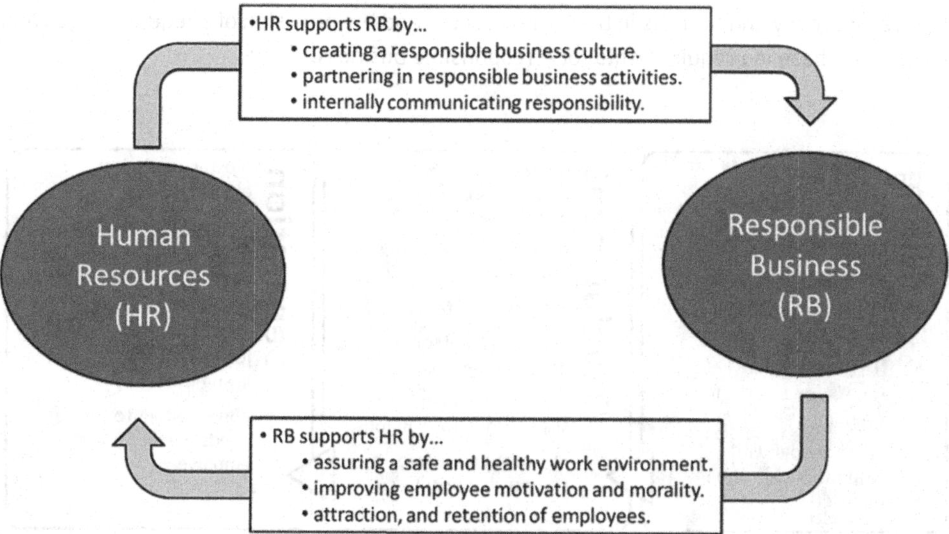

Figure 16.7 Symbiosis of Human Resources and Responsible Business.

employee life cycle. As a result, companies, if managing the responsible human resources process right, have the potential to, at the same time, increase employee welfare, improve the quality of their human resources, and reduce costs (SHRM, 2007).

How does HR support responsible business? "CSR – HR = PR" (SHRM, 2011) is a formula used by the Society for Human Resources Management to describe the importance of HR management to implementing responsible business. The message is that if HR is not involved in responsible business activities, it can only result in superficial, weakly integrated public relations talk. Such public relations work for sure fulfills an important function in responsible business, but can easily result in accusations of greenwashing, if not based on sound implementation through human resources activities. As a matter of fact, the HR department is crucially instrumental for implementing successful responsible business activities. Why? HR is a crucial partner in implementing responsible business activities, from functions as broad as hiring employees with the right attitudes values and skill set, to functions as specific as conducting volunteering programs. HR is also crucially important when it comes to credibly communicating business responsibility internally. Last, but not least, employees are the critical entity in creating a responsible corporate culture, a situation which is often called "embedding responsible business into the DNA of the company".

Companies successfully implementing a responsible human resources culture do so throughout all stages of the "*employee life cycle*" as described in Figure 16.8.

The *hiring* stage begins even before a concrete job opening. Employer branding, a measure of promoting the company's responsible image among potential employees, aims at generally attracting employees to the company beyond individual job openings. Some companies even heavily invest in external education programs at public schools and universities, in order to actively qualify future employees, who otherwise would not have a possibility of being hired. The creation of job profiles focusing on responsible business may additionally attract employees. It may also attract employees with the right competences necessary for the company's shift towards responsible and sustainable business. It goes without saying that transparency and fairness in the hiring process and the provision of adequate wages and benefits are baseline requirements for a responsible business.

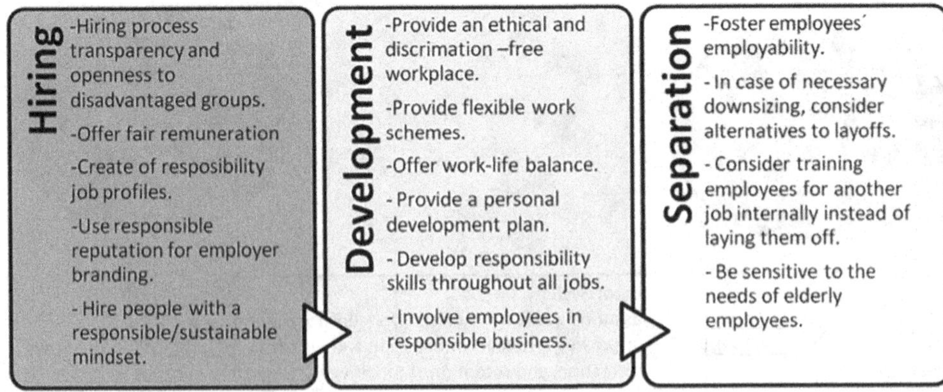

Figure 16.8 Simplified "Employee Life Cycle".

The employee *development* stage describes the time of productive engagement between employees and the company. The underlying goal during this time is to simultaneously increase employee welfare and increase the value of the overall human capital involved in the company. Activities to reach those goals are to provide an ethical and discrimination-free workplace, to provide flexible work schemes such as telework or flexible work hours; to provide an attractive personnel development plan including feedback schemes; and to offer the right prerequisites to develop a healthy work-life balance. In order to develop responsibility competences throughout the company, it is also important to empower employees to contribute to and participate in responsible business. Active development of sustainability job skills is also an important contribution of HR management to the development of responsible business.

Work-life balance, good for employee and employer?

Should it be of any concern to a business if employees are able to live a life, balanced between professional and private life? According to the British *HR Magazine*, it pays off for businesses to support such a balance, as a work-life imbalance is the number one reason for workplace absence. A healthy work-life balance instead contributes to motivation and increases productivity. Thus, it is not surprising that as much as 38% of employers participating in a UK survey mentioned improving their employees' work-life balance as a top priority(HR Magazine, 2012).

The *separation* stage deals with the point in time where employees leave the company for whatever reason. In the case of downsizing responsible companies might consider options different from laying people off. Alternatives might be part-time employment or temporal leaves. Separation due to a redundancy of employees' competences can be avoided by training employees in other competences valuable to the business. An irresponsible practice in some companies is to fire employees before their old-age benefits, to be paid by the company, grow too big. To avoid such irresponsible practices, of course, is the minimum baseline of responsible business during the separation phase. Companies may offer an active outplacement support, which prepares employees to succeed in the labor market. Even before people are outplaced, responsible business should take care of building up employees' employability, their ability to succeed in the labor market, long before they need to or want to switch jobs.

Research, Development, and Innovation

R&D, technology, and innovation are important building blocks towards the development of responsible and sustainable processes, products, and organizations. The process of innovating for a better social, environmental, and economic performance is called *sustainable innovation*. Examples might include changes from integrating a material produced by a poor community into the production process to fully powering your production facilities using renewable energies and to changing the formula of your beverage product to not use industry sugar any more or to switch from producing a product to producing a less resource

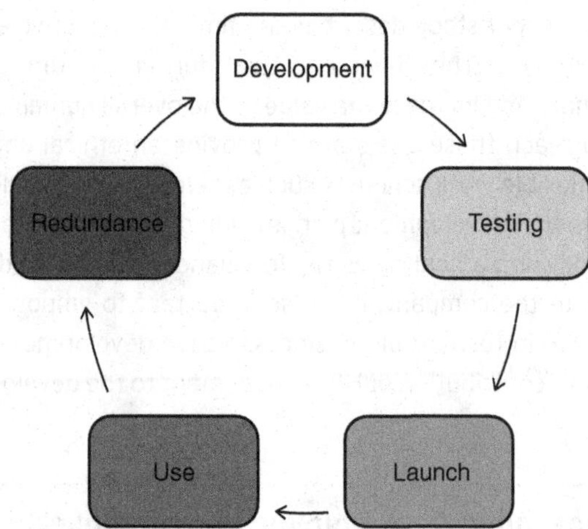

Figure 16.9 The Business Life Cycle of Innovations.

intensive service. As with any other innovation process, sustainable innovation follows the basic steps of the innovation business life cycle as illustrated in Figure 16.9.

What usually comes to mind when thinking of research and development is the *development* process, which is only the first step of the overall R&D process. It is an important step, however. The basic question to be asked for sustainable innovation is: How can we change processes and products in order to improve the social, environmental, and economic performance and sustainability of companies' activities? During the development process it is crucially important to thoroughly assess the social, environmental, and economic impacts of the innovation to be implemented throughout the products' physical life cycle, and to involve stakeholders in the development process. Social and environmental issues have been proven to inspire business innovations and to open access to new markets. Sustainable innovation supports marketing through the products and helps to shaper those with improved social and environmental impact while simultaneously accessing new markets such as the LOHAS and BoP markets. The *testing* stage might use "the social sector as betasite" (Kanter, 1999), a place where prototypes can be honed to perfection. A win-win practice is to provide communities that usually would not be able to afford buying with the not perfect (but safe) product or process for free and, in return, ask for feedback. The testing stage also is where products can be scrutinized in terms of potential real-life implications that question their sustainability.

The *launch* stage is critical for positioning the product in the market segment where it truly adds sustainable value and to make sure that the *use* given to the product is truly sustainable. It needs to be ensured, that consumers (product innovations) and employees (process innovations) use the product in the adequate way to realize its full potential to make a positive impact. The interconnection with marketing again plays an important role. However, as sustainable as a product might be, if it is marketed to be over-consumed, its potential positive impact is limited, through the negative environmental impact piling up through over-consumption. The last stage in the business life cycle of innovations is *redundancy* of the product or process. Redundancy in mainstream business occurs when a product has lost its market potential or when a process can be replaced by a more efficient one. For sustainable innovation two additional questions have to be added to assess redundancy. Is the product or process still socially and environmentally viable or should it be abandoned? Is there a more responsible and sustainable alternative to the product or process?

The above description is focused on product and process innovation as part of a company's research and development efforts. However, this setting is not always the dominant one. For instance, a distinct subject of innovation efforts, apart from product and process, is a form of organizational innovation – *business model innovation*. However, we are not going much deeper into such innovation in this chapter, as it is typically not part of the activities of the support functions; including R&D. Business model innovation as outlined in the strategy and innovation chapters implies a much more exhaustive change. Business models are the underlying logic and the very essence of what a business is and does. Thus, it has to be a company-embracing process which "changes everything". Accordingly, products and processes may be changed as part of a business model innovation.

Exercises

A. KNOW

Use the below multiple-choice questions to test your knowledge. Each answer may be wrong or right and there may be zero to four right or wrong answers per question:

1. Responsible management in the law and compliance and in the accounting functions...
   a. ...involves the compliance with soft law. Soft law refers to formal legislation that only applies to a small, specific set of companies.
   b. ...involves areas of hard law, such as environmental legislation, consumer protection, and labor rights.
   c. ...in the sustainability accounting process involves measurement and documentation of social, environmental, and economic activities and performance.
   d. ...involves the development of indicators to measure social, environmental, and economic performance and activity. In order to reduce complexity, such indicators should exclusively focus on company-internal business activities, the so-called sphere of influence.
2. Responsible management in finance, organizational structure, and governance...
   a. ...involves three activity areas for responsible management in finance; transforming financial management in businesses, implementing responsible finance tools such as microfinance, and transforming financial institutions.
   b. ...involves establishing a responsible financial management framework. An important point to be paid attention to in such a framework is integration. Integration here refers to the necessity to integrate finance and accounting.

c. ...includes structural change towards responsible business, such as creating institutions and ensuring that the business structure allows for criticism, innovation, and even disruptive change.

d. ...the topic of corporate governance, which describes the rules, mechanisms, and institutions that regulate and control businesses. Corporate governance fulfills the one and only function to ensure that the organization is governed in the best interest of shareholders.

3. Responsible management in human resources...
   a. ...can be seen as a one-sided relationship for the unique benefit to human resources.
   b. ...often leads to a situation where responsible business supports human resources management by, for instance, improving employee motivation and morale and by supporting the attraction and retention of employees.
   c. ...involves implementing a culture of responsibility in human resources, which in turn may influence the whole employee life cycle.
   d. ...builds upon the assumption that the responsibility for employees ends at the time when it is clear when the employee will leave the business.

4. Research and development in responsible business...
   a. ...involves sustainable innovation as the process of innovating with the goal of a better social, environmental, and economic performance of products and processes.
   b. ...involves adjustments throughout the business life cycle of innovations, integrating sustainable innovation into this life cycle.
   c. ...involves eco-innovation, which always refers to the application of green technologies in businesses.
   d. ...involves the social innovation approach, which aims at creating processes and products with an improved social impact

B. THINK

Rethink one of the following concepts by asking how it relates to responsible business, and how it would need to be re-conceptualized to fit well into a responsible business world: a) shareholder value maximization; b) human resource; c) bottom line.

C. DO

Design and implement a small-scale sustainability accounting process for something you do.

D. RELATE

Think about one organization you know well, or identify one that has much information publicly available. Whom would you need to speak to in this organization to change it towards more sustainability? What motivations and interests might people have to join your cause or oppose it? Who might become your allies and opponents in the process? What would your game plan look like?

E. BE

In human resources assessment situations, you might find questions like the following. Answer the one that best reflects your attitude to moral goals at work (Spurgin, 2004):

a. It is important for me to use prudential judgment in making decisions at work.
b. When engaged in action, I do not typically consider how virtuous my motives are as I move to accomplish objectives.
c. I think about my motives when achieving the mission, to ensure they are based upon moral ends.

Feedback

A. KNOW

Feedback 1

a. Wrong: Soft law refers to voluntary norms and standards, such as the ISO norms.
b. Right: These areas of hard law are exemplified in the overview figure of typical hard laws.
c. Right: These are central elements of the sustainability accounting process as illustrated in the figure describing such a process.
d. Wrong: The sphere of influence to be included in indicator development usually involves much more than only company-internal activity.

Feedback 2

a. Right: All three are illustrated in the section on responsible management in the finance function.
b. Wrong: Integration refers to integrating social and environmental factors into the frameworks used in financial management.
c. Right: These elements have been described as part of the organizational structuring process for responsible business and management.
d. Wrong: Corporate governance may also be understood as managing to the best of a broad set of stakeholders, not only shareholders (see Box on Corporate Governance).

Feedback 3

a. Wrong: Responsible management in human resources co-exist in a mutually benefitting symbiotic relationship.
b. Right: Responsible management practices supporting the goals of HR management are part of the symbiotic relationship between both topics.
c. Right: Responsibility may become a cultural aspect of a company that leads to a set of responsible practices in all different parts of the employee life cycle.
d. Wrong: Responsible human resources management includes responsibility in the so-called separation phase, after it is clear when the employee will leave the business.

Feedback 4

a. Right: Improved triple bottom line performance is the unifying goal for sustainable innovation.
b. Right: Sustainable innovation may impact the business life cycle of a product or process innovation at several stages.
c. Wrong: The green technology movement is only one possible approach to reducing the negative environmental impact through innovation.
d. Right: The improvement of social impact is the desired outcome of social innovation.

B. THINK

Level	*Rethinking business concepts and principles*	*Notes*
+	Appreciation of conceptual issues when applied in a responsible business world and convincing proposals for reconceptualization.	
=	Appreciation of the issues of the concept in a responsible business world.	
–	No appreciation of the need for the concept to change in a responsible business world.	

C. DO

Level	*Implementation skills*	*Notes*
+	Designed and implemented.	
=	Feasible sustainability accounting process has been designed.	
–	No sustainability accounting process.	

D. RELATE

Level	Political skills	Notes
+	Promising game plan for change based on convincing understanding of the inner workings of the organizations.	
=	Insight into political structures, but no feasible game plan.	
–	Little insight into "political structures" of the organization.	

E. BE

Level	Enacting moral goals	Notes
+	a) I think about my motives when achieving the mission, to ensure they are based upon moral ends.	
=	b) It is important for me to use prudential judgment in making decisions at work.	
–	c) When engaged in action, I do not typically consider how virtuous my motives are as I move to accomplish objectives.	

Note

1 Rankings of Global Reporting Initiative (GRI) reports are based on quality criteria, defined by the GRI and checked by GRI-accredited auditing organizations.

References

Ambito.com. (2011). *Gas Natural Fenosa consigue la máxima calificación de GRI por segundo año consecutivo [Gas Natural Fenosa achieves the maximum GRI ranking for the second year in a row]*. Retrieved January 22, 2012, from https://www.ambito.com/noticia.asp?id=597801

BBC. (2011). *Australia Senate backs carbon tax*. Retrieved January 22, 2012, from BBC News Asia: https://www.bbc.co.uk/news/world-asia-15632160

Bent, D., & Richardson, J. (2003). *Sustainability accounting guide: The Sigma guidelines toolkit*. London: Sigma Project.

Carroll, A. B. (1991, July-August). The pyramid of corporate social responsibility: Toward the moral management of organizational stakeholders. *Business Horizons*, 225–235.

Corporate Responsibility Magazine. (2010). *Corporate responsibility best practices: Setting the baseline*.

Erhardt, M. C., & Brigham, E. F. (2010). *Financial management: Theory and practice*. Mason: Cengage.

Freeman, R. E., & Reed, D. L. (1983). Stockholders and stakeholders: A new perspective on corporate governance. *California Management Review*, *15*(3), 88–106.

Gas Natural Fenosa. (2011). *Informe de responsabilidad corporativa 2010*.

GRI. (2006). *Sustainability reporting guidelines*. Amsterdam: Global Reporting Initiative.

GRI. (2011). *Rethink. Rebuild. Report.: The Amsterdam global conference on sustainability and transparency*. Amsterdam: Global Reporting Initiative.

Hitt, M. A., Ireland, R. D., & Hoskisson, R. E. (2007). *Strategic management: Competitiveness and globalization* (7th ed.). Mason: Thomson Southwestern.

HR Magazine. (2012). *Work/life balance ranks higher than stress as the biggest health concern for employers, says GRiD*. Retrieved January 23, 2012, from https://www.hrmagazine.co.uk/hro/news/1020665/work-life-balance-ranks-stress-biggest-health-concern-employers-grid

Ioannou, I., & Serafeim, G. (2011). The consequences of mandatory corporate sustainability reporting. *Harvard Business School Working Paper Series, 100*(11).

Kanter, R. M. (1999). From spare change to real change: The social sector as beta site for business innovation. *Harvard Business Review, 77*(3), 122–132.

Keeble, J. J., Topiol, S., & Berkeley, S. (2003). Using indicators to measure sustainability performance at corporate and project level. *Journal of Business Ethics, 33*(2/3), 149–158.

Naess, A. (1973). The shallow and the deep, long run ecology movement: A summary. *Inquiry, 16*, 95–100.

OECD. (2004). *OECD principles of corporate governance*. Retrieved from OECD principles for corporate governance: https://www.oecd.org/dataoecd/32/18/31557724.pdf

SHRM. (2007). *2007 Corporate social responsibility: United States, Australia, India, China, Canada, Mexico and Brasil*.

SHRM. (2011). *Advancing sustainability: HR's role*.

Sobczak, A. (2006). Are codes of conduct in global supply chains really voluntary? From soft law regulations of labour regulations to consumer law. *Business Ethics Quarterly, 16*(2), 167–184.

Spurgin, E. W. (2004). The goals and merits of a business ethics competency exam. *Journal of Business Ethics, 50*(3), 279–288.

Starik, M. (1995). Should trees have managerial standing? Toward stakeholder status for non-human nature. *Journal of Business Ethics, 14*(3), 207–217.

Stone, C. D. (1972). Should trees have standing? *Southern California Law Review, 45*.

Thielemann, U., & Wettstein, F. (2008). *The case against the business case and the idea of "earned reputation"*. St. Gallen: Institute for Business Ethics.

UNEP; KPMG. (2006). *Carrots and sticks for starters*. Parktown: KPMG Global Sustainability Services.

Vives, A. (2011). *Chief Reputation Officer, Chief Sustainability Officer… ¿Y el Chief Responsibility Officer?* Retrieved January 22, 2012, from Expok: https://www.expoknews.com/2011/07/11/chief-reputation-officer-chief-sustainability-officer%E2%80%A6-y-el-chief-responsibility-officer/

Weaver, G. R., & Treviño, L. K. (1999). Compliance and values oriented ethics programs: Influences on employees'attitudes and behavior. *Business Ethics Quarterly, 9*(2), 315–335.

17 Supply Chain Management

While the preceding chapters illustrated how to conduct responsible business throughout the internal functions of a business, now the focus will shift to how to multiply responsible business throughout a company's external supply chain relations. The reality is much more complex and the **sustainable supply chain management** process is much more than a simple copy-and-paste of responsible businesses' practices. Supply chain management today often confronts the two main issues; the complexity of globalization and numerous ethical issues that are encountered in global supply chains (Svensson, 2009).

> **Dangerous supply chain**
>
> The list of costly supply chain scandals is long. One of the most prominent examples is the ongoing struggle betweeen Nike and activitsts about working conditions in the factories supplying the sports shoes giant. Another scandal that cost its reputation was encountered by Mattel. The company had to recall millions of toys that had been painted by Chinese manufacturers using highly toxic lead paint. (Barboza D., 2007a). In 2011, a contractor of the fashion retailer Zara was accused of employing slave labor in the production process (Pereira & Alerigi, 2011). In the same year Apple faced the existence of fake Apple stores in China, that even the local employees thought were real (Lee M., 2011b). As we can see dangers in the supply chain can take many forms.

What is supply chain management and what is it not? Supply chain management serves the purpose of managing and integrating a series of companies into a supply chain that jointly delivers a value proposition through a product or service to end customers. To understand supply chain management in responsible business and in general it is crucial to consider the following three points.

- **External supply chain versus internal value chain**: Supply chain management deals with managing inter-company relationships along the supply chain, while value chain management aims at optimizing the value creation intra-company; from the inside of a business through its value chain.

DOI: 10.4324/9781003544074-23

- **Beyond procurement**: Supply chain management should not be misunderstood as being a task of merely the procurement or purchasing department. While those departments play a crucial role in establishing a relationship with suppliers, true engagement throughout the supply chain goes much further than an economic exchange of goods for money.
- **NOT merely about suppliers**: Managing a company's suppliers is only the so-called upstream part of supply chain management. The often-forgotten downstream part consists of managing the relationships from direct clients to the final end-consumer.

A life-or-death matter

Increasingly, supply chain issues are a matter of life or death. Consider just three out of many more examples during the recent years. In 2009, six children got killed and almost 300,000 got sick from poisoned milk powder, tainted with Melanin, manufactured by the company Sanlu in China. The boss of the workshop responsible for the disaster was sentenced to death by Chinese authorities (Branigan, 2009). The factory of Apple's provider Foxconn in 2009 was the stage of seven young Chinese worker's suicide in the midst of the Apple I-Pad boom (Chamberlain, 2011). Even more bizarre, the company is reported to have installed nets at the factory walls for employees who might try to jump to their death. They also have forced workers to sign "no-suicide pledges" to keep them from killing themselves (Lee A., 2011a). The boss of a Mattel provider, responsible for the company's scandal around lead-poisoned toys, hanged himself in a warehouse of his company Lee Der Industrial (Barboza J., 2007b).

Figure 17.1 illustrates the basic components of a supply chain, integrating sustainability features, which will be explained at a later point in time, when the framework of sustainable supply chain management will be explained. Supply chains consist of a series of companies that are jointly involved in producing a product or service. Depending on the section of the supply chain they are located in, companies are traditionally classified as suppliers, manufacturers, distributors, and retailers. Between those different businesses, a constant flow of inputs, products, money, and information creates a connectedness, which is the object of supply chain management. A business might have vertically integrated more than one supply chain stage into its structure. A dairy product business might for instance own all stages from dairy farming (supplier) to stores (retailers), or merely focus on the production and branding of dairy products (manufacturing) and leave the other stages to other companies. Considerations about supply chain stage and degree of integration of a company are important to defining the **focal point** for subsequent supply chain management activities. The focal point helps to define *upstream supply* chain management activities, which aim at the company's suppliers and *downstream* activities, which focus on the company's clients.

Defining Sustainable Supply Chains

How to make a specific supply chain sustainable? The ultimate goal of sustainable supply chain management is to ensure that the respective supply chain contributes to sustainable

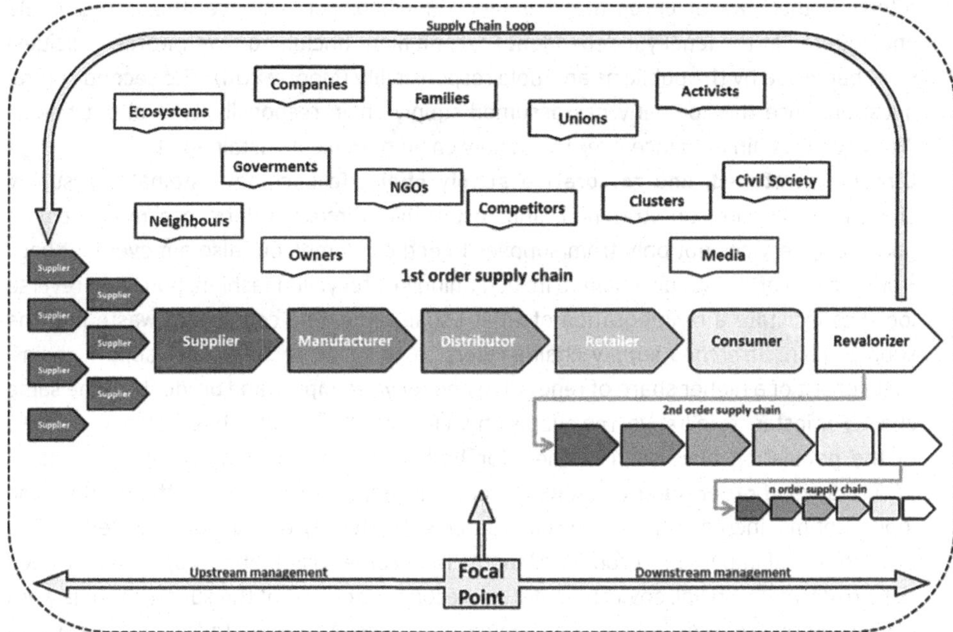

Figure 17.1 Sustainable Supply Chain Management Model.

development in the long run. To do so, the overall supply chain has to integrate measures aimed at assuming the responsibility to reach this ultimate goal. In the following paragraph, a list of central characteristics on the way to creating a *sustainable supply chain* (SSC) is provided:

- **Triple bottom line supply chain management**: Sustainable supply chain management (SSCM) needs to optimize the overall *triple bottom line* from first supplier to consumer and needs to pay special attention to the complex interdependences between the supply chain's social, environmental, and economic performance (Carter & Rogers, 2008). SSCM also needs to identify and solve *ethical dilemmas* throughout the supply chain (Svensson, 2009). When, for instance, the European Union decided on ambitious goals to increase the usage of biofuels, the decision-makers apparently did not consider the negative environmental and social consequences further up the supply chain. The increased demand for palm oil as one of the top biofuels, created devastating effects for the rainforest and local communities when big areas became cleared, to create monocultures for palm oil production.
- **Extended chain of responsibility**: The term **extended chain of responsibility** describes how responsibilities migrate from single company's stakeholders to all stakeholders along the supply chain. We see the "Evolution from Corporate Social Responsibility [CSR] to Supply Chain Responsibility [SCR]" (Spence & Bourlakis, 2009, p. 291). Two central questions are to be answered by management. The question, "How far into the supply chain do our responsibilities reach?" is a tricky one to answer. While companies might not have extended legal responsibilities for their supply chain, there often is a moral responsibility. General stakeholders will hold companies responsible for realities,

often off the map of corporate managers' thinking. For instance, the issues Apple encountered at the legally independent Foxconn plant (including seven worker suicides) were perceived by the public as an Apple responsibility (Moore, 2011). The second central question, once the company has assumed supply chain responsibility is about power: "How can we gain influence over the supply chain to make it sustainable?"

- **Circular, stretched, and restorative supply chain**: To become sustainable a supply chain must be circular, stretched, and restorative. *Circular* refers to a movement of goods and services not only from supplier to end consumer, but also a movement back from the end of the supply chain to its beginning in a recycling fashion. So-called reverse logistics facilitate a re-integration of what usually would be considered waste into the supply chain. *Stretched* supply chains refers to so-called second order supply chains, that consist of a higher share of renewable and recycled inputs and products in the same chain. For instance, in Kenya, the supply chain for second-hand clothes is strong, as 80% of the population buys such clothes, for both price and fashion reasons (Svensson, 2007). **Second order supply chains** are crucially important, to extend the product and input lifetime, increase the value that can be extracted by consumers, and reduce the environmental impact per product or input. To become sustainable supply chains, need to be *restorative*. Social, environmental, and economic capital of the supply chain is worn off in the process of establishing a product or service. According to the law of **entropy** there will always be energy losses through processes, which will lead to the reduction of certain capital during its usage. This becomes clearer, through three simple examples: The amount of materials recyclable from a product will always be smaller than the inputs used to the product (environmental capital). Employees will get exhausted, if not living a healthy work-life balance (social capital). Production facilities, if not taken care of, will lose their value (economic capital). A central task of SCM is to restore these capitals.

A n-order downstream supply chain business model

The North American company Rent-a-Center (RAC) has successfully integrated several supply chains (n-tiered supply chains) into the same business model. If you enter a RAC branch, it first looks like a normal department store. Products presented range from furniture to TV sets. Not so familiar is the business model, which aims at renting out products instead of selling them. Customers of RAC may either rent out a new (first tier) product for a monthly fee or do the same with a product that had been rented out before (first, second, n-order supply chain). RAC customers may give back the product at any time, without any final payment attached. The company also provides maintenance service throughout the useful life of a product (RAC, 2012). It can be assumed that primary motivation for this business model is not sustainability. Nevertheless, the overall environmental impact of the product may be reduced drastically for several characteristics of this business model. One of the major reasons is that customers have strong incentives to not use two products of the same kind at the same time, which means the use of each product is more efficient. Also, the same product is used by more people, which creates the potential to drastically reduce the environmental footprint per person.

In order to integrate the three preceding characteristics mentioned, the sustainable supply chain model includes numerous stakeholders throughout all stages of the supply chain. It also features supply chain loops to ensure circularity. The model also introduces a new supply chain function, which is to "revalorize". A company revalorizing adds new value to products that traditionally would be considered worthless, by either channeling them into recycling through the feedback loop, or to second order supply chains, where such products can still be used. A **revalorizer** typically performs tasks such as recovering, repairing, reusing, refurbishing, recycling, or in the most preferable case **upcycling** (Pauli, 1999).

Stages of Sustainable Supply Chain Management

The actual practice of responsible and sustainable supply chain management differs widely, depending on what section of the supply chain a company operates in. Above, this supply chain position has been called the focal point. Companies depending on their supply chain position can also be categorized into supply chain sustainability leaders or followers. For instance, Walmart as a company on the retail stage of its supply chain, requires preceding supply chain stages to comply with a basic supplier code of conduct. The same goes for HP from a manufacturer supply chain position. Both can be called sustainability leaders in their respective supply chain. While sustainable *supply chain leaders* proactively facilitate change towards more sustainability, sustainable *supply chain followers* might react to pressure for more responsible practices in many different modes of responsiveness. In the best case, supply chain followers might react proactively and become supply chain leaders themselves.

The steps for developing responsible supply chain leaders illustrated in Figure 17.2 are a cooking receipt for progressively maximizing a single company's contribution to developing truly sustainable supply chains.

- **Be a responsible business**: For a company to credibly foster responsible business practices throughout its supply chain, it is of crucial importance to first make sure to excel internally in becoming a responsible business.

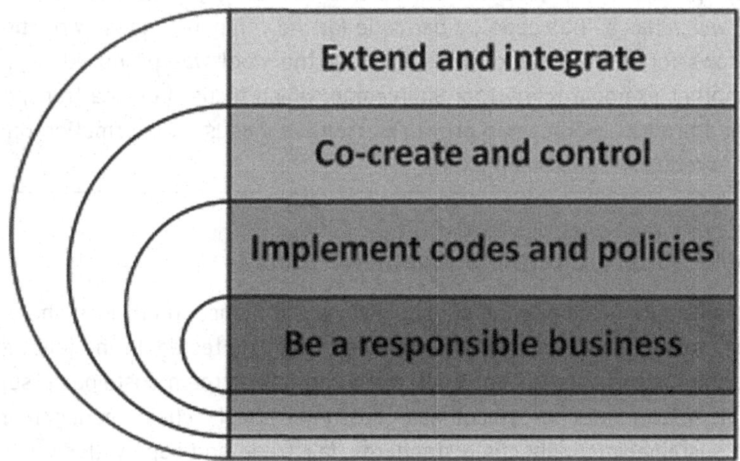

Figure 17.2 Steps for Developing Sustainable Supply Chain Management Leaders.

- **Implement codes and policies**: Installing a sustainable procurement and purchasing program helps to communicate a company's stance in terms of upstream supplier ethics and sustainability (Roloff & Aβlander, 2010; Saini, 2010). While less common, companies might also draft policies for downstream supply chain stages, determining the basic requirements that clients have to fulfill. A weapons producer for instance might establish a strict code of ethics, defining to whom to sell.
- **Co-create and control**: Most businesses do have well-drafted codes and policies, but those cannot ensure compliance and much less sustainable supply chain excellence. Nevertheless, those documents are an excellent basis for assuming co-responsibility with supply chain partners and to co-create solutions to social, environmental, and ethical issues. Those solutions have to be re-checked against policies established and effective control mechanisms have to be installed.
- **Extend and integrate**: Once supply chain partners inside a company's direct sphere of influence have been encouraged towards becoming responsible, it is time to extend the company's influence. Companies can aim to influence deeper tiers of suppliers, far upstream, clients of clients, and finally even second-tier supply chains downstream. The ultimate goal is to influence the complete supply chain until it becomes truly sustainable from first raw material to the final end-consumer.

Without a trace?

One of the big trends in SSCM is traceability. Traceability refers to the ability to exactly understand the route taken by products throughout the complete production process from extraction of the first raw material to the final end-product. One promising technology is the use of radio frequency identification (RFID) tags, which store this information (Kelepouris, Pramatar, & Doukidis, 2007). A future scenario would be to go shopping with a reading device that is able to decipher all supply chain data, from miles traveled, to information of companies involved, such as concrete social and environmental practices. An excellent example is the company Icebreaker from New Zealand, which has a "Baa code", a bar code for the company's sheep wool products, which shows for every product bought where the wool was produced (Icebreaker, 2012). Another example is the tool Sourcemap, which focuses on the transportation impact of a product. Sourcemap provides extensive, hands-on information on a wide variety of products (Sourcemap, 2012).

Sustainable Supply Chain Management Tools

For companies aiming at improving supply chain performance, there is a whole variety of instruments, most of which have extensively been tried and tested. In the following, we will briefly describe instruments for both upstream and downstream sustainable supply chain management. Instruments for sustainable upstream supply chain management can be divided into sustainable supply chain standards, fair trade and supply chain inclusiveness, and green supply chain management.

- **Sustainable supply chain standards** aim at assuring that social and environmental issues typically encountered in international supply chains are addressed in a responsible way. Such standards in the social dimension usually cover working conditions, health and safety, wages and benefits, and ethical issues such as child labor and overtime. In the environmental dimension, good environmental management practices, such as emission and waste management are key topics and often exceed standards given by local legislation (Reed, 2002). Such standards are a valuable tool in both evaluating existing and identifying new suppliers (Ehrgott, Reimann, Kaufmann, & Carter, 2011).
- **Fair trade** and **inclusive supply chains** are both about the inclusion of poorer suppliers into a company's supply chain. In practice, both approaches are closely connected. Minor differences lie in the underlying approaches for involvement. Fair trade focuses on providing distribution channels for "third world" products in the "first world" under a characteristic value set of trust, fairness, and equity (Raynolds, 2002; Renard, 2003). Under fair trade regimes, producers are usually paid a "fair" price, which is higher than the normal market price. Inclusive supply chain management includes many characteristics of fair trade, but highlights addressing social exclusion through supply chain participation (Hall & Matos, 2010) by the active involvement with small producers. This involvement exceeds a pure trade relationship. Supply chain inclusion often involves active collaboration and education to jointly improve small producers' production methods, quality standards and often even their communities. The Oxfam stores, a world-wide distribution channel for products purely from small communities in developing countries, is a classical fair-trade company, while the French retail giant Carrefour can be characterized as a highly inclusive business. The company sells more than 400 products produced in cooperation with small communities with an overall sales volume of over US$70 million (Carrefour, 2012).
- **Green supply chain management** focuses on the environmental impact of supply chains in both production and transportation. The environmental impact of transportation and the topic of responsible logistics have been covered extensively in earlier sections of this book. Improving the environmental impact of production activities throughout the supply chain is often described by the term "green and lean supply chains". It has proven successful to collaborate with suppliers in order to simultaneously increase their overall efficiency and eco-efficiency, by linking those efforts to suppliers' education in lean manufacturing (Simpson & Power, 2005; Mollenkopf, Stolze, Tate, & Ueltschy, 2010). Indicators typically used to evaluate suppliers' environmental performance are the production of solid and hazardous waste, air and water pollution, and natural resource usage (Beamon, 1999). Many companies also require their suppliers to develop an ISO 14000 certified environmental management system.

Know your main impact!

Controlling upstream supply chains with all its different types of social and environmental impacts is an almost impossible task, if a company aims at optimizing all impacts simultaneously. Sustainable supply chain management can make the biggest difference where the company's supply chain has the biggest impact. For a furniture company such as the Swedish IKEA, the main resource input is wood. The sourcing of wood may have immense negative environmental impacts on biodiversity, forests, and the communities living in them. As a consequence, IKEA has developed a highly sophisticated and effective four-stepped staircase model for the sourcing of the wood used by the company. The model aims at improving the social and environmental performance of the company's suppliers until they comply with the highest level of sustainable practices, which fulfills the most advanced standards of the Forest Stewardship Council (IKEA, 2003; Andersen & Skjoett-Larsen, 2009).

Sustainable downstream supply chain management tools used most often are related to the customer relationship management (CRM) function. As main tools and techniques of responsible CRM have been illustrated previously, we will merely highlight several specific points of engagement with the downstream supply. First, in order to create demand for responsible products, companies jointly with other market incumbents might aim at actively changing market demand towards such products. Online retailers such as Amazon and e-bay with their immense markets for second-hand products have already done so. Second, educating consumers how to use products and to recycle them is another field of action. Third, companies might also start to create, scrutinize, or even manage markets in secondary supply chains, in order to increase the overall lifetime of products and inputs. Finally, the creation of revalorization mechanisms downstream of the supply chain is a critically important task if the overall supply chain is to become sustainable.

Life Cycle Assessment

Life Cycle Assessment (LCA) is a methodological framework that assesses the environmental impacts associated with all the stages of a product's life from raw material extraction through materials processing, manufacture, distribution, use, repair and maintenance, and disposal or recycling. This 'cradle-to-grave' approach is pivotal in understanding and mitigating the environmental impacts of products and services, particularly in the context of sustainable business practices in supply chain management. LCA methodologies involve several key stages: goal and scope definition, inventory analysis, impact assessment, and interpretation (Guinée, 2021). These stages ensure a comprehensive evaluation of a product's environmental footprint, encompassing a wide range of impact categories such as climate change, resource depletion, and ecosystem degradation. The process begins with a clear definition of the LCA's objectives and the system boundaries, which is crucial for guiding the assessment and ensuring its relevance to the intended application.

Inventory analysis is the data collection phase of LCA, where inputs (like raw materials and energy) and outputs (such as emissions and wastes) throughout the product's life cycle are quantified. This stage requires meticulous data collection and often involves the use of life cycle inventory (LCI) databases. LCI is a critical component of LCA, providing the quantitative basis for the subsequent impact assessment (Heijungs & Sun, 2002).

The impact assessment phase evaluates the potential environmental impacts associated with the inputs and outputs identified in the inventory analysis. This stage is crucial for identifying the most significant environmental issues related to a product or process. This phase often involves translating inventory data into impact scores using various impact assessment methodologies, which can range from simple, single-issue methods to more complex, multi-issue methods (Finnveden et al., 2009).

Finally, the interpretation phase involves analyzing the results, drawing conclusions, and making recommendations based on the LCA study. This phase is critical for decision making in business and policy contexts, as it provides a comprehensive understanding of the environmental aspects of products or processes. Interpretation also includes the identification of limitations and the provision of an overall assessment that reflects the accuracy and reliability of the LCA study (Hauschild, 2018).

In the context of responsible business, LCA is increasingly recognized as a valuable tool for guiding product design, improving process efficiency, informing policy decisions, and communicating environmental performance to stakeholders. Companies are using LCA to identify hotspots in their supply chain, develop more sustainable products, and communicate the environmental credentials of their products to consumers (Cooper, 2022, Figure 17.3).

In summary, Life Cycle Assessment is a comprehensive approach that enables businesses and policymakers to evaluate the environmental impacts of products and services across their entire life cycle. By providing a detailed and quantitative analysis of environmental impacts, LCA plays a crucial role in the pursuit of sustainable development and responsible business practices.

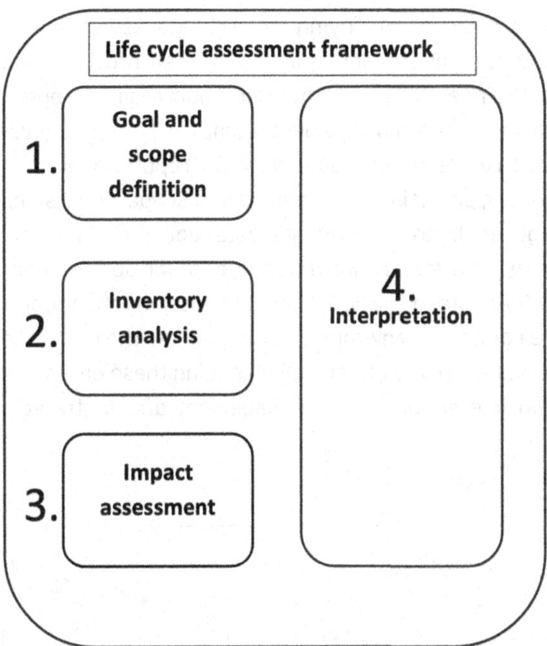

Figure 17.3 Life Cycle Assessment.

Based on ISO (2022)

Supply Chains and Carbon Emissions

Scope 3 emissions, a term that has gained substantial attention in the discourse of corporate sustainability, refer to indirect emissions not produced by the company itself but related to its value chain. These emissions are an integral part of a business's overall carbon footprint and encompass a wide range of sources, including both upstream and downstream activities. Understanding and managing Scope 3 emissions is increasingly recognized as a critical component of effective supply chain management and corporate environmental responsibility. Scope 3 emissions are distinguished from Scope 1 and 2 emissions, which represent direct emissions from owned or controlled sources and indirect emissions from the generation of purchased energy, respectively. Scope 3 emissions can be more challenging to measure and manage due to their indirect nature and the complexity of modern supply chains (Benoît-Norris, 2020). These emissions typically include, but are not limited to, business travel, procurement, waste generated in operations, leased assets, and the use of sold products and services.

The relevance of Scope 3 emissions in business is highlighted by their potential magnitude. For some companies, especially those in the manufacturing and retail sectors, Scope 3 emissions can constitute a significant majority of their total greenhouse gas emissions (Goldstein, 2021). This underscores the importance for companies to extend their carbon management strategies beyond direct emissions to encompass these indirect emissions. Effective management of Scope 3 emissions requires a comprehensive approach that includes robust data collection, stakeholder engagement, and the integration of carbon management into business decision making. This involves not only tracking and reducing emissions but also collaborating with suppliers and customers to achieve broader environmental goals (Matthews, 2019). Companies are increasingly employing life cycle assessment (LCA) methodologies to understand and mitigate the environmental impact of their products and services across the entire supply chain (Guinée, 2022). Furthermore, addressing Scope 3 emissions is becoming a key factor in corporate risk management. Companies are recognizing that failure to manage these emissions can result in regulatory risks, reputational damage, and increased operational costs. However, proactive engagement with Scope 3 emissions can offer businesses a strategic advantage, enabling them to anticipate regulatory changes, meet consumer demands for sustainability, and foster innovation in product development and supply chain management (Jackson & Apostolidis, 2021). Scope 3 emissions then represent a significant and complex aspect of a company's environmental impact. As the discourse on corporate sustainability evolves, understanding and effectively managing these emissions is becoming a crucial element of responsible supply chain management and a strategic imperative for businesses.

Exercises

A. KNOW

Use the below multiple-choice questions to test your knowledge. Each answer may be wrong or right and there may be zero to four right or wrong answers per question:

1. Sustainable supply chain management...
   a. ...in the chapter was defined as a responsible management of company's supplier relationship.
   b. ...involves the concept of an extended chain of responsibility, which means that companies should extend their responsibilities to suppliers beyond the contractually agreed responsibilities.
   c. ...can be developed in stages, of which the first stage is for a company to become a responsible business and the last step, to co-create solutions in collaboration with immediate supply chain partners.
   d. ...involves the usage of sustainable supply chain management tools, such as supply chain standards, fair trade, and green supply chain management.
2. A chocolate company pays their cocoa suppliers more than the market price. This is an example of...
   a. ...green supply chain management.
   b. ...fair trade.
   c. ...inclusive supply chains.
   d. ...revalorization.
3. The German fashion chain store Humana exclusively sells second-hand clothing under the slogan "first class second hand". Most of the clothing sold is sourced through donations. This example involves elements of ...
   a. ...fair trade.
   b. ...reverse logistics.
   c. ...an extended chain of responsibility.
   d. ...a secondary supply chain.

B. THINK

Imagine you are a sourcing manager in charge of assuring your company's global supply chain does not further any morally questionable practices. You have learnt that one of your suppliers employs children, which in itself appears morally critical. Moreover, your company has just made a public commitment to not employ child labor. However, you learn that the same supplier gives these children access to education through their in-house secondary school, which they wouldn't have otherwise. Also, you personally speak to some of the children and learn that their family depends on their income to survive. What do you think should you as company representative decide to do?

C. DO

Pick a product of your choice. Identify and use a (probably web-based) tool to estimate the CO_2 emitted through its global supply chain.

D. RELATE

Work to get in touch with someone who is working in a factory in a developing country. Ask this person about her/his experience and try to understand how it relates to you. If this person wants to, help her/him to be heard by others.

E. BE

Think about one product or service you use. What social, environmental, economic, and moral impacts do you think are triggered by your use?

Feedback

A. KNOW

Feedback 1

- a. Wrong: Supply chain management involves managing both suppliers (upstream supply chain) and clients (downstream supply chain) of a company.
- b. Wrong: The term extended chain of responsibility refers to the ideal situation where company's take responsibility not only for their direct stakeholders, but for stakeholders along the whole supply chain of their product.
- c. Wrong: The last step and highest level of responsible supply chain management is to extend the company's influence through the supply chain to co-create solutions with suppliers and clients that could not be reached before.
- d. Right: All tools mentioned are typical examples of SSCM tools.

Feedback 2

- a. Wrong: There is no direct environmental impact visible in the description.
- b. Right: Paying higher than average market prices is the main element of fair trade.
- c. Wrong: The example does not show any inclusion of marginalized suppliers or efforts to develop supply practices to make them eligible for inclusion into a greater supply chain.
- d. Wrong: Revalorization refers to recovering, repairing, reusing, refurbishing, recycling activities that add value to a product after its use.

Feedback 3

- a. Wrong: As far as we know from the description, no higher than average prices are paid to any marginalized group.
- b. Right: Reverse logistics is necessary to bring the products from an end-user back to the company.
- c. Wrong: An extended chain of responsibility refers to an appreciation of responsibility that moves from a single company's stakeholders to all stakeholders along the supply chain.

d. Right: Humana is entirely built upon a secondary supply chain, after the primary supply chain of newly produced clothing has been closed.

B. THINK

Level	*Dealing with moral complexity*	*Notes*
+	A decision has been made considering all aspects of the moral setting.	
=	A decision has been made, but parts of the information on the moral situation have not been dealt with in the decision-making process.	
–	No reduction of complexity visible in the answer.	

C. DO

Level	*Green technology skills*	*Notes*
+	Feasible estimation of CO_2 transport footprint has been conducted.	
=	Tool and product have been identified, but the analysis was not conducted correctly.	
–	Either product or tool has not been identified.	

D. RELATE

Level	*Facilitating voice for typically unheard groups*	*Notes*
+	Factory workers' experience has been heard by others.	
=	Personal account of the factory worker's experience.	
–	No contact has been established.	

E. BE

Level	*Appreciating impacts of own actions*	*Notes*
+	Wide and deep appreciation of impacts made throughout the product's or service's supply chain.	
=	Only impacts very proximate to the individual and its action have been considered (e.g. the water used when using toothpaste).	
–	No appreciation of impacts.	

References

Andersen, M., & Skjoett-Larsen, T. (2009). Corporate social responsibility in global supply chains. *Supply Chain Management: An International Journal, 14*(2), 75–86.

Barboza, D. (2007a). *Scandal and suicide in China: A dark side of toys*. Retrieved January 18, 2012, from The New York Times: https://www.nytimes.com/2007/08/23/business/worldbusiness/23suicide.html?pagewanted=all

Barboza, J. (2007b). *Owner of Chinese toy factory commits suicide*. Retrieved January 23, 2012, from New York Times: https://www.nytimes.com/2007/08/14/business/worldbusiness/14toy.html

Beamon, B. M. (1999). Designing the green supply chain. *Logistics Information Management, 12*(4), 332–342.

Benoît-Norris, C. (2020). Understanding and managing Scope 3 emissions. *Journal of Environmental Management*, 265.

Branigan, T. (2009). *China to execute two over poisoned baby milk scandal*. Retrieved January 23, 2012, from The Guardian: https://www.guardian.co.uk/world/2009/jan/22/china-baby-milk-scandal-death-sentence

Carrefour. (2012). *Responsible sourcing*. Retrieved January 19, 2012, from Carrefour: https://www.carrefour.com/cdc/responsible-commerce/our-commitment-to-the-environment/responsible-sourcing/

Carter, C. R., & Rogers, D. S. (2008). A framework of sustainable supply chain management: Moving toward new theory. *International Journal of Physical Distribution & Logistics Management, 38*(5), 360–387.

Chamberlain, G. (2011). *Apple factories accused of exploiting Chinese workers*. Retrieved January 23, 2012, from https://www.guardian.co.uk/technology/2011/apr/30/apple-chinese-factory-workers-suicides-humiliation

Cooper, J. S. (2022). Life cycle assessment in industry and business: Adoption patterns, applications, and implications. *Journal of Industrial Ecology, 26*(4), 678–691.

Ehrgott, M., Reimann, F., Kaufmann, L., & Carter, C. R. (2011). Social sustainability in selecting emerging economy suppliers. *Journal of Business Ethics, 98*, 99–119.

Finnveden, G., Hauschild, M. Z., Ekvall, T., Guinée, J., Heijungs, R., Hellweg, S., Koehler, A., Pennington, D., & Suh, S. (2009). Recent developments in life cycle assessment. *Journal of Environmental Management, 91*(1), 1–21.

Goldstein, B. (2021). Scope 3 emissions evaluation in corporate value chains. *Sustainable Production and Consumption, 27*, 392–405.

Guinée, J. B. (2021). Handbook on life cycle assessment: Operational guide to the ISO standards. *International Journal of Life Cycle Assessment, 28*(2), 153–158.

Guinée, J. B. (2022). Life cycle assessment for sustainable supply chain management. *Journal of Cleaner Production, 291*.

Hall, J., & Matos, S. (2010). Incorporating impoverished communities in sustainable supply chains. *International Journal of Physicial Distribution & Logistics Management, 40*(1/2), 124–147.

Hauschild, M. Z. (2018). *Life cycle assessment: Theory and practice*. Springer.

Heijungs, R., & Sun, S. (2002). The computational structure of life cycle assessment. *The International Journal of Life Cycle Assessment, 7*(5), 314–314.

Icebreaker. (2012). *Baa code*. Retrieved January 23, 2012, from https://baacode.icebreaker.com/site/baacode/index.html

IKEA. (2003). *IKEA's position on forestry*. Ikea Services AB.

ISO. (2022). *ISO 14040:2006*. ISO. https://www.iso.org/standard/37456.html

Jackson, T., & Apostolidis, C. (2021). Corporate strategy and the management of Scope 3 emissions. *Journal of Business Ethics, 169*(2), 335–352.

Kelepouris, T., Pramatar, K., & Doukidis, G. (2007). RFID-enabled traceability in the food supply chain. *Industrial Management & Data Systems, 107*(2), 183–200.

Lee, A. (2011a). *Apple manufacturer Foxconn makes employees sign 'no suicide' pact*. Retrieved January 23, 2012, from Huffingtonpost: https://www.huffingtonpost.com/2011/05/06/apple-foxconn-suicide-pact_n_858504.html

Lee, M. (2011b). *Fake Apple store in China even fools staff*. Retrieved January 18, 2012, from Reuters: https://www.reuters.com/article/2011/07/21/us-china-apple-fake-idUSTRE76K1SU20110721

Matthews, H. S. (2019). Managing carbon footprints in supply chain management. *International Journal of Production Economics, 214*, 102–113.

Mollenkopf, D., Stolze, H., Tate, W. L., & Ueltschy, M. (2010). Green, lean and global supply chains. *International Journal of Physical Distribution & Logistics Management, 40*(1/2), 14–41.

Moore, M. (2011). *Inside Foxconn's suicide factory*. Retrieved January 20, 2012, from The Telegraph: https://www.telegraph.co.uk/finance/china-business/7773011/A-look-inside-the-Foxconn-suicide-factory.html

Pauli, G. (1999). *UpCycling: Wirtschaften nach dem Vorbild der Natur für mehr Arbeitsplätze und eine saubere Umwelt*. Munich: Riemann.

Pereira, V., & Alerigi, A. (2011). *Zara supplier accused of slave labor in Brazil*. Retrieved January 18, 2012, from Reuters: https://uk.reuters.com/article/2011/08/17/zara-brazil-idUKN1E77G18N20110817

RAC. (2012). *How Rent-A-Center works*. Retrieved January 25, 2012, from Rent-A-Center: https://www6.rentacenter.com/How-RAC-Works/How-Rent-A-Center-Works.html

Raynolds, L. T. (2002). Consumer/producer links in fair trade coffee networks. *Sociologia Ruralis, 42*(4), 404–424.

Reed, D. (2002). Employing normative stakeholder theory in developing countries: A critical theory perspective. *Business and Society, 41*(2), 166–207.

Renard, M.-C. (2003). Fair trade: Quality, market and conventions. *Journal of Rural Studies, 19*, 87–96.

Roloff, J., & Aßlander, M. S. (2010). Corporate autonomy and buyer-supplier relationships: The case of unsafe Mattel toys. *Journal of Business Ethics, 97*, 517–534.

Saini, A. (2010). Purchasing ethics and inter-organizational buyer-supplier relational determinants: A conceptual framework. *Journal of Business Ethics, 95*(3), 439–455.

Simpson, D. F., & Power, D. J. (2005). Use the supply relationship to develop lean and green suppliers. *Supply Chain Management, 10*(1), 60–68.

Sourcemap. (2012). *Sourcemap: Where things come from*. Retrieved January 19, 2012, from https://sourcemap.com/

Spence, L., & Bourlakis, M. (2009). The evolution from corporate social responsibility to supply chain responsibility: The case of Waitrose. *Supply Chain Management: An International Journal, 14*(4), 291–302.

Svensson, G. (2007). Aspects of sustainable supply chain management (SSCM): Conceptual framework and empirical example. *Supply Chain Management: An International Journal, 12*(4), 262–266.

Svensson, G. (2009). The transparency of SCM ethics: Conceptual framework and empirical illustrations. *Supply Chain Management: An International Journal, 14*(4), 259–269.

F Communicating

18 Communication in Responsible Business

It is a common prejudice that companies are managing responsible business as a public relations exercise, that there is a lot of talk, but little walk. The role given to communication in the context of this book is a different one. Communication here is taken as a tool to support the implementation of responsible business and management throughout three phases of the implementation process. Only the very last of those phases is to share information about responsible business and management - talking the walk. Phases one and two are about walking the talk. In order to create a sound knowledge base about communicating for responsible business, one needs to understand the role of stakeholders in communication, to get to know a basic toolset of related communication formats, and to differentiate between external and internal communication. The next three sections will prepare you for those important background topics.

> **Reputation again?**
>
> The most frequent answer that you will get when asking why companies behave responsibly is reputation; no matter if you ask stakeholders inside or outside the company. A recent study can even provide a solid estimate. Forty percent of the factors influencing reputation are highly related to businesses' responsible management activities (Boston College; Reputation Institute, 2010).

Communicating with Stakeholders

If responsible business is about assuming the various responsibilities towards a multifaceted set of stakeholders, communicating with those stakeholders must be a crucial aspect of managing the responsible business. Each stakeholder is provided with a unique set of attitudes, interests, values, and communication needs. This is why communicating with stakeholders is a highly complex task. Before beginning the communication process, serious consideration must be given to understanding the stakeholder groups involved in future communication.

Why communicate with stakeholders? The Accountability Stakeholder Engagement Standard characterizes the following set of basic questions to define why a communication is desired: Is there a mutual dependency? Does the business have a responsibility towards

DOI: 10.4324/9781003544074-25

the stakeholder? Is there tension because of a company-related issue that the stakeholder is involved in? Does the stakeholder have the power to influence the company? Does the stakeholder provide a diverse perspective? (AccountAbility, 2011). Either of those communication motives is legitimate, and it is important to know what the mutual communication motivation is in order to tune in the communication process to it.

- **Personal characteristics** of stakeholders influence how they receive and assimilate the message and also how the stakeholder responds. Personal characteristics might be, for instance, basic attitudes. Maybe, the stakeholder has a very negative attitude towards companies in general and wants to avoid contact. The opposite situation might be the case, too. Profession also matters. An engineer may be inclined to process information differently from a business major or somebody trained in law or philosophy. Also, demographic factors such as age, income, gender, religion, and education, are basic factors helping to understand to whom the company is communicating.
- Potential **communication barriers** may prevent stakeholders from receiving, understanding, or answering the message sent. Barriers may include personal characteristics, but also physical or technical inhibitors, such as missing access to communication channels, and conflicting responsibilities or scheduling issues. It is worth reminding that there are also stakeholders that "do not have a voice", such as the natural environment, animals, or future generations.

Those communication criteria can be used to draft a basic stakeholder segmentation, which in turn can help to plan and customize communication activities for those segments.

MTV broadcasting about what, to whom, and why?

If you worked for a music and lifestyle broadcaster such as MTV and you received the task of designing a campaign to spark civic action for the environment among your audience, what do you need to know? This is a stakeholder assessment question. Here are some answers: 41% of kids and teens worry about the environment and 34% worry specifically about animal extinction. When asked about what they believe the greatest issues are, 47% mention global warming and pollution, 45% environmental protection. You might also want to know that 94% say they are most motivated to take action, because helping is fun and only 34% say they might be motivated by celebrities. The result was the MTV Switch campaign, a fun-based campaign, focused on climate change (von Walter, 2012).

Responsible Communication Formats

Is more frequent communication always better communication? A survey (Morsing & Schultz, 2006) found out that more frequent communication is not always best. It is quality that counts. The survey, conducted in the Nordic countries of Denmark, Sweden, and Norway, asked how companies should communicate their responsible business. The results were astonishing and challenging in several ways. First of all, 9% of the survey respondents were convinced that companies should not publicize their responsible business efforts at all, 51% stated that companies should focus on minimal releases only, such as reports and information on corporate websites, and merely 40% supported extended communication activities through the formats of corporate advertising and press releases. While those percentages might look different in other countries, there is still an important conclusion in this survey: Communication frameworks and formats cannot follow the-more-the-better paradigm but need to be closely tuned in to stakeholders' expectations about the overall amount of communication activities and the means used. Successfully communicating responsible business requires a prudent deployment of communication formats aligned with each respective communicative situation, focused on the communication's purpose and characteristic of primary stakeholders. Table 18.1 provides an overview of such communication formats applied in responsibility communication.

Table 18.1 Overview Responsibility Communication Formats

Format	*Process*	*Stage/Purpose*	*Primary stakeholders*
Stakeholder dialog	Establish a constructive moderated dialog with stakeholders involving extensive interaction and co-creation of messages and real-life impacts	Direction giving, sense-making, consensus creation, inspiration (Preparation, control)	Stakeholders involved vary depending on each respective consultation topic
Persuasion	Usage of arguments to convince communication partners	Create approval and support for responsible business (Preparation, implementation)	Management and general employees, internal and external key decision-makers
Vision, mission, values statements	Draft guidance documents, for long-run strategy and short run behavior	Provide guidance for decision making and behavior (Implementation)	Management and general employees
Training	Educate and train for knowledge, skills, and attitudes	Equip key stakeholders with the necessary prerequisites to support responsible business conduct (Implementation)	Employees, suppliers, customers
Design	Design organizational structure, processes, and products that implicitly reflect responsible business conduct	Send an intrinsic message about how deeply implemented responsible business is (Implementation)	Users of designs, such as customers, employees, or suppliers
By example and action	Show role-model responsible management conduct of exemplary individuals, leaders, groups, and the organization as a whole	Inspire, create trust, and credibility of implementation (Implementation)	Employees, general public

(Continued)

Table 18.1 (Continued)

Format	*Process*	*Stage/Purpose*	*Primary stakeholders*
Social marketing	Use marketing as a tool to evoke individuals' behavior change with a positive effect on society and environment	Behavior change (Implementation)	Customers, employees
Lobbying	Influence the political decision-making process	Political decisions conducive to responsible business (Implementation)	Governments, politicians
Policies, codes, handbooks	Create concise guidelines for operational decisions in processes critical for responsible business	Provide guidance for operational decisions and activities influencing responsible business (Implementation)	Employees, specific departments, suppliers
PRs (Press Releases)	Communicate responsible business activities and achievements	Raise awareness about and highlight responsible business activities (Share)	Media and broader public
Endorsements	Achieve public endorsement by high credibility individuals or organizations	Credibility catalyst effect (Define, implement, share, control)	Any stakeholder targeted
Certification and labeling	Align your responsible business activities to compliance with responsible business labels and certifications for products, processes, or the complete organization	Credibility catalyst effect	End consumers, business clients, government agencies
Reporting	Establish an extensive, factual, and neutral account of social, environmental, and economic business performance and activities	High-quality information provision (Share, control)	Investors, employees, prospective employees, suppliers, industry analysts, competitors, general public
Newsletters	Publish a (usually company-internal) newsletter covering responsible business events, policies, highlight individuals, or provide information to topical responsible business issues	Inform, motivate, and inspire for responsible business activities	Employees
Advertising	Start an advertising campaign, communicating responsible business activities and performance	Use marketing methods to inform and inspire people about your responsible business	Customers, general public

(*Continued*)

Table 18.1 (Continued)

Format	*Process*	*Stage/Purpose*	*Primary stakeholders*
Cause-related marketing and branding	Integrate a good cause into your marketing and branding activities	Increase product sales or brand positioning (Implement, share)	Customers
Speeches and forewords	Use speeches to define the company's tone from the top, interpreting responsible business activities	Provide leadership interpretation and perspective (Prepare, implement, share)	Depending on communication intention
Internet and social networks	Establish internet- and intranet-based communication platforms such as social networks, corporate blogs, micro-blogs, wikis, podcasts, or video blogs	Reach the broad internet public and capitalize on enhanced communication characteristics such as speed, low-cost, and interactiveness (Prepare, implement, share)	Internet public, employees, activists, consumers
Issues and crisis communication	Protect and provide guidance and vision when faced with issues and crises threatening the business	Mitigate negative effects (e.g. negative publicity) of issues and crises (Share)	Investors, employees, general public, activists
Hotlines and whistle blowing mechanisms	Establish formal feedback channels	Create feedback for improvement (Control)	Consumers, employees
Audits and assurance	Conduct internal or external audits, reviewing responsible business activities, outcomes, and reports	Create feedback for improvement (Control)	Management, corporate headquarters, clients
Testimonials	Communicate the experience of stakeholders involved in or related to your responsible business conduct	Create credible and largely unfiltered insider information and perceptions	Employees, customers, etc.

The table can only be a rudimentary overview, a toolset with the goal of revealing a broad spectrum of formats for potential use. We will later provide a more extensive description on how to deploy those to answer a specific communication purpose. Every one of the formats mentioned just represents an entry gate to an entire world of theoretical and practical information, which is highly recommended for deeper study, but which exceed the scope of this book. What are the important basics that need to be understood to put these communication formats to use? First of all, it is important to understand the basic process involved in using each format. *Stakeholder consultation and feedback*, for instance, usually requires a complex social process of exchange and mutual sense-making, while the process of the *reporting* format consists of internal information gathering and external communication one-way stakeholder information. Also formats and their respective processes may be combined. A company can, for instance, conduct a stakeholder consultation in combination with the *internet and social network* format or as it is typically done, a sustainability report would include a foreword, applying the *speech as* format.

Second, communicators need to understand the purpose and desired outcome of each format. A common mistake is to confuse social- and cause-related marketing. While they are highly related in their application processes of marketing each respective purpose is distinct. *Social marketing* aims at creating behavior change in people for the good of society, while *cause-related marketing* aims at increasing product sales.

A third essential characteristic of tools is determining in the communication with which stakeholder they are most relevant. For instance, *lobbying* usually aims at the narrow and limited stakeholder group of politics and governmental institutions, while *issues and crisis communication* has a broader aim, consisting of shareholders, employees, customers, and the general public. A professional working in responsible business needs to be able to understand and use all the different tools, understanding that each provides different solutions. The following section will show how to reach an integrated communication strategy by combining those tools in a holistic and responsibility communication plan, which conveys an overall impression of consistency and integrity.

Integrated Stakeholder Communication

There is no such thing as purely internal or purely external communication. Most messages freely cross the boundaries of companies. The effect becomes even more distinct, when scrutinizing communication processes in responsible business. Responsibility communication is stakeholder communication. Stakeholders cross borders, communicate among each other, and often have roles inside and outside the company. Imagine a Google employee who learns from a supposedly "internal" newsletter about his company's algorithm to identify dissatisfied employees (M3, 2011), which becomes the main scandalous topic at a party with his friends. Is that internal or external communication? Clearly, the effects of the communication transcended the company's boundaries. There is a growing overlap between the external and the internal sphere of communication (see Figure 18.1). This is the reason why, in this book, communication will be considered an integrated external and internal process, producing a consistent and congruent message outside and inside the company borders, so called **integrated communication**. Creating such a message requires that all communication tools and all organizational communicators become tuned in to this joint message.

What does it mean to harmonize external and internal messages? If, for instance, the ice-cream company Ben and Jerry's promotes its new flavor HubbyHubby in support of marriage diversity (Ben & Jerry's, 2011), harmonization of messages would require that the company is also internally committing to diversity activities, for instance by diversity policy, including support for causes of the Lesbian, Gay, Bisexual, & Transgender (LGBT) community (Cohen, 2011). In theory, such a harmonization is a reasonable strategy to enhance the overall credibility of responsible business. In practice, departmental responsibilities and borders impede such efforts. Traditionally, external communication has been covered by the public relations or communications department and marketing. Internal messages have rather been handled by the human resources department. Who should be in charge of integrated

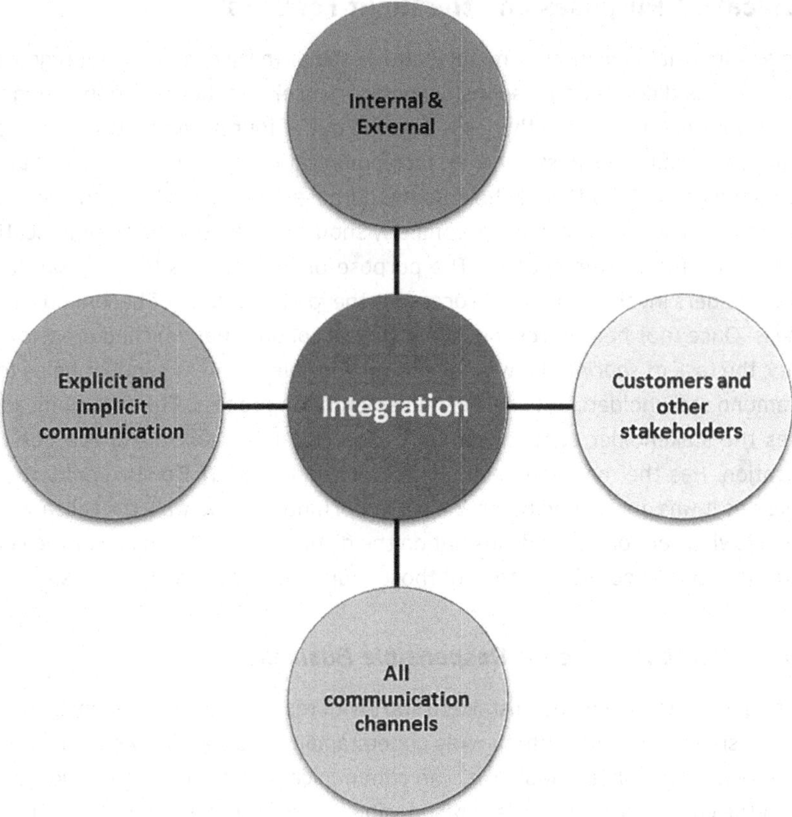

Figure 18.1 Integrated Communication.

stakeholder communication? Truly integrating a company's communication requires extensive coordination efforts beyond departmental borders. Many companies have communication departments for this task. Nevertheless, company departments in charge of responsible business might be the most adequately equipped institutions. They usually are highly connected to most of the company's departments and to stakeholders.

Integration at the movies

The movie chain Cinépolis' "love gives birth to eyesight" [Del amor nace la vista] campaign relies on a broad set of communication channels and tools integrating their communication efforts internally and externally and involving a diverse set of stakeholders. The campaign is communicated to customers through clips before movies start, addressed through staff at ticket and candy sales, and through transparent bathroom mirror stickers imitating the experience of cataract patients. To employees Cinépolis communicated through internal competitions ("who saved the most eyes?"), and the so-called eye-meter, which was used to keep count of fundraising and what it means for beneficiaries. Those are just a few of the communication channels used (Laasch & Conaway, 2011).

Communication Purposes and the Right Formats

Why does a responsible business communicate? Is the primary communication goal sharing the message of good deeds and responsible performance? It is, but communicating the outcomes of responsible business activities is just one out of four primary purposes of communication in responsible business. The first communication task illustrated in Figure 18.2 consists of *defining* jointly with stakeholders the purpose, values, and basic characteristics of what responsible business for a specific company should be. The second communication task is communication for *implementation*. The purpose of this stage is to bring on board and enable stakeholders involved into the process for the joint endeavor of becoming a responsible business. Once (not before) responsible business conduct has reached a basic maturity and quality, the task of *sharing* the word about responsible business conduct helps to create goodwill among stakeholders outside the implementation process. The communication task that closes the stakeholder communication cycle consists of *controlling* the outcomes of communication. Has the message been shared and understood? Do stakeholders perceive the business as it was envisioned before? Most importantly: Do we walk the talk and walk the talk? The following sections provide insight on the distinct practice and use of the communication tools introduced before, for each of those four communication purposes.

Communication to Prepare for Responsible Business

It is an easy and commonly made mistake to start with responsible business by incrementally doing that "responsible stuff" without truly understanding and defining what the responsible business to be created should look like. The communication tool of stakeholder dialog can enrich all of the communication tasks in responsible business, but it is most powerful in drafting a first picture of what a business should become in the long-run. The goal is to reach a consensus between internal and external stakeholders and to develop responsible business based on this initial vision. How can a company reach this consensus? Interestingly, the two

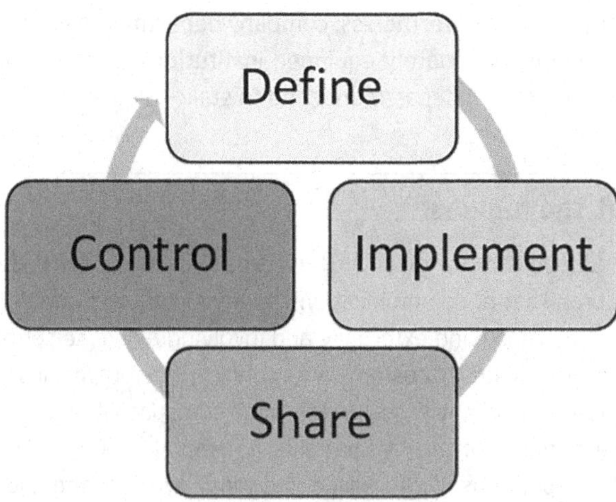

Figure 18.2 Communication Purposes in Responsible Business.

main approaches to reaching consensus and defining a responsible business vision supported by all stakeholders of a company, stakeholder dialog and persuasion are often seen as opposing.

Stakeholder dialog is the part of the stakeholder management process which aims at establishing an exchange at eye level with a broad set of organizational stakeholders. Such a dialogue might be conducted using several forms, such as meetings, broad stakeholder forums, surveys, social-network-based interactions, and many more. Whatever form is chosen for the process, it needs to be designed to make sense of the business. **Sense-making** (Weick, 1995) refers to the process of jointly constructing consensus about responsible business and defining what the responsible business is supposed to be, to do, and to represent. Sense-making is based on recurrent, interconnected action and communication and making sense of both. So, it cannot be a one-time communication effort. It is important for the success of such a sense-making process that it establishes a so-called **ideal speech situation** (Bohman & Rehg, 2011; Habermas, 2005), facilitating an optimum outcome of the communicative process. When applying the four basic conditions that establish such an ideal speech situation (see Figures 18.3 and 18.4) on stakeholder engagement, it becomes clear that first of all, stakeholder dialog must include all stakeholder groups that are capable of making a relevant contribution. For instance, companies may make the mistake of only inviting the stakeholders that share their opinion. The process is likely to be more fruitful if diverging opinions are represented. Second, it is also important to not only invite diverging stakeholder profiles, but also to give them an equal right to speak. Third, the process should facilitate a platform in which

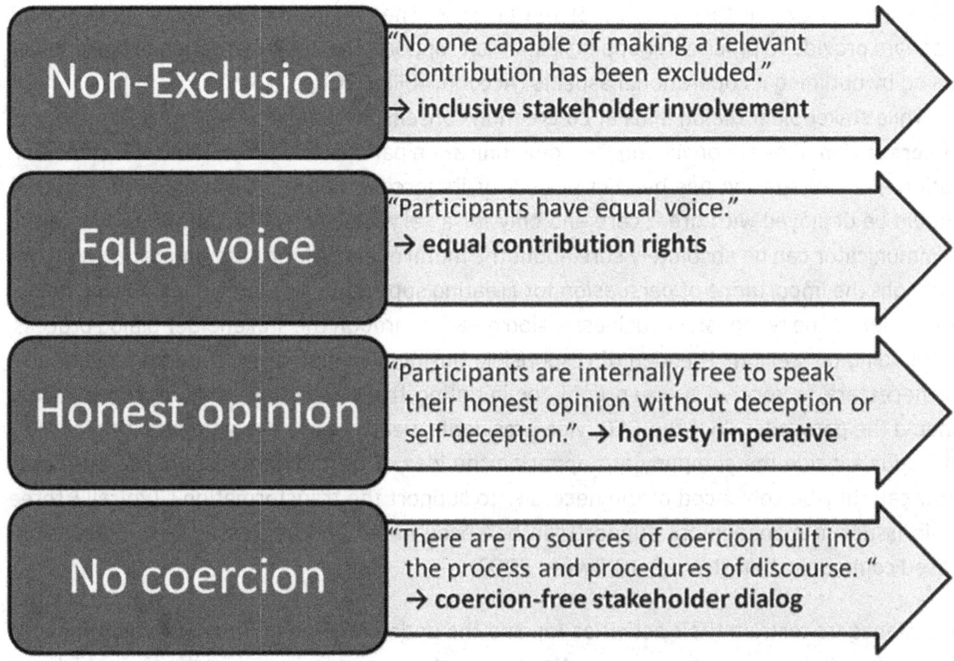

Figure 18.3 Approaches to Creating Successful Stakeholder Dialog - Ideal Speech and the Accountability Stakeholder Engagement Standards (part 1).

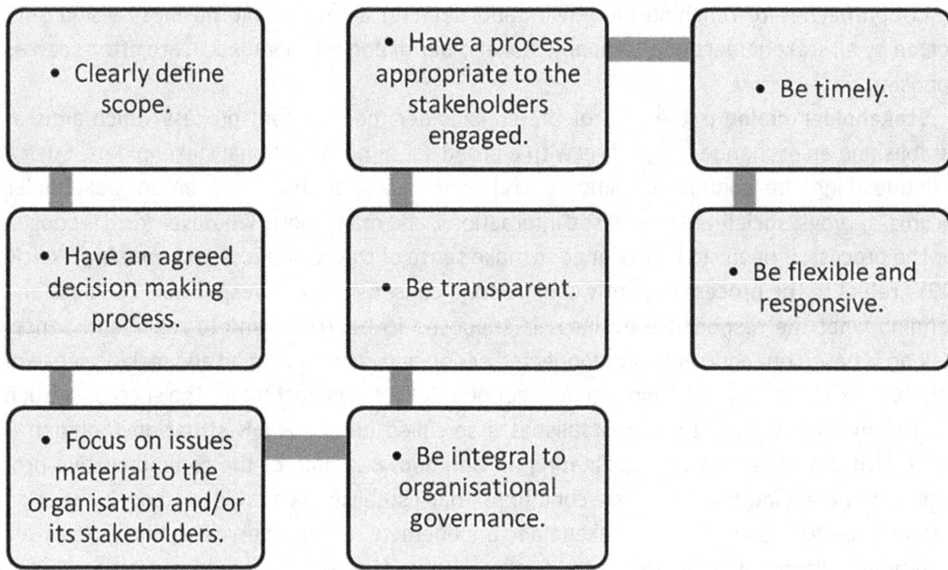

Figure 18.4 Approaches to Creating Successful Stakeholder Dialog – Ideal Speech and the Accountability Stakeholder Engagement Standards (part 2).

participants are able to provide a honest opinion and where they are coerced neither to action nor to abstain from action. Those general presuppositions provide a valuable framework for assessing the overall functionality of the process. The AA 1000 stakeholder engagement standard provides a practical shopping list, which supports the implementation of stakeholder dialog by outlining its operational aspects (AccountAbility, 2011, p. 45).

While stakeholder dialog aims at co-creating consensus by a democratic process, the tool of **persuasion** aims at convincing the communication partner of a pre-established communication goal. Persuasion has been criticized for its forceful nature. It is a powerful tool that should be deployed with great care and only for a very specific set of situations, where the communicator can be absolutely sure about the moral quality of the communication goal. We highlight the importance of *persuasion* for creating support by key individuals for the implementation of the responsible business vision created through the stakeholder dialog process. Persuading or "selling" the idea of responsible business to high-level leadership might also be necessary to receive a green light for initiating the stakeholder dialog process. What should the persuader do if the CEO, vice-presidents, heads of key departments, or other key individuals inside the company are opposing the idea of becoming a responsible business? How can they be convinced of the necessity to support the transformation? Typically, three main issues in management support can be encountered and addressed by a persuasion-based communication strategy (O'Dwyer, 2003).

- Managers restrain their activities for, and the understanding of, responsible business to a **shareholder wealth maximization rationale**. They can impede activities, which are necessary to become a responsible business, but which are not easily identified as shareholder value maximizing.

- Managers form **"pockets of resistance"** opposing the change towards responsible business.
- Managers are not able to form a clear **understanding of responsible business**, due to conflicting definitions and usages of related terminologies.

Central in persuasion are **arguments**, attaching to people's motivations and supporting the change in attitude aspired by the communication purpose. It is helpful to group arguments to persuade managers for the adoption of responsible business on three fundamental rationales (Aguilera, Rupp, Williams, & Ganapathi, 2007; Shiraishi, et al., 2009).

- **Instrumental arguments** attach to individuals' self-interest. Managers need to understand what is in it for them or the organization. Typical arguments are the business case for responsible business, or the congruence between performance indicators and responsible business.
- **Relational arguments** attach to every individual's need for social belonging. Arguments that could be applied refer to support for becoming a responsible business by the manager's peers, or to highlight how an organization's internal community will thrive from responsible business.
- **Moral arguments** attach to individuals' need for meaningful and moral existence. Managers often need to feel they can do a moral good by supporting responsible business. Arguments could be to highlight the manager's potential contribution to the solution, presenting a pressing moral issue, or by getting the manager in touch with people benefitting from responsible business conduct.

The persuasion framework proposed in this section has been illustrated in the application for managers. It is as instrumental for persuading any high-influence individual that needs to be convinced of the necessity of developing responsible business. This persuasive process is especially important for the transformation of business to more responsible ways as covered in the chapter on organizational change.

Communication to Implement Responsible Business

Many communication tools exist for supporting the implementation of responsible business. The following section will highlight merely three high-impact communication instruments for the implementation phase. The tool policies, codes, and handbooks provide a set of rules, decision mechanisms, often values, that need to be complied with, in order to become a responsible business. **Social marketing** aims at changing or creating behaviors conducive to responsible business, by using typical marketing mechanisms as a tool, while sustainability education aims at providing stakeholders with the necessary competences to contribute to responsible business conduct.

Policies, codes, and handbooks are characterized by many different formats, scope, scale, and tones. Policies are usually broadest in the formulation of guidance, while codes are rather concise and handbooks meticulously provide operational details on how to behave in a responsible business. Codes related to responsible business can be subdivided in distinct groups. The broadest in scale and scope are general company-wide codes of conduct, separate codes of ethics, environmental policies, and responsible business policies. Rather narrow in scale are codes covering specific issues, such as human rights or diversity, or specific departments such as purchasing or finance codes. There are also codes governing stakeholders' interaction with the company, such as supplier codes or shareholder policies (Preuss, 2010).

Codes of conduct - pleasure or pain?

When Walmart (2009) published its supplier code of conduct for ethical sourcing, many stakeholders were overwhelmed by the social and environmental opportunities. What would happen if Walmart, the world's biggest retailer, enforced codes with all its suppliers and this way pushes them towards becoming responsible businesses? The power of codes of conduct may be enormous, but establishing a code requires extensive due diligence. The same company, Walmart, ran into serious problems in Germany, when they were sued because the company's employee code of conduct aimed at regulating the love life of the employees and was judged to violate the very basic personal rights of the employees, particularly the very personal freedom guaranteed in Article 1 of the German constitution (Darsow, 2005).

The goal of *social marketing* is to create behavior change, a format which was traditionally used by public organizations to promote behavior changes. Social marketing campaigns were, for instance, centered on stopping smoking or starting to use condoms. Social marketing increasingly finds application by business actors. Implementing responsible business requires extensive behavior change of stakeholders inside and outside the business. Lines of action for social marketing among employees might be, for instance, a green office program that requires employees to actively switch lights off and to reduce the amount of paper used for printing. A recycling business might be interested in social marketing to promote behavior change towards waste separation. Alcoholic beverage companies may market responsible consumption and "don't drink and drive" behavior change.

Social marketing uses mainstream marketing tools, such as the four Ps of marketing to plan, conduct, and evaluate campaigns. Social marketing is often paraphrased as awareness campaigns, a framing that stands in the way of seeing the tool's full potential. Creating awareness is only the first out of five steps to reach and sustain new behaviors (Diclimente & Prochaska, 1998). A crucially important task in social marketing is to assess at what stage of behavior change the target audience is, and to design social marketing campaigns based on this initial assessment. Table 18.2 summarizes the five stages of behavior change, typical stakeholder statements per stage, and a brief description of characteristics of marketing campaigns based on the respective stage.

Table 18.2 Stages of Behavior Change

Stage	*Description*	*Marketing strategies*	*Exemplary message to facilitate change*
1) Pre-contemplation	Denial or missing information about necessity for change	Inform and convince individuals about necessity to change	"The UN's Food and Agriculture Organization has estimated that meat production accounts for nearly a fifth of global greenhouse gas emissions. These are generated during the production of animal feeds, for example, while ruminants, particularly cows, emit methane, which is 23 times more effective as a global warming agent than carbon dioxide" (Jowit, 2008)
2) Contemplation	Considering change by weighing costs and benefits of change	Inform about the actions necessary for change and the full costs and benefits	"(...) health benefits of eating less meat. The average person in the UK eats 50g of protein from meat a day, equivalent to a chicken breast and a lamb chop – a relatively low level for rich nations but 25–50 percent more than World Health Organization guidelines" (Jowit, 2008)
3) Preparation	Preparing a serious adoption of change by experimenting with small changes	Provide information and support for first experiences of success	"Give up meat for one day [a week] initially and decrease it from there" (Jowit, 2008)
4) Adoption	Adoption of new behavior	Provide guidance on how to conduct the new behavior in all situations of life	"Making delicious vegetarian meals is easy once you know where to start. The following are a few recipes and meal suggestions that are perfect for the new vegetarian: Breakfast, Lunch, Dinner, Snacks" (PETA, 2012)
5) Maintenance	Maintaining new behaviors	Help to make the new behavior crisis proven	"When you're away from home: Restaurant options for vegetarians keep getting better, and many hosts now prepare for vegetarian guests, even when they don't phone ahead. No matter what the occasion, we can help you figure out what to eat away from home: The restaurant connoisseur, the traveler, the house guest, the wedding crasher" (PETA, 2012)

A textbook example for social marketing

The animal protection NGO, PETA, offers a web-based tool for marketing the behavior change towards becoming a vegetarian. The tool exactly follows the five steps of behavior change by starting from a general "meet your meat" section, aimed at creating awareness (pre-contemplation), through a "Making the transition" section (preparation), and a section where new vegetarians can find tips to how not to quit the vegetarian lifestyle while travelling (maintenance) (PETA, 2012).

Responsible business education aims at creating necessary responsibility competences among company stakeholders. Competences are primarily developed among employees and can be classified into the three categories: Knowledge, skills, and attitudes (KSA). Competences required for responsible business vary widely depending on the structure of a company's human capital, the company's approach to responsible business, and external factors such as the industry and the company's location of operations. Table 18.3 provides examples for each competence type and delivers a first insight on the educational means available to build those competences. Educational designs for responsible business education might be based on external or in-company trainings and involve formats such as mentoring, on-the-job training, computer-based trainings, single workshops, continuous programs, and even complete external degree programs, such as a master program in responsible management.[1]

Additional communication tools applied in implementing responsible business are business vision, mission, and value statements as "light tower documents", that provide broad guidance, and lobbying as a tool specifically tuned in to political stakeholders. Communication by design and example might not traditionally be considered communication instruments but are crucially important in conveying a message about the seriousness of commitment (Conaway & Laasch, 2012).

Communication to Share the Responsible Business Performance

Imagine a company that has done considerable work to become a responsible business. It is at the forefront of responsible businesses in its market, its industry, and its region. The main communication task now is to cash-in on the work done in the form of stakeholder goodwill. Stakeholders are likely to reward responsible business with tangible benefits. To grasp the

Table 18.3 Competences for Responsible Business

Competence type	*Exemplary competences*	*Educational means*
Attitudes and values	Honesty, responsibility, environmental and social sensitivity, etc.	Moral dilemma training, social and environmental immersions, discussion and imaginative exercises, feedback circles, etc.
Skills	Stakeholder engagement skills, systemic thinking, change skills, etc.	Coaching, simulations, on-the-job trainings, etc.
Knowledge	Cross-functional knowledge, responsible management tools, etc.	Classroom education, e-learning-based programs, etc.

potential of such benefits, one only needs to scrutinize how the three most important stakeholder groups in companies' perceptions (Lacey, Cooper, Hayward, & Neuberger, 2010), consumers, employees, and owners, may reward responsible businesses. Consumers might buy more and pay higher prices. Employees might be attracted to work with a responsible business, and get motivated to be more productive, while working for the business. Shareholders might consider a responsible business an attractive investment for manifold reasons, including higher profit potential and lower investment risk. All three groups are likely to develop a higher loyalty to the business due to the additional bond made from the perception of dealing with a "good business" (Bhattacharya & Sen, 2010; Du, Bhattacharya, & Sen, 2007). The main task during the sharing phase is to let stakeholders know about performance and to create goodwill. The goal of communication at this stage is "maximizing the returns" on responsible business (Bhattacharya & Sen, 2010, p. 8). In the following we will describe three main tools proven to be highly effective in sharing the word about responsible business. The tool cause-related marketing connects product sales with a good cause. The tool certification and labeling signals compliance with external standards, and reporting provides extensive information about social, environmental, and economic business performance and activities to a broader set of stakeholders.

"What is the message?" might be the question of someone who stumbles over Google's newly-established website extensively disclosing the search engine's energy usage. While the most likely intended message was: "We make the planet a little greener" (Google states to run one of the most energy efficient technical infrastructures). The message that many stakeholders received would rather read "So much energy?" To hear that only the company's data center uses as much energy as 200,000 households (260 million watts) came as a surprise to many. Google's Urs Hoelzle, senior vice president for technical infrastructure, offers in defense that a Google search uses up less CO_2 than driving to the library to retrieve the same information there (Glanz, 2011; Google, 2011). How much of the information found on Google would we otherwise move our car for? That is hard to tell. The lesson: If you want to spread a message, be concise about what you want to say and anticipate your audience's reactions.

The tool of *cause-related marketing (CRM)* connects sales of a prody2uct to a good cause. CRM connects the implementation of a responsible business activity (the donation) with simultaneously spreading the word about the responsible business. The traditional form of CRM involves donating a certain percentage of sales revenues to a civil society organization, which then channels the money towards furthering the cause. The credit card business American Express is said to be the inventor of CRM in the early 1980s. American Express donated money for the renovation of the Statue of Liberty with every credit card issued and every payment made (Atkins, 1999). Nowadays CRM has been established in many different variants, the most important of which are described in Table 18.4 For businesses CRM is often perceived as a very attractive tool due to its direct and tangible financial benefit from increased product sales and easy implementation. For the same reason, some stakeholders may criticize CRM as unconnected to issues in the core business and purely profit-motivated. The chapter on communication challenges and greenwashing provides further guidance on how to address such criticism.

Table 18.4 Types of Cause-Related Marketing

Type	*Description*	*Example*
Classic	A fraction of the sales revenue of a certain product is channeled to a civil society organization (CSO) that supports a good cause.	As the pioneering classic cause-related marketing campaign, American Express still conducts cause-related marketing campaigns by donating lump sums for new credit cards issued and percentages for card usage to the World Monuments Fund and the National Trust for Historic Preservation (American Express, 2012).
In-kind donation	Based on the quantity of a product sold, a certain quantity of in-kind donation is realized.	Following the one for one (buy one, donate one) movement, the toothbrush company **Smile Squared** donates a toothbrush for every one bought and even provides a "zero for two" option, where people buy both brushes to donate both.
Total process management	The company conducting the cause-related marketing campaign also manages the follow-up process of channeling the donation to the beneficiary instead of outsourcing it to a CSO.	The movie theater chain **Cinépolis** is managing every activity of their "love gives birth to eyesight" campaign, from fundraising to cataract eye surgery, including fundraising, and the collaboration with doctor's, beneficiaries, and volunteers (Laasch & Conaway, 2011).
Cause-related branding	Instead of selling a specific product through a cause, cause-related branding connects a whole product line or brand to the cause.	The Mexican pharmacy chain **Farmacias del Ahorro** [The Savings Pharmacy] through their corporate foundation, employs doctors in a small doctor's office right next to their branches. Doctors provide for-free medical orientation. The cause covered is health promotion and has a direct sales-increasing effect for the majority of products sold by the company (Farmacias del Ahorro, 2012).
Rotating causes	Causes rotate in a fixed period of time, while the general possibility to donate is a constant offer.	The restaurant chain TOCKS manages its 12-month, 12 causes campaign changing causes every month of the year.
Multi-company cause brands	The same cause is used as a label that can be used by several companies.	**Product RED** (cause = AIDS) has provided a branding effect that has been harnessed for cause-related marketing campaigns of many companies from **Apple** to **Nike**.
Special cause editions	Companies offer a special edition of their product, which often has a visual connection with the cause.	The **Pink Ribbon International** (cause = breast cancer) organization has teamed up with many companies such as **Fiat**, which issued a special edition of its 500 model, with a dark pink stripe and small ribbon as a design feature. Every car sold accounts for US$1000 donation for breast cancer research (Tokic, 2011).
Virtual product	Companies provide a "decoy product" usually not bought, to raise awareness for a classic donation campaign.	The food chain **Chili's** offers customers to buy a color-book style Chili's logo for any price up from one dollar; 100% of the donation goes to the St. Jude Hospital to sponsor medical research (Alden Keene, 2007).
Product as cause	There are products that further a cause just by being bought and used and do not involve an additional donation.	The US American company Whole Foods Market has a whole product line branded as "locally grown". Through the consumption of those products a number of positive effects such as the reduction of CO_2 emissions and biodiversity protection are achieved (Whole Foods Market, 2012).

Certification and labeling provide a signal for stakeholders who search for easy to grasp information on the compliance with responsible business principles. Labels are visual symbols or brief texts placed on products or in company facilities, signaling compliance with a certification process, membership in a responsible business network, or support of a certain cause. Some labels such as the Latin American *ESR* label [ESR stands for socially responsible enterprise in Spanish] cover the overall activity of a business, while others, such as the *Great place to work* or the *Forest Stewardship Council (FSC)* labels focus on smaller sub-sections of the company and on particular good causes. Labels find wide use and come in an almost confusing variety.

While labeling aims at communicating with the minimum depth of information, *reporting* has the opposite purpose of providing extensive, detailed, and high-quality information for sophisticated stakeholders, highly interested in the details of businesses' responsible management activities. The best-known reporting standard is the Global Reporting Initiative (GRI), which has been illustrated extensively earlier in this book. Reports do not necessarily need to be aimed at an external public, nor do they need to cover a company's overall activity. Internal management reports and reports of individual responsible management activities are less frequent forms of reporting but can be valuable communication instruments. Recent trends in reporting are annual reports that integrate economic, environmental, and social business activities and performance and the provision of extensive reporting information online.

Additional popular tools for sharing the message on responsible business are press releases, classical public relations work, advertising, web-based communication, external and internal newsletters, and testimonials. A special role in sharing the message about irresponsible business is attributed to issues and crisis communication, which aims at communicating topics related to difficult issues and communicating in times of crises. While the tools mentioned beforehand rather focus on sharing messages about company's positive performance, issues and crisis communication focuses on communicating negative or critical socio-environmental performance.

Yes they do!

Companies do spread their responsible business message. Corporate responsibility managers answered that 67% of their companies' products rely on responsible business messages. Also, 42% published corporate responsibility reports and 75% of those followed the guidelines of the Global Reporting Initiative, including 84% doing so on a yearly basis. Out of the big multinational corporations with revenues of above US$50 billion, 95% publish such a report (Corporate Responsibility Magazine, 2010).

Communication to Control Responsible Business

When the responsible business message has been shared, it is crucially important to receive feedback and to control responsible management activities based on the feedback received. Has the message been understood as intended? Does the responsible business make up to stakeholder expectations? Do all parts of the business comply with the goals and standards set? The tool stakeholder dialog, which has been introduced as a tool for preparing responsible business, is very fitting for the control purpose.

Hotlines and ombudsmen provide institutional structures for providing feedback on specific issues, such as product quality for customers, and labor practices for employees. Employee hotlines also facilitate the so-called **whistleblowing** process, in which employees report misconduct related to any kind of social, environmental, or ethical issue from sexual harassment to corruption. Centrally important good practices for establishing effective whistle blowing mechanisms include protection mechanisms for whistleblowers and institutional reactions mitigating criticized conditions. While not used to its full potential yet, social network platforms such as Facebook and YouTube, allow for group-based and dynamic opinion building processes.

An external review of responsible business activities by trustworthy organizations and individuals fulfills a double purpose. On the one hand, it might be used to enhance credibility throughout all other stages of the responsible business communication process. On the other hand, external opinions are a valuable input into the review and control process of responsible business. **Endorsement and assurance** statements can both fulfill those functions but are different in the implementation process and focus of review. The assurance process is a highly structured, often standardized review of a company's responsible business activities by an external third party. Assurance is used to identify the quality of reports. Endorsements usually are less rigorous in the review process and can be provided for the company's activity as a whole, single departments or programs, or even single documents, such as a report. Endorsement contents are a short introduction of the endorser, information on the points reviewed and a personal statement of the endorser. An endorsement by a person involved in a specific responsible business activity in practice is called a testimonial. Testimonials provide feedback on the experience of the person involved, which may help to continuously improve the process.

Exercises

A. KNOW

Use the below multiple-choice questions to test your knowledge. Each answer may be wrong or right and there may be zero to four right or wrong answers per question:

1. Communicating with Stakeholders...
   a. ... is a task of low-complexity as most stakeholders are very alike when communicating to them.
   b. ...can be based on an interest of the company to communicate with the stakeholder or of the stakeholder to communicate with the company.
   c. ...might make it necessary to conduct a survey of stakeholders' access to different communication channels.
   d. ...must pay attention to potential communication barriers, which impede the stakeholder communication process. A barrier might, for instance, be that the company has not established a feedback channel for stakeholders to communicate back to the company.

2. Responsible business communication tools...
   a. ...are diverse. In order to understand each, it is important to know 1) the process involved in using the tool; 2) purpose and desired outcome of the tool; 3) primary stakeholders at which the tool aims.
   b. ...include frameworks as diverse as lobbying, reporting, certification, and labels.
   c. ...each should be used alone. It does not make sense to combine those tools, as they are too different.
   d. ...each are unique in terms of the primary stakeholder group to which they apply. For instance, lobbying primarily is applied to the customer and employee stakeholders, while hotlines and whistleblowing mechanisms primarily apply to governmental stakeholders.

3. Integrated communication...
   a. ...refers to integrating external and internal communication channels.
   b. ...aims to better separate the communication to internal and external stakeholders.
   c. ...aims to communicate a consistent message throughout all communication tools.
   d. ...requires that each communicating department, such public relations, marketing, and human resources management, communicate their own message separately.

4. Communication purposes in responsible business...
   a. ...can be divided into two basic tasks. First, communication to increase sales, and second, communication to increase brand value.
   b. ...during the "define" task includes, as the main goal, to convince stakeholders about how "good" the company is in its responsible business activities and performance.
   c. ...during the "implementation" task, one of the main goals is to achieve stakeholders' contribution to responsible business activities.
   d. ...during the "control" task, the main goal is to convince stakeholders about responsible business performance.

5. Communication to implement...
   a. ...may involve social marketing, the main tool to sell green products to customers.
   b. ...typically involves hotlines as a central communication tool.
   c. ...may involve both social marketing and responsible business education. The difference between both is that social marketing aims at behavior change, while responsible business education aims to create competences for responsible business.

d. ...responsible business education can aim to transmit a wide variety of different competences required to responsible business implementation by employees. An example might be the skills to manage a new recycling machine in a bottling plant.

6. Communication to control...
   a. ...exclusively aims to control that stakeholders really translate their good image of the company into tangible benefits.
   b. ...can involve feedback mechanisms, such as an ombudsman or an ethics hotline.
   c. ...can involve a whistleblowing mechanism (helps stakeholders to give positive feedback on companies' excellent activities) and testimonials (stakeholders "testifying" about what the company is doing wrong).
   d. ...may involve assurance and endorsements both of which involve external evaluations of the company's responsible business performance.

B. THINK

Pick one company of your choice. Imagine you are in charge of developing a company slogan that captures what the company is or wants to become to their four main stakeholders.

C. DO

Identify one label or certification related to responsible business (e.g. Blauer Engel in Germany, ESR in Mexico, or the international Great Place to Work) and familiarize yourself with the criteria and steps to be taken for a company/product to be certified or labelled. Draft an action plan of the steps to be taken to get there.

D. RELATE

Identify one company whose (ir)responsible business practices you consider questionable. Search for the company's social media presence, and write a short reply to the company, explaining convincingly why you are not OK with what they do/did.

E. BE

Think about one of your strongly-held personal beliefs. How could you express this belief in one sentence? What do you think this sentence means to four of your personal stakeholders? How would they react to you saying this sentence to them? What would they think? How would they reply?

Feedback

A. KNOW

Feedback 1

a. Wrong: Each stakeholder is provided with a unique set of attitudes, interests, values, and communication needs, which makes stakeholder communication a highly complex task.

b. Right: Stakeholder communication is based on open bidirectional communication.

c. Right: Access to different communication channels is a stakeholder characteristic, important to consider for successful stakeholder communication.

d. Right: There are a number of communication barriers that might impede effective stakeholder communication.

Feedback 2

a. Right: The diversity of stakeholder communication tools makes appreciating their different characteristics crucial for their effective use.

b. Right: All mentioned frameworks are tools for stakeholder communication.

c. Wrong: Responsible business communication tools are frequently combined. A prominent example is sustainability reports, which are offered with an interactive online navigation.

d. Wrong: The stakeholder groups mentioned are swapped around between the two tools. Lobbying primarily applies for governmental actors and whistleblowing for employees.

Feedback 3

a. Right: The integration of external and internal communication channels is the main characteristic of integrated communication.

b. Wrong: Internal and external stakeholder communication cannot be separated. The goal is rather to send a consistent message that works as much for internal as it does for external stakeholders.

c. Right: Shaping a consistent/integrated overall message is a main characteristic of integrated stakeholder communication.

d. Wrong: Integrated stakeholder communication requires coordinating the messages of those departments in order to send a joint message.

Feedback 4

a. Wrong: Increase in sales and brand value might both be motivations to communicate in responsible business. Nevertheless, in this chapter, we divided the communication purposes into four (defining responsible business, implementation, sharing, control).

b. Wrong: Such behavior would endanger the "define" task's main goal of defining what the responsible business should be.
c. Right: Active contribution of stakeholders is a crucial input to the implementation task.
d. Wrong: Such behavior would conflict with the "controlling" task's main goal of checking on the communication outcomes.

Feedback 5

a. Wrong: Social marketing during the "implementation stage", will rather support necessary behavior changes among stakeholders in general. There might be behavior changes that might support sales, but this is not the main function of social marketing.
b. Wrong: Hotlines are typically applied as part of the communication "control" task.
c. Right: Social marketing focuses on behavior change, while education aims at creating competences for responsible management.
d. Right: Skills such as the one mentioned are part of the competences to be created for responsible management.

Feedback 6

a. Wrong: The goal of the control task is much broader and involves checking on the effectiveness of the communication process and to ensure congruence between communication and implementation of responsible business.
b. Right: Ombudsmen and ethics hotlines help to control as they provide feedback on where responsible management might have gone wrong.
c. Wrong: The descriptions of both whistleblowing and testimonials are incorrect.
d. Right: Assurance and endorsements are distinct external evaluation mechanisms.

B. THINK

Level	*Reconciling diverging perspectives*	*Notes*
+	Slogan appreciates that it is directed at four main stakeholders and elegantly integrates their perspectives.	
=	Slogan only integrates some of the four stakeholder relationships.	
–	No slogan was established, or main stakeholders were not identified.	

C. DO

Level	*Complying with standards*	*Notes*
+	Feasible action plan, including areas to be improved before labelling has been established based on a solid understanding of the criteria of the standard.	
=	Criteria have been understood, but no feasible or superficial action plan has been established.	
–	Label/certification standard has not been identified.	

D. RELATE

Level	*Expression of difference*	*Notes*
+	Clear argument convincingly and consistently expressing the critical position regarding the company practice(s).	
=	Argument has been made, but leaves room for improvement in terms of argument structure, tone, or similar aspects.	
–	Company and/or their social media outlet have not been identified.	

E. BE

Level	*External orientation*	*Notes*
+	Belief clearly captured in sentence and an in-depth appreciation of stakeholder reactions.	
=	Belief expressed in sentence and basic appreciation of main stakeholders' reactions.	
–	Major difficulties in describing belief, in translating it into a sentence, or in identifying personal stakeholders.	

Note

1 The exercises at the end of every chapter of this book are based on a competence-based approach to responsible management education with the sub-competency areas of knowing, thinking, doing, relating, and being.

References

AccountAbility. (2011). *AA1000 Stakeholder Engagement standard 2011: Final exposure draft*. London: AccountAbility.

Aguilera, R. V., Rupp, D. E., Williams, C. E., & Ganapathi, J. (2007). Putting the S back into corporate social responsibility: A multilevel theory of social change in organizations. *Academy of Management Review*, *32*(3), 836–863.

Alden Keene. (2007). *Chili's and St. Jude Children's Research Hospital*. Retrieved January 19, 2012, from Cause Marketing: https://causerelatedmarketing.blogspot.com/2007/08/chilis-and-st-jude-childrens-research.html

American Express. (2012). *American Express partners in preservation*. Retrieved January 19, 2012, from American Express: https://about.americanexpress.com/csr/pip.aspx

Atkins, S. (1999). *Cause related marketing: Who cares wins*. Oxford: Butterworth-Heinemann.

Ben & Jerry's. (2011). *Flavors: HubbyHubby*. Retrieved January 19, 2012, from Ben & Jerry's: https://www.benjerry.com/hubbyhubby/

Bhattacharya, S. D., & Sen, S. (2010). Maximizing business returns to corporate social responsibility (CSR): The role of CSR communication. *International Journal of Management Reviews*, *12*(1), 8–19.

Bohman, J., & Rehg, W. (2011). Jürgen Habermas. In E. N. Zalta (ed.), *The Stanford Encyclopedia of Philosophy (Winter 2011 Edition)*. Retrieved January 19, 2012, from https://plato.stanford.edu/archives/win2011/entries/habermas/. Retrieved January 19, 2012, from https://plato.stanford.edu/entries/habermas/#HabDisThe

Boston College; Reputation Institute. (2010). *The 2010 corporate social responsibility index*. Boston.

Cohen, E. (2011). CSR for HR. *Course human resources management*. Berlin: Insitute of Corporate Responsibility Management, Steinbeis University.

Conaway, R., & Laasch, O. (2012). *Communication in responsible business*. New York: Cengage.

Corporate Responsibility Magazine. (2010). *Corporate responsibility best practices: Setting the baseline*.

Darsow, I. (2005). Implementation of ethics codes in Germany: The Wal-Mart case. *IUSL Labor*, *3*. Retrieved January 25, 2012, from https://www.upf.edu/iuslabor/032005/art11.htm

Diclimente, C. C., & Prochaska, J. O. (1998). Toward a comprehensive, transtheoretical model of change. In W. R. Miller, & N. Heather, *Treating addictive behaviors*. New York: Plenum Press.

Du, S., Bhattacharya, C., & Sen, S. (2007). Reaping relational rewards from corporate social responsibility: The role of competitive positioning. *International Journal of Research in Marketing*, *24*, 224–241.

Farmacias del Ahorro. (2012). *Rol del médico de Farmacias del Ahorro [The role of the physician at The Savings Pharmacy]*. Retrieved January 19, 2012, from fahorro.com: https://www.fahorro.com.mx/fundacion.php?id=8

Glanz, J. (2011). *Google details, and defends, its use of electricity*. Retrieved January 25, 2012, from New York Times: https://www.nytimes.com/2011/09/09/technology/google-details-and-defends-its-use-of-electricity.html

Google. (2011). *Data centers*. Retrieved January 25, 2012, from Google.com: https://www.google.com/about/datacenters/

Habermas, J. (2005). *Zwischen Naturalismus und Religion [Between naturalism and religion]*. Berlin: Suhrkamp.

Jowit, J. (2008). *UN says eat less meat to curb global warming*. Retrieved January 17, 2012, from The Guardian: https://www.guardian.co.uk/environment/2008/sep/07/food.foodanddrink

Laasch, O., & Conaway, R. (2011, March). "Making it do" at the movie theatres: Communicating sustainability at the workplace. *Business Communication Quarterly*, *74*(1), 68–78.

Lacey, P., Cooper, T., Hayward, R., & Neuberger, L. (2010). *A new era of sustainability: UN global compact-Accenture CEO study 2010*. Accenture Institute for High Performance.

M3. (2011). *Google's approach to employee engagement: Surprise! It's an algorithm*. Retrieved January 19, 2012, from My strategic plan: https://mystrategicplan.com/resources/googles-approach-to-employee-engagement-surprise-its-an-algorithm/

Morsing, M., & Schultz, M. (2006). Corporate social responsibility communication: Stakeholder information, response and involvement strategies. *Business Ethics: A European Review*, *15*(4), 323-338.

O'Dwyer, B. (2003). Conceptions of corporate social resonsibility: The nature of managerial capture. *Accounting, Auditing & Accountability Journal*, *16*(4), 523–557.

PETA. (2012). *PETA's vegetarian starter kit*. Retrieved January 17, 2012, from People for the Ethical Treatment of Animals: https://features.peta.org/VegetarianStarterKit/

Preuss, L. (2010). Codes of conduct in organisational context: From cascade to lattice-work of codes. *Journal of Business Ethics, 94*, 471–487.

Shiraishi, M., Washio, Y., Takayama, C., Lehdonvirta, V., Kimura, H., & Nakajima, T. (2009). Using individual, social and economic persuasion techniques to reduce CO_2 emissions in a family setting. *Proceedings of the 4th International Conference on Persuasive Technology*. New York: Association for Computing Machinery.

Tokic, A. (2011). *Fiat 500 pink ribbon limited edition cars support a great cause*. Retrieved January 19, 2012, from Autoguide: https://www.autoguide.com/auto-news/2011/09/fiat-500-pink-ribbon-limited-edition-cars-support-a-great-cause.html

von Walter, B. (2012). *MTV Switch: A global climate change campaign*. Berlin: MTV Networks Germany.

Walmart. (2009). *Standards for suppliers*.

Weick, K. E. (1995). *Sensemaking in organizations*. Thousand Oaks: Sage.

Whole Foods Market. (2012). *Locally grown: The whole foods market promise*. Retrieved March 1, 2012, from Whole Foods Market: https://www.wholefoodsmarket.com/products/locally-grown/

19 Communication Challenges

Why are there cases where companies use a broad set of communication channels extensively and reach all important stakeholder groups, but still are not able to create goodwill among them? One reason why the company cannot communicate credibly may be that it is actually not doing a good job in implementing responsible business. In this case the task is not to communicate better, but to review and improve responsible business and management activities. A second reason is that using responsibility communication to its full potential does not only require the company to get the message through to stakeholders, but also reach a situation where stakeholders make positive attributions to this message (Bhattacharya & Sen, 2010; Du, Bhattacharya, & Sen, 2007). While the previous chapter provided powerful tools to communicate, this chapter aims at enhancing the credibility of messages and at dealing with stakeholders' attitudes that might impede the creation of trust and goodwill.

Dear Company, who are you really?

The communication formats illustrated throughout the preceding sections, if not applied skillfully may lead to many conflicting messages and impressions about a company. Stakeholders may easily get confused about how responsible or sustainable a company really is. Are you one of those stakeholders? If so, you might fall into two negative, but typical habits. Either you believe that all companies are basically good, or bad, without being able to justify such a verdict. Either verdict is equally dangerous. The first one may harm the responsible business and the other falsely endorses irresponsible businesses. A good starting point for stakeholders is to begin with a company's Global Reporting Initiative report, which provides the most complete, extensive and if well-rated, highest quality impression. Afterwards, it is recommended to cross-check this report with other communication channels, and finally if there are still doubts about a specific practice, to shoot an e-mail with a direct question. Most companies are surprisingly open to answering such personalized requests about their responsible business activities.

DOI: 10.4324/9781003544074-26

Dealing with Critical Attitudes

Critical attitudes come in many forms and occur in the most different types of stakeholders. Criticism in most cases does not come from the stereotypical aggressive NGO or the activist consumer advocate group trying to harm the company. Table 19.1 describes commonly occurring negative attributions and communication strategies for each situation. First step in all those types of criticism is to take the question posed seriously and see if there is a factual necessity to change the point criticized. If not so, or after making the change, it is a communication task to transform negative attributions to positive ones.

There are many frameworks for reaching effective communication. The following checklist is a simple, but effective one. To avoid negative attributions and criticism, companies

Table 19.1 Negative Attributions to Responsible Business Conduct

Object of skepticism	*Question posed*	*Communication strategy*
Sincerity	Do they really mean it?	Communicate motivation of responsible business activities.
Impact	Are they really making a difference?	Focus on communicating on results of responsible business activity.
Fittingness	What does it have to do with their core business?	Communicate interrelatedness between responsible business activity and core business.
Egoism	Are they only doing it for the money?	Communicate openly if the main motivation is or is not the money.
Incongruence activity - company "character"	How does that go in line with their history and reputation?	Communicate either how responsible business is in line with the company's established "character" or how the character of the company will change to fit the responsible business activity.
Incongruence activity - company stakeholder	Is the company in-line with my values and ideology?	Communicate communalities between stakeholder and company characteristics.
Cause justification	Shouldn't they spend their money on more important things?	Communicate how the cause addressed is most important for the company, for stakeholders, and for society in general by comparing it to other causes that might be perceived as more important.
Efficiency	Are they wasting money?	Communicate transparently about the usage of money and the results achieved by spending it.
Cause quality	Is that a good cause?	Explain why the cause chosen should be addressed and what results can be achieved by addressing the cause.
Capitalism and corporations	I am against whatever they do!	Educate to clarify prejudices and to show how responsible business conduct is having positive impacts independently from what system it is conducted in.

should always communicate responsible business in four categories: Input, output, motives, and fit (Bhattacharya & Sen, 2010).

- Communicating both **input and output** and long-run results of responsible business conduct, provides a factually substantiated complete picture, answering the questions "What does the business do?" and "What has the business achieved?" Such communication helps to erase doubts about a company's real effort, impact, and the effectiveness of activities, all of which might lead to unfavorable stakeholder attitudes if left unattended.
- Communicating **motives and fit** answers stakeholder's doubts about the company and its relationship to the respective responsible business communication. The question of *fit* between responsible business activities and core-business refers to the question of how the cause chosen relates to core business. It is intuitively reasonable that car companies reduce product emissions and paper companies use recycled paper; it is less understandable and needs additional explanation why, for instance, an educational institution is involved in reforestation. To understand the company's intentions, stakeholders need to know the *motives* leading to responsible business activities.

Communicating about... Bloody Chocolate

How about this: You bite into your favorite chocolate bar and what happens is that blood splashes out - a horrifying idea. The situation described is the plot of a Greenpeace YouTube video clicked more than 500,000 times. The clip is aimed at keeping the company Nestlé from buying palm oil from companies destroying the orangutans' habitat. The palm oil is one of the ingredients of the famous Kit Kat brand. Especially painful for the company is that the Greenpeace clip resembled a popular TV ad and the long-established slogan "Have a break, have a Kit Kat" (Greenpeace UK, 2012). The damage to the company and its brand is difficult to estimate.

Greenwashing

Stakeholders tend to call any communication that leads to negative attributions such as the ones mentioned in Table 19.1 **greenwash**. Unfortunately, the term often is only understood superficially and, accordingly, used in the wrong way. The essence of the many definitions of greenwash is that of a communication overstating the true social and environmental performance of a product, an initiative, a person, or a whole company, and therefore, creating a *misleading impression*. Referring to greenwash suggests a relationship to purely environmental performance, but in absence of a better intuitively graspable terminology, it is also being used to describe misleading communication on social performance. Avoiding greenwash is about balancing a company's communication efforts with the impact truly made. For instance, the popular criticism, of questioning a company's motives for responsible business activities would not fall into this definition and accordingly should not be called greenwash. There is a confusing flurry of terms that relates to greenwash. Figure 19.1 provides insight into some of the commonly used expressions.

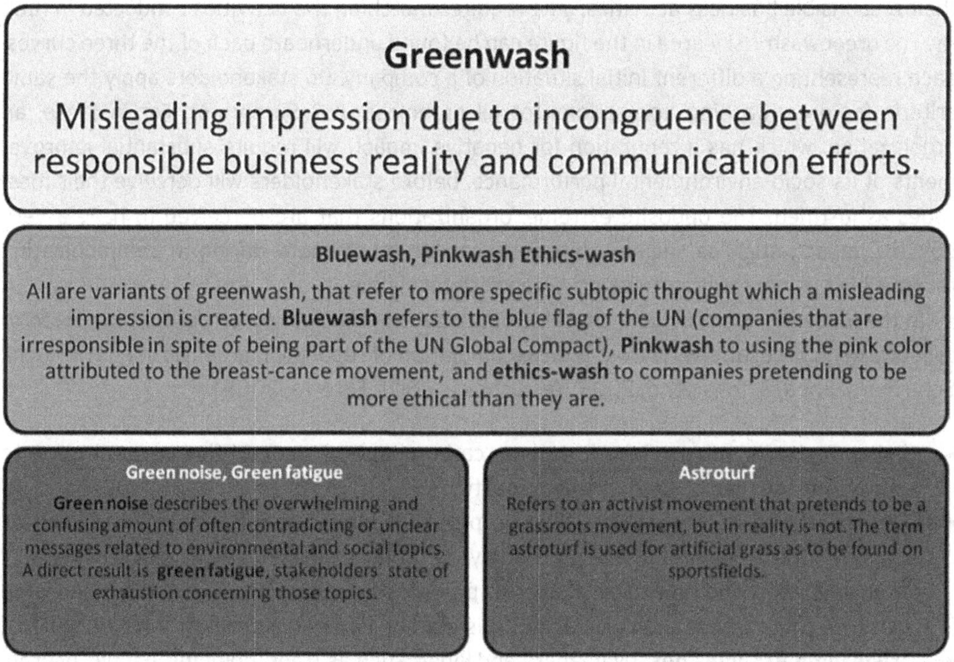

Greenwash

Misleading impression due to incongruence between responsible business reality and communication efforts.

Bluewash, Pinkwash Ethics-wash

All are variants of greenwash, that refer to more specific subtopic throught which a misleading impression is created. **Bluewash** refers to the blue flag of the UN (companies that are irresponsible in spite of being part of the UN Global Compact), **Pinkwash** to using the pink color attributed to the breast-cance movement, and **ethics-wash** to companies pretending to be more ethical than they are.

Green noise, Green fatigue

Green noise describes the overwhelming and confusing amount of often contradicting or unclear messages related to environmental and social topics. A direct result is **green fatigue**, stakeholders' state of exhaustion concerning those topics.

Astroturf

Refers to an activist movement that pretends to be a grassroots movement, but in reality is not. The term astroturf is used for artificial grass as to be found on sportsfields.

Figure 19.1 Cognates of the Term Greenwash.

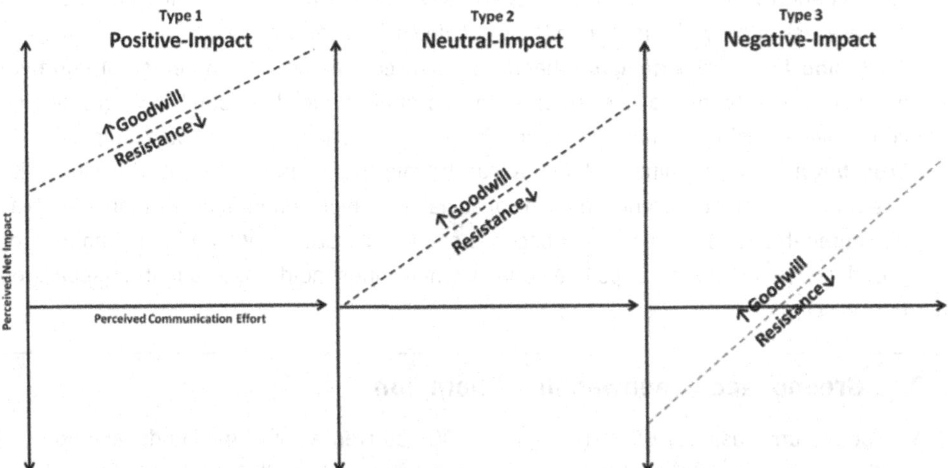

Figure 19.2 Stakeholder Perceptions and Subsequent Outcomes.

How to avoid being accused of greenwash? A very basic prerequisite for stakeholders to evaluate the congruence between communication claim and actual responsible business performance is to transparently communicate input and output as proposed in the preceding section. This way, consumers can factually compare walk and talk. Figure 19.2 is aimed at illustrating how companies should substantiate their communicative efforts by performance. In order to avoid greenwashing accusations, companies should communicate as much about their responsible business activities, as it requires matching the activities conducted in reality. The greenwash-risky area in the figure can be found underneath each of the three curves, each representing a different initial situation of a company. Do stakeholders apply the same criteria for greenwashing accusations for all organizations? Surely not. For instance, an organization, which has a reputation for negative impact, will require substantial improvements of its socio-environmental performance, before stakeholders will perceive their messages as justified. The opposite extreme, organizations that are perceived to have a very positive impact, such as social enterprises, can be much more daring in communicating responsible business, without risking greenwashing claims.

In the following, we provide a checklist of typical communication errors that may lead to greenwashing accusations. The list is an accumulation of reports on greenwashing (Horiuchi, Schuchard, Shea, & Townsend, 2009; Terrachoice, 2007; Futerra, 2008).

- **Lying**: Factually untrue claims, such as "carbon-neutral" or "certified as great place to work", if those "facts" do not reflect reality.
- **Unsubstantiated messages**: Giving no proof for claims about performance, such as claiming 100% environmentally friendly, without explaining what environmentally friendly means, and how to calculate this percentage, or claiming to be "the greenest in class", without explaining by what fact this market leadership position can be justified.
- **Misleading associations**, by imagery and labels such as trees, dolphins, happy children, the color green, logos, etc., which are not backed up by performance.
- **Hidden trade-off**, in actions that look responsible, but come with hidden side-effects such as energy-saving light bulbs that come with toxic mercury, or fair-trade products that are less energy efficient than their non-fair-trade counterparts.
- **Confusing less bad with good**, happens when communicating incremental improvements to bad outcomes as a solution such as organic cigarettes, "safe" weapons, and oil companies focusing on marginal efforts in renewable energies are good examples.
- **True, but irrelevant** claims highlight a truthful fact that sounds nice, but which in reality does not make any difference in terms of social and environmental performance such as biodegradable tobacco (usually tobacco is smoked before it ends up in any landfill), or recyclable yogurt plastic cups in a country where household waste is neither separated nor recycled.

The Greenpeace Greenwashing Champion

The petroleum business BP in the early 2000s started a multi-million-dollar public relations campaign to show how green the company supposedly was. For instance, in 2008 BP made 93% of their investment in oil, but merely 2.79% in biofuel and 1.39% in solar initiatives. The slogan "beyond" petroleum does not match the numbers and was therefore perceived as greenwash. Also, the company's flower-like logo, and the catchphrases "from the earth to the sun and everything in between" and "the best way out of the energy fix is an energy mix" encountered strong critical reactions. In 2009, Greenpeace activists tried to award BP CEO Tony Hayward with a greenwashing award (a green paintbrush) for the company's overall campaign, which the company declined to receive (Walker, 2010).

Sports Washing

The concept of "sports washing" is becoming increasingly relevant in the business context, particularly as corporations seek to enhance their reputational image through association with sports. This strategy involves sponsoring sporting events, teams, or individual athletes to divert public attention from controversial practices or to improve corporate image, especially in areas of environmental, social, and governance (ESG) concerns. From a business ethics perspective, sports washing is a form of impression management, a strategy where organizations attempt to influence the perceptions of various stakeholders through calculated associations with positive and high-profile activities like sports. Elsbach and Sutton (2021) explore impression management in organizations, highlighting the strategic use of symbolic actions to shape public perception. In the context of sports washing, this involves leveraging the universal appeal and positive public sentiment towards sports to overshadow less favorable aspects of a company's operations.

The efficacy of sports washing as a corporate strategy is a topic of debate in academic circles. On one hand, it can provide short-term reputational benefits, as noted by Kumar and Christodoulides (2022), who discuss the immediate positive impact of sports sponsorships on brand image and customer perception. However, this strategy can also attract criticism and increased scrutiny, especially from informed consumers and activists who are aware of the underlying ethical issues. For instance companies involved in environmental controversies might sponsor sports events or teams, but this can lead to accusations of hypocrisy and greenwashing if their core business practices are not aligned with the values promoted through their sponsorships (Wagner et al., 2022).

A notable example in recent years has been the involvement of energy companies in sponsoring major sporting events. These sponsorships are often seen as attempts to divert attention from environmental concerns associated with their primary business activities. Whist such sponsorships might enhance short-term visibility and positive association, they do little to address the underlying ethical and environmental concerns (Davidson, 2020). The role of social media and digital platforms in amplifying or countering the effects of sports washing is also significant. Digital platforms can both promote and expose sports washing activities, leading to a more informed and critical audience (Carter & Buraimo, 2023). This dual role of digital media means that while sports washing can reach a wider audience more effectively, it also faces greater risks of being publicly challenged and scrutinized. The practice of sports washing in the business context highlights the complexities and ethical considerations in corporate sponsorship strategies. While it can offer short-term reputational benefits, it poses long-term risks, including heightened scrutiny and potential backlash, especially in an era where consumers are increasingly aware and critical of corporate practices.

Exercises

A. KNOW

Use the below multiple-choice questions to test your knowledge. Each answer may be wrong or right and there may be zero to four right or wrong answers per question:

1. Critical attitudes...
   a. ...might lead to a situation where the companies communicate their responsible business message well, but stakeholders still do not make a positive attribution to the business.
   b. ...might for instance exist in an employee, who just cannot "believe" the company's external philanthropic attitude as he feels badly treated in his workplace.
   c. ...might be avoided, if the company communicates both inputs and outputs of responsible business conduct and this way provides a factually substantiated and complete picture.
   d. ...might be avoided, if the company communicates both the motivation to evolve into a responsible business and how the activities fit with their core business.
2. Greenwashing...
   a. ...refers to offering "green products".
   b. ...stakeholders apply the same criteria for greenwashing accusations for all organizations.
   c. ...should be avoided by increasing the quantity of communication.
   d. ...can occur due to communication errors, such as lying, not communicating hidden trade-offs, and communicating that something is good for the environment or society, while it is just less harmful than other alternatives.
3. Bluewashing...
   a. ...refers to the misuse of a United Nations association.
   b. ...is a form of greenwashing.
   c. ...is a synonym for green noise.
   d. ...is the opposite of greenwashing.

B. THINK

Go to your local supermarket and identify three products you believe could be accused of greenwashing. Test your suspicion by locating more detailed information on the product and comparing your findings to the description of different types of greenwashing or possibly by communicating with the company.

C. DO

Write a brief text on typical thinking and behavior patterns you think lead to greenwashing. Then provide a shopping list of three points someone in marketing and communication can adhere to in order to avoid falling into the greenwashing trap.

D. RELATE

Think about one product that you consider to be a clear example of greenwashing. Design an alternative communication strategy for the product that avoids greenwashing and send it to the company. Be prepared to discuss your idea if they should answer back to you.

E. BE

Greenwashing is about walking the talk. This is very similar to one aspect of personal integrity, where what we say should reflect our values, and what we do should reflect both values and our statements. Which of the following statements best reflects you? Briefly mention an example from your own life where you see the statement reflected.

a. I have no difficulty to communicate my values and most of the time I act upon them.
b. Most of the time I feel I cannot translate my values into words or actions.
c. I mostly can clearly articulate my values, but often find it difficult to act upon them.

Feedback

A. KNOW

Feedback 1

a. Right: The attribution of responsible business to a company's communication also depends on the context such as a preconceived negative attitude towards the company not only on the communication itself.
b. Right: We have a classic misleading imbalance between walk and talk here.
c. Right: In this case the company would communicate a factually true picture reflecting the business reality. However, this truthfulness might not always be enough to avoid greenwash accusations.
d. Right: Communicating motivation and fit are good practices for avoiding greenwashing accusations.

Feedback 2

a. Wrong: Offering "green products" is only greenwashing, if the products are not as ecologically viable as the marketing and communication concerning those products suggest.
b. Wrong: How sensitive stakeholders are to perceiving companies as greenwashing depends on stakeholders' often biased perception of the company's overall social and environmental performance, and the general attitude towards the business.

c. Wrong: Even increasing the amount of communication, while not improving responsible business activities, will lead to stakeholders' perception of even stronger greenwashing.
d. Right: All of the mentioned communication errors are typically subsumed under greenwashing.

Feedback 3

a. Right: Bluewashing typically refers to a company that behaves irresponsibly in spite of being a member of the United Nations Global Compact initiative.
b. Right: Bluewashing also falls under the same definition to that of greenwashing as incongruence between responsible business reality and communication activity.
c. Wrong: Green noise refers to the overwhelming and often confusing amount of messages related to environmental and social topics.
d. Wrong: It is a form of greenwashing specifically referring to the misleading perception created by a company that communicates its Global Compact membership, but that does not adhere to the ten Global Compact principles.

B. THINK

Level	*Critical discernment...*	*Notes*
+	Greenwashing suspicions have been refuted or corroborated, based on a sound investigation.	
=	Greenwashing candidates have been identified based on concrete evidence and understanding of the characteristics of greenwashing.	
–	No or weak identification of greenwashing candidates.	

C. DO

Level	*Breaking action patterns*	*Notes*
+	Very feasible and pragmatic plan to break patterns leading to greenwashing behavior.	
=	You are on to something. Patterns have been identified, but the list does not seem effective in getting to the root of the behavior.	
–	Thinking and behavior pattern could not be identified.	

D. RELATE

Level	*Giving advice...*	*Notes*
+	Feasible alternative strategy has been communicated to the company. Possibly, even a dialogue has been established.	
=	Convincing non-greenwashing communication strategy has been designed. It constitutes a feasible alternative.	
–	No non-greenwashing communication strategy has been designed.	

E. BE

Level	*Personal integrity*	*Notes*
+	I have no difficulty in communicating my values and most of the time I act upon them.	
=	I mostly can clearly articulate my values, but often find it difficult to act upon them.	
–	Most of the times I feel I cannot translate my values into words or actions.	

References

Bhattacharya, S. D., & Sen, S. (2010). Maximizing business returns to corporate social responsibility (CSR): The role of CSR communication. *International Journal of Management Reviews, 12*(1), 8–19.

Carter, J., & Buraimo, B. (2023). Digital media and sports washing: The dual role of social platforms. *Media, Culture & Society, 45*, 134–150.

Davidson, L. (2020). Corporate sponsorship in sport and environmental controversies: A case study of the energy sector. *Sport in Society, 23*(4), 632–647.

Du, S., Bhattacharya, C., & Sen, S. (2007). Reaping relational rewards from corporate social responsibility: The role of competitive positioning. *International Journal of Research in Marketing, 24*, 224–241.

Elsbach, K. D., & Sutton, R. I. (2021). Building reputations through impression management: A theoretical overview. *Academy of Management Review, 46*(2), 357–373.

Futerra. (2008). *The greenwash guide*. London: Futerra Sustainability Communications.

Greenpeace UK. (2012). *Have a break?* Retrieved January 25, 2012, from YouTube: https://www.youtube.com/watch?v=VaJjPRwExO8

Horiuchi, R., Schuchard, R., Shea, L., & Townsend, S. (2009). *Understanding and preventing greenwash: A business guide*. San Francisco: BSR.

Kumar, A., & Christodoulides, G. (2022). Sports sponsorship and brand perception: A quantitative analysis. *Journal of Brand Management, 29*(3), 275–288.

Terrachoice. (2007). *The "Six Sins of Greenwashing": A study of environmental claims in North American consumer markets*. Ottawa: Terrachoice.

Wagner, U., Lutz, R. J., & Weitz, B. A. (2022). Corporate sponsorships in sports: Ethical perspectives and implications for practice. *Journal of Business Ethics, 159*(1), 95–112.

Walker, H. (2010). *Recapping on BP's long history of greenwashing*. Retrieved January 24, 2012, from Greenpeace USA: https://www.greenpeace.org/usa/en/news-and-blogs/campaign-blog/recapping-on-bps-long-history-of-greenwashing/blog/26025/

20 Responsible Business Certification

The increased interest in responsible business practices has precipitated a corresponding surge in adopting reliable business certifications. Such certifications are designed to operationalize the principles of sustainability and ethics within the corporate ambit, serving as both a framework for implementation and a beacon for corporate identity in the marketplace (Schaltegger & Burritt, 2010). As vehicles for translating the abstract concepts of ethical conduct and sustainability into tangible business practices, responsible business certifications are increasingly perceived as an integral component of contemporary business strategy (Beske & Seuring, 2014). The genesis of responsible business certification is inextricably linked to the broader sustainability movement, which has seen a shift from voluntary corporate social responsibility initiatives to more structured and formalized processes (Montabon et al., 2007). Certifications crystallize the ethos of responsible business by stipulating clear, auditable criteria against which companies can be evaluated and held accountable. This evolution in sustainability practices mirrors the heightened expectations of stakeholders, who now demand greater transparency and verifiability in corporate claims of responsibility and sustainability (Delmas & Blass, 2010).

Within this domain, the *raison d'être* for businesses to seek certification is multifaceted. On the one hand, certifications can unlock economic benefits by streamlining operations and improving market positioning. On the other hand, they serve as a testament to a company's commitment to societal values, potentially enhancing reputation and engendering trust among consumers and other stakeholders (Castka & Corbett, 2015). The dual promise of internal operational efficiency and external reputational benefits positions responsible business certifications as ornamental and a strategic imperative (Orlitzky et al., 2011). As the contemporary business landscape continues to evolve under the influence of globalization, digitalization, and increasing societal expectations, the role of responsible business certifications is likely to become ever more central. They are not just tools for compliance but are stepping stones towards a new paradigm of business conduct where the imperatives of profit, people, and the planet are inextricably linked (Aguinis & Glavas, 2012).

The introduction of responsible business certifications marks a significant stride in the journey towards sustainable development. By formalizing the principles of ethical behavior and sustainable practices, certifications offer a pathway for businesses to contribute meaningfully to the Sustainable Development Goals (SDGs) outlined by the United Nations (UN Global Compact, 2014). In this context, responsible business certifications are not the

DOI: 10.4324/9781003544074-27

destination but a conduit through which sustainable development aspirations find practical expression in the business world (Bansal & Song, 2017).

What is Responsible Business Certification?

As a concept and practice, Responsible Business Certification manifests an evolving corporate consciousness that seeks to anchor business operations within an ethical and sustainable framework. This certification encapsulates a set of criteria and standards a business must meet to be considered socially responsible, environmentally sustainable, and ethically managed. It is not merely an accolade but a metric of a company's commitment to responsible business conduct.

The historical development of Responsible Business Certification schemes is an illustrative narrative of the business world's response to the evolving landscape of societal values, environmental concerns, and ethical imperatives. In the nascent stages, certification schemes were predominantly focused on environmental stewardship, with pioneering initiatives such as the ISO 14001 environmental management standards introduced in 1996. These provided a template for organizations to systematize and improve their environmental management efforts (Melnyk et al., 2003). The trajectory of these certification schemes over time reflects a growing sophistication and diversification. The Forest Stewardship Council (FSC), established in 1993, was one of the first to offer certifications that guaranteed the sustainable origin of forest products - a response to public concern over deforestation and its ecological impacts (Cashore et al., 2004). Similarly, the inception of the Marine Stewardship Council (MSC) in 1997 signaled a recognition of the need to address sustainable fishing practices in response to declining global fish stocks. Moving into the new millennium, the scope of certification has broadened significantly. The early 2000s saw the rise of the fair-trade movement, encapsulated by organizations like Fairtrade International, which certified products that adhered to standards designed to support producers in developing countries. This trend indicated an emerging consciousness that responsible business practices encompass environmental, social, and economic dimensions (Raynolds et al., 2007).

The historical narrative of certification schemes is also one of regional- and sector-specific responses. For instance, the European Union's Eco-Management and Audit Scheme (EMAS), introduced in 1995, is a management tool for companies and other organizations to evaluate, report, and improve their environmental performance. It reflected the EU's commitment to enhancing environmental protection (Szymanski & Tiemann, 2004). Similarly, sector-specific schemes like the Responsible Jewelry Council, established in 2005, sought to certify the ethical production and sourcing within the gemstone and precious metals industry, responding to concerns about conflict diamonds and mining impacts (Gilbert, 2010).

The evolution of certification schemes has been accompanied by a transition from niche markets to mainstream adoption. As consumer awareness and demand for sustainable products have grown, so has the number of companies seeking certification. This indicates a broader shift in market dynamics, where sustainability has become a competitive parameter (Darnall et al., 2010). Moreover, the development of these schemes has occurred in collaboration. It has been influenced by the dialogue among businesses, non-governmental organizations (NGOs), academia, and policy-makers, reflecting a multi-stakeholder approach to sustainable development (Perez-Aleman & Sandilands, 2008). This collaborative process has been fundamental in shaping the criteria and governance of certification schemes, ensuring they remain relevant and rigorous. The historical development of Responsible Business Certification is thus a complex tapestry woven from a confluence of environmental activism, social justice movements, market forces, and regulatory developments. It represents a collective endeavor to harmonize business operations with sustainability principles, demonstrating an ongoing commitment to a future where corporate success is intrinsically linked to ethical and responsible conduct.

Eco-Labelling

Eco-labels serve as a critical tool in promoting sustainable consumption and production by providing consumers with clear, verifiable, and readily understandable information on the environmental impact of their purchases. These labels are applied to products and services that meet specific environmental standards, covering a broad range of criteria including energy efficiency, resource conservation, reduction of harmful chemicals, and the promotion of recycling. The emergence of eco-labels responds to growing consumer demand for environmentally friendly products and the need for transparency in environmental claims. The concept of eco-labelling originated in the late 20th century, with the first eco-label, the "Blue Angel," introduced in Germany in 1978. Since then, the use of eco-labels has proliferated globally, with numerous countries and independent organizations developing their own certification schemes to address various environmental issues. These labels can be found across different industries, including food, cosmetics, clothing, and electronics, to name a few. Eco-labels can be broadly categorized into three types:

Type I: Voluntary labels awarded by third-party organizations, based on a set of predetermined environmental criteria. These are considered the most stringent and reliable eco-labels.

Type II: Self-declared environmental claims made by manufacturers, importers, or distributors, which are not independently verified.

Type III: Quantitative environmental data provided by the manufacturer, verified by a third party. This category includes life cycle assessments and is often presented in the form of an Environmental Product Declaration (EPD).

Eco-labels play a pivotal role in guiding consumer choices towards more sustainable options, thereby encouraging manufacturers to adopt greener practices. They contribute to environmental awareness and education, helping consumers make informed decisions that align with their values. However, the proliferation of eco-labels also presents challenges, such as label confusion among consumers due to the multitude of certifications and standards. According to the Ecolabel Index, a global directory of eco-labels, as of 2024 there are some 456 ecolabels in 199 countries, and 25 industry sectors (Ecolabel Index, 2024). Moreover, the credibility of eco-labels depends heavily on the rigor of the certification process and the transparency of the criteria used, highlighting the importance of third-party verification and international standards.

Whole Business Certification

The typology of Responsible Business Certifications reflects an intricate mosaic of standards, each tailored to different sectors and objectives within the corporate sustainability domain. Among the plethora of certifications, Benefit Corporation certification stands out as a comprehensive framework for companies dedicated to social and environmental performance, accountability, and transparency.

Benefit Corporations

Benefit Corporation certification is a legal status and a certification that extends beyond product- or service-level assessments. It encapsulates a company's entire operation, subjecting it to rigorous social and environmental performance standards. Companies certified as Benefit Corporations are legally required to consider the impact of their decisions on their workers, customers, suppliers, community, and the environment, representing a shift towards a more inclusive and sustainable economy (Clark & Babson, 2012). This certification embodies the movement towards embedding sustainability into a company's legal and financial framework. It mandates the integration of stakeholder interests into corporate governance, thereby operationalizing the triple-bottom-line concept - people, planet, and profit - within corporate structures (Sisodia et al., 2014). Benefit corporations represent a significant evolution in the corporate landscape, primarily in the United States, as they integrate societal and environmental goals into their legal corporate framework. This legal structure is distinctive because it expands the fiduciary duty of directors from focusing solely on financial interests to also considering the broader impacts on society and the environment.

The genesis of benefit corporations can be traced to a legislative movement beginning in Maryland in 2010, rapidly spreading to most US states (Vranka, 2013). This adoption signifies a growing recognition of the role of corporations in addressing societal challenges. A defining characteristic of benefit corporations is their commitment to creating public benefit. This is a legally defined goal that includes a positive impact on society, workers, the community, and the environment. This broader view of purpose distinguishes benefit corporations from traditional corporations, which primarily focus on maximizing shareholder value. Legally, benefit corporations are required to consider the impact of their decisions not only on shareholders but also on other stakeholders, including employees, customers, and the community, as well as the local and global environment. This requirement represents a shift from the traditional shareholder primacy model and aligns corporate decision making with broader societal and environmental considerations (Hiller, 2013). Furthermore, benefit corporations are mandated to report on their social and environmental performance using a comprehensive, credible, independent, and transparent third-party standard. This reporting requirement enhances transparency and accountability, ensuring that these corporations are genuinely committed to their stated goals (Sabeti, 2011).

The rise of benefit corporations can be seen as part of a larger movement towards sustainable business practices. As public concern over environmental issues and social inequalities has grown, so has the interest in corporate models that can address these issues. Benefit corporations provide a legal framework that facilitates and legitimizes the pursuit of social and environmental objectives alongside financial profitability (André, 2012). However, despite the promise and growth of benefit corporations, some critics argue that the legal structure may be more symbolic than transformative, as the enforcement mechanisms and legal implications of failing to meet social or environmental objectives are still unclear (Tyler, 2015). Nevertheless, the emergence of benefit corporations marks a significant step towards integrating ethical considerations into the core of corporate governance and operations.

Laureate Education, Inc.: Benefit Corporation

Laureate Education, Inc. is a global network of private, higher education institutions dedicated to making quality education accessible. Founded in 1998, it operates universities in multiple countries, emphasizing workforce development and social change through education. In 2015, Laureate became the first publicly traded company to adopt Benefit Corporation status, committing to high standards of purpose, accountability, and transparency. Their Benefit Corporation status enables Laureate to align its operations with its social mission without sacrificing financial objectives and serves as an example as to how an organization can integrate social goals with responsible business models.

Inspired by the US benefit corporation model, several other nation states have sought to develop similar certifications for example:

Canada's British Columbia Benefit Company: Similar to the US, British Columbia in Canada has introduced legislation for Benefit Companies, allowing businesses to include a commitment to conduct business responsibly and sustainably in their articles of incorporation (BC Centre for Social Enterprise, 2020).

Italy's Società Benefit: Italy has introduced a legal status for "Società Benefit", which is similar to the Benefit Corporation model in the US. These companies integrate the goal of having a positive impact on society and the environment into their corporate purpose, in addition to profit (Società Benefit, 2016).

Colombia's BIC (Benefit and Collective Interest) Companies: Colombia became the first country in Latin America to introduce legislation for BIC companies, which are similar to Benefit Corporations, requiring them to commit to higher social and environmental standards (Villamizar, 2023)

B-Corps

B Corporations, commonly referred to as B-Corps, constitute a global movement of companies voluntarily committing to higher standards of social and environmental performance, accountability, and transparency. Unlike benefit corporations, which are a legal structure, B-Corps are certified by B Lab, a non-profit organization, based on their adherence to these stringent standards. The concept of B-Corps emerged from the recognition that while traditional businesses focus primarily on profit maximization, there is a growing need for companies to address societal and environmental issues. B-Corps seek to demonstrate that businesses can be both profit-driven and socially responsible (Honeyman & Jana, 2019).

To become a certified B-Corp, companies must undergo a rigorous assessment process conducted by B Lab. This assessment evaluates the company's impact on all its stakeholders, including workers, customers, community, and the environment. The evaluation criteria are comprehensive and cover areas such as governance, workers' rights, community engagement, environmental impact, and customers. Companies must score a minimum of 80 out of 200 points to qualify for certification and are required to recertify every three years, ensuring ongoing compliance and improvement (B Lab, 2024). An essential aspect of B-Corp certification is the requirement for companies to amend their corporate governance structures to reflect their commitment to stakeholder interests. This often involves incorporating the interests of workers, the community, and the environment into their decision-making processes, thereby aligning business practices with social and environmental objectives (Stubbs, 2017).

B-Corps are part of a broader movement towards responsible business practices and sustainable development. They represent a shift in the business paradigm from focusing solely on financial performance to integrating social and environmental considerations into the core business strategy. This shift is driven by increasing consumer awareness, investor interest in sustainable and responsible businesses, and a growing recognition of the role of businesses in addressing global challenges such as climate change and social inequality (André, 2012; Honeyman & Jana, 2019). Critically, the B-Corp certification is seen as a powerful tool for building credibility and trust among consumers, investors, and other stakeholders. It signals a company's commitment to not just being the best in the world but being the best for the world. As such, B-Corps often use their certification as a differentiator in the marketplace, appealing to a growing segment of socially and environmentally conscious consumers and investors (Clark & Babson, 2012). B-Corps represent an innovative model for businesses that seek to balance profit and purpose. Through rigorous standards and a comprehensive certification process, B-Corps demonstrate that it is possible to use business as a force for good, addressing societal and environmental challenges while maintaining financial viability.

As of 2024, there are nearly 8,000 Certified B Corporations (B-Corps) across 160 industries in 93 countries. Figure 20.1 illustrates the year-on-year increase in the number of Certified B Corporations from 2010 to 2024. As depicted, there has been a significant and consistent rise in the number of B-Corps, reflecting a growing global commitment to sustainable business practices. The data highlights a marked acceleration in recent years, underscoring the increasing importance placed on social and environmental performance by companies worldwide.

Elvis & Kresse: Innovating for sustainability and social impact

Elvis & Kresse, a UK-based Certified B Corporation, stands out for its innovative approach to sustainability in the luxury fashion industry. Founded in 2005, the company has built its business model around rescuing decommissioned London firehoses and repurposing them into high-end accessories, alongside other reclaimed materials. By adopting circular economy principles, Elvis & Kresse not only reduces waste and promotes sustainable consumption but also supports charitable causes, donating 50% of the profits from its fire-hose range to the Fire Fighters Charity. This initiative exemplifies how businesses can integrate environmental stewardship and social purpose, setting a benchmark for ethical practices in the industry.

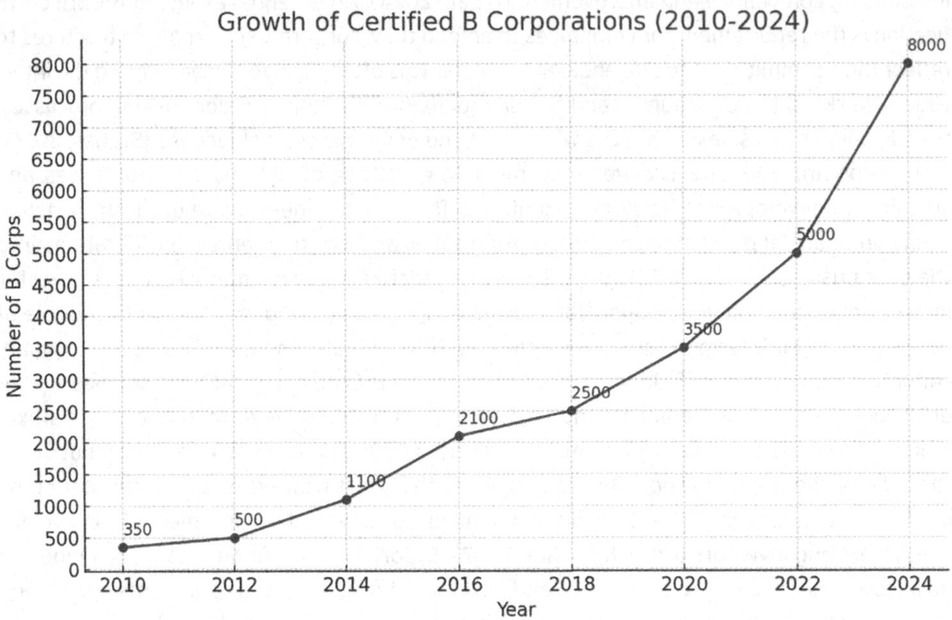

Figure 20.1 Growth of Certified B Corporations (2010–2024).

Differences between Benefit Corporations and B-Corps

Benefit corporations and B-Corps, while often confused due to their similar nomenclature, represent distinct concepts within the realm of sustainable and ethical business practices. A "benefit corporation" is a legal form of organization in the United States and several other countries. It differs from traditional corporations in its core legal structure and purpose. The defining characteristic of a benefit corporation is its dual mission: To generate profit and to create a positive impact on society, workers, the community, and the environment. This dual mission is embedded in its legal framework, making it a part of its fiduciary duty to consider the impact of their decisions not only on shareholders but also on other stakeholders and the public good. This incorporation model was first enacted in Maryland in 2010 and has since been adopted in a majority of US states (Clark & Babson, 2012).

In contrast, a B-Corp, or a B Corporation, is a certification conferred by the non-profit organization B Lab. B-Corps are certified by B Lab to meet rigorous standards of social and environmental performance, accountability, and transparency. This certification does not change the legal status of a company but serves as a third-party validation of its social and environmental practices. The B-Corp certification applies globally and includes an assessment that measures a company's impact on its workers, customers, community, and environment. B-Corps are required to undergo verification every three years to maintain their certification (Honeyman & Jana, 2019).

The key difference between the two lies in their legal status and scope. A benefit corporation is a legal form in certain jurisdictions, mandating the consideration of stakeholder interests in their operations. On the other hand, B-Corp certification is a voluntary, private certification that any business, regardless of its legal form, can achieve if it meets the standards set out by B Lab. Both benefit corporations and B-Corps are part of a broader movement towards more responsible business practices, addressing the growing concern about the role of business in society and the environment. They reflect an increasing recognition that businesses can and should play a positive role in addressing social and environmental issues. However, it is crucial to distinguish between the legal structure and commitments of benefit corporations and the voluntary, certification-based approach of B-Corps (André, 2012; Stubbs, 2017).

Etsy, Inc.: A fusion of social purpose and craft

Etsy, Inc., renowned for its global online marketplace for handmade and unique items, stands out as both a registered Benefit Corporation and a Certified B Corporation, embodying a commitment to social responsibility and environmental sustainability. Founded in 2005, with headquarters in Brooklyn, New York, Etsy champions the cause of small businesses and artisans, promoting economic empowerment and sustainable practices. By becoming a Benefit Corporation and achieving B-Corp Certification, Etsy has institutionalized its mission to "keep commerce human", demonstrating its dedication to balancing profit with purpose. The company's initiatives, from offsetting carbon emissions to supporting community engagement, highlight its role in fostering a more inclusive and sustainable economy, making Etsy a model for integrating business success with societal and environmental stewardship.

Better Business Act

The Better Business Act (BBA) represents a significant reform initiative aimed at updating the Companies Act in the United Kingdom (Better Business Act, 2023). The primary objective of the BBA is to amend Section 172 of the Companies Act, thereby shifting the paradigm of corporate governance towards a more inclusive and responsible framework. This initiative is driven by the understanding that the alignment of business operations with the broader interests of society and the environment is not only ethically imperative but also beneficial for long-term business success. The core principles of the BBA include:

Aligned Interests: This principle seeks to advance the interests of shareholders alongside those of the wider society and environment. It establishes a new norm of fiduciary duty within Section 172 of the Companies Act, thereby mandating directors to consider the impact of their decisions on stakeholders beyond just shareholders.

Empowering Directors: The Act aims to empower company directors, enabling them to exercise judgment in balancing and advancing the interests of all stakeholders. This empowerment is crucial for directors to navigate the complex interplay between financial performance and societal impact.

Default Change: The BBA proposes that these changes apply to all businesses by default, making it a standard practice rather than an optional one to consider broader stakeholder interests.

Reporting Requirements: Post-amendment, businesses would be required to report on how they align the interests of people, planet, and profit. This reporting, either in the form of a strategic or impact report, would ensure transparency and accountability in how companies address their broader societal and environmental impacts.

As of 2023, over 2500 companies have joined the coalition supporting the BBA, indicating a growing corporate acknowledgment of the importance of sustainable and responsible business practices (Better Business Act, 2023).

Triodos Bank. Supporting the BBA

Triodos Bank is a European bank known for its pioneering efforts in sustainable banking. Founded in 1980 in the Netherlands, the bank has built its operations around the principles of transparency, sustainability, and using money to bring about positive social, environmental, and cultural change. As a supporter of the Better Business Act, Triodos Bank emphasizes the alignment of its foundational mission with the BBA's objectives. Its backing of the BBA reflects its longstanding commitment to ethical banking and finance, where the consideration of people and the planet stands on equal footing with profit. The bank's involvement in the BBA is a natural extension of its business model, which focuses on financing companies and projects that have a positive impact on society, culture, and the environment reinforcing its vision of a banking sector that serves humanity's long-term needs and aspirations (Triodos Bank NV, 2021).

The Role of Third-Party Verification

The role of third-party verification in the context of responsible business certification is pivotal in establishing the credibility and authenticity of a company's commitment to ethical and sustainable practices. This verification process is conducted by an independent entity that assesses the company's adherence to specific standards, thereby providing an objective validation of the company's claims. Third-party verification serves several critical functions:

Objective Assessment: Unlike self-assessments, which can be biased, third-party verification provides an objective evaluation of a company's operations, ensuring that they meet the established standards for certification.

Credibility and Trust: Certifications from recognized and reputable third parties lend credibility to a company's sustainability claims, fostering trust among consumers, investors, and other stakeholders.

Market Differentiation: In a crowded marketplace, third-party certification can serve as a differentiator, signaling to consumers that a company's products or services meet high ethical and sustainability standards.

Continuous Improvement: Most third-party certifications require regular re-assessment to maintain certification status, encouraging companies to continually improve their practices and operations.

Transparency and Accountability: Third-party verification ensures transparency in how companies report their practices and holds them accountable to stakeholders for their performance.

Risk Management: By adhering to the standards required for certification, companies can identify and mitigate potential risks associated with environmental, social, and governance (ESG) factors.

The utilization of third-party assurance companies like Veritas in the certification of business sustainability initiatives represents a pivotal element in the discourse on sustainable development and corporate responsibility, resonating deeply within the academic realm. This approach is rooted in the principle of enhancing credibility and trust, a notion extensively discussed in the literature. Darnall et al. (2022) emphasize that the independent verification of sustainability claims by external entities devoid of vested interests significantly augments the authenticity of these claims. This is particularly crucial in an era marked by heightened consumer and investor skepticism towards self-reported corporate sustainability initiatives, often referred to as "greenwashing" (Laufer, 2003).

The objectivity and expertise offered by these third-party entities are another critical dimension. Assurance companies specialize in audit and certification processes, bringing a level of expertise and understanding of specific standards and sustainability frameworks that is typically beyond the scope of internal corporate resources (Boiral, 2013). This expertise is not only instrumental in ensuring compliance with international standards but also in imbuing corporate sustainability initiatives with a degree of legitimacy and rigor. Moreover, the role of third-party assurance in risk management and compliance is increasingly acknowledged in the academic discourse. Such entities aid in identifying and mitigating risks related to sustainability practices, ensuring adherence to a rapidly evolving regulatory landscape around environmental, social, and governance (ESG) issues (Kolk & Perego, 2010). This aspect of third-party assurance aligns with the proactive approach to risk management that is becoming essential in contemporary business practices.

In the context of market differentiation and competitive advantage, third-party certifications serve as a critical tool. As argued by Delmas and Burbano (2011), in a marketplace where numerous companies assert their commitment to sustainability, certification by a respected third party can significantly enhance a company's market position. It signals a genuine commitment to sustainable practices, potentially leading to a competitive edge. The transparency and clarity provided by third-party certifications are pivotal in stakeholder engagement and communication. Such certifications offer a standardized and reliable method of communicating a company's sustainability performance, addressing stakeholders' growing demands for detailed and trustworthy information about corporate sustainability practices (Hahn & Kühnen, 2013). Finally, the continuous improvement aspect of third-party certification, necessitating regular audits and reviews, fosters an environment of ongoing enhancement in sustainability practices. This facet is crucial in ensuring that companies not only adhere to current standards but also evolve with new developments and best practices in the field (Boiral, 2012).

Exercises

A. KNOW

Use the below multiple-choice questions to test your knowledge. Each answer may be wrong or right and there may be zero to four right or wrong answers per question:

1. What is the primary purpose of responsible business certifications?
   a. To increase the CEO's personal reputation.
   b. To operationalize sustainability and ethics within companies.
   c. To eliminate all forms of corporate regulation.
   d. To solely boost short-term profits.
2. Which of the following certifications was one of the first to guarantee the sustainable origin of forest products?
   a. ISO 14001.
   b. Marine Stewardship Council (MSC).
   c. Forest Stewardship Council (FSC).
   d. Fairtrade International.
3. What key difference distinguishes Benefit Corporations from B-Corporations?
   a. Benefit Corporations are a legal status; B-Corps are certified by a non-profit.
   b. B-Corps do not focus on social and environmental performance.
   c. Benefit Corporations do not require third-party certification.
   d. B-Corps are a form of legal status in the United States.
4. Which type of eco-label is awarded by third-party organizations based on environmental criteria?
   a. Type I.
   b. Type II.
   c. Type III.
   d. None of the above.
5. What is the primary benefit of third-party verification in responsible business certification?
   a. Reducing operational costs for businesses.
   b. Eliminating the need for corporate governance.
   c. Enhancing the credibility and trust in corporate sustainability claims.
   d. Guaranteeing corporate profits.

B. THINK

Pick one company of your choice. Imagine you are tasked with selling the value of perusing Benefit or B-Corp certification to the board. How would you persuade them?

C. DO

Identify one responsible business certification discussed in this chapter and research the criteria and steps required taken for a company/product to be certified or labelled. Draft an action plan of the steps to be taken to get there.

D. RELATE

Take a look at the B-Corp website https://www.bcorporation.net/en-us/ and investigate the range of companies who are certified. Consider the products and services which you use on a daily basis in both your professional and personal lives. Could you be using a B-Corp instead? Can you generate a list of those you would be able to award your custom/business to?

E. BE

Consider how you feel about companies that claim to be responsible businesses. Do you believe them all? Are you sensitive to false claims and "greenwashing"? Do you feel that third-party certification provides you with more assurance as a consumer or client? Would you consider moving your custom or business to a certified company or not and why?

Feedback

A. KNOW

Feedback 1

a. Wrong: Leading a certifiable responsible business may increase a senior leader's reputation in some ways, however on its own it is unlikely to lead to any significant personal benefits.

b. Right: Responsible business certifications are designed to translate the abstract concepts of ethical conduct and sustainability into tangible business practices, serving as both a framework for implementation and an identity marker in the marketplace.

c. Wrong: Corporate regulation has an important part to play in the basket of available tools through which companies may be held accountable.

d. Wrong: Whilst obtaining a responsible business certificate may lead to improved profitability over time for example by enabling access to new markets, short-term profit focus in rarely a sustainable business strategy.

Feedback 2

a. Wrong: ISO 14001 focuses on environmental management systems.
b. Wrong: MSC on sustainable fishing focuses on supporting producers in developing countries.
c. Right: The FSC, established in 1993, offered certifications guaranteeing the sustainable origin of forest products, addressing public concern over deforestation and its ecological impacts.
d. Wrong: Fairtrade International focuses on supporting producers in developing countries.

Feedback 3

a. Right: Benefit Corporations have a legal status requiring them to consider broader societal and environmental impacts, whereas B-Corps undergo a third-party certification process by B Lab.
b. Wrong: B-Corps do indeed focus on social and environmental performance.
c. Wrong: This answer is a little misleading as the differentiation between the two concepts is not about the requirement for third-party certification but their fundamental nature and scope.
d. Wrong: B-Corps certification does not in itself confer a legal status.

Feedback 4

a. Right: Type I eco-labels are voluntary and awarded by third-party organizations based on a set of predetermined environmental criteria, making them the most stringent and reliable eco-labels.
b. Wrong: Type II involves self-declared environmental claims.
c. Wrong: Type III relates to quantitative environmental data.
d. Wrong: Type I clearly fits the description.

Feedback 5

a. Wrong: Third-party verification is not directly about cost reduction.
b. Wrong: Third-party verification is not related to the elimination of corporate governance.
c. Right: Third-party verification plays a critical role in establishing the credibility and authenticity of a company's commitment to ethical and sustainable practices, fostering trust among consumers, investors, and other stakeholders.
d. Wrong: Third-party verification is not directly related to profit generation; however, organizations may be able to improve profitability through the increased trust building that it can generate.

B. THINK

Level	*Selling responsible business certification*	*Notes*
+	Able to articulate the reasons or benefits associated with adopting a responsible business certification for the specific business selected.	
=	Able to articulate the reasons or benefits associated with adopting a responsible business certification but not related to a specific business case.	
–	Unable to articulate the reasons or benefits associated with adopting a responsible business certification.	

C. DO

Level	*Certification process*	*Notes*
+	Feasible action plan, including areas to be improved before labelling has been established based on a solid understanding of the criteria of the standard.	
=	Criteria have been understood, but no feasible or superficial action plan has been established.	
–	Label/certification standard has not been identified.	

D. RELATE

Level	*B-Corp research*	*Notes*
+	Clear identification of B-Corp certified companies who may offer the same or similar services and products to those you use in your personal and professional life with a list.	
=	Investigation of the website but no generation of a list of relevant companies.	
–	Not investigated the B-Corp website or engaged with the exercise.	

E. BE

Level	*Trust in responsible business*	*Notes*
+	Thoughts clearly captured in an in-depth appreciation of how responsible business certification may improve trust in a brand.	
=	Basic capture of thoughts and adequate explanation as to the perceived value of responsible business certification in your view.	
–	Major difficulties in capturing and articulating your thoughts relating to responsible business certification.	

References

Aguinis, H., & Glavas, A. (2012). What we know and don't know about corporate social responsibility: A review and research agenda. *Journal of Management, 38*, 932–968.

André, R. (2012). Assessing the accountability of the benefit corporation: Will this new gray sector organization enhance corporate social responsibility? *Journal of Business Ethics, 110*(1), 133–150.

B Lab. (2024). *B Corp Certification demonstrates a company's entire social and environmental impact*. https://www.bcorporation.net/en-us/certification/

Bansal, P., & Song, H.-C. (2017). Similar but not the same: Differentiating corporate sustainability from corporate responsibility. *Academy of Management Annals, 11*(1), 105–149.

BC Centre for Social Enterprise. (2020, June 11). *Benefit Company BC*. BC Centre for Social Enterprise. https://www.centreforsocialenterprise.com/benefit-company/

Beske, P., & Seuring, S. (2014). Putting sustainability into supply chain management. *Supply Chain Management. An International Journal, 19*(3), 322–331.

Better Business Act. (2023, June 15). *About*. Better Business Act. https://betterbusinessact.org/about/

Boiral, O. (2012). ISO certificates as organizational degrees? Beyond the rational myths of the certification process. *Organization Studies, 33*(5–6), 633–654.

Boiral, O. (2013). Sustainability reports as simulacra? A counter-account of A and A+ GRI reports. *Accounting, Auditing & Accountability Journal, 26*(7), 1036–1071.

Cashore, B., Auld, G., & Newsom, D. (2004). *Governing through markets: Forest certification and the emergence of non-state authority*. Yale University Press.

Castka, P., & Corbett, C. J. (2015). Management systems standards: Diffusion, impact and governance of ISO 9000, ISO 14000, and other management standards. *Foundations and Trends in Technology. Information and Operations Management, 7*(3–4), 161–379.

Clark, W. H., & Babson, E. K. (2012). How benefit corporations are redefining the purpose of business corporations. *William Mitchell Law Review, 38*.

Darnall, N., Henriques, I., & Sadorsky, P. (2010). Adopting proactive environmental strategy: The influence of stakeholders and firm size. *The Journal of Management Studies, 47*(6), 1072–1094.

Darnall, N., Ji, H., Iwata, K., & Arimura, T. H. (2022). Do ESG reporting guidelines and verifications enhance firms' information disclosure? *Corporate Social Responsibility and Environmental Management, 29*(5), 1214–1230.

Delmas, M., & Blass, V. D. (2010). Measuring corporate environmental performance: The trade-offs of sustainability ratings. *Business Strategy and the Environment, 19*(4), 245–260.

Delmas, M. A., & Burbano, V. C. (2011). The drivers of greenwashing. *California Management Review, 54*(1), 64–87.

Ecolabel Index. (2024). *All ecolabels*. https://www.ecolabelindex.com/ecolabels/

Gilbert, D. U. (2010). The transformation of the jewellery market through certification and supply chain regulation. *Accounting, Auditing & Accountability Journal, 23*(4), 530–550.

Hahn, R., & Kühnen, M. (2013). Determinants of sustainability reporting: A review of results, trends, theory, and opportunities in an expanding field of research. *Journal of Cleaner Production*, *59*, 5–21.

Hiller, J. S. (2013). The Benefit Corporation and corporate social responsibility. *Journal of Business Ethics: JBE*, *118*(2), 287–301.

Honeyman, R., & Jana, T. (2019). *The B Corp handbook: How you can use business as a force for good*. Berrett-Koehler Publishers.

Kolk, A., & Perego, P. (2010). Determinants of the adoption of sustainability assurance statements: An international investigation. *Business Strategy and the Environment*, *19*(3), 182–198.

Laufer, W. S. (2003). Social accountability and corporate greenwashing. *Journal of Business Ethics*, *43*(3), 253–261.

Melnyk, S. A., Sroufe, R. P., & Calantone, R. (2003). Assessing the impact of environmental management systems on corporate and environmental performance. *Journal of Operations Management*, *21*(3), 329–351.

Montabon, F., Sroufe, R., & Narasimhan, R. (2007). An examination of corporate reporting, environmental management practices and firm performance. *Journal of Operations Management*, *25*(5), 998–1014.

Orlitzky, M., Siegel, D. S., & Waldman, D. A. (2011). Strategic corporate social responsibility and environmental sustainability. *Business & Society*, *50*, 6–27.

Perez-Aleman, P., & Sandilands, M. (2008). Building value at the top and the bottom of the global supply chain: MNC-NGO partnerships. *California Management Review*, *51*(1), 24–49.

Raynolds, L. T., Murray, D., & Wilkinson, J. (2007). Fairtrade: The challenges of transforming globalisation. *Journal of International Development*, *19*(7), 933–942.

Sabeti, H. (2011). The for-benefit enterprise. *Harvard Business Review*, *89*(11), 98–104.

Schaltegger, S., & Burritt, R. L. (2010). Sustainability accounting for companies: Catchphrase or decision support for business leaders? *Journal of World Business*, *45*(4), 375–384.

Sisodia, R., Wolfe, D. B., & Sheth, J. N. (2014). *Firms of endearment: How world-class companies profit from passion and purpose*. Pearson Education.

Società Benefit. (2016). *Benefit Company Information Site*. Società Benefit. https://www.societabenefit.net/english-information/

Stubbs, W. (2017). Sustainable entrepreneurship and B Corps. *Business Strategy and the Environment*, *26*(3), 331–344.

Szymanski, M., & Tiemann, I. (2004). The EU Eco-Management and Audit Scheme (EMAS). *Corporate Social Responsibility and Environmental Management*, *11*, 130–141.

Triodos Bank NV. (2021). *Business Principles*. https://www.triodos.com/binaries/content/assets/tbho/corporate-governance/triodos-bank-business-principles.pdf

Tyler, A. R. (2015). The Benefit Corporation's role in corporate law jurisprudence. *The Journal of Corporation Law*, *40*(3), 817–840.

UN Global Compact. (2014). *Guide to corporate sustainability*. United Nations Global Compact Office. https://d306pr3pise04h.cloudfront.net/docs/publications%2FUN_Global_Compact_Guide_to_Corporate_Sustainability.pdf

Villamizar, F. R. (2023). Social enterprises and benefit corporations in Colombia. In *The international handbook of social enterprise law* (pp. 535–552). Springer International Publishing.

Vranka, W. H. (2013). The need and rationale for the Benefit Corporation: Why it is the legal form that best addresses the needs of social entrepreneurs, investors, and ultimately, the public. *University of Pennsylvania Journal of Business Law*, *2*.

G Innovating

21 Innovation for Change

Up to now the chapters of this book were aimed at providing a map of the known territory of responsible business and management. However, the magnitude of the social, environmental, and ethical challenges faced by businesses and humanity is calling for solutions beyond what we know - off the map and out of the box. For tackling these challenges, "business as usual" and to keep doing the things as they were always done will not create the change necessary. Or as Albert Einstein famously stated, "*We can't solve problems by using the same kind of thinking we used when we created them*". Innovation is often used as a buzzword to describe ideas that lead to change.

Innovation describes "the successful exploitation of new ideas" (DTI, 2003, p. 8). Looking at the idea of innovation a bit closer we find that there are two main elements to it: Novelty (new ideas) and use (exploitation). Accordingly, a brilliant novel idea is no innovation if it is not used. Innovation begins with but goes far beyond creativity which helps to generate ideas. However, there is a very practical component of putting these ideas to use, which make the innovation. Corporate sustainability, responsibility, and ethics represent an immense opportunity for companies and managers to be innovative, with all of the potential advantages that go with it, such as access to new markets, cost savings, or competitive advantage (Nidumolu, Prahalad, & Rangaswami, 2009). It has even been suggested that we are at the beginning of a wave of innovation with sustainability at its heart. This innovation, at the beginning of a sixth wave of innovation with previous waves as prominent as steam power and electricity in the 1850s, and information technology in the 1990s (see Figure 21.1). For businesses it appears that this evolves into a game-changing megatrend equal in magnitude as mass production and electrification before them (Lubin & Esty, 2010). However, this time of dramatic innovation does not necessarily only provide opportunities for businesses. It also may lead to the demise of companies, possibly whole industries that cannot adopt to a swiftly changing business environment. A sustainable world might not be a place for unsustainable dinosaurs, and this might lead to the "creative destruction of industries", possibly to "corporate suicide" (Hart & Milstein, 1999; Kelso & Hetter, 1973).

DOI: 10.4324/9781003544074-29

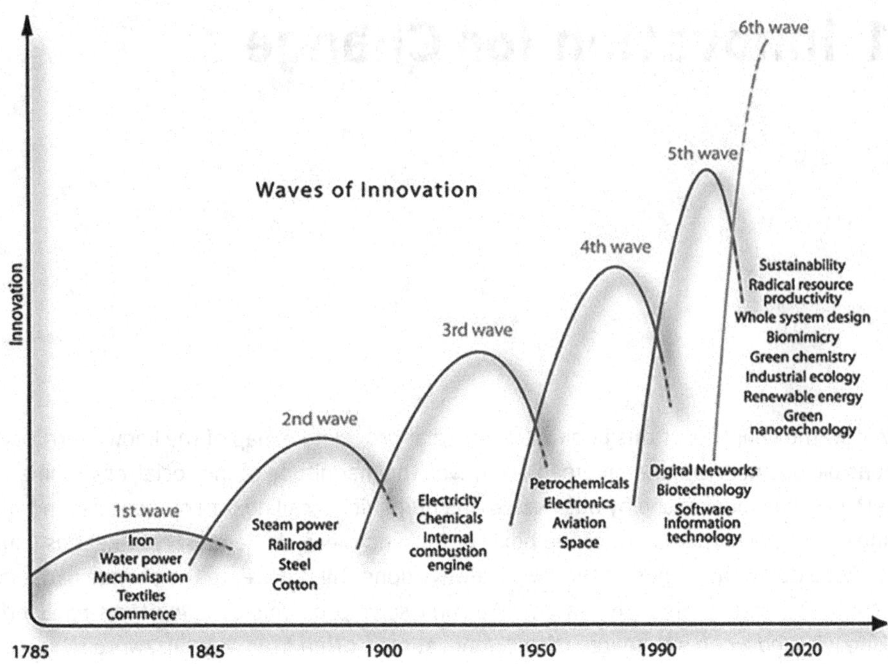

Figure 21.1 Waves of Innovation Diagram, Showing the Latest Sustainable Development Wave. (*Hargroves & Smith, 2006*)

In the context of innovation for sustainable development and corporate social responsibility, it is particularly important to distinguish divergent approaches to innovation and the related discussions:

- **Maslow (restraint) versus Solow (technology)**: An ongoing discussion is on different approaches as to how cope with the environmental resource scarcity as a root cause of the current unsustainable situation (Martin & Kemper, 2012). On the one hand, the theories of Abraham Maslow (see Chapter 2) call for restraint, in resource consumption and a curbing of population growth – a call for a strategy of austerity. Solow on the other hand, advances the view that any resource can be substituted by some new technology and no resource is irreplaceable.
- **Disruptive versus incremental innovation**: A related, but different discussion lies in the distinction between incremental and disruptive innovation. Incremental innovation, for instance, for resource consumption would innovate to make existing "things" better. A good example is more eco-efficient production methods. Disruptive innovation, on the other hand, would lead to things radically different from what they used to be and substituting old things (Christensen, 2013; Christensen, Baumann, Ruggles, & Sadtler, 2006).

What is your innovation strategy? What do you think is the most promising strategy for reaching business sustainability, and ultimately global sustainable development? What are arguments for and against the austerity and technology strategies? Do you think we rather need disruptive or incremental innovation?

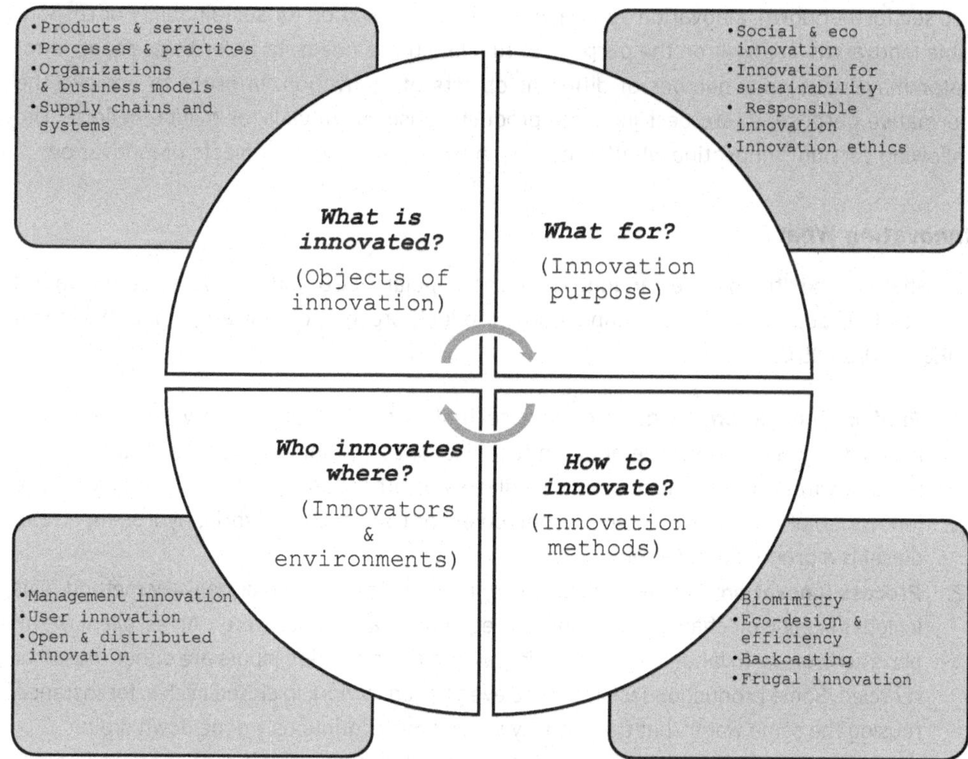

Figure 21.2 Concepts of Innovation Covered in this Chapter.

This chapter features contents related to both discussions, about restraint versus technology fix, and incremental versus disruptive innovation. The purpose of this chapter is to provide a mental map of innovation concepts related to the areas of responsible business for sustainable development. As outlined in Figure 21.2 we will first provide an overview of "the things" to be innovated, the objects of innovation, then introduce different innovation frameworks aimed at distinct purposes, such as social innovation, or innovation for sustainability. We will then introduce innovation methods, such as frugal innovation or biomimicry especially tuned in to business responsibility for sustainable development. In a last step, we will look at frameworks that help us to better understand who innovates in what environment, such as management innovation or open innovation.

Objects and Purposes of Innovation

From our definition of innovation above we have learnt that it is about both new ideas and their exploitation. In the context of responsible business, what kind of ideas are these, and what is their exploitation? We have to ask ourselves: Innovating what and what for? These two fundamental questions gain special importance in innovation for sustainability, responsibility, and ethics. All three topics have a strong normative orientation. They are based on ideas of what *ought to* happen and be. We ought to ensure the survival of humanity on planet Earth (sustainability). We ought to be responsible towards our stakeholders (responsibility). We ought to make sure we do the right thing and abstain from doing wrong (ethics). As you will see further down, innovation approaches, such as innovation for sustainability or responsible innovation, are built on the purpose of fulfilling these needs. In order to do so, an innovator may focus on a number of different objects of innovation. In order to achieve the normative purpose, do we best innovate products, business models, or maybe beliefs? The following section "innovating what" provides an overview of typical objects of innovation.

Innovating What?

So, what are the "things" we can innovate? The popular OECD understanding of innovation outlines four objects or areas of innovation, product, process, organization, and marketing (OECD; EU, 2005):

1. **Product innovation**: "A good or service that is new or significantly improved. This includes significant improvements in technical specifications, components and materials, software in the product, user friendliness or other functional characteristics". The innovation of alternative engine technologies for cars, such as hybrid, hydrogen, or biodiesel is a product innovation.
2. **Process innovation**: "A new or significantly improved production or delivery method. This includes significant changes in techniques, equipment and/or software". An excellent example is zero-waste to landfill manufacturing, where all production inputs are either reused or recycled. Some production facilities have even begun to work in closed cycles, for instance, reusing the same water that traditionally would have continuously gone down drain.
3. **Marketing innovation**: "A new marketing method involving significant changes in product design or packaging, product placement, product promotion or pricing". For instance, in the pharmaceutical industry, there used to be the same (rather high) price for drugs all over the world. Some companies have innovated their pricing to provide drugs at lower prices, sometimes below production cost, in developing countries.
4. **Organizational innovation**: "A new organizational method in business practices, workplace organization or external relations". An example is the inclusion of small and/or marginalized suppliers as part of a fairtrade scheme.

While the above objects of innovation cover many of the types of innovation typically found, there is a number of additional, partly overlapping areas of innovation that have become increasingly important, especially in the realm of responsible business:

- **Business model innovation**: The underlying logic of businesses may have to change to address responsible business challenges and to become sustainable. As outlined in the strategy chapter, the company TOMS has invented a completely new business model for a shoe company which both sells and donates shoes at the same time.
- **Supply chain innovation**: While often subsumed under organizational innovation, especially in the context of sustainability it deserves highlighting. As illustrated in the chapter on supply chains, a company can only claim to be sustainable if the whole supply chain impact is sustainable. The company Icebreaker's "Baa Code" which allows one to trace back where your sweater came from to the original farm the wool was produced at is a supply chain innovation.

- **Systems innovation**: Often single elements cannot change alone, but the whole system has to change. An attempt at such systems innovation are local currencies, such as the "Bristol Pound" in the UK, which are typically aimed at creating independence from potential issues in the larger economic system, and to support the local economy (Grover, 2013).
- **Practice(s) innovation**: The repeated meaningful actions, or practices both in business and private life are of great relevance for business sustainability, responsibility, and ethics. For instance, the practice of always giving a plastic bag with any purchase has created a waste problem of global scale, and discriminatory employment practices create ethical and social problems.
- **Institutional innovation**: Institutions as structures and mechanisms that create social order and govern behavior may both be helpful or harmful to achieving responsible business purposes. The increasing social and legal acceptance of same-sex marriage is an institutional innovation, changing the institution of marriage.

Innovating What For?

A number of distinct innovation approaches has emerged, explicitly addressing goals related to responsible business. Innovations for sustainability can broadly be subdivided into two main innovation frameworks, social innovation, which aims at creating social value and eco-innovation that reduces negative environmental impacts through innovation.

- **Social innovation** has been developed from a non-profit organizations perspective and often has been related to social entrepreneurship. Nevertheless, social innovation has an enormous potential to deliver scalable solutions to social issues, when applied in long-established for-profit companies (Phills, Deiglmeier, & Miller, 2008). It is important not to confuse the understanding of social innovations as innovations with social value added (understanding applied in this book) with the traditional definition which understands social innovations as big societal changes resulting from a shift in society.
- **Eco-innovation** has been approached from many angles. *Eco-efficiency* for instance aims at small, so-called *incremental innovations* throughout existing systems, while the *green technology* movement aims at inventing new technological solutions to environmental issues, *disruptive innovations*. The framework of *Design for Environment (DfE)* provides a meta tool, which combines both types of impact, and offers clear design principles to be followed for planned eco-innovation (Fiksel, 2010).

Table 21.1 illustrates examples for both social and eco innovations in processes and products. It is important to mention that in practice a sustainability-oriented innovation has to be viable in all dimensions in the long run socially, environmentally, and of course economically (Hansen, Grosse-Dunker, & Reichwald, 2009). Such sustainable innovation often serves as a basis for social or environmental entrepreneurship ventures, which will be described in more detail in the chapter on individual change.

While the above frameworks focus on the intended output of innovation, another stream of thinking is centered on the precautionary thinking of unintended consequences of

Table 21.1 Exemplary Innovations Combining Distinct Purposes and Objects

Object of Innovation→ Purpose↓	*Process*	*Product*
Social	The international **cement producer** CEMEX has innovatively included low-income community members into their production process by establishing so-called "Blockeras", cement block making machines in rural communities. Community members can use the machine and material for free; 50% of the blocks become property of the community member, 50% are sold (CEMEX, 2012).	**Video game console producers** increasingly substitute traditional games by motion-controlled gaming (Steinberg, 2011). This innovation has the potential to transfer the negative health effects of excessive gaming into the positive effects associated with physical activity, very similar to sports; to transform console users from "couch potatoes" to superjocks.
Ecologic	**Supermarkets** have encountered solar energy as an attractive and timely resource. As a matter of fact, supermarket energy usage peaks correspond to the highest productivity times for solar energy production. Refrigeration and air-conditioning (main energy consumers) are running when most needed at the same time as the most sun is received. An excellent match!	**Promotional products producers**, produce in masses and distribute often without due care and thus are usually not included in role models for responsible businesses. The company EarthImprints was the first one to focus on promotion products with environmental value added. How about a biodegradable pen with integrated seed? Take it out, put it into earth and with some watering you may grow everything from cherry tomatoes to grey pine (EarthImprints, 2012).

innovation, and the broader, potentially detrimental impact on society. Two examples of such frameworks are innovation ethics, and responsible innovation. *Innovation ethics* centers on the multiple ethical issues that may arise during the innovation process, and as a result of a successful innovation. Such issues may be animal testing when developing a new drug, the ethical use of patents and other intellectual property rights, or also potential negative side-effects of a new product. The list is endless and open, mostly related to direct ethical issues and consequences. *Responsible innovation* instead is rather concerned about the larger ethical implications in a societal context. Typical questions would be, what are, for instance, the societal dangers and potential side-effects of innovations in nanotechnology or biofuels? (Sutcliffe, 2014). While innovation ethics issues may be addressed one-by-one, responsible innovation is aimed at creating the larger conditions that make sure an innovation is responsible, such as building responsible innovation capabilities, future oriented learning, and institutional change (Randles, Gee, & Edler, 2015).

E-cigarettes, a socially responsible innovation? Around the world, e-cigarettes have become a phenomenon substituting for traditional cigarettes. Proponents argue that these cigarettes may be less hazardous to health than traditional cigarettes, but also admit that we know little about the long-term consequences (Reinberg, 2014). What do you think? Are e-cigarettes a responsible innovation?

Who Innovates and How?

Now that we have had a look at what may be innovated for what purpose, there is a question about the "how" of innovation. Who innovates where, and what are innovation frameworks and methods that may be of value in the process?

Who Innovates Where?

Not too long ago innovation was primarily considered an activity carried out by either "scientists" or "product developers" in companies' research and development departments. While other innovators in distinct environments were always existent, there has been a recent focus on these distinct innovators and their environments. We will look at the two larger frameworks of open innovation and management innovation to develop an appreciation of who innovates where.

The term **open innovation** was first coined by Henry Chesbrough (2003) and refers to an approach to innovation where innovators inside and outside the company work together in the same innovation process. Such an approach is particularly helpful in responsible business, where stakeholder groups, inside and outside the company, play an important role in defining what the company is and should become. Innovation processes and their actors are "distributed" inside and outside the company and bring together the distinct capabilities of all involved (Metcalfe & Coombs, 2000). In such distributed and open innovation processes, the company moves away from being the innovator, towards a coordination and integration role for the open innovation process. Open innovation may involve co-innovators from many different groups, such as suppliers, competitors, or NGOs. A particularly powerful outside innovator group appears to be users. User innovation and creation products often result in situations where innovations emerge outside company boundaries and are freely accessible in the public domain (Hippel, 2005).

A second crucial group we would like to focus on in this book are managers. Managers may both be originators of novelties, and pioneers in finding exploitation opportunities for innovations. In other words, they may be creators of novelties, "management innovations" (Birkinshaw, Hamel, & Mol, 2008), and they may be pioneers in applying them in "innovative management" practices (Khandwalla, 1987). As we have learnt earlier in this chapter, both novelty and exploitation are constituting parts of an innovation. The idea of **management innovation** "as the invention and implementation of a management practice, process, structure, or technique that is new to the state of the art and is intended to further organizational goals" (Birkinshaw, Hamel, & Mol, 2008, p. 825). The most impactful management innovations do not stay within one company but become part of the repertoire of companies in general. For instance, the balanced scorecard most companies are using nowadays started as a management innovation of Art Schneiderman a manager in the company Analog Devices (Schneiderman, 2006). The innovation of the Toyota production system has become the basis for most of the management systems used worldwide. In the realm of responsible business, for instance, it was marketing managers at American Express who created the tool of cause-related marketing, and Muhammad Yunus at The Grameen Bank innovated group

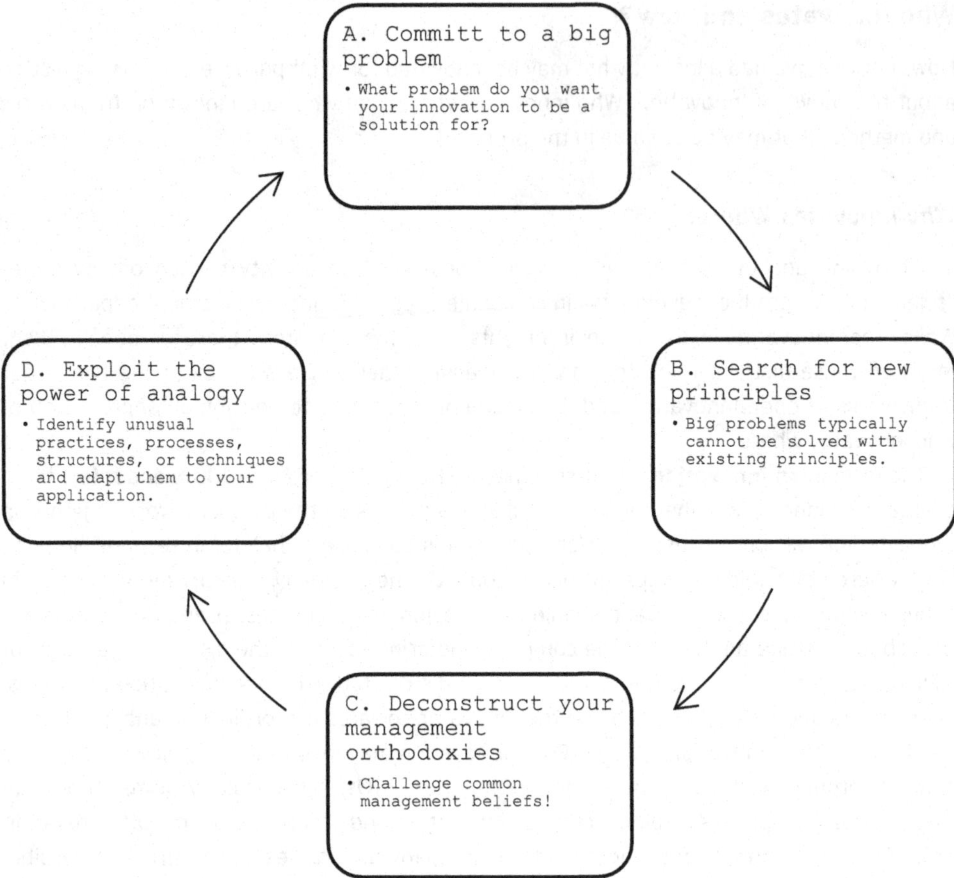

Figure 21.3 How to Become a Serial Management Innovator?

lending as a managerial banking practice, and life-cycle assessment started out as a project at The Coca Cola Company. Imagine you could become a management innovator, transforming how companies around the world do business – more sustainably, responsibly, and ethically. In Figure 21.3, you find a summary of the main steps for becoming a management innovator as outlined by management guru Gary Hamel (2006).

How to Innovate?

Now we know everything about innovation, but how do we actually innovate? In this last section we will review a number of innovation methods that are especially relevant for innovating for sustainability, responsibility, and ethics. As you will see in the following list, most of the innovation methods are especially geared towards innovations with an environmental impact. What all of these motivations have in common is a leitmotiv, a theme that serves as orientation for innovation measures.

1. The method of *biomimicry*, also called biomimetics, for instance, follows the theme of "learning from nature" (Benyus, 2002). This is especially relevant for environmental sustainability as we can argue that nature is inherently sustainable, as it sustains itself. When we encounter a problem, the question guiding the innovation process is "what would nature do?" What examples can we find where nature solved a similar problem and how can we learn from these examples?
2. *Backcasting* (as opposed to forecasting) relies on the question "what innovations do we need today, so that a desired future becomes real?" This question becomes especially relevant for sustainability, as we are trying to do the right thing today to achieve a sustainable future (Holmberg & Robèrt, 2000).
3. The *frugal innovation* method is guided by the question "How would/do we innovate under limited resources?" The idea is to develop a mindset where you see resource constraints not as a limitation, but as an opportunity to innovate differently (Radjou & Prabhu, 2014). Frugal innovation is especially relevant for two reasons. First, innovations that work under resource scarcity are likely to be tuned in to a world where the once abundant natural resources are increasingly depleted. Second, frugal innovation often produces less pricy, but still functional products tuned in to the needs of lower income consumers.
4. The long-established method of *eco-efficiency*, which was described in previous chapters, is an approach to incremental innovation that aims to improve the ratio between natural resources used and output achieved. Reviewing a production process guided by the question, "how can we do more with less?" often leads to amazing reductions in resource consumption.
5. The *design-for-environment* method tackles environmental issues by asking "how can we design things" that are better for the environment. It is guided by the four subquestions of "how can we use less material? How less toxins? How can we make sure the product is recycled? How can we make sure the overall product life cycle renews environmental, social, and economic capital, instead of depleting it?" (Fiksel, 2010).

Humanize versus naturalize and biomimicry versus humanism? The idea of biomimicry builds upon learning from nature. However, human beings are quite a special animal and do many things differently from what you would typically expect from other living beings. Humanism connects to this idea and the movement around humanistic business builds upon our collaborative social nature, compassion, human dignity, and freedom (Kimakowitz, Pirson, Spitzeck, Dierksmeier, & Amann, 2011; Melé, 2003). There may be trade-offs and conflict situations between both philosophies. The most humane thing to do is not always the most natural thing. To think of an extreme example, a global disaster wiping the majority off the face of planet Earth would be great for the planet, and a natural mechanism often observed when there is an overpopulation of one species in its habitat, but it would be a humanitarian catastrophe. What do you think? Should we innovate inspired by the idea of achieving "natural" outputs or "human" outputs? Do you see a potential compromise? What might such a compromise look like?

Exercises

A. KNOW

Use the below multiple-choice questions to test your knowledge. Each answer may be wrong or right and there may be zero to four right or wrong answers per question:

1. The Korean company Biocera has invented "washing balls" that work entirely without detergent. The company highlights its positive effect in terms of less water pollution, economic savings due the saved money for buying detergent, and less skin irritations due to residual detergent in clothes. We may consider this an example of...
   a. ...frugal innovation, as it provides an answer to the question "how would we innovate if we had limited freshwater resources?"
   b. ...design for environment, as it provides an answer to the question "how can we use fewer toxins"?
   c. ...biomimicry, as nature wouldn't use detergent either.
   d. ...of backcasting, as it might be an answer to the question "for a future where we want to be able to live without contaminating water, what innovations do we need?"
2. Who innovates where? Questions to this answer may be...
   a. ...in open innovation the R&D department innovates, but openly tests the results involving external stakeholders.
   b. ...in management innovation, company managers innovate new practice, process, structure, or techniques for their own company, but often these innovations are then used across many companies.
   c. ...that it used to be the R&D department driving innovation, but nowadays we typically see a more distributed innovation process.
   d. ...user innovation, where users primarily are involved in pilot testing to tweak new products.
3. The innovation of e-cigarettes involves the innovation of what? Innovation objects are...
   a. ...product innovation, as electronic cigarettes are radically different from traditional cigarettes.
   b. ...the practice of smoking a cigarette.
   c. ...processes.
   d. ...the supply chain.

B. THINK

Identify one strongly held management belief that you think might provide a toehold for criticism. Then deconstruct where the belief comes from and what might be wrong with it and why.

C. DO

Follow the four steps of the management innovation process described in this chapter to come up with one concrete management innovation idea. Then put this novelty to use in order to make it a realized innovation.

D. RELATE

Start a small advocacy campaign for an innovation that you think deserves spreading in order to make an impact for sustainability, responsibility, and/or ethics. Choose whatever medium you think is best, possibly including social networks, mails, involvement in groups, personal conversations, etc.

E. BE

Inform yourself about the story behind one responsible business innovation and the person realizing the innovation. This could be, for instance, how Blake Mycoskie came up with the one-for-one idea, or how Ann Makosinski invented a flashlight powered by the heat in your hands. How does the story relate to you? Do you think you can ben an innovator? What would you have done differently? What kind of innovator could you be?

Feedback

A. KNOW

Question 1

a. Right: We clearly see the frugal innovation theme of "innovating under scarcity" in this example.
b. Right: Both the emission of toxins into the water and the skin irritating characteristics of detergents are examples of the toxicity of conventional detergents, which are to be substituted by the washing balls innovation.
c. Right: In nature, cleaning typically happens with pure water and with mechanical forces - no detergent - this is how the washing balls work.
d. Right: The washing balls innovation might have come out of a backcasting exercise.

Question 2

a. Wrong: The innovation itself is an open innovation which involves a network of inside and outside innovators, not only testing the results in such a network afterwards.
b. Right: This sentence is a rephrasing of the paragraph describing management innovation.

c. Right: While there are still R&D departments, innovation has become distributed to many more locations and innovators.
d. Wrong: Pilot testing might be one activity under the umbrella of user innovation, but primarily user innovation refers to users innovating freely, sometimes even without any relationship to a company at all.

Question 3

a. Right: While both e-cigarettes and traditional cigarettes are ultimately smoked, the product used for smoking is technically entirely different. For instance, tobacco in traditional cigarettes is burnt, while e-cigarettes vaporize a fluid.
b. Right: The way a cigarette is smoked can be considered a practice, which is innovated through e-cigarettes. For instance, smoking a traditional cigarette involves a lighter and is typically only permitted in open spaces, both of which are less relevant for an e-cigarette.
c. Right: Given the entirely different product, also the production processes have to be innovated.
d. Right: Given the distinct inputs for the e-cigarette, these inputs are supplied by distinct types of companies, some of which (e.g. the vaporization liquid) did not exist before e-cigarettes, which makes supply chain innovation necessary.

B. THINK

Level	*Challenging assumptions and mindsets*	*Notes*
+	A strong critical argument has been developed, based on a deep understanding of the management belief.	
=	A management belief has been identified and an appreciation of its roots has been developed.	
–	No management belief worth criticizing has been identified.	

C. DO

Level	*Innovation-implementation competence*	*Notes*
+	A complete management innovation has been realized, including the idea and putting it to use.	
=	An innovative idea has been developed, based on elements of the management innovation process.	
–	Neither an innovative idea, nor implementation activities have been documented.	

D. RELATE

Level	*Advocacy skills*	*Notes*
+	Evidence of proactive advocacy for the innovation worth promoting.	
=	Identification of innovation worth promoting.	
–	No innovation worth promoting identified.	

E. BE

Level	*Developing innovative attitude*	*Notes*
+	Clearly displayed appreciation of own identity as a particular type of innovator.	
=	Evidence of emerging own particular attitude to being an innovator.	
–	No evidence of developing an innovative attitude.	

References

Benyus, J. M. (2002). *Biomimicry: Innovation inspired by nature*. New York: William Morrow Paperbacks.

Birkinshaw, J., Hamel, G., & Mol, M. J. (2008). Management innovation. *Academy of Management Review, 33*(4), 825–845.

CEMEX. (2012). *Centros productivos de autoempleo [Productive self-employment centers]*. Retrieved January 17, 2012, from CEMEX construyendo el futuro: https://www.cemexmexico.com/DesarrolloSustentables/CentrosProductivos.aspx

Chesbrough, H. W. (2003). *Open innovation: The new imperative for creating and profiting from technology*. Boston: Harvard Business Press.

Christensen, C. (2013). *The innovator's dilemma: When new technologies cause great firms to fail*. Cambridge: Harvard Business Review Press.

Christensen, C. M., Baumann, H., Ruggles, R., & Sadtler, T. M. (2006). Disruptive innovation for social change. *Harvard Business Review, 84*(12), 94–102.

DTI. (2003). *Competing in the global economy: The innovation challenge*. London: Department of Trade and Industry.

EarthImprints. (2012). *EarthImprints*. Retrieved January 17, 2012, from https://www.earthimprints.com/

Fiksel, J. (2010). *Design for environment*. McGraw Hill.

Grover, S. (2013, March 20). *Why one English town created its own currency*. Retrieved March 25, 2015, from https://www.mnn.com/money/sustainable-business-practices/stories/why-one-english-town-created-its-own-currency

Hamel, G. (2006). The why, what, and how of management innovation. *Harvard Business Review, 84*(2), 72–88.

Hansen, E. G., Grosse-Dunker, F., & Reichwald, R. (2009). Sustainability innovation cube—A framework to evaluate sustainability-oriented innovations. *International Journal of Innovation Management, 13*(4), 683–713.

Hargroves, K., & Smith, M. H. (2006). *The natural advantage of nations: Business opportunities, innovations and governance in the 21st century*. Earthscan.

Hart, S. L., & Milstein, M. B. (1999). Global sustainability and the creative destruction of industries. *Sloan Management Review, 41*(1), 23–33.

Hippel, E.V. (2005). *Democratizing innovation*. Cambridge: MIT University Press.

Holmberg, J., & Robèrt, K. H. (2000). Backcasting–A framework for strategic planning. *International Journal of Sustainable Development & World Ecology*, *7*(4), 291–308.

Kelso, L. O., & Hetter, P. (1973). Corporate social responsibility without corporate suicide. *Challenge*, *16*(3), 52–57.

Khandwalla, P. N. (1987). Generators of pioneering-innovative management: Some Indian evidence. *Organization Studies*, *8*(1), 39–59.

Kimakowitz, E. V., Pirson, M., Spitzeck, H., Dierksmeier, C., & Amann, W. (2011). *Humanistic management in practice*. New York: Palgrave Macmillan.

Lubin, D. A., & Esty, D. C. (2010). The sustainability imperative. *Harvard Business Review*, *May 2010*, 1–9.

Martin, R., & Kemper, A. (2012). Saving the planet: A tale of two strategies. *Harvard Business Review*, *90*(4), 49–56.

Melé, D. (2003). The challenge of humanistic management. *Journal of Business Ethics*, *44*, 77–88.

Metcalfe, J. S., & Coombs, R. (2000). Organizing for innovation: Co-ordinating distributed innovation capabilities. In N. Foss, & V. Mahnke (Eds.), *Competence, governance, and entrepreneurship: Advances in economic strategy research* (pp. 209–231). Oxford: Oxford University Press.

Nidumolu, R., Prahalad, C. K., & Rangaswami, M. R. (2009). Why sustainability is now the key driver of innovation. *Harvard Business Review*, *87*(9), 56–64.

OECD; EU. (2005). *Oslo manual: Guidelines for collecting, and interpreting innovation data* (3rd ed.). Paris: OECD Publishing.

Phills, J. A., Deiglmeier, K., & Miller, D. T. (2008). Rediscovering social innovation. *Stanford Social Innovation Review*, *6*(4), 34–43.

Radjou, N., & Prabhu, J. (2014, December 10). *What frugal innovators do*. Retrieved March 26, 2015, from https://hbr.org/2014/12/what-frugal-innovators-do

Randles, S., Gee, S., & Edler, J. (2015). *Governance and the institutionalisation of responsible research and innovation in Europe: Transversal lessons from an extensive programme of case studies*.

Reinberg, S. (2014, July 30). *Benefits of e-cigarettes may outweigh harms, study finds*. Retrieved March 25, 2015, from https://consumer.healthday.com/cancer-information-5/smoking-cessation-news-628/benefits-of-e-cigarettes-may-outweigh-harms-study-finds-690268.html

Schneiderman, A. (2006). *Analog devices: 1986-1992 the first balanced scorecard*. Retrieved March 26, 2015, from https://www.schneiderman.com/Concepts/The_First_Balanced_Scorecard/BSC_INTRO_AND_CONTENTS.htm

Steinberg, S. (2011). *The future of motion controlled gaming*. Retrieved January 17, 2012, from CNN Tec: https://articles.cnn.com/2011-01-21/tech/motion.controls.steinberg_1_avatars-killzone-playstation-network?_s=PM:TECH

Sutcliffe, H. (2014). *Responsible innovation in business*. London: Matter.

22 Individual Change

The preceding chapters focused on what businesses can do to contribute to sustainability. The sobering reality is that businesses can actually not do that much without people. It is single individuals or groups of people who demand goods, often in a highly unsustainable fashion. It is people who work in companies and make unsustainable decisions, and it is people who, in their citizen function, vote for governments that do not move quickly enough towards a sustainable infrastructure. For this reason, this chapter looks at who we are as individuals and what we need to do to contribute our share to a sustainable world. The constant question in this chapter is "What does our individuality mean for responsible business?" The chapter illustrates approaches of responsible business that aim at fostering the creation of sustainable lifestyles and activism and showing how to benefit from those trends.

The first section takes a close look at what characteristics of human nature are the roots of unsustainable behavior, to understand how we make decisions, and what human traits lead us to make decisions contradicting the logic of sustainable development. The second section aims to develop a basic idea of what sustainable lifestyles, consumption, and work patterns might lead to an optimum sustainable lifestyle for the world population. The third section covers how individual activism, actively trying to change the status quo, can make an important change towards sustainability.

What do sustainability experts think about sustainable consumption?

The consultancy SustainAbility asked more than 500 sustainability experts worldwide about their opinions on sustainable consumption. Interesting outcomes include the following (SustainAbility, 2011):

1) **Sustainable product lines**: "Businesses have a duty to offer sustainable product lines instead of, rather than in addition to, unsustainable ones" (yes: 78%; no: 9%).
2) **Sustainable consumption = less consumption**: "Sustainable consumption must mean less consumption" (yes: 53%; no: 27%).
3) **Sustainable consumption = degrowth**: "There is an inherent conflict between economic growth and sustainable consumption" (yes: 40%; no: 43%)

DOI: 10.4324/9781003544074-30

4) **Sustainable consumption in emerging countries**: "Consumers in emerging countries will adopt sustainable consumption behaviors at a faster pace than in developed countries" (yes: 31%; no: 40%).
5) **Sustainable consumption = impossible**: "Sustainable consumption is impossible to achieve" (yes: 11%; no: 69%).

Unsustainable Attitudes, Behaviors, and Their Origins

Why is it so hard for us contemporary human beings to show sustainable behavior? One could dodge the question and blame "politics", "businesses", or even "the system" for today's global **unsustainability**. In the following paragraph, we will ignore such criticism and focus on the root cause, human nature. Why do we ignore or even deny the disastrous situation humanity is steering towards? Why don't we act? Why don't we protest? Why don't we change our consumption behavior towards more sustainable ways?

Individuals' inertia in accepting the challenge of sustainable development can be attributed to defining elements of human nature. The psychologists Maslow and Kohlberg, have both provided staged models, aiming to explain human action and inaction (see Figure 22.1). Abraham *Maslow* explains human behavior by the **needs** creating the intrinsic **motivation** for their actions. The most basic needs are physiological needs such as hunger, thirst, sex and safety needs, such as stability and routine. Those are followed by social needs such as love and belonging and esteem by others. The ultimate stage of Maslow's needs pyramid is self-actualization. It is in this last stage where human beings' greatest need is to fulfill their potential beyond the other four stages. Maslow suggests that human beings fulfill their most basic needs first. (Maslow, 1943). Thus, knowing what needs hierarchy an individual is on, knowing the individual's primary motivation is crucially important for understanding an individual's actions.

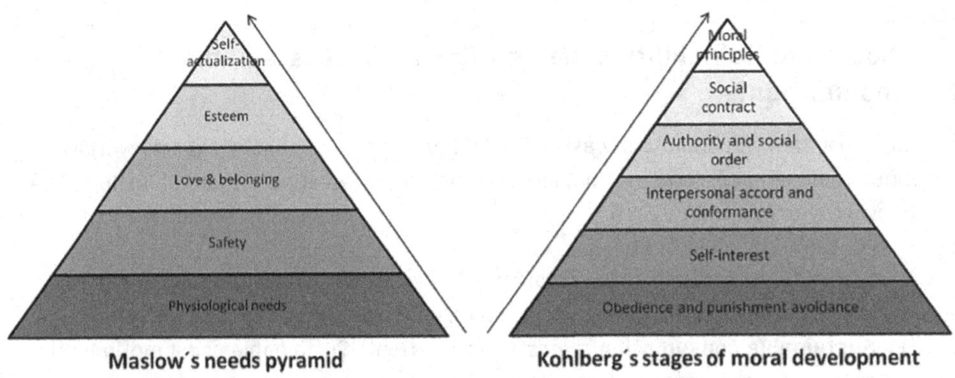

Figure 22.1 Classic Approaches to Explaining Human Behavior.

Adapted from Maslow, 1943 & Kohlberg, 1985

Laurence *Kohlberg*'s pyramid of moral development can be used to explain behaviors not by their motivation, but by their capability of **moral reasoning**. Kohlberg, in contrast to Maslow, does pose the question, "What do people want to do?", but asks what they are morally capable of doing. Kohlberg's lowest stages of moral reasoning are motivated by avoidance of punishment and self-interest. Then follow the moralities motivated by intrapersonal accord (satisfying the direct social group's expectations) and social order (aligned with the existing social order and authority). The final and highest two stages of moral reasoning are the social-contract morality, which searches for the greatest happiness possible, and stage six, on which individuals make decisions on higher ethical principles. Kohlberg also suggests that human beings usually move from the lower to the higher stages as they develop (Kohlberg, 1985).

How does sustainability come into the picture? Maslow's needs pyramid is based on peoples' motivation, asking, "Why do people *want* to do the things they do?" Most of the behaviors related to sustainable development are rather related to higher stages of the needs pyramid, especially self-actualization. It is on this last stage where individuals might start to ask themselves "What am I really here for?" On the one hand, the world's over four billion *poor* might rather be motivated by short-run physiological needs, by safety, love, and belonging. Survival, savings, building family, and community life come first, before sustainable lifestyles on the poor's needs pyramid. The world's *middle class*, on the other hand, to a large degree is driven by the need for esteem, which often is satisfied by showing off the newest phone, the biggest car, and the nicest shoes. Such unsustainable consumerism mostly leads to a highly unsustainable footprint. Critics believe that the formerly poor, new middle classes are likely to follow the western role-models seeking esteem by falling into unsustainable consumerist patterns. The two main change tasks arising from interpretation of the needs pyramid are the following:

1) **Improve the lives of the poor** people up to the esteem level, where they are on the brink of worrying about nothing, but their own self-actualization.
2) Show individuals who are searching for esteem by consumerist habits how to first win the very self-esteem while **adopting more sustainable behavior** patterns, and then migrate to the next level of self-actualization.

While Maslow answers the question about peoples' wants, Kohlberg's pyramid answers questions about what people are able to do, if they *can* actually make moral decisions leading to sustainable living. Maslow explains behavior with the intrinsic satisfaction of basic needs, while Kohlberg explains behavior with active moral choices made by individuals. Unsustainable behavior is usually not punished by law (level 1). Sustainable behavior in most cases is not in individuals' direct self-interest (level 2) and society typically does neither require (level 3) such behavior, nor is it a fully implemented element of social order (level 4). Thus, sustainable behavior is most likely to be found among individuals on the two highest levels of moral development. On the social contract level, individuals make their decisions based on welfare thinking (level 5). Sustainable development with its concept of intergenerational equity is welfare optimization between current and future generations. People on level 6, aligning their decisions and behavior with higher principles, may accept sustainability as a higher principle to be adopted with urgency. Necessary actions for sustainable development, resulting from those observations are the following:

3) **Support moral development** of individuals mostly in economically developed countries.
4) Show how **sustainable behavior makes sense** on each of the stages of moral development.

In addition to the explanations given by those two models mentioned in the last section, single characteristics of human nature are impeding sustainable living patterns.

- **Greed** and the insatiable **thirst for growth**: It seems human beings have a strong propensity to own more and constantly grow in all aspects of our lives. Unfortunately, both characteristics are hard to align with sustainable development on a finite and crowded planet.
- **Mental disconnect**: People tend to feel isolated from the negative results of unsustainable development. Catastrophes always seem to happen somewhere else to someone else. Also, contemporary human beings feel disconnected from nature, and are often not aware of how severe the consequences of their lifestyles are.
- **Present value focus**: People have the tendency to value the present state of affairs more than the future one. Crisis scenarios of an unsustainable future, including the consequences of climate change or an economic meltdown, are usually given less weight than a convenient and sacrifice-free life today. Future events are not perceived as grave enough to make people leave their comfort zone.
- **Herd-animal man**: It is hard to swim against the current, which means that single individuals will hardly change their behaviors to more sustainable ways, if the rest of the group doesn't. Sustainable living has to become a cultural trait, before the majority adheres to it.

The psychology of greed

It has been suggested that greed, wanting more than we really need, is the root cause of human beings' unsustainability. If that is true, to foster sustainable behaviors in us and others, we first need to understand greed. A *Harvard Business Review* article frames greed in the business world and cites Sigmund Freud, the grandfather of psychoanalysis. As the author interprets Freud, there are three types of greed, corresponding to the different phases of infant development, oral, anal, and phallic. In the oral phase people just want to swallow as much as they can. Greedy people corresponding to the anal phase find pleasure in piling up or splashing around needlessly. The phallic phase is about comparing what you have with others (Coutu, 2003). Do you see some of those behaviors in the way you consume, make your job, or maybe run your business? Only if we are able to control all three kinds of greed, we will be able to consume corresponding to our true need and in a sustainable manner.

What Can Business Do?

The impediments for sustainable living mentioned in the preceding section are for sure strong, but can be overcome by several tools, most of which work well in a business context. It is important to keep in mind that those human characteristics do not only pose big questions, but also provide immense opportunities for businesses. The following fields of action are just a few salient points to begin with:

- **Responsible marketing** has an immense potential to make an impact. If traditional marketing would be able to question its role as consumption increaser, to stop fueling consumerism and unsustainable behavior patterns, much will be achieved. People would be enabled to make their own decisions on how much and what kind of consumption they need. Interestingly, Kotler (Kotler & Levy, 1971), the grandfather of marketing already in the early 1970s described the possibility of de-marketing as a legitimate strategy. If marketing then not only stops fostering unsustainable behavior patterns, but even actively fosters sustainable behavior patterns (by using social marketing), its contribution to sustainable behavior can be very powerful.
- **Education**: Of course, businesses are not ethics schools. Nevertheless, businesses have an enormous potential to teach sustainable, responsible, and moral competences. Many of the positive learnings from the workplace can be transferred to private life. Competences as simple as separating trash or as complex as solving moral dilemmas can be learned on the job and applied throughout private life.
- **Human development**: Businesses are no development agencies either, but they do automatically contribute to human development. Businesses provide income and healthcare, often improve infrastructure themselves or with the tax money paid and provide or support education. Companies can also engage in community involvement and make **social investments** to strengthen society. The Human Development Index (HDI) provided by the United Nations Development Program (UNDP) includes all the factors that business can influence as mentioned before. The higher the human development, the higher people climb on Maslow's needs pyramid and the closer they come to a situation where they can truly live a sustainable lifestyle.

Sustainable Development, Lifestyles, and Income

An important question that has been touched upon only superficially in the preceding sections is: What happens if economic development eradicates poverty to the over two-thirds of the world's population who are still poor today? What if they decide to live a rich, but unsustainable lifestyle as we find in most fully developed countries? Another crucial question is, what happens to individuals and whole countries' footprint on the way to full economic development? The concept of the **Kuznets curve**, named after its inventor Simon Kuznets, provides a powerful analysis tool for both questions (Kuznets, 1955).

The Kuznets curve has been applied to both income inequalities and environmental degradation during the economic development process. Both topics are central considerations in sustainable development. First, income inequality (the gap between rich and poor) is a

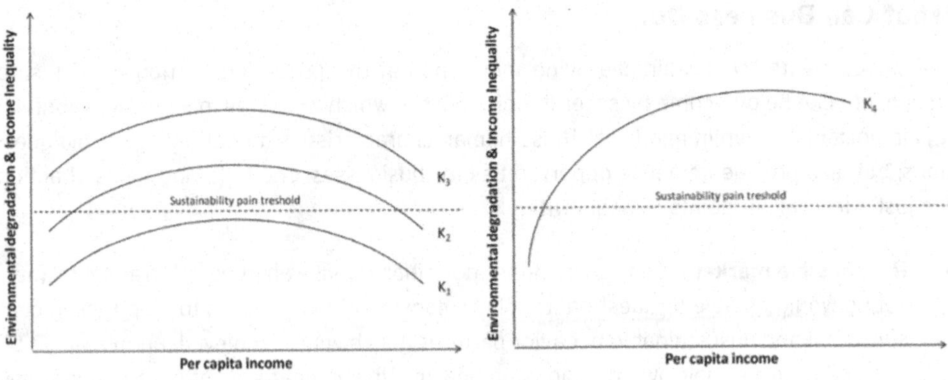

Figure 22.2 Kuznets Curves and Sustainable Development.

powerful proxy for the degree of poverty, which in turn is the central factor of socially sustainable development. Poverty and its consequences, such as exploitation, human rights abuses, and poor health conditions are crucial issues to be tackled in order to reach socially sustainable development. Second, environmental degradation, such as water and air pollution, or deforestation are central factors to environmentally sustainable development.

As illustrated in Figure 22.2 the Kuznets curve suggests an inverted U-shaped development of income inequality and environmental degradation, along with economic development, measured by the average per capita income of a country. This means that countries with a low average income will suffer higher environmental degradation and social inequality once they start developing but will improve both factors once reaching a high level of average income. Thus, the average sustainability footprint of an inhabitant of those countries would first be increased and finally be reduced. In the best case, the reduction would lead back to a low average individual footprint, while maintaining higher income, and an accordingly higher individual welfare as described by the curve K_2.

The important question when applying Kuznets curves on sustainable development are two. First: Will the planet be able to sustain the very negative impact during the economic development process? Second: Will the average footprint of the country's citizens, when reaching the point of maximum economic development, end up above or below the threshold of the planetary carrying capacity? We can imagine three possible scenarios as illustrated in the figure above. The curve titled K_1 describes the optimum situation, where a country develops fully without ever crossing the sustainability threshold. K_3 depicts the opposite extreme of a country whose inhabitants never (during the development process and after its end) are able to live within planetary resource limits. The global situation of developed countries looks more like K_4. The citizens of none of such so-called "developed" countries have achieved a footprint corresponding to the planetary sustainability pain threshold. While being considered economically developed, they are by no means developed sustainably.

Why does this feel odd?

It sounds too good to be true. If we only make people rich enough, we will solve all our global problems. Unfortunately, there are many reasons why such a beneficial scenario might never be reached. There is much criticism about the theory of the curve itself (Stern, 2004; Yandle, Bhattarai, & Vijayaraghavan, 2004). If we assume that the curve properly reflects reality, what are the reasons why countries might not all end-up in a sustainable development situation. One salient reason is that the Kuznets curve primarily refers to the situation inside the country. Highly developed countries with little internal inequality and environmental degradation, might be *outsourcing the negative effects* of their wealth to other countries. Another danger is *a stuck-in-the-middle situation*, where countries get stuck in economic development half-way. Such a country and its inhabitants then would constantly exert an unsustainable influence.

What can be learned for sustainable development and how individuals must develop and change in order to reach it? Most urgently, citizens in "developed" countries (see K_4) must learn how to reduce their footprint to a level within the world's resource limits. Second, citizens of "developing" countries must find a personal socio-economic development path that either never exceeds the planet's carrying capacity (K_1) or that at least minimizes the length of the unsustainable development section (K_2). To reach those goals cannot be the mere task of single individuals, there is the need for sound public policies to support those developments, following the clues derived from the Kuznets curve (Panayotou, 2002). The following section "changing lifestyles and consumption" will aim at finding ways to reach both.

Changing Lifestyles and Consumption

Is it really necessary to change lifestyles? Isn't there a less painful way to reach sustainable development? Western consumerist lifestyles are bound to be unsustainable. The annually published Global Footprint Atlas measured the average footprints of citizens of 156 countries in 2010. The worldwide average footprint was of 1.5 times Earth' bio-capacity per person. The figure widely varies from country to country. Citizens of the United Arab Emirates use up 5.9 Earths. For US Americans and Australians, the figure is 4.4. Even developed citizens of countries considered very advanced in environmental protection, countries score high. Germans for instance use up 2.8 Earths, almost the double of the world average. Only countries like India with a population of 2.4 billion people living on an average of 0.5 of Earth's bio-capacity, keep the worldwide environmental footprint from skyrocketing. But what will happen once those countries reach their development goals and join the club of unsustainable consumers? The *World Footprint Atlas* defines affluence, as "consumption per person" and identifies it as one of the three main drivers of the footprint explosion. New lifestyles and alternative consumption patterns are crucial for solving the puzzle of sustainable development (Moore, Goldfinger, Oursler, Reed, & Wackernagel, 2010).

What is an Optimum Sustainable Lifestyle?

A crucial challenge if sustainable development is to be achieved, is to reach a situation where the average person on Earth is living a lifestyle that is in line with both meeting human needs and the natural carrying capacity of the planet: A footprint of 1.0. It is also imperative that countries with high and low environmental footprints will need to meet in the middle. Low-footprint citizens such as the Indian population will only have a minimal margin for increasing their footprints, while high footprint countries such as the USA and Germany will need to reduce it drastically. We are in search of a new sustainable lifestyle for 9 billion people on planet Earth, the population estimate for 2043 (Rosenberg, 2011). What lifestyle might that be? More sustainable lifestyles have always existed in a wide variety of forms, albeit no globally significant quantity of people lives by them.

The power of awareness, priority, and framing

A young violinist stands in a subway station, playing six classical pieces in 43 minutes. Passers-by hardly noticed. Just one person stopped, some threw a coin walking by with an impression of guilt. The financial outcome is US$23, which you might consider decent for a street musician. Just, that this man is not an ordinary street musician. The 1057 people passing by just missed a for-free concert of the star-violinist Joshua Bell. One of the tunes played was Bach's "Chaconne" one of the most difficult violin pieces on Earth. Bell played on a 3.5-million-dollar violin. Just a few days before, thousands of people had paid an average US$100 for a concert performed by the same person in the same city (Weingarten, 2007). Does the money we need to earn for consumption leave us time to see the for-free beauty that is surrounding us? If we could only see and cherish the beauty of things that surround us, would we be able to forfeit costly consumption and slow down hectic and unsustainable lifestyles? Would we start to consider protecting the world that surrounds us?

Figure 22.3 provides a basic overview of some lifestyles alternative to the classic consumerist life. The figure assumes that the environmental footprint caused by a certain lifestyle depends on both the quantity and quality of consumption. **Quantity of consumption** refers to how much a person consumes overall. A person owning two cars instead of one will consume more natural resources for the vehicles' production and possibly also for their use. The individuals' footprint will be increased by the quantity of consumption. Other examples for changes in quantity of consumption can be seen in reduced transportation by moving a residence closer to the workplace and replacing the cell phone every four instead of every one-and-a-half years. **Quality of consumption** makes reference to the degree of sustainability in an individual's consumption patterns. For instance, a vegetarian and a non-vegetarian both would eat until feeling full (same quantity). Nonetheless, the consumption of the vegetarian is of a more environmentally sustainable quality. Producing meat creates an environmental footprint (greenhouse gases, energy, water, etc.) far beyond the footprint of most vegetarian food alternatives. Thus, a vegetarian's footprint would be decreased due to the quality of consumption. Other examples for improvements in the quality of consumption would be

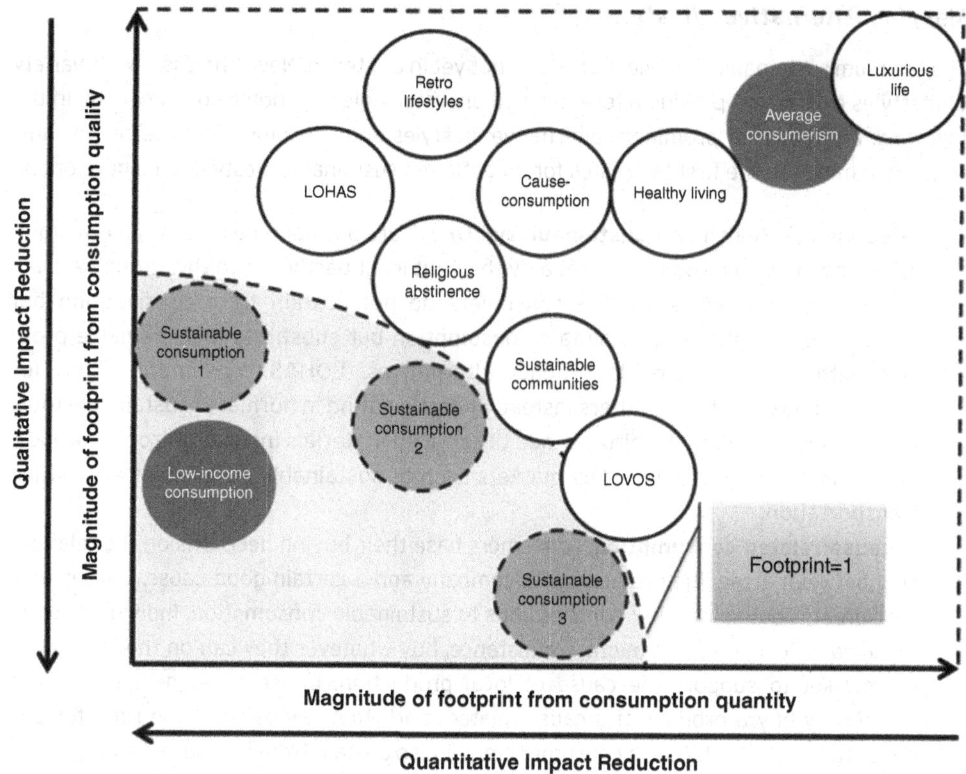

Figure 22.3 Sustainability of Lifestyle and Consumption Styles.

buying organic goods instead of non-organic ones; to drive a solar car instead of one with a traditional combustion engine; or buying airplane tickets including a carbon offsetting fee. The figure illustrates different lifestyles, such as the lifestyle of a person in a developing country, a LOHAS consumer, or the lifestyle of a person living in a sustainable community. Each lifestyle scores differently in terms of the environmental impact of their consumption quality and quantity. While the figure is an intuitive and therefore superficial estimate of what different lifestyles might mean in terms of sustainability it might still provide valuable food for thought and stimulate discussion.

The key criterion for sustainable lifestyles that should be developed for the future is that their impact per person must be close to a footprint of 1. In the figure, this situation is indicated by the dotted semi-circular line. Sustainable lifestyles must not trespass this sustainability frontier. In the figure, two circles inside the sustainability frontier are the lifestyles of developing countries, and two types of new sustainable lifestyle to be developed. Type 3 represents a lifestyle with highest-possible impact reduction by quality of lifestyle, which allows for the highest quantity of consumption, while still being sustainable. Also Types 1 and 2 illustrate sustainable consumption choices, but on a lower sustainability quality level and quantity level than Type 3. Thus, Type 3 sustainability might be the preferred solution: An **optimum sustainable lifestyle**. It provides higher consumption quantity and quality for consumers in currently developing countries and a higher quality, but much lower, and the highest possible sustainable consumption in quantity.

Mapping Alternative Lifestyles

The optimum sustainable lifestyle is probably not yet in existence. Nevertheless, a wide variety of lifestyles exists, that provide alternatives to unsustainable traditional consumerism. In the following, a brief list of prominent alternative lifestyles and consumption patterns will illustrate what might be the first templates for an optimum sustainable lifestyle to be developed.

- **Lifestyles of Health and Sustainability LOHAS** are possibly the most-visible sustainable consumption movement. Probably this is at least partly due to this group's attractiveness for marketers. LOHAS consumers do not abstain from consumption but consume differently. They maintain consumption but substitute unsustainable products with more sustainable product alternatives. LOHAS consumers might, for instance, book eco-tourist offers instead of participating in normal unsustainable tourism, or they would buy furniture made of recycled materials instead of tropical woods. LOHAS is often characterized by markets such as sustainable energies or alternative transportation.
- In **cause-related consumption**, consumers base their buying decisions on the relationship between a specific product or its company and a certain good cause. Causes may vary greatly, but so do their contributions to sustainable consumption. Individuals practicing cause consumption might, for instance, buy whatever they can on the local farmers market to support the cause of local production. Cause consumers might also specifically buy a product of a cause-related marketing campaign, if the right topic is benefitted through it. Cause consumers might also abstain from buying certain products that are considered derogatory for the cause supported. Resulting consumer boycotts are typical outcomes of cause-motivated consumption or non-consumption.
- Individuals following **Lifestyles of voluntary simplicity (LOVOS)** make a conscious choice to reduce the complexity of western consumption-based lifestyles (Brown & Kasser, 2005). Typical reasons are dissatisfaction with consumerism and the search for non-material benefits, such as personal fulfillment, spirituality, or simply rest. LOVOS usually reduce their consumption drastically and often also aim at jobs that are low in stress and rather distant from the consumerist system. Also, the *slow living* movement is a variant of a LOVOS lifestyle, where individuals aim at leaving the "rat race" and reducing complexity by slowing down life's pace (The World Institute of Slowness, 2012). LOVOS lifestyles' main contribution to sustainable development is the reduction in overall consumption per individual.
- **Religious lifestyles** often lead to sustainable behavior patterns. For instance, the Amish Christian group is known for their rural lifestyle, characterized by simple living, plain dress, and the refusal of many modern technological comforts. Buddhist belief is based on a simple life, avoiding the distractions represented by consumption. Many animist beliefs and Chinese Taoism base their practices on nearness to nature.
- **Sustainable communities** are formed of groups of individuals, jointly building and running a community that focuses on **sustainable community** infrastructure and community practices. In the most extreme case, sustainable communities try to become completely independent from the outside world, produce their own food, clothing, shelter, and live from local water and energy resources.

Strategic sustainable consumption

The German UTOPIA platform for strategic consumption provides consumers with a Web 2.0 tool for supporting sustainable practices by their purchasing decisions. The platform is branded as a tool for "strategic consumption", meaning strategic purchasing decisions for a more sustainable world. The platform offers a community of over 60,000 subscribers, direct contact to leading responsible businesses ("changemakers"), and extensive background facts making cause-consumption easier (Utopia Foundation, 2012).

Responsible Business and New Lifestyles

It seems like the shift towards one or several sustainable global lifestyle patterns, pursued by the majority of the world's population is inevitable; either to reach sustainable development (in an optimistic scenario) or to survive the consequences of un-sustainable development. How can business connect to this development? Business can have a part in both, fostering and harvesting the fruits of new sustainable lifestyles. Adapting to sustainable lifestyles requires substantial transitions in businesses' most protected "sanctuaries"; products, core-business processes, and even underlying paradigms, such as growth. The following three points are crucial prerequisites for achieving a business transition along with the new sustainable lifestyles to be developed.

- Provide **higher-sustainability-quality products** and services. As the slogan "LOHAS means business" (Emerich, 2000, p. 1) suggests, this prerequisite is probably the most pleasant to be fulfilled. Improving the **sustainability quality** of products and the processes leading to those products can be a highly attractive product differentiation feature in order to win new customers, or even whole new markets.
- Be prepared to **degrow the quantity of production** together with your consumers. As we realized above, the quantity of global production and consumption is already by far exceeding the ecological capacity of the planet. Considering how eco-systems decay, and with them their ecological capacity decreases, while population continues to grow, it becomes clear that a purely quality-based reduction in impact from consumption will not lead to sustainable development. The quantity of consumption per capita and as a (planetary) whole needs to be degrown. This will only happen if companies prepare for the transition to lower production volumes. To provide a very rough estimation, the reduction in production would need to be least one-third[1] of a company's overall production. What are the consequences? Does this mean companies need to shut down a major part of their operations and lay off millions of people? If the quantity reduction is based on a well-planned process, the negative effects might not be as drastic. Much of the decreased production activity might be absorbed by increased activity in boosting products' sustainability quality. Also, a reduction of quantity might be achieved by increased servitization, substituting higher-impact products, and by lower impact and labor-intensive services. Those are just two examples of mechanisms enabling a smart transition. Companies should be highly involved in searching for such solutions and facilitating a smooth transition to a low-quantity, low-production economy.

- Create a mutually benefitting and flexible **symbiosis with individuals** in both their roles as consumers and employees, sensitive to the needs of new lifestyles. Many of the movements towards sustainable living also involve a change in work patterns and professional preferences. For instance, people searching for voluntary simplicity and a slow life might be very willing to work for a lower salary in less-time intensive and more flexible schemes, that support their lifestyle, and at the same time enable companies to deploy a mutually appreciated reduction of employment, going in accordance with both the need for degrowth and the new lifestyle.

Activism and Change Agency

The animal protection activist Ric O'Barry once said "*To me you are either an activist or an inactivist*" (Psihoyos, 2009). The last section addressed consumption and the work aspects of changing an individual's lifestyle towards sustainability. It was about "minding one's own business". This section goes beyond "minding one's own business". **Activists** focus on actively leaving the boundaries of their own life and aim at changing individuals, social groups, and whole systems around them. In light of the necessity to become a truly sustainable global society, including businesses, governmental systems, and individuals, activism is an important catalyst for change.

> **After-death-activism**
>
> The Austrian branch of the World Wildlife Fund (WWF) offers specialist support for drafting peoples' last will for the environment. WWF has even published a last will guide including sound advice from legal to ethical issues (WWF, 2012).

What is an Activist for Sustainable Development?

When we think of activists, very different individuals may come to mind. One might think of famous leaders such as Mahatma Gandhi, Martin Luther King, Che Guevara, or Nelson Mandela. For being an activist, one does not need to be or become famous. Activists share three common characteristics. They display a commitment to a cause as a goal of activist activity. Activists feel nonconformity with the status quo and actively challenge structures, authorities, institutions, and beliefs. Activists can be subdivided as belonging to **grassroots activism**, which emerges naturally and spontaneously from among the society and **organizational activism** that uses and follows established institutions as vehicles for activism.

As illustrated in Figure 22.4, individuals can be activists in many different roles in life. Even some of the *consumer* movements, such as cause-consumption and related boycotts, can be classified as activism in the individual's role as consumer. They follow a common cause, are non-conforming with the way companies deal with this cause, and challenge the companies by not buying their products. *Employees* can also be activists inside their employing organization. They can act as so-called **intrapreneurs** and leaders facilitating change towards more

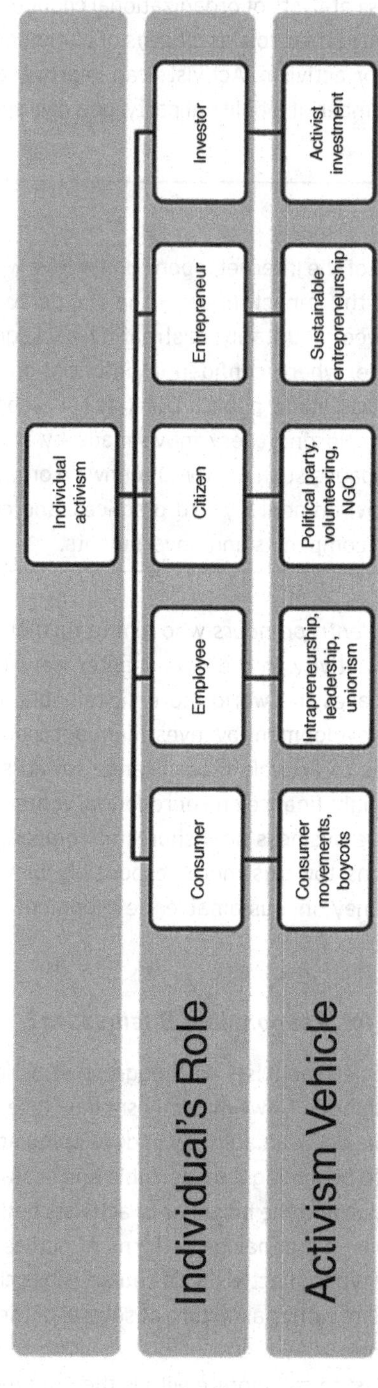

Figure 22.4 Individual Activism, Roles, and Vehicles.

responsibility from within. Activists, especially in the responsible business jargon, are also called **change agents**. In the next chapter we will extensively describe what leaders and change agents can do to serve as catalysts of organizational change towards responsible business from within an organization. In their role as *citizens* of communities, states, or the world, individuals find many vehicles for activism. Activists can improve local structures by volunteering, fight for change as a member of a political party, or a civil society organization (CSO).

Activism 2.0

Web 2.0, the interactive form of the internet, opens up a whole world of potential activist engagement. Think about the impact made by the one person who uploaded a clip of a parcel services' employee voluntarily mistreating packages to YouTube. Think about the Wikileaks webpage, where confidential information about corporate and governmental misbehavior was made public. Think about webpages that call themselves online watchdogs, scrutinizing every move made by potentially irresponsible companies. Think about webpages such as www.regenwald.org, where you can, with a few clicks, pledge against environmentally bad practices, and channel your personal pledge to decision-makers in companies and governments.

Some individuals might become *entrepreneurs* who aim to further the cause of sustainable development through business activity. In the next chapter we will illustrate how to create and manage a business that makes the world more sustainable. A minority of individuals might also further sustainable development by investment decisions. As an *investor*, an individual has manifold possibilities to actively drive change towards more sustainability. So-called private **angel investors** might finance entrepreneurial ventures for more sustainability. Activist investors for responsible business hold shares of companies in order to be able to actively influence their decisions towards more responsible behavior. Even small private investors can invest their money in sustainable development in green technology or microfinance-based funds.

What Does Activism Mean for Responsible Businesses?

Business managers might associate activists with aggressive actions, such as Greenpeace collaborators climbing their chimneys. However, activism may take much more collaborative forms than that. Activists may be an invaluable ally in developing new perspectives and even concrete solutions on the way to becoming a responsible and sustainable business.

In order to understand activism and the behavior of activists better, it is important to have an insight into basic motivations and behavior patterns of activist individuals. Figure 22.5 describes four commonly found types of activists. Of course, those classifications are extreme stereotypes. In reality, activists are rather a mixture of several of the four and even additional types not considered in the figure.

The activist type probably best to collaborate with is the *Pragmatist*, one who is primarily driven by the willingness to solve a pressing social or environmental problem. The pragmatist

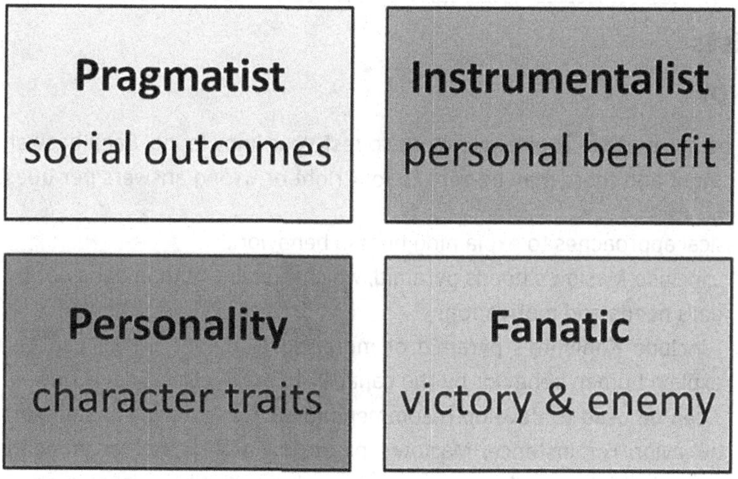

Pragmatist social outcomes	**Instrumentalist** personal benefit
Personality character traits	**Fanatic** victory & enemy

Figure 22.5 Activist Types and Common Motivations.

is highly results-oriented, and will happily collaborate with a business, if there is a good chance of mitigating or solving the cause addressed. In contrast, the *Instrumentalist* uses activism to achieve a personal benefit. Politicians are often accused of preying on a good cause to impress voters, which is one example for an instrumental activist. Instrumentalists have an interest in furthering the cause, but always when it helps them to reach their personal goals. The *Personality* possesses character traits, such as high critical skills, or a leader personality, which intrinsically make him an example of pursuing activist behavior. The Personality type activist might not be as interested in furthering the cause as he is in maintaining his role as a "born activist". It is almost impossible to collaborate with *Fanatics*, unless you share their motivation of ultimate victory against a self-declared enemy. Fanatics tend to be very uncompromising. With them it is all or nothing - defeat or victory. Collaboration if wanted requires substantial diplomacy and confidence building as prerequisites.

"The beginning is near" reads the sign held up by one of the activist protesters of the Occupy movement in late 2011. Can activism and protest really be the beginning of a new more socially responsible and environmentally sustainable economic system? The Occupy movement with its criticisms of capitalism, greed, and the banking systems in particular, in just a few months had spread out to more than 700 cities in over 80 countries worldwide (Rogers, 2011). A worldwide opinion poll revealed that there was minimum opposition to the movement. Only 12% did not sympathize with the movement's ideology, while 34% of respondents were undecided, and 53% supported the movement's opposition to "social and economic inequality, corporate greed, the power of the financial sector and the global financial system" (IPSOS, 2012). Could that be the world citizens' vote for a new industrial revolution?

Exercises

A. KNOW

Use the below multiple-choice questions to test your knowledge. Each answer may be wrong or right and there may be zero to four right or wrong answers per question:

1. Classical approaches to explaining human behavior...
   a. ...include Maslow's needs pyramid, which explains human behavior by individual's needs and motivation.
   b. ...include Kohlberg's pyramid of moral development, which can be used to explain human behavior by the capacity to make ethical decisions.
   c. ...can be used to develop recommendations for fostering sustainable human behavior. For instance, Maslow's pyramid leads to the recommendation to focus on the moral development of people especially in developing countries.
   d. ...features Kohlberg's pyramid describing moral development. Kohlberg. for instance, might explain the fact that well-endowed people use big cars in spite of the negative environmental impact with their existence on the esteem level, where the actions are led by the necessity to be esteemed by others. In this case, people would aim to achieve this esteem by showing off their wealth in the form of an expensive car.
2. Characteristics of human behavior impeding sustainable living...
   a. ...include greed, as always wanting more does not go in accordance with a planet of finite resources, limiting growth.
   b. ...include the characteristic of mental disconnect, describing that people are not able to understand the worldwide social and environmental issues on an intellectual level.
   c. ...include the characteristic of present value focus, which keeps people from leaving their comfort zone and move towards more sustainable behaviors.
   d. ...include that individual behavior often does not change before collective behavior does.
3. What business can do to influence peoples' behavior...
   a. ...includes responsible marketing. Responsible marketing here refers only to selling more sustainable products.
   b. ...always creates costs and can hardly be harnessed as opportunities.
   c. ...includes the possibility to educate people in the workplace towards more sustainable behaviors, which then might be transferred to sustainable behavior in private life.
   d. ...does not include contributing to human development, as businesses should not assume the role of development agencies.

4. Sustainable lifestyles...
   a. ...are necessary in order to both reduce the footprint of individuals with medium-to-high incomes and to find viable future consumption styles for the upcoming new middle class in developing countries.
   b. ...need to develop to one or several optimum sustainable lifestyles with a footprint of exactly two per person.
   c. ...may be evaluated by the quantity (e.g. vegetarian meal versus meat-eater's meal) and the quality (e.g. one flight per year versus five flights per year) of consumption of an individual.
   d. ...include the idea that in order to develop a worldwide sustainable lifestyle for the future, the quality of consumption of an average individual has to be increased, independently from the individual's current income level in order to reach optimum sustainable lifestyles.

5. Activism...
   a. ...can be defined by its constituting elements of an individual's commitment to a certain cause, the nonconformity with the actual status quo, and an action to change the situation.
   b. ...always comes in the form of a single individual's effort to change the status quo.
   c. ...includes so-called grassroots activism, which refers to activists who exclusively tackle ecological issues.
   d. ...for sustainable development can be conducted in many of the roles we fulfill as individuals. In responsible business jargon, activists are often called change agents.

6. Activist roles and vehicles...
   a. ...describe the reality that individuals can be activists in many different ways throughout the different roles taken in their life.
   b. ...do not include individuals' role as investor.
   c. ...do not include individuals' engagement in political parties.
   d. ...include an individual's role as an employee, actively changing the workplace towards more sustainability.

B. THINK

View a movie on successful activists such as "The yes men fix the world", or "The Cove". Analyze how the activists in the movie identify a problem and then search for an opportunity to solve it. Think hard to identify one such problem-solving opportunity yourself and plan an action to seize the opportunity.

C. DO

Browse the many causes on online petition sites (e.g. ipetitions, avaaz, change.org), decide on one petition you find worth supporting, and make sure you have enough background information beyond the information given on the site to cast your vote.

D. RELATE

Think about whom in your sphere of influence might benefit most from something you could do. Try to truly understand what the other person's situation and needs are, and how s/he feels. Then do it!

E. BE

Inform yourself deeply about a lifestyle different to your own (e.g. being a vegetarian or vegan, living a no-waste life, living LOHAS or LOVOS). Organize yourself to lead a life after the principles of this lifestyle for a predetermined period of time. Then do it!

Feedback

A. KNOW

Feedback 1

a. Right: Maslow's pyramid is one of these classical approaches we have used in this chapter to explain unsustainable human behavior.
b. Right: Kohlberg's pyramid is one of these classical approaches we have used in this chapter to explain unsustainable human behavior.
c. Wrong: The recommendation given is related to Kohlberg's pyramid rather than Maslow's.
d. Right: This is an adequate description of an argument based on Kohlberg's pyramid of moral development.

Feedback 2

a. Right: Greedy behavior by definition will make ones' footprint exceed the planetary boundaries.
b. Wrong: Mental disconnect refers to the psychological phenomenon that people know about the issues, but do not feel their personal connection to them.
c. Right: The present value focus makes us value the current comfortably unsustainable lifestyle more than the future suffering in an unsustainable world.
d. Right: Individuals' behaving against the dominant cultural behavior patterns will most likely have it difficult.

Feedback 3

a. Wrong: Responsible marketing refers to a drastic shift in marketing from promoting consumerism to promoting consumers' independence and mature decision making for consumption.
b. Wrong: Businesses can find immense opportunities in influencing peoples' behavior.
c. Right: Such transfer might be one way of how businesses may contribute to changes towards more sustainable lifestyles among their employees and their families.
d. Wrong: Businesses independently, from an official assignment to contribute to human development, do so in many different ways.

Feedback 4

a. Right: Sustainable lifestyles are the solution in both cases.
b. Wrong: A sustainable lifestyle, to be sustainable, has to result in a footprint of one or less.
c. Wrong: The examples for quality and quantity have been switched.
d. Right: An increased sustainability quality will help current low-income consumers to not cross the sustainability threshold, and current high-income consumers to move back into the sustainability threshold of their consumption.

Feedback 5

a. Right: These are the defining elements of activism.
b. Wrong: The form of activism does not always need to find its form in a single individual's effort. Organizational activism, such as in the case of the environmental activist organization Greenpeace is another form of activism.
c. Wrong: Grassroots activism refers to activism that emerges naturally and spontaneously in society, without being initiated by existing institutions.
d. Right: Activism and change agency can be rooted in many different roles, such as being an employee, a consumer, or an entrepreneur.

Feedback 6

a. Right: Activism and change agency can be rooted in many different roles, such as being an employee, a consumer, or an entrepreneur.
b. Wrong: Investors can be activists for sustainable development. Examples are so-called angel investors and activist shareholders.
c. Wrong: Engagement in political parties is the longest-established vehicle for activism. An excellent example for party activism for sustainable development is the Green Party movement, which has reached important change in many countries.
d. Right: This is a description of possible activism from the employee role.

B. THINK

Level	*Social problem and opportunity analysis*	Notes
+	Promising action plan grounded in unique social, environmental, or ethical opportunity.	
=	Opportunity identified, but no promising action plan outlined.	
–	No opportunity identified.	

C. DO

Level	*Acting with adequate amount of information*	Notes
+	Petition decision was made based on sufficient, balanced information from the petition site and other external sources.	
=	Decision to sign or not sign the petition was primarily based on information given on the petition website.	
–	Specific petition was not identified, or decision to sign or not sign was not made.	

D. RELATE

Level	*Acting upon empathy*	Notes
+	Action fits the benefitted person due to the developed empathy.	
=	Credible evidence of empathy for another person.	
–	Little evidence of empathy development.	

E. BE

Level	*Self-organization for action*	Notes
+	Lifestyle was lived authentically for the planned period of time.	
=	Solid understanding of lifestyle and feasible self-organization efforts.	
–	Little appreciation of the lifestyle principles and practices, or little self-organization efforts to live it.	

Note

1 Based on reducing the current ecological footprint of 1.5 to 1 by reducing the quantity of products produced and the optimistic assumption that the increase in environmental impact from consumption related to population growth and the new middle class in developing countries can be absorbed by improving the sustainability quality of consumption.

References

Brown, K. W., & Kasser, T. (2005). Are psychological and ecological well-being compatible? The role of value, mindfulness and lifestyle. *Social Indicators Research, 74*, 349–368.

Coutu, D. L. (2003). I was greedy too. *Harvard Business Review, 81*(2), 38–44.

Emerich, M. (2000). LOHAS means business. *The LOHAS Journal.*

IPSOS. (2012). *As 'Occupy' protesters promise new strategies for 2012: Global citizens are in the dark but sympathetic*. Retrieved January 27, 2012, from https://www.ipsos-na.com/news-polls/pressrelease.aspx?id=5487

Kohlberg, L. (1985). Kohlberg's stages of moral development. In W. C. Crain (Ed.), *Theories of development* (pp. 118–136). Prentice-Hall.

Kotler, P., & Levy, S. J. (1971). Demarketing, yes demarketing. *Harvard Business Review, 79*(6), 74–80.

Kuznets, S. (1955). Economic growth and income inequality. *The American Economic Review, 45*(1), 1–28.

Maslow, A. H. (1943). A theory of human motivation. *Psychological Review, 50*(4), 370–396.

Moore, E. B., Goldfinger, S., Oursler, A., Reed, A., & Wackernagel, M. (2010). *The ecological footprint atlas 2010*. Oakland: Global Footprint Network.

Panayotou, T. (2002). Demystifying the environmental Kuznets curve: Turning a black box into a policy tool. *The Review of Economics and Statistics, 84*(3), 541–551.

Psihoyos, L. (Director). (2009). *The cove* [Motion Picture].

Rogers, S. (2011). *Occupy protests around the world: Full list visualised.* Retrieved January 27, 2012, from The Guardian: https://www.guardian.co.uk/news/datablog/2011/oct/17/occupy-protests-world-list-map

Rosenberg, M. (2011). *Current world population.* Retrieved January 19, 2012, from About.com: https://geography.about.com/od/obtainpopulationdata/a/worldpopulation.htm

Stern, D. I. (2004). The rise and fall of the environmental Kuznets curve. *World Development, 32*(8), 1419–1439.

SustainAbility. (2011). *Survey on sustainable consumption.* London: SustainAbility.

The World Institute of Slowness. (2012). *What is slow living?* Retrieved January 19, 2012, from The World Institute of Slowness: https://www.theworldinstituteofslowness.com/whatisslowliving

Utopia Foundation. (2012). *Utopia*. Retrieved January 18, 2012, from https://www.utopia.de/

Weingarten, G. (2007). *Pearls before breakfast.* Retrieved February 19, 2012, from Washington Post: https://www.washingtonpost.com/wp-dyn/content/article/2007/04/04/AR2007040401721.html

WWF. (2012). *Ihr Testament für die Umwelt [Your last will for the environment]*. Retrieved January 18, 2012, from World Wildlife Fund: https://www.wwf.at/de/testament/

Yandle, B., Bhattarai, M., & Vijayaraghavan, M. (2004). Environmental Kuznets curves: A review of findings, methods, and policy implications. *Property and Environment Research Center (PERC), 2*(1).

23 Organizational Change

The earlier chapters on responsible business and management illustrated how to make incremental changes, or baby-steps, towards the assumption of first responsibilities. Baby steps are important, but not enough. In order to reach a situation where businesses are truly sustainable, it requires disruptive change, a creative destruction and reconstruction of what businesses are and how they work. As early as 1927, Donham (1927, p. 406) wrote in *Harvard Business Review* "Unless more of our business leaders learn to exercise their powers and responsibilities with a definitely increased sense of responsibility toward other groups (...) our civilization may well head for one of its periods of decline." Two years later he warns about the dangers of irresponsible economic growth and materialism (Donham, 1929). Have we learned anything since then? We have had the last 90 years for baby steps and theories. It is time for changing business! This chapter provides guidance on how to achieve this disruptive innovation of businesses in two basic ways. Either businesses might be transformed by strong leaders to more sustainable ways, or old unsustainable businesses might increasingly be substituted by newly created sustainable businesses. Entrepreneurial business creations boosted by the worldwide sustainability trend have the potential to quickly grow to a size offering sustainability solutions on a global scale. Of course, there are also hybrid forms between transformation and entrepreneurship, such as corporate social entrepreneurship and social intrapreneurship that will be covered in this chapter.

The first section describes what an optimum sustainable business may look like. The section provides a basic classification scheme along the dimensions impact (unsustainable, sustainable, restorative) and level of responsiveness (from defensive to civic). It also provides clear guidance on what kind of business every organization should finally become. The second section focuses on the transformation of established business through leadership, change management, and sustainability project management. Section three then turns to entrepreneurial approaches to create completely new sustainable businesses or sustainable actions from either inside or outside established businesses. Entrepreneurial approaches covered are social and environmental entrepreneurship, intrapreneurship, and corporate social entrepreneurship.

DOI: 10.4324/9781003544074-31

Developing Sustainable Business

The responsibility trend among businesses has led to a situation where many businesses and their leaders decide to participate in responsible business, often unknowing of what makes a successful responsible business. What should change towards responsible business look like? What should the goal of responsible business be? How do we know how good the business is in its responsibility activities? Answering those questions is instrumental for successfully implementing responsible business. Before responsible business, decision making for business leaders was comparatively easy. Following profit, mostly without breaking the law was the fundamental criterion for business activity and development. Now that the sole-leadership of the profit motive is questioned, many businesses in their responsible business activities seem to be drifting aimlessly across the landscape, trying to find their way around in a confusing world of responsible business norms, trends, and activities. The following section will structure a basic development path for responsible business, providing clear steps and goals.

Eco-bank versus Retro bank

Seeing the flurry of different business models and supposedly sustainable ways of doing business, it is often hard to find out which one is actually responsible or is a sustainable alternative to business as usual. Make up your own mind: Here are two competing examples from the German banking business. The German "Umweltbank", which roughly translates as Eco-bank, exclusively invests their clients' money into opportunities with double profit, a financial one for clients, and an environmental one through the positive environmental impact of investment projects. The bank has had these goals from its foundation in 1997. In 2011 it had a working capital of 1.6 billion Euro and employed 150 people (UmweltBank, 2012). The competing model is the Raiffeisenbank in the small southern German town of Gammesfeld, which we call the Retro-bank. This bank operates very much like it would have several decades ago, no computer (but an electrical typewriter and a calculating machine) and offices that remind one of a museum. The bank's only employee, Peter Breiter, who at the same time fulfills the job positions of cleaning staff, back-office and front-desk manager, and only member of the bank's board of directors, describes "his" bank as the counter-design to what he calls "turbo-capitalism". The banks investment strategy is rather conservative. The only type of investment made is in safe, but not very profitable fixed-term deposits. The bank has total assets of 25 million Euro with which it achieves an annual profit of 40,000 Euros. During the financial subprime crisis, Mr. Breiter received requests from people all over Germany who wanted to deposit their money at the "safest bank of Germany". All were rejected. The bank, represented by its only employee, does not want to grow. Neither does Breiter want to get rich at the cost of others. Another operating principle includes that any customer is treated exactly the same, no matter if he deposits a few Euros or millions (Die Welt, 2012). Which bank do you think is more responsible and closer to becoming a role model for a sustainable banking business? What criteria can we apply to understand how advanced a business is on the way to becoming truly sustainable and how it is doing in comparison to its peers?

Sketching the Sustainable Business

Throughout the preceding chapters, the focus was on responsible business, as a commitment and first actions to increase the assumption of business responsibilities with the ultimate goal of becoming a sustainable business. Now the focus will be on developing a roadmap towards the final goal of being a sustainable business. What would be the perfect version of a sustainable business? This ideal business would be one that is not only **neutrally sustainable** (an overall impact of 0), but even **restoratively sustainable** with an overall positive impact, replenishing Earth's resources. The ideal business following the sustainability paradigm would act as *multiplier* that inspires sustainability in other actors inside its industry, throughout the supply chain, and among its broader set of stakeholders.

Figure 23.1 is a roadmap for developing such an *optimum sustainable business*. The horizontal axis of the chart describes a succession of **modes of implementation** of responsible business practices. Zadeck (2004) described those modes of implementation as stages in the organizational learning process towards becoming a more responsible business. Previous

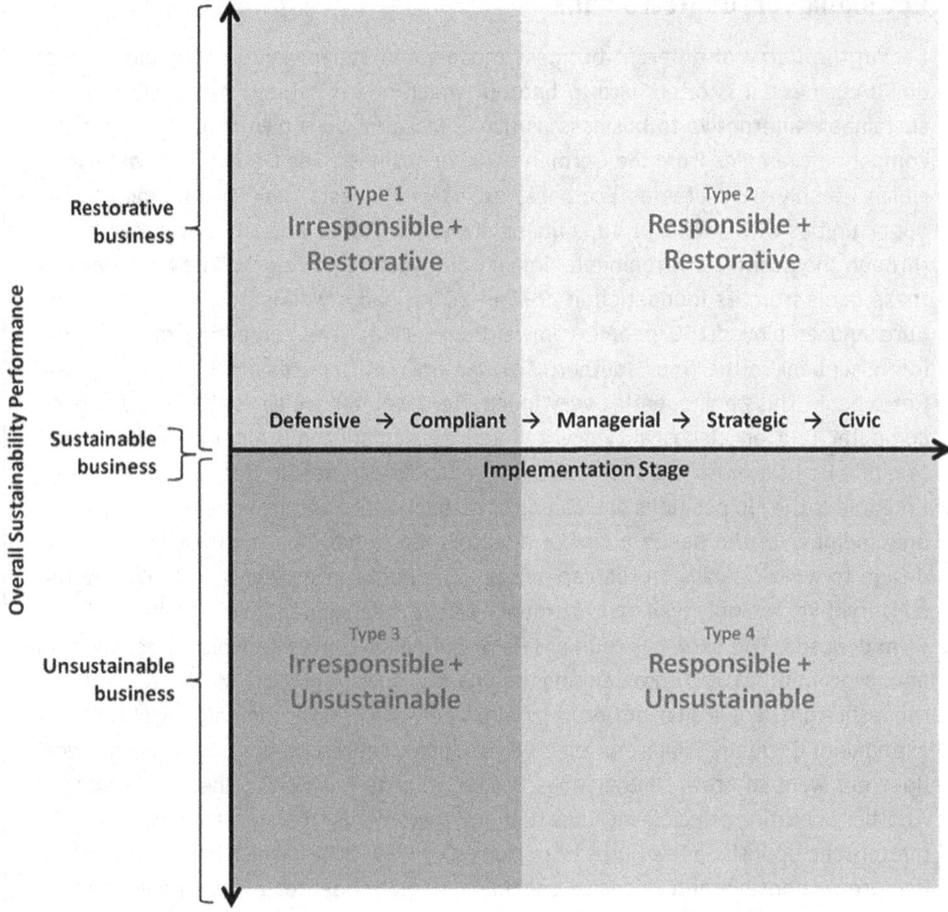

Figure 23.1 Sustainable Business Practice and Overall Output.

stages include later stages. Thus, a business can only be counted as having achieved the managerial stage, if also fulfilling the conditions of the compliance stage. The highest, civic responsibility stage, can only be considered achieved if a company has also become a responsible business in its core management and strategic processes. The stages are loosely based on the corporate responsiveness framework, as introduced in the chapter on responsibility.

- **Defensive** stage: Businesses deny responsibilities to defend the business from reputational damage.
- **Compliance** stage: Businesses assume all responsibilities that are required by law, norms, and minimum stakeholder expectations by implementing basic policies.
- **Managerial** stage: Businesses embed responsible management into the core management processes and daily operations.
- **Strategic** stage: Businesses integrate responsible business into core strategies to enhance economic and sustainable value.
- **Civic** stage: Businesses work as multipliers for sustainability, promoting it among other actors inside its industry, value chain, and among its broader set of stakeholders.

Charging up the sustainability ladder

Global Compact (GC) businesses seem to be quick on the path to responsibility. The 2010 GC CEO survey revealed that 64% of CEOs see their companies in the highest, "civic" mode of responsibility, involving in industry collaborations and multi-stakeholder partnerships. In 2007, only 43% were at this stage. In 2007, only 50% of CEOs stated that responsible business is fully embedded into operations and strategy, which corresponds to the "managerial" and "strategic" responsibility implementation stages. In 2010, this number had showed an impressive 30% increase to 80%. Based on this number, the majority of GC businesses appears to be either on the managerial or strategic level of responsible business (Lacey, Cooper, Hayward, & Neuberger, 2010).

The stages of implementation of responsible business can be seen as the input a business provides in order to first become a responsible and then a sustainable business. The outcome of this input, depending on additional external and internal factors, will be an impact, which is reflected in the overall sustainability performance of the business. The chart's vertical axis depicts the sustainability performance of a business, which might either be negative (unsustainable), neutral (neutral sustainability), or positive (restorative sustainability). Classifying a company as belonging to one of the responsible business implementation stages above is less complex than estimating a company's overall sustainability performance. In the chapter on individual change the footprint of individuals was compared to the Earth's environmental carrying capacity. A footprint equal or lower to 1 was defined as sustainable. Assessing and evaluating the footprint of a whole company, throughout the whole product life cycle, requires an intensive life-cycle assessment and sustainability accounting process as described in the preceding chapters. Once done so, the sustainability performance can be divided into three basic degrees of sustainability for any given business.

- An **unsustainable businesses** is characterized by a negative overall life-cycle impact exceeding the planet's resource limits.
- A **sustainable business** is characterized by a neutral overall life-cycle impact, matching the planet's resource limits.
- A **restorative business** is characterized by a positive overall life-cycle impact, replenishing the planet's resource limits.

A restorative business?

The eco-tourist business Amazonia Expeditions organizes tours from a lodge located in the Peruvian Amazon near to the city of Iquitos. A more extensive assessment might reveal that the venture is a great example of a restorative business. A superficial analysis shows strong evidence. Not only is the lodge solar powered, most food is locally harvested and fished, but also the lodge is one of the economically, politically, and organizationally sustaining factors of the surrounding natural reserve. It provides employment and healthcare to local communities through the foundation Angels of the Amazon. Lodge staff also are crucially involved in the creation of micro-enterprises, protection and restoration of the local eco-system, and the creation of sustainable agricultural opportunities (Amazonia Expeditions, 2011).

The figure does not propose any growth pattern of a businesses' overall sustainability performance, depending on the improvement of modes of implementation. A more responsible business is not necessarily a more sustainable business. A business on the highest stage of responsibility (the civic stage) is not necessarily also a restorative business. Generally, it can be assumed that the more businesses develop their modes of implementation for responsible business, the more they move towards becoming a sustainable business in their overall performance. Nevertheless, there can be no direct relation between stakeholder responsibilities taken and sustainability performance, as too many other mediating external and internal factors play a role in truly achieving the status of a responsible or sustainable business. A business at the ultimate, civic stage mode of implementation will not automatically have achieved sustainability. There might be some businesses, which are in their basic characteristics so unsustainable, that will never, with whatever good implementation practice, be able to become completely neutral in their impact. Thus, business leaders aiming at creating a responsible business need to understand their organizations' potential and limits. Only with this preparation will it be possible to draft a realistic and effective plan for responsible business development. The following section will provide insight into the two alternative implementation vehicles, potential drivers and inhibitors on the way to becoming a responsible business.

Barriers, Drivers, and Vehicles on the Road to Sustainable Business

What does the road to sustainable business look like? What are typical obstacles and enablers? What are the processes and vehicles available for creating a responsible business? When asking more than seven hundred CEOs about the main challenges of company-wide

Table 23.1 Barriers on the Way to Sustainable Business

Barrier	*Percentage of CEOs encountering this barrier among their top-three obstacles*	*Approaches to overcoming the barrier*
Complexity of implementing sustainability strategy across functions	49%	See chapters on main and support functions.
Competing strategic priorities	48%	See chapters on strategizing.
Lack of recognition from financial markets	34%	See finance section in the support functions chapter.
Differing definitions of responsible business	31%	See chapters on sustainability, responsibility, and ethics.
Difficulty in engaging with external groups	30%	See chapter on the responsible management process for its stakeholder engagement section, and the communication chapters for stakeholder communication.
Failure to recognize a link to value drivers	30%	See the box on the business case.
Lack of skills/knowledge among middle-senior management	24%	See the training-related contents in the communication chapter.
Lack of effective communication structure	15%	See the communication chapters.
Employee resistance	7%	See the communication chapters, and the change management section of this chapter.
Lack of board support	5%	See the persuasion section in the communication chapters.

transformation of their business, the *barriers* to implementation turned out to be as varied as illustrated in Table 23.1 (Lacey, Cooper, Hayward, & Neuberger, 2010).

Implementation *barriers* encountered by practitioners can be supplemented by a brief list of *bad practices* that inhibit transcendental changes towards sustainable business. Visser (2010) calls those bad practices "curses" of responsible business.

- **Incremental** responsibility: Businesses focusing on incremental possibilities, such as successively improving codes of compliance or continuous improvement in eco-efficiency, might miss the necessary big transformative changes.
- **Peripheral** responsibility: Businesses focusing on responsible business activities outside the core business will not be able to reach the maximum possible scale and maturity in their activities, thwarting sustainability performance.
- **Immediately profitable** responsibility: Companies only implementing responsible business activities that pay off immediately in the short run, will miss many crucial changes that enable becoming a sustainable business and that pay off in the long.

It is important to interpret the word "curse" right. As a matter of fact, each of those bad practices has a place and valuable function in responsible business and are legitimate practices on the road to becoming a sustainable business. Bad practices are only curses when businesses are not able to go beyond them. Important to successfully going along the path towards sustainable business are *enablers* catalyzing successful change. The before mentioned CEO survey identifies three main *enabling practices*.

- Develop and launch **sustainable products and services** for both business-to-business customers and end-consumers. Creating an embedded implementation throughout internal processes and the external supply chain provides both short and long-run financial incentives, and it is likely to increase competitiveness.
- Making use of new **sustainability technologies and innovation** fuels the development of new solutions for sustainable business and development inside and outside the business.
- Excelling at **collaboration** with all kinds of stakeholders helps to tap resources for change inside and outside the company.

Focusing on these three good practices for change towards sustainable business promises truly transformative responsible business implementation. These three practices are mutually reinforcing. A company should not focus on one practice alone because synergies are lost. For instance, Procter and Gamble heavily relies on its "open innovation program" (collaboration) to develop new sustainable innovation products (product and services) and to achieve more sustainable production methods (technology) (Dogdson, Gann, & Salter, 2006).

Responsible business is growing!

During a survey among company's chief responsibility officers (CROs) it was revealed that 77% of them expect their corporate responsibility implementation to expand in a three-year period. Only 7% disagreed. Of the CROs answering in the affirmative, 19% believed they will mainly grow through an increase in staff, 21% through a higher budget, and 57% believe implementation to grow through more coverage of additional areas (Corporate Responsibility Magazine, 2010).

In the following two sections there is a description of the main *vehicles for developing responsible business*, which will provide hands-on insight on the process of creating a responsible business. While the vehicle **change management** transforms long-established businesses, **sustainable entrepreneurship** creates new businesses which contribute to sustainable development.

Transformational Approaches

Transforming organizations of any size is a complex process. The process involves all systems and sub-systems and the interconnections between systems. For a business to become sustainable, drastic change is often required in spheres as different as the company's organizational structure (power, decision making, information, etc.), processes, products values, vision, and even the most basic assumptions the business and its management is based

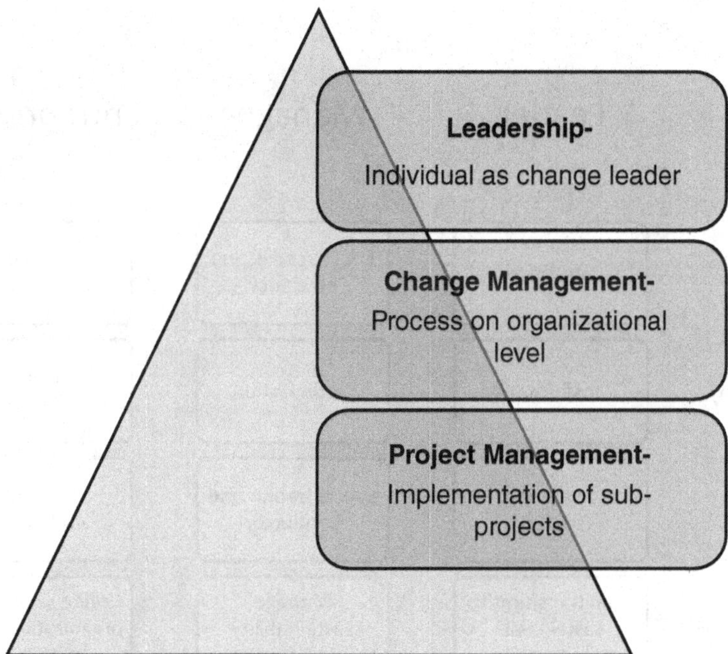

Figure 23.2 Elements of the Transformation Process.

upon. Imagine a business that realizes its most important input needs to be substituted, because it is highly unsustainable. Imagine a different business that is forced to re-invent two thirds of its products. Imagine a third business that realizes its core production technology can never become sustainable and needs to be replaced. Those challenges sound overwhelming, even catastrophic, but can be overcome with a well-managed transformational process.

This section illustrates three central elements of transition processes (see Figure 23.2). First, the central role of **leadership** in times of transition will be described. Second, **change management** will be introduced as the tool for managing the overall transition process. Third, we present an illustration of critical elements of sustainability *project management* for successfully managing the manifold sub-projects of organizational transitions towards becoming a sustainable business.

Leadership

What is a leader? Can managers be leaders? Aren't entrepreneurs also leaders? It is important to understand differences and similarities between leaders, managers, and entrepreneurs. It is also important to understand the different ways how all three groups play central roles in creating sustainable businesses. Figure 23.3 profiles all three groups. *Leaders* for sustainable business follow the basic target of providing guidance for transformation. Important traits of leaders are a clear vision of the sustainable business to be created and power to lead others in achieving this vision. *Managers* instead are in charge of the operational aspects of creating effective and efficient departments, resulting in an attractive triple

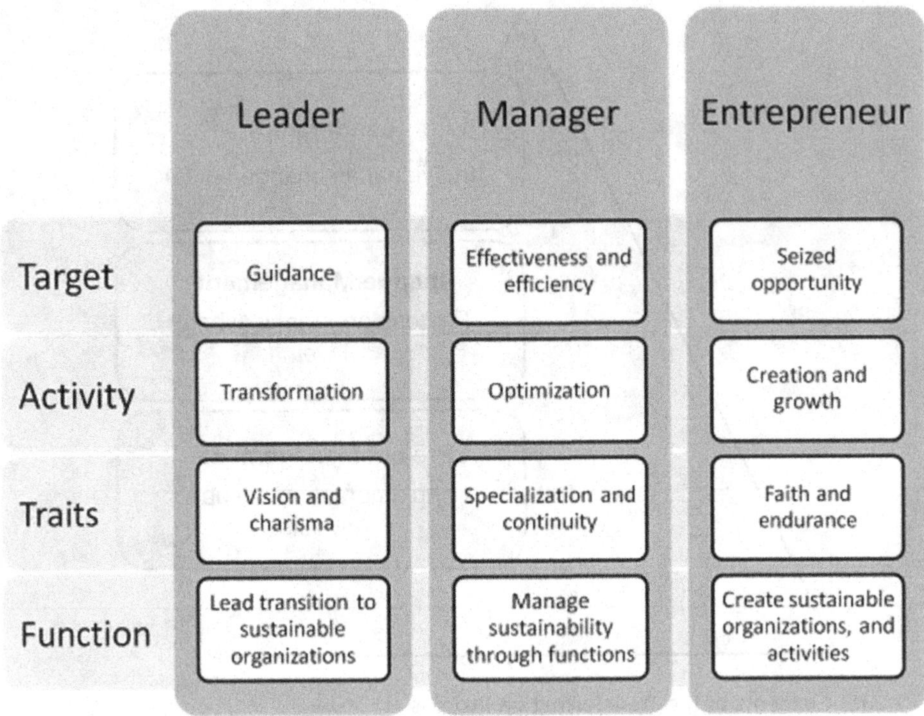

Figure 23.3 Profiles of Leaders, Managers, and Entrepreneurs.

bottom line. To do so they require specialized knowledge in their respective areas of expertise and endurance for the continuous learning and improvement involved. *Entrepreneurs* for sustainable business take advantage of social, environmental, and economic opportunities to create new sustainable activities or new organizations.

No followers, no leader

For the task of leadership, it is crucial to understand the "*followers*" of sustainability leadership and how they can contribute to shifting the company towards sustainable development. There are typically four types of followers as described by Visser (2008). *Experts* possess technical skills needed for responsible business implementation. *Facilitators* provide excellent interpersonal skills necessary for bringing key stakeholders onboard. *Catalysts* have political skills important for assuring progress through times of hardship and opposition. *Activists* usually possess excellent critical skills that keep the change agenda real and transformative.

Those roles may overlap, but do not necessarily have to do so. For a sustainability leader, both certain managerial and entrepreneurial traits will be enriching for her transformational task. It is important to not misunderstand leaders as purely defined by their job position and institutional power. Some CEOs, who are usually understood as leaders may rather be managers. Individuals at the base of organizational hierarchies may turn out to be great leaders of their respective group. Leaders for sustainability may rise at all levels of organizational hierarchy (Ferdig, 2007). Such leaders might be the "enlightened" janitor who functions as operational leader of the company's waste separation, the human resources manager inspiring change towards enhanced employee well-being, or the chief sustainability officer. Change happens in many parts of the company with manifold leaders. Leaders are the most salient actors of the change management process towards sustainable businesses and are crucial for its success (Gill, 2003). The following section will highlight the process itself by illustrating the tool of change management.

Change Management Process

Good news first: The **change management** process towards sustainable business tends to be easier than other big organizational changes, at least from the following perspective: Typically, *employee resistance* to change is perceived as the main obstacle to a swift and effective change process, but not so in creating a sustainable business. Only 5% of CEOs report employee resistance among their top-three obstacles (Lacey, Cooper, Hayward, & Neuberger, 2010). It seems like employees are enthusiastically inclined to making their business sustainable. Nevertheless, many other *obstacles* are to be overcome. Kotter (1995) has provided the best-established tool for managing organizational change, which will be applied in the following steps for highlighting the most crucial practices in transforming businesses in order to make them responsible and sustainable. The tool consists of eight steps going from the first step of convincing people, to creating institutions, to anchoring the sustainable business in the organizational structure. The eight steps for organizational change management can be subdivided into three phases: Preparation, implementation, and maintenance of change.

The first step during the *preparation phase* is to (1) "establish a sense of urgency". Key decision-makers (and later all individuals involved in the change) in the organization need to understand and feel that it is not only important, but urgent to transform the organization; that there is no alternative and that consequences of failure would be devastating. Establishing sense of urgency for becoming a sustainable organization, for instance, can be achieved by translating the negative consequences of non-sustainable development to every decision-maker's individual situation. Marketers might understand that their job depends on not losing one-third of customers to a competitor, who is offering a sustainable product alternative. The CEO might feel threatened by an immense drop in company reputation that can only be fixed by making people perceive his company as a sustainable business. Many individuals might even have caught a grasp of the planetary urgency to move towards sustainable development and will not necessarily need individual cues. Once the leader has achieved the buy-in of key decision-makers, it is time to (2) *"form a powerful guiding coalition"* in the form of a key change management team. Such a coalition requires individuals fulfilling manifold roles. There must be high-power individuals, knowledge-leaders, and representatives of the most important areas affected by the change. Members of the guiding coalition must also make a credible commitment to fulfill their function by channeling sufficient resources and personal effort to the sustainable business transformation. Next, the guiding coalition, informed by a broader stakeholder dialog, must (3) *"create a vision"* for the transformation, which in the best case conveys both the sense of urgency and contents of the sustainability shift. General Electric's *Ecomagination* (General Electric, 2012) or Marks and Spencer's "Plan A - Because there is no plan B" (Marks and Spencer, 2012) visions are excellent examples.

During the following *implementation phase* the first step is to broadly and credibly (4) *"communicate the vision"* of a sustainable business. The main goal is to motivate not only employees, but also other internal and external stakeholders to do their part in the transformation. In the communication process, it is crucial that the vision is communicated personally by the company's highest leaders and, by each employee's superior not only once, but periodically. Employees must understand that the sustainability transformation is there to last. Once employees and broader stakeholders are motivated to contribute to the shift, the task is to provide them with the necessary tools and power to make a difference. (5) *"Empowering others to act"* may involve activities such as assigning paid work time, allocating budgets or complete job profiles to work on the change and to install communication channels, committees and temporary institutions that provide an infrastructure to make a difference. Once employees are able to and work on transforming the organization, it is crucially important to make them see and feel the progress made towards becoming a sustainable business. (6) *"Planning for and creating short-term wins"* aims at providing employees with a sense of achievement that increases motivation and fuels future efforts. In order to credibly communicate those wins, it is important to have started into the implementation phase with clear and measurable indicators that can be used to communicate tangible improvements.

During the *maintenance and consolidation phase* companies should build on the first results that were achieved during implementation to (7) *consolidate improvements and create still more change*. Only when the first wave of change management activities can be translated into a medium to long-run priority activity can the goal of becoming a responsible and sustainable business be reached. Companies might define best practices and create working groups with the task to transfer new approaches to scalable results. At the last stage, the salient task is to (8) *institutionalize new approaches*, to anchor them in the organization's institutional structure. Institutionalization might consist of the creation of job positions, centers, hotlines, periodical events, and budgets exclusively dedicated to responsible business. Institutionalization might also include periodic sustainability reports, sustainability scorecards, and the inclusion of sustainability-related indicators into every employee's performance evaluation as common good practices.

Those eight steps to organizational change towards responsible business provide a crude cooking recipe, which needs to be refined by extensive practice and customized to each company's peculiarities. As in any good cooking recipe, all steps are important. Leaving out just one step will inevitably be detrimental to the overall result. Many change initiatives towards sustainable business fail as early as the preparation stage, when, for instance, they do not establish a sense of urgency. Others make the mistake of thinking the change is done with implementation and do not ensure the maintenance; the business falls back into old unsustainable patterns.

Watch out, PUMA charging...what exactly?

The sneaker and sportswear company PUMA has been in the headlines for its creative and progressive responsible business conduct in 2010. The company's CEO Jochen Zeitz called it "a transformative year (...) in many ways" and explicitly refers to the next stage of the company's sustainability strategy (Puma, 2011a). Did the company actually follow the change management process? Let's go step-by-step:

(1) Urgency: PUMA states that "we feel the one can't go without the other. Sustainability is a necessary lifestyle and not a luxury anymore and is therefore central to our long-term future–not only for PUMA's business success, but also for the environment upon which we all rely. Sustainability is key to PUMA's long-term progress as much as Sport and Lifestyle are part of the essence of our brand" (Puma, 2011a, p. 7).

(2) Coalition: Responsible business leadership at PUMA involves the company's CEO, support from the company's majority shareholder, the French PPR (other labels include Gucci and Yves Saint Laurent) group's sustainability team, and external experts (Liggett, 2011).

(3) Vision: The company's vision/mission statement, renewed in 2008, reads as follows: "Our mission to be the world's most desirable and sustainable Sportslifestyle company is driven by the 4Keys: Fair, Honest, Positive and Creative that guide our work on a daily basis" (Puma, 2011a, p. 14).

(4) Communication: The mission mentioned under the last point as being the company's mainstream mission, centrally including sustainability is communicated constantly throughout internal and external communication channels

(5) Enablers: PUMA states: "PUMA is committed to living these Keys and is focused on empowering employees and suppliers on all levels to take action towards our collective sustainable goals–ultimately helping to provide an authentic and informed customer experience" (Puma, 2011a, p. 14). An excellent example for practice implementation of this enabling purpose is the close collaboration with suppliers and the measures following, which enable consumers to consume more sustainably.

(6) Wins: The years 2010 and 2011 brought a series of sustainability wins for PUMA, consisting of impressive developments towards responsible business, which constantly reinforced stakeholders' faith in the overall sustainability efforts of the company. In April 2010, PUMA launched its highly innovative new shoe package design, substituting the classic shoe box and plastic bag, by a re-usable design, that uses "65 percent less cardboard, has no laminated printing, no tissue paper, takes up less space and weighs less in shipping" (Gould, 2010). The company's 2010 annual report innovatively included an environmental-profit-loss account, including water and CO_2 footprints, not only in PUMA, but also of several tiers of suppliers, a worldwide novelty that made history (Puma, 2011b). Early in 2011 the

company announced it will launch biodegradable products, promising to revolutionize the waste impact of the "recycling nightmare" sneakers (Chua, 2011).

(7) Consolidation: It seems like PUMA is able to keep innovating top-notch responsible management activities. This is very likely a sign that responsible business has become a part of the company's culture. PUMA now has to show that it also is able to use the managerial activity to create real-life results for business, society, and the environment.

(8) Institutionalization: The company has long been creating institutions and reinforcing their sustainability performance. Examples include the code of ethics and code of conduct for both employees and suppliers, the company-wide sustainability scorecard, and the mother company PPR's "Creative Sustainability Lab" with an annual budget of US$14.1 million (Liggett, 2011).

There is no doubt that PUMA's transformative efforts have gone a long way in establishing the company as a leader in responsible management practices, but is the company truly on the way to becoming a sustainable business? Based on the company's vision ("the world's most sustainable Sportslifestyle company"), PUMA takes a best-in-class approach to evaluate their sustainability performance relative to industry peers. The company seems to be successful in the parameters of this strategy, being ranked as the most sustainable company in its industry by the Dow Jones Sustainability Index in 2010. The goals set in the company's so-called long-run sustainability strategy 2010-2015 are absolute goals, not relative to competitor performance (Puma, 2011a). But where is PUMA going afterwards? What is the final goal? What does a sustainable company mean in the sports and lifestyle industry? What is the long-run motivation and development strategy for becoming a sustainable or even restorative business? How could such goals possibly go in accordance with the company's aggressive global expansion plans?

Change towards sustainable business cannot only be conducted as a top-down process, where high-level management decides, and lower hierarchies follow. Involving stakeholders on all hierarchy levels, inside and outside the company is imperative to developing business responsible in all its stakeholder relations and sustainable in its impact. As Figure 23.4 illustrates, a high-level management-driven *top-down* change strategy is just one of many change approaches that, in the optimum case, each do their part in effecting change throughout the company. A so-called *bottom-up* change strategy is driven by momentum from the lower hierarchical levels of the company and has strong similarities to the grassroots activism introduced before. *Nuclei* strategies consist of many "cells" of change that effect change in their sphere of influence. Nuclei can be located on any hierarchical level. The *wedge* change strategy broadly targets middle managers and enables them to become change agents. For change towards sustainable business, it is important to complement those internal change initiatives by an *outside-in* change strategy that allows external organizational stakeholders to participate in change. Also, an *inside-out* change strategy where company representatives act as change agents in the company's environment is complementarily important. Changing a company towards sustainable business requires extensive adaptation of its environment,

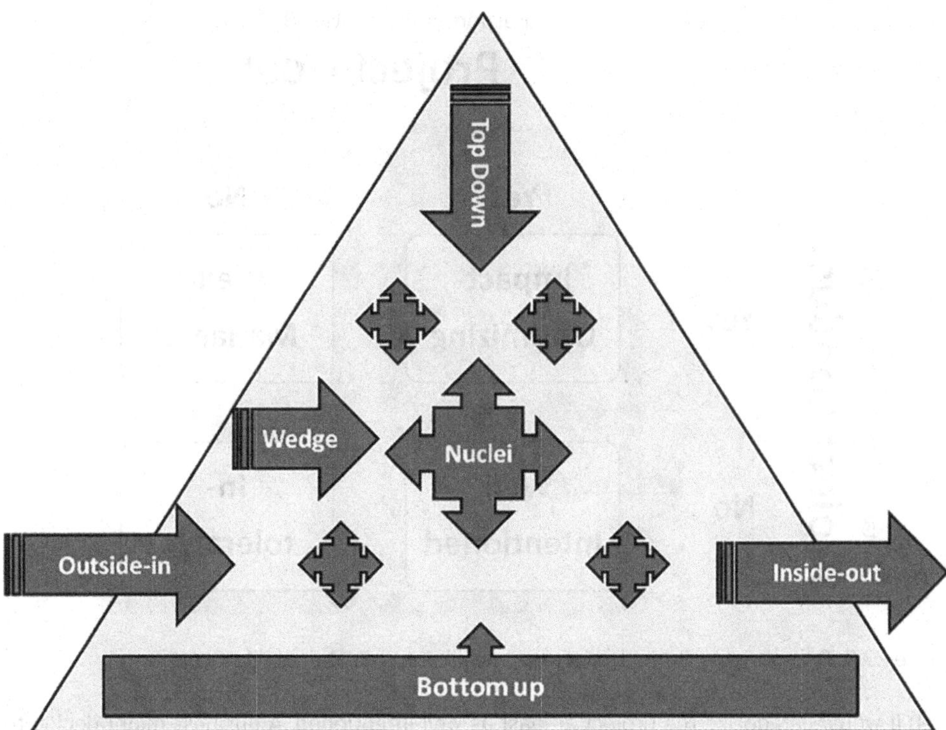

Figure 23.4 Complementary Change Approaches.

Adapted from Vaupel (2011)

from technological change to legislation, to a shift in mindset in external stakeholders such as customers and suppliers. The goal is to embed the sustainable company in a sustainable system, which enhances stability and resilience of both.

Responsible Project Management for Sustainable Business

Changing a business towards sustainability involves a myriad of sub-projects, each important for the overall process. Projects are different from the overall task to sustainable development in that they are usually much shorter in their time to completion, and they are reduced in scale and scope as they focus on sub-goals of the overall change to sustainable business (Wysocki, 2009). As illustrated in Figure 23.5 such projects can be classified by the primary project goal (related or unrelated to responsibility and sustainability of the company) and by the impact made throughout the conduct of the project (responsible/sustainable or not). For instance, if a cosmetics business develops a new skin cream, the primary goal of the project would not be related to the responsibility or sustainability of the business. Nevertheless, the project conduct might or might not involve animal testing as an environmentally irresponsible practice. If it does, for a responsible business, it would be a non-tolerable project. If it does not, from a responsibility point of view, it would fall into the project category well-managed. If another company used animal testing (conduct) to create a cure for a deadly disease (project

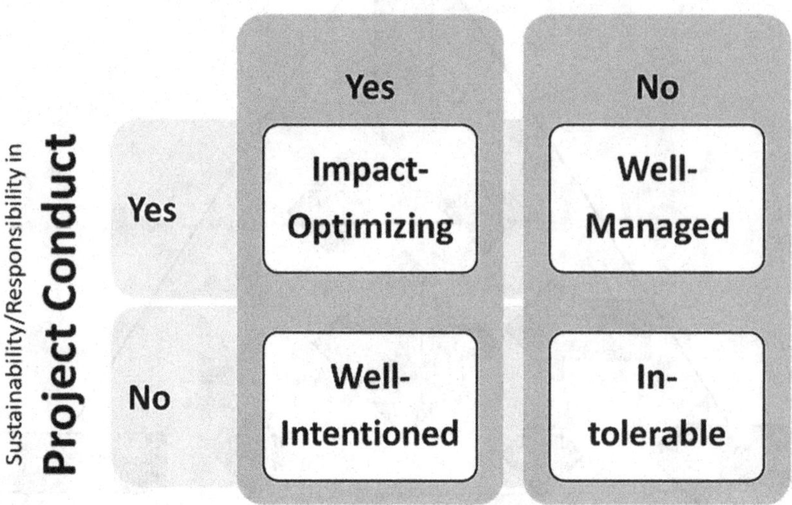

Figure 23.5 Categorizing Projects by Responsibility and Sustainability Criteria.

goal) it would categorize the project at least as well-intentioned. A business might decide to conduct well-intentioned projects with a negative conduct for the sake of the final goal. The preferable project type in responsible business is the impact optimizing project, which pursues the goal of furthering the company's responsibility and sustainability, while honoring both also through the project conduct. In the following section we will refer to responsible and sustainable projects management when talking about the project's conduct, and about responsibility and sustainability projects when referring to the primary project goals.

Managing projects in responsible business and for sustainable business requires some consideration that is different from mainstream project management. The following description will provide a quick primer for sustainability project management throughout the three phases of project management, preparation, implementation, and closing of a project as illustrated in Figure 23.6 (Wysocki, 2009).

The project *preparation phase* determines the potential *scope and quality* of project goals. For sustainability projects, the project quality especially needs to include concise indicators

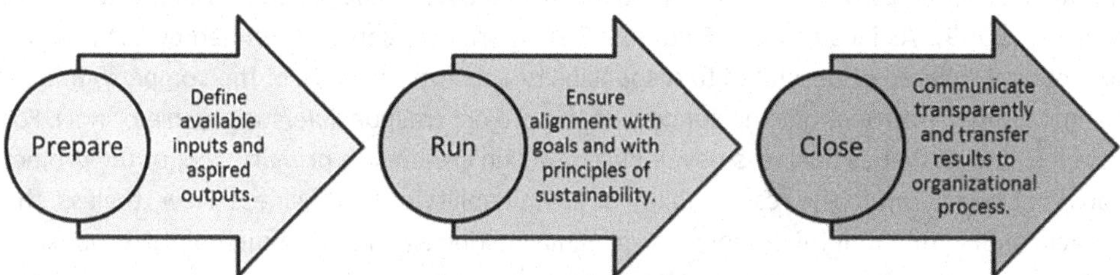

Figure 23.6 Stages and Tasks of Responsible Project Management.

for not only economic, but also social and environmental project results. The main goal at this preparation stage is to harmonize inputs available and desired outputs. Three main inputs need to be considered when preparing a sustainability project. First, the *time* to completion of the project must be defined. In this context it is important to make sure that even when projects are of rather short duration, a lasting impact contributing to long-run sustainability is achieved. Second, the economic *cost* of the project needs to be defined and reflected by assigning an ensured budget for all three phases of the project management process. Cost items to be considered specifically in a sustainability project include costs of assessing social and environmental impacts, costs of skill development for sustainability, or of hiring external experts. Third, defining *resources* available might require the hiring of external staff and the reduction of responsibilities for internal staff assigned to the project, including office space assignments, and also communication channels and power given to the sustainability project. As sustainability projects often involve far-reaching change, which may in turn create resistance, the assignation of sufficient resources to ensure change in spite of adversity is even more important than in mainstream projects. An important intangible resource is to know exactly where the project goal is ranked on the company's priority list (Wysocki, 2009) (Figure 23.7).

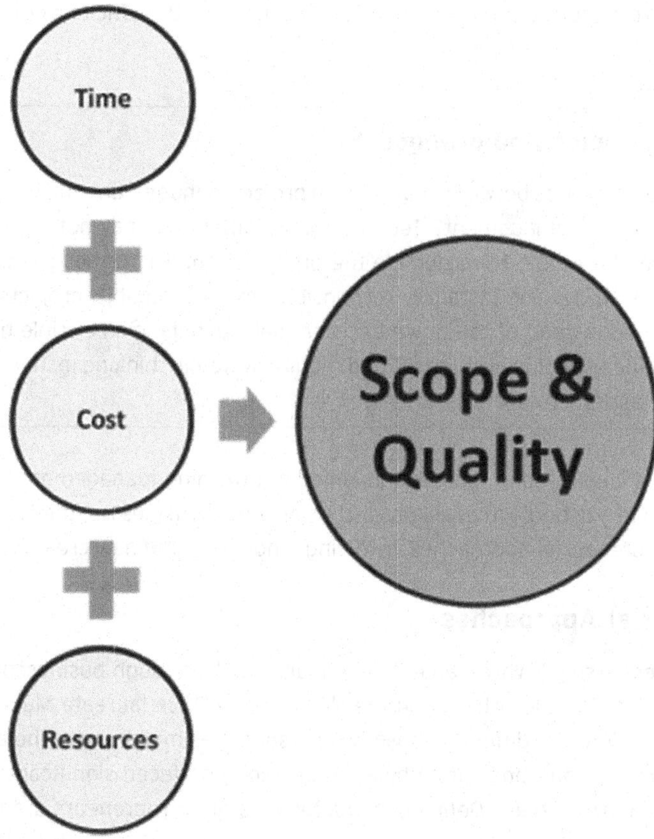

Figure 23.7 Inputs and Outputs of Projects.

To *run* a sustainability project, the most important task that is different from mainstream projects is ensuring the *alignment* of all details of the project implementation with values related to responsibility and sustainable development. Negative social and environmental impacts have to be avoided. In sustainability projects, neglecting "details" of sustainability in project conduct may cost valuable credibility among internal collaborators and the external public. Simple bad practice examples are excessive printing (paper footprint), traveling (CO_2), socially irresponsible work conditions (e.g. overtime, contractual issues, hiring and firing), or the morally irresponsible behavior of employees (e.g. mobbing or embezzlement). The implementation of the project must be a role-model for the practices of what the sustainable business is expected to become.

To *close* the sustainability project, special attention needs to be paid to transparently communicating the process and assuring that project results can be translated into change towards sustainability on an organizational level. *Communicating* the process, unlike mainstream projects, requires establishing extensive stakeholder dialog, including all groups related to project conduct and outcomes, and organization both internally and externally. Projects in this last stage require *reconnecting* to the organizational change task of becoming a sustainable business. Project outcomes can be used to communicate short term wins stimulating the organizational change process (stage six of the organizational change process). Learning from project conduct can be used to increase the efficiency of other sustainability projects.

Comparing apples and oranges

So, what's the difference between mainstream project management and responsible or sustainable project management? Technically, the difference may not be too big, and might not even be visible from outside the organization. It is rather the details that matter on the inside. For instance, responsible and sustainable projects focus on consensus-based instead of top-down decision making, balancing a triple bottom line with a pre-defined set of project goals, and require systemic thinking instead of a linear one-outcome approach (Griffiths, 2007).

While approaches illustrated in this section aimed at providing management tools, to effect a transformation of existing activities, products, and whole businesses, the following section focuses on entrepreneurial approaches, involving innovation and new creation.

Entrepreneurial Approaches

What is entrepreneurship? Who is an entrepreneur? What do tough businesspeople such as Facebook founder Mark Zuckerberg and the Nobel Peace Prize laureate Muhammad Yunus have in common? However different those two personalities might seem; the answer is simple: They both tackled an opportunity by an innovation and faced significant complexity in bringing their venture to scale. *Defining characteristics* of entrepreneurs are exactly those:

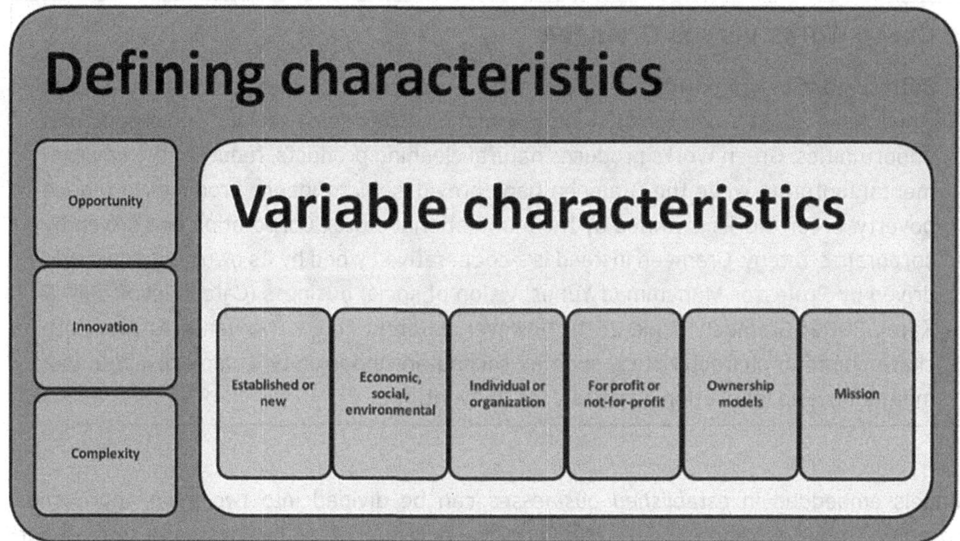

Figure 23.8 Characteristics of Entrepreneurship.

Entrepreneurs perceive an *opportunity*, which does not necessarily need to be an economic opportunity. In the case of Muhammad Yunus, it was a social opportunity, to improve the life of poor women. Both entrepreneurs then seized the opportunity by an *innovation*, Zuckerberg with his new social networking technology, Yunus with micro-credit. The ambiguity involved in creating and implementing innovation, automatically brings about more *complexity* than would typically be encountered in a management activity. Figure 23.8 summarizes those three defining characteristics of entrepreneurship but adds another list of variable characteristics.

It is the *variable characteristics* that open up an endless nexus of opportunities for entrepreneurship to contribute to creating sustainable businesses and furthering sustainable development. The *motivation* of entrepreneurial ventures might be either classic economic value creation or social and environmental causes that contribute to sustainable development, or possibly a mixture of both. The realized *impact* of a venture might be a social, environmental and/or economic one. The *profit* motivation might be either for-profit, or a not-for-profit focus, re-investing profits made into the venture. The *origin or point of departure* of ventures might be from an established business or NGO or from an individual person. The entrepreneurial models resulting from the different combinations of those characteristics can be summarized into two broad types; models embedded in an existing business, and models for the creation of new business. The *ownership* of an enterprise might lie with single individuals, a broad group (e.g. a cooperative), or it might be owned by an established company or other type of organization.

Green Works versus Grameen

Both companies are entrepreneurial ventures, which could not be more different, but which have at least one major thing in common. They seize social or environmental opportunities. Green Works produces natural cleaning products, reducing the environmental footprint, while the Grameen Bank provides microfinance products to reduce poverty. Green Works is owned by the multinational Clorox Corporation and driven by corporate strategy. Grameen instead is a cooperative owned by its own customers and driven by Professor Muhammad Yunus' vision of social business (Cate, Pilosof, Tait, & Karol, 2009; Grameen Bank, 2011). However different those two ventures are, both share common characteristics, such as seizing an opportunity, complexity in implementation, and innovation as a basis for the venture.

Models embedded in *established businesses* can be divided into two main approaches. *Corporate social entrepreneurship* highlights the potential of big businesses to seize opportunities for sustainable development in a powerful and scalable way (Austin & Reficco, 2009). *Social intrapreneurship*, instead of focusing on the overall business as entrepreneurial actor, sheds light on individuals and their potential to make a difference for sustainable development. These individuals seize opportunities from the inside of a business and use the organization as a vehicle for a social cause (SustainAbility, 2008).

Several other entrepreneurial approaches for business creation have been proposed. **Social entrepreneurship** is associated with creating a business, which has a social cause as its main motivation, and/or which with its main business activity creates considerable social value. *Environmental entrepreneurship* is very similar but focuses on creating solutions to environmental causes. *Sustainability entrepreneurship*, sometimes called "sustainopreneurship" takes a more holistic perspective and aims at furthering one or a set of causes contributing to sustainable development (Abrahamsson, 2007).

Managing Entrepreneurship for Business Creation

The *stages of entrepreneurial ventures* are the same in mainstream entrepreneurship as they are in entrepreneurship for sustainable business (see Figure 23.9). After an initial conceptual phase, of planning the venture, and an implementation and growth phase, the enterprise may reach the last phase, maturity. Throughout these stages, typical tasks and necessary competences of the entrepreneur are changing considerably. Crucial to long-run success is that entrepreneurs are able to either make the transition from one stage to the other themselves, or to hire people with the skills needed. The majority of enterprises never reach maturity. Understanding those different phases is vital for the venture. In the following paragraphs, readers will find a brief characterization of each stage, with special focus on peculiarities of entrepreneurship to create a sustainable business.

During the *concept stage* the entrepreneur's main task is to identify a social, environmental, or economic opportunity and to develop a detailed strategy for seizing this opportunity. Problems become opportunities when one holds the key to a solution (or mitigation).

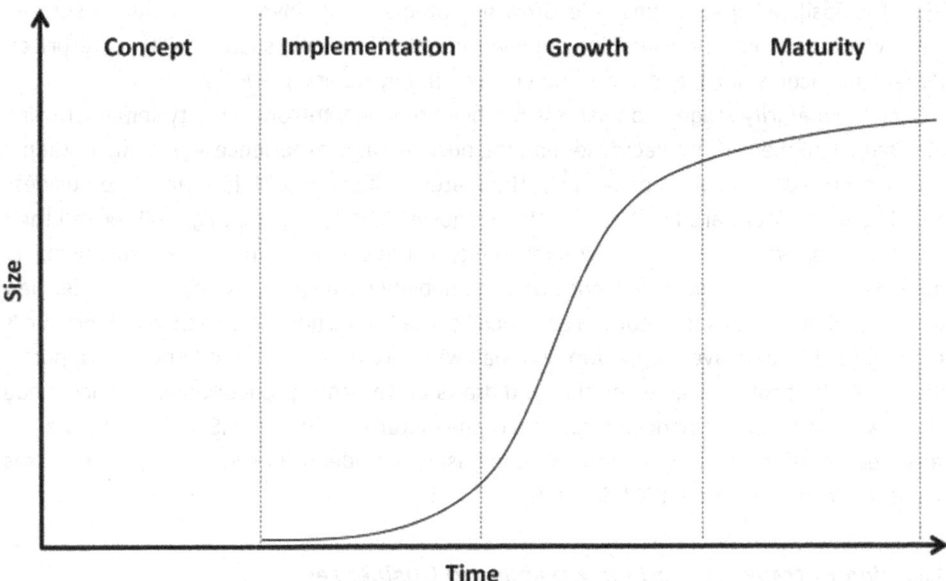

Figure 23.9 Stages of Entrepreneurial Ventures.

The more pressing the problem and the higher the economic potential of the venture, the more likely it is that there will be somebody financing the entrepreneurial solution. Social and environmental entrepreneurs often use sustainable innovations (see R&D section of the chapter on support functions) as a means to seize opportunities. Unlike mainstream entrepreneurial ventures, the main source of income for sustainability ventures does not necessarily have to be customers. Such ventures appeal to a greater group of stakeholders, due to the social good and environmental benefits created. Governmental institutions, foundations, interest groups, and other stakeholders are often interested in supporting in cash and in kind. Any of the social, environmental, and economic issues related to sustainable development has the potential to be an excellent basis for a venture. The conceptual stage is usually centered on the development of a **business model** (see strategic management chapter), the basic logic of the venture, and a **business plan**, which illustrates all aspects of the planned venture in detail. Both business model and business plan are key reference documents for managing venture implementation and for finding support.

During the *implementation* phase, the business plan is transferred into practice. During the conceptual stage, the main entrepreneurial skill was vision and the ability to plan. For implementation, entrepreneurs must be able to show endurance, flexibility, and a strong will to succeed. First, implementing a venture is an iterative process, which necessarily comes with highs and lows. A main challenge is financial survival, while productive processes and structures are subject to constant change until a working system is implemented. Acquisition of customers and standardization of processes are key activities during the implementation process.

The *growth* stage involves drafting a strategy for bringing the business to scale. Apart from financial advantages of company size (e.g. economies of scale), there is a striking argument for quick growth in ventures for sustainable development. The bigger the venture, the bigger the positive impact to be made. Growth strategies might involve, for instance, sustainability venture capital, partnerships between corporations and sustainability enterprises, mergers and acquisitions, and social franchising (Tracey & Jarvis, 2007).

Once the *maturity* stage of a business has been reached, the opportunity, initially fueling quick growth of the venture decreases and the business may experience less growth, stagnation, or even a decline. The challenge in the maturity stage is to define what the business should become. There are two basic strategic choices. Entrepreneurs might either sell their business or innovate to seize a new opportunity. A critical factor in selling a sustainability enterprise is to ensure the persistence of sustainability performance and values under new ownership. Role-model social enterprises such as The Body Shop (sold to L'Oreal) and Burt's Bees (sold to Clorox) have gone down this road with mixed results. Identifying new opportunities might be another viable solution and draws on the entrepreneurial experience made before, while leveraging financial resources of the mature venture. TOMS shoes, for instance, translated its successful buy-one-donate-one business model from shoes to now eyeglasses as a new stream of revenue (TOMS, 2012).

Managing Entrepreneurship in Established Businesses

Entrepreneurial approaches to managing responsible business are a promising tool for effecting dynamic change. Such approaches can be subdivided into **corporate social entrepreneurship (CSE)**, which highlights the potential of big corporations to proactively bring about scalable solutions to major sustainability challenges (Austin & Reficco, 2009). The tool of social intrapreneurship or more generalized sustainability intrapreneurship instead focuses on how individuals can solve sustainability issues from the inside of a company, deploying the entrepreneurial process and mindset. Both tools exist in a mutually reinforcing relationship. A company needs Intrapreneurs to develop CSE and a company-wide CSE approach may create a favorable environment for single individuals' intrapreneurial activity for sustainable development.

The intrapreneurial animal kingdom

The *SustainAbility Guide for Entrepreneurs* compares social intrapreneurs with four kinds of inhabitants of the animal kingdom, each contributing different important characteristics to the intrapreneurial task. Intrapreneurs must be like donkeys with the capability of carrying the weight of transformation and being able to plod along with it. Intrapreneurs must also be like giraffes, with the head in the clouds (vision to create sustainable business), and feet firmly on the ground to step over obstacles when encountered. Social Intrapreneurs must endure times of loneliness like a wolf, in the times that their vision of responsible businesses is not shared. Finally, intrapreneurs must be like beavers, reshaping their company's landscape, creating lakes and cascades of opportunities for the business to be changed (SustainAbility, 2008).

The company-internal venture process basically runs through the same stages as external ventures described above and therefore does not require repeated illustration. A factor that deserves heightened attention, though, is the *collaboration strategies* for sustainable intrapreneurship. A guide for social Intrapreneurship proposes three salient strategies to facilitate intrapreneurship, which companies might deploy alternatively, depending on business and venture structure and purpose (SustainAbility, 2008).

- The *island* strategy allows intrapreneurs to work isolated from the main business while being on the payroll. Isolation supports the development of innovative, disruptive or even radical ideas, far away from the usual business rationale, values, and practices. Island strategies require special attention to re-integrating outputs into the mainstream business.
- A *bridges* strategy provides the intrapreneur with great autonomy, while allowing for some well-defined links for support. Bridges might be communication channels, access to resources and information. The bridges strategy facilitates entrepreneurial outcomes with direct support of the main business.
- The *symbiosis* strategy aims at locating the intrapreneurial venture right inside the main business, in order to facilitate as many synergetic relationships as possible.

Exercises

A. KNOW

Use the below multiple-choice questions to test your knowledge. Each answer may be wrong or right and there may be zero to four right or wrong answers per question:

1. The different types of sustainable, responsible, and irresponsible business...
   a. ...include an ideal type of sustainable business, that is restoratively sustainable (it even replenishes the Earth' natural capital). Additionally, such a business would work to multiply its good practices among other actors.
   b. ...is a basic classification, involving the businesses' overall impact (from defensive to civic) and stage of implementation (from very negative to very positive).
   c. ...are related to the business' mode of implementation, describing the different ways a business might manage its responsibilities. A business, for instance, might be defensive (fiercely defending its stakeholders and their claims) or strategic (implementing a strategy to avoid responsibilities).
   d. ...is related to a business' overall sustainability performance. Companies can be classified as unsustainable (exceeding the global footprint), sustainable (exactly matching the planet's resource limits), or a restorative business (replenishing the planet's natural resources).
2. Leaders...
   a. ...be it managers, and entrepreneurs all fulfill the same function.
   b. ...for sustainable business primarily need a clear vision of what the sustainable business should look like and the power to lead others towards this vision.

c. ...of a sustainable business might, at the same time, also be managers or entrepreneurs.
d. ...for sustainable business are always representatives of high-level management.

3. Change management...
   a. ...to create a responsible business is always impeded by very high resistance to change by employees.
   b. ...has been described by Kotter's tool of eight steps for successful change management.
   c. ...ends with the last step of enabling others to act upon the vision of sustainable business. From this point on, change will happen automatically.
   d. ...includes creating institutional structures such as budgets, fixed job positions, and official communication channels.

4. Entrepreneurship...
   a. ...always refers to creating a new business.
   b. ...among its defining characteristics has complexity, innovation, and seizing opportunities for profit.
   c. ...can contribute to sustainable business both from the inside of an established business, and through the establishment of new businesses.
   d. ...in both of its forms, social entrepreneurship and corporate social entrepreneurship aims at the creation of new businesses with a social purpose.

5. Entrepreneurship in established businesses...
   a. ...may take the form of corporate social entrepreneurship, where single individuals try to change the company from the inside towards more sustainable ways.
   b. ...may take the form of intrapreneurship.
   c. ...is related to the island strategy, where social intrapreneurs work in isolation from the main business to develop sustainability ideas for it.
   d. ...may be achieved by the symbiosis strategy, where businesses aim to establish a mutually reinforcing relationship with a social or environmental cause.

6. Entrepreneurship for creating new sustainable businesses...
   a. ...can be divided into four main stages, ranging from the conceptualization of the venture to its maturity.
   b. ...once entered into the growth stage finds the possibility of magnifying its positive social and environmental impact.
   c. ...in the maturity stage includes the example of The Body Shop, which was sold to the company L'Oreal.
   d. ...the only possible action during the maturity stage of an entrepreneurial sustainable business venture is to sell it off.

B. THINK

Imagine you were in charge of managing the transformation towards sustainability of a company of your choice. Envision what (radical) changes the company would have to go through to become truly sustainable. Then prepare a change management plan according to Kotter's change management process.

C. DO

Conduct a mini project for sustainability, responsibility, or ethics either in your private or professional life.

D. RELATE

Observe the activity of someone you find "outside" (for instance, inside a shop, an office, a restaurant, etc.) and identify one practice/activity that appears to be unsustainable to you. Engage the person in a conversation, aiming to both develop an appreciation for why the person does this practice and trying to find more sustainable alternatives. Make sure the person does not feel bothered, pushed, or cornered through the conversation.

E. BE

How do you feel about the possibility of being an entrepreneur? Could you imagine launching and managing an enterprise? Do you feel motivated to drive new ventures, possibly inside an existing company? Are you generally motivated to innovate and pursue opportunities?

Feedback

A. KNOW

Feedback 1

a. Right: Such a business combines the civic stage of business responsibility with a restoratively sustainable output.
b. Wrong: The description of overall impact and stage of implementation have been switched.
c. Wrong: The descriptions given for defensive and strategic are wrong.
d. Right: This is a correct description of the different levels of outputs in relationship to sustainability.

Feedback 2

a. Wrong: While leaders fulfill the function of leading the transformation of an existing business, mangers manage sustainability throughout different business functions, and entrepreneurs create sustainable organizations and activities.

b. Right: Vision and power to lead are the two main characteristics necessary for leadership.

c. Right: Leaders may emerge in all parts of the company.

d. Wrong: Leaders can arise on all levels of the organizational hierarchy.

Feedback 3

a. Wrong: Employees have been found to mostly be very supportive to change for becoming a responsible business.

b. Right: Kotter's change management process perfectly summarizes the main elements of making large-scale change in a company happen.

c. Wrong: Enabling others to act is not the last step of change management.

d. Right: The institutionalization of the change, making it stick, is part of the change management process.

Feedback 4

a. Wrong: For instance, intrapreneurship and corporate social entrepreneurship describe entrepreneurial activities from inside an established business.

b. Wrong: Opportunities do not necessarily have to be for-profit opportunities, but can also be of a social, environmental, or ethical nature.

c. Right: Entrepreneurial ventures may be either embedded into an established business, or lead to the creation of a new business.

d. Wrong: Corporate social entrepreneurship uses existing businesses to tackle a social opportunity.

Feedback 5

a. Wrong: Corporate social entrepreneurship does not refer to changing the business, but to using the business as a vehicle to seize external opportunities to make a difference for society and the environment.

b. Right: Intrapreneurship and corporate social entrepreneurship are both types of entrepreneurships located in an established business.

c. Right: The island strategy helps to create entrepreneurial solutions without the restrictions resulting from being deeply embedded into the company.

d. Wrong: The symbiosis strategy refers to a constellation in which intrapreneurs work in close union with the business, in order to achieve synergies.

Feedback 6:

a. Right: The entrepreneurial venture runs through distinct stages, often requiring different entrepreneurial competences per stage.

b. Right: The impact of a business is multiplied through growth and expansion.

c. Right: The Bodyshop being sold to L'Oreal is an example of what might happen with sustainability ventures in the maturity stage.
d. Wrong: An alternative action is to newly enter into the entrepreneurial process and use the established business to seize another sustainability opportunity.

B. THINK

Level	*Strategic thinking*	*Notes*
+	Vision and change process appear deeply thought-through and very feasible.	
=	A basic vision has been developed, based on the current position of the company, and a basic change process has been outlined.	
–	No or a little feasible change management plan has been developed.	

C. DO

Level	*Project management skills*	*Notes*
+	Project has come to successful closure both from a mainstream management and from a responsible management perspective.	
=	Project has been planned and initiated based on solid project management skills both from a mainstream management and from a responsible management perspective.	
–	Project has been planned superficially or conducted feebly.	

D. RELATE

Level	*Engaging in meaningful conversation*	*Notes*
+	Conversation has led to learning for sustainability in one or both conversation partners.	
=	Conversation has taken place but did not prove meaningful to learning for sustainability or to improving practices.	
–	Conversation has not happened.	

E. BE

Level	*Entrepreneurial motivation*	*Notes*
+	Strong motivation towards entrepreneurial action.	
=	No strong drive towards being entrepreneurial, but it is a possibility.	
–	Being entrepreneurial does not appear attractive, or even "scary".	

References

Abrahamsson, A. (2007). Sustainopreneurship: Business with a cause. *Master Thesis*. Växjö University.

Amazonia Expeditions. (2011). *Amazonia Expeditions*. Retrieved January 18, 2012, from https://www.perujungle.com/

Austin, J., & Reficco, E. (2009). Corporate social entrepreneurship. *HBS Working Paper Series, 101*(9).

Cate, S. N., Pilosof, D., Tait, R., & Karol, R. (2009). *The story of Clorox Green Works TM – In designing a winning green product experience Clorox cracks the code*. Retrieved May 28, 2011, from Product Development Consulting, Inc.: https://www.pdcinc.com/files/Visions_March09.pdf

Chua, J. M. (2011). *Will Puma be launching compostable clothing, footwear next?* Retrieved January 28, 2012, from Ecouterre: https://www.ecouterre.com/will-puma-be-launching-compostable-clothing-footwear-next/

Corporate Responsibility Magazine. (2010). *The state of corporate responsibility: Setting the baseline*. Retrieved September 4, 2011, from Corporate Responsibility Magazine: www.thecro.com

Die Welt. (2012, January 7). Die Bank in der die Zeit stehengeblieben ist [The bank in which the time stands still]. *Die Welt*, p. 21.

Dogdson, M., Gann, D., & Salter, A. (2006). The role of technology in the shift towards open innovation: The case of Procter & Gamble. *R&D Management, 36*(3), 333-346.

Donham, W. B. (1927). The social significance of business. *Harvard Business Review, 5*(4), 406–419.

Donham, W. B. (1929). Business ethics: A general survey. *Harvard Business Review, 7*(4), 385–394.

Ferdig, M. A. (2007). Sustainability leadership: Co-creating a sustainable future. *Journal of Change Management, 7*(1), 25–35.

General Electric. (2012). *Ecomagination*. Retrieved January 19, 2012, from https://www.ecomagination.com/

Gill, R. (2003). Change management - Or change leadership? *Journal of Change Management, 3*(4), 307–318.

Gould, D. (2010). *Puma re-invents the shoe box*. Retrieved January 28, 2012, from PSFK: https://www.psfk.com/2010/04/puma-reinvents-the-shoe-box.html#ixzz1kmhUMMw7

Grameen Bank. (2011). *Breaking the vicious cycle of proverty through microcredit*. Retrieved October 15, 2011, from Grameen Bank: https://www.grameen-info.org/index.php?option=com_content&task=view&id=25&Itemid=128

Griffiths, K. (2007). Project sustainability management in infrastructure projects. *2nd International Conference on Sustainability Engineering and Science*. Auckland.

Kotter, J. P. (1995). Leading change: Why transformation efforts fail. *Harvard Business Review, 73*(2), 59–67.

Lacey, P., Cooper, T., Hayward, R., & Neuberger, L. (2010). *A new era of sustainability: UN global compact-Accenture CEO study 2010*. Accenture Institute for High Performance.

Liggett, B. (2011). *PPR group launches sustainability scheme for Gucci, Yves Saint Laurent, Stelle Mc Cartney brands*. Retrieved January 28, 2012, from Ecouterre: https://www.ecouterre.com/ppr-group-launches-sustainability-scheme-for-gucci-yves-saint-laurent-stella-mccartney-brands/

Marks and Spencer. (2012). *Plan A doing the right thing*. Retrieved January 19, 2012, from https://plana.marksandspencer.com/

Puma. (2011a). *Annual report 2010*. Herzogenaurach.

Puma. (2011b). *Puma completes first environmental profit and loss account which values impacts at € 145 million*. Retrieved January 27, 2012, from https://about.puma.com/en/newsroom/news/puma-completes-first-environmental-profit-and-loss-account-which-values-impacts-eu

SustainAbility. (2008). *The social intrapreneur: A field guide for corporate change makers*. London: SustainAbility.

TOMS. (2012). *TOMS eyeglasses*. Retrieved March 2, 2012, from https://www.toms.com/eyewear/

Tracey, P., & Jarvis, O. (2007). Toward a theory of social venture franchising. *Entrepreneurship Theory and Practice*, *31*(5), 667–685.

UmweltBank. (2012). *Geschichte und Philosophie [History and philosophy]*. Retrieved January 27, 2012, from https://www.umweltbank.de/umweltbank/index_geschichte.html

Vaupel, M. (2011). *Sustainable leadership. Course sustainable leadership*. Berlin: Institute of Corporate Responsibility Management.

Visser, W. (2008). CSR change agents: Experts, facilitators, catalysts and activists. In *CSR inspiration series, No. 2*.

Visser, W. (2010). *The age of responsibility: CSR 2.0 and the new DNA of business*. Chichester: Wiley.

Wysocki, R. K. (2009). *Effective project management*. Indianapolis: Wiley.

Zadeck, S. (2004). The path to corporate social responsibility. *Harvard Business Review*, *82*, 125–132.

24 Systemic Change

Isn't it enough to change people and businesses, and the economic system will change itself? Or will it be "visionary companies" that lead to a "creative destruction of industries" to create a more sustainable overall system? (Hart & Millstein, 1999). It might be more complex than either one of these two ideas. According to systems theory, a system is more than the sum of its elements. Systems have complex internal mechanisms that in the case of the economic system can either impede or facilitate the sustainable development of the system as a whole. Businesses and individuals in their various roles are parts of the system. The economic system is like a machine that needs right handling to produce the aspired output: sustainability. This chapter on systemic change aims to show the rusty wheels that need oiling and helps to spot the right buttons and levers to speed up the process. However, systems are much more complex than most machines and they are typically not designed like machines, but naturally grown. So, even the most intelligent attempts at systems change might not succeed due to this immense complexity. Accordingly, systems change will always have rely on repeated attempts and trial and error learning.

The first section highlights salient characteristics of the economic system sabotaging sustainable development. It shows why the economic system is highly resilient to change. The section also illustrates alternative approaches to traditional capitalism. The second section focuses on transforming sub-systems, such as supply chains, industries, or local industry clusters towards sustainability, as one potential strategy to make the overall system more sustainable. The third section takes the opposite approach. Instead of changing sub-systems, it shows how to change the basic conditions and rules of the overall system through public policy instruments.

Changing Systems

A different economic reality

"Economic growth has been decoupled from ecosystem destruction and material consumption and re-coupled with sustainable economic development and societal well-being. Society has redefined the notion of prosperity and successful lifestyles, as well as the bases of profit and loss, progress and value creation to include more long-term considerations such as environmental impacts and personal and societal well-being" Vision 2050 (WBCSD, 2010, p. 6).

DOI: 10.4324/9781003544074-32

The economic system has been blamed extensively as the root cause of unsustainable development. But isn't the system a mere outcome of the actions of single individuals and organizations? Will it therefore change automatically if people live sustainable lifestyles and when companies become sustainable businesses? In the following section, an economic system will be considered an entity in its own right, with the whole being more than the pure sum of its elements. System elements may be either considerable impediments or leverage for achieving sustainable development.

From GNP to GNH for a happy planet

In 2005 the government of Bhutan decided to measure national success by happiness, not merely by economic measures. The Gross Happiness Index (GNH) was born. It covers nine indicators from Indicator 1, psychological well-being to Indictator 9, time use and happiness (Centre for Bhutan Studies, 2012). The links between economic wealth and happiness are weak. So maybe a move from countries' GDP focus to a GNH focus might be the starting point for economic systems that truly serve peoples' well-being instead of their moneybags. The Happy Planet Index, illustrates the "(...) relative efficiency with which nations convert the planet's natural resources into long and happy lives for their citizens" or in short: "How much happiness do we get for the resources we use?" (New Econmics Foundation, 2012).

What is an **economic system** and what are its mechanisms? An economic system consists of interconnected mechanisms and institutions aimed at the allocation of resources to the creation and use of goods and services. A **sustainable economic system** would lead to an allocation that is socially, environmentally and economically sustainable in the long run. Reaching this goal implies that, on the one hand, elements of the system are sustainable and that, on the other hand, the connections between the elements are also sustainable. As illustrated in Figure 24.1, elements of the economic system are businesses, governmental and non-governmental organizations, and individuals as consumers and employees. Connections of the economic system's elements consist of moving flows, such as financial, material, and information flows. Elements of the economic system are also connected by comparatively stable relations such as legal responsibilities, norms, values, culture of the system, and power structures. Also, the system is not closed. It requires inputs (such as natural resources, labor, and ideas) from the outside and delivers outputs (such as waste, welfare, and innovation) to society and the environment. As will be illustrated in the following sections, it may be the system-inherent stable relations, that dominantly characterize a system. Accordingly, these relations need to be understood, influenced and changed, to reach the final goal of a resilient and sustainable economic system.

Characteristics worth Changing

Is the current global economic system that bad for sustainable development? What needs to be changed and how do those changes relate to sustainable business? The unsustainability of the current economic system and its historic roots have been described in the first

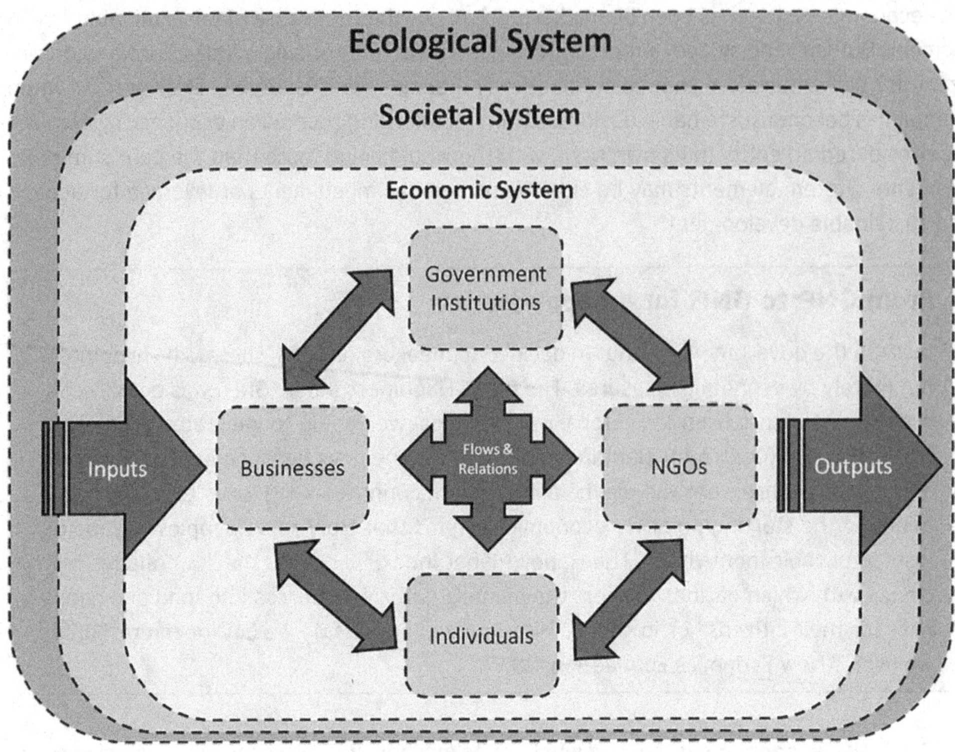

Figure 24.1 Elements, Interrelations, and Embeddedness of the Economic System.

chapters of this book. In the following we will focus on three of the root characteristics of the economic system's unsustainability.

- The **growth imperative** applies to most economic activity inside the system. More is better. Growing a country's GDP, company's revenue, an individual's income and consumption are just a few examples. Economic growth comes with increased resource consumption, further exceeding the planet's ecological resource-production and waste absorption capacity. The required systemic change is to *degrow* its planetary impact to a sustainable level of 1, while providing the growing world population with employment, goods and services necessary for living a decent life.
- Neglecting **external effects** creates unsustainable situations as outcomes of the market mechanism. Imagine a fast-food company that would be forced to pay the direct and future environmental cost of destroying the Brazilian rainforest for meat production. This company, then, would need to include this cost in the price of a hamburger, which would then increase to US$50 per piece. Imagine the average price of a car at US$70,000. Those figures are fiction but might not be very far from reality. The change task is to *internalize external costs* in market mechanisms, such as pricing, so that many unsustainable decisions will not be made anymore.

- An old-established prejudice is that social **inequality** is built in through the global economic system, that it will always make the rich richer and the poor poorer. That statement might not be completely true. Analyzing recent global developments (e.g. HDI/MDG Reports) it seems like there is a sluggish development towards more global wealth equality. Nevertheless, it does not go fast enough. The change task is to create a global economic system that re-distributes wealth and includes helping the poor in their economic activity and its benefits. This new feature of the economic system might be the remedy to unsustainable population growth as has been illustrated in the chapter on individual change.

Economics primer

To understand the intersection between the economic, social, and environmental systems, a basic working knowledge of central concepts related to economics is crucial. Those concepts can be subdivided into the field of environmental economics (intersection of economy and environment) and welfare economics (intersection of economy and society). Links in the following text connect the theoretical concepts to their applications throughout this book.

The field of **Environmental Economics** comprises a wide variety of economic analysis instruments mostly related to idea of external effects (externalities). The idea of differentiating between *externalities and internalities* was introduced by Pigou (1920/2005) who promoted the idea that any action has a private cost (internal cost) to the actor and a social cost, incurred by society in general (external cost). External costs may be social, but are primarily environmental, such as pollution through a factory's wastewater that is channeled into a river. A so-called *Pigouvian tax* aims at a reduction of negative internalities by *internalizing* them. Companies are forced to pay a tax, which corresponds to the size of the social costs (externality) created by their activity. As the company incurs this cost, decision-makers have an incentive to avoid the cost of the tax and to reduce the creation of externalities. The opposite case is a *Pigouvian subsidy*, where companies are rewarded for the positive externalities created. For instance, the European Union strongly subsidizes renewable energies. This type of internalization provides companies with the incentive to create more positive externalities.

Another way to control externalities is the introduction of a *market for externalities*, where external effects are traded. The idea has its roots in the work of Coase, who proposed that an introduction of property rights for externalities would lead to an efficient overall number of externalities. For instance, in the European Union Emissions Trading Scheme, companies are given the right to emit a certain maximum amount of CO_2. This right becomes a property of the company, which it can then sell as any other property. Those property rights could then be traded in a market. The *Coase Theorem* states that such a market will create efficient results, no matter the initial allocation of property rights for externalities, in the absence of transaction costs (Coase, 1960).

The frequently used term *tragedy of the commons* has been coined by Hardin (1968) and is widely used in environmental economics. Thus, property rights could lie either with polluters or with the party injured by the negative externalities. *A commons good* is a resource that is *non-excludable*, meaning that anybody can use it. It is also *rival*, meaning that the more people use it, the less value can be extracted by each user. An example for such a good is fish stock in the open sea or air quality. Nobody can be kept from using those, but the more they are used, the less there is left for each user. The tragedy of the commons describes the human behavior, which leads to the over-usage and final depletion of any commons good, a mechanism which has largely fueled today's unsustainability.

Environmental economics should not be confused with **ecological economics**, which integrates most concepts mentioned before, but criticizes long-established economic thinking in many ways. While environmental economics conform to neo-classic economic theory, ecological economics is rather "revolutionary", in the sense that it rejects many traditional assumptions of neo-classic economics such as the growth paradigm, and the understanding of humans as an egoist, rational homo economicus (Daly & Farley, 2004; Farley, Erickson, & Daly, 2005).

Welfare economics describes the relationship between economic factors and social welfare. Subject of study is the interrelationship between the overall wealth created by economic activity and how it is distributed. A picture illustrating those two main criteria of welfare economics is that of a cake at a birthday party. The cake should be as big as possible (wealth creation), and the slices should be evenly enjoyed by all attendees (distribution). *Pareto efficiency* is the criterion by which to achieve maximum wealth creation. The Italian Economist Pareto (Samuelson & Nordhaus, 2005) defined efficiency of economic activity by a situation where no individual involved in a certain situation can improve his or her personal welfare without decreasing the welfare of somebody else. This reasoning is called the *Pareto criterion*. This criterion is in line with the Utilitarian Greatest Happiness Principles, which aims to maximize the utility and happiness of all parties involved. The Pareto criterion falls short in assessing equality or the well-being of individuals inside a group of people (e.g. a country), as it cannot analyze the distribution of wealth in a country.

The *Lorenz curve* (Lorenz, 1905) instead describes how equally wealth is distributed inside a given group, by plotting the percentage of households on x axis and the percentage of total income on the y axis. The reality in countries lies somewhere between two extremes, the most unequal distribution, where one individual owns all wealth and the most equal situation, where every person has exactly the same wealth. The *Gini coefficient* is a quantitative measurement of income inequality based on the Lorenz curve (Todaro & Smith, 2006). One important question related to income distribution and economic growth is how income equality develops along with economic development. The *Kuznets curve* (Kuznets, 1955) is an instrument that describes the relationships between economic development and income equality as an inverted U curve (see chapter on individual change). At the beginning of economic development, the possibilities for single individuals to make a fortune (e.g. as an entrepreneur) are big, which increases inequality. The more advanced and mature economic development is, the smaller are those possibilities and the stronger are the mechanisms redistributing fortunes made before. The Kuznets curve has found application in both welfare and environmental economics, where it is applied on the amount of pollution depending on the degree of economic development.

System Resilience

The Kyoto protocol, the United Nations Global Compact, and the Global Reporting Initiative, are just some of the manifold powerful global initiatives for making the economic system more sustainable. In spite of all their effort, change is at best sluggish. One characteristic of systems is to display certain resilience. Resilience means that a system will be prone to "bounce back" to its original state after an external force has ceased to influence the system. Resilient systems are highly resistant to change. Resilience in a sustainable system would be very desirable. However, in an unsustainable system, resilience leads to a stable reproduction of the same unsustainable system features. In order to change the economic system to more sustainable ways system resilience needs to be understood and overcome. There are three main reasons for why systems are hard to change.

- Systems exist in a dynamic **equilibrium**. The relationships existing between system elements stabilize the status quo. Examples are values, such as the profit imperative or an irresponsible business morality, which the system reinforces internally.
- Systems experience **path dependence**, meaning that past decisions influence the decisions to be made in the present and future. For instance, the past development of a carbon-based economic system goes against current efforts to re-orient the economic system towards alternative energy sources. In the most drastic case, the path to carbon dependence can even lead to a lock-in situation, where decision-makers are completely dependent on one alternative. For instance, the enormous initial investment and complicated, time-intensive switch-off procedure for a nuclear power plant has led to a technological lock-in of nuclear energy production.
- **Power** reinforces power. Powerful players with unsustainable impact use their power to prevent or slow down changes towards costly or even business-harming sustainability initiatives and regulation. Lobbying by the tobacco and petroleum industries, or the agricultural sector in Europe, has led to considerable delays in tackling those industries' sustainability issues.

System resilience is not always bad news. A sustainable economic system, once created, may develop self-reinforcing resilience which stabilizes the new system. The crucial question is if it will be possible to change the planetary socio-economic system before it is too late? The set of convergent crises illustrated in the chapter on the status quo of the planet leads us to assume that it is likely that we will not be able to avert such a global mega-catastrophe. To make the best of it, even if the global community cannot avert the crises, it is very likely to de-stabilize the unsustainable economic system to a degree that it can be changed or rebuilt in more sustainable ways afterwards. If systems are very resilient, the most reliable force for system change is an external shock.

Symptoms of resilience and setback?

Is our economic system really moving towards sustainability? Anecdotal evidence exists that cast doubt that it can happen. For instance, in October 2011, British Petroleum regained permission for drilling additional oil wells in the Gulf of Mexico, not long after having caused the death of eleven workers and a spill of millions of barrels of crude oil into the gulf of Mexico, one of the biggest environmental disasters of the new millennium (Krauss, 2011). Can the system become sustainable, if we easily renew the "social license to operate" of a company that has failed so hard? In December of the same year, Canada pulled out of the Kyoto protocol, because the country could not meet the goals set (The Guardian, 2011). Is a sustainable economic system possible if we allow an important player to easily bail out of such a crucial commitment? In December 2011, Brazil changed its forest code, which now reduces the protection of the Amazon rainforest drastically in comparison to the former legislation that was substituted (Black, 2011). Can we reach a sustainable economic system, if we accept such drawbacks in legislation?

Envisioning a New System

New economic systems would need to solve at least the three core issues of the old system as illustrated above. There are several approaches for alternative economic systems that have been developed in the past, each addressing a different sustainability issue of the economic system. The *ecological economics* approach aims at creating a market system that deeply includes environmental factors, such as external environmental effects to reach environmental sustainability of the overall system (Common & Perrings, 1992). *Eco-socialism* attributes current social and environmental problems to the capitalist system and globalization and aims at tackling the problems by common ownership of the people and providing general access to the commons (Pepper, 1993). The *social market economy* model, which had been created in Germany, takes a middle stance between socialism and laissez-faire economic liberalism by assuring strong social welfare through state intervention, with minimum possible obstruction of market mechanisms.

Masters of transition

The "New Economics Foundation" in collaboration with the business school at the University of Plymouth, offers a unique master program that exclusively focuses on topics related to achieving a transition towards a sustainable economic system (Schumacher College, 2012).

The optimum sustainable economic system might not have been envisioned yet, but whatever system it should become in the end, it is important to start change into the right

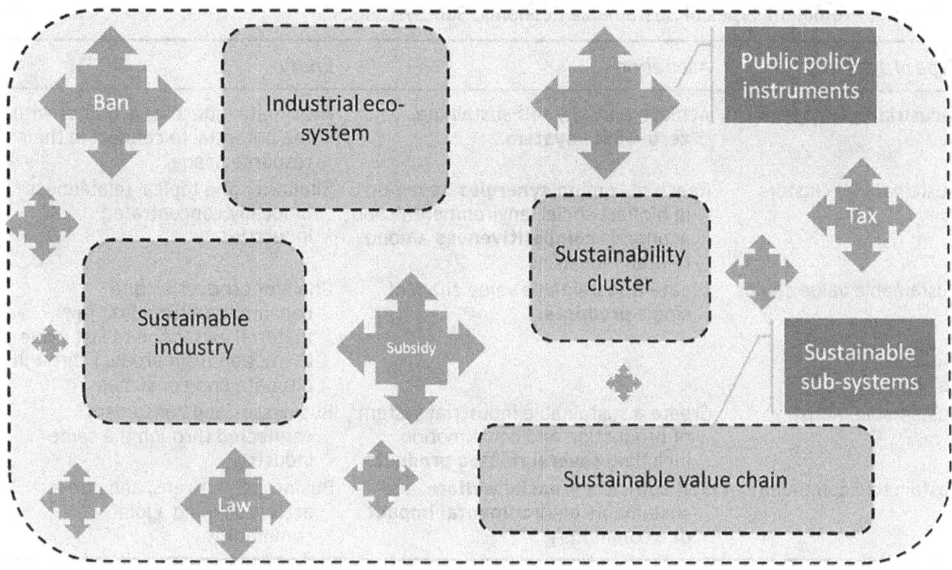

Figure 24.2 Approaches to System Change for Sustainability.

direction right now. In the following two sections, two approaches (see Figure 24.2) to changing the system will be illustrated. The first approach is to create sustainable sub-systems through sustainability clusters, industrial eco-systems, or sustainable supply chains and industries. Those sustainable sub-systems are supposed to change the system from within. The second approach is to leverage public policy instruments to change the rules of the overall system, which then should force the system to adapt to more sustainability. Both approaches are complementary.

Transforming Sub-Systems

The WBCSD (2010, p. 70), in the Vision 2050 strategy for creating a sustainable economic system, states that "our findings suggest that there is no simple, single path, but rather the need to design, build and transform complex systems". Such a bottom-up strategy for changing the overall system is to change economic sub-systems in a first step. In a second step, the task is to grow those sub-systems in number and size to transform the overall system from within. In preceding chapters such sub-systems have been introduced on several occasions. For instance, the sustainable value chain model can be considered a system of economic actors, coordinating their efforts to become jointly sustainable. Also, sustainable living communities, touched upon in the chapter on individual change can be considered socio-economic sub-systems of social, economic, and political actors, coordinating their varied contributions to make the community system sustainable. Industry sustainability initiatives, such as the Extractions Industry Transparency Initiative (see chapter on norms) are aimed at changing industries. Table 24.1 summarizes prominent types of sustainable economic sub-systems, their aspirations, the basic unit of analysis (entity), and examples of prominent practice implementation of each respective system. In the following two sections, the two specific forms of industrial eco-systems and sustainability clusters will be illustrated with greater detail.

Table 24.1 Prominent Types of Sustainable Economic Sub-Systems

Type of system	*Aspiration*	*Entity*
Industrial eco-systems	Achieve a locally self-sustaining, **zero-waste system**.	Proximate industrial activities with the potential to connect in their resource usage.
Sustainability clusters	Reach maximum **synergies**, resulting in highest social, environmental, and economic **competitiveness** among related industries.	Similarity and topical relatedness of locally concentrated industries.
Sustainable value chains	Create a sustainable value chain of single **products**.	Chain of production and consumption from first raw-material extraction to last value extraction from product through ultimate end-consumer.
Sustainable industry	Create a sustainable industrial system of production and consumption including **several related products**.	Businesses and consumers connected through the same industry.
Sustainable community	Self-sufficiency, **social welfare**, and sustainable **environmental impact** of a community.	Businesses, citizens, and public actors, shaping a joint community.

Industrial Eco-Systems

Doesn't the term *industrial ecology* sound like an oxymoron, like an inherent contradiction? Often industry and ecology are perceived as opposing concepts (Erkmann, 1997). Interestingly, the conjunction of those two terms has given birth to the industrial ecology approach and its main practice application, so-called **industrial eco-systems**. An industrial eco-system takes natural eco-systems as an ideal model for industrial organization. Natural eco-systems are usually very resilient and, more importantly, exist in a restoratively sustainable manner; they are circular (perfect recycling), do not create any waste, and are usually able to work with solar power as the only energy input. Even if we would be able to create only a few of those features in an industrial eco-system, we would have solved many of the environmental problems caused by economic activity.

The highest art of biomimicry

Biomimicry (Benyus, 2002) describes the process of inspiring human design by designs in nature. Biomimicry has been applied in many ways, mainly for the development of products. Examples are high-speed trains whose aerodynamic characteristics were inspired by the head of sharks; hammers that absorb shocks like woodpeckers; and buildings that "breathe" like termite hives. Biomimicry is ready for the next stage. The big task of biomimicry is now to not only copy single features of inhabitants of eco-systems, but to design the whole economic system and its sub-systems following the principles of eco-systems. Such systems would restore capital instead of using it up, eliminate waste, and work in the resource limits of the planet. Reaching such a state of the economic system can be called "the highest art of biomimicry".

Figure 24.3 illustrates the basic mechanisms and aspirations of an industrial eco-system. In steep contrast to global approaches, such as sustainable supply chain management,

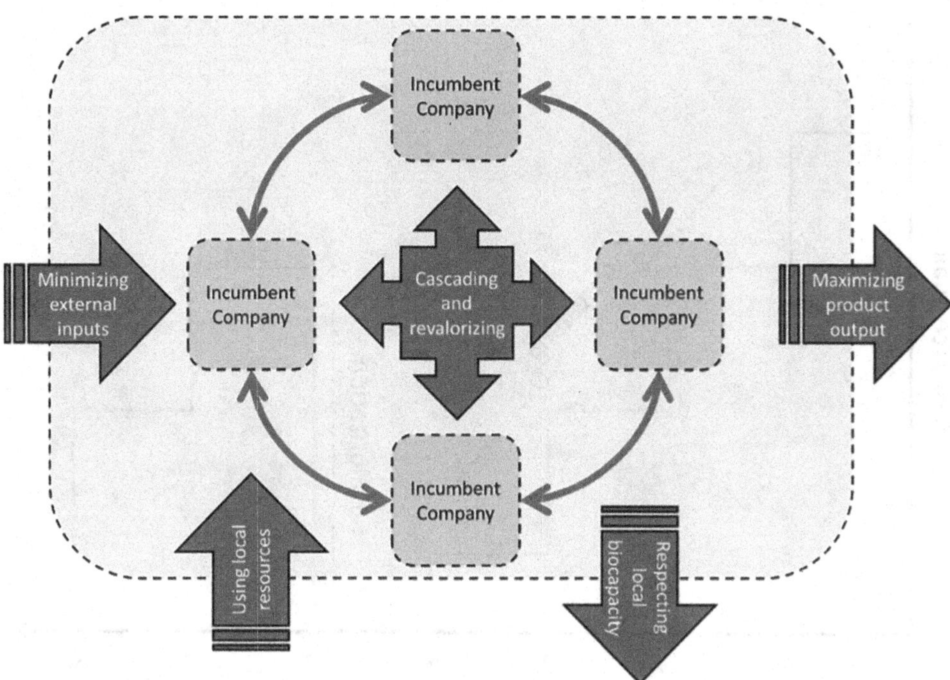

Figure 24.3 Industrial Eco-System Mechanisms.

industrial eco-systems, exist on a local scale with strong local connections. Thus, industrial eco-systems aim at using as many local resources as sustainably possible to avoid environmental impact from transportation. Industrial eco-systems also aim at minimizing waste to a degree that can be absorbed and processed by the surrounding local eco-system. How can those goals be achieved? Companies forming part of an industrial eco-system develop close links to reach a maximum efficiency in the joint resource usage (**eco-efficiency**).

The two main mechanisms for achieving such efficient resource usage are cascading and revalorizing (see Figure 24.4). **Resource cascading** refers to using the same resource several times until all value has been extracted and it is useless. The underlying pattern is to use the resource first for the process that requires the highest resource quality. After every usage the quality of the resource is reduced and can only be used for processes that suffice with a lower resource quality. For instance, a coal (higher quality resource) energy plant might capture the fly ash left over after burning (lower quality resource) and sell it to a gypsum factory, which uses the ash as main input for its production process. An interesting example for energy cascading can be developed from the same coal energy plant. Coal (highest energy intensity) is used to heat up water in the power generation process. The heated water (lower energy intensity) can be used for fish farming, which requires warm water all the year round. One can imagine this process as a cascade, where the highest-level quality is the highest level of the cascade, and the material flows down to lower-quality usage. While cascading only involves the allocation of lower quality resources to the right use, **revalorization** involves an additional process increasing the resources quality: Its value. For instance, paper will be usable again after recycling. Waste-water after being treated can be used for many purposes.

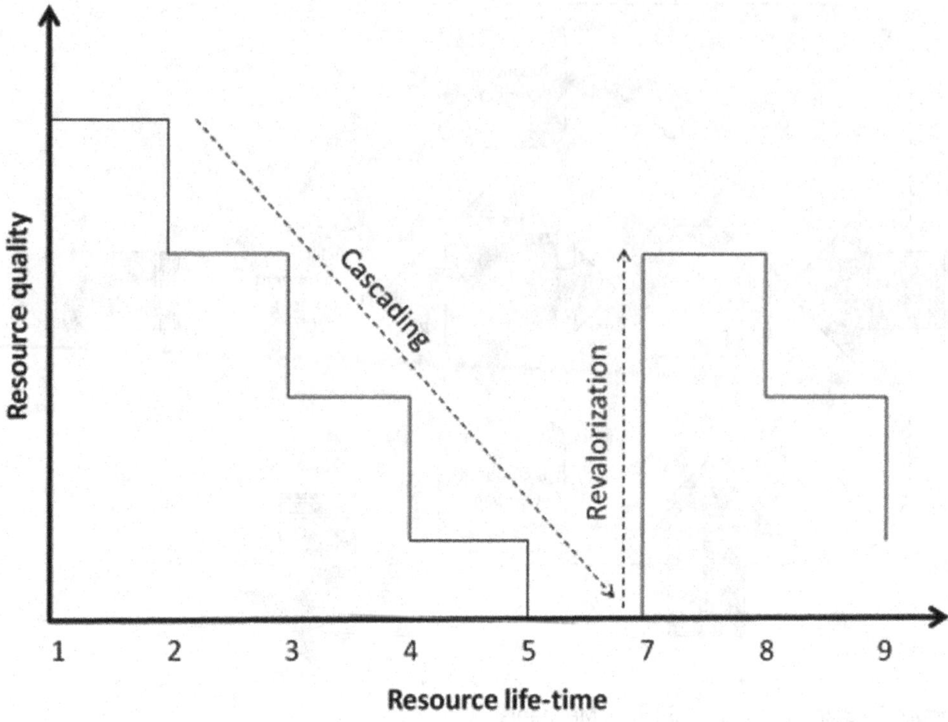

Figure 24.4 Resource Cascading and Revalorization.

Cascading and revalorization have the strongest effect when combined. Therefore, an industrial eco-system needs an industrial diversity of different companies, facilitating both processes cascading and revalorization.

Industrial eco-systems have a strong environment focus, but social value creation is barely considered. A future task to be accomplished is to include the social dimension of sustainability into industrial eco-system development. The cascading and revalorization concepts have the potential to be broadened to cover social resource quality. Industrial ecology in many of its elements is positively aligned with economic value creation, as increased efficiency in environmental resources usually saves companies money.

Growing an industrial eco-system

The industrial eco-system in the Danish city of Kalundborg, approximately 100 kilometers from Copenhagen, has been described as role-model for an industrial ecosystem. The system began forming in 1976 when local farmers started using sludge from the town's Novo Nordisk plant as fertilizers (Ehrenfeld & Gertler, 1997). By 2007 the industrial eco-system involved efficiency-increasing relationships between more than 20 companies. Examples are the exchange of heat, water, fly-ash, biomass, all waste for the emitter, but valuable input for the receiver. The industrial eco-system is intimately connected with the local natural eco-systems of a fjord and lake (Cervantes, 2007).

Sustainability Clusters

Business **clusters** "(...) are geographic concentrations of interconnected companies, specialized suppliers, service providers, firms in related industries, and associated institutions (e.g., universities, standards agencies, trade associations) in a particular field that compete but also cooperate" (Porter, 2000). A finance cluster exists in London, a technology and entrepreneurship cluster in California's Silicon Valley and a diamond cluster in Rotterdam. Clusters support companies and whole regions in developing a competitive advantage. Clusters hone a business' capability to excel in the market by, for instance, providing strong local competition, highly specialized cluster suppliers, and sophisticated local customers (Porter, 1990). Developing clusters for responsible business is a promising approach, as it involves a direct economic benefit from the increased cluster competitiveness, for both companies and governments involved. Simultaneously, developing *responsible business clusters* also increases social and environmental competitiveness, jointly creating a responsible competitiveness (Zadeck, 2006). We can differ between the following two types of clusters centrally important for responsible business:

- In **sustainability industry clusters**, companies and industries, group locally around a certain sustainability cause, technology, or industry type. A sustainability consulting cluster exists in London, an eco-tourism cluster in the Mexican Riviera Maya, and a sustainable construction cluster around Lisbon.
- **Responsible mainstream clusters** involve old-established industries that have taken a local turn towards sustainability. The Southern-German car-manufacturing cluster has developed to a center of excellence for sustainable mobility with companies such as BMW, Audi and Mercedes shaping a local, more sustainable cluster infrastructure.

Figure 24.5 illustrates the elements of a cluster from a company perspective. According to Porter, important *cluster elements* defining the size and quality of a cluster are factor conditions (inputs), demand conditions (customers), a network of related and supporting industries, and the context for firm strategy and rivalry (local laws regulations, incentives, values) (Porter, 1990; Porter & Kramer, 2006). To learn how to create responsible business clusters, it is crucial to understand how each of the cluster elements may contribute to the sustainability of the overall cluster.

- **Factor conditions** or inputs determine the functionality of sustainability cluster in many ways. In order for a food retailer to offer locally grown organic food, this very special input needs to be available locally at competitive prices. For a responsible mainstream businesses cluster, it is crucial to find local human resources trained in responsible business.
- **Demand conditions** for responsible business clusters are related to customers' attitudes towards responsible business and the degree of sustainability of customers' lifestyles and consumption patterns. When migrating from a mainstream to a responsible business cluster, it is increasingly important to perceive business stakeholders as an important "customer" of the social and environmental component of responsible business performance. Demanding stakeholders are an additional condition serving to hone responsible business competitiveness.

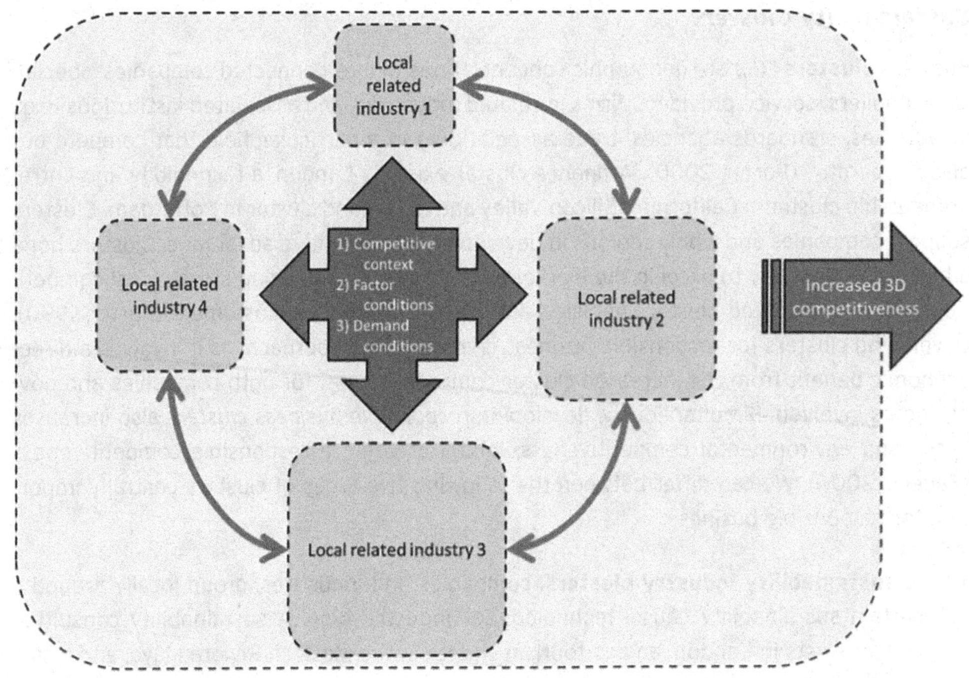

Figure 24.5 Structure of a Sustainability Cluster System.

- **Related and supporting industries** and businesses include both antagonistic and cooperative relationships. Imagine a green tech cluster. It might for instance be highly beneficial for a solar technology company inside such a cluster to have direct competitors near, and maybe even to engage in coopetition (cooperation with competitors), to join forces for new technology development, industry initiatives or lobbying. At the same time, the same cluster might include companies developing alternative engine technologies. It might be possible to develop a joint solar-powered engine technology, or to jointly invest into battery-systems, which are critical to both industries.
- The **Context for strategy and rivalry** for responsible business clusters consists of local public policy factors, such as subsidies for responsible businesses, or high taxation for irresponsible firms. Also, the context factor of local business culture can have a strong influence.

Which city is the world's responsible business capital?

London would definitely be in the list of potential candidates. The city is home to some of the most powerful consultancies and centers dealing with responsible business, such as the consultancy SustainAbility or AccountAbility. London is also the world's main hub for socially responsible investments, home to the FTSE4Good Index, a stock exchange, listing responsible enterprises. The UK's public policy structure is reportedly the world's most advanced (Bertelsmann Stiftung; GTZ, 2007), which gives additional incentives for responsible business development. Both customers and providers in the UK are used to and highly sensitive to social and environmental issues. A wide variety of highly renowned universities such as the London School of Economics, and Oxford and Cambridge Universities have developed specialized degree programs for related topics and fuel the city's thriving sustainability industries with highly qualified human resources. All the points mentioned contribute to a beneficial climate for the development of clusters related to sustainability and responsibility. No wonder that the city now has become the breeding ground for one of the world's most advanced responsible business clusters, the Green Enterprise District, which is aimed at showing "the world what the future should look like". This district accumulates businesses and organizations with a social or environmental purpose and provides the infrastructure for low carbon and waste elimination for those businesses (London Development Agency, 2010).

How to *build and grow* responsible business clusters? Zadeck (2006) lists many factors leading to the creation and fueling growth of such clusters, which are all routed in one or another of the cluster's elements mentioned above. Examples include stakeholder pressure (demand conditions), the statutory environment (context for strategy and environment), and business initiative (related and supporting industries). Once established, a healthy cluster tends to self-reinforce favorable conditions for its growth. A high concentration of similar, related enterprises and industries tends to attract a wider variety of specialized factor conditions and vice versa. As illustrated in Figure 24.6, to actively grow a cluster, organic growth processes are required, simultaneously improving all four cluster conditions. Increasingly, governments become active in creating the necessary context for responsible business cluster creation and growth. The following section will provide a quick overview on how public policies can create a favorable environment for not only responsible business clusters, but also a transition to a sustainable economic system.

The Role of Public Policy in Systems Change

While the preceding section has illustrated several ways of creating sustainable sub-systems of the overall economic system, this section focuses on changing the economic system's normative ("the rules of the game") infrastructure. Main *actors* in such infrastructure change are governments (e.g. the London municipality administration, Chinese government, European Union Commission), supra-governmental institutions (e.g. United Nations and World Bank) and NGOs with normative "soft" power (e.g. Global Reporting Initiative and the International Organization for Standardization). While traditionally only governments are seen as actors of public policies, we will take on a broader perspective. As a matter of fact, it is not only governments that are able to change the rules of the game, but also all of the other actors mentioned before. NGOs are increasingly able to be normative political actors of their own and make "world civic politics" (Wapner, 1995). Responsible business and the sustainability of the world economic system can be achieved by creating efficient institutions governing business conduct (Vanberg, 2007). Creating those institutions will be the primary

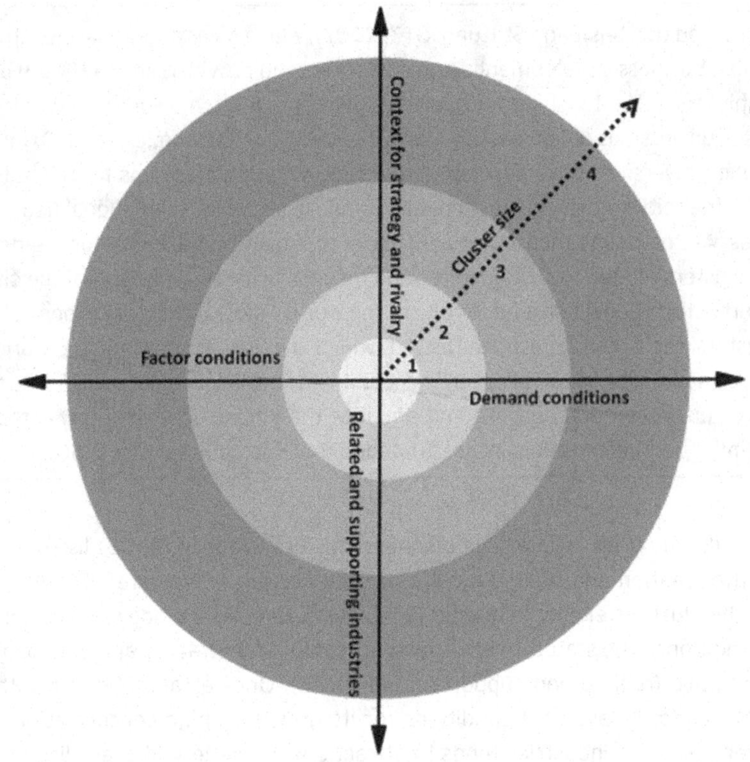

Figure 24.6 Cluster Growth.

Loosely based on Porter, 1990

goal to be achieved when designing **public policies** for sustainable world development. In the context of this book, the term public policies will serve as a wide umbrella term, including all policies for the creation of an institutional infrastructure, the rules of the game, for a sustainable economic system. Actors of those policies may be all the formerly mentioned political actors. Figure 24.7 illustrates the interconnection between policies and political actors for sustainable development.

Change of the economic system's normative context may be affected on the following four different levels, all of which include different interaction between the actors mentioned before. The goal of globally sustainable development is allocated on a *global policy level*. A global issue requires global policies to develop solutions. As there is no all-embracing, coherent global governance system, policies for sustainable development on a global level are fragmented and little binding. In absence of a global government, supra-national and global non-governmental institutions have taken the lead in developing global policies. The United Nations are leading, for instance, political efforts in poverty reduction and environmental protection. NGOs like the Global Reporting Initiative and the World Wildlife Fund press hard to achieve participation in and compliance with global standards of sustainable business and living. *Goals* for the institutionalization process on a global level are to both create a higher degree of coordination of efforts and to achieve a binding character.

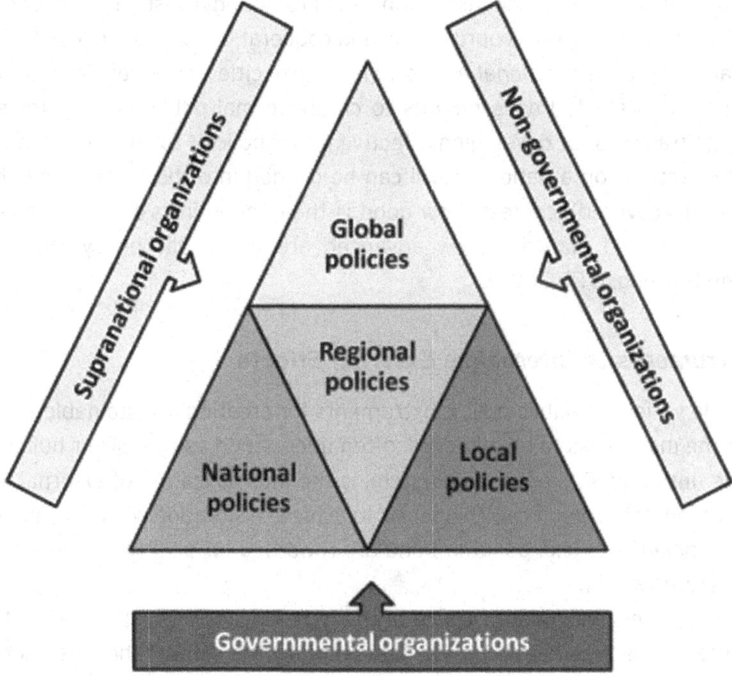

Figure 24.7 Policies and Political Actors for Sustainable Development.

A world government for sustainability?

Sustainable development, especially environmental issues do not know national borders. Global warming, water scarcity, ecosystem damage, and poverty are all problems that require resolute and legally binding actions on a global level. The topic of a potential world government has been both emphasized and criticized. Before the 1993 Rio conference, even voices of a potential conspiracy of the world's money elite to use the environmental topic to reach out for world-domination were heard. The Rio+20 congress in 2012 declared the strengthening of an "institutional framework for sustainable development" as one of the two main goals of the event (United Nations, 2012). Maybe the congress was another move towards a world government for sustainable development?

Regional policies for sustainable development aim at creating a sustainable economic system for major global regions such as Latin America or Europe. Due to differing levels of regional organization, regional policies differ greatly in their achievements for sustainable development. The European Union is a role-model for regional public policies for sustainable development with many policy packages, fostering sustainability clusters, technologies, and sustainable consumption. One prominent landmark document is titled "Making Europe a pole of excellence on CSR" (Commission of the European Communities, 2006). The foremost task for the development of public policies and institutions and promoting a sustainable economic system is to create higher-level regional coordination and cooperation for sustainable development.

The big advantage on a *national and local level* (e.g. cities, counties, federal state) is the increasing power of elected governments to create formal public policies for sustainable development. Strategies for developing effective public policies for the creation of sustainable economic systems on a national level can be divided into the three elements *contents* (what causes are covered), *context* (how good is the general infrastructure for sustainable economic system) and *maturity* (how advanced are the public policy measures taken) (Bertelsmann Stiftung; GTZ, 2007).

Policy Instruments to Internalize External Effects

There is a wide variety of public policy instruments for creating a sustainable economic system. One of the main tasks to be achieved, often understood as the "silver bullet" for bringing down the unsustainable economic system, is the internalization of external effects (see box on environmental economics). The goal is to achieve a situation where companies pay for negative external effects (e.g. pollution) and are rewarded for positive external effects they create (e.g. reforestation).

The following three instruments all aim at the internalization of external effects. They are of varying effectiveness and applicability, depending on the context they are used in. To better understand the underlying justifications and mechanisms have a look at the box environmental and welfare economics. The practice examples given for the three policy measures prohibition, taxation, and introduction of markets all refer to public policies related to air emissions, mostly in European Union and member states. The following policy instruments might serve to fulfill two basic purposes. First policy instruments are aimed at changing behavior towards a creation of less negative or more positive external effects. Second, the remediation effect of policy instruments is aimed at mitigating the negative consequences of external effects (e.g. to clean up pollution, or to pay the healthcare costs of affected individuals) or to reward the creators of positive externalities.

- **Prohibition and permission** are aimed at controlling negative external effects by eliminating the sources of the effects. Examples include the prohibition of socially and environmentally harmful products, production methods, or even whole industries. A weaker form of prohibition is to only provide permission to operate in the case of compliance with certain requirements that avoid or minimize negative environmental effects. Cars, for instance, only receive market access to the European Union if complying with emission standards. Many major European cities do not allow cars of non-residents into the city centers. Most types of factories do not receive a permission to operate if not applying up-to-date filter technologies.
- **Taxes and subsidies** are aimed at putting a price on negative externalities (taxes) and a reward on positive ones (subsidies). An example is the German eco-tax on fuels. The height of the tax or subsidy should in the optimum situation correspond to the exact size of the cost caused by the externality for two reasons. First, the externality is "internalized", meaning that the company pays the full price or receives the full benefit of its

actions. The other argument is that especially in the case of negative externalities, the harm done can be remediated through the tax income. Unfortunately, it is very difficult to define and attribute the complete and exact external costs and benefits to the actor causing them. Also, the tax income is often not explicitly and exclusively (if at all) dedicated to remediation efforts. Countries such as Denmark, the United Kingdom and Germany apply a so-called eco-tax on the use of energy to reduce related CO_2 emissions. Many countries, such as Japan offer eco-subsidies for fuel-efficient cars (Kim, 2011).

- **Introducing a market** on which external effects are traded is the least mature public policy instrument but has shown great potential and first tangible results. The mechanism is simple and follows the "cap and trade" principle. The government decides on the overall number of external effects (e.g. 500,000 tons of CO_2 emissions), the so-called cap. Then an allowance for a maximum number of external effects is distributed to the main polluters. If they pollute less than their allowed individual cap, they are allowed to trade the difference between actual emissions and allowed emissions to other companies that exceeded their emission limit. These companies can literally buy the right to pollute. However, the overall pollution level would never exceed the initial cap. Regulators may consider subsequently reducing the overall cap in order to reduce the overall number of external effects in the long run. The most extensive and well-known example for introducing a market for external effects is the European Emission Trading Scheme (ETS).

Trading whales and thick air?

Introducing markets to control external effects may lead to strange schemes. Trading the right to emit CO_2 for instance is literally trading (thick) air. A little "heavier" is the good traded in the market proposed by an economist and two marine scientists in 2012. The idea is to allocate property rights to whales, which means whaling countries could buy the right to hunt whale (catch quota) from anti-whaling countries. Vice versa, anti-whaling countries could buy the right to hunt whales from whaling countries and would then not make use of them (Eilperin, 2012).

Inhibitors of Public Policies for Sustainable Development

If there is such a broad choice of effective instruments, why are public policies for sustainable development and a sustainable economic system not yet reaching a far broader level of deployment? An interesting answer might lie in the decision-making process of political actors. The so-called Overton window illustrates that political action in the form of implemented policies is only taken if the general citizen's opinion on the intended policy is very favorable. The policy to be implemented has to be popular. As illustrated in Figure 24.8 many key issues for reaching sustainable development are not on the popular stage yet; such as the idea of degrowth might be perceived as outright radical or unthinkable (e.g. a world government for sustainable development). Accordingly, an explanation of political action and inaction may be given by political actors taking their representation role of citizens seriously. Politicians might argue they will only act in an interest that is reflected in popular opinion.

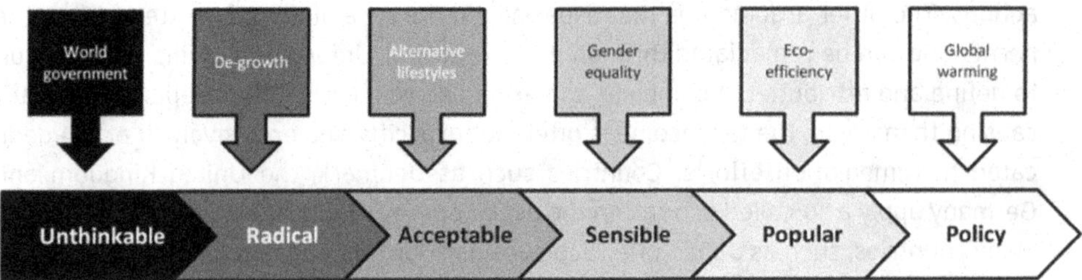

Figure 24.8 The Overton Window for Selected Responsible Business Topics.

Another, less favorable, but understandable explanation is the so-called blame-avoiding mechanism. Political actors might fear to "lean too far out of the window", when implementing necessary, but not commonly accepted policies for sustainable development (Joseph Lehman, 2010; Weaver, 1986). What does this mean for the goal of a sustainable economic system as a crucial pillar for reaching sustainable development? In order to reach a transformation of the world's economic system to become truly sustainable, all actors for sustainable development need to actively engage. The goal is promoting and educating ourselves, the planet's citizens to make it a popular conviction to take big steps towards the sustainability of human beings on Earth.

Another inhibitor of the legislative progress for sustainable development may be lobbying. For instance, the petroleum or tobacco industries have a long history of slowing down political progress towards sustainable development to protect their industries from harsh regulation. Interestingly, some companies also have been observed to lobby for stricter sustainability regulation. For leading businesses in social and environmental topics, especially, that makes sense, as it benefits them in their competition against sustainability laggards.

Ready for the next wave?

Changes towards more sustainability do not happen in a linear pattern, but rather in "waves". Such waves sweep over business and society and effect considerable change in little time. After each wave, there is a down phase, during which change might not seem as drastic, but which serves as preparation time for the next wave to build up. The *first pressure wave* rolled through in the early 1960s and brought about most of the environmental legislation in place today. The *second wave* was observed throughout a long period from the 1970sto the 1990s and triggered large scale criticism of specific companies' misconduct and the creation of most of the international NGOs for responsible business, such as the Global Compact and the Global Reporting initiative. The *third wave* in the early 2000s, was characterized by criticism of globalization and multinational business, and a rapid improvement of supply chain conditions. Now, in the 2010s, the *fourth wave* sees a rapid increase in entrepreneurial and proactive solutions to global challenges (SustainAbility, 2008). What will be the next wave that finally brings a true sustainability and profound transformation to the global economic system?

Exercises

A. KNOW

Use the below multiple-choice questions to test your knowledge. Each answer may be wrong or right and there may be zero to four right or wrong answers per question:

1. Changing the economic system...
   a. ...may be a very complex task, as a system is more than the pure sum of its elements.
   b. ...involves changing the elements of a system, such as the flows of resources.
   c. ...involves also influencing the connections between the elements of the system. Examples might be laws, values, and responsibilities between elements.
   d. ...involves considering the embeddedness of the society and environment into the economic system.
2. Root causes of the economic system's unsustainability...
   a. ...include that the economic system is geared towards growth.
   b. ...require among others the change task of creating mechanisms to internalize external effects.
   c. ...include external effects. External effects if internalized may lead to a situation where people pay the full price for products and this way include external effects into their buying decision.
   d. ...includes inequality in a sense, that companies should treat all employees equally.
3. System resilience...
   a. ...refers to systems' high instability.
   b. ...can among others be explained by equilibriums inside the system that are self-reinforcing.
   c. ...can among others be explained by path dependency, which is when organizations inside a system aim at following the goals recently chosen and therefore leave the system.
   d. ...can among others be explained by power mechanisms. For instance, a powerful corporation with an unsustainable product may have the power to stabilize the system in which it sells such a product.
4. Transforming sub-systems of the overall economic system...
   a. ...includes the idea of creating industrial eco-systems, which are aimed at connecting a single business with its surrounding natural eco-system.
   b. ...includes sustainable value chains and clusters. The difference between both is that sustainable value chains aim to create a local network of companies related to responsible business, while sustainability clusters aim to make all processes involved into producing a single product sustainable.
   c. ...might include creating sustainable communities, involving local individuals, government and companies jointly creating a sustainable community life.

   d. ...might include changing a whole industry towards sustainability performance. For instance, the car industry is currently in an industry-wide shift towards more sustainable solutions.

5. Mechanisms for the efficient use of natural resources...
   a. ...can be subdivided into resource cascading and revalorization. Both increase the overall useful lifetime of a natural resource.
   b. ...include resource cascading, such as in the case of a PET plastic bottle that gets recycled to T-shirts.
   c. ...include revalorization, which requires an additional transformation process, before the resource can be re-used, while resource cascading only requires reallocating the resource to a use which requires lower resource quality.
   d. ...revalorization and resource cascading cannot be applied to the same resource.

6. Changing the economic system infrastructure...
   a. ...is necessary to provide public policies, such as legislation, taxation, or subsidies that support the creation of a sustainable economic system.
   b. ...by public policies can only be done by governments.
   c. ...may be done by mainly three types of political actors, supra-governmental organizations (e.g. Greenpeace), non-governmental organizations (e.g. European Union), and local governments (e.g. German government).
   d. ...on a global level urgently requires additional coordination of efforts and a local abidingness to global norms.

B. THINK

The subprime mortgage financial crisis was an excellent example of a malfunctioning of the global financial system. Identify the main forces at play and prepare a causal loop diagram (CLD) explaining "the big picture" of the forces causing and sustaining the crisis. You will find many examples for CLDs online and advice on how to prepare them online.

C. DO

Practice either the principle of degrowth or of the internalization of external costs in one aspect of your personal or professional life.

D. RELATE

Identify at least two people who have very different disciplinary backgrounds from yourself (e.g. a mixed group of people from natural sciences, philosophy, politics, business). Engage in a discussion with them on what would need to be changed to the economic system to become truly sustainable.

E. BE

Think about one thing that you would like to change towards more sustainability in the very local production and consumption system surrounding yourself (e.g. to stop your street food stall from using Styrofoam, or your mother from keeping the fridge door open). Attempt to change this aspect until you succeed. If it works with the first try, find another change project that requires a more continuous effort.

Feedback

A. KNOW

Feedback 1

a. Right: Systemic complexity is based on this very characteristic of systems.
b. Wrong: Resource flows are not the elements (e.g. organizations and individuals) of a system, but a connection between these elements.
c. Right: Both influencing system elements and relationships between these elements are necessary activities for systemic change.
d. Wrong: The economic system is embedded into the society and environment system, not the other way around.

Feedback 2

a. Right: The growth imperative of the economic system causes problems when considering that we are living on a finite planet with finite resources. So infinite growth is not an option.
b. Right: The internalization of external effects is a main systemic change challenge for creating a sustainable economic system.
c. Right: The underlying idea is that higher (real) prices of products including all negative external effects throughout the product life cycle will create a situation where less people buy and use the product, which in turn reduces the negative impact.
d. Wrong: Inequality in this chapter refers to the economic system maintaining or even increasing inequalities between rich and poor.

Feedback 3

a. Wrong: System resilience refers to systems' high stability against forces of change.
b. Right: Dynamic equilibriums lead to situations where the system "bounces back" to its original state after it has been influenced externally.
c. Wrong: Path dependency refers to how past actions define present actions.
d. Right: Power structures with a vested interest in the system may work to maintain the status quo.

Feedback 4

a. Wrong: Industrial eco-systems aim at creating a network of connected companies that function like a natural eco-system.
b. Wrong: Descriptions of sustainable value chains and sustainability clusters have been switched.
c. Right: A sustainable community is an example of a subsystem transformed to become sustainable.
d. Right: A sustainable industry is an example of a subsystem transformed to become sustainable.

Feedback 5

a. Right: This is a correct interpretation of the figure and explanation of resource cascading and revalorization.
b. Wrong: As recycling requires an additional transformation process, it is resource revalorization.
c. Right: This is a correct interpretation of the figure and explanation of resource cascading and revalorization.
d. Wrong: Combining both mechanisms can extend the lifetime of resources drastically.

Feedback 6

a. Right: Such public policies are a necessary precondition for creating the global and local infrastructures for responsible and sustainable business and management.
b. Wrong: Increasingly, NGOs create their own public policies as relevant to enterprises as government-made public policies.
c. Wrong: The examples for Greenpeace and European Union do not correspond to the organization types mentioned.
d. Right: Global coordination is a crucial task for creating a global infrastructure for sustainable development.

B. THINK

Level	*Non-linear thinking*	*Notes*
+	Diagram convincingly captures the main causal loops responsible for the financial crisis, while providing an accessible overview.	
=	Feasible causal loop diagram.	
–	Diagram does not appreciate the multiple causal mechanisms involved.	

C. DO

Level	*Principled action competence*	*Notes*
+	Principle has been actioned flawlessly.	
=	Principle has partly been converted into action, but still lacks more attention to details that still are not in line with the principle.	
–	Principle has either not been understood or not practiced.	

D. RELATE

Level	*Interdisciplinary problem solving*	*Notes*
+	Multi-disciplinary discussion has led to an integrated solution more feasible than the individual solutions of each individual discipline.	
=	Discussion reflects multiple disciplinary backgrounds, but an integrated solution approach could not be reached.	
–	Discussion has not taken place or reflects a narrow disciplinary background.	

E. BE

Level	*Endurance*	*Notes*
+	Evidence of multiple tries to change the same issue with ultimate success.	
=	Giving up after multiple tries of changing the same issue.	
–	Not tried or giving up after first try.	

References

Benyus, J. M. (2002). *Biomimicry: Innovation inspired by nature*. New York: William Morrow Paperbacks.

Bertelsmann Stiftung; GTZ. (2007). *The CSR navigator: Public policies in Africa, the Americas, Asia and Europe*. Eschborn: GTZ.

Black, R. (2011). *Climate targets 'risk' from Brazil's forest changes*. Retrieved February 2, 2012, from BBC: https://www.bbc.co.uk/news/science-environment-16074628

Centre for Bhutan Studies. (2012). *Gross national happiness*. Retrieved January 2012, from https://www.grossnationalhappiness.com/

Cervantes, G. (2007). A methodology for teaching industrial ecology. *International Journal of Sustainability in Higher Education*, *8*(2), 131–141.

Coase, R. (1960, October). The problem of social cost. *Journal of Law and Economics*, 414–440.

Commission of the European Communities. (2006). *Making Europe a pole of excellence on CSR*.

Common, M., & Perrings, C. (1992). Towards an ecological economics of sustainability. *Ecological Economics*, *6*(1), 7–34.

Daly, H. E., & Farley, J. (2004). *Ecological economics: Principles and applications*. Washington: Island Press.

Ehrenfeld, J., & Gertler, N. (1997). Industrial ecology in practice: The evolution of interdependence at Kalundborg. *Journal of Industrial Ecology*, *1*(1), 67–79.

Eilperin, J. (2012). *Market proposed to end feud over whale hunting*. Retrieved February 2, 2012, from Property and Environment Research Center (PERC): https://www.perc.org/articles/article1455.php

Erkmann, S. (1997). Industrial ecology: A historical overview. *Journal of Greener Production*, *5*(1/2), 1–10.

Farley, J., Erickson, J. D., & Daly, H. E. (2005). *Ecological economics: A workbook for problem-based learning*. Washington: Island Press.

Hardin, G. (1968). The tragedy of the commons. *Science*, *162*, 1243–1248.

Hart, S. L., & Millstein, M. M. (1999). Global sustainability and the creative destruction of industries. *Sloan Management Review*, 23–33.

Joseph, L. (2010). *The Overton window*. Retrieved January 19, 2012, from Mackinac Center for Public Policy: https://www.mackinac.org/12887

Kim, C.-R. (2011). *Japan auto lobby cheers subsidies, says tax change not enough*. Retrieved January 30, 2012, from Reuters.com: https://www.reuters.com/article/2011/12/15/japan-autos-idUSL3E7NF00520111215

Krauss, C. (2011). *BP to drill again in the Gulf of Mexico*. Retrieved February 2, 2012, from New York Times: https://green.blogs.nytimes.com/2011/10/26/bp-to-drill-again-in-the-gulf-of-mexico/

Kuznets, S. (1955). Economic growth and income inequality. *The American Economic Review*, *45*(1), 1–28.

London Development Agency. (2010). *Green enterprise district East London*. London: London Development Agency.

Lorenz, M. (1905). Methods of measuring the concentration of wealth. *Publications of the American Statistical Association*, *9*(70), 209–219.

New Econmics Foundation. (2012). *The happy planet index*. Retrieved January 18, 2012, from https://www.happyplanetindex.org/

Pepper, D. (1993). *Eco-socialism: From deep ecology to social justice*. London: Psychology Press.

Pigou, A. C. (1920/2005). *The economics of welfare: Volume 1*. New York: Cosimo.

Porter, M. E. (1990). The competitive advantage of nations. *Harvard Business Review*, *68*(2), 73–93.

Porter, M. E. (2000). Location, competition, and economic development: Local clusters in a global economy. *Economic Development Quarterly*, *14*(5), 15–34.

Porter, M., & Kramer, M. (2006). Strategy and society: The link between competitive advantage and corporate social responsibility. *Harvard Business Review*, *84*(12), 78–92.

Samuelson, P. A., & Nordhaus, W. D. (2005). *Economics (18th edn.)*. New York: McGraw-Hill.

Schumacher College. (2012). *MA economics for transition – achieving low carbon, high well-being, resilient economies*. Retrieved January 18, 2012, from Schumacher College: https://www.schumachercollege.org.uk/courses/ma-in-economics-for-transition

SustainAbility. (2008). *The social intrapreneur: A field guide for corporate change makers*. London: SustainAbility.

The Guardian. (2011). *Canada pulls out of Kyoto protocol*. Retrieved February 2, 2012, from https://www.guardian.co.uk/environment/2011/dec/13/canada-pulls-out-kyoto-protocol

Todaro, M. P., & Smith, S. C. (2006). *Economic development (9th edn.)*. Harlow: Pearson.

United Nations. (2012). *Rio +20: United Nations conference on sustainable development*. Retrieved January 18, 2012, from https://www.uncsd2012.org/rio20/index.html

Vanberg, V. J. (2007). Corporate social responsibility and the 'game of catallaxy': The perspective of constitutional economics. *Constitutional Political Economy*, *18*(3), 199–222.

Wapner, P. (1995). Politics beyond the state: Environmental activism and world civic politics. *World Politics*, *47*(3), 311–340.

WBCSD. (2010). *Vision 2050: The new agenda for business in brief*. Geneva: World Business Council for Sustainable Development.

Weaver, R. K. (1986). The politics of blame avoidance. *Journal of Public Policy*, *6*, 371–398.

Zadeck, S. (2006). Responsible competitveness: Reshaping markets through responsible business practices. *Corporate Governance*, *6*(4), 334–348.

Glossary

A

Accountability Refers to both assuming a company's responsibilities and being held accountable for those.

Accounting Refers to the process of measuring and documenting an activity and performance.

Activist Is committed to a certain cause and shows nonconformity with the status quo by challenging structures, authorities, institutions, and beliefs.

Actors of responsible management activities Are the individuals (managers) and/or organizations carrying out a particular responsible management process. Organizational actors can be subdivided into the three groups businesses, civil society organizations (CSOs), and governmental organizations.

Angel investors (also business angels) Are private investors that use their financial resources to fund entrepreneurial start-ups.

Anthropogenic Greenhouse Gases Gases that contribute to the greenhouse effect by absorbing infrared radiation, produced by human activities such as burning fossil fuels and deforestation.

Assurance Refers to a third-party approval statement of responsible business communications (especially of reports).

B

B-Corp Certification A certification for businesses that meet high standards of verified social and environmental performance, public transparency, and legal accountability to balance profit and purpose.

Belonging The sense of being an accepted and integral part of a community or organization, which goes beyond mere presence to include being valued and affirmed.

Biomimicry Refers to efforts to imitate designs from nature in order to develop solutions for humanity.

Bottom of the Pyramid (BoP) Is a term coined by Prahalad that refers to (often the market constituted by) the approximately four billion people of low-income at the bottom of the socio-economic pyramid.

Brundtland Report A seminal document that defined sustainable development as development that meets the needs of the present without compromising the ability of future generations to meet their own needs.

Business case for responsible business Describes the manifold advantages that a business can gain when acting responsibly; the business or money sense of responsible business.

Business ethics Is the study of morally right or wrong decisions in a managerial and business context. Making morally right decisions is a fundamental pre-condition for becoming a responsible business. Business ethics is intimately interwoven with the responsible management process and provides the basis for successful ethics management.

Business model Reflects a company's realized strategy by describing the essence of a business, the underlying logic of everything it does.

Business philanthropy Is defined by voluntary altruistic contributions of businesses "for the good of mankind". In practice businesses often call philanthropic activities those that are not directly related to its main operations such as donation or volunteering campaigns.

Business plan Extensively describes the most important characteristics of an entrepreneurial venture.

Business unit strategy Aims at finding a strategic position inside one core market. Main positions are cost leadership or differentiation. Responsible business activities have the potential to create or support both types of position.

C

Carbon Dioxide (CO_2) A naturally occurring greenhouse gas, levels of which have increased significantly due to human activities like the burning of fossil fuels and deforestation.

Cause A cause is an issue that a company has started to mitigate or solve.

Cause-related consumption Aims at contributing to a certain cause by strategically consuming or boycotting products furthering or obstructing the achievement of the cause objective.

Cause-related marketing Is a responsible management tool that connects sales of a product to contributions to a good cause.

Certifications Are external approvals of fulfilling pre-defined criteria.

Change agents Are individuals successfully contributing to a change process.

Change management Is a management tool to achieve organizational transitions.

Circular Economy A model that moves away from the traditional linear "take, make, dispose" system, promoting a closed-loop system where resources are reused, remanufactured, and recycled to minimize waste and reduce environmental impact.

Civil Rights Act of 1964 US legislation that prohibited employment discrimination based on race, color, religion, sex, or national origin, marking a pivotal point in legal workplace equality.

Climate Adaptation Adjustments in ecological, social, or economic systems in response to actual or expected climatic stimuli and their effects or impacts.

Climate Feedback Loops Processes that can either amplify or diminish the effects of climate forcings, potentially leading to significant environmental changes.

Climate Mitigation Efforts to reduce or prevent emission of greenhouse gases; mitigation can mean using new technologies, making older equipment more energy efficient, or changing management practices or consumer behavior.

Climate Models Mathematical models that simulate the interactions of the important drivers of climate, including atmosphere, oceans, land surface, and ice. They are used to understand past climate and predict future climate changes.

Cluster Refers to a local accumulation of economic actors, sharing joint characteristics.

Communication barriers Are circumstances that impede successfully sending, receiving, and understanding a message.

Communication tools in responsible business Are manifold frameworks, all with the joint purpose of communicating social and environmental business activity and performance to stakeholders.

Compliance officers Are the highest-ranking officials in a company in charge of compliance with hard law and soft law.

Contact Hypothesis A theory suggesting that under certain conditions, increased contact between diverse groups can reduce prejudice and increase acceptance.

Corporate citizenship (CC) Considers companies citizens of the community/communities in which they operate. Being another citizen businesses have citizen rights, but also the duty to act for the well-being and development of the overall community.

Corporate Ethics The ethical principles and standards that guide behavior and decision making within an organization.

Corporate governance Refers to the rules and institutions governing corporate decision making. The need for corporate governance stems from principle-agent relationships.

Corporate level strategy Is developed for businesses competing in more than one core market with several strategic business units. The main strategic decision on the corporate level is degree and type of diversification. Responsible businesses often aim at reducing the corporation's negative impact by acquiring or developing strategic business units with a very positive social and/or environmental impact.

Corporate social entrepreneurship (CSE) Describes how whole businesses can apply entrepreneurial activities to tackle social and environmental problems.

Corporate social responsibility (CSR) The object of CSR is a business conduct that acts upon the various social responsibilities a business has towards its' stakeholders.

Customer relationship management (CRM) Is a management function that is in charge of managing the relationship with customers and unites the traditional functions of marketing, sales, and service.

D

Degrowth A concept advocating for a reduction in production and consumption to protect the environment, promote social equity, and sustain natural resources, challenging the traditional focus on economic growth.

DEIB (Diversity, Equality, Inclusion, and Belonging) An expanded framework of EDI that includes the psychological and emotional aspects of inclusion through the addition of "Belonging".

Development objectives for responsible business Describe the underlying development strategy a business chooses for its responsible business activities. Development activities can broadly be divided into growth and non-growth objectives.

Diversity The practice of acknowledging, valuing, and leveraging differences within the workforce, which include race, gender, age, ethnicity, sexual orientation, physical abilities, and other dimensions.

Diversity management Refers to the company's inclusion of often marginalized groups, such as elderly employees, women, racial minorities, disabled people, and gay-lesbian-transgender people.

Doughnut Economics A visual framework that outlines a "safe and just space for humanity" between the social foundation and the ecological ceiling, suggesting economic activity should occur within these boundaries to ensure planetary and societal health.

E

Eco-efficiency Is a management tool developed by the World Business Council for Sustainable Development (WBSD) that aims to increase the efficiency in the usage of natural resources.

Eco-innovation Describes an innovation that leads to an improved environmental impact.

Ecological Ceiling Part of Doughnut Economics, it represents the ecological limits beyond which humanity should not go to avoid detrimental impacts on the planet.

Economic capital Can be expressed in monetary terms. It comprises tangible assets such as machines or production facilities, intangible assets such as customer loyalty or brand value, and financial resources such as cash flows or a certain revenue margin. Economic capital can be attributed to an individual company or to the economic system as a whole.

Economic system Consist of elements (such as businesses, private and governmental organizations, and individuals) and interrelations between those elements (such as contracts, values, laws, power, information flows).

Ecosystem services Are services provided by ecosystems to humanity. Examples include the provision of water, timber, and food, climate regulation, recreational and spiritual functions of nature and elementary supporting services such as photosynthesis and nutrient cycling.

Employee life cycle Describes the different stages of a relationship between employee and company.

Endorsements Are external statements, supporting a company's responsible business activities or performance.

Entrepreneur Is an individual applying entrepreneurship, including environmental entrepreneurship, social entrepreneurship, or sustainability entrepreneurship

Entropy Refers to the fact that resources lose energy (or quality) the more they are used.

Environment, health, and safety (EHS management) Is a management tool that in many countries is required by law in order to ensure the physical integrity of employees and ensure the avoidance of environmental contingencies.

Environmental, Social, and Governance (ESG) Criteria Standards for a company's operations that socially conscious investors use to screen potential investments.

Equality Ensuring that all individuals are given the same opportunities and are not subjected to discrimination based on aspects like gender, race, age, disability, sexual orientation, religion, or other characteristics.

Equality Act 2010 UK legislation that consolidated previous anti-discrimination laws and provides a modern framework for equality by protecting specific characteristics.

Ethics management That aims of fostering ethically "right decisions" among the actors of responsible management. Main phases of the ethics management process are the mapping of ethical dilemmas, defining desirable decisions for every dilemma, understanding why people do or do not reach those desirable decisions, and implement management tools to foster desirable decisions.

Extended chain of responsibility Refers to the necessity for a responsible business to assume stakeholder responsibilities beyond their factory gate along the upstream and downstream supply chain.

External effects Are effects of an action that are not incurred by the actor. A smoker, for instance, does not need to pay directly for the damage caused to passive smokers. The opposite term is internal effects, which are incurred by the actor.

F

Fair trade Refers to a just distribution of the financial benefits of trade between the initial (often "third-world") producer and the (often "first world") distributers of a product.

Financial management Refers to the process of managing financial resources.

Focal point Refers to the specific starting point of interest of an analysis. For instance, in supply chain management the focal point is the company of interest in a specific section of the supply chain from where the supply chain analysis starts.

Functional departments (= business functions; = departments) Refer to certain functions fulfilled by a business, which are anchored in organizational structure by specific departments fulfilling this function, such as human resources management, accounting and financial management. Functional departments usually use encounter specific functional issues and deploy function-specific management instruments.

Functional issues Are social, environmental, and ethical issues that are specifically occurring in a certain function, such as unethical sales practices in the customer relations management function and air pollution in logistics.

Functional strategy Describes the activities in specific business functions such as marketing or human resources, which aim at supporting the chosen business unit strategy.

G

Gaia Hypothesis The Gaia Hypothesis was first proposed by James Lovelock proposes to see the planet as a mother system of interconnected sub-systems that behave similar to a living organism. The term Gaia has been borrowed from its eponym, the ancient Greek Earth goddess.

Global Indicator Framework A set of indicators approved by the United Nations Statistical Commission that are used to monitor the progress of the SDGs globally.

Global Reporting Initiative (GRI) An independent organization that provides the world's most widely used standards for sustainability reporting and disclosure.

Grassroots activism Refers to activist activities that occur on a societal level, not coordinated by existing organizations.

Green Economy Advocates for economic activities that promote environmental health, resource efficiency, and social inclusivity, focusing on sustainable consumption and production, low-carbon technologies, and green infrastructure.

Green supply chain management Is a management instrument for to improving the environmental impact of complete supply chains of a product.

Greenwashing Refers to a misleading impression about companies' social and environmental performance, created by an imbalance in a company's activities and communication.

H

Hard law Refers to formalized legislation and is often compared to soft law, which refers to informal norms.

Human development Refers to a series of indicators (e.g. education, health, income, ...) aiming to assess a human being's overall development.

Human resources management Is the functional department fulfilling the function of managing employee relations.

I

Ice-Albedo Feedback A climate feedback loop involving changes in the Earth's albedo caused by the melting of ice; reduced ice cover decreases albedo, increasing absorption of solar energy and further warming.

Ideal speech situation Refers to a high-quality communication situation, which serves to reach optimum outcomes of the communication process.

Immediate responsibilities Immediate responsibilities of responsible businesses aim at fulfilling the needs of stakeholders currently alive in a humanistic approach of maximizing stakeholder welfare and also include the rights of natural living beings, objects, and systems.

Inclusion The creation of an environment where all individuals feel valued, respected, and supported, enabling them to contribute fully to the organization's objectives.

Inclusive supply chains Including marginalized groups (mostly poor people) into supply chain activities, for instance, through the roles of suppliers, employees, or customers.

Incremental responsibility Refers to making small moves towards responsible business that do not transform the business as a whole.

Indivisibility A principle of the SDGs which suggests that the goals and targets are interlinked, and that success in one affects success in others.

Industrial eco-system Describes a local accumulation of businesses that jointly imitate (biomimicry) the functionality of a natural eco-system to jointly reduce the businesses' environmental impact. Industrial eco-systems are art of the industrial ecology approach.

Innovation Describes "the successful exploitation of new ideas" (DTI, 2003, p. 8). (See Chapter 21 for reference).

Institutions Refer to taken-for-granted norms guiding behavior. Institutions may come for instance, in the form of a value, a certain way of doing things, a social structure (such as the family), or an organization giving norms.

Integrated communication Refers to a holistic communication concept integrating communication with all stakeholders, internal and external communication, manifold communication tools, and the activities of many communicating functional departments such as the marketing, public relations, and human resources departments.

Integration This principle emphasizes understanding and recognizing the interconnections between the goals for sustainable development.

Inter-Agency and Expert Group on SDG Indicators (IAEG-SDGs) A group responsible for developing and implementing the global indicator framework for the SDGs, which are used to measure progress towards the goals.

Intergenerational responsibilities Responsible businesses aim to ensure humanity's survival on Earth and to maintain today's resources for future generations. Intergenerational responsibilities pragmatically follow the question: "What do we need for the future?".

Intersectionality A framework for understanding how various social identities (e.g., race, gender, class) intersect to create unique modes of discrimination and privilege.

Intrapreneurs Aim at using entrepreneurial measures to either changing an organization from within or using their position in an organization as instruments to achieve external change.

Irresponsible business Is a business, which in its mode of responsibility does not go beyond the compliance stage.

ISO 26000 An international standard that provides guidance on how businesses and organizations can operate in a socially responsible way, helping them contribute to sustainable development.

Issues and crisis communication Is a communication tool aimed at effective communication of critical contingencies, such as issues encountered by the business or during the involvement into crises.

Issues in responsible management Are understood as areas of potential action to either avoid the destruction or foster the creation of social, environmental, economic value. An issue being addressed is called a cause. An upcoming synonym for issue is subject area as first proposed the by the ISO standard on social responsibility.

K

Kuznets curve Suggests that, with increasing economic development, the income inequality and environmental degradation of a country follows an inverted u-shaped curve. With initial increasing average income, the income inequality and environmental degradation increase and decrease with high average income.

L

Labeling Refers to the usage of visual symbols to communicate compliance with a predesigned set of criteria.

Leader In the responsible business context provides vision and guidance for the transformational process towards sustainable business.

LEED Certification Leadership in Energy and Environmental Design (LEED) is a widely used green building certification program that recognizes best-in-class building strategies and practices.

License to operate Describes society's willingness to accept a company's activities. When societal opposition to a company's activity reaches a degree at which the business is not able continue operation, society withdraws the license to operate.

Life cycle impact assessment Is a specialized responsible management instrument that aims at an integrated measurement and management of social, environmental, and economic issues and impacts related to a certain product's life cycle. The three main product life cycle phases are "production" (from raw material extraction to first use by the end-customer), "use" (by the end consumer) and "end of useful lifetime" (disposal or revalorization).

Lifestyle Describes the way people live, including private and professional life.

Lifestyles of voluntary simplicity (LOVOS) Describe a lifestyle characterized by actively making life simpler by reducing consumption and professional workload. LOVOS should not be confused with LOHAS.

Logistics Refers to making inputs available to the production process (inbound logistics) and outputs available to customers (outbound logistics).

M

Mainstream responsible management instruments Are traditional management instruments that have been reinterpreted to additionally to economic performance create social and/or environmental performance. Examples are cause-related marketing, social accounting, and sustainable innovation.

Management innovation Is "the invention and implementation of a management practice, process, structure, or technique that is new to the state of the art and is intended to further organizational goals" (Birkinshaw, et al., 2008, p. 825). (See Chapter 21 for reference).

Management instrument (= tool) Refers to frameworks used for a specific management task. For instance, social marketing is used to create behavior change. Management tools can be deployed throughout one or several functional departments. For instance, social marketing may be deployed in both the human resources department and the marketing department.

Manager In the responsible business context fulfils the task of managing sustainability, responsibility, and ethics in an organization.

Materiality Describes the overall importance of a certain issue and is a compound value of the importance for an organization's stakeholders and the organization itself.

Methane (CH_4) A potent greenhouse gas with a global warming potential far exceeding that of carbon dioxide, primarily emitted through agricultural practices and fossil fuels.

Metrics Are quantifiable indicators.

Microfinance Is a management tool that provides financial services to a low-income population.

Millennium Development Goals (MDGs) Predecessor to the SDGs, these were eight international development goals that all United Nations member states agreed to achieve by 2015, focusing primarily on reducing extreme poverty.

Mode of implementation In responsible business describes the quality and degree to which responsible business assumes stakeholder responsibilities. The five stages of the mode of implementation are defensive, compliance, managerial, strategic, and civic implementation.

Monetarization Refers to the process of expressing non-monetary (social and environmental) values in money terms.

Moral development Refers to an individual's capacity of moral reasoning, of making ethical decisions. According to Kohlberg there are six stages of moral development.

Motivation Is an individual's reason for action. In the context of sustainable lifestyles, we described needs and moral reasoning (moral development) as two main motivational factors.

N

Natural (environmental) capital Comprises both renewable and non-renewable natural resources. Resources here should not be narrowly misunderstood as material production inputs, but also as non-material services provided by the natural environment such as the recreational value, realized while enjoying nature or flower pollination by bees.

Needs Describe human beings' predominant necessities in a certain situation. According to Maslow, needs are organized hierarchically, with the higher needs (e.g. self-actualization) driving individual behavior only after the lower needs (e.g. physiological needs) have been fulfilled.

Net Zero The balance between the amount of greenhouse gases emitted and the amount removed from the atmosphere. Achieving net zero means the total emissions are equivalent to the emissions removed.

Neutrally sustainable Refers to activities that are exactly within the planet's resource limits; neither unsustainable, nor restoratively sustainable.

Nitrous Oxide (N_2O) A powerful greenhouse gas produced by soil cultivation practices, especially the use of commercial and organic fertilizers, fossil fuel combustion, and biomass burning.

O

Ombudsman Is a neutral person who helps to mitigate conflicts of interest and represents stakeholder interests.

Open innovation Refers to an approach to innovation where innovators inside and outside the company work together in the same innovation process.

Operations management Refers to the operational (non-strategic) level of management. The term is often confused with production management.

Organizational activism Describes activist behavior deployed through an organization as vehicle.

Organizational structure and design Refers to the organization institutions and their interrelatedness through for instance power structures, and information channels.

Overton window Explains political decision making by the congruence of the decision to be made with the maturity and public acceptance of the decision topic.

Ozone (O_3) A gas composed of three oxygen atoms, occurring naturally in the Earth's stratosphere, and acting as a protective layer absorbing the sun's ultraviolet radiation. In the lower atmosphere (troposphere), it is a secondary pollutant in smog.

P

Path dependence Refers to a situation where the breadth of current decisions is delimitated by decisions made in the past.

Performance indicators For responsible business performance are social, environmental, and economic performance measures, jointly constituting an organization's triple bottom line. Responsible business indicators may be summarized through a sustainability scorecard.

Peripheral responsibility Refers to the assumption of primarily responsibilities that are unrelated to the core business and main business activities.

Persuasion Is a communication tool aiming at convincing communication partners of a predefined communication goal.

Planetary boundaries The critical values that our Earth system should not exceed for humanity to be able to live on Earth in the long run.

Political actors (in the context of this chapter) Are all organizations and individuals that shape public policies.

Primary functions (= main functions) in the value chain model Refer to the functional departments of a business that are primarily and directly involved into the value creation through a product or service.

Primary motivations Primary motivations for responsible business describe the main driving forces for a particular businesses' involvement in responsible practices. Motivations can broadly be divided into profit and non-profit motivations.

Principal-agent relationships Are situations, where an agent conducts a certain action for an agent (e.g. the manager (agent) for the owner of a business or stakeholders (principals)). In the management of such a relationship special attention has to be paid to information asymmetries and diverging interests between both principals and agents.

Production management Refers to the management of the production process. The term is often confused with operations management.

Public policy (in the context of this book) Refers to any measure by political actors actively and purposefully changing the infrastructure of the current economic system.

Q

Quality of consumption Describes the sustainability quality of a particular consumption pattern.

Quantity of consumption Describes the amount of goods and services consumed by an individual.

R

Regenerative Economy Goes beyond sustainability by aiming to restore and revitalize sources of energy and materials, focusing on systems that contribute to the regeneration of ecosystems and communities.

Representative Concentration Pathways (RCPs) Scenarios that include time-dependent projections of atmospheric greenhouse gas concentrations used for climate modeling and research.

Resilience Refers to a system's stability and resistance to change.

Resource cascading Refers to using the same resource several times until all value has been extracted and it is useless.

A responsible business Is one that in its mode of implementation assumes responsibilities going beyond the compliance stage.

Responsible business (RB) Is a business that has committed to ultimately becoming a sustainable business by improving its social, environmental, and economic impacts among its various stakeholders. RB applies responsible management activities to follow up on the commitment made.

Responsible Business Certification Certification programs designed to assess and recognize businesses that meet specific standards of ethical, environmental, and social responsibility.

Responsible business portfolio Is a list of issues and causes of an enterprise, including an analysis of factors relevant to their management.

Responsible business SWOT analysis Is a methodology to analyze the internal and external strategic factors related to social and environmental topics.

Responsible management (RM) Is a process involving tools for managing social, environmental, and economic capital and impact throughout discrete activities and functions. RM aims at the achievement of sustainable business by influencing its triple bottom line. A synonym for responsible management is three-dimensional management.

Responsible management instruments Manage the three constituting elements of the responsible management process and aim at the creation of three-dimensional value. Sub-groups are specialized and mainstream responsible management instruments.

Responsible management process Consists of the three basic elements actor, stakeholder, and issue (also called the trinity of responsible management) and one or several responsible management instruments connecting and manipulating those elements to create a well-balanced triple bottom line.

Responsible management systems Are sets of rules, values, and procedures, leading to responsible management practices.

Restoratively sustainable Refers to activities that are not only within the resource limits of the planet, but even contribute to restoring the planet's environmental capacity.

Revalorization Is the process of increasing the quality of a resource so that it can be used again.

Revalorizer Is a type of business or business function that in its core operations gives back value to formerly depleted resources. Revalorizers are for instance maintenance departments or recycling businesses.

Rio+20 The United Nations Conference on Sustainable Development held in Rio de Janeiro in 2012, which resulted in a focused political outcome document that contains clear and practical measures for implementing sustainable development.

S

Second order supply chains Are characterized by higher percentages of renewable and renewed resources used than first order supply chains. For instance, second-hand clothing or recycled paper is managed through a second order supply chain.

Sense-making Refers to the process of creating individual meaning through a communication activity.

Servitization Describes the substitution of a product by a service. Services often have a lower environmental impact and open up employment opportunities.

Shared Socio-economic Pathways (SSPs) Scenarios of projected socio-economic global changes up to 2100. They are used to derive greenhouse gas emissions scenarios with different climate policies.

Shared Value A management strategy where companies find business opportunities in social problems, aligning business success with social progress.

Social Accountability International (SA8000) A social certification standard for factories and organizations across the globe that ensures ethical working conditions.

Social capital Is any capital directly embodied in human beings. Social capital on the one hand comprises individual, so-called human capital including among others knowledge, skills, values, and even physical health and personal well-being. On the other hand, social capital also comprises capital collectively created by interaction inside groups of human beings, such as joint values, culture, and collective welfare.

Social entrepreneurship Entrepreneurship with a social purpose and/or following a social opportunity.

Social Foundation Also part of Doughnut Economics, it represents the minimum social standards according to the United Nations' Sustainable Development Goals.

Social Identity Theory A theory that suggests individuals derive their identity from the groups to which they belong, influencing intergroup behavior.

Social innovation Refers to an innovation with added value for society.

Social investment Is the use of financial resources to strengthen social infrastructure.

Social license to operate Refers to society's acceptance of a specific businesses' operations.

Social marketing Employs marketing instruments to create a behavior change for the good of society in individuals. Examples include non-smoking or recycling campaigns.

Socially responsible investment (SRI) Refers to investment practices with an added value for society.

Soft law Refers to norms to be obeyed by companies that are not written down in formal law (hard law).

Specialized responsible management instruments Are three tools specially designed for responsible management. One each of the constituting elements of the responsible management process.

Sphere of influence Refers to the area and decisions inside and outside a company that can be influenced directly by the company's actions.

Stakeholder Are all individuals, groups, living and even non-living entities that have a relationship to an organization; that are affected by the organization and/or affect it. Also, individuals or even single activities may have stakeholders. Typical stakeholders of businesses are for instance employees, communities, customers, and shareholders.

Stakeholder dialog Refers to a two-way communication with a diverse set of stakeholders.

Stakeholder management Is a specialized responsible management instrument that aims at the management of a company's stakeholder relations. Stakeholder management can be subdivided into the phase of stakeholder assessment and the stakeholder engagement phase.

Supply chain Consists of a series of companies connected through the joint creation of a product. The supply chain runs from the extraction of first raw material to the use of the product through the final end-consumer. The supply chain should not be confused with a company's value chain.

Support functions (= staff functions) Describe all functional departments in a company's value chain that are not primarily and directly involved into the value creation through product or service.

Sustainability accounting Is a management tool used to measure and document social, environmental, and economic activities and impacts.

Sustainability entrepreneurship Refers to various types of entrepreneurship that leads to the creation of businesses that contribute to sustainable development.

Sustainability Indexes Benchmarks that assess the sustainability performance of companies based on environmental, social, and governance (ESG) criteria.

Sustainability indicators Are qualitative and quantitative (metrics) categories, aiming at documentation and control of social, environmental, and economic business activity and performance.

Sustainability quality Refers to the degree of sustainability of an entity (e.g. a product, a consumption style, a company).

Sustainability reporting Is a communication tool that aims to neutrally, concisely and completely communicate social, environmental and economic business activity and performance.

Sustainability scorecard Is a conglomerate of social, environmental and economic performance indicators serving to manage and control an organization's sustainability strategy.

Sustainability scorecard Uses a set of sustainability indicators to document and control social, environmental, and economic business activity and performance.

Sustainability strategy Describes an integrated set of social, environmental, and economic strategies jointly aiming at achieving the goal of becoming a sustainable business.

Sustainable business (SB) Refers to a single business, industry or a whole economy that has reached a harmonization of its overall social, environmental, and economic capital and which has achieved sustained neutral to positive impact in all three dimensions. SB is the business sector contribution to sustainable development.

Sustainable community Is a local group of people, companies, and governmental entities that jointly pursues a sustainable overall impact of the community.

Sustainable development (SD) Is a development that achieves a harmonization of economic, social, and environmental capital throughout all sectoral contributions of business, civil society, and governmental sector. SD ensures long-run quality of life and survival of the human race on Earth. SD refers to both the process and the achievement of SD.

Sustainable Development Goals (SDGs) A set of 17 global goals set by the United Nations in 2015 to end poverty, protect the planet, and ensure prosperity for all as part of a new sustainable development agenda.

Sustainable Economics An economic system prioritizing long-term viability, environmental stewardship, and social well-being, striving to meet present needs without compromising future generations.

Sustainable economic system Operates in the limits of the Earth's natural carrying capacity.

Sustainable governance (SG) Refers to governmental activities creating an at least neutral or even positive impact in the social, environmental, and economic dimensions. SG is the governmental and public sector contribution to sustainable development.

Sustainable lifestyle Is a lifestyle not exceeding the planet's resource limits.

Sustainable living (SL) Describes an individual or collective lifestyle characterized by an at least neutral or even positive impact on business, society and economy. SL is the civil society sector contribution to sustainable development.

Sustainable supply chain management Aims at the creation of supply chains that contribute to sustainable development through paying attention to the supply chain's triple bottom line, assuming an extended responsibility for stakeholders along the supply chain, and creating circular resource flows.

Strategic guidance statements Define the general parameters for strategy development. Main statements are vision, mission, values, and codes of conduct.

Strategy evaluation and control Mechanisms aimed at tracking performance and ensure the achievement of predefined goals of the strategy developed.

Systems Thinking A holistic approach that recognizes the complex interconnections within business operations and the broader environmental and social contexts.

T

Task Force on Climate-related Financial Disclosures (TCFD) An organization that develops voluntary, consistent climate-related financial risk disclosures for use by companies in providing information to investors, lenders, insurers, and other stakeholders.

Testimonials Are a communication tool involving experience reports of stakeholders involve into a responsible business activity.

Three-dimensional management Is a characteristic of responsible management that is aimed at highlighting the multidimensional (social, environmental, economic) elements of the responsible management process. It also aims at creating a neutral term that is not yet taken by contradictory definitions ad understandings. Three-dimensional management is the management process leading to the desired outcome of a well-balanced triple bottom line.

Total responsibility management Refers to a responsibility management system that aims at achieving maximum quality, for a broad set of stakeholders in responsible management, out of all operations of an organization.

Trade-off Refers to what one has to give up receiving something else.

Trinity of responsible management Refers to the omnipresent elements, actor, stakeholder, and issue that are of central importance to any responsible management activity.

Triple bottom line (TBL) Refers to balancing the social, environmental, and economic outcome of an activity. In order to contribute to sustainable development any activity needs to achieve an at least neutral or even positive TBL. The TBL is the main object of responsible management. Achieving a sustainable TBL is the main characteristic of a sustainable business and the final goal of responsible business.

2030 Agenda A plan of action for people, planet, and prosperity, which seeks to strengthen universal peace and ensure no one is left behind. It integrates and balances the three dimensions of sustainable development: economic, social, and environmental.

U

Universal Declaration of Human Rights An international document that was influential in shaping global norms relating to equality and non-discrimination.

Universality In the context of SDGs, it refers to the universal application of the goals, meaning they are relevant for all countries and people.

Unsustainability Refers to a situation, practice, or object whose negative impact puts a strain on the resource of the planet.

Upcycling Refers to a recycling process that increases the value of the recycled resource above the value before the first usage.

V

Value chain Describes how all functional departments of a company jointly create value through a product or service. The value chain should not be confused with the supply chain, which can be seen as a series of value chains.

Voluntary National Reviews (VNRs) Reviews conducted by national governments to follow-up and review the progress of countries towards the SDGs, which are presented at the High-Level Political Forum on Sustainable Development.

W

Whistleblowing Refers to a stakeholder (mostly employees) who communicates misconduct.

Work-life balance Refers to creating an equilibrium between private and professional life.

Index

Page numbers in *italics* refer to figures and those in **bold** to tables.

Printed in the United States
by Baker & Taylor Publisher Services

Printed in the United States
by Baker & Taylor Publisher Services